Novell® GroupWise® 6.5

Administrator's Guide

Tay Kratzer

800 East 96th Street, Indianapolis, Indiana 46240 USA

Novell GroupWise 6.5 Administrator's Guide

International Standard Book Number: 0-7897-2982-2

Library of Congress Catalog Card Number: 2003402953

Printed in the United States of America

First Printing: October 2003

06 05 04 4 3 2

Trademarks

Warning and Disclaimer

Bulk Sales

Que Publishing offers excellent discounts on this book when ordered in quantity for bulk purchases or special sales. For more information, please contact

U.S. Corporate and Government Sales
1-800-382-3419
corpsales@pearsontechgroup.com

For sales outside of the U.S., please contact

International Sales
1-317-428-3341
international@pearsontechgroup.com

Acquisitions Editor
Jenny Watson

Development Editor
Emmett Dulaney

Managing Editor
Charlotte Clapp

Project Editor
George E. Nedeff

Copy Editor
Kezia Endsley

Indexer
John Sleeva

Proofreader
Kathy Bidwell

Technical Editor
Eric Raff

Team Coordinator
Vanessa Evans

Designer
Gary Adair

Page Layout
Eric S. Miller

Contents at a Glance

Table of Contents

Part II Administration Interface

Part IV Practical Administration

Welcome to Novell Press

Novell Press, the world's leading provider of networking books, is the premier source for the most timely and useful information in the networking industry. Novell Press books cover fundamental networking issues as they emerge—from today's Novell and third-party products to the concepts and strategies that will guide the industry's future. The result is a broad spectrum of titles for the benefit of those involved in networking at any level: end user, department administrator, developer, systems manager, or network architect.

Novell Press books are written by experts with the full participation of Novell's technical, managerial, and marketing staff. The books are exhaustively reviewed by Novell's own technicians and are published only on the basis of final released software, never on pre-released versions.

Novell Press at Que Publishing is an exciting partnership between two companies at the forefront of the knowledge and communications revolution. The Press is implementing an ambitious publishing program to develop new networking titles centered on the current versions of NetWare, GroupWise, ZENworks, BorderManager, and networking integration products.

Novell Press books are translated into several languages and sold throughout the world.

Darrin VandenBos
Publisher
Novell Press, Novell, Inc.

Foreword

About a decade ago, I began my career as a GroupWise guy on what most people would rightly consider the bottom rung—I did front-line technical support. I won't pretend for a moment that those were "the good old days," but I do remember the heady exhilaration I got from learning something new every day. We trained each other back then, and one of the guys I learned the most from was Tay Kratzer.

By the mid-90s I felt like I could write the book on GroupWise. I'd cranked out hundreds of technical information documents for Novell's Web site, and numerous white papers for support's consulting arm. So, I did a quick stint as a technical editor for other authors who were writing an end user guide, and I cheated a little bit by using Tay as a resource without paying him. (Well, I let him listen to some of my CDs at work, but that shouldn't count.)

In the late 90s I DID write the book on GroupWise, but the publishers only let me in on the deal because they had Tay Kratzer signed up already. We roped in a third guy (Hi, Ross!), and the three of us wrote a GroupWise 5.5 book. Somehow I got top billing. I suspect it's because I cheated again.

In the intervening years between our first book and today, Tay wrote two more books, while I took my self-promotional skills in another direction and usurped control of the entire GroupWise product line at Novell. Predictably, I got a lobotomy along with my management position, and I can barely write my own emails, let alone technical documents (this foreword required three days, two dictation machines, and the help of my six-year-old). And what do you know? With all the resources of Novell's mighty GroupWise team at my disposal, I still turn to a long-trusted source for the best technical help—Tay Kratzer.

For the last ten years, he's committed himself to making GroupWise work in complex environments out in the real world. He's a superstar in the GroupWise community, and a darn nice guy besides. People pay tens of thousands of dollars for the privilege of talking to him on the phone for a few minutes each week, and they get in line to do it. But for you, dear reader, he's gone and done a complete brain-dump, asking only for some chump change in return.

So pay up. Head to the checkout counter and buy this book before turning the page.

Thanks,

—Howard Tayler
Collaboration Product Line Manager
Novell, Inc.

About the Author

Tay Kratzer works as a Novell Premium Service-Primary Support Engineer for some of Novell's larger customer sites. He is the author and co-author of five other GroupWise-related books and writes for *Novell Connection Magazine, Novell AppNotes,* and *GroupWise Advisor Magazine*. He has supported Novell GroupWise for 11 years, is a Novell Master CNE, and is the recipient of the Software Support Professional Association's Year 2000 "Outstanding Superstar" award. He lives in Utah with his wife, Dr. Irina Kratzer, and their four children, Anastasia, Lindy, Dallin, and Wesley. Tay maintains a Web site to support this book and GroupWise topics at `www.taykratzer.com`.

Dedication

To my wife, Irina Kratzer. You are simply the best! *Thank you for gracing me every day with your friendship and love. Thanks for putting the current needs of our family above ambitions that you are so well suited for.*

To my mother and father, Venice and LeRoy Kratzer. Dad, thanks for teaching me things such as Basic programming before PCs ever hit the market. Mom, thanks for teaching me word processing in the WordStar days.

Acknowledgments

Thanks to the following people for their major contributions to this book:

Greg Hinchman (`http://www.hinchmanconsulting.com`) A.K.A The GroupWise Document Management Guru, for writing Chapter 14.

Erno de Korte (`http://www.clarify.nl`) for co-authoring Chapter 30.

Roel van Bueren (`http://www.rovabunetworks.nl`) for co-authoring Chapter 30.

Scott Kunau for major contributions to Chapter 31.

Eric Raff for major contributions to Chapters 16 and 18.

Thanks to the following people for their contributions to this book:

Howard Tayler

Ross Phillips

Frank Gioffre

Ed Hanley

Ira Messenger

Chuck Sisson

Thanks to the following people who have patiently worked with me while GroupWise 6.5 was in its development phase:

Eva Cornish

Glenn Brown

Thanks to the management team at Novell, which has willingly supported me in my efforts to inform GroupWise administrators:

Barry Haug

Todd Abney

Dave Cutler

Thanks to my technical editor, Eric Raff, who shares my passion for learning new things.

Thanks to my production staff Jenny Watson, Emmett Dulaney, and George Nedeff for all their attention to detail.

We Want to Hear from You!

As the reader of this book, you are our most important critic and commentator. We value your opinion and want to know what we're doing right, what we could do better, what areas you'd like to see us publish in, and any other words of wisdom you're willing to pass our way.

You can e-mail or write directly to let us know what you did or didn't like about this book—as well as what we can do to make our books stronger.

Please note that we cannot help you with technical problems related to the topic of this book, and that due to the high volume of mail we receive, we might not be able to reply to every message.

When you write, please be sure to include this book's title and author as well as your name and phone or e-mail address. We will carefully review your comments and share them with the author and editors who worked on the book.

Email: `feedback@quepublishing.com`

Mail: Que Publishing/Novell Press
800 East 96th Street, 3rd Floor
Indianapolis, IN 46240 USA

Reader Services

For more information about this book or others from Novell Press or Que Publishing, visit our Web site at `www.quepublishing.com`. Type the ISBN (excluding hyphens) or the title of the book in the Search box to find the book you're looking for.

Introduction

Novell GroupWise is an *integrated* e-mail and collaboration tool with a rich feature set and hundreds of options. The GroupWise clients appeal to first-time users along with power users, because administering a GroupWise system can be quite straightforward.

GroupWise 6.5 administration is simple for several reasons, but mostly because GroupWise is stable and easy to troubleshoot. This book makes that troubleshooting much easier by helping you understand the structure of the data you'll be working with, as well as the tools you'll have at your disposal. Very few administrators are needed to administer large GroupWise systems. This fact is one of the major reasons why Novell GroupWise continues to have a strong presence in organizations that take productivity, cost-effectiveness, and return-on-investment factors into account when evaluating collaboration solutions.

As users and administrators look to wireless and Windows-independent solutions, GroupWise 6.5 is unparalleled by any competitor in its offerings. GroupWise 6.5 is also strongly integrated with Novell's eDirectory. With GroupWise 6.5 and LDAP-directory authentication, users simply need to remember the Novell eDirectory password. I appreciate that if I access my GroupWise account on my PalmPilot, or on a Macintosh-, Linux-, or Windows-based computer, I need to remember only one password: my Novell eDirectory password.

I learned a long time ago that if I write something down, and I know where I put it, I don't have to memorize a lot of information. I don't enjoy trying to remember mundane facts, so I just write them all down. Over the 11 years that I have supported Novell GroupWise, I have had to cook up some elaborate solutions in an effort to modify or fix my customer's systems. You are the beneficiary of my efforts to document hundreds of facts and solutions, which I just did not want to have to keep in my head!

When I sit down to a technical book, I like specifics. That's what I have provided to you in this book; I try to be specific. The other thing that makes this book unique is that it explains how to do many tasks that programmatically there are no solutions for. For example, moving a GroupWise post office is a popular theme from a customer's standpoint, but nothing in the GroupWise administration allows for this task.

I am sure you will appreciate the in-depth information in this book, written in a style that breaks complete tasks into step-by-step task lists. I want to make this book a dynamic resource and so I have established the site `www.taykratzer.com`, as discussed in Appendix A of this book, to make this book even more valuable.

Enjoy!

—Tay Kratzer

PART I

Architecture

CHAPTER 1

GroupWise Architecture: Basics

CHAPTER 1

This chapter examines the Novell GroupWise architecture. The chapter defines some terms and discusses the way some of the components interact. This chapter will prepare you for a more thorough discussion of architecture in the next chapters. This chapter also discusses the evolution of the GroupWise product, to help you understand some of the naming conventions.

Understanding a Basic GroupWise 6.5 System

To truly understand GroupWise, it is imperative to have a basic knowledge of the terms used to describe it. In the following section, the key terminology behind it is explored.

GroupWise

The word *GroupWise* is a Novell, Inc. trademark. It refers to a collection of applications and datastores that, taken together, provide e-mail (and a lot more) to a community of computer users. GroupWise is properly categorized as collaboration software, or as a "GroupWare" product.

GroupWise User

The term *GroupWise user* (or sometimes just *user*) refers to a mailbox that has been assigned to an end-user on a GroupWise system. As an analogy, think of the United States Postal Service (USPS); a GroupWise user is similar to a P.O. box. Just as various mail items are delivered to a P.O. box, e-mail and other items are delivered to a GroupWise user.

GroupWise Post Office

Just as a P.O. box exists at a USPS post office, a GroupWise user exists at a GroupWise post office. A post office can also contain resources, libraries, and other GroupWise objects.

Physically, every GroupWise post office exists as a collection of directories and data files on a file server. One of the most important attributes of a post office is the path to the root of these directories, known as the UNC (Universal Naming Convention) path, as shown in Figure 1.1.

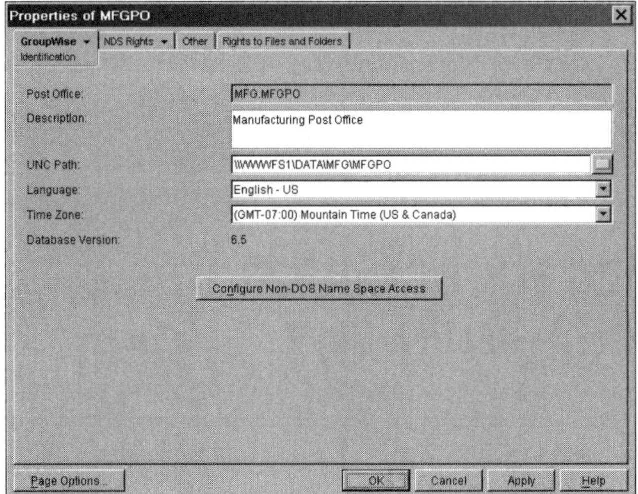

FIGURE 1.1
The details of a GroupWise post office.

GroupWise Domain

If GroupWise users are like P.O. boxes, and GroupWise post offices are like USPS post offices, the GroupWise domain is like the distribution center at the airport where trucks shuttle mail to various USPS post offices. At this point, the analogy gets a little difficult to follow, and domains will be discussed in terms of their functions. Domains exist to

- Transfer items between GroupWise post offices
- Transfer items to other GroupWise domains (which in turn deliver to their post offices)

- Provide a point of administration for all GroupWise objects, such as users, post offices, and libraries

Although post offices see most of the action, GroupWise domains are necessary because post offices cannot be administered by themselves. Just as you saw with post offices, every GroupWise domain has a physical location, or UNC path. This *domain directory* is the root of a complex directory structure containing files that are critical to the administration and proper functioning of a GroupWise system. Figure 1.2 shows the properties of a GroupWise domain, the *primary domain* in this instance.

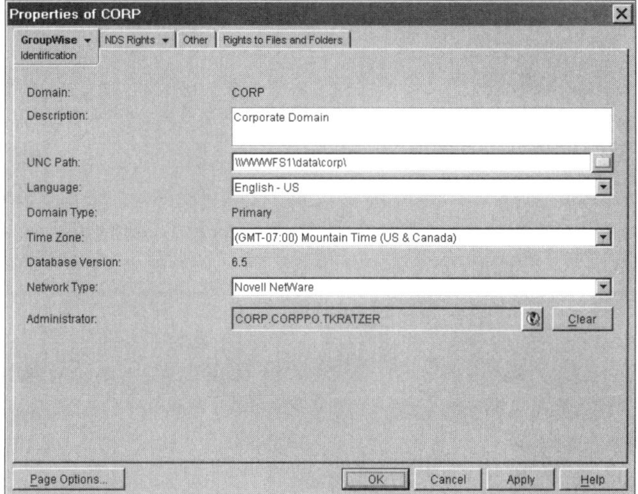

FIGURE 1.2
The details of a GroupWise domain.

Primary Domain

Every GroupWise system must have a GroupWise primary domain. There can only be one primary domain in a GroupWise 6.5 system. All other domains established within a GroupWise system are either secondary domains or external domains. There's also a thing called an *IDOMAIN* or an *Internet Domain*. The IDOMAIN refers to the Internet domain name for your organization (for example: `worldwidewidgets.com`). When you create IDOMAINs in your GroupWise system, they are not synonymous with the regular GroupWise domains discussed in this chapter. IDOMAINs do not have a physical location (UNC path) associated with them as a primary and secondary domain(s) do. They are strictly used to help facilitate Internet style addressing within a GroupWise system. The first domain you create in a GroupWise system must be your primary domain.

The primary domain can function like any other GroupWise domain with post offices, users, and so on. The difference is that the primary domain is the "supreme authority" within a GroupWise system. This means that any change made from any domain in a GroupWise system must be cleared through that system's primary domain. The GroupWise primary domain is responsible for replicating changes to all other domains, and in the event that a secondary domain database is damaged, the primary domain can be used to rebuild it.

Secondary Domain

After the primary domain has been established, most GroupWise systems require secondary domains to accommodate large numbers of users. When an administrative change is made from a secondary domain, that change must be transmitted to the primary domain before it can be replicated to the rest of the GroupWise system.

In the event that the primary domain database is damaged, a secondary domain can be used to rebuild that primary domain's database.

The GroupWise System

The GroupWise system is basically the name assigned to the collection of domains, post offices, and users (and more) that are managed from a particular primary domain. It is not a physical object with its own directory structure, or even its own object screen like domains and post offices. The icon shown in Figure 1.3 is used to represent the system.

FIGURE 1.3 The GroupWise system level object.

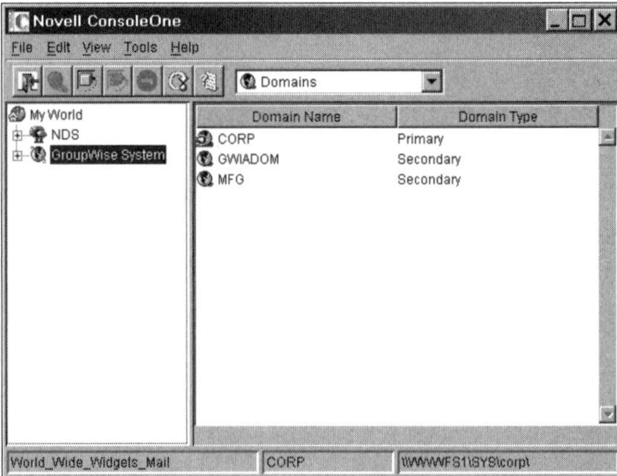

Although a GroupWise system is not an object that you can physically administer, it exists so that you can define actions that will affect both the primary domain and all of the secondary domains.

To understand the idea of a GroupWise system, imagine this analogy of a family. A family is not a tangible object, but an entity that defines a group of people that are related to one another. A GroupWise system is a family of GroupWise domains, with a primary domain and, usually, additional secondary domains. The administrator of a GroupWise system can make changes that affect the entire "family" of GroupWise domains (the GroupWise system).

GroupWise Client

The GroupWise client is an application that enables a computer user to access a GroupWise mailbox. There are three types of GroupWise 6.5 clients: the Windows client, which runs on any Windows 32-bit platform (shown in Figure 1.4), the GroupWise WebAccess client (shown in Figure 1.5), and GroupWise Wireless clients, which can run on a variety of browser platforms. The GroupWise Windows Client typically talks to a post office agent (POA) in order to access the mailbox.

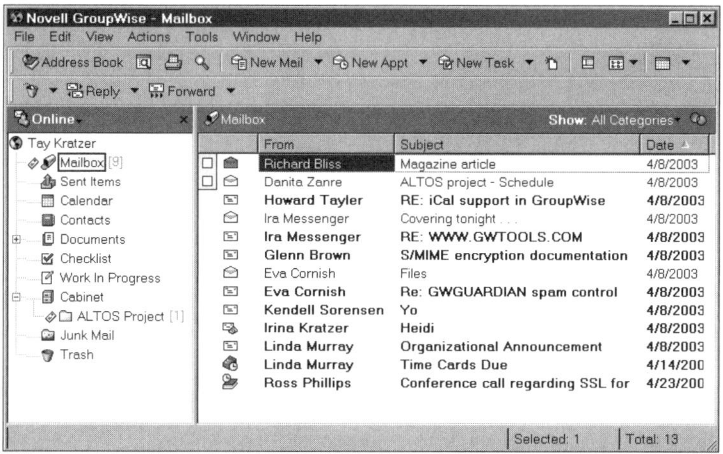

FIGURE 1.4
The GroupWise 6.5 32-bit client interface.

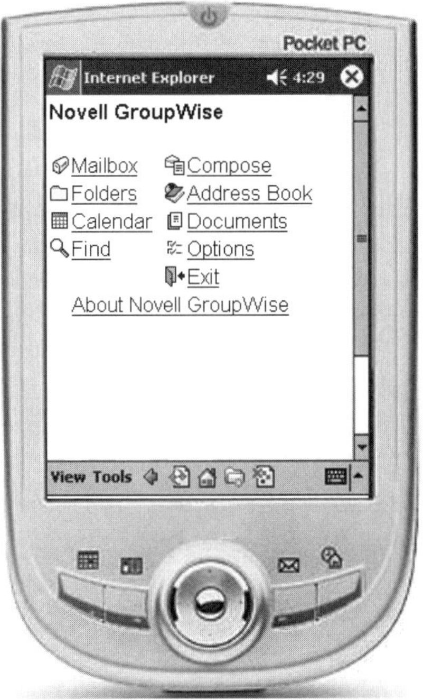

FIGURE 1.5 The GroupWise 6.5 WebAccess client for the Pocket PC/ Windows CE platform.

POA

Every GroupWise 6.5 post office must have a POA associated with it that updates user mailboxes on that post office. A POA is a software process that typically runs on the same file server that houses the GroupWise post office. It also updates its GroupWise post office with administrative changes made from a domain in the GroupWise system; these might be address book changes or changes relevant to end users' interaction with the GroupWise system (such as rights to libraries or membership in distribution lists). The POA is discussed in more detail in Chapter 8, "Configuring the Post Office Agent." Figure 1.6 shows a GroupWise POA object.

MTA

Every GroupWise 6.5 domain must have a *message transfer agent* (MTA) associated with it. The MTA services the domain and each of the entities (post offices or gateways) associated with that domain. It is a software process that typically runs on the same file server that houses the GroupWise domain.

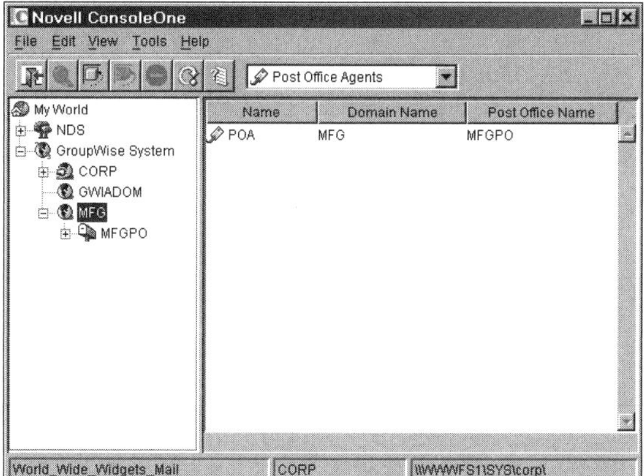

FIGURE 1.6
A GroupWise POA object.

The MTA is the agent that transfers messages between the post offices and gateways owned by the domain. It also transmits and receives messages with other domains on the GroupWise system—or even with domains outside of your GroupWise system, if you let it. The MTA does not deliver messages to user mailboxes, but drops messages off to the POA at a post office. The POA then delivers to the user mailbox databases. Figure 1.7 shows a GroupWise MTA object.

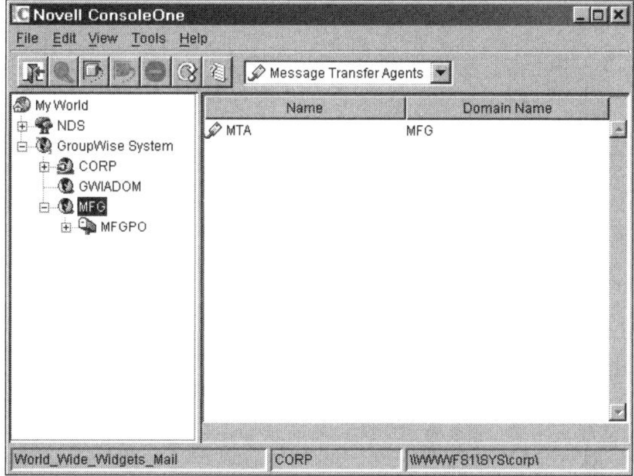

FIGURE 1.7
The GroupWise MTA object.

GroupWise Administrator

The GroupWise Administrator application is a collection of snap-in modules for ConsoleOne. Because the GroupWise Administrator requires ConsoleOne, the GroupWise system must include at least one server with Novell eDirectory. GroupWise uses eDirectory for a portion of its administrative directory. Figure 1.8 shows GroupWise Administrator and the several GroupWise objects that can be configured for GroupWise.

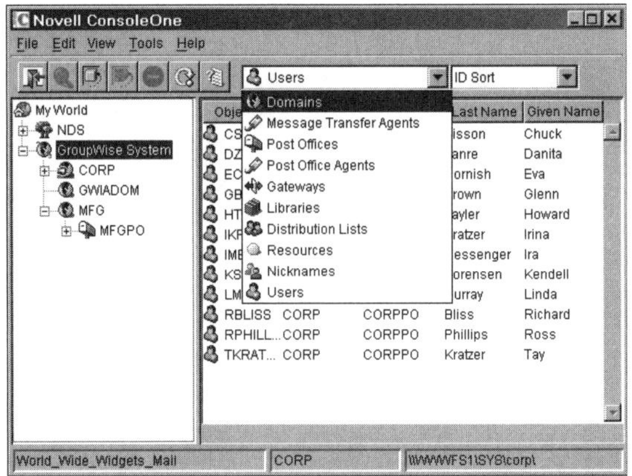

FIGURE 1.8 The GroupWise view in ConsoleOne.

The GroupWise Directory

The GroupWise directory is the collection of databases that define the GroupWise system's domains, post offices, users, and other objects. The GroupWise directory has two major components:

- eDirectory/Novell directory services
- GroupWise domain and post office databases

eDirectory/Novell Directory Services

Novell eDirectory is the leading network directory solution. eDirectory is what Novell Directory Services (NDS) has evolved into. Throughout this book, NDS and eDirectory will be referred to simply as "eDirectory." eDirectory is commonly used to define user accounts on file servers across enterprise networks, and it provides for simple, centralized administration. eDirectory has become an open solution beyond the Novell NetWare platform and as such, NDS is now merely referred to as eDirectory.

eDirectory provides GroupWise administrators with the capability to manage their user's GroupWise mailboxes and network accounts from the same interface, ConsoleOne.

GroupWise Domain and Post Office Databases

The largest portion of the GroupWise directory is in the GroupWise domain and post office databases. These database files are named WPDOMAIN.DB and WPHOST.DB. Every domain has a WPDOMAIN.DB file, which is that domain's database. Every post office has a WPHOST.DB file, which is that post office's post office database.

When ConsoleOne is loaded with GroupWise Administrator, the GroupWise Administrator snap-ins update the WPDOMAIN.DB file. When a GroupWise domain's MTA is loaded, it must be pointed at the domain's WPDOMAIN.DB file. The WPDOMAIN.DB is the brain of the MTA and instructs the MTA how to route messages.

Every post office POA must have the path to the WPHOST.DB database in order to load. The WPHOST.DB database is often referred to as the *address book*. This is the database GroupWise clients read in order to see other users and objects in their GroupWise system.

The GroupWise Message Store

A GroupWise message store is contained at each GroupWise post office. This is where a user's mailbox, with all its attendant messages and other data, is contained. The message store is the heart of what users interact with while they are running the GroupWise client.

A GroupWise message store can also exist in the form of a GroupWise "caching" mode mailbox, remote e-mail, or in a GroupWise archive mailbox. Chapter 4, "Understanding the GroupWise Information Store," discusses the message store in much more detail.

Novell Messenger/GroupWise Messenger

Starting with the GroupWise 6.5 release, an Instant Messaging (IM) solution is bundled with GroupWise. The Novell Messenger/GroupWise Messenger Instant Messaging solution is its own independent collaboration solution, independent of GroupWise. The integration between GroupWise and Novell Messenger is only at the client level. Chapter 29, "Configuring a GroupWise Messenger (Instant Messaging) System," focuses on how to configure a Novell Messenger/GroupWise Messenger solution.

Other GroupWise Objects and Services

This chapter has discussed users, post offices, domains, and systems, and it's also touched on the agents and the directory. The discussion of the basic GroupWise architecture is complete, but there are several types of

GroupWise objects that have not been discussed. Subsequent chapters will also discuss

- Gateways
- Libraries
- Resources
- Distribution lists
- Nicknames

GroupWise Evolution

GroupWise 6.5 is a sixth-generation product. The original ancestor of GroupWise 6.5 was called WordPerfect Office 1.0. When Novell bought WordPerfect Corporation, and later sold it to Corel, Novell retained the GroupWise product line. Prior to GroupWise 6.5, there were six revisions of GroupWise that are of interest in this book: GroupWise 4.1, GroupWise 5.0, GroupWise 5.2, GroupWise 5.5, GroupWise 5.5 Enhancement Pack, and GroupWise 6.

It's helpful to understand that GroupWise evolved from WordPerfect Office, because the current product retains some of the earlier naming conventions for files and directories. Anywhere you see WP or OF, you are looking at the legacy of WordPerfect Office:

- WP—The GroupWise domain database is called WPDOMAIN.DB. You will also find WPHOST.DB, WPGATE, WPCSIN, and WPCSOUT.
- OF—All GroupWise post offices have directories called OFUSER, OFFILES, and OFMSG.

The reason Novell retained the WordPerfect and the Office naming conventions was to provide backward compatibility with older versions of GroupWise and WordPerfect Office. As new components have been added to GroupWise, the names of these components have followed the new GroupWise or Novell GroupWise names. For example

- GW—The name of a GroupWise 6.5 domain dictionary file is GWDOM.DC. Look for GW in the names of GroupWise NetWare loadable modules, too.
- NGW—Every GroupWise post office has an important file called NGWGUARD.DB.

Summary

A GroupWise system is a combination of logical and physical components that work in harmony with one another. These components are

- *GroupWise Administrator:* The snap-in software in conjunction with ConsoleOne
- *The GroupWise Directory:* The combination of GroupWise domains and post offices, and Novell eDirectory
- *The Message Transfer System:* The GroupWise MTA and POA
- *The GroupWise Message Store:* The collection of files and directories in a GroupWise post office that contains all of the mail messages and other items in user mailboxes
- *The GroupWise Client:* Your end-users' tools for reading mail, sending new mail, and collaborating with each other

Chapters 2, "Creating a GroupWise System," 3, "Understanding the GroupWise Directory," and 4 will expose you to each of these components from an architectural standpoint.

For More Information

The GroupWise online documentation discusses the components of a GroupWise system. Have a look at the Administration section of this documentation found at `www.novell.com/documentation/lg/gw65`.

CHAPTER 2

Creating a GroupWise System

This chapter traces the creation of a GroupWise system. The goal is to explore the architecture in a way that will better help you understand it. There are some aspects of GroupWise architecture that are easier to explain as a GroupWise system evolves; these aspects will be explored in later chapters.

For the purposes of this chapter, GroupWise 6.5 is going to be installed at the fictional WorldWide Widgets Corporation. This fictional company is used for many examples throughout the book.

NOTE

Don't take this chapter as license to start installing your GroupWise system yet! First learn the architecture. You will want to carefully plan your system using the considerations offered throughout this book, and especially in Chapter 19, "Building Your GroupWise System Correctly." Chapter 19 gives you pointers on how to build your system correctly.

Installing GroupWise

WorldWide Widgets has a mixture of NetWare 5x, NetWare 6x, Windows NT, and Windows 2000 servers on its network. The company also has met one of the most important criteria for installing GroupWise 6.5, which is that its network supports Novell eDirectory. To install GroupWise, follow the steps in the following sections.

Creating the Master GroupWise 6.5 Software Distribution Directory

The GroupWise CDs should be copied onto a network drive. This way you can easily apply patches and make configuration changes to files as needed.

1. Insert the GroupWise 6.5 Administration CD. The screen shown in Figure 2.1 appears.

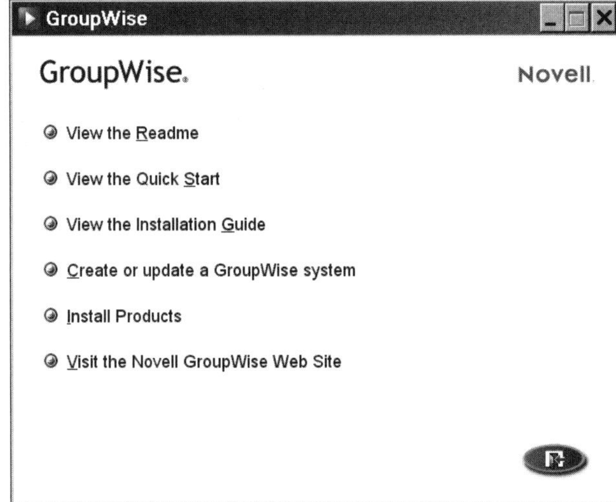

FIGURE 2.1 The GroupWise 6.5 installation screen.

2. Close the GroupWise 6.5 Install Screen if it appears (it will not appear if autorun is not enabled on your PC).
3. Create a location for a new GroupWise 6.5 Software Distribution Directory (SDD). Do not try to overwrite a GroupWise 5.x Software Distribution Directory. For example, you might create `F:\GW65SDD` as your new SDD.
4. Copy the entire GroupWise 6.5 Administration CD contents to the GroupWise 6.5 SDD location that you created in step 3.
5. Delete the directory called `CLIENT` from the GroupWise 6.5 SDD.
6. Insert the GroupWise 6.5 Client CD.
7. Copy the entire `CLIENT` directory on the GroupWise 6.5 Client CD to the <GroupWise 6.5 SDD> directory. There should now be a `CLIENT` within the <GroupWise 6.5 SDD> directory, as there was before the deletion in step 5.

8. Remove the read-only property from the <GroupWise 6.5 SDD>. To do so in Windows Explorer, highlight the <GroupWise 6.5 SDD> (GW65SDD in our example) and select File, Properties. Remove the check mark next to the read-only attribute. When you select OK, you will be asked how much further to apply this attribute—apply the change to the folder, subfolders, and all files.

You are now ready to actually install GroupWise to your network.

Extending the eDirectory/NDS Schema and Install Administration for GroupWise 6.5

In this section you will add new attributes to existing eDirectory objects, such as user objects, and you will add definitions to eDirectory for new object types. This is called *extending the eDirectory schema*.

Novell eDirectory comes with a basic set of definitions for objects and their attributes. When GroupWise extends the schema of eDirectory, it adds new definitions, allowing eDirectory to contain new objects and new attributes for existing eDirectory objects. Novell GroupWise (NGW): Post Office is a new object type that the GroupWise schema extension defines. The NGW: Object ID is a new, GroupWise-specific attribute that is added to the existing eDirectory user class object.

The eDirectory schema definitions are added to eDirectory via standard developer APIs. You can find the GroupWise schema definition information in an ASCII file in the ADMIN folder of the GroupWise 6.5 CD. The name of the file is GwSchema.sch.

If you do not have administrative rights to the root of your eDirectory tree, another administrative user can perform the steps in this section for you. You cannot proceed until the schema has been extended.

The following steps enable you to install the GroupWise Administration software:

1. You must be logged into your Novell eDirectory tree as a user with administrative rights to the tree in order to extend the schema of the eDirectory tree. Supervisor rights are required at the `[Root]` of the eDirectory tree in order to extend the tree schema.
2. If you have ConsoleOne installed on your computer, run ConsoleOne and choose Help, About ConsoleOne to determine the version of ConsoleOne you are running. The version of ConsoleOne that comes

with first shipping version of GroupWise 6.5 is version 1.3.4. If the version of ConsoleOne you are running is older than 1.3.4, you must install the ConsoleOne version that comes with GroupWise 6.5. The process to do so is explained in step 6.

3. Go to the <GroupWise 6.5 Software Distribution Directory>\ADMIN directory and run INSTALL.EXE.

4. Proceed to the Administration Options screen, uncheck the options "Create a new system or update an existing system" and "Copy files to a software distribution directory" (as shown in Figure 2.2), and then click Next.

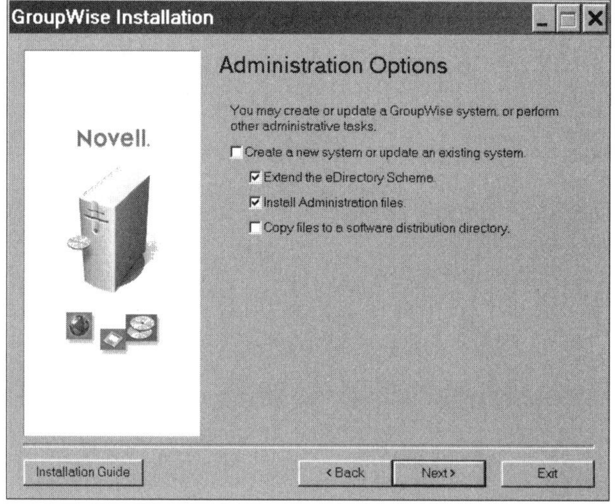

FIGURE 2.2 The GroupWise 6.5 administration installation screen.

5. Select the eDirectory tree in which you intend to create your GroupWise system. Select Next and proceed to extend the schema of your eDirectory tree.

6. Now you need to install ConsoleOne to the GroupWise administrator's computer. Assuming you left the "Install Administration files" check box checked as instructed earlier, you should now be at the Select Languages screen. At the Select Languages screen, check the languages that you want to install for the administration files. Click Next.

NOTE **If you have ConsoleOne and it is newer than ConsoleOne version 1.3.4, which is the version that ships with GroupWise 6.5, skip step 7 that follows. Do not install ConsoleOne; just install the GroupWise 6.5x Snap-ins to ConsoleOne.**

7. (You might already have ConsoleOne 1.3.4 installed. If you do, you do not need to reinstall it.) You will now be at the ConsoleOne Path screen. Verify that this is the path where you want to install ConsoleOne. Select the Install ConsoleOne button. A Java installation routine will be launched. Proceed through the ConsoleOne installation. Even though the ConsoleOne version you are installing is 1.3.4, it defaults to an install path of `C:\Novell\ConsoleOne\1.2`; this does not affect the version of ConsoleOne.
8. After ConsoleOne has been installed (or ConsoleOne is already installed and you are skipping step 7), you will be returned to the ConsoleOne Path screen. Verify that the path to ConsoleOne is correctly indicated, and then select the Next button.
9. At the Ready to Install screen, click Install to begin the GroupWise 6.5 ConsoleOne Snap-in installation.

The following section will establish a new GroupWise system.

Creating a GroupWise System

To create a GroupWise system, you must launch ConsoleOne. To create the GroupWise system and GroupWise primary domain for WorldWide Widgets Corporation, the administrator chooses Tools, GroupWise Utilities, New System.

There is a set of prompts that asks the administrator for information regarding the creation of a GroupWise system. The following sections take a close look at the prompts that are relevant to understanding GroupWise architecture.

Selecting the Software Distribution Directory

Fill in the software distribution directory prompt shown in Figure 2.3, with the path where you installed the GroupWise software (earlier in this chapter, you copied the GroupWise 6.5 CD manually to a directory on a file server). The location where you copied the GroupWise 6.5 CD is the location you should select for the software distribution directory. For example GW65SDD is shown in Figure 2.3.

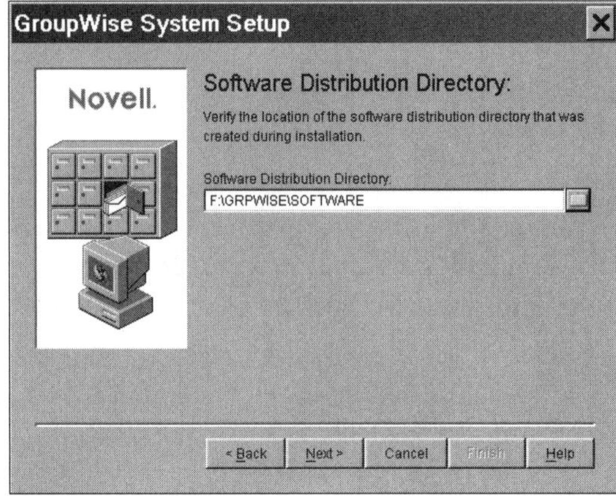

FIGURE 2.3 Prompting for the software distribution directory.

Selecting an eDirectory Tree

You can create GroupWise only in an eDirectory tree that has had its schema extended with the GroupWise schema extensions, as explained earlier. You will be prompted for an eDirectory tree to install GroupWise to, as shown in Figure 2.4. Select the eDirectory tree that you extended the schema for earlier in this chapter.

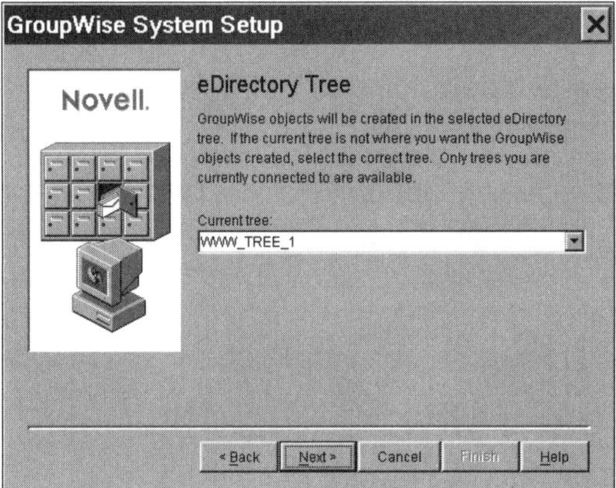

FIGURE 2.4 Prompting for the eDirectory tree.

Choosing a System Name

Now you need to decide on a name for your GroupWise system (see Figure 2.5). The GroupWise system name is rarely referenced again, but it will always be visible in the GroupWise system view in ConsoleOne. If WorldWide Widgets ever wants to enable a feature called *external system synchronization,* it has to share its GroupWise system name with its partner.

Chapter 6, "Using GroupWise System Operations," talks more about external system synchronization.

Beyond external system synchronization, the GroupWise system name rarely becomes a point of interest.

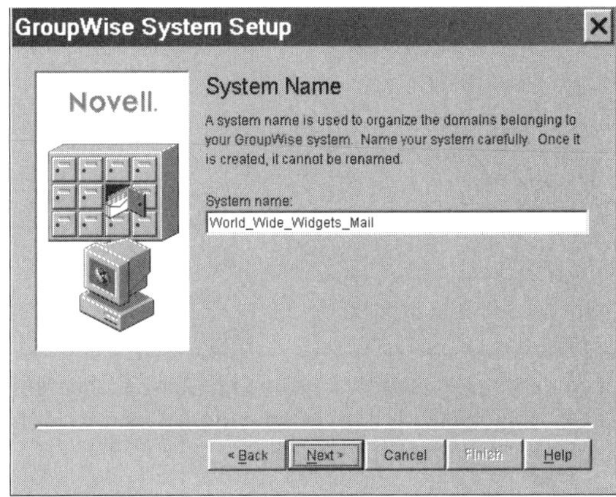

FIGURE 2.5
Prompting for the system name.

Creating the GroupWise Primary Domain

The primary domain is the first thing that actually denotes the physical creation of a GroupWise system.

The primary domain serves as the following:

- The "master" of the GroupWise system.
- An object in eDirectory.
- A set of files and directories/folders needed for any GroupWise domain, physically located at a specific UNC path on a file server.

Choosing Your Primary Domain Name

Choose domain names carefully, because you cannot change them once you've created them. Figure 2.6 shows the prompt for the primary domain name. I suggest using naming conventions that adhere closely with those used in your eDirectory tree and server environment. WorldWide Widgets will call its primary domain **CORP**. Don't use any of the following invalid characters when naming the domain:

- ASCII characters 0-13
- The at sign @
- Braces {}
- Parentheses ()
- A colon :
- A comma ,
- A period .
- A space
- A double quote "

TIP

If possible, keep domain and post office names equal to or shorter than eight characters in length. This makes it easy to have directory names that match the name of the domain and helps avoid confusion.

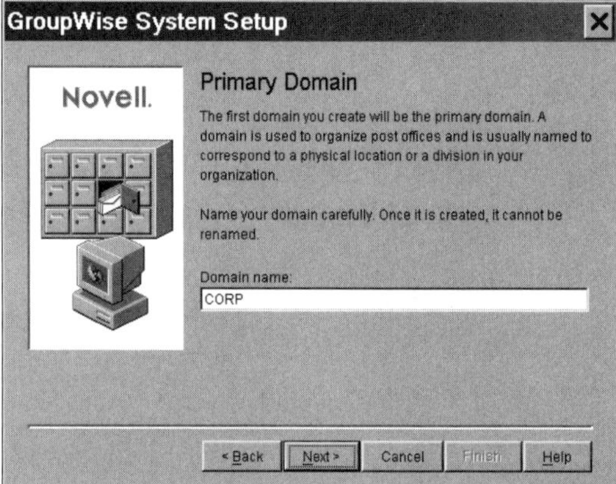

FIGURE 2.6 Naming a primary domain.

Selecting a Primary Domain Directory

This is where the primary domain will physically reside. This directory must be on a file server. It need not be on a NetWare server though; it can also be on a Windows NT/2000 server. Specify a path that is no longer than eight characters in length. The path should not contain spaces or periods. The path should only be made up of letters, numbers, and dashes or underscores.

Never give your users file access to a domain directory. They don't need it, and if they arbitrarily delete files, you might be in a world of hurt.

Specifying the Domain Context

This is where you place the GroupWise primary domain object in your eDirectory tree. The domain context is important only from an administration standpoint. If your company implements security controls on eDirectory objects, for example, you might want to have a container for GroupWise objects. You might want to use organizational role objects to administer trustee assignments to the GroupWise system. In this way, you can control which of the system administrators can perform GroupWise administration operations.

WorldWide Widgets has decided to make its GroupWise domain structure match its eDirectory Organization Unit (OU) structure. In large systems, where operators all over the network are making changes in eDirectory, creating a GroupWise OU helps non-GroupWise administration personnel understand the separate purpose of the GroupWise objects. As shown in Figure 2.7, you will be prompted for the eDirectory OU to place the Primary Domain object into.

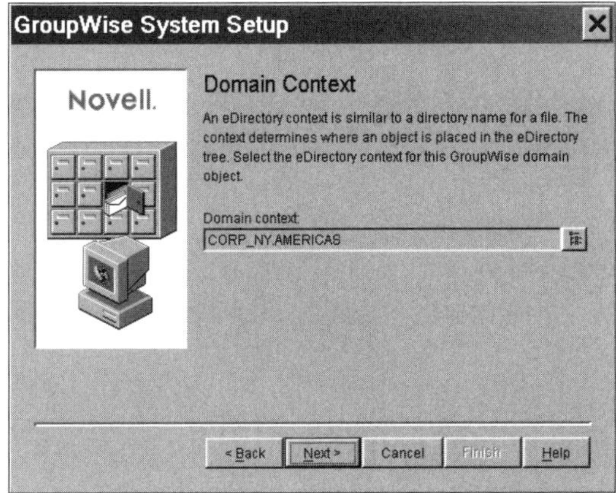

FIGURE 2.7 Primary domain eDirectory context.

If you need to move a GroupWise domain or post office to a new eDirectory container, refer to Chapter 21, "Moving Domains and Post Offices."

Letting GroupWise Know Your Timezone

By specifying the timezone a GroupWise post office or domain is in, you affect how appointment and status message timestamps are created. Make sure to specify the correct timezone information or people will miss appointments. The timezone for the primary domain will be the timezone for the location where the file server is that will house the GroupWise primary domain. Chapter 6 covers timezone administration in more detail.

Giving the Post Office a Name

Although you might not want to create a post office yet, the installation wizard requires you to do so. The name of a post office cannot be changed, so choose wisely!

Giving the Post Office a Home: The Post Office Directory

The post office directory is the physical location for the GroupWise post office. A GroupWise post office is a set of files and a directory structure that denotes a GroupWise post office. All GroupWise post offices have the same kind of structure.

Establishing the Post Office Context

This is where the post office object will be placed in your eDirectory tree. This context is important to your users, for reasons explained further in Chapter 12, "Administering the GroupWise Client." The GroupWise client can use eDirectory to authenticate users to their mailboxes; having the post office in the same context as your users speeds up authentication. If you place post offices in contexts where users have no trustee assignments, you will create administration headaches for yourself later.

NOTE **There is no security risk inherent in allowing users to have browse, read, and compare rights to post office objects in the eDirectory tree.**

Defining a Post Office Link

Each post office communicates with the rest of the GroupWise system through the domain's MTA. In order for the MTA to "talk" with a post office, it needs a way to hand messages to the post office. An MTA can either drop off and pick up files at the post office via a UNC connection, or it can transmit files via TCP/IP to the POA servicing the post office. Figure 2.8 shows the post office link prompt. A UNC link is called a *direct link* in this figure. A TCP/IP link is just as direct, however, and almost always preferred.

- *Direct link:* This method of linking a domain to a post office requires that the MTA have file system rights to the UNC path where the post office is. A direct link is sometimes used, particularly if your GroupWise post office is on the same file server that houses the domain that owns the post office. In most cases, even if a domain and post office are on the same file server, it is better to configure a TCP/IP connection between the MTA and the POA.
- *TCP/IP link:* This is the preferable method for linking the domain's MTA with a post office's POA.

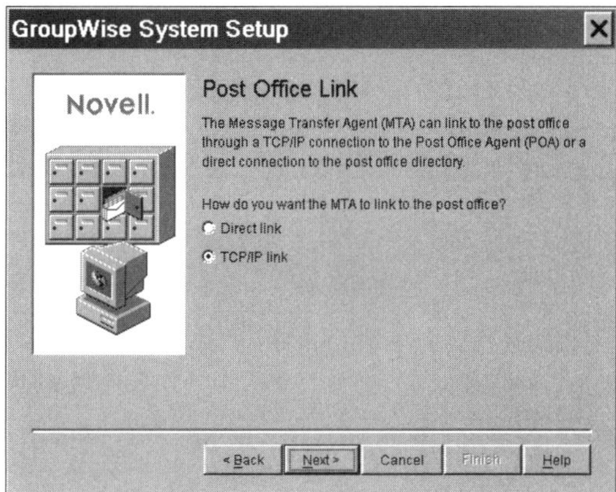

FIGURE 2.8
Post office link.

Selecting Post Office Users

You can select users to be associated with this post office at this point. You also can do this later as you create additional users.

TIP

One advantage to not selecting users for the post office at this point is that GroupWise 6.5 enables you to set a system-wide default password. By not selecting users to add to the GroupWise system at this point, you can set up this default password feature and then add the users to the GroupWise system. You learn more about setting a default system password in Chapter 6.

Summary

This chapter walked you through the creation of a GroupWise system. This chapter also discussed creating a GroupWise system, domain, and post office. You should now be fairly secure in your understanding of the general architecture of a GroupWise system. The next chapter explores the GroupWise directory in greater detail.

CHAPTER 3

Understanding the GroupWise Directory

This chapter explores how the various components of the GroupWise directory fit together. It examines some principles of administration and the flow of administrative messages through the GroupWise system, and it lays the groundwork for a very detailed discussion on troubleshooting and fixing the GroupWise directory in Chapter 22, "Fixing the GroupWise Directory." The GroupWise directory refers to the databases used to manage GroupWise objects.

GroupWise Directory Components

As mentioned in earlier chapters, the GroupWise directory uses both eDirectory and the GroupWise domain and post office databases. eDirectory and the GroupWise domain database (WPDOMAIN.DB) together provide the administration-level directory databases. The portion of the GroupWise directory that is replicated for GroupWise clients to use is the post office database (WPHOST.DB).

GroupWise domain, post office, and message store databases use an underlying architecture called *FLAIM*, which allows for billions of extensible records. Until 1999, eDirectory used a different architecture that was also extensible, but did not work as well for large numbers of records. In 1999, Novell released eDirectory Version 8, which also uses FLAIM as its underlying architecture. Despite the fact that the lowest-level structures are now similar, the two systems are still separate.

Figure 3.1 shows some important architectural concepts that need to be explored:

- When administering GroupWise objects, most of the information goes into the GroupWise FLAIM databases.
- Information in eDirectory is moderately important to GroupWise administration.
- Every GroupWise domain database is essentially identical to every other record in other GroupWise domain databases.
- GroupWise post office databases only accept information that has first flowed through their owning domain.
- Not all information written to a domain database is written to a GroupWise post office database.
- GroupWise post office databases are not modified by GroupWise administration.

FIGURE 3.1 The GroupWise directory databases.

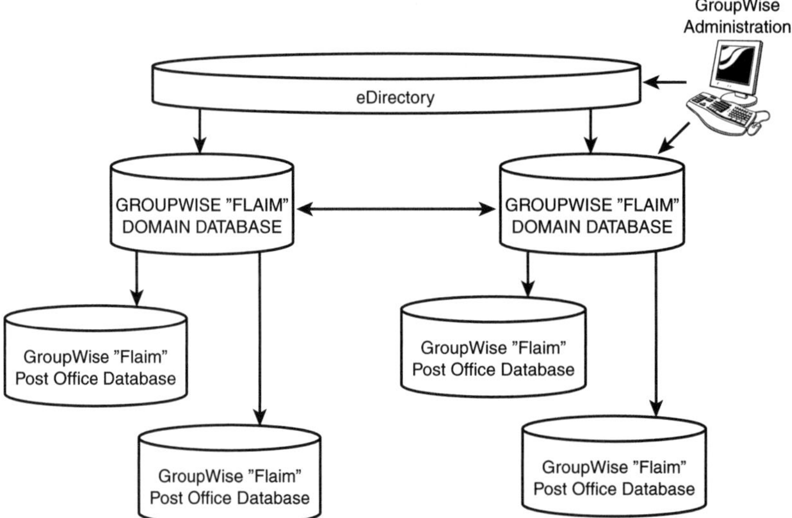

How eDirectory Is Used

It is important to understand that GroupWise evolved from WordPerfect Office. Before a heavy-duty, industry-recognized directory such as eDirectory came along, many applications had to have their own directory. With the release of GroupWise 5x, Novell began the process of merging the GroupWise directory with eDirectory. GroupWise administration requires eDirectory, but the primary domain database is still the ultimate authority in a GroupWise system.

Channeling GroupWise administration through eDirectory gives GroupWise administration two major improvements over versions that did not support eDirectory/Novell Directory Services (NDS) (and over many other applications that do not leverage eDirectory):

- *Authentication security:* In older versions of GroupWise, if users could get into GroupWise administration, they could exert control over any object. Now, access to individual GroupWise objects and their properties can be controlled through eDirectory.
- *Single point of administration:* Most GroupWise customers have already implemented an eDirectory directory tree. Having GroupWise mailboxes associated with their eDirectory user objects makes administration much easier. A phone number change or a name change has to be done only once.

Grafting GroupWise Objects with eDirectory

The process of controlling GroupWise objects through eDirectory is referred to as *grafting*. There are menu options in GroupWise administration that enable administrators to graft a domain, post office, or user into the eDirectory tree. The term *graft* might build a mental image in which a branch is taken from one tree and put on another tree.

Grafting GroupWise objects creates new objects in eDirectory, but those objects are fully contained in the WPDOMAIN.DB file. Most GroupWise objects in an eDirectory tree should be regarded as *aliases,* or *pointers,* to the actual object in the GroupWise FLAIM databases. Grafting objects into eDirectory allows objects to then be controlled through eDirectory.

The GroupWise directory is largely contained in GroupWise FLAIM databases. GroupWise FLAIM databases have their own repair and analysis tools, which are discussed in Chapters 17, "Maintaining the GroupWise System," and 22, "Fixing the GroupWise Directory." Rarely is a GroupWise directory problem fixed by running the eDirectory repair tool—`DSREPAIR`.

The GroupWise Domain Database

A GroupWise domain directory contains a critical file, WPDOMAIN.DB, shown in Figure 3.2. This is the domain database.

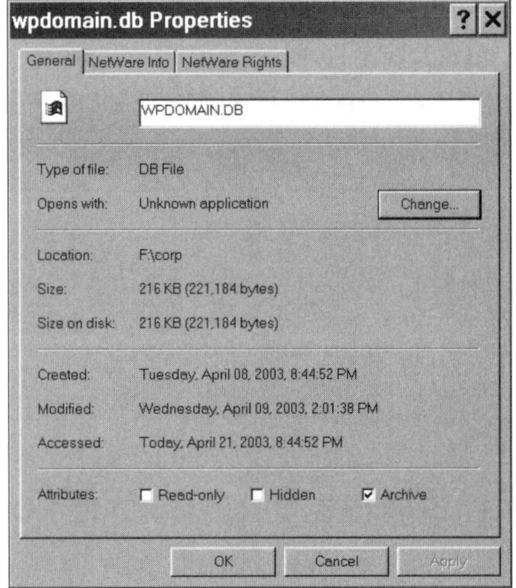

FIGURE 3.2 A GroupWise WPDOMAIN.DB file in a domain directory.

Creating the First WPDOMAIN.DB File (the Primary Domain)

When a GroupWise system is created, a WPDOMAIN.DB file for the primary domain is created based upon the following:

- Information that the administrator inputs
- Information from eDirectory
- Information from the domain structure, or *dictionary file,* called GWDOM.DC

The GWDOM.DC file is located at the root of any domain's directory. The GWDOM.DC file is an ASCII text file that defines the structure for all GroupWise 6.5 domain databases. The GWDOM.DC file should never be edited or modified.

Creating Secondary Domains

When a GroupWise secondary domain is originally created, it is created from information in the WPDOMAIN.DB file from the primary domain and the generic GWDOM.DC file. The information in a GroupWise secondary domain is an exact duplicate of the information in the primary domain. The only thing that makes a primary domain "primary" is that the Domain Type field, shown in Figure 3.3, reads as follows:

```
Domain Type: Primary
```

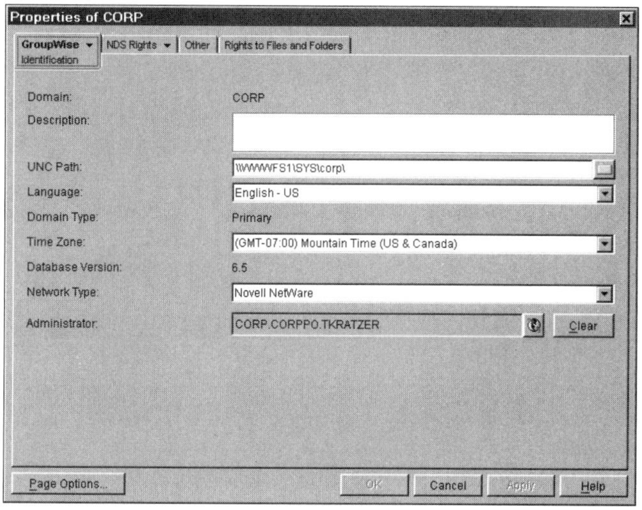

FIGURE 3.3
The domain type for the primary domain.

A secondary domain's domain type, shown in Figure 3.4, reads like this:

```
Domain Type: Secondary
```

How a WPDOMAIN.DB File Changes and Increases in Size

As new objects and users are added to a GroupWise system, those objects are replicated to every WPDOMAIN.DB file in a GroupWise system. Deletions of objects are also replicated to every WPDOMAIN.DB file in a GroupWise system. The only two entities that write to a WPDOMAIN.DB file are the following:

- GroupWise administration snap-ins in ConsoleOne
- The *admin* thread of the GroupWise MTA

Suppose a GroupWise directory update message is sent from the `CORP` domain to the `MFG` domain. The administrator who makes the change is connected to the **CORP** domain, so GroupWise administration snap-ins write the changes to WPDOMAIN.DB for **CORP**. The CORP MTA sends the update to **MFG**. Now the MFG domain's MTA will be responsible for updating the MFG domain database (WPDOMAIN.DB) file.

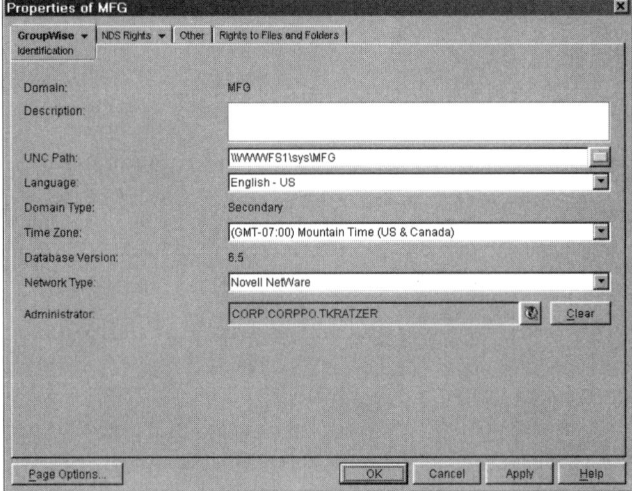

FIGURE 3.4
The domain type for a secondary domain.

The Role of Domain Databases and Information Replication

Ideally, each GroupWise domain database has a record for every object in the GroupWise system. When a GroupWise domain adds an object, it transmits a copy of that object to the primary domain, to be replicated to all other domains. Larger GroupWise systems are in a constant state of change. A change to a GroupWise object should take a short while to replicate to all other domains, but on a large system, "a short while" might mean 15 minutes or more.

This means that if for some reason one of your domain databases is damaged, you should recover it from tape backup or rebuild it, which is always done from the primary domain's database. Recovering a domain database from a backup tape that is more than a day old can result in serious synchronization problems with other domains.

Understanding the Directory Role of the Domain Database

The administration role of the WPDOMAIN.DB is to contain GroupWise objects in a database. With the help of GroupWise administration snap-ins, GroupWise objects in the WPDOMAIN.DB file can be created and modified. Whenever you administer your GroupWise system, GroupWise administration is connected to any one of the WPDOMAIN.DB files in your system. One WPDOMAIN.DB file exists for each domain. GroupWise administration enables you to connect to any one of your domains.

The GroupWise directory is a fully replicated directory. This means the following:

- Every object that `DOMAINA` has ownership of is replicated to `DOMAINB` and `DOMAINC`.
- Every object that `DOMAINB` has ownership of is replicated to `DOMAINA` and `DOMAINC`.
- Every object that `DOMAINC` has ownership of is replicated to `DOMAINA` and `DOMAINB`.

If GroupWise administration is connected to `DOMAINA`, you can still modify almost all of the objects that `DOMAINB` owns (as long as you have the eDirectory rights to that object). This process is explained in the section entitled "Understanding Object Ownership." For those familiar with eDirectory, this object modification model might seem different. The GroupWise replication model is different from eDirectory in these two ways:

- eDirectory uses a partitioned architecture. Although a server might contain eDirectory databases, the objects in those databases do not necessarily represent all the objects in an eDirectory tree.
- eDirectory requires that only servers with replicas of a particular partition be allowed to accept changes to the objects.

Understanding Object Ownership

Every user must be associated with a post office. Every GroupWise post office must be associated with a GroupWise domain. Consider the following scenario:

DOMAINA owns a post office called POST1, and POST1 has Eva Cornish associated with it. In this scenario, the following information can be extrapolated:

- DOMAINA owns POST1.
- Eva Cornish is associated with POST1.
- DOMAINA must own the object Eva Cornish.

Ownership is an important role because it plays a key part in ensuring that an object is properly synchronized across all domain databases (WPDOMAIN.DB files).

How GroupWise Objects Stay Synchronized

Only the GroupWise domain that owns a particular object can officially approve a change to an object. Another domain might propose a change to an object, but that proposal must be approved by the object's owning domain. Here's an example in which the whole process of GroupWise directory changes is drawn out.

Consider the following scenario: DOMAINB owns Eva Cornish. The GroupWise administration snap-ins for ConsoleOne are connected to DOMAINC (a domain that does not own the object being modified) and change the phone number for Eva Cornish.

- DOMAINC—Secondary domain
  - Eva Cornish's phone number is changed.
  - The record for Eva Cornish in DOMAINC's WPDOMAIN.DB file is changed from "safe" to "modify".
  - The proposed change is sent to DOMAINB by DOMAINC's MTA.
  - The proposed change is viewable to the administrator while connected to DOMAINC by selecting Tools, GroupWise System Operations, Pending Operations.

- DOMAINB—Secondary domain
  - DOMAINB's MTA receives the change information from DOMAINC and accepts the change. It changes the user object's phone number in its WPDOMAIN.DB

    - DOMAINB increments the *record version* of this object from version 1 (version 1 was initial creation) to version 2. The fact that the record version value increments to "2" is not propagated to other domains.
    - DOMAINB's MTA creates a message destined to the primary domain telling the primary domain about the change to the object Eva Cornish.
    - DOMAINB's MTA creates a message destined for the post offices that it owns, indicating the change to the object Eva Cornish.

- DOMAINA—Primary domain
    - DOMAINA's MTA receives from **DOMAINB** the change to object Eva Cornish to its WPDOMAIN.DB file.
    - DOMAINA's MTA creates a message and sends this message to all other domains (except **DOMAINB**), telling all other domains to rewrite this entire user object record with the information that the primary domain is sending about this object record.
    - DOMAINA's MTA creates a message and sends this message to each of its own post offices indicating the change to Eva Cornish.
- DOMAINC—Secondary domain
    - DOMAINC's MTA receives from **DOMAINA** the change to object Eva Cornish to its WPDOMAIN.DB file.
    - DOMAINC changes the record on object Eva Cornish from "modify" to "safe".
    - DOMAINC sends a message to each of its own post offices indicating the change to the object Eva Cornish.
- All other secondary domains
    - DOMAINX's MTA receives from **DOMAINA** the change to object Eva Cornish to its WPDOMAIN.DB file.
    - DOMAINX's MTA sends a message to each of its own post offices indicating the change to object Eva Cornish.

From the preceding synchronization detail, the following conclusions can be drawn about how objects are synchronized to the GroupWise directory:

- If an administrator has eDirectory rights to do so, he/she can be connected to any domain in the system and modify objects associated with another domain.
- The only domain that can approve an object change is the domain that owns the object.
- The only domain that can propagate object changes to an entire GroupWise system is the GroupWise primary domain.
- Each domain is responsible for propagating directory changes to the post offices that it owns.

Knowing the Agent Information Role of the Domain Database

When a GroupWise MTA loads, it must point to the root of the domain directory, which contains the WPDOMAIN.DB file. The WPDOMAIN.DB file provides three basic types of information to the MTA:

- *Configuration information:* When to connect, how many threads to load, and so on
- *Link information:* How to establish a connection with the other domains on the system
- *Routing information:* Discovering the correct route to use to send messages to their destinations

The MTA specifically reads the MTA object record associated with the domain that the MTA points to. Under Tools, GroupWise Diagnostics, Record Enumerations, this record is found in the "Message Transfer Agents by domain" section.

The other processes that access the WPDOMAIN.DB file directly are the GroupWise Internet Agent (GWIA), the WebAccess Agent, and the various GroupWise gateways. They all need the same basic kind of information:

- *Configuration information:* When to connect, how many threads to load, and so on
- *Addressing information:* Looking up users to deliver inbound mail to them

The GroupWise Post Office Database

Every GroupWise post office must have a WPHOST.DB file. The WPHOST.DB file for a post office provides the following:

- The GroupWise client address book
- Lots of information for the GroupWise client and post office agent (POA) that aren't readily apparent to a user

A GroupWise WPHOST.DB file is created when a post office is created. The WPHOST.DB file is created using the following:

- Information from the WPDOMAIN.DB file of the GroupWise domain that owns the post office
- The dictionary file called GWPO.DC located in all GroupWise domain and post office directories

How a WPHOST.DB File Is Modified

When a change needs to be replicated down to a post office, the domain MTA for the domain that owns the post office needing the replication sends the object update information to the POA servicing the post office. The POA has an admin thread that updates the WPHOST.DB file with the change.

The only entity that updates a WPHOST.DB file is the GroupWise POA. This is different than how a WPDOMAIN.DB file is modified. The WPDOMAIN.DB file is modified by the GroupWise MTA and by GroupWise administration. So when an administrator makes changes that affect GroupWise, those changes are written to the WPDOMAIN.DB that the GroupWise administration is connected to. The administrator's workstation actually commits those changes to the GroupWise WPDOMAIN.DB. In the case of post offices, an administrator's workstation does not touch the WPHOST.DB file. The only time an administrator's workstation would touch a WPHOST.DB file is when the administrator uses Tools, GroupWise Utilities, System Maintenance to run routines on a post office.

Contents of a WPHOST.DB File

A WPHOST.DB file is not a mirror of the entire GroupWise system. There are records related to domains that do not need to be replicated to a WPHOST.DB file. Because the WPHOST.DB file is not a general depository file like the WPDOMAIN.DB file, the content of a WPHOST.DB file is far tighter than a WPDOMAIN.DB file.

WPHOST.DB as an Address Book

When users go into the GroupWise address book and access the Novell GroupWise address book (otherwise known as the system address book), they are accessing information contained in the WPHOST.DB file. The information accessible in any of the other tabs of the GroupWise address book is not contained in the WPHOST.DB file.

WPHOST.DB for Identity Purposes

The WPHOST.DB file is read by the GroupWise client in order to help the GroupWise client create an appropriate environment for the users. The WPHOST.DB file helps the client and the POA identify which USERXXX.DB file in the message store is the user's database. The WPHOST.DB file helps to hold administrator-defined settings that control how GroupWise preferences are configured. A WPHOST.DB file has a hidden password within it; that password is given to all databases below a post office. The password read from the WPHOST.DB file helps a GroupWise POA gain access to all the other message store databases in a post office. This adds a level of security to the GroupWise system. It prevents someone from creating their own GroupWise system and simply copying the message store databases into a different GroupWise post office.

What the WPHOST.DB File Provides to the POA

The POA reads its configuration information from the WPHOST.DB file. So when a POA is configured in ConsoleOne, those changes are replicated down to the WPHOST.DB file for the POA to read.

The POA discovers other information from the WPHOST.DB, including the following:

- The administrator for the domain that owns this post office, which is important so that problems can be reported by the POA to the administrator.

- The IP addresses and ports of the POAs that service the other post offices in the GroupWise system. This helps when a POA needs to hand a user off to another post office so that it can proxy into a user's e-mail on a different post office.
- The names of all mail recipients (users and resources), gateways, domains, and post offices. This way, if a user types an incorrect name, the POA can immediately tell the user of the error.
- The TCP/IP port and address of the domain MTA that owns this post office.

Summary

The GroupWise directory is a fully replicated directory. All objects are broadcast to all other GroupWise domains. The GroupWise directory is separate from eDirectory, but is integrated with eDirectory to use the administration strengths of eDirectory. For example, without eDirectory rights to the primary domain, a secondary domain administrator can be excluded from being able to make system-wide changes in the GroupWise system.

CHAPTER 4

Understanding the GroupWise Information Store

The GroupWise information store consists of messages in post offices and documents in libraries. The GroupWise information store follows a *distributed* or *partitioned* model, in which different store files contain different portions of the entire store.

This chapter looks at these store files individually. It also details their relationships and considers the information store as a whole, spanning multiple post offices. The objective of this chapter is to help you understand GroupWise architecture well enough to effectively troubleshoot your system. The concepts discussed in this chapter will be applied in Parts IV, "Practical Administration," and V, "Applied Architecture," and especially in Chapter 17, "Maintaining the GroupWise System."

The Post Office Directory Structure

The information store is entirely contained in the post office directory and its subdirectories. If you have more than one post office, your information store spans post offices, with each local store containing items particular to the users belonging to that post office. Figure 4.1 shows a post office directory.

There are four types of directories relevant to the discussion of the GroupWise information store, as follows:

- Input and output queues
- The OFUSER and OFMSG directories

- The OFFILES directories
- The GWDMS (GroupWise document management system) directory structure

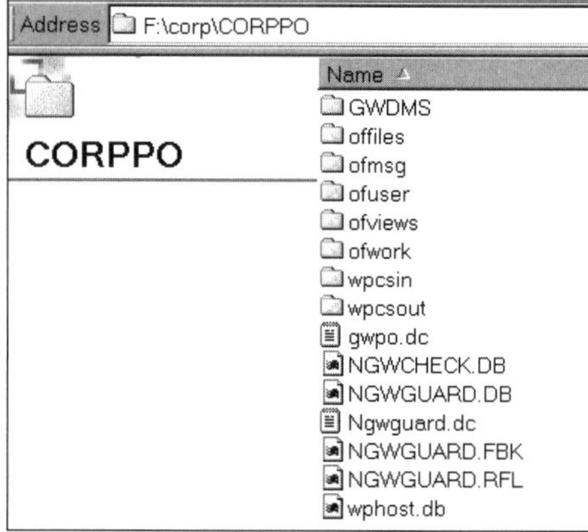

FIGURE 4.1 Post office directory structure as viewed through Windows Explorer.

How Input and Output Queues Are Used

There are three queue directory structures in a GroupWise post office. These queues store message files that are coming into the post office from another location, or that are outbound to another location.

The WPCSIN Directory

The WPCSIN directory, whether you see it at the post office level or under a domain directory, always does the same thing. It is the input queue for a GroupWise MTA; see Figure 4.2.

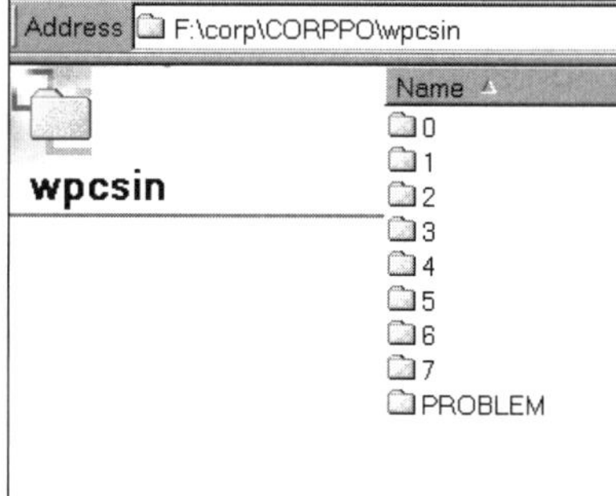

FIGURE 4.2 The WPCSIN directory under a GroupWise post office.

The 0-7 directories under WPCSIN hold message transport files that need to be transferred to another location (domain, post office, or gateway). This means all the files here are outbound messages, from the perspective of the post office.

The naming convention is a holdover from the old WordPerfect Office days. This directory name is really an abbreviation for WordPerfect Connection Server INput.

The queue directories were named from the perspective of the MTA. So no matter at which level you see the WPCSIN or WPCSOUT directories, think of their functions from the perspective of the MTA. Hence, the WPCSIN directory at the post office level is the MTA's input queue, and the WPCSOUT directory is the MTA's output directory.

Aside from the 0-7 queues, you will see a PROBLEM directory. This directory contains files that could not be processed for some reason, with the exception of files that could not be processed because a link was down. These files go into a holding queue elsewhere.

The 0-7 Directory

Following is an explanation of the subdirectories of WPCSIN. Each of these numbered directories serves a different purpose:

0: Live, interactive request messages (busy searches, remote library queries, and agent restart)

1: GroupWise remote mode (mailbox synchronization requests, shared folder and shared address book replication messages)

2: Administration updates and high-priority mail messages

3: Status messages from high-priority mail

4: Normal priority mail messages

5: Status messages from normal priority mail

6: Low priority mail messages

7: Status messages from low priority mail

You will find these directories in many places on the GroupWise system. Everywhere you find them, the queue assignments for each directory remain the same.

The WPCSOUT Directory

The meaning behind the name of the WPCSOUT directory is **W**ord**P**erfect **C**onnection **S**erver **OUT**put. This directory, as shown in Figure 4.3, contains things that the MTA (long, long ago known as the *connection server*) has transmitted to the post office. This directory contains messages that are inbound for the post office.

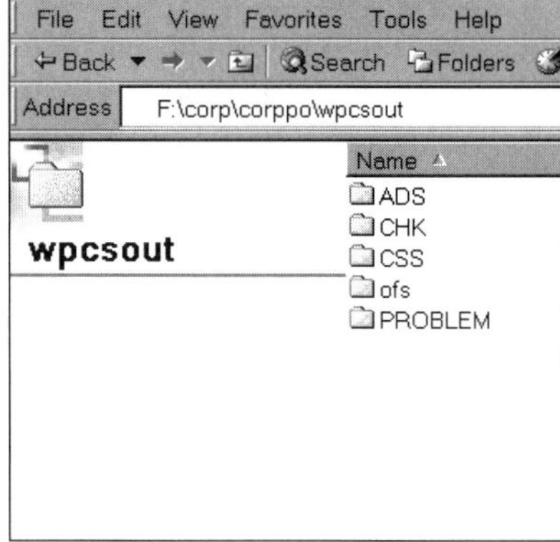

FIGURE 4.3 The WPCSOUT directory under a GroupWise post office.

There are five subdirectories off of WPCSOUT: ADS, CHK, OFS, CSS, and PROBLEM. The ADS, CHK, and OFS directories contain the familiar 0-7 queues. The CHK directory is new with GroupWise version 6 and later. It only has directories 0-3 and the DEFER directory.

- ADS: Administration updates
- CHK: GWCHECK jobs sent to the POA (Post Office Agent)
- OFS: Information store updates (user e-mail, notes, tasks, and so on)
- CSS: Messages that tell the POA to restart
- PROBLEM: Where problem messages go

Remember, though, that these are queues. User e-mail does not exist in the OFS/0-7 structure for very long. It is dropped there by the MTA, or by the POA's MTP thread, and then the POA processes the item further.

The OFWORK Directory

The only directory off of the OFWORK directory is the OFDIRECT subdirectory. The OFWORK\OFDIRECT directory is used by the GroupWise remote client. Queue directories are created for each remote user, and these directories serve as input and output queues for remote requests, which then move through the WPCSIN\1 or WPCSOUT\OFS\1 directories for processing.

The GroupWise 6.5 versions use the OFWORK\OFDIRECT directory much less now when the GroupWise client is in remote mode. Updated remote technology (live remote) bypasses this directory most of the time, which facilitates much quicker access for remote users. The only time the OFWORK\OFDIRECT queues are used is when the GroupWise client is using an older *batch* remote mode to communicate with the post office.

The Function of the OFUSER and OFMSG Directories

The core of the GroupWise information store is found in the OFUSER and OFMSG directories. These directories contain the user and message databases in which all mail items are stored as database records. The section of this chapter titled "The Core of the Messaging System" covers the user and message databases.

The Purpose of the OFFILES Directories

In most GroupWise systems, the majority of the disk space (often up to 80 percent) that is used by the information store is actually used by attachment files and BLOB files (***B***inary ***L***arge ***OB***jects) in the OFFILES directory structure. The OFFILES directory has up to 248 subdirectories, hexadecimally numbered. Figure 4.4 shows a portion of an OFFILES directory structure.

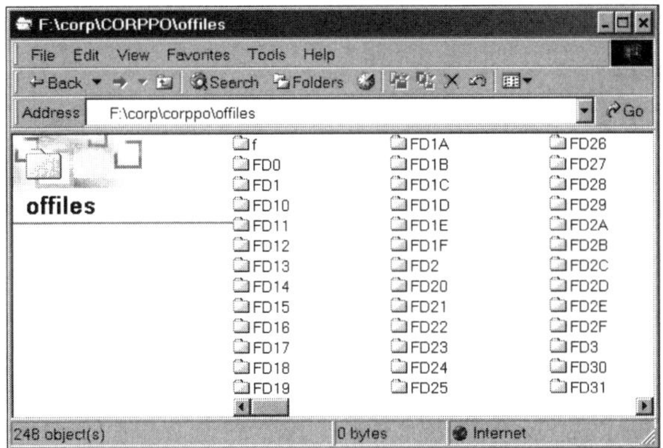

FIGURE 4.4
The OFFILES directory structure found under a GroupWise post office.

Storing Libraries in the GWDMS Directory Structure

The GWDMS directory and its subdirectories are the home for any GroupWise libraries that have been created under this post office. Figure 4.5 shows one library created under this post office's GWDMS directory.

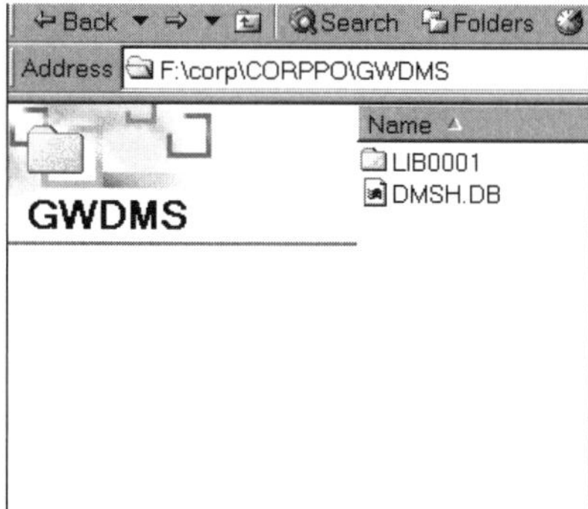

FIGURE 4.5 The GWDMS directory structure found under a GroupWise post office.

In Figure 4.7, the GWDMS directory structure has been expanded to illustrate the deeper structure. More discussion about the GroupWise document management system is in the section titled "The GroupWise Document Management System."

The Core of the Messaging System

The exploration of the post office directory structure earlier in this chapter glossed over the relationships between the various files. This section covers these relationships in detail.

The User Database

Every user mailbox in the GroupWise system is assigned to a unique user database per post office. These files are found in the OFUSER directory. They follow the naming convention USER*xxx*.DB, where *xxx* is replaced with the three-character file ID for the user.

Customers who have migrated from WordPerfect Office days might on occasion have users with a two-character file ID.

This *file ID,* or *FID,* is alphanumeric, which means that you can have up to 46,656 uniquely named user databases on each GroupWise post office. The FID must be unique at the post office level, but no such restrictions exist system-wide. Users are also assigned a *globally unique ID,* or *GUID,* to ensure uniqueness system-wide, but this string is far too long to be conveniently used as part of a filename.

Contents of a User Database

The user database contains the following types of records:

- Pointers
- Personal items
- Personal address books
- Preferences

These four record types are explained in the sections that follow.

Pointers

When you open a user mailbox with a GroupWise client, you will see a list of folders, and in each folder you will see different items. These are simply database records. Each item record contains enough data to make the display meaningful, but the item itself usually exists in a different database. The item records found in the user database serve as *pointers* to the items in message databases. There are also special pointers, called *document references,* that point to records in GroupWise libraries. Chapter 14, "Library and Document Administration," talks more about document references.

Personal Items

Some items are completely contained in the user database, however. These *posted* or *personal* items do not have recipients or senders. Personal notes, tasks, and appointments, as well as posted items, fall into this category.

Personal Address Books

Addresses that users enter and groups that users create exist in the *personal address books.* One such book is the *frequent contacts list,* which is populated automatically with the addresses of individuals with whom you send or receive e-mail.

Preferences

Many user settings and preferences are kept in the user database. These include rules, send options, categories, button bars, proxies, signature options, and the user password. Other settings, such as window positions, are kept in the Windows Registry.

What Is Contained in the Message Databases

On every GroupWise post office, you find up to 25 message databases. These files follow the naming convention MSGn.DB, where *n* is a number from 0 to 24. Message databases contain group items—items that have been sent from one user to another user or users.

When a message is delivered to a user, that user gets a pointer in his/her user database. The pointer points to the actual message item record in a message database. When a user reads a subject line from the Mailbox folder, the text comes from the item record in the user database. When that user double-clicks the message to open it, the pointer is followed, and the resulting window is populated from the appropriate item record in a message database.

The User Database/Message Database Relationship

When a GroupWise user sends a message, the complete item record is first written to the sender's message database (which is shared with other users). Next, a pointer is written to the sender's user database. This shows up as a sent item. If the message was sent to a user in the same post office as the sender, the recipient's user database gets a pointer to the message, which exists in the message database. If the recipient exists in a post office different than the sender's, when the message arrives at the destination, it is written first to the same message database as the sender's. The destination user's user database then receives a pointer to the local message database.

Every message a user sends will be written to the same message database. Each user is assigned to a message database for sending based on the user

FID. This means that the 46,656 possible FIDs map to 25 possible message databases.

Item records in message databases contain all data pertaining to that item, including status information—when it was delivered, opened, deleted, or any other action performed against it. If items are attached to a message, they will also be included as part of that item record, unless the item is larger than 2KB. Attachments, message bodies, or other item fields that exceed 2048 bytes in length are written as separate records called *binary large objects* (*BLOBs*).

Binary Large Objects (BLOB Files)

In the OFFILES directory, there are 248 subdirectories. Each of these can contain binary large object files. These BLOB files are stand-alone records. They are referenced as records by pointers in user and message databases, and they contain any field data for item record fields that exceed 2048 bytes in length. Following are just a few examples of how BLOB files are created:

- **With attachments:** If you attach a 2MB file to a mail message, you end up creating a BLOB file in the OFFILES structure, as well as a message record in your assigned message database. If your attachment is less than 2KB, however (say, a 1000-byte autoexec.bat file), the attachment is encoded as a field in that message record, and it exists entirely within your assigned message database.
- **With long messages:** If you type a 10-page message and send it, your mail item exists as a record in the message database you are assigned to, but the text of that message is now in a BLOB file somewhere in the OFFILES structure. This is simply because the length of your message exceeds the 2KB limit stored in each record of the message database.
- **With multiple addressees:** If you address a message to every user in your company, your TO: field will very likely exceed 2048 bytes in length. Thus, your message body record could exist in your assigned message database (if it's under 2KB), but the distribution list for that message will be in a BLOB file.

BLOB files are given hexadecimal names with alphanumeric extensions. They are encrypted using GroupWise's native 40-bit encryption, and they are compressed as well. BLOB files in the OFFILES structure cannot be read independently; they must be opened by following the appropriate item pointers via the GroupWise client.

The Purpose of the Deferred Message Database

In the OFMSG directory, there is a 26th database, used for delayed delivery messages and for special item lists used by the system when GroupWise mailboxes are moved between post offices. This file is named NGWDFR.DB, and is called the *deferred message database.*

There are two operations a user can perform that will result in records being written to this database:

- Sending a message with Delay delivery checked
- Sending a message with Expiration date checked

Both of these options can be checked for individual items from the Send Options tab of a message you are composing. These settings can be made for all items by choosing Tools, Options, Send from the GroupWise client.

Delayed Delivery

When delayed messages are sent, GroupWise must write to four places:

- *Message database:* The message database, assigned to this user for send operations, gets the item record.
- *User database (of the sender):* The user database gets a pointer, as usual.
- *Deferred message BLOB:* The message in its entirety is kept in a special BLOB file. These BLOB files are kept in the OFFILES\FD0–FDF directories.
- *Deferred message database:* NGWDFR.DB gets a pointer to that item record, along with a date indicating when the item should be delivered to its recipients.

The reason the message is placed in its entirety as a BLOB file is because the message should not show up in the recipient's mailbox until the delivery time. Entries in the NGWDFR.DB tell the POA when to deliver a message, as well as which BLOB file corresponds to that message.

Messages with Expiration Dates

When a message is sent with an expiration date, it is sent normally. That is, records exist in the sender's user database, the recipient's user database, and the sender's assigned message database. An additional record is placed in

NGWDFR.DB: a pointer to the message database record, along with the date that record should be deleted if it has not yet been opened by the recipient.

Although you can set expiration date options globally, this is a very poor way to manage mailbox size. Expired items are deleted only if they are unread, and the NGWDFR.DB database file will grow to be quite large if it must keep track of every sent message.

How Prime User Databases Are Made

To explain the function of a prime user database, this section uses variables, like in high school algebra.

A prime variable is one that represents a new iteration of the original variable. A prime user database is a new iteration of the original user database, containing only a subset of the contents of that original database.

Now, if you are not mathematically inclined, that example might not work. Here's an approach to the prime user database in terms of functionality.

When a user shares a folder or address book with a user on another post office, a prime user database will be created on that post office. This database will contain any shared folders or address books the user has shared with anyone on that post office.

The items that go into a shared folder are written either to the appropriate message database on the sharee's post office, or, in the case of personal and posted discussion items, are written directly to the prime user database.

Prime user databases cannot be named the same way user databases are. On large systems, the capability to create uniquely named databases would be compromised. Thus, they are named as follows: PU*nnnnnn*.DB, where *nnnnnn* is a six-digit number. This number is in two-byte hexadecimal pairs, beginning with 020101.

The first shared folder to arrive at a post office will arrive in PU020101.DB, regardless of which user shared the folder. The next user who shares a folder or an address book with that post office will end up creating PU020102.DB.

PU databases are created only for folders or address books that are shared across post offices. If they are shared with users on the same post office only, they will be accessed through the sharing user's USERxxx.DB file.

Using the Mailbox Index to Find Mailbox Items

Every item on the GroupWise system is full-text indexed. This allows the powerful Find feature of the GroupWise client to locate items in your mailbox, even if you have forgotten which folder you filed them in. This full-text index is created by the POA during the QuickFinder Indexing process.

There are actually two sets of indexes in a GroupWise post office. The *mailbox index* is found in OFUSER/INDEX. There is a *library index* as well, which will be discussed later in this chapter.

In the OFUSER/INDEX directory, there are two types of files:

- **.IDX:* The *permanent index files.* They are updated and renamed at the end of each day. There is typically one of these for each user mailbox.
- **.INC:* The *incremental index files.* They are created during each QuickFinder Indexing run, and at the end of each day they are appended to the appropriate *.IDX files.

The names of these files are based on the time they were created or updated. The filenames are in hexadecimal format, so the file 000000F1.INC was created before the file 000000FF.INC. Index files are discussed further when GroupWise document management is fully explained in Chapter 14.

Keeping Track of Databases with the Guardian Database

With all the various files floating around in a GroupWise post office directory, a central naming authority is required. The NGWGUARD.DB file, or the *guardian database,* is the central naming authority. This file contains a catalog of every database in the GroupWise information store on this post office. Any process that needs to work with a GroupWise database must first hook into the guardian database.

Because NGWGUARD.DB represents a potential single-point-of-failure, the GroupWise POA backs this file up each time it loads, as well as at midnight. Here's how the process works:

1. The POA loads and checks the structure of NGWGUARD.DB.

   If it checks out okay, go to step 5.
2. The POA renames the bad NGWGUARD.DB to NGWGUARD.DBA.

3. The POA copies the last backup, NGWGUARD.FBK, to NGWGUARD.DB.
4. The POA writes all transactions from NGWGUARD.RFL (the guardian roll-forward log) to NGWGUARD.DB.

   The POA now has a clean NGWGUARD.DB, with all transactions made since the last backup rolled back into it.
5. The POA copies NGWGUARD.DB to NGWGUARD.FBK and to OFMSG\GUARDBAK\NGWGUARD.FBK.
6. Delete NGWGUARD.RFL and create a fresh, blank version of this file.
7. When changes are made to NGWGUARD.DB, write these changes to NGWGUARD.RFL.

This is how the changes between guardian backups are stored for recovery.

The User and Message Database Relationship

It might be helpful at this point to illustrate the way the user and message databases work together. Figure 4.6 shows the relationship between user and message databases.

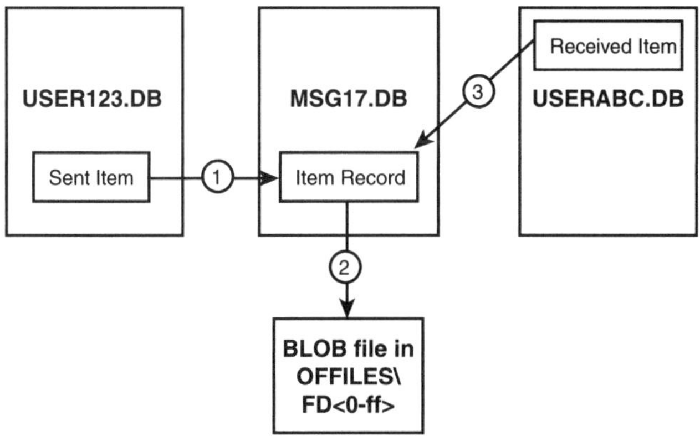

FIGURE 4.6 The relationship between user and message databases.

In the example in Figure 4.6, the user assigned to USER123.DB has sent a message to another user. USER123.DB is assigned to send through MSG17.DB, and has sent to USERABC.DB. The following numbers correspond to the numbered arrows in Figure 4.6:

1: In the USER123.DB file, there is a record for a sent item. This record has a pointer to the message item record in MSG17.DB.

2: In MSG17.DB, there is an item record that was created by USER123. This item contains an attachment that is larger than 2048 bytes, so that attachment data is written to a BLOB file. The item record contains a pointer to this BLOB file in the OFFILES directory structure.

3: In USERABC.DB, there is a record for the item received from USER123. This record contains a pointer to the message item record in MSG17.

From this simplified illustration, you can see that even if a dozen users on a post office have a copy of a message in their inbox, that message record exists only once in the appropriate message database. An attachment sent to several people is written to only one BLOB file.

The GroupWise Document Management System

If a GroupWise post office has no libraries, the GWDMS directory will not contain any data. Once libraries have been created, though, the structure beneath GWDMS becomes fairly complex.

Shared Document Management Services Database (DMSH)

This file, DMSH.DB, exists at the root of the GWDMS directory structure. It contains lookup tables for document type and other administrator-defined document property fields, as well as a list of the libraries defined under this post office. It does not contain any document data, but it is critical to the functionality of the document management system on this post office.

Library Directories and Naming Conventions

Regardless of what you name your library, the library directories created under the GWDMS directory follow a numeric naming convention, beginning with LIB0001 and hexadecimally numbered through LIB00FF.

The last two characters of the directory name become the *library number.* As you can see in Figure 4.7, this number is used throughout the library directory structure for the naming of files found in library directories.

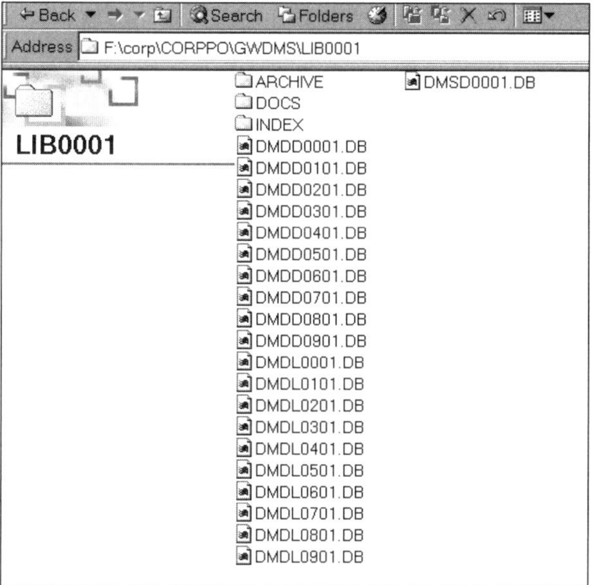

FIGURE 4.7
The library directory name is reflected in the name of each of the files contained therein.

In Figure 4.7, the last two characters of every file in the LIB0001 directory are 01 (excluding the .DB extensions, of course). Following is a look at each of these databases in turn.

Library Database

DMSD00*xx*.DB is the library database, where *xx* is replaced with the two-digit hexadecimal library number. This database contains the table of document numbers, as well as property-sheet field layout information for this library. It contains no document data but is critical to the function of the library.

Document Properties Database (DMDD)

There are 10 document properties database files; they should be treated as a single database that has been partitioned into 10 files. The naming convention is DMDD*ppxx*.DB, where *pp* is replaced by the partition number 00 through 09, and *xx* is replaced by the library number.

The document properties database contains all information entered into document property sheets. This includes document subject, author, type, associated application, and much more. The property sheet is one of the key benefits to the GroupWise document management system, because it allows information about the document to be stored and searched for independently of the document itself, while maintaining a relationship to the document.

Each document record contains three kinds of pointers. The first is to the document BLOB file (discussed later in the section "Document BLOB Files"). The second is to the document's activity log (discussed in the next section). The third pointer points to any user database that contains a document reference to this document. This pointer is used to provide the mailbox indexing process with a word-list file for this document. In this way, a search for full-text of the document returns the document reference, even if the user did not specify a search of GroupWise libraries.

The last digit of the document number indicates in which DMDD partition the document's property sheet record resides. For example, document 1762 in this library is referenced in DMDD0201.DB, and document 21265's properties are in DMDD0501.DB.

Document Logging Database (DMDL)

There are also 10 document logging database files. Again, they should be treated as a single database spread across 10 partitions. The naming convention is DMDL*ppxx*.DB, where *pp* is the partition number 00 through 09, and *xx* is the library number.

The document-logging database contains all activity logs for documents in the GroupWise libraries. Any action that affects a document is logged in this database, including opening, closing, viewing, downloading, uploading, and deleting. Also recorded in the DMDL files is the file name for the document BLOB upon which the logged action was performed. When a document is viewed, the BLOB filename does not change, but any action that changes document content (closing it and, hence, checking it back in with possible changes) results in a new BLOB file being created.

Document BLOB Files

Although the DOCS directory structure is very similar to OFFILES, the contents of the 255 DOCS subdirectories are very different from the OFFILES BLOBs.

Document BLOB files are created for every document, regardless of document size. Whereas OFFILES BLOBs are created only when field data exceeds 2048 bytes in length, document BLOBs are created even for a 0-byte document.

Word-List Files

There is another kind of BLOB in the DOCS subdirectories. *Word-list files* are created for each document when that document is indexed. These files contain, as their name suggests, a list of every word in that document. These files are used to build the .INC files (incremental index files), and are also used to provide mailbox indexes with the full-text information for any document references they might contain.

Document Compression

Document BLOB files are encrypted and compressed, just like OFFILES BLOBs, but they contain information that allows them to be manually opened by certain GroupWise users. The GroupWise client can read a BLOB file directly and determine whether the GroupWise user is supposed to have access to this BLOB (a user with the manage right for this library, or a user who has edited the document in the past). If the user is cleared for the document, it will be re-imported, and a new BLOB and property sheet created. This might be useful for restoring documents that have been deleted, but whose BLOB files exist on backup media.

Document BLOB files are typically around 50% smaller than the documents in their native formats. Pure text documents can be reduced to 10% of their original size, whereas compressed graphic formats (such as GIF or JPEG documents) cannot be reduced.

Document Index

All documents are full-text indexed. This is another selling point of GroupWise document management as a solution for document storage. Documents can be found using the GroupWise client to search for words they contain, or for field data recorded in their property sheets.

Inside the INDEX subdirectory, there are 10 active and permanent index files. These files have an .IDX extension. There are also many .INC files containing the incremental indexes. Just like the mailbox index, the POA QuickFinder Indexing process creates the document index. The .INC files are created from the word-list BLOB files discussed earlier. At the end of the day, all .INC file content is written into the .IDX files, and the .IDX filenames are updated.

Document Reference Relationships

Figure 4.8 explores the relationships between the various GroupWise information store databases when document references are being employed.

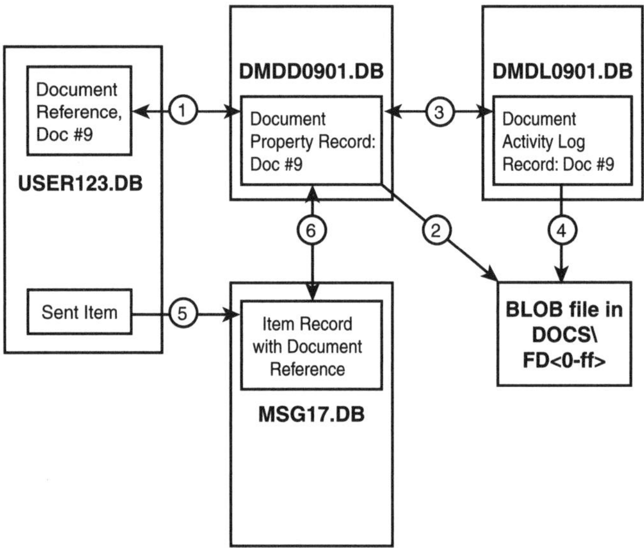

FIGURE 4.8 The complex system of pointers created when document references are employed.

The following is a discussion of Figure 4.8:

- The user assigned to USER123.DB creates a document in a GroupWise library. It is the ninth document created in this library, and it has been assigned document number 9.
- This library is the first one created on this post office, and it is in the LIB0001 directory.
- USER123 has also created a document reference, a pointer in his Documents folder enabling him to quickly find document number 9.
- USER123 attaches this document reference to a mail message and sends it to another user.

The following numbered items correspond to the numbered arrows in Figure 4.8.

1: The document reference is a pointer to the document property record. The document property record has a back link to this document reference (the arrow points both ways). Because this is document number 9, library 1, its property sheet is in DMDD0901.DB.

2: The document property record has a pointer to the actual document BLOB file in the DOCS directory structure.

3: The document property record has a pointer to the activity log record for this document. The activity log has a back link to the property record (again, the arrow points both ways).

4: The activity log record for this document is in DMDL0901.DB, because this is document number 9 in library 1. This record has a pointer to the BLOB file for this document.

5: When the user sends the document reference, a message item record is created in MSG17.DB. USER123.DB has a pointer to this item record.

6: The item record in MSG17.DB contains a document reference, which means it has a pointer to the document property record in DMDD0901.DB. That document property record has a back link to MSG17.DB.

NOTE

For simplicity's sake, the recipient's mailbox is not shown in Figure 4.8. That mailbox would have only a pointer to MSG17.DB for the received item.

The document property record "knows" more about this document than any other database or record shown. When the POA needs to index this document, it reads this property record to find all document references and makes sure that the word-list generated for this document is accessible when the mailboxes containing those references are indexed.

Summary

The GroupWise information store employs a mixture of strategies. Partitioning is used on user mailboxes so that message items are not unnecessarily replicated. A different sort of partitioning is used on document property and activity databases, in order to keep these files at manageable sizes even on large libraries. A third type of partitioning is used for document files and for long strings of field data; the binary large object files can be considered partitions of the message databases or the document databases, depending on their content.

Replication is used across post offices. Shared folders and address books are replicated to prevent unnecessary network utilization when users access these items. Messages sent between post offices are replicated once per post office, again, so users reading these messages do not need to open client/server connections to the sender's post office.

This replication across post offices is managed through database record numbers (DRNs) and GUIDs. Items replicated to other post offices are linked back to the original item record. When users are moved, or folders are shared, and another copy of an item ends up on a post office, the duplicate DRN or GUID tells the delivery process to create a pointer to the existing item, instead of writing the item again.

PART II

Administration Interface

CHAPTER 5

Working with GroupWise Objects

This chapter looks at how some of the GroupWise entities—domains, post offices, and so on—are represented as objects in ConsoleOne. ConsoleOne is the tool you use for most of your GroupWise administration.

The GroupWise View

From ConsoleOne, you access GroupWise view by doing the following:

1. Choose Edit, Preferences.
2. Check the Show View Title option.

   By doing this, it is easy to distinguish when you are in GroupWise view.
3. Now select the GroupWise System icon, which displays the window shown in Figure 5.1.

This window displays your GroupWise system and does so in a way that clearly illustrates the relationships between domains, gateways, post offices, and other objects. The window is divided into two side-by-side panes.

The System pane, on the left in Figure 5.1, displays the GroupWise system and the domains and post offices. The display follows the GroupWise domain and post office hierarchy: domain icons are at the first level, and post offices are at the second level.

The Object pane, on the right in Figure 5.1, displays all possible GroupWise objects, including domains and post offices. Because either a domain or a post office must own all GroupWise objects in the GroupWise view, these objects are only viewable on the Object pane on the right.

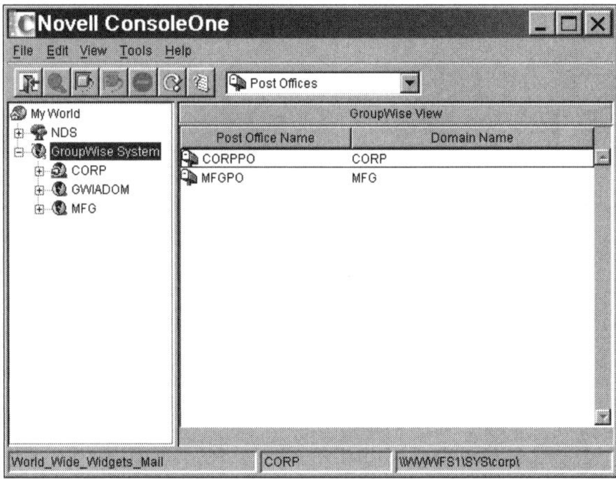

FIGURE 5.1 The GroupWise view.

Filtering the GroupWise View

The Object pane cannot display all types of GroupWise objects at once, however. An object filter drop-down menu determines the types of objects that are viewable.

The drop-down filter shown in Figure 5.2 provides up to 10 types of filters for easily maneuvering between GroupWise objects.

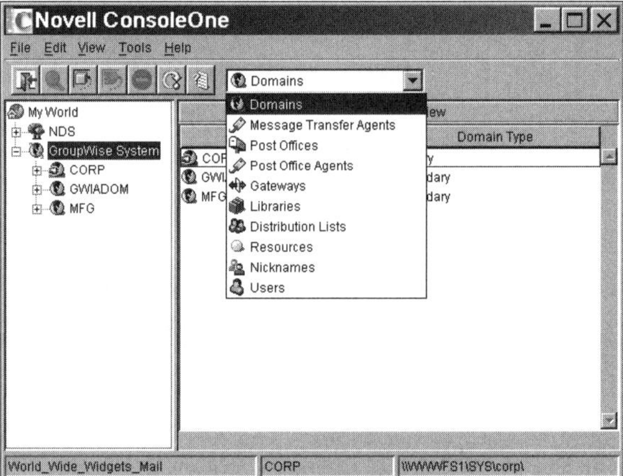

FIGURE 5.2 The GroupWise view drop-down filter.

Creating GroupWise Objects

You can create GroupWise objects, especially user objects, from either the GroupWise view or the eDirectory view in ConsoleOne.

To create a GroupWise object from the GroupWise view, do the following:

1. Highlight the GroupWise System or a domain or post office. Click the right mouse button (right-click) and select New.

   For example, you might want to create a new user and immediately associate that user with the CORPPO post office.

2. Select the CORPPO post office, and right-click.
3. From the New menu item, select User.
4. Proceed through the object-specific dialog boxes.

This method enables you to create an eDirectory user and assign the user to a post office with a mailbox in essentially one step.

Viewing the Domain Object

Generally, you do not administrate the domain object much after you have initially configured it. However you will often find that when you are troubleshooting, you will go back to the domain object to confirm how it is configured.

If you highlight a domain, right-click, and select Properties, you get a window such as the one shown in Figure 5.3.

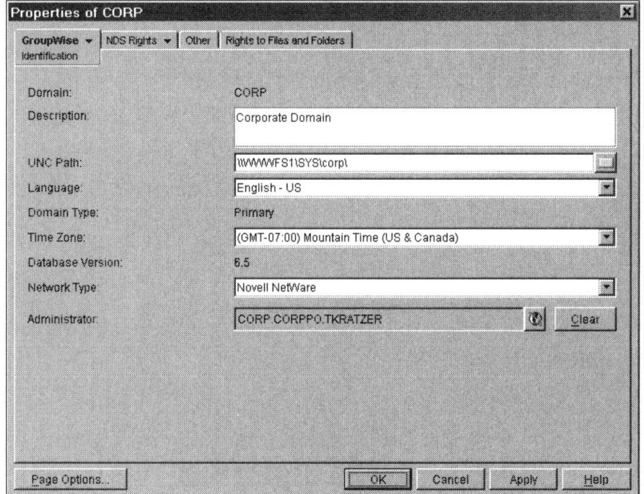

FIGURE 5.3
The domain object properties window.

The domain object properties window has six properties pages, selectable by clicking the word on the GroupWise tab. These properties pages are the following:

- Identification
- Post offices
- Address book
- Addressing rules
- Internet addressing
- Default WebAccess

The following sections offer a discussion of each of these pages in turn.

The Domain Identification Property Page

This page displays all the general information about this domain. There are nine fields, as shown in Figure 5.3, but only six of them can be edited.

- *Domain:* The domain name cannot be changed once the domain has been created. If naming conventions at your organization require you to change a domain name, you must create a new domain by that name and move users to it. Refer to Chapter 13, "Moving Users," for more information.
- *Description:* The optional text you place in this field can be used to help other administrators contact you. This text is never visible to users, or from the server console.
- *UNC Path:* This field should be populated with the Universal Naming Convention (UNC) path to the domain database for this domain. The syntax for a UNC path is `\\<server name>\<volume>\<path to domain database>`. When you use the System Connection tool to switch domains (covered more fully in Chapter 6, "Using GroupWise System Operations"), ConsoleOne requires the UNC path value.
- *Language:* This drop-down menu is populated with the available languages.
- *Domain Type:* A domain that is part of your GroupWise system will show either as Primary or Secondary (and only one domain will be the primary). Domains belonging to other systems that your system sends messages to will show as External or perhaps Foreign.

- *Time Zone:* This field is populated from a drop-down menu containing all of the widely recognized timezones worldwide. This field is critical if your organization spans multiple timezones, or if you share e-mail with organizations in other timezones.
- *Database Version:* In this field, you will either see 4.1, 5.0, 5.5, 6, or 6.5. A 4.1 identifies a GroupWise 4.1 domain, whereas a value of 5.0 applies to any version of GroupWise 5.0, 5.1, or 5.2. If a domain is running GroupWise 5.5 or GroupWise 5.5 Enhancement Pack, this field reads 5.5. A GroupWise 6 domain reads 6. For a GroupWise 6.5 domain, this field reads 6.5. This field is important to keep an eye on if you are upgrading from an earlier version of GroupWise.
- *Network Type:* This field is a holdover from WordPerfect Office 4.0 days and can be ignored.
- *Administrator:* The Browse button for this field enables you to choose an eDirectory user object to serve as the GroupWise administrator. The object you select must have a valid GroupWise mailbox associated with it. Any error messages generated by GroupWise agents are e-mailed to this user.

The next property page that you can select from the GroupWise tab is the Post Offices Property Page.

The Post Offices Property Page

Simply put, this tab lists the post offices that belong to this domain. Post offices cannot be moved or renamed, however, so the information in this tab is not editable. Post offices can be deleted from this page, however. Post offices can be deleted only if they do not own any objects (such as users, resources, distribution lists, libraries, POAs, and so on).

If you want to know what post offices a particular domain owns, it is often easier just to expand the hierarchy under this domain in the System pane of the GroupWise view. All the post offices will appear there.

The Domain Address Book Property Page

This is the interface for administering the way the system address book appears to your users. In the Windows client, this address book appears under the Novell GroupWise Address Book tab, as shown in Figure 5.4.

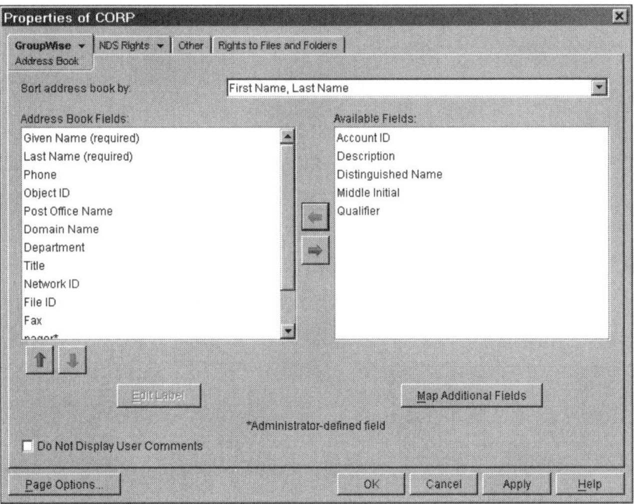

FIGURE 5.4
The domain object address book property page.

Using this tab, you can change the sort order, the field order, and the field labels in the address book for this domain. You can also add fields to the GroupWise address book.

WARNING

This feature set is somewhat limited, though. For example, if you change the sort order from a system level, users can change the sort order to whatever they like, and you can't dictate what they choose.

- *Sort address book by:* This tool has only two available values: Last Name, First Name or First Name, Last Name. As expected, the first option would put "Zachary Abrams" above "Allan Zane" (sorting alphabetically by last name). The second option would put "Allan Zane" above "Zachary Abrams."
- *Address Book Fields and Available Fields:* The interface here is a little tricky.
    - The left- and right-pointing arrows move fields into and out of the address book, respectively.
    - The up- and down-arrows change the order of the fields by moving the selected field up or down, respectively.
    - The Edit Label button enables you to change the field label of the selected field. Note: The only fields that you can edit are Administrator defined fields.

- The Map Additional Fields button opens a new window. This feature enables you to define additional fields for user objects, which are then available in the GroupWise address book. Chapter 6 talks in detail about how you might use this powerful feature to extend the capabilities of the GroupWise address book.

The next property page that you can select from the GroupWise tab is the Post Offices Property Page.

The Domain Addressing Rules and Internet Addressing Property Pages

The Addressing Rules property page enables you to set and test existing addressing rules. It does not allow for the creation of addressing rules, however. You create addressing rules from the System Operations window. Chapter 6 goes into more detail on creating addressing rules.

The Internet Addressing property page enables you to override system-wide Internet addressing settings at the domain level. It also lets a GroupWise system use native Internet style addresses for GroupWise users and resources. This page allows for wide ranges of flexibility in regards to how users' Internet style addresses are maintained and used. At this point, it is important to know that Internet addressing is a very powerful tool, and like any good power tool, it can take your fingers off. Chapter 16, "Internet Addressing," discusses Internet addressing. For now, leave it unplugged and put it back down between your table saw and your lathe.

The Default WebAccess Property Page

Use this property page to select the default WebAccess agent (gateway) that processes requests for users located in this domain. This page applies only if you have multiple WebAccess agents installed in your GroupWise system. If you have only one WebAccess agent, that WebAccess agent services users in all domains. Chapter 11, "Configuring GroupWise WebAccess," discusses how to use this feature for practical purposes.

The following bulleted items explain the purpose of the different selections on this property page.

- *Default WebAccess:* When you have multiple WebAccess agents and a user logs in to GroupWise WebAccess, the GroupWise WebAccess Application (running on the Web server) determines whether a default

WebAccess agent has been assigned to the user's post office (Post Office object, GroupWise tab, Default WebAccess page). If so, the WebAccess Application connects to the assigned WebAccess agent. If not, it connects to the default WebAccess agent assigned to the post office's domain that you define from this page.

If possible, you should select a WebAccess agent that has the best network level access to the domain's post offices to ensure the best performance. Each post office will use the domain's default WebAccess agent unless you override the default at the post office level (Post Office object, GroupWise tab, Default WebAccess page).

- *Override:* Check this box to indicate that you want to assign a default WebAccess agent to the domain.
- *Default WebAccess Gateway:* Browse for and select the WebAccess agent you want to use as the default.

This section explained how settings can be made at the domain level. Some of these settings can also be made at the post office level. The value of making a setting change at the domain level is that several post offices can be changed at the same time. The notion of a domain administration model helps GroupWise to be administered at a higher level. By administering GroupWise at a higher level, post office administration can be less taxing.

There are many more property pages to administer under a GroupWise post office versus a domain. However the purpose for this is flexibility. For example, if you wanted a post office to be configured differently from other post offices in a domain, some of the defaults that are specified at the domain level can be customized to the requirements of a particular post office.

Viewing the Post Office Object

Figure 5.5 shows a detailed look at the post office details window.

As with the domain properties window, the post office properties window has several properties pages. In order, they are

- Identification
- Post office settings
- Client access settings
- Membership

- Resources
- Distribution lists
- Libraries
- Gateway aliases
- Internet addressing
- Security
- Default WebAccess

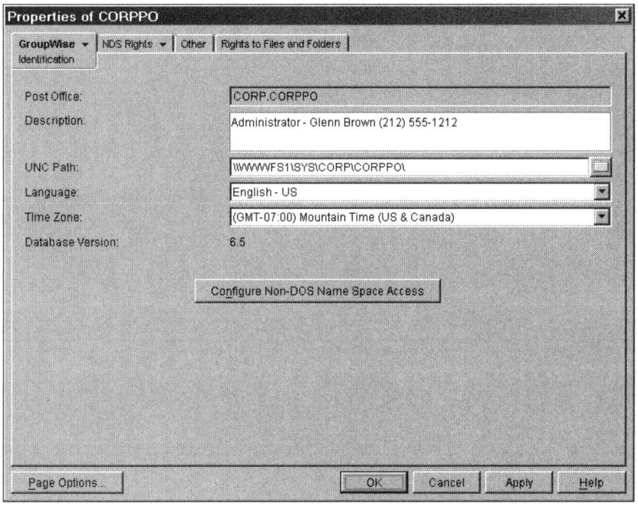

FIGURE 5.5
The post office object properties page.

The fields on this property page are shown in Figure 5.5. Only two fields are non-editable. The remaining four fields on this identification property page will generally stay the same.

- *Post Office:* This field displays the post office's GroupWise object ID (or "name" to you and me). Post offices cannot be renamed once they have been created. As with domains, if you need to rename one for some reason, you will have to create a new post office and move your users between the two. Moving users is covered in Chapter 13.
- *Description:* This optional field might be a good place to enter your pager number, or perhaps special instructions for system operators. The text here is visible through this window only.
- *UNC Path:* This field shows the path to the post office database, WPHOST.DB. Incorrect information here can foul network links and can prevent you from successfully running system maintenance on the post office database.

- *Language:* This field shows the language for this post office.
- *Time Zone:* This is the timezone for this post office. Changing this setting will result in chaos among the users on this post office, as all the appointments on their calendars at the time of the change will move. Timezones should be carefully selected when you create the post office, and then you should leave them alone.
- *Database Version:* As explained in the section entitled "The Domain Information Property Page," this will be 4.1, 5.0, 5.5, 6, or 6.5.
- *Configure Non-DOS Name Space Access:* If you are running in direct access mode, *and* if you have GroupWise clients running on platforms that do not recognize UNC paths, *and* you want those clients to obtain the post office path from eDirectory, you'll need to use this button. Enter the path style that your clients prefer into the appropriate field in the resulting dialog box. This setting is really here to be backward compatible to GroupWise 5.x level post offices and is rarely used anymore.

The next property page that you can select from the GroupWise tab is the Post Office Settings Property Page.

The Post Office Settings Property Page

The Post Office Settings page is packed with features specific to a post office. Here's an explanation of each of the options you see on this page:

- *Network Type:* This field is obsolete and can be ignored.
- *Software Distribution Directory:* This pull-down menu is populated with the names of each of the software distribution directories (SDD) you have created in this system. Assigning an SDD to a post office provides the GroupWise client with a UNC path for client updates. Chapter 12, "Administering the GroupWise Client," discusses software distribution directories in more detail.
- *Access Mode:* There are three options here. Novell recommends the first option, Client/Server Only, be used almost exclusively.
    - *Client/Server Only:* The client "talks" via IP (Internet protocol) to the POA. The POA handles all message store transactions. Users do not need any file system rights to the message store to run in client/server mode. (This is the preferable mode for running the GroupWise client.)

- *Client/Server and Direct:* The client attempts a client/server connection, and if that fails, attempts to connect in direct access mode. This mode is not a hybrid. Clients always connect in only one manner. All this mode offers is the flexibility to support a mix of machines with and without IP addresses.
- *Direct Only:* The client performs all mailbox transactions directly on the message store. It does not talk to the POA at all but will access the message store directly. This is not a recommended mode to run your GroupWise clients in.

- *Delivery Mode:* This setting applies only if users are allowed to use the direct connection. For users with direct access connections, the setting applies as follows:
  - *Use App Thresholds:* The client writes to the sending user's USER and MSG databases, and if the threshold is not exceeded, will also write to each recipient's USER database.
  - *Client Delivers Locally:* The client writes to the sender's USER and MSG databases, as well as to the USER database for every recipient on the local post office.

WARNING

Novell recommends that clients only connect to the post office in client/server mode. Direct mode, regardless of the delivery mode selected, poses a security and a stability risk to the message store. In direct mode, users must have file system rights to the message store, and store files are subject to corruption if a workstation has a GPF (Windows General Protection Failure—Windows crashes) or is cold-rebooted.

- *Disable Live Mode:* Select Disable Live Move to turn off the improved move-user capabilities available in GroupWise 6.5.

  A live move uses a TCP/IP connection to move a user from one post office to another. In general, it is significantly faster and more reliable than earlier move-user capabilities in GroupWise 5.x. However, it does require that both post offices are running GroupWise 6 or 6.5 POAs, and that TCP/IP is functioning efficiently between the two post offices. Moving users and live mode user moves are both discussed in Chapter 13.

- *Exempt this post office from the Trusted Application routing requirement:* This feature is made available for third-party integration with the GroupWise POA and MTA. It's an obscure feature that you should check only if you are instructed to do so when installing software that integrates with the GroupWise POA. An example is a server-based virus scanning utility that integrates with GroupWise.

- *Remote File Server Settings:* Use the remote file server settings to provide the POA a login ID to use when connecting to another file server. This is used in order to access a remote machine where a GroupWise library, document storage area, or restored post office databases are located. The POA might also connect to a GroupWise Software Distribution Directory on another server using this same login information. The Remote File Server Settings are not needed unless the POA will need to connect to a remote file server for any of the aforementioned purposes.
- *Remote User Name:* Specify the network userID for the POA(s) of this post office to use when accessing a remote file server. For example, GWMAIL.EMAIL.ACME identifies the eDirectory userID that the POA will use to authenticate to the remote server.
- *Remote Password:* Specify the password associated with the login ID provided in the Remote User Name.

NOTE

The Remote User name and password must have the necessary rights to access the remote file server and perform whatever action the POA has been instructed to perform.

The GroupWise Post Office Settings page is not a page where you will be making frequent changes. Most of your post offices will be configured in the same manner under the post office settings page.

The Post Office Client Access Settings Page

This property page allows you to lock out older clients, or users that might be trying to get into another user's account without authorization.

- *Minimum Client Release Version (x.x.x):* This is a great way of keeping users with an older GroupWise windows client out of your post office. However, if a user is denied the ability to connect to your post office because their GroupWise client is too old, they are not prompted to upgrade their client in any manner. To determine the Client Release Version of a GroupWise client, select Help, About GroupWise within the GroupWise Windows client. Look at the program release; it will read "6.5.0", or something similar.

- *Minimum Client Release Date:* This feature is very similar to the Minimum Client Release Version. A GroupWise client has both a release version and a release date. This is a great way of keeping users with an older GroupWise windows client out of your post office. However, if a user is denied the ability to connect to your post office because their GroupWise client is too old, they are not prompted to upgrade their client in any manner. To determine the Client Release Date of a GroupWise client, select Help, About GroupWise within the GroupWise Windows client. Look at the program release; it will read similar to "2/3/2003".
- *Disable Logins:* If checked, users cannot log in to their GroupWise mailboxes on this post office. This option does not kick users out, however, if they are already logged in.

If you need to kick users out in order to perform server or system maintenance, it helps if you are in client/server only mode. In this mode, you can simply unload the POA from the server console to kick everyone off—another reason to choose client/server only mode over the alternatives.

- *Enable Intruder Detection:* Select Enable Intruder Detection to configure the POA for the post office to detect system break-in attempts in the form of repeated unsuccessful logins. For example, when someone repeatedly tries to log in but is using the incorrect password.
- *Incorrect Logins Allowed:* Specify how many unsuccessful login attempts trigger a lockout. The default is 5. Valid values range from 3 to 10.
- *Incorrect Login Reset Time:* Specify how long unsuccessful login attempts are counted. The default is 30 minutes. Valid values range from 15 to 60 minutes.
- *Lockout Reset Time:* Specify how long the user login is disabled. The default is 30 minutes. Valid values range from 15 to 60 minutes.

If a user account is locked out because it tripped the Intruder Detection code, you can go to the user's account and uncheck the Disable Logins check box on the GroupWise Account property page.

The Post Office Membership Property Page

This page provides a list of those users assigned to this post office. This tab comes equipped with tools to add existing eDirectory users to this post office, delete users from the post office, and move users between post offices.

The Post Office Resources, Distribution Lists, and Libraries Property Pages

These pages provide lists of the various non-user objects associated with this post office. None of these objects can be created from the post office details window, so there are no Add buttons.

Creating Gateway Aliases for a Post Office

Post office aliases provide one way for a post office to be given a different Internet address than the rest of your organization. The Post Office Alias is generally only useful when you have defined an external post office. External post offices are explained in more detail in Chapter 19, "Building Your GroupWise System Correctly."

The Internet Addressing Property Page

Just like on the domain details screen, this tab exists to enable you to make exceptions to the system Internet addressing configuration. Chapter 16 covers Internet addressing in detail.

The Security Property Page

There are two possible security values for a post office:

- *Low:* Users' network logins are not checked to determine whether they correspond to the mailbox they are using. In this mode, mailboxes should be password protected. If they are not, any user can log in as any other user by placing the `/@u-<userID>` switch on the GroupWise command line (without the greater than and less than symbols).
- *High:* Users' eDirectory passwords are checked before enabling users to access their GroupWise mailbox. There are two methods that GroupWise can use to get the eDirectory password. They are *eDirectory authentication* and *LDAP authentication.* Here's a discussion of both of these options:
    - With eDirectory authentication enabled, if a user has a Novell client that is authenticated to an eDirectory tree, the GroupWise 32-bit client queries the Novell client using the WnetGetUser network API call. If a user is logged in as one person, but trying to open GroupWise as someone else, that user will be prompted

for the mailbox password, which is not contained in eDirectory and requires that the mailbox truly have a GroupWise password.

- With LDAP authentication enabled, if users do not have the Novell client on their computers, or a user is using GroupWise WebAccess through a Web browser, they can still use an eDirectory password. The POA queries eDirectory via LDAP on behalf of the user. A prerequisite to this functionality is that your implementation of eDirectory be version 8.5 or better, with LDAP services enabled. Setting up LDAP authentication for the POA is explained in detail in Chapter 26, "Configuring GroupWise Authentication via LDAP."

The Default WebAccess Property Page

Use this property page to select the WebAccess agent (or gateway) that will process requests from this post office's users. Use this property page to select the WebAccess agent (gateway) that processes requests for users located in this domain. This page applies only if you have multiple WebAccess agents installed in your GroupWise system. If you have only one WebAccess agent, that WebAccess agent services users in all domains. Chapter 11 goes into more detail about how to use this feature for practical purposes.

The following are the choices you can make on the Default WebAccess page.

- *Default WebAccess:* When you have multiple WebAccess agents and a user logs in to GroupWise WebAccess, the GroupWise WebAccess Application (running on the Web server) checks to see whether a default WebAccess agent has been assigned to the user's post office (Post Office object, GroupWise tab, Default WebAccess page). If so, the WebAccess application connects to the assigned WebAccess agent. If not, it connects to the default WebAccess agent assigned to the post office's domain.

  If possible, you should select a WebAccess agent that has the best network level access to this post office to ensure the best performance. Each post office will use the domain's default WebAccess agent unless you override the default at the post office level.
- *Override:* Check this box to indicate that you want to assign a default WebAccess agent to the post office.
- *Default WebAccess Gateway:* Browse for and select the WebAccess agent you want to use as the default.

Configuring Library Objects

If you want to use document management, you will be creating *library objects.* To find any Libraries that are already created, highlight the GroupWise System object in ConsoleOne, and then in the GroupWise view change the drop-down filter to Libraries. When you highlight a GroupWise library and view its properties, you will see a screen similar to Figure 5.6 (which shows the Library Identification property page).

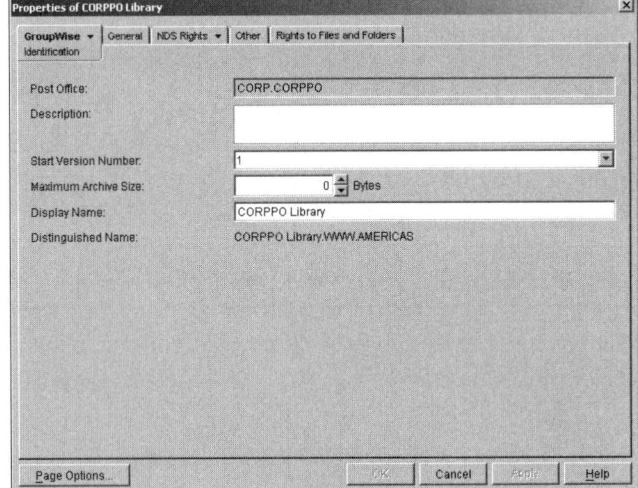

FIGURE 5.6
The library identification property page.

The Library Identification Property Page

This section includes a discussion of the fields that appear in the property page, as shown in Figure 5.6:

- *Post Office:* This field is the GroupWise domain and post office to which this library belongs. Libraries cannot be moved from one domain and post office to another, but with mass-change operations, the documents in one library can be moved to another. This topic is discussed in Chapter 14, "Library and Document Administration."
- *Description:* This is an optional field. The text here is not visible to users and is useful as a way to describe the library object to other system administrators.
- *Start Version Number:* Document version numbers can begin at either 0 or 1. If you enter 0, the first version of each document will be 000. If

you enter 1, the first version number will be 001. Most people count in ordinal terms, so it might be better to enter 1 here.

- *Maximum Archive Size in Bytes:* This is the number of bytes per library archive directory. The value you enter should be compatible with your backup medium. For example, you could make it 90% of the tape backup's capacity to allow for the tape's file storage data. Then you can back up one archive directory per tape.
- *Display Name:* Like domains and post offices, GroupWise libraries cannot be renamed. Fortunately, the display name for a library can be changed. This is visible to users when they select a library to save documents in.
- *Distinguished Name:* This is the name and context of the GroupWise library object in eDirectory.

All of what you see on this property page will make more sense when you read Chapter 14.

The Storage Areas Property Page

As described in Chapter 4, "Understanding the GroupWise Information Store," GroupWise libraries are made up of document property databases (and other databases), and the documents themselves are stored as compressed, encrypted files called BLOB (binary large object) files. By default, all of the databases and BLOBs are kept in subdirectories of the post office directory.

The storage areas page enables you to choose other locations, whether they are on different volumes or even different servers, for the BLOB files. The document databases will always remain under the GWDMS (GroupWise document management system) structure, however.

By default, the box labeled Store Documents at Post Office is checked. You must uncheck it in order to add a storage area for documents. You cannot add document storage areas while this box is checked. Make sure to read Chapter 14 before deciding how you will store your documents.

Administering User Objects

Administering GroupWise user objects is the most common task you will be doing with GroupWise administration in ConsoleOne. This section fully explains all the attributes that can be administered on a GroupWise object.

The User Object's GroupWise Account Property Page

If you have worked at all with Novell Directory Services and ConsoleOne, you are probably quite familiar with the User Object Details window. With GroupWise 6.5 installed in your tree, the user object has some new property pages available to it. The one you'll likely use the most is the GroupWise Account property page. Figure 5.7 shows this page.

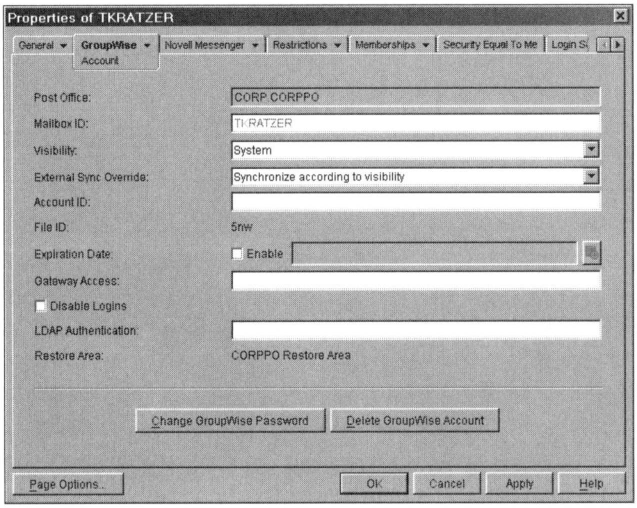

FIGURE 5.7
The user object's GroupWise account page.

Note: There is a special kind of user object that you may or may not see in your GroupWise system. It's what's called a "GroupWise External Entity". A GroupWise External Entity is a full GroupWise user, with an eDirectory object, but the eDirectory object is not a typical "red shirt" type user object. External Entity users have a green shirt. These users cannot authenticate to eDirectory, but they have an eDirectory object in order so that administrative rights can be assigned to the object.

This tab offers three major administrative tools:

- Changing GroupWise information for this user
- Changing this user's GroupWise password
- Deleting the user's GroupWise account

The following offers a discussion of each of the fields:

- *Post Office:* This is the name of this user's post office, with the name of the domain tacked on before the post office name with a period delimiting the domain and post office names.
- *Mailbox ID:* This is the user's GroupWise user ID for accessing the user's mailbox.
- *Visibility:* This field defines which users elsewhere in the GroupWise system can find this user in the GroupWise address book. The options for this pull-down menu are as follows:
    - *System:* Anyone on this GroupWise system can see this user in the address book.
    - *Domain:* This user can be seen only by users in the same domain.
    - *Post Office:* This user can be seen only by users in the same post office.
    - *None:* This user does not appear in the GroupWise address book.

    Just because a user cannot be seen in the address book does not mean that user cannot be sent to. If you know the domain, post office, and user ID, you can enter those items in the TO field (for example, `corp.corppo.tkratzer`), and the e-mail will reach the user.

    Similarly, if GroupWise Internet addressing is enabled, you can reach this user by entering the user's user ID and IDOMAIN (that is, `tkratzer@wwwidgets.com`) in the TO field.
- *External Sync Override:* If you have connected your GroupWise system to another organization's GroupWise system, and are using external system synchronization, you might want to make some users invisible outside of your GroupWise system. This field enables you to override the setting in the Visibility field for this user.
- *Account ID:* This field is used for GroupWise gateways that offer accounting features so that users can be charged for, say, sending faxes or transmitting data across an expensive line.
- *File ID:* This is the three-character string that uniquely identifies this user's USER database in this post office directory. In the example in Figure 5.7, the File ID is *5nw,* which means that the mailbox for user TKRATZER is in USER5NW.DB.

- *Expiration Date:* If you have temporary or contract employees, you can choose to set an expiration date for them. After the date has passed, the user cannot log in to his or her GroupWise mailbox. Other users can still send mail to an expired user, however. Clearing the date out of this field after that date has passed will, in effect, un-expire the user, allowing them to log in again.
- *Gateway Access:* This is an obscure feature that was used in older GroupWise gateways. Use this field if instructed to do so when configuring a specific GroupWise gateway.
- *Disable Logins:* If you need to prevent a user from logging in, you can check this box. Note that this change, as with any changes made in ConsoleOne, takes time to propagate down to the post office. Try to plan a few minutes ahead in order to ensure that the user doesn't successfully log in before the update takes place. If the post office that this user is a member of has Enable Intruder Detection enabled, when a user is locked out of their account, you should see a check mark in this box. By unchecking the box, the user's mailbox will no longer be locked out.
- *LDAP Authentication:* This option applies only if you are using LDAP to authenticate users (see "The Security Property Page" section earlier in this chapter) and the LDAP server is not the Novell LDAP server, or if the eDirectory tree that you are using for LDAP authentication is a different tree than the one the users are in. Chapter 26 talks more about how you might use this field.
- *Restore Area:* This option displays the restore area, if any, that the user can access to restore deleted items from backup.

  To set up a restore area, choose Tools, GroupWise System Operations, Restore Area Management. Restore area management is covered more in Chapter 28, "Restoring Deleted GroupWise Users."
- *Change GroupWise Password:* Clicking this option displays the Security Options window shown in Figure 5.8. The GroupWise password (managed with this Security Options window) is independent of the user's eDirectory password. So changing this password will not change the user's eDirectory password. It offers the following options:
  - *Enter new password:* If a user forgets a GroupWise password, you can provide the user with a new password to access GroupWise. You should advise the user to change the new password to a personal one.

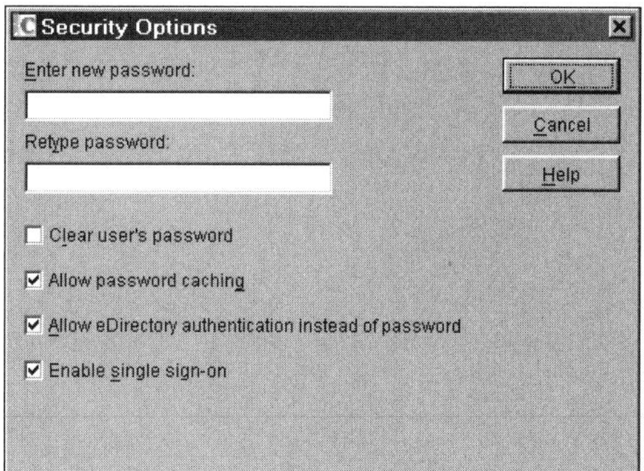

FIGURE 5.8
The security options window.

- *Retype password:* If you retype the password correctly, it is set; otherwise, you need to reenter the password in both fields.
- *Clear user's password:* If a user forgets a personal password, check this box to clear the password. The user can then enter a new password at his or her discretion. In a high-security post office, it might be necessary to set a new password after clearing the old one.
- *Allow password caching:* This option is selected by default, enabling the user to select the Remember My Password option under Tools, Options, Security in the GroupWise client. This option lets the user restart GroupWise without reentering the password. The password is stored in the Windows password list on the current computer.
- *Allow eDirectory authentication instead of password:* This option lets users select the No Password Required with eDirectory option under Security options in the GroupWise client. When selected, this option lets the user access his or her mailbox without requiring a password if he or she is already logged in to eDirectory. Mailbox access is granted based on eDirectory authentication, not on password information.
- *Enable Novell Single Sign-on:* This check box lets the user select the Use Novell Single Sign-on option under Tools, Options, Security in the GroupWise client. When selected, this option lets the user access his or her mailbox without reentering the password. The GroupWise password is stored in eDirectory for the currently logged-in user.

Novell Single Sign-on must be installed on user workstations in order for this option to take effect. The Single Sign-on options are not applicable if LDAP authentication is enabled.

- *Delete GroupWise Account:* This selection deletes a user's GroupWise account, but not the user's eDirectory account.

The user password portion of the user account page is a very popular destination in ConsoleOne, unless you have enabled LDAP authentication at the post office. This section listed all of the ways you can approach mailbox authentication security with GroupWise.

The User Distribution Lists Property Page

To find this page, click the GroupWise tab, and click Distribution Lists. This page displays all of the distribution lists that this user appears in, and it enables you to add this user to additional GroupWise distribution lists.

The Participation button enables you to specify whether the user is a TO, CC, or BC (blind copy) recipient of messages sent to the distribution list you are highlighting.

The User GroupWise Internet Addressing Property Page

Internet addressing exceptions can be configured at the domain, post office, and user level. On the user object's details window, this tab enables you to make exceptions at the user level. Most particularly, you can even change the USER ADDRESS portion of the <USER ADDRESS>@<INTERNET DOMAIN NAME>. This feature is new to GroupWise 6.5. Figure 5.9 shows an example in which the default Internet Addressing scheme has been changed at a user level.

In the example shown in Figure 5.9, when Tay Kratzer sends messages to the Internet, the recipient will see Tay's address as `taykratzer@wwwidgets.com`. For incoming messages destined for Tay, the GroupWise Internet Agent (GWIA) will accept messages addressed to `taykratzer@wwwidgets.com` or `tkratzer@wwwidgets.com`. Because of the check marks that have been removed under Allowed Address Formats, the GWIA will not allow messages sent to `tay.kratzer@wwwidgets.com`, `kratzer.tay@wwwidgets.com`, or `tkratzer.corppo@wwwidgets.com`.

Chapter 16 goes into depth on Internet addressing.

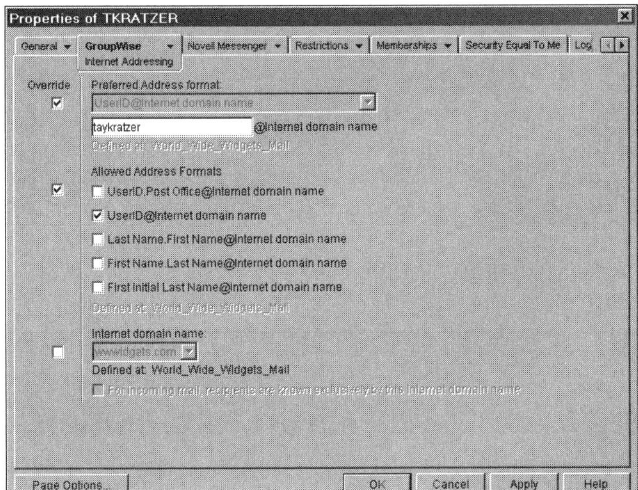

FIGURE 5.9
Defining Internet addressing at the user level.

The post office must be version 6.5 in order to see the "free form" Internet address override option on the user object. The GWIA must also be version 6.5 to use this feature.

The User Gateway Aliases Property Page

A user alias can be used to change the "user" field for a single user's Internet address. It can also be used to change the entire address.

If you set the gateway alias address to a value with no @ sign, you are only changing the user portion of the Internet address. If you include the @ sign, you have changed the entire address for that user.

If you assign a gateway alias to a user, that alias appears as the reply-to address on all mail he or she sends through that particular gateway. In an example mentioned in Chapter 3, "Understanding the GroupWise Directory," Eva Cornish wants inbound e-mail that is addressed to `webmaster@wwwidgets.com` to come to her. If you create a gateway alias called "webmaster" for her, not only will she get mail addressed to "webmaster," but also all the mail she sends will appear as if it is *from* "webmaster." This is most likely not the desired effect. And so in this scenario a gateway alias is not the best choice. It is probably better to create a nickname of "webmaster" for Eva, covered next.

The User Nicknames Property Page

A nickname is a way for a user to exist in two places at once. It is also a way for one user to have more than one identity. Nicknames added through this tab can be placed in any GroupWise post office. This is a handy way to overcome some of the limitations of the visibility feature, and can also enable the user to be known by more than one user ID.

Assume, for example, that Eva Cornish is the webmaster for WorldWide Widgets. If you create a nickname for Eva Cornish of "webmaster", when someone sends a message to `webmaster@wwwidgets.com`, it will reach Eva.

The User GroupWise X.400 Information Property Page

If you need to connect your system to an X.400 system, each of your users might need an X.400-style address. In most situations, however, it is much more convenient for X.400 systems and GroupWise systems to communicate via the SMTP, or *Internet e-mail* protocol.

If your users do need X.400 addresses, the X.400 system's administrator can assist you as you populate these fields.

Understanding Resource Objects

A GroupWise resource is nothing more than a mailbox used to represent a physical entity, such as a conference room or a data projector. Resources are typically used to allow GroupWise users to schedule the use of these physical entities such as a conference room in the GroupWise calendar. The Resource Identification property page, with the Identification tab shown, is in Figure 5.10. The fields this page presents include

- *Distinguished Name:* This is the eDirectory name of the resource object, complete with the object's context. This field is not editable, but the resource can be moved to another eDirectory context using the eDirectory console view.
- *Post Office:* This shows the GroupWise domain and post office that contain the resource. You cannot change the post office that a resource is a member of from this window. But if you go to the GroupWise

view, you can right-click the resource and use the Move option. Resource moves are very similar to (and every bit as complex as) user moves. Chapter 13 talks about moving users.

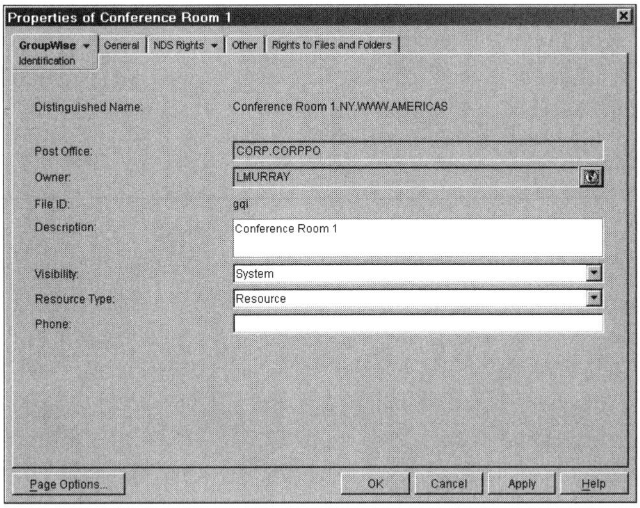

FIGURE 5.10
The resource object identification property page.

- *Owner:* This is the GroupWise user ID of the owner of this resource. This user is responsible for assigning proxy rights for the resource, managing the resource's calendar, and responding to mail received by the resource. All of these tasks will be performed through the GroupWise client's proxy function. The owner of the resource automatically has proxy rights to the resource object.

  A resource owner should be someone who is comfortable using GroupWise, and who has responsibility over the actual physical entity. For instance, the secretary who keeps the overhead projector at his desk should own that projector's resource object.

- *File ID:* This is the three-character string that uniquely identifies this resource's USER database in this post office directory. In the example in Figure 5.10, the File ID is `gqi`, which means that the database for Conference Room 1 is in USERGQI.DB.

- *Description:* This description field is unlike several of the others discussed in this chapter in that it is actually very useful to your user community. The text entered here will appear in the Comments field in the GroupWise address book's entry for this resource. For instance, for a conference room resource, you could populate this field with directions to the room, descriptions of the seating and white-board arrangements, and the telephone number of the individual with the key to the room.

- *Visibility:* This field works exactly like it does for the user object. Restricting visibility prevents the resource from appearing in some users' address books. This is a good way to prevent users from trying to schedule a resource that they should not have access to.
- *Resource Type:* There are two possible entries in this field:
  - *Resource:* Used to denote all types of physical objects that can be checked in or out by employees, from handheld radios to company cars.
  - *Place:* Used to denote conference rooms or other locations at your physical plant. When you schedule an appointment for a group of people and include a place resource, the appointment's Place field will be populated with the name of the resource.
- *Phone:* If the resource is a location, such as a conference room, you can put the phone number for the conference room in this field, and it will display in the GroupWise address book. You might also put the phone number of the resource owner, particularly if the resource type is not a place.

The best thing you can do is ensure that the Identification Property Page is completely filled out. This will ensure that users can schedule the correct resource, and do so more quickly.

The Resource Distribution Lists Property Page

Just like you saw in the User Object's Details window, this tab provides a list of the GroupWise distribution lists that this resource is included in. (See "The User Distribution Lists Property Page" earlier in this chapter.) The resource can be added to or removed from a mailing list using this tab.

The Resource Nicknames Property Page

This also works exactly like the nicknames interface for the user object (see "The User Nicknames Property Page" earlier in this chapter).

The Resource GroupWise Internet Addressing Property Page

Internet addressing exceptions can be configured at the domain, post office, and resource level. On the resource object's details window, this tab enables you to make exceptions at the resource level. Most particularly, you can even change the RESOURCE ADDRESS portion of the <RESOURCE ADDRESS>@<INTERNET DOMAIN NAME>. This is a feature that is new to GroupWise 6.5. With the example object shown in Figure 5.11, the resource's Internet address will be known as `CONFERNCEROOM1@WWWIDGETS.COM`.

If the override has not been specified, the resource's Internet address would have been `CONFERENCE_ROOM_1@WWWIDGETS.COM`.

Or worse yet, if the default Internet addressing scheme for the GroupWise system is <FIRST.LAST>@<INTERNET DOMAIN>, the default Internet address for the Conference Room would be `CONFERENCE_ROOM_1.CONFERENCE_ROOM_1@WWWIDGETS.COM`.

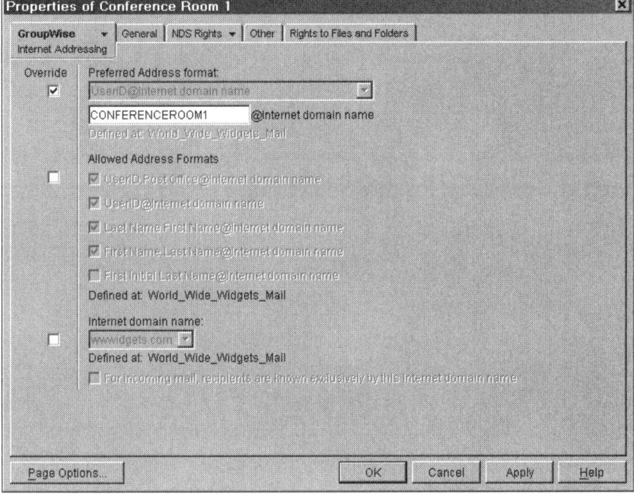

FIGURE 5.11
The resource object Internet addressing window.

The Distribution List Object

The GroupWise distribution list is simply a mailing list, and is sometimes called a *group*. eDirectory group objects can also be used like GroupWise distribution lists. An eDirectory group object functions in the normal manner in which users can inherit rights. A GroupWise distribution list does not give users eDirectory rights. GroupWise distribution lists are more flexible as mailing lists than eDirectory groups though. For example, with a GroupWise distribution list, you can specify whether recipients are TO, CC, or BC recipients; with eDirectory groups, you cannot.

Like every other GroupWise object, the distribution list has an identification window in ConsoleOne. See Figure 5.12.

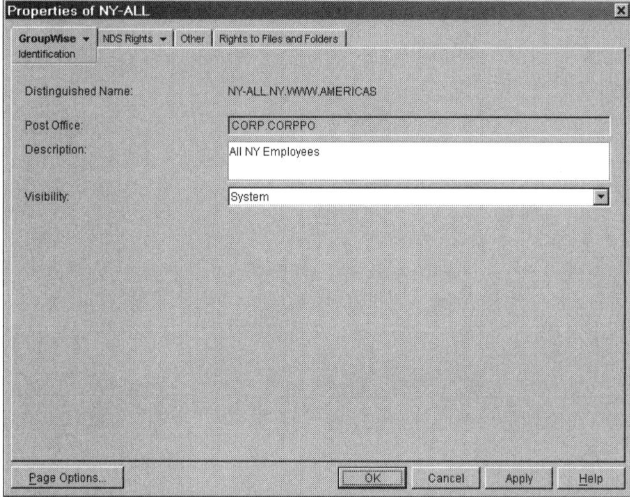

FIGURE 5.12 The distribution list object properties window.

The Distribution List Identification Property Page

As shown in Figure 5.12, this page has only a few fields to examine:

- *Distinguished Name:* This is the eDirectory name and context for this distribution list object.
- *Post Office:* This is the name of the GroupWise domain and post office that contains this distribution list. This field cannot be edited.
- *Description:* This field appears in the GroupWise address book, and might therefore be very helpful to your users. Distribution list descriptions can explain the purpose of the mailing list, and even whom to contact to change the membership list.
- *Visibility:* Distribution list visibility, although populated with the same values as the visibility for users and resources, works a little bit differently. If you know the GroupWise address of a user, you can send mail to that user even though the user does not show up in the address book. A distribution list cannot be sent to in this way.

  The Visibility field is extremely useful for preventing unauthorized users from using a single distribution list to send to the entire company. Simply restrict the visibility to Post Office and only users on the same post office as the distribution list can send to the list.

Distribution lists are a powerful means of communicating to a lot of people. Just make sure you've configured them correctly so that they are not abused within your GroupWise system.

The Distribution List Internet Addressing Property Page

The Internet address of a distribution list is not visible to users outside the GroupWise system. However, if on the GWIA, you have the Expand Groups on Incoming Messages option enabled, this dialog box helps you to define the name of the distribution list. Generally it is not recommended that you enable this option. The ramification of having this feature enabled is that senders on the Internet can potentially flood your system with e-mail.

The Distribution List Membership Property Page

From this page you can see all of the users currently associated to a distribution list and make changes to the list. Figure 5.13 shows the interface you use to change a distribution list.

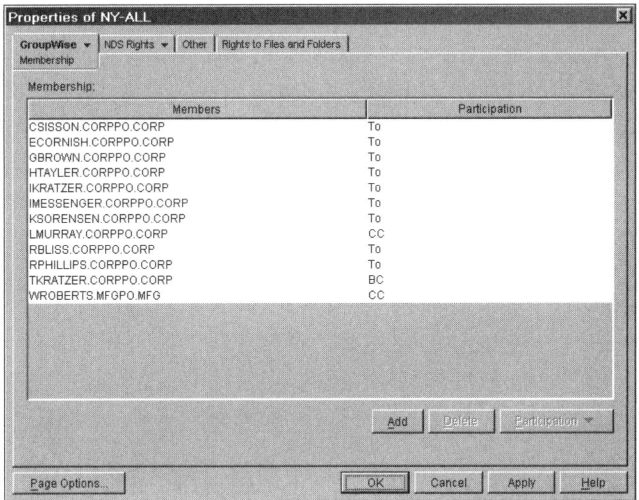

FIGURE 5.13
The distribution list membership property page.

Clicking the Add button gives you a browser dialog box from which you can add users to a list. The Participation button enables you to change a user's participation in the list from TO to CC or even BC. The Delete button removes the selected user or users from the distribution list.

As with almost all details window operations, membership changes are not committed to the domain database until the details window is dismissed with the OK button.

The Distribution List Nicknames Property Page

If you have restricted visibility to a distribution list, you might find it inconvenient that only users in a single post office can use the list. The Nicknames tab enables you to work around this. By adding a nickname for this list in another post office, you can allow users on that post office to use the list as well. The nickname will not grant visibility to the distribution list, just the capability to send to the distribution list.

Summary

This chapter focused on the GroupWise view and GroupWise object interfaces. Each of the objects has a different purpose, and each identification window is a little different, but they all work in much the same way.

A large portion of your time as a GroupWise system administrator will be spent working with the objects described in this chapter.

CHAPTER 6

Using GroupWise System Operations

System operations can potentially affect all other domains or post offices in a GroupWise system. Because of this you must have eDirectory object rights in order to access all of the menu choices from the GroupWise system operations menu. If your organization has several people who administer the GroupWise system from different domains, you might consider who should have eDirectory object rights to the primary domain, and thus have access to all of the GroupWise system operations menu choices.

Accessing System Operations

Selecting GroupWise System Operations from the Tools menu will present the menu shown in Figure 6.1.

These operations all have one thing in common: They affect GroupWise objects system-wide (the only menu option that does not affect all domains is the Select Domain menu option). This means they can affect multiple domains, post offices, and users, and it is important to know what is being done before you experiment. These operations will be discussed in turn.

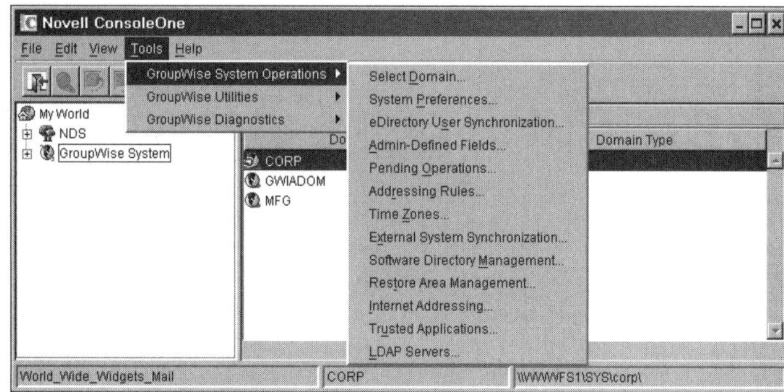

FIGURE 6.1
The GroupWise system operations menu.

Changing Connections with Select Domain

The GroupWise System Connection window enables you to change ConsoleOne's connection to a different GroupWise domain's WPDOMAIN.DB file, or even to a completely different GroupWise system.

This "connection" is simply the GroupWise domain database that ConsoleOne is reading from and writing to. This window shows the path for the domain to which ConsoleOne is currently connected.

Some administrative operations are best performed from the primary domain. When performing system operations, it is best to be connected to the system's primary domain. When adding users to a secondary domain, however, you might want to be connected to the domain to which the user will belong; the select domain window offers this flexibility.

System Preferences

The window shown in Figure 6.2 enables you to set administrative preferences. From the first tab, it is possible to set preferences pertaining to user creation.

- *Set access rights automatically; When creating a GroupWise user:* By checking the box labeled When creating a GroupWise user, you allow ConsoleOne to make trustee assignments automatically for new users. These assignments include rights to the Post Office (PO) and Post Office Agent (POA) objects hosting the user's mailbox, as well as file-system rights if you are using direct access mode (which should not be done, as discussed in Chapter 5, "Working with GroupWise Objects"). If the post office is set to allow only client/server connections, the GroupWise client always chooses a client/server connection, even if the user has file-system rights. The problem with choosing this is that users could have file-system rights to places where they don't need it. As a general rule, don't check this option.

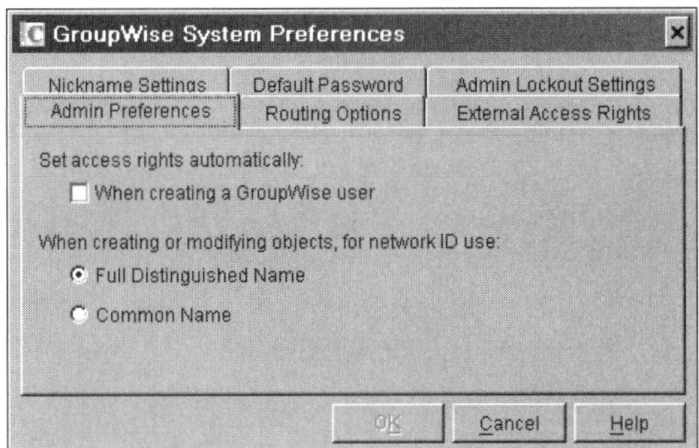

FIGURE 6.2
The GroupWise Admin Preferences tab.

- *When creating or modifying objects for network ID use:* The two options here apply only to objects created after this preference has been set. To modify the network ID for existing GroupWise users, open their user object and make the change. Any modification will do—the network ID will be changed in the background. Do not change this option unless you really know what you are doing. It is generally best to keep the setting at Full Distinguished Name.
- *Full Distinguished Name:* The GroupWise post office records the fully-distinguished eDirectory name for users, and it associates that name with the appropriate GroupWise user ID. Use this setting on post offices whose users authenticate to eDirectory.
- *Common Name:* The GroupWise post office records only the common name for users, and it associates that name with the appropriate GroupWise user ID. Use this setting for post offices whose users do *not* authenticate to eDirectory. (Generally, the Common Name selection need not be used.)
- *Routing Options:* This enables you to specify a default routing domain. Chapter 16, "Internet Addressing," provides a full discussion of how to use this option. Figure 6.3 shows the routing options tab.

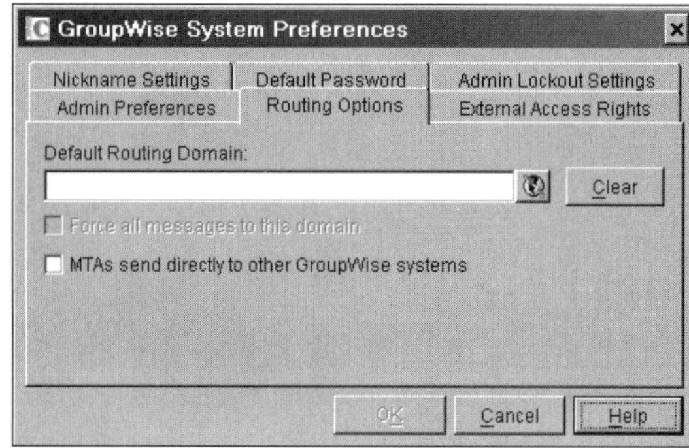

FIGURE 6.3 The Routing Options tab.

- *External Access Rights:* The GroupWise MTA can be enabled to send messages across the Internet to another GroupWise system. By doing this, GroupWise messages can retain their native GroupWise format. This feature was introduced in GroupWise 5.5. The only flaw to this feature was that in GroupWise 5.5, with MTA to MTA connectivity, outside Internet users could do busy searches and status tracking even if you did not want to allow for that. This system preference was created to control that. Figure 6.4 shows the External Access Rights tab.

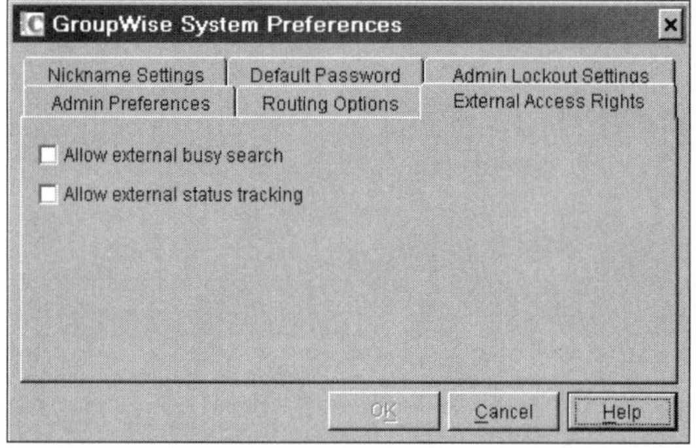

FIGURE 6.4 The External Access Rights tab.

- *Nickname Settings:* This feature, shown in Figure 6.5, can be helpful, particularly when moving a lot of people. When you move a user to a new post office, under certain circumstances or with older GroupWise clients, users might send a message to the user at their old post office location. Without a nickname tied to the old post office, the sender might get a `"D101 - User not found"` error, because the user is no longer on the old post office. However, with a nickname in place, the message will be redirected to the new place where the user resides.

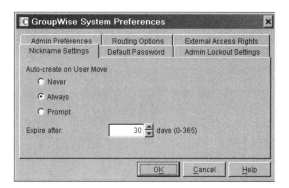

FIGURE 6.5
The Nickname Settings tab.

- ▶ *Auto-create on User Move:* Choose whether or not nicknames are to be created automatically, or if it is necessary to be prompted.
- ▶ *Expire after:* Nicknames do not need to be in place forever; generally the fact that a user has moved will replicate everywhere within time. Choose a time that seems acceptable for the environment. Take into account how often caching or remote users update their copies of the system address book.

▶ *Default Password:* By choosing a default password, shown in Figure 6.6, you know that users immediately have a GroupWise password. GroupWise WebAccess requires that all users have a password, so having a default password is particularly attractive to those sites with users who only use WebAccess. If LDAP authentication is enabled, this password will not be in effect, but the eDirectory (or other LDAP directory) password will be the authentication password. LDAP authentication works only for users who have an account in your directory; LDAP does not work for users who are *external entities*.

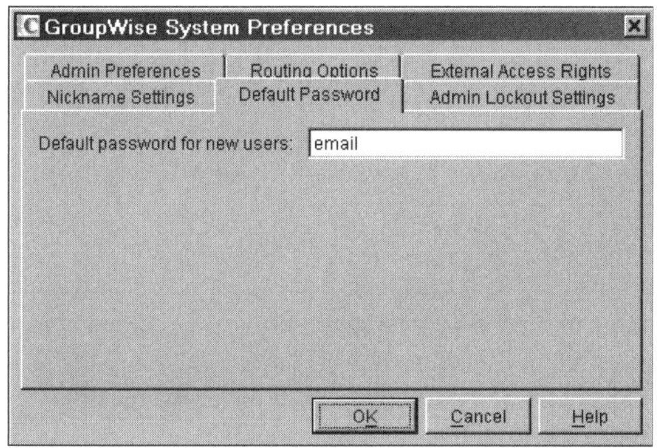

FIGURE 6.6
The Default Password tab.

- *Admin Lockout Settings; Restrict System Operations to Primary Domain:* Figure 6.7 shows this great new feature to GroupWise 6.5. If you have a GroupWise Administrator that is responsible for some secondary GroupWise domains, but do not want him or her to make system level changes, this feature makes that possible. If Restrict System Operations to Primary Domain is enabled, when anyone is connected to a Secondary domain, the only options available are Select Domain, Pending Operations, and Restore Area Management.

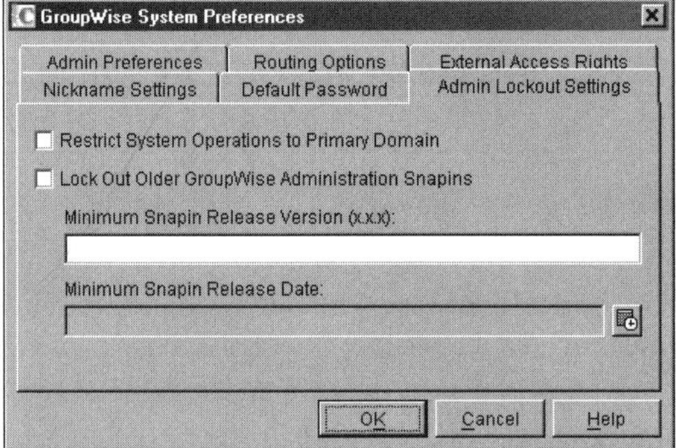

FIGURE 6.7 The Admin Lockout Settings tab.

NOTE **The GroupWise Administration developers can change what this setting allows in the future. The ramifications of this setting can change based upon the GroupWise 6.5 Support Pack that you are using.**

- *Admin Lockout Settings; Lock Out Older GroupWise Administration Snapins:* This setting is only available in GroupWise 6.5 Support Pack 1 or later SNAPins. You can force all administrators with older GroupWise 6.5 SNAPins to upgrade, or they will not be able to use the GroupWise 6.5 SNAPins to ConsoleOne. You can choose the date or the revision of the GroupWise 6.5 SNAPins. An example of a revision is 6.5.1.

  Figure 6.8 shows the effects on the System Operations menu by using this option.

NOTE **This setting is not enforced if an administrator is using NWAdmin with GroupWise 5.5x SNAPins installed or ConsoleOne with the GroupWise 6.0x SNAPins. It is only honored when ConsoleOne has GroupWise 6.5 SNAPins installed.**

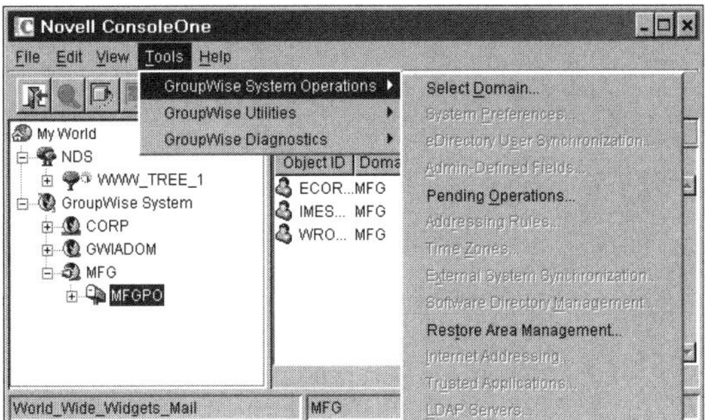

FIGURE 6.8
System operations are grayed out.

There are two other system-level operations not on the GroupWise System Operations menu that are also restricted when Restrict System Operations to Primary Domain is enabled. They are scheduled events. Scheduled events are configurable under the Message Transfer Agent (MTA) and the POA. These scheduled events will be grayed out for a Secondary domain administrator. Chapters 8, "Configuring the Post Office Agent (POA)," and 9, "Configuring the Message Transfer Agent (MTA)," talk about scheduled events.

eDirectory User Synchronization

eDirectory user synchronization is a process by which information is pulled from eDirectory into the GroupWise directory. Ordinarily, it is not necessary to set this preference. When running ConsoleOne with the GroupWise snap-ins, changes are written to both directories simultaneously.

Suppose, however, that the administrators in human resources do not have file-system rights to a GroupWise domain database. They can change phone numbers, mail-stops, or titles for users, and the changes will never propagate into the GroupWise address book where they will be really useful—unless eDirectory user synchronization is correctly configured. Furthermore, if you were to create admin-defined fields, which is discussed just a little later in this chapter, enabling eDirectory user synchronization is particularly valuable.

By default, eDirectory user synchronization is not enabled. To change the eDirectory synchronization status, click Configure Agents, which will bring up the box shown in Figure 6.9.

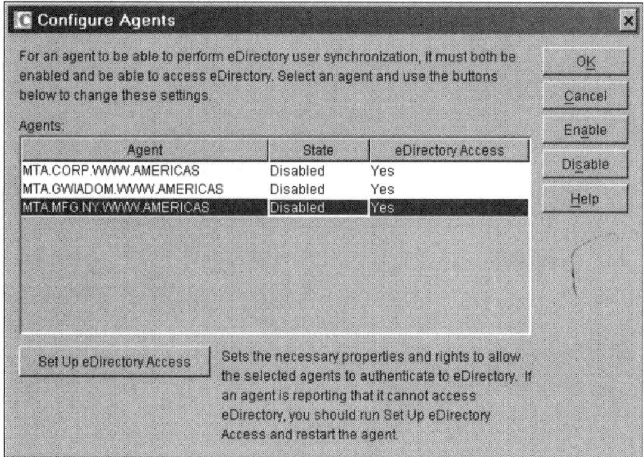

FIGURE 6.9 The Configure Agents window displays every MTA object in the GroupWise system.

This window displays every MTA object in the GroupWise system. The state of each agent is either Enabled or Disabled. Before an agent can be enabled as an eDirectory Sync agent, it must have rights to read information from eDirectory.

Clicking Set Up eDirectory Access gives the highlighted MTA object the necessary trustee assignments to authenticate to and read from eDirectory. Before the rights are effective, however, the agent must be restarted.

With one or more agents enabled for eDirectory sync, you can make agent assignments. From the eDirectory User Synchronization Configuration window, highlight a domain and click Change Assignment.

TIP

It is interesting to note that an MTA can perform synchronization for more than one domain. Configuring an MTA this way can result in unnecessary GroupWise administration traffic. Novell recommends that every MTA be assigned to perform eDirectory synchronization for the domain to which it belongs, unless it is not possible for that MTA to authenticate to eDirectory for some reason.

Two more things must be configured before eDirectory user synchronization can occur. An event must be activated under the MTA's Scheduled Events tab. Chapter 9 talks about the eDirectory user synchronization event in more detail.

Admin-Defined Fields

This tool is part of a solution that enables you to define new fields for the GroupWise address book. Extending the schema of both the GroupWise and eDirectory directories does this. This tool is also available by clicking Map

Additional Fields from the Address Book tab of the domain object's details window. This section will explain the entire process to take in order to add a new Address book field that can be viewed within the GroupWise 6.5 client's address book.

In this scenario, the administrator wants to add a field called Employee Cost Center Number, which will be viewable in the GroupWise Address book. Here are the steps required:

NOTE

This procedure was written using eDirectory 8.6.2 and ConsoleOne 1.3.4 with the GroupWise 6.5 Administration Snap-ins to ConsoleOne.

TIP

When making changes to eDirectory, be prepared for a possible time lag that comes with creating new attributes.

1. Make sure you are logged into Novell eDirectory as a user with rights to extend the eDirectory tree.
2. Load ConsoleOne.
3. Highlight an eDirectory Organization or Organizational Unit and select Tools, Schema Manager.
4. Select the Attributes tab.
5. Click the Create button, and select the Next button.
6. Name the attribute. Click the Help button for helpful information about naming this field. In this example, the name of the attribute is `www: emp cost center number`.

NOTE

The assigned name cannot be over 32 characters. That's part of the reason for a somewhat cryptic name. Also, the `www:` portion of the attribute name is added so that World Wide Widgets eDirectory administrators know that this is a custom attribute added by an internal eDirectory administrator.

   Figure 6.10 shows the attribute name. Click Next to define the syntax of the attribute.

7. In the Syntax window, select in the drop-down list, Case Ignore String, and select the Next button.
8. From the Set Flags screen, select Single valued; keep all other check boxes unchecked (unless there is a special purpose for checking them). Click the Next button.

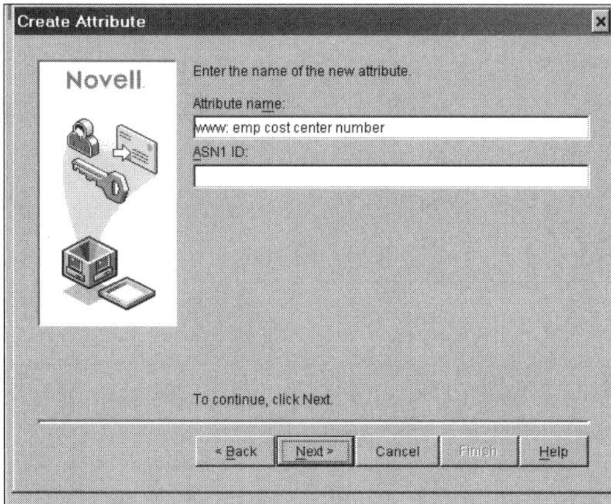

FIGURE 6.10
Naming a new attribute.

9. From the summary screen, review the selections and click the Finish button.
10. Exit the Schema Manager.
11. Go back into the Schema Manager by selecting Tools, Schema Manager.
12. From the Classes column, select the object type of User. Click the Info button. You should see a window similar to the one in Figure 6.11.

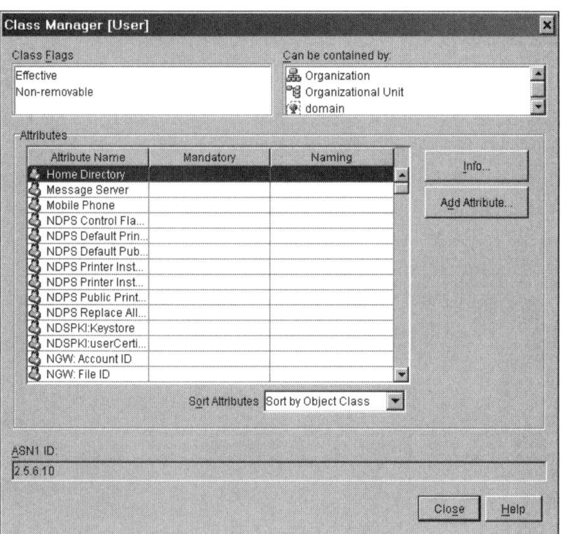

FIGURE 6.11
Adding an attribute to the user object.

13. Select the Add Attribute button.

14. From the Available Attributes column in the Add Optional Attribute window, scroll down to the attribute created earlier. In the example scenario this is the `www: emp cost center number` attribute. With the attribute highlighted, select the arrow pointing to the right, which places the attribute in the Add These Attributes column. Figure 6.12 shows that the attribute `www: emp cost center number` has been added to the User object.

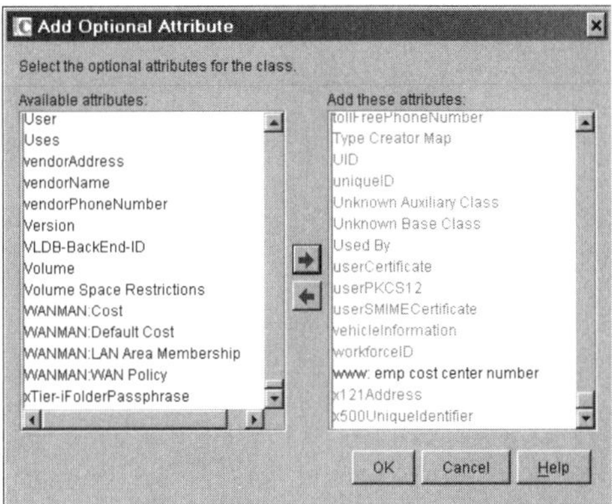

FIGURE 6.12
Selecting the attribute.

15. Select the OK button. Exit the Schema Manager utility.
16. In ConsoleOne, go to the GroupWise view. Make sure that you are connected to the GroupWise primary domain.
17. Select Tools, GroupWise System Operations, Admin Defined Fields.
18. From the Administrator-Defined Fields window, highlight an unused admin-defined field, and then click the Edit button.
19. From the Select eDirectory User Property window, select the attribute `www: emp cost center number`, and select the OK button. You should see the attribute mapped to an admin-defined field as shown in Figure 6.13. Click the OK button to dismiss the Admin-Defined Fields utility.

    To add admin-defined fields to the address book of a post office, you must define the attribute to the domain that owns that post office. Therefore, the steps described going forward must be performed on every GroupWise domain.
20. Highlight the domain containing post offices whose address book you want to display this new field in.
21. Edit the domain by right-clicking it and selecting the Properties menu option.

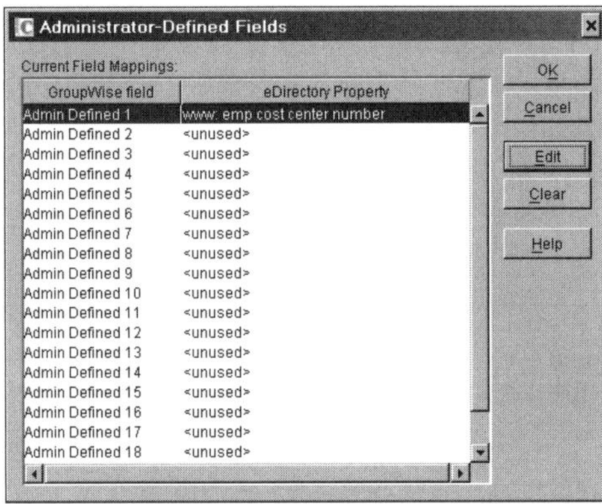

FIGURE 6.13 Assigning an eDirectory attribute to an admin-defined field.

22. On the GroupWise tab from the Properties of the domain, select the address book property page.
23. From the Available Fields column, select `www: emp cost center number` and click the arrow pointing to the left. This adds `www: emp cost center number` to the Address Book Fields column.
24. With the `www: emp cost center number` attribute highlighted in the Address Book Fields column, select the Edit Label button.
25. In the Address Book Label field, give the field a more intelligible name; this name is the name users will see within their GroupWise 6.5 client. Figure 6.14 shows a fully configured Address Book field.

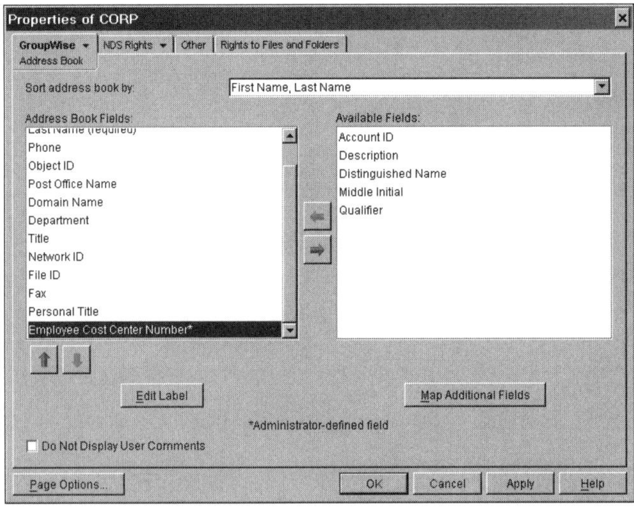

FIGURE 6.14 Configuring the address book to contain an admin-defined field.

26. Exit the domain properties of the domain you just modified. Then with the domain highlighted, select Tools, GroupWise Utilities, System Maintenance. From the GroupWise System Maintenance window, select Rebuild Indexes for Listing and then select the Run button. Then exit the GroupWise System Maintenance window.

27. In ConsoleOne, highlight a post office where you want the Address Book field to show. Select Tools, GroupWise Utilities, System Maintenance. From the GroupWise System Maintenance window, select Rebuild Indexes for Listing and then select the Run button. Then exit the GroupWise System Maintenance window.

NOTE

Repeat step 27 for each post office where you want the new Address Book field to show.

Assign the Employee Cost Center Number to a user. The instructions given here are instructions for how to populate the attributes for one user. If you had a mechanism for bulk loading the newly created eDirectory field, it could be used as well. You must, however, have eDirectory User Synchronization enabled to ensure that the GroupWise Domain MTA replicates to the GroupWise directory the information that was put into eDirectory. When populating the `www: emp cost center number` field for a user, you do so with the GroupWise 6.5 Snapins to ConsoleOne installed. The GroupWise Administration Snapins know to grab the contents of the `www: emp cost center number` field and add it to the GroupWise Address Book as the field called Employee Cost Center Number. If you bulk load information into eDirectory, however, there's not necessarily a mechanism to determine that the information in eDirectory then gets populated over to the GroupWise directory (WDOMAIN.DB and WPHOST.DB files). With eDirectory User Synchronization enabled and configured, the GroupWise MTA will extract the values from the eDirectory field `www: emp cost center number` and push it into the GroupWise directory into the GroupWise Employee Cost Center Number field.

28. Edit the properties for a user object that is on a post office configured to allow the new Employee Cost Center Number attribute to be displayed in the address book.

29. Go to the Other tab on the user object.

30. Select the word *Attributes* and then select the Add button.

31. Find the attribute `www: emp cost center number` from the list of available attributes, and select the OK button.

32. Populate the entry field below the new attribute, and select the Apply button. Figure 6.15 illustrates the results of adding this attribute and populating the entry field.

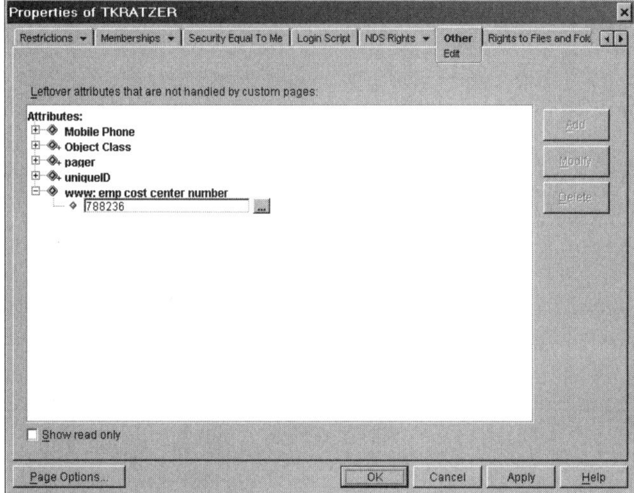

FIGURE 6.15
Editing information for an attribute.

33. Log into the GroupWise as a member of the post office that allows for the addition of Address Book fields, and view the user. To do this, run the GroupWise 6.5 client and go into the address book. Select the user, and select View, Details. You should see something similar to Figure 6.16.

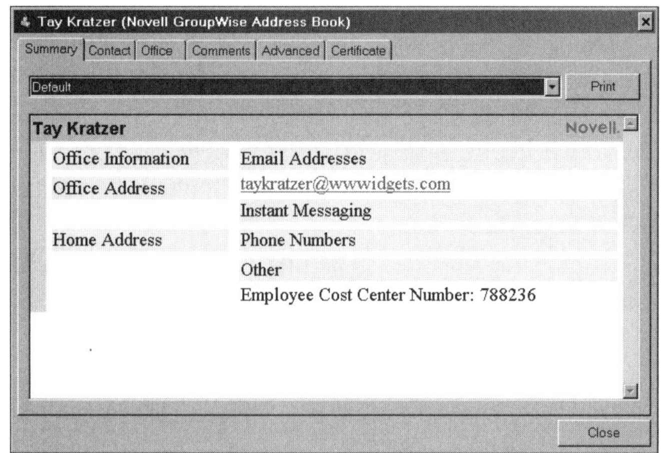

FIGURE 6.16
Viewing details on a user with a custom attribute.

Although the steps to configure admin-defined fields are many, once you have it all configured, you have a powerful way to add eDirectory information into the GroupWise address book.

Pending Operations

When changes are made that involve multiple domains, it is possible for these changes to take several minutes to complete. While connected to a particular domain, the Pending Operations box lists all operations that this domain still has marked as unsafe.

Consider an example where a change was made to the phone number on a user that is owned by DOMAINA, but the person making the change is connected to DOMAINB. DOMAINB must wait for DOMAINA to acknowledge the change to the user whose phone number changed. Until an acknowledgement is returned to DOMAINB, the operation performed will show up in the Pending Operations box from the perspective of DOMAINB.

If you suspect synchronization problems, try using some of the buttons in this window to solve the problem. Unfortunately, this seldom works. Typically, when an operation is pending for an extended period, the problem is not a simple one. Try these actions to resolve a pending operation.

- *Undo:* Restores the object record in this database to its original state and sends a request to the other domain or domains to do the same.
- *Retry:* Resends the transaction request. This is likely to work only if the original request somehow got lost in transit—something that seldom happens—or if domain databases have been rebuilt to repair problems.
- *View:* Displays the transaction in more detail.
- *Refresh:* Rereads the list of pending operations.

You can certainly try and retry the item listed in Pending Operations. However in my experience, you are generally better off using the Undo operation, and then redoing it, and keeping a close eye on the GroupWise agents to see whether the change goes through.

Addressing Rules

Addressing rules are find-and-replace operations that act on the addresses that users enter in the TO, CC, and BC fields in mail messages they send. This feature was introduced in earlier versions of GroupWise so that Internet-style addresses could be entered without adding a gateway prefix.

In GroupWise 4.1 and 5.2, a user sending to `glennbrown@novell.com` had to enter a string such as `<domain>.<smtp gateway name>: tkratzer@wwwidgets.com` or `INTERNET:glennbrown@novell.com`. With addressing rules, the prefix can now be added automatically by the system, making things simpler for the user. Configuring the addressing rules correctly is anything but simple, however.

Fortunately, from GroupWise 5.5 going forward, there is a much better alternative to using addressing rules: native Internet addressing. If you have a need for an addressing rule for other conditions, you will want to set up addressing rules for your users. For example, if your users send a message to FAX:5551212, perhaps you'll want to have the FAX: changed to GATEWAYS_DOM.GWFAX:5551212. This can be done with an addressing rule (see Figure 6.17).

FIGURE 6.17
Thee New Addressing Rule box.

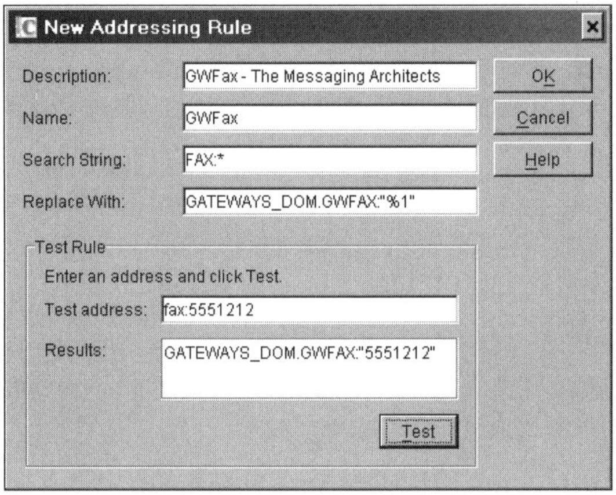

The following is a list of fields you fill out when defining an addressing rule:

- *Description:* Enter a brief description of the rule.
- *Name:* Name the rule.
- *Search String:* Enter the search string that will trigger the rule.

  For example, `FAX:*` searches for any address that is preceded with `FAX:`.

- *Replace With:* Enter the string to replace the address line. Be sure to include all necessary elements of the original address string, as in the following example:

  ```
  GATEWAYS_DOM.GWFAX:"%1"
  ```

- *Test address:* Enter an address that a user might enter, for testing your rule, such as the following:

  ```
  FAX:5551212
  ```

- *Results:* After clicking the test button, this field will be populated automatically:

  ```
  GATEWAYS_DOM.GWFAX:"5551212"
  ```

NOTE

When you create an addressing rule from system operations, it is not enabled at the domain level yet. You must then go to the properties of the domain, and from the GroupWise tab, select the Addressing Rules option. From here, you will see all addressing rules that have been defined from system operations. You can now enable them at the domain level and they will be active. Addressing rules are activated or deactivated at a domain level only. They are created at the system level through system operations.

When Internet addressing is enabled, any addressing rule that you create which contains an @ symbol in the search field, and a : in the replace field will be ignored by any GroupWise 5.5 or newer client. The reason for this is that these types of rules were in older GroupWise systems to provide the functionality that Internet addressing now provides. These rules are no longer needed unless you still have users using a GroupWise client older than 5.5x.

TIP

Addressing rules are processed in order from top to bottom. If you have multiple addressing rules defined, be aware that the format might have been altered by a previous addressing rule by the time it is acted upon by a lower addressing rule. You can rearrange the order of the addressing rules by clicking the up and down arrows.

Timezones

In a GroupWise system with post offices in more than one timezone, it is critical that the timezones be correctly configured. If you do business via e-mail with users on the Internet, you will also want to make sure your timezones are configured correctly so that timestamps on your e-mail messages reflect reality.

The timezones that are predefined in GroupWise 6.5 should cover every real timezone on the planet. Most GroupWise 6.5 shops find that once the correct timezone has been selected at the domain or post office level, timestamps system-wide are accurate.

Suppose, though, that you have a need to edit this timezone (Novell does not recommend this, but the functionality is here). Clicking Edit calls up a new dialog box in order to edit the timezone. All aspects of the timezone are available to be edited, including the rather tricky algorithm for determining when Daylight Saving Time begins and ends.

Numerous administrators have made a mistake using this interface. Suppose you have offices in Las Vegas and Phoenix. Las Vegas observes Daylight Saving Time, and Phoenix does not, but both cities observe the same offset from GMT. You have assigned both domains to the Mountain Time timezone. If you connect to the Phoenix domain and edit this timezone (to turn Daylight Saving Time off, of course), you are making that change system-wide. You have just turned Daylight Saving Time off for Phoenix and for Las Vegas.

TIP

The mistake was a simple one, and the solution is equally simple. Don't edit timezones. Put Phoenix in a different timezone than Las Vegas. There is even a predefined timezone, Arizona, which suits your needs perfectly in this case. Remember, you are performing system operations in this chapter—if you edit a timezone, you do so for the whole system.

WARNING

Do not edit timezones, unless you really intend to do so. Editing timezones affects any other entities in the timezone that you edited.

External System Synchronization

If your organization has partners that use GroupWise, you might want to synchronize your address books with theirs. This synchronization must be set up on both sides, and requires you to choose a single domain on the external system as your point-of-contact.

When configured correctly, external system synchronization is a powerful collaborative tool. Users in your organization will see members of the external system as entries in the Novell GroupWise address book and can communicate and share with those users just like they do with users on their home system. The process of defining an external system, and then synchronizing with that external system, is fully explained in Chapter 15, "Administering Multiple GroupWise Systems."

Software Directory Management

The software directory management feature (see Figure 6.15) is a powerful tool. A software distribution directory object represents a directory on a file server that contains GroupWise software. These objects can be assigned to post offices, but each post office can be assigned to only one software distribution directory.

Your scheme for managing software distribution directories can have a huge impact on your successful rollout of the GroupWise client, or on upgrading the GroupWise client. Chapter 12, "Administering the GroupWise Client," goes into a significant amount of detail on leveraging the software distribution directories to your advantage.

There are several things you might want to do with software distribution directories as part of your GroupWise administration:

- Create a new directory
- Move an existing directory to a new path
- Patch or update an existing directory
- Delete an existing directory

Creating a software distribution directory is straightforward. Chapter 12 will give you a better understanding as to why you should create a software distribution directory.

Creating New Software Distribution Directories

Clicking the Create button results in the dialog box in Figure 6.18. Software distribution directories describe a directory that typically exists. When you first installed GroupWise 6.5 you most likely established a Software Distribution Directory (SDD). The purpose for defining a SDD is to associate the SDD to post offices so that the users of that post office can update their GroupWise clients when upgrades happen.

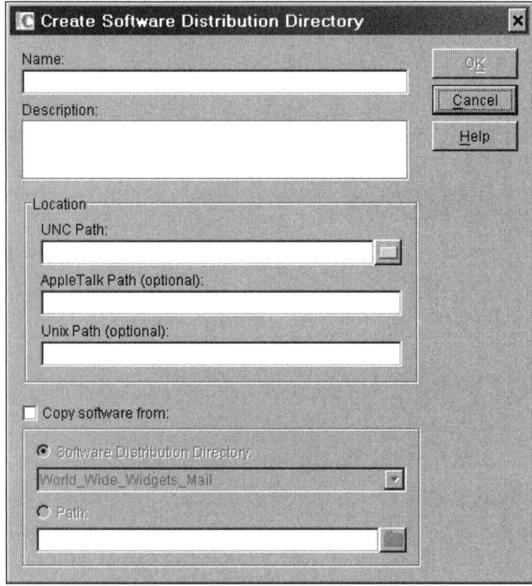

FIGURE 6.18 Defining a software distribution directory.

The following are the fields that you fill in when defining a software distribution directory.

- *Name:* You must assign a unique name to each software distribution directory object. You might choose to name the object based on the server upon which it will reside.
- *Description:* This optional field can be populated with the name and number of the individual responsible for maintaining the software in this directory. Input a detailed description. This description is used when assigning a software distribution directory to a GroupWise post office.
- *UNC Path:* This is the path to the directory. If a drive has been mapped already, you can browse to the directory. The field will be populated with a drive-based path, but when you click OK, GroupWise administrator converts that path to UNC format.
- *AppleTalk Path:* This optional path will be used only by users of the GroupWise 5.2 Macintosh client who cannot browse to UNC paths.
- *Unix Path*: Only users of the GroupWise 5.2 Unix client who cannot browse to UNC paths will use this optional path.

- *Copy Software From:* If you check this box, you're indicating that you want to populate the UNC path that you specified from another software distribution directory. If you do not already have a GroupWise 6.5 Software Distribution Directory, run SETUP.EXE from the GroupWise 6.5 Administration CD.

NOTE

The process responsible for this copy operation is ConsoleOne, running on your workstation. It might not be wise to use this feature to populate software distribution directories across a wide area network (WAN). In these cases, you should not use the Copy software from feature. Instead, have someone local to that server manually copy the GroupWise 6.5 Admin & Client software from CDs into the directory you specified.

Editing or Moving Existing Directories

Moving a software distribution directory is simple:

1. Using Explorer or a command prompt, move or copy the software from the current location to the new location.
2. Edit your existing Software Distribution Directory and change the UNC path field and the Name field, if needed.

NOTE

Be careful about editing SDDs; this causes a number called the *bump number* to be incremented on all post offices that point to this defined SDD. This could cause users to start receiving prompts that there is new GroupWise software available. More about this is covered in Chapter 12.

Deleting Existing Directories

This interface can be used to delete the SDD object, but the directory itself must be deleted manually. This action prevents accidental deletion of software in cases where SDD objects share physical directories.

Patching or Updating Existing Directories

The Update tool (shown in Figure 6.19) is used only *after* a patch or upgrade has been applied to a SDD somewhere on the system. For instructions regarding applying patches, refer to the readme file or files associated with that particular patch.

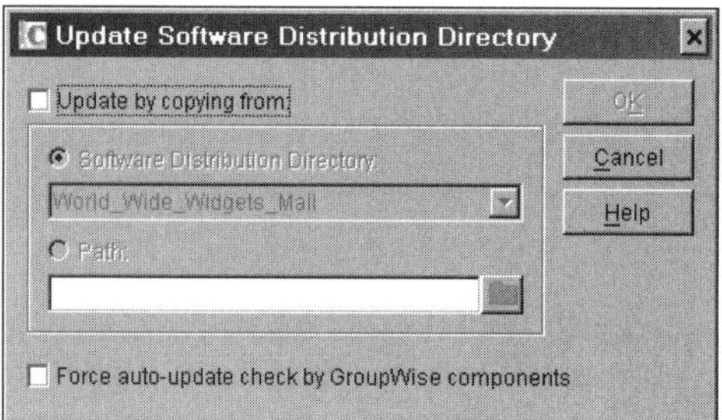

FIGURE 6.19 The Update Software Distribution Directory dialog box.

Once one directory on the system has been updated, you can use this interface to copy the updated files from the updated directory to other directories.

NOTE **Again, be careful about using this to distribute software across the WAN. It is probably a wiser use of bandwidth to patch or update remote SDD while on location.**

The Force auto-update check by GroupWise components check box exists to alert the GroupWise client that new software is available. When you check this box and click OK, the new software bump number associated with this SDD is incremented by one. Therefore, this is not something to be undertaken lightly! Every GroupWise client that attaches to any post office assigned to this SDD must browse to the UNC path and determine whether the code in the directory is newer than the code on the user's workstation. If the UNC path is not available (that is, the user has no rights to the directory), and SETUPIP is not configured, an error will be reported.

This subject, along with SETUPIP, is covered in Chapter 12.

Using Restore Area Management

A *restore area* is a location where a post office has been restored from backup. There's no set procedure on how you configure restore areas. You might want to create one per post office. Or you can just create restore areas on demand. When there's a need to restore something, and you've brought a post office off of backup, you come here to define a restore area.

The following are the fields available in the Restore Area Management configuration window:

- *Restore Area Directories:* Displays the directories in your GroupWise system that have been designated as restore areas for post offices.
- *Description:* Select a restore area directory to display any information entered in the Description field when the restore area was created. To modify or add a description, click Edit.
- *Create:* To create a restore area, click Create. You can create multiple restore areas.
- *Edit:* Select a restore area directory and then Edit to modify the name, description, or location of the restore area.
- *Delete:* Select a restore area directory and then click Delete to delete the restore area.

Figure 6.20 shows the window for Restore Area Management and an example restore area. Restore areas is part of a backup and restore system that is fully explained in Chapter 28, "Restoring Deleted Users."

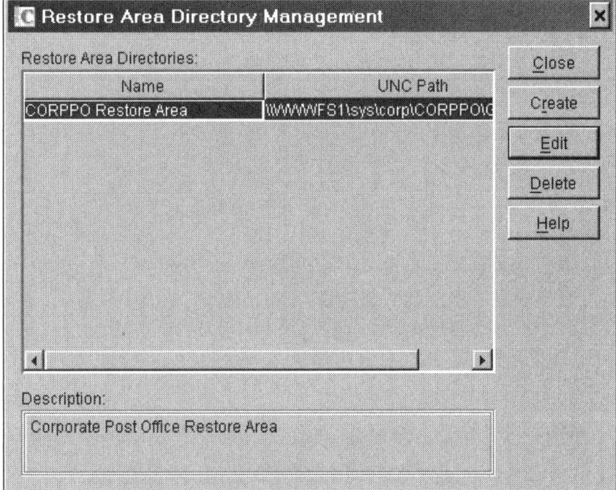

FIGURE 6.20 Restore area directory management.

Internet Addressing

Since the early 1990s, GroupWise has used a proprietary addressing format, commonly called *UPD format* for `User.PostOffice.Domain`. With GroupWise 5.5, Novell made it possible for the administrator to change the internal addressing algorithms. GroupWise 5.5 and GroupWise 6.5 can be configured to use Internet-style addresses

Because of the significant impact of this change, there's an entire chapter devoted to Internet addressing. Refer to Chapter 16 for more information.

Trusted Applications

Trusted applications is a new feature to GroupWise 6.5. A trusted application is not something you create in ConsoleOne, nor is it configured from ConsoleOne. A trusted application is an object that is created by software that might integrate with GroupWise. An example might be GWAVA's (`www.beginfinite.com`) post office message store scanning features (shown in Figure 6.21). There is one other place where you can disable certain trusted applications. If you edit a post office, and select the Post Office Settings property page, you have the option to Exempt This Post Office from the Trusted Application Routing Requirement.

Because a trusted application is really a registry for a third-party software solution of some type, consult the documentation for that software for configuration procedures.

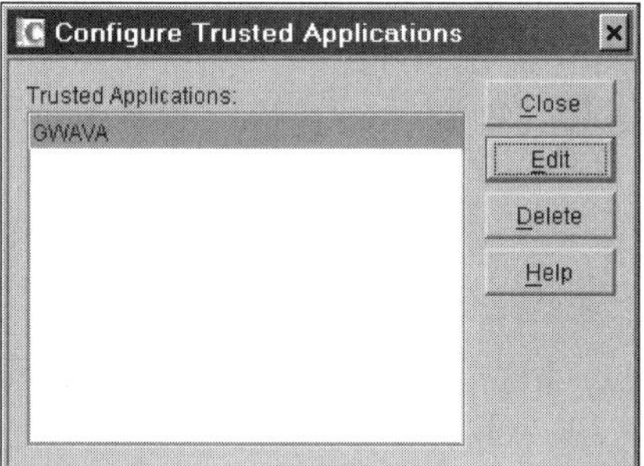

FIGURE 6.21
GWAVA as a trusted application.

LDAP Servers

Both GroupWise 6 and GroupWise 6.5 support user authentication to the post office via LDAP. It's only in GroupWise 6.5 Administration that the LDAP servers can be configured from ConsoleOne. With LDAP authentication there are some distinct advantages; here are some of them:

- Users no longer need to remember an eDirectory and a GroupWise password.
- Even if users use GroupWise WebAccess or GroupWise Wireless, their passwords will be the same as their eDirectory passwords.
- When users change their password in GroupWise, it can also change their eDirectory passwords.
- Password expiration in GroupWise is now feasible because it's really just an eDirectory password.

The process of creating LDAP servers should be well thought out and well configured. Because of this, I have dedicated an entire chapter (Chapter 26, "Configuring GroupWise Authentication via LDAP") to configuring GroupWise authentication via LDAP.

Summary

This chapter explored how to use a number of tools that apply changes to your entire GroupWise system. Now that you are familiar with each of them, it is time to move to the GroupWise utilities, which is the topic of Chapter 7, "GroupWise Utilities and Diagnostics."

CHAPTER 7

GroupWise Utilities and Diagnostics

Even though this is the seventh chapter of the book, there are still quite a few GroupWise administration tools that need to be introduced. This chapter discusses the GroupWise Utilities menu and the functionality it presents. This chapter also discusses the GroupWise diagnostics.

The GroupWise Utilities Menu

Much of the work performed in administering the GroupWise system is done from the GroupWise Utilities menu, shown in Figure 7.1. On this menu are the tools used to maintain and repair libraries and user mailboxes, set global defaults for users' GroupWise client preferences, define links between GroupWise servers, and more.

NOTE

The GroupWise Utilities menu is context-sensitive. The available menu items change depending on which view is active and what type of object has been selected.

The GroupWise Utilities menu shown in Figure 7.1 illustrates the functions that can be performed on a particular object.

For some of the options on the GroupWise Utilities menu, this chapter gives only a brief description, because these utilities are discussed in other chapters.

FIGURE 7.1
The GroupWise Utilities menu.

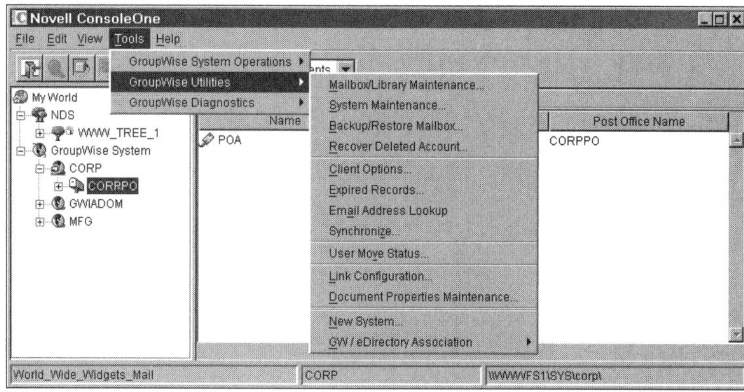

Mailbox/Library Maintenance

These are the tools used to repair the GroupWise information store. Mailbox/Library Maintenance is just another name for the GroupWise check utility, or GWCHECK. When you issue a Mailbox/Library Maintenance job from ConsoleOne, the selections you make are sent to the Post Office Agent (POA) for the selected post office. The POA then runs the job using the GWCHECK code, which is embedded in the POA. In Chapter 17, "Maintaining the GroupWise System," Mailbox/Library Maintenance is covered in more detail.

System Maintenance

These tools are for the repair of the GroupWise directory domain and post office databases. Chapter 17 gives practical circumstances under which to use System Maintenance.

Backup/Restore Mailbox

This is a menu item that is a piece of the Smart Purge and Backup/Restore system in GroupWise 6.5. This feature enables you to manually specify that a post office's user databases have been backed up, and to add a backup timestamp into the user databases. Selecting this menu option, and selecting Backup or Restore, will send a message to the POA to complete this function. Chapter 28, "Restoring Deleted GroupWise Users," contains a thorough explanation on how to use this Backup/Restore Mailbox, along with other features related to the Backup/Restore Mailbox.

Recover Deleted Account

This is a great new feature of GroupWise 6.5. If a user has been deleted accidentally, the user's user object can be added back to the WPDOMAIN.DB and eDirectory with all the original information. Most importantly, the user retains his/her FID, which is a three-character identifier, and his/her GUID (Globally Unique Identifier), which is another unique identifier that is particularly important with document management in GroupWise. In order to use this utility you must have a backup of the primary domain's WPDOMAIN.DB file. Do the following to recover a deleted account:

1. Select the Recover Deleted Account menu item.
2. Select the browse button next to the Backup Domain Path field and select the WPDOMAIN.DB for the primary domain, which you have brought back from backup. The WPDOMAIN.DB file must be from a time before the user was deleted.
3. Select the Browser button next to the Account to Restore field, filter for the user, and then select the user. Proceed through the rest of the Recover Deleted Account wizard.

NOTE

Restoring a user's object won't bring back his/her mail. Further steps must be taken to restore the user's mail messages. Chapter 28 goes into detail on how to restore a user's mailbox. Here are a couple of field notes on this feature: I have had this feature work several times, and fail a few times. So you might need to use the Import/Export feature to restore a user. This is also explained in Chapter 28. I have been able to use Recover Deleted Account feature when specifying the path to a secondary domain's WPDOMAIN.DB, so although the instructions say to use the primary domain, in my experience a secondary domain works fine as well.

Client Options

Figure 7.2 shows that the Client Options window looks very similar to the interface found under the Tools, Options interface in the 32-bit GroupWise client. Settings here can be made and specified as defaults or even locked down as defaults for users, post offices, and entire domains.

NOTE

As a general rule, it is best to allow most client options to stay at the system default. When you have a specific business need to make the GroupWise client, or GroupWise mailboxes, behave in a certain manner, you will want to utilize the Client Options features.

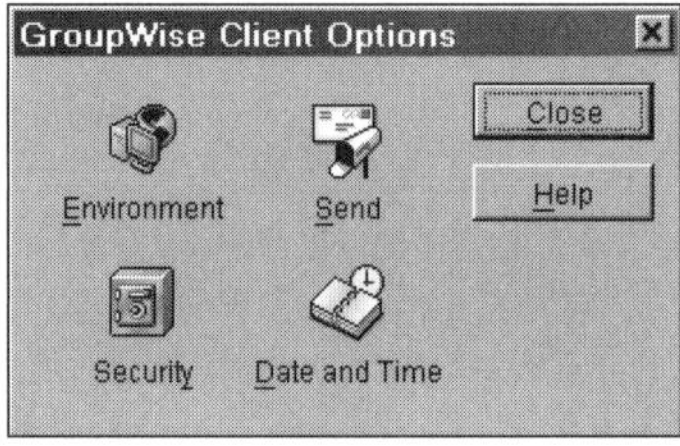

FIGURE 7.2 The GroupWise Client Options dialog box in ConsoleOne.

Double-clicking the Environment button causes the dialog box in Figure 7.3 to appear.

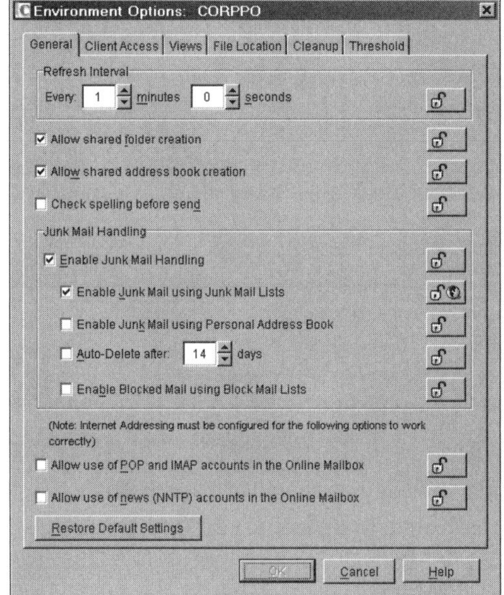

FIGURE 7.3 Administering GroupWise client environment options in ConsoleOne.

Client Environment Options

The dialog box shown in Figure 7.3 looks somewhat similar to the Tools, Options, Environment dialog box as seen from the GroupWise 32-bit Windows client. Imagine, for example, that you did not want the users' mailboxes to refresh every minute; but instead every two minutes by default. Changing the Refresh Interval to a value of 2 would accomplish your design. Users can change this back to 1 or to 3 or whatever else they would like. Take note, however, of the set of padlock buttons on the right side. To make sure that the users' mailboxes refresh only every two minutes, you can set the padlock button, which locks this setting so that users cannot make changes.

TIP

Client options can be set, and/or locked, on a user, post office, or domain level. If you want to set an option on an entire post office, make sure to highlight that post office, and then choose Tools, GroupWise Utilities, Client Options. If you want to set the client options for an entire domain, you highlight the domain object, and then choose Tools, GroupWise Utilities, Client Options.

Any setting listed in this dialog box can be changed, which will effectively change the default options for users who have not changed their defaults. Clicking the adjacent padlock puts a locked setting in place. This will prevent users from changing their individual default, and it will also force the setting down to users who might have already changed it. If a user were to view these settings after the administrator has locked them down, they would be grayed out, and they would not be able to modify them.

Some of the settings shown in Figure 7.3 are not available under Tools, Options in the GroupWise client. For example, if you uncheck the option Allow Shared Folder Creation, when a user goes to create a folder, the option to create a shared folder will be grayed out.

NOTE

The settings you configure in client options do not carry over for GroupWise users who are in GroupWise remote mode or GroupWise caching mode.

General—Allow Shared Folder Creation

This option takes away the capability— or enables the capability—for users to share folders. This option should generally be enabled.

General—Allow Shared Address Book Creation

This option takes away the capability—or enables the capability—for users to share address books. If you are using another address book solution, you should take away the capability to share address books. This will encourage users to use another address solution for sharing addresses. For example, if you were to implement Reach for eDirectory by Concentrico.net, you would most likely want to disable shared address book creation. Appendix A, "Using the taykratzer.com Web Site," introduces Concentrico.net's Reach for eDirectory product.

General—Check Spelling Before Send

This option is not enabled by default, but because good spelling is a dying art in this modern era of spell-checking computers, it might be a good idea to enable it.

General—Enabled Junk Mail Handling

By default, Junk Mail Handling is enabled; you might, however, want to consider if your organization is going to use Junk Mail Handling or not. At its best, Junk Mail Handling is a feature that gives users the satisfaction of zapping junk mail. At its worst, users can flag thousands of junk mail addresses (SPAMmers), only to find that they continue to get SPAM from differing addresses on the Internet. The impact on the GroupWise system is that whenever a user gets a message from the Internet, the POA must go through the Junk Mail Handling list to see whether the message to be received matches any of the addresses in the list. Chapter 25, "Configuring a SPAM/Junk Mail Control System," goes into a lot more detail on how to manage junk mail and SPAM mail. Consult Chapter 25 further to see whether you will keep the Junk Mail features enabled.

Allow Use of POP/IMAP/NNTP Accounts in the Online Mailbox

This option is not enabled by default, which is a good idea. If you allow users to POP their mailboxes from other e-mail accounts, they could bloat your message store beyond what you expect. The same goes for IMAP and NNTP. Generally, you will want to enable this feature on a user-by-user basis. If you enable the POP/IMAP feature, your users will see the Accounts menu option right next to the Tools menu in their GroupWise client. From the Accounts menu, users can define a POP3 or IMAP server to retrieve messages from.

If NNTP is enabled, when a user goes to create a folder, one of the options on that folder will be to enable them to define NNTP specific information.

If a user is in caching mode or remote mode, that user can access POP3, IMAP4, and NNTP accounts, even if you have locked those features down. The reason for this is that the GroupWise POA cannot exert control over a GroupWise information store that is on a user's hard drive. So these features cannot be controlled.

Client Access—Client Licensing

Under the Client Access tab shown in Figure 7.4, you will see two different kinds of client licensing. They are

- Full license mailboxes—Windows client access
- Limited license mailboxes—Non–Windows client access, such as WebAccess/Wireless, POP3, and IMAP4

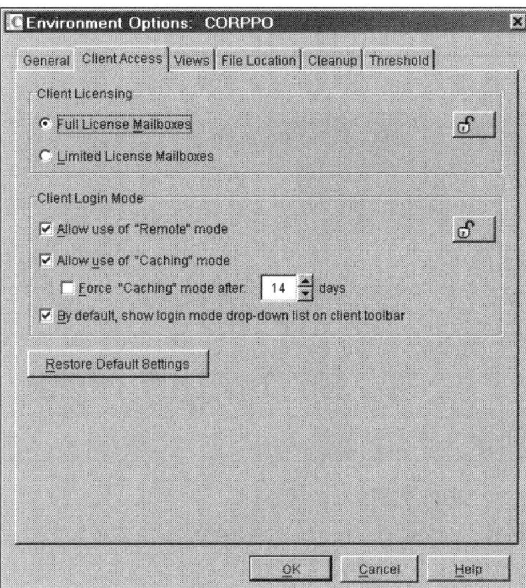

FIGURE 7.4
The Client Access menu.

NOTE

If you are using a client that uses the Windows client to access the GroupWise message store, for example the Nexic sync client for Palm OS devices, this is still considered a full license mailbox. Novell will soon release Java client that will include support for the Macintosh and Linux platform. The licensing model for those clients has not been determined at the time of the writing of this book.

GroupWise is licensed per mailbox. However, Novell licenses the mailboxes in such a manner that there are two access methods (and two prices of mailboxes); they are Windows client access or non-Windows client access. When a mailbox is accessed via the GroupWise Windows client, the mailbox is stamped in the GroupWise system as a full license mailbox. Once the Windows client accesses a mailbox, that mailbox is considered a full license mailbox for its life (even if you rename the user). If a user only accesses a mailbox via a non-Windows client, for example Outlook Express as a POP3 client, that mailbox is considered a limited license mailbox.

The notion of the mailbox types is relevant for customers who must determine how many licenses of GroupWise they need to report to Novell or a Novell partner in order to assess the correct licensing and maintenance fees. By default, all mailboxes are considered full license mailboxes. If you were to create a new mailbox for a user whom you do not want to use the Windows client (in an effort to decrease the cost of the mailbox), it would be wise to do the following:

1. Create the user.
2. In ConsoleOne, highlight the user and select Tools, GroupWise Utilities, Client Options, Environment, Client access.
3. Change the Client Licensing selection to limited license mailbox.

The process of determining how many of your current users are using limited license mailboxes requires a GWCHECK job, and looking at the right place to gather the information. This process is explained in Chapter 17.

Client Access—Client Login Mode

With this selection in this section of the Environment options, you can control how much flexibility GroupWise has to make copies of a user's mailbox for additional speed or functionality. GroupWise has always had a remote mode. With GroupWise 6.0x and GroupWise 6.5, caching mode has been added. The caching mode does all that remote mode ever did, and more. The caching mode allows the GroupWise client to receive regular automatic updates to the caching mailbox, as well as keep a live connection with the GroupWise POA, which is necessary for functions such as busy search or cross-post-office proxy. Another advantage to caching mode is that the GroupWise client needs to chat far less with the GroupWise POA in order to read data from the GroupWise information store. Also, if the POA goes down for some reason, when the GroupWise client is in caching mode, the GroupWise client doesn't even blink.

WARNING

The caching mode feature replicates a user's entire mailbox down to that user's local hard drive. If in your GroupWise system you do not have a message expiration policy, and the GWCHECK-Mailbox/Library Maintenance procedures to enforce the expiration policy, your users could have more data than can be contained on their local hard drive.

The GroupWise 6.5 client can interact with the GroupWise user's mailbox when it is in one of three locations. These locations are the following:

- The post office (the standard GroupWise client mode)
- A copy of the user's mailbox in remote mode
- A copy of the user's mailbox in caching mode

If you do not want your users to use remote mode or caching mode, you can disable these modes.

Almost always, if you need your users to have remote connectivity to their mailboxes, you will want to encourage your users to use caching mode. Here are some reasons that support using caching mode. Imagine that you have a couple of users who connect over a slow WAN link to their post office. Because the caching mode is much less chatty than a normal client/server connection to the POA, you could force some users to use caching mode. To do this, highlight the individual, and then go into Tools, GroupWise Utilities, Client Options and select the check box, Force "Caching" mode after: X days. A value of 0 means that the next time users log in they will be forced to caching mode, and they will be kept in caching mode going forward.

The feature, By Default, Show Login Mode Drop-Down List on Client Toolbar, is useful for this reason. If your users were previously GroupWise 5x users, they never saw the online or caching options in their GroupWise client. Rather than confuse your GroupWise 5x users, or leave them to make the decision to go to caching mode, you can just hide this feature by unchecking this option.

The GroupWise client is capable of establishing a *live remote* connection with a Message Transfer Agent (MTA). This MTA opens a link to the user's post office, and the POA accesses the user's mail.

Views

On the Views tab there are three options, as follows:

- Views—Read next after accept, decline, or delete. Generally you want to enable this feature, as it makes browsing messages easier.
- Views—Open new view after send. This feature is generally best kept unchecked, to allow users to make their own choice as to how the GroupWise client behaves.
- Views—Disable HTML view. There is good support for disabling HTML viewing. The HTML viewing enables features from Microsoft Internet Explorer. With this design, HTML viewing could possibly

enable browser-based viruses or browser-based security breaches. The downside to enabling this is that you take away a major feature that might be necessary for users to receive legitimate communication.

How users view messages is an important part of the users' productivity. Make choices that work for your environment; however, generally you do not want to lock these preferences down.

File Location—Archive Directory

From the File Location tab in the Environment Options box, GroupWise users can archive their messages to a location other than their mailbox. If there is a message expiration policy of 90 days, users who archive will have recourse for saving messages that are important enough to them to retain beyond those 90 days. It should be noted that there are some organizations that don't want, or cannot accept, the legal liability with archived messages. If your organization does not want users to archive, keep the path blank, and click the padlock button.

NOTE **If your users have defined their own archive paths, and then you lock the archive path with a blank path, when the users log back in, they will not be able to archive anything, nor will they have access to any previous archives.**

Many organizations find they do need an archiving solution, but that solution must be centralized. Appendix A of this book introduces third-party solutions for archiving.

File Location—Custom Views

File Location—Custom Views is part of a somewhat obscure but useful feature. If a user has a standard message, or even a template message that they often send, that user can save that message in the form of a "custom view" file. The File Location tab simply indicates where custom views should be saved and retrieved by default.

Cleanup

In this tab in the Environment Options box, you can specify just how mail messages should be cleaned up. The options in this tab can be useful for implementing a message retention policy. Using Mailbox/Library

Maintenance jobs (GWCHECK) is a more effective method for implementing a message retention policy. All of the cleanup options set here, except the archive options, are performed by the POA during a process called *nightly user upkeep* (nightly user upkeep is enabled by default on the POA). If the auto-archive feature has been selected, the archiving operation takes place when the GroupWise client logs in each day. The client must do the archiving because the POA usually does not have rights or even access to the user's archive path.

Cleanup—Allow Purge of Items Not Backed Up

With GroupWise 6.0x and 6.5 and the Smart Purge and Backup/Restore system, GroupWise can be configured to not automatically purge items that are deleted from the trash. Thus, before a backup has been done, nothing will truly be purged from the information store.

This is a powerful feature, but if your organization does not intend to use this, it's useless to have this feature enabled. In fact, with this feature enabled and used incorrectly, the information store will grow at an exponential rate. It's best to leave this option checked, until you are sure you've completely implemented the software for the Smart Purge and Backup/Restore system. Configuring and using these options is explained in Chapter 28.

Threshold

The Threshold tab in the Environment Options box has to do with when users are connected directly to their post office via direct mode, which is a connectivity mode you can set on any post office. When a user is connected in direct mode, the threshold value determines the number of recipients of a message, within the post office the sender is on, will have their user databases written to by the sender's GroupWise client.

WARNING

Do not regularly allow your users to connect directly to their post office via direct mode; this opens you up for all kinds of corruption if used on a regular basis.

Send

Almost all of the features under the Send client options mirror 32-bit Windows client's options. Most of the features should not be administered, unless you have some special business reason that requires you to administer or lock down a feature of the GroupWise client. Rather than explain all of these GroupWise client-based features, this section discusses the client options under Send that are not available to the Windows client, or that are particularly noteworthy.

Send—Send Options—Allow Use of Reply to All in Rules

This option is unchecked by default. This is a good default that will cut down on vacation rules users might make that reply to all recipients of a message.

Send—Send Options—Allow Use of Internet Mail Tracking

Internet mail tracking is a feature that will work if your GWIA has Delivery Status Notification enabled. The Delivery Status Notification feature is discussed further in Chapter 10, "Installing and Configuring the GroupWise Internet Agent." If you have not enabled this feature on the GWIA, you might as well not tease users with a feature that will not work.

Send—Send Options—Wildcard Addressing

Wildcard addressing can allow users to send a message to a lot of other users. Fortunately there is no dialog box in the GroupWise client that prompts or coaches users to use wildcard addressing. Generally this is a feature you will want to disable company-wide, and then enable it for a few select people. For more information on how to use wildcard addressing, use the Help feature in the GroupWise client, and then read up on how to send a message with a wildcard address.

Wildcard addressing can be configured to enable users to send to the following:

- Post office—All users on the sender's same post office

- Domain—All users on the post offices in the same domain as the sender's post office
- System—All users on all post offices in all internal GroupWise domains in the GroupWise system
- Unlimited—All users on all post offices in all internal GroupWise domains in the GroupWise system; all users on all external domains that you might have defined

Send—Send Options—Allow Reply Rules to Loop

Starting with GroupWise 6.0x, there is some rule loop detection intelligence in the GroupWise POA that was designed to not allow reply rules to loop. Sometimes though, the rule loop detection intelligence goes too far, and the result is that your users might complain that a rule fires off only once, and then never works beyond that. If you enable the Allow Reply Rules to Loop feature, your users should no longer experience this problem.

TIP

The customers that I support have chosen to use the Allow Reply Rules to Loop feature. We have found that too often the POA turns off rule processing prematurely unless we do so.

Send—Security—Require Password to Complete Routed Item

When a user creates a message into a routing slip and recipients of the routing slip mark the slip as completed, the recipient will be prompted to enter the same password they used to authenticate to GroupWise.

Send—Disk Space Mgmt

With this feature, you can specify just how much disk space users' mailboxes can use, as well as the largest message that users can send.

- Mailbox Size Limits—This is the maximum amount of space allocated to users for their messages and the attachments associated with those messages.

NOTE **Mailbox size is made up of anything in the users mailbox, including items in shared folders and document references to documents in a GroupWise library.**

- Threshold for Warning Users—When a user is getting close to the quota of disk space, the GroupWise client warns the user that allocated disk space is getting low.
- Maximum Send Message Size—Good when you don't want your users to send messages over a certain size. This option is one way to prevent users from using e-mail as an FTP utility.

Understanding the Architecture Behind the Client Options Interface

As Chapter 3, "Understanding the GroupWise Directory," of this book noted, the GroupWise administration SNAPins write changes directly to the GroupWise domain database to which it is connected. For client options to take effect, however, the changes must propagate all the way down to the GroupWise user database, USERxxx.DB. Here is the flow of events:

1. The administrator makes a change to client options.

   For example, imagine that you have unchecked the box labeled Allow Shared Folder Creation, and then locked that setting. Assume that the post office object was selected at the time you made the change. This means that the setting will apply to the entire post office.
2. The GroupWise administrator SNAPins write the change to the GroupWise domain database and creates an administration update file to propagate this change to the post office.
3. The MTA transmits this file to the POA.
4. The POA administration thread writes this change to the post office database.
5. A POA writes (or merges) the change to the preferences capsule of the user database, or to the user databases that are affected by the changes in client options.

The GroupWise client reads the preferences capsule of the user database when the client initially logs in. This means that if you make a client option change, the users will not normally see this change until they have logged out and back in with the GroupWise client.

Using Client Options to Lock Down the GroupWise Archive

The following scenario walks through the process of editing a client option. A company policy has been established that all GroupWise mailbox archives must be created on the network. All users have home directories mapped to the root of drive `U:`, and GroupWise administrators need to enforce the policy and force all archives for all users into their home directories. Here are the actions required to fulfill this scenario:

1. From ConsoleOne, select a domain object.

   If there are multiple domains in this system, perform steps 1-7 for each domain.

2. Pull down the Tools menu and choose GroupWise Utilities, Client Options.
3. Click the Environment button.
4. Click the File Location tab to get to Figure 7.5.

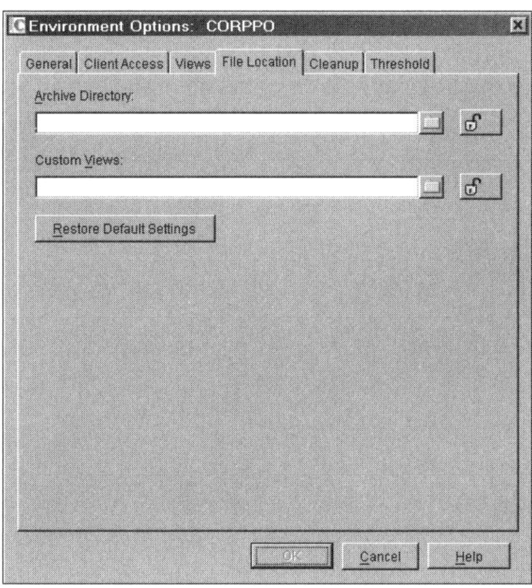

FIGURE 7.5
File location—archive path.

5. In the Archive Directory field, enter the following:

   `U:\archive`

6. Click the padlock button to lock this option.

   Because you are doing this with a domain selected, the option will be locked for all users on this domain.

7. Click OK and close out of the Environment Options dialog box.

At this point, all you need to do is wait for this option to propagate. The next time users log in, they will find that their archives must be created in their home directories.

Now, suppose users already had archives on the local drives. In this case, you have to move the archives manually, visiting each workstation. There is no central administration tool for working with existing GroupWise archives. If you want to administer an archive location, it is wise to decide this before users begin using the archive feature of GroupWise. Otherwise, they might lose access to the archives on their local drives.

WARNING

If the user's archive path does not exist, the GroupWise client will not be able to run the auto-archive operation. In other words, using the preceding example, when the administrator defines the archive path to `U:\archive` and locks this down, the end-user's client will not auto archive the first time they log in. This is because their unique archive directory does not exist under the `U:\archive` directory. They will simply need to manually archive something, or go to File, Open Archive, and then close the archive. This will create the unique user directory with a couple of archive databases in the `U:\archive\ofFIDarc directory`. The next time the user logs into GroupWise from the GroupWise client, the auto-archive function will run. Remember that this applies only if you have enabled auto archiving from the Cleanup tab. Any manual archives will work just fine, of course.

Expired Records

GroupWise administration allows you to set an expiration time on a GroupWise user's account. The Expired Records tool allows you to easily see accounts that have expired (see Figure 7.6).

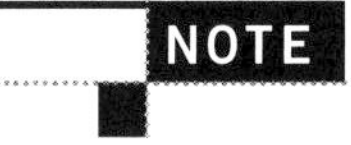

Users who have expired can still receive mail, but they cannot open their mailboxes. Expiration is a useful way to deal with temporary or contract employees without having to commit to deleting their mailboxes.

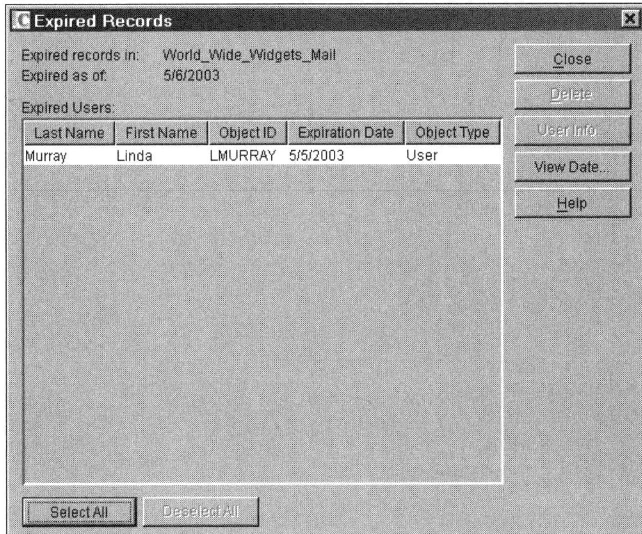

FIGURE 7.6
The Expired Records window.

Email Address Lookup

Many organizations want to make sure that their GroupWise user IDs are unique throughout the system. With this nifty feature (shown in Figure 7.7), you can type your proposed Mailbox ID/User ID to see whether it has already been used. You can search for a user ID in the following manner:

- User ID—`ECORNISH`
- Portions of the user ID with a wildcard—`EC*`
- The user ID at the user's Internet domain—`ECORNISH@WWWIDGETS.COM`

TIP

The Email Address Lookup option will also find alias records. The search window must match exactly what a user has defined as an alias, however (for example, `EVA_THE_EMAIL_QUEEN@WWWIDGETS.COM`). This will be helpful to quickly search for an address that you think might be coming from an alias record.

Also know that when creating a new user, the GroupWise snap-ins will automatically ensure the user ID is unique within the GroupWise system. If this user ID already exists you will receive an error stating that the e-mail address conflicts with the address of an existing user (db57).

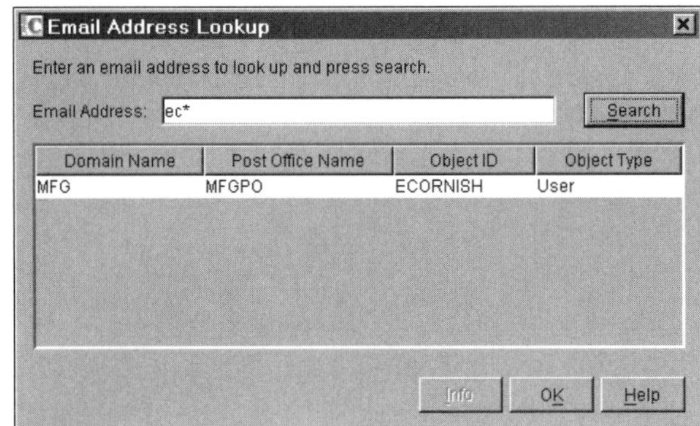

FIGURE 7.7 The Email Address Lookup window.

Synchronize

The synchronization process is nowhere as simple as the description in this synchronize dialog box. Assuming that ConsoleOne is connected to the primary domain, and the administrator synchronizes a user belonging to a secondary domain, this is what happens:

1. eDirectory-specific information in the user object is rolled into the synchronization request.
2. The synchronization request is sent to the secondary domain that owns this user.
3. The secondary domain updates the user object with information that was extracted from eDirectory.
4. The secondary domain bundles the GroupWise-specific information about the user object into another synchronization request.
5. The secondary domain propagates the new information to its post offices.
6. The secondary domain sends the request from step 4 to the primary domain.
7. The primary domain propagates this information to all other secondary domains.
8. All other secondary domains propagate the information to their post offices.

NOTE

Synchronize only synchronizes the object that you have highlighted. For example, if you highlight a post office, it sends a message to the entire system regarding the post office object itself. All of the users on that post office are not synchronized, just the post office object itself.

The synchronization process initiated here is nearly identical to the process of updating or creating objects—the only difference being that no "new" information is created. The record is simply being repropagated through the GroupWise directory.

User Move Status

The User Move Status utility allows you to track the progress of moved resources or distribution lists. Chapter 13, "Moving Users," talks more about utilizing this utility.

Link Configuration

This tool allows you to define the connections and routes for messages on your GroupWise system. Connections and routes such as how a post office connects to its domain, or how one domain connects to another domain.

The Link Configuration tool is used to define the connections, or links, between the domains and post offices on your GroupWise system. These links govern the way that the GroupWise MTA routes messages.

Before exploring the Link Configuration interface, you need to be familiar with some terms:

- *Link type:* Link types describe the type of route between two domains. A link type can be direct, indirect, gateway, or undefined.
- *Direct:* A direct link between two domains means that those domains' MTAs "talk" directly to each other. There is no domain or gateway intervening.
- *Indirect:* An indirect link between two domains means that a third domain is involved in any communication between them. For instance, if Domain A has an indirect link with Domain C through Domain B, the Domain A MTA will send to the Domain B MTA, and then it is up to Domain B's MTA to route the message to Domain C.
- *Gateway:* A gateway link between two domains indicates that the domains must communicate through a gateway, such as Async or GWIA. In this case, both domains must have the same type of gateway installed at their systems. For instance, if Domain A has a gateway link to Domain B through the Async gateway, the Domain A MTA will

hand the message to the Async gateway. This gateway will then dial Domain B's Async gateway to hand the message off again. Finally, Domain B's Async gateway will hand the message off to the Domain B MTA.

- *Link protocol:* Link protocols describe the type of connection between two domains. Differentiating between link type and link protocol is easy. Think of a trip on a U.S. highway. Link type is like your route—your choice of roads. Link protocol is like your choice of vehicles—it is your transport mechanism. The protocol choices offered are mapped, UNC, and TCP/IP.
  - *Mapped:* A mapped link is typically used by an MTA on an NT box. That machine must have a drive mapped to the link target. Mapped links to post offices require the MTA to actively poll the post office WPCSIN queues for mail to be transported. Mapped links take the form of `<drive letter>:\path`.
  - *UNC:* A UNC link is similar to a mapped link, in that an MTA with a UNC link to a post office must poll the post office WPCSIN queues. UNC links do not require drive mappings, however, and for that reason are preferred over mapped links. UNC links take the form of `\\<server>\<volume>\<path>`.
  - *TCP/IP:* TCP/IP links are preferred over both UNC and mapped links. With TCP/IP, the MTA need not poll post office directories. The POA will poll the structure and will open a connection with the MTA only when there are items to be transferred.

No link type is better than another. For some organizations lots of indirect links will work well. For others, all domains will be linked directly. The size of your system will dictate your link types. UNC links should be eliminated, even in instances in which the two agents that must talk with one another are on the same server. The best link type is TCP/IP.

The window shown in Figure 7.8 has four main components:

- The toolbar
- The Domain drop-down menu
- The Outbound Links pane
- The Inbound Links pane

From this window, you can edit links and drag and drop links in order to change how agents link to one another.

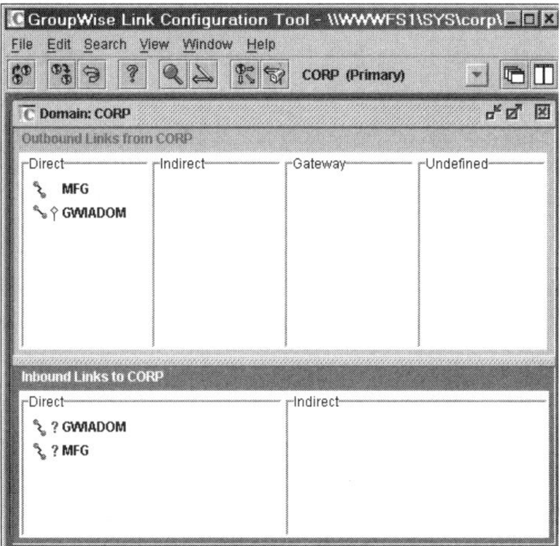

FIGURE 7.8
The Link Configuration utility.

If you have created your domains and post offices properly, assigning IP addresses and ports right away, you do not have to worry about the actual configuration of the agents. All you have to worry about is how the domain-to-domain links work. By default newly created domains link to one another via the Primary domain, and have an indirect link to all other domains. This isn't necessarily the best design for your system.

The Link Configuration Toolbar

This toolbar has eight action buttons on it. These buttons allow you to perform operations without accessing menu items. Here's a description of these buttons from left to right:

- *Open:* The first button is the Open button. It allows you to connect to a different domain database for configuring links. You will be prompted for the path to a domain database.
- *Save:* The second button is the Save button. This saves all changes you have made to link configuration in the current domain database.
- *Undo:* If you have made changes but have not saved them yet, you can use the third button to revert to the original link configuration.
- *Help:* The fourth button opens the help file to the Link Configuration Contents page.
- *Find:* The fifth button allows you to find a domain link by entering a domain name. This is useful for very large systems.

- *Link:* The sixth button opens the highlighted link for viewing or editing. This is discussed further in Chapter 9, "Configuring the Message Transfer Agent (MTA)."
- *Domain Links:* The seventh button changes the display of the tool so that only domain links are displayed.
- *Post Office Links:* The last button changes the display of the tool so that only post office links are displayed.

You can accomplish each of the tasks shown on the buttons either through menu choices or by right-clicking and choosing from the menu.

The Domain Drop-Down Menu

In Figure 7.8, this menu reads "Corp (Primary)". This means that the primary domain's links are being examined. Changing this to another domain does not change the system connection, however. Remember that all domains have copies of each other's records—you can be connected to one domain and change the links for a different domain.

To change the system connection, use the first button on the toolbar, or go to the File menu and select Open.

The Outbound Links Pane

This pane displays each of the outbound links, or "send" connections for this domain. Notice that domains displayed here are listed by link type, which is either direct, indirect, gateway, or undefined. The View menu can also be used to display links to this domain's post offices instead of links to other domains.

The Inbound Links Pane

This pane displays each of the inbound links, or "receive" connections for this domain. The sales domain's outbound link to Corp will be the same as the Corp domain's inbound link from sales. Outbound links can be edited—inbound links are edited by changing the corresponding outbound link somewhere else.

Again, use the View menu to expand this display to include gateway and undefined links, or to switch to post office links.

Document Properties Maintenance

This menu option is available only when a post office is selected, and it allows you to customize default property sheets for documents in GroupWise libraries. Chapter 14, "Library and Document Administration," goes into much more detail on how and when to use the document properties maintenance tool.

If document management figures in to your GroupWise strategy, you will want to become familiar with this tool. With a post office object selected, the menu item is available under the GroupWise Utilities menu.

This tool allows you to do the following things:

- Change the property sheet fields for documents for each GroupWise library
- Create or edit lookup tables for populating certain property sheet fields
- Add or edit document types to fit your document retention strategy
- Create relationships between fields and between lookup tables

Don't venture into these selections in this menu without first reading Chapter 14. Some of the things you select from this menu are not reversible!

New System

If you have already created a GroupWise system, it is unlikely that you will want to use this tool. Most organizations fare better with a single GroupWise system spanning multiple domains than with multiple GroupWise systems.

When you launch ConsoleOne for the first time after installing the GroupWise snap-ins, this wizard loads automatically. It walks you through the process of creating a GroupWise system, gathering domain and post office names from you, creating those objects, and then installing the necessary agent software.

This chapter does not discuss this interface, but you can find information about it in Chapter 2, "Creating a GroupWise System."

GW/eDirectory Association

This section discusses your options when you select the GW/eDirectory Association option under the GroupWise Utilities menu.

Graft GroupWise Objects

The Graft Wizard helps you add GroupWise attributes to eDirectory user objects, and add GroupWise objects to the eDirectory tree. Recall that GroupWise has its own directory independent of eDirectory. The graft function is used on the occasions that a GroupWise object isn't in eDirectory, or is somehow not associated with its eDirectory object. Throughout this book, you can find instances in which you will be told to use the graft function.. If you are creating a GroupWise 6.5 system from scratch, you will not need to use this tool, because your eDirectory user objects will automatically be grafted to the GroupWise mailboxes you create.

Invalid Associations

This utility allows you to identify whether you have any invalid associations between your GroupWise directory store and eDirectory. Here are the steps you should take to use this utility:

1. Highlight an eDirectory OU in ConsoleOne with users in it whom you are searching through in order to find invalid associations.
2. Select Invalid Associations.
3. The utility will look for objects in that eDirectory OU that have the following type of a problem:
   - eDirectory says that it has an object GBROWN.OU1.ACME that points to the GroupWise object GBROWN.PO1.DOMAIN1.
   - GroupWise reports that GBROWN.PO1.DOMAIN1 is associated with GBROWN.OU2.ACME.

The Invalid Association utility will then come up with a wizard that helps you to resolve this potential issue. This issue could likely happen if you have regrafted objects, and somehow you grafted the users into an OU in which they did not originally exist, or your GroupWise system spans multiple eDirectory trees and there are user objects that GroupWise is pointing to in the wrong tree.

Disassociate GroupWise Attributes

The Disassociate GroupWise Attributes feature is the opposite of a graft. This feature is used when you want to disassociate a GroupWise object from its eDirectory object. This is often used for troubleshooting purposes. For example, you suspect that an eDirectory object has some corruption in it, and you want to delete the object from eDirectory, but not from GroupWise. This is a perfect scenario to disassociate the eDirectory object from its GroupWise object.

As illustrated in Chapters 3 and 5, "Working with GroupWise Objects," when GroupWise is first installed into a network, it adds attributes to, or *extends,* the eDirectory user object. This makes administration of user accounts much simpler.

Unfortunately, the synchronization between eDirectory and the GroupWise domain and post office databases is not perfect. Sometimes, particularly after a user moves, the eDirectory user object contains inaccurate GroupWise attributes, and the user mailbox can no longer be administered from ConsoleOne.

Here is where the Disassociate GroupWise Attributes tool comes into the game. This tool strips all of the GroupWise information from the highlighted user's eDirectory object.

Using the Disassociate GroupWise Attributes Tool

This tool has no interface window of its own. To remove GroupWise attributes from a user, do the following:

1. Select the user object in either the eDirectory or the GroupWise view.
2. Pull down the Tools menu and choose GroupWise Utilities, GW/eDirectory Association, Disassociate GroupWise Attributes.

If you were to use Display Object on a user whose GroupWise attributes had been removed, you would find that none of the attributes with NGW in their names (the GroupWise schema extensions) were populated. Also, "GDS" (GroupWise directory services) information appears. The eDirectory object would no longer be linked to a GroupWise object.

When GroupWise attributes have been removed, the user's mailbox still exists. All that has happened, in practical terms, is the link between the GDS and eDirectory systems has been broken for this user.

Convert External Entity to User

The Convert External Entity to User tool allows you to take a GroupWise external entity user who does not currently have an eDirectory account and convert that user to a GroupWise user with an eDirectory account. By converting an external entity into a full eDirectory user, the user can leverage services from eDirectory; for example, LDAP authentication or password expiration.

TIP **You can select multiple external entities in eDirectory and convert them all to full eDirectory users in one step.**

Convert User to External Entity

The Convert User to External Entity feature allows you to take a GroupWise user who also has an eDirectory account and convert that user and eDirectory account so that it's an external entity. External entities have a green shirt (rather than a red shirt on a typical eDirectory user object), and external entities have no eDirectory rights. External entities do not use an eDirectory license, which is typically the motivation behind making a user an external entity. So if you are sure this user does not need eDirectory rights or services, go ahead and make the user an external entity.

TIP **You can select multiple eDirectory user objects and convert them all to external entities in one step as well.**

NOTE **If you are using LDAP authentication, external entity users cannot authenticate to eDirectory via LDAP. That being the case, you must assign a GroupWise password to external entities to allow them to get into GroupWise.**

GroupWise Diagnostics

This section discusses your options when you select the GroupWise Diagnostics option under the GroupWise Utilities menu. You probably won't use GroupWise Diagnostics often, but it sure is handy when you are doing hard-core troubleshooting.

Display Object

One of the most useful tools the developers have for debugging is the Display Object tool shown in Figure 7.9. This window bypasses the usual object details windows and displays all record data as straight text.

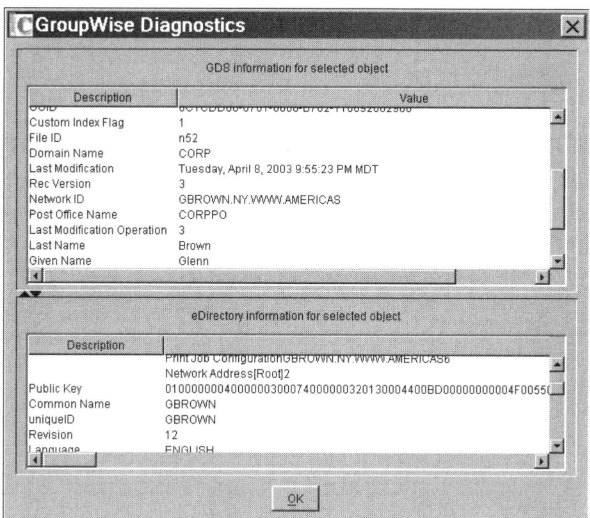

FIGURE 7.9
Displaying an object in GroupWise Diagnostics.

This is a useful tool for viewing all the information about any object in your GroupWise system in one simple view. GroupWise Diagnostics is particularly helpful because it allows you to see some information that is not available any other place. GroupWise Diagnostics is an information-gathering tool, but it in no way does a health-check type diagnosis of a GroupWise system or object. At various points throughout this book, you'll be told to use GroupWise Diagnostics to garner some little piece of information.

In the example in Figure 7.9, a user named Glenn Brown has been highlighted when selecting the Display Object menu. The top pane shows the GDS (GroupWise Directory Store) information. The bottom pane establishes the context and class of this object record in eDirectory. Then you are given a flat list of attribute names and values.

Record Enumerations

This tool is similar to the display object tool, but it only shows information from the GDS system, as read from the connected GroupWise domain database. Also, the record enumeration tools reference objects via several record type indexes available as a drop-down list.

Unlike Display Object, Record Enumerations shows the same information regardless of what was selected when the tool was activated. Record Enumerations is a window into the "guts" of the domain database, and from the Record Enumerations window in Figure 7.10, any record can be selected.

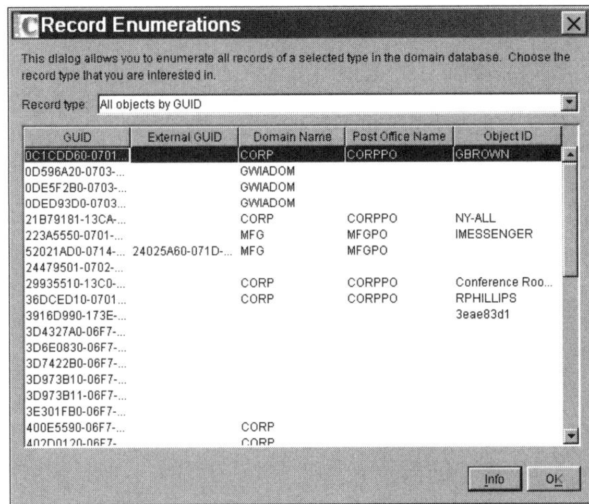

FIGURE 7.10 Record Enumerations window in GroupWise diagnostics.

Like the display object tool, Record Enumerations is typically useful when troubleshooting synchronization problems.

Information

This tool, shown in Figure 7.11, is available when highlighting the GroupWise system, a GroupWise domain, or a GroupWise post office.

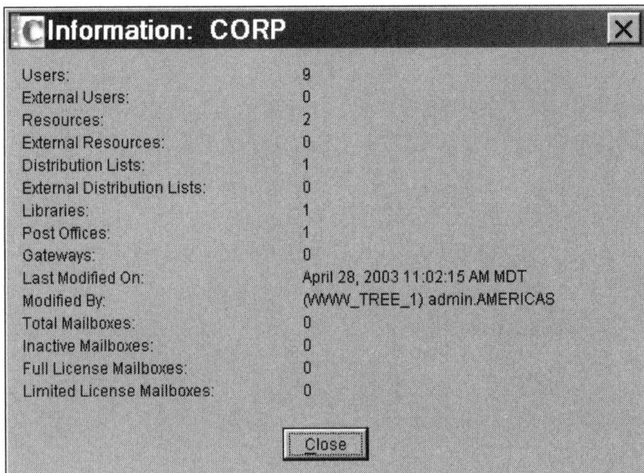

FIGURE 7.11 The Information dialog box.

This is a quick way to find out how many of which kinds of objects exist in a GroupWise system, domain, or post office.

Summary

This chapter covered the GroupWise Utilities and GroupWise Diagnostics menus. During the rest of this book, you will weave in and out of many of these tools, using them for maintenance, troubleshooting, and all kinds of configuration.

PART III

Agents and Clients

CHAPTER 8

Configuring the Post Office Agent (POA)

The post office agent (POA) is the workhorse of the GroupWise system. It is responsible for delivering mail to users, providing them with access to their mailboxes in client/server mode, indexing mailboxes and libraries, maintaining and repairing the message store, and redirecting users to other post offices for proxy or login.

It can be complicated to correctly configure the POA. After all, there is a lot for it to keep track of, and if your POA cannot accomplish everything with the CPU cycles the server gives it, your users will notice. This chapter explores all of the settings and console commands for the POA, and offers you some best practices to help you design and configure your system correctly.

Loading the POA

The GroupWise POA requires certain information before it will load properly. Simply typing `LOAD GWPOA.NLM` from the server console will result in an error message stating that the required parameters are missing. There are two ways to provide the required parameters, as described next.

Using the Startup File

When the GroupWise agent installation program ran on your server, you were prompted for some information. The install wizard, in order to create a startup file with all the information the POA needs, used this information. The name of this file is the name of the post office, truncated to eight characters, followed by the .POA extension (for example, CORP_PO1.POA).

If the installer ran more than once, the extension of the startup file was changed to .PO1, .PO2, and so on (depending on how many times you installed it).

To use the startup file, load the POA with the @ switch as follows:

```
LOAD GWPOA @<filename.POA>
```

For the CORPPO1 post office, the command is

```
LOAD GWPOA @CORPPO1.POA
```

TIP **This command assumes that the GroupWise POA software is installed into the SYS:SYSTEM directory, and the CORPPO1.POA file is also in the SYS:SYSTEM directory. The name of the *.POA file is not particularly important—it could be called MICKEY.POA or MICKEY.TXT—the POA doesn't care.**

Using Command-Line Switches

Another way to provide the POA with the information it needs is to use command-line switches. These switches take the general format of /<*parameter*>=<*value*>. Neither the parameter nor the value strings are case sensitive. Any number of switches can be placed on the command line used to load the POA, and they can even be used in conjunction with the @ switch described in the preceding section.

The only required switch for the POA is the /Home switch, which gives the agent the path to the post office to be served. The syntax is as follows:

```
LOAD GWPOA /HOME=<volume>:\<path>
```

For a post office residing in the PO directory on the MAIL volume of this server, the command line would look like this:

```
LOAD GWPOA /HOME=mail:\po
```

Learning the Switches

Almost all of the switches the POA will recognize are listed in the startup file. There is a blank startup file on your GroupWise 6.5 Administration CD, in the \AGENTS\STARTUPS\LANGUAGE\STRTUPUS.POA file. By now you've probably figured out that the startup file is just a shortcut for passing ≥command-line switches to the POA. Any switch found in this file can be entered on the command line used to load the agent.

There are some undocumented POA switches described in the section titled "Undocumented POA Commands and Switches." Included in that section are switches to enable diagnostic logging, detailed IP logging, specification of the message transfer port, and more.

TIP

You can discover most of the switches for the GroupWise NLM POA by loading the GroupWise POA with the /? switch, as in the following example:

```
LOAD GWPOA /?
```

When to Use Switches

When loading a GroupWise POA, you usually do so with a command line such as this:

```
LOAD GWPOA @CORPPO.POA
```

The CORPPO.POA file is just an ASCII file that contains a listing of all the documented GroupWise POA switches that can possibly be enabled. Ideally, the only switch that should be enabled is the `/home` switch:

```
/home-vol1:\CORPPO
```

Most of the switches map to a location in ConsoleOne where the functionality that the switch is mapping to in the GroupWise POA code is configurable from ConsoleOne. For those switches, use ConsoleOne. For example, rather than have the `/HTTPPORT-8300` switch enabled in the startup file of the POA, you edit the POA in ConsoleOne and configure the HTTP port field on the Network Address property page of the POA. By managing the features that are mapped to settings in ConsoleOne, it's much easier to make changes to the POA. Most of these changes can happen on the fly when you make changes from ConsoleOne. With the GroupWise POA, however, when you make a change to the startup file (CORPPO.POA, in this example), you must manually bring down the POA and restart it.

Configuring the POA

The numerous startup switches are probably a poor choice of tools for configuring the POA. You must have file-system access to the `SYS` volume to apply them, and the values they represent will be visible only to those with server console or `SYS` volume access.

The solution is to administer the POA through ConsoleOne. Each post office object has a child object representing its POA. Double-clicking this object from the GroupWise view (or selecting Properties from the right-click menu) opens the window shown in Figure 8.1.

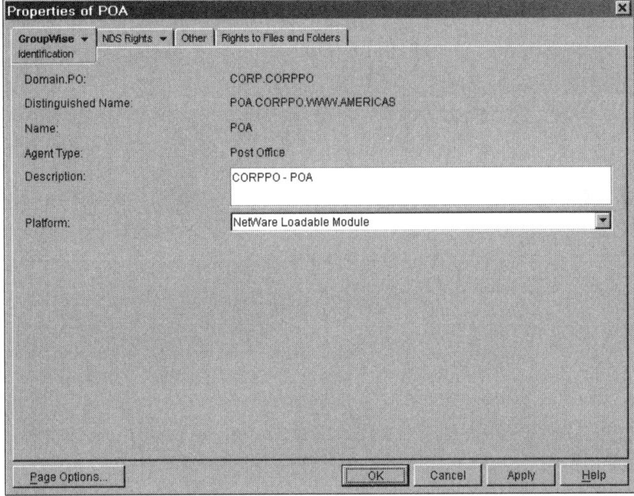

FIGURE 8.1
The POA property page in ConsoleOne.

The rest of this section examines each of the eight property pages on the GroupWise tab of the POA: Identification, Agent Settings, Network Address, QuickFinder, Maintenance, Log Settings, Scheduled Events, and SSL Settings.

The Identification Property Page

The information on the Identification property page is not critical to the tuning of the POA, but it does help identify the POA as a unique object within the system. This page is the one that is visible when the POA object is first opened, and it is shown in Figure 8.1.

- **Description:** The string entered in this field is visible at the top of the POA screen on the server console.
- **Platform:** The pick list here offers four choices, as follows:
  - **NetWare Loadable Module:** Use this if you have GWPOA.NLM running on a NetWare file server.
  - **Windows:** Use this if you are running GWPOA.EXE on a Windows NT, Windows 2000, or Windows XP box.

- **Unix:** GroupWise 6.5 does not have Unix agents. In April of 2003, Novell announced that there would be Linux-based agents some time in the future.
- **Other:** There is probably no need for you to use this entry. It is here for possible future compatibility.

You really cannot configure this page wrong. I recommend that you fill in the description field with something useful that will display on the POA's console screen.

The Agent Settings Property Page

This is where you find most of the POA settings that directly affect POA's performance, and thus the end-user performance, in their GroupWise client. The following list explains these settings:

- **Message File Processing:** There are four available settings here. They roughly correspond to the `WPCSOUT` queues, and determine which priorities of messages this POA will process.
  - **All:** This default setting makes the POA poll all `WPCSOUT` queues for message files.
  - **Low:** The POA will only process messages in the 4, 5, 6, and 7 (normal and low priority) queues.
  - **High:** The POA will only process messages in the 0, 1, 2, and 3 (high priority) queues.
  - **Off:** The POA will not perform any message-file processing.

  In most customer environments, the POA should be set to process all. In the case of a dedicated QuickFinder indexing POA though, you might want to change this to "Off". Chapter 14, "Library and Document Administration," talks about the concept of a dedicated QuickFinder indexing POA.
- **Message Handler Threads:** This setting determines the number of threads the POA will devote to the message file processing. This should not be more than half the number of TCP handler threads (see the next bullet). Generally, one message handler thread for every 50 users on the post office is sufficient. The lowest number of message handler threads you should allocate is three.
- **Enable TCP/IP (for Client/Server):** When checked, this allows the POA to listen and respond to client/server requests. This is required

for the client/server access mode, which is more fully described a little later in this chapter.

TIP

If you disable TCP/IP (for client/server) on the POA, you must shut down the POA and restart it for this to take effect. This is because the POA must stop listening for client/server requests on its client/server port, and to do this, it must be shut down and restarted. The same rule applies if you have it disabled and then enable it.

- **TCP Handler Threads:** This determines the number of threads the POA will devote to handling client/server requests. Increasing this number might improve client/server performance, but only to a point. As a rule of thumb, you should have one TCP handler thread for every 25 users on the post office. The lowest number of TCP handler threads you should allocate is six. Setting the TCP handler threads beyond about one thread per user will not necessarily improve the performance of the POA. In fact, the POA might take up more CPU cycles than is currently needed if this is set too high. From moment to moment, the POA uses fewer TCP handler threads to support users who are using the GroupWise client in caching mode. However, use the same rule of thumb for threads to users as explained earlier.

TIP

If you have allocated too few TCP handler threads, the POA will dynamically allocate more if needed. You can configure a maximum of 99 TCP handler threads.

- **Max Physical Connections:** This is the maximum number of physical connections, or ports, that the POA will allow to be open simultaneously. If this number is reached, and a new user attempts to log on, that user will receive an error message and will not be able to connect. Set this to be equal to or slightly higher than the total number of users on this post office. Be sure to take into account users running GroupWise from more than one machine, or users who are proxied to or from other post offices.
- **Max App Connections:** This is the maximum number of application, or virtual, connections that the POA will allow to be open at any given time. If this number is reached and a client attempts to open another application connection, the oldest connection in the table will be dropped. The client whose connection has been dropped might attempt to re-open it, however, so reaching this threshold can cause a serious performance hit as dropped connections cascade through the clients. One GroupWise client has the capability to use a few

application connections. Set this to be equal to about four application connections per user associated with the post office.

- **Enable Caching:** When checked, the POA will store the last several database files it has "touched" in memory for quick access. This is in addition to any caching done by the operating system, and it typically improves agent performance.

NOTE

This setting is not be confused with the "caching" mode of the GroupWise client. If you are looking to control whether users can switch their GroupWise client to caching mode, edit the Client options of the Post Office object. Select Environment, Client Access and make changes to the caching mode settings.

TIP

If you disable caching of databases on the POA, the POA does not dynamically "un-cache" the databases that it currently has cached in memory. The POA must be shut down and restarted.

- **CPU Utilization:** This value is a trigger based on server utilization, and it is used in conjunction with *delay time* (discussed next). Should utilization climb above this number, the POA waits for the specified delay time before spawning a new thread. This throttles back the POA, perhaps preventing server utilization from sticking at 100% for extended periods. This setting applies to the POA only when it is running on the NetWare platform.
- **Delay Time:** Used with CPU utilization, this is the amount of time, in milliseconds, that the POA waits before spawning a new thread. This setting applies to the POA only when it is running on the NetWare platform.
- **Max Thread Usage for Priming and Moves:** This is an interesting setting that you might want to move beyond the default of 20%. For example, if you were moving many users off of a post office, you could tweak this setting to 50% during the user moves. Or if you had a post office that was largely dedicated to users in caching mode, you should also consider changing this setting to 50% during the original time that users are establishing their caching mailboxes.
- **Enable IMAP:** If checked, the POA will allow users to access the GroupWise POA via an IMAP client. The IMAP protocol has a rich feature set, and so it is quite feasible to allow IMAP clients, such as Microsoft Outlook Express, to access the GroupWise system via IMAP.

NOTE

The IMAP protocol defines the method for handling the display and deletion of messages in an IMAP user's mailbox. The IMAP protocol does not support sending messages. Any IMAP client that must send messages must do so using an SMTP relay server. So if you enable IMAP at the POA, make sure that you have configured a GroupWise Internet Agent (GWIA) in your GroupWise system to allow message relaying, or have the IMAP client authenticate to the GWIA in order to send mail. It is generally best not to allow message relaying on a GWIA that is accessible to the Internet. Chapter 10, "Installing and Configuring the GroupWise Internet Agent," talks more about configuring the "Allow message relaying" option on the GWIA.

- **Max IMAP Threads:** This is the number of IMAP clients that can be requesting an IMAP session with the POA at one time. If a user's IMAP session is inactive for a few minutes, the IMAP session times out. Set this to one IMAP thread per potential IMAP client that will access the post office.
- **Enable SNMP:** If checked, the POA will "publish" SNMP information for any management agents that are listening.
- **SNMP Community "Get" String:** The fields for SNMP community strings are not required unless you are using a third-party simple network management protocol (SNMP) product.
- **HTTP Username/Password:** This is the password you intend to use when monitoring your POA through a Web browser. There are monitoring features of the POA that you cannot get from the POA's console screen; but you can get from the HTTP monitoring screen of the POA. So it is a good practice to define the HTTP username and password. The username and password do not need to correlate to an eDirectory user. This feature of monitoring the POA with a browser is discussed toward the end of this chapter.

Outside of server performance, the settings on the Agent Settings page have the most significant impact on the performance of the POA. Make sure to tune your POA according to the recommendations in this section.

The Network Address Property Page

The fields in this window, shown in Figure 8.2, are needed for the GroupWise POA to listen for client/server connections from a GroupWise client, and for the POA to listen for messages from the MTA servicing the domain above the post office the POA is running for. The SSL portions of this screen are not discussed in this chapter. Chapter 27, "Securing Your GroupWise System via SSL," gives detailed information on how to enable SSL on the POA.

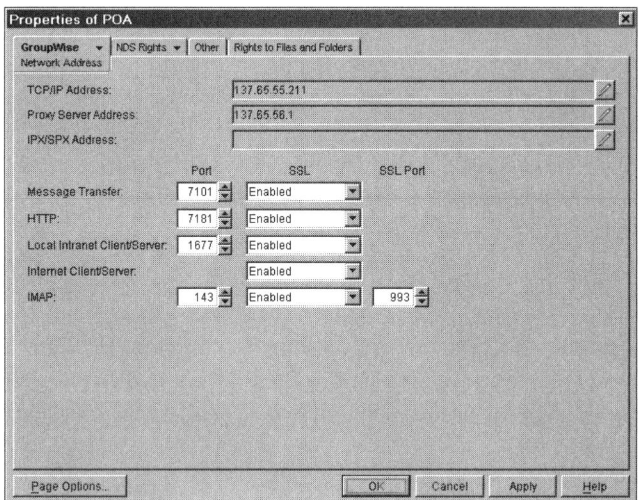

FIGURE 8.2
The POA Network Address property page in ConsoleOne.

The fields that appear are

- **TCP/IP Address:** This field should display the TCP/IP address or DNS address for the server where the POA is running.

NOTE

If your server happens to have two or more IP addresses bound to it, using this field to define the TCP/IP address you want the POA to listen on is not sufficient. You must add the following switch into the startup file of the POA:

```
/IP-<IP address bound to the server that you want the POA to
listen on.>
```

For example:

```
/IP-137.65.55.211
```

TIP

If the POA needs to be moved to another server, or the server's IP address must be changed, be sure to change the IP address for this POA to match the IP address of the server.

- **Proxy Server Address:** This setting is relevant if you intend for your users to use caching or remote modes, and you want to enable access to the post office when these users are connected to your system via an Internet connection. The proxy IP address must be a public class IP address, and this address will actually map (or be bound) to an IP address on a proxy server or L4 switch (Layer 4 network switch).

NOTE **Your proxy server or L4 switch should be configured to use NAT (Network Address Translation) in order to send traffic to the proxy server address back to the TCP/IP address defined (or bound) on the POA. The GroupWise client will speak to the proxy server or L4 switch—at the same client/server port that the POA is configured to listen to for "normal" client server sessions. This is typically port 1677.**

- **IPX/SPX Address:** This setting is relevant only if you use SNMP software that can access an IPX address.
- **Message Transfer Port:** The Message Transfer Port field identifies the port that will be used for communication from the domain MTA for the domain that owns this post office, down to the POA process that is running for this post office. If this field is not populated, the MTA will require direct file access to the post office directory structure. If there is a port number here, however, the MTA can transfer files to the POA using a TCP connection.

  The default value for message transfer port is 7101. If there are multiple post offices on this server, each of them must be assigned a unique message transfer port. You might use sequential numbering in cases like this (for example, 7101, 7102, and so on). Also, if there is an MTA running on the same server as the POA, the MTA by default will listen on port 7100. You would need to use a port other than the default 7100 for the POA when the MTA is running on the same server as the POA.
- **HTTP Port:** The HTTP port is used by the POA and the GroupWise monitor utility. This port tells the POA which port to listen to when monitoring Web browsers. This GroupWise monitor utility reads the HTTP port value from the domain database, in order to monitor the POA.

TIP **If you enable HTTP monitoring, you will also want to enable the HTTP username and the HTTP password. To do this, go to the Agent Settings property page and fill in the HTTP username and HTTP password fields. Without defining the HTTP username and password, anyone can access the POA's HTTP port; they are not prompted for authentication. Not a good thing to have wide open.**

- **Local Intranet Client/Server Port:** Enter the client/server port for this POA at the bottom of this window. If you are unsure of this value, use the default port, 1677. If there are multiple post offices on a single server, each of the POAs will need a unique port. You might use sequential numbering in this case (for example, 1677, 1678, 1679, and so on).

NOTE

To fully configure the POA for client/server connections, make sure that the Enable TCP/IP (for client/server) check box is checked on the Agent Settings property page.

- **Internet Client/Server:** This field is relevant to the Proxy Server Address field mentioned earlier in this chapter. You cannot change the port with the shipping GroupWise 6.5 snap-ins, so the port for the Internet Client/Server is the same as the local intranet client/server. However, if you're running the GroupWise 6.5 sp1 and later ConsoleOne snap-ins, you can edit this port. This allows administrators to use the same proxy server address for all of the POA agents in the GroupWise system, and then simply define different Internet client/server ports per POA. As discussed earlier, the proxy server would NAT (Network Address Translation) the proxy IP address *and* Internet client/server port to the appropriate POA's IP address and client/server port on the company's backbone.
- IMAP Port: If you intend to enable IMAP connectivity to the POA, it is advisable to keep the IMAP port at 143, because this is the default port for the IMAP protocol.

NOTE

To fully configure the POA for IMAP client connections, make sure that the Enable IMAP check box is checked on the Agent Settings property page.

You might have also noticed that each port has the option to enable SSL. This option is discussed in Chapter 27.

The QuickFinder Property Page

The GroupWise message store can be fully indexed. Indexing is an essential part of the Find feature in the GroupWise client. You will want to make sure that QuickFinder Indexing is enabled. If it is not, the GroupWise POA will have to do real-time indexing when the user uses the Find feature. By requiring the POA to do real-time indexing, the POA's performance is degraded.

Following is an explanation of the settings on this page, and some recommendations regarding these settings:

- **Enable QuickFinder Indexing:** If enabled, the QuickFinder indexing process launches at the interval specified under the QuickFinder Interval setting. The first launch takes place as scheduled under Start QuickFinder Indexing.
- **Start QuickFinder Indexing:** Because the QuickFinder process is CPU-intensive, it might be useful to schedule it to occur only outside of business hours. The number you set in this field is in the form of hours after midnight. For example, if you set Start QuickFinder Indexing to 4, and set QuickFinder Interval to 12, the first indexing run will execute at 4 a.m., and the second will execute at 6 p.m. The second run will be more intensive than the first, catching all of that day's mail. The next 4 a.m. run will pick up any messages that were created in the late evening or early morning.
- **QuickFinder Interval:** This is the number of hours and minutes the POA will delay between spawning the QuickFinder index update process. This setting is best used in conjunction with Start QuickFinder Indexing, discussed in the previous bullet. Generally, the default of 24 hours is the best setting. By setting the QuickFinder interval for every 24 hours, and coupling the Start QuickFinder Indexing setting to happen in the nighttime or early morning hours, the CPU-Intensive QuickFinder indexing process will not kick in during business hours.

  It is essential that you do not turn off QuickFinder indexing completely. It is best to run it once a day, during off-peak hours.

TIP

The GroupWise POA indexes only around 500 items in a QuickFinder pass, even if the user has more items to index. Generally, if QuickFinder runs every night, this default is sufficient. However if a user's database is rebuilt, or if the user has moved to a new post office, the user's entire mailbox must be re-indexed. If your QuickFinder indexing isn't taking too long to run at night, it might be best to add the undocumented switch `/QFLEVEL=3` in the startup file of the POA. This tells the POA to process 2,000 items to be indexed before moving to the next user, if there are that many items that must be indexed.

The Maintenance Property Page

From the Maintenance Property Page of the POA, shown in Figure 8.3, you can define some of the daily routines that the GroupWise POA should run. It is best to design these routines to execute during off-peak hours.

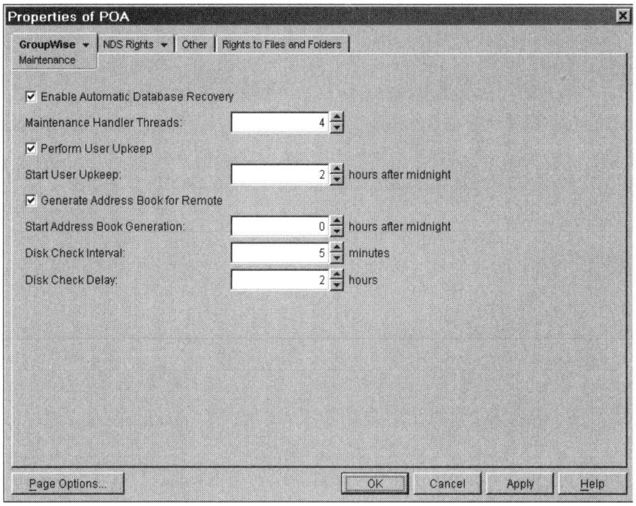

FIGURE 8.3
The POA Maintenance property page.

- **Enable Automatic Database Recovery:** When checked, this setting allows the POA to rebuild damaged databases it encounters while processing messages or client/server requests. It is highly recommended to leave this setting enabled. If it is disabled, you are setting yourself up for potentially serious database corruption issues and performance problems.
- **Maintenance Handler Threads:** These are the threads that can be spawned when the POA must run a Mailbox/Library Maintenance (GWCHECK) job on the message store. The default is 4; if you generally keep your Mailbox/Library Maintenance jobs running after business hours, you can set this to the maximum of 8.
- **Perform User Upkeep:** If enabled, this allows the POA to do the following:
  - Advance uncompleted tasks to the next day.
  - Delete expired items from users' mailboxes.
  - Delete mail, appointments, tasks, and notes that are older than what's defined in client options when client options have been set to automatically delete these types of items.
  - Empty the trash based on client options.
  - Synchronize users' frequent contacts books with the system address book.
  - Clean address book indexes.
  - Expire references from the document folder.

NOTE

When the POA actually executes the Perform User Upkeep code, the upkeep happens in two passes. In the first pass the POA advances uncompleted tasks and synchronize users' frequent contacts books with the system address book. In the second pass, the POA deletes expired items from users' mailboxes, cleans address book indexes, and expires invalid references from the document folder (if you are using GroupWise Document Management).

- **Generate Address Book for Remote:** If enabled, this allows the POA to generate a WPROF50.DB file for GroupWise caching and remote users. This file is the system address book for caching and remote users. This setting is used with the Start Address Book Generation setting.

NOTE

The WPROF50.DB file is found in the `<post office UNC path>\WPCSOUT\OFS` **directory.**

TIP

When caching or remote users download the remote address book, it is placed on the remote machine with a filename WPROF.DB instead of WPROF50.DB, as it appears in the post office directory.

- **Start Address Book Generation (Hours After Midnight):** A value of 2 results in a 2 a.m. run, whereas a value of 22 results in a 10 p.m. run.

TIP

Address book generation usually takes less than five minutes to complete; it is a very quick process.

- **Disk Check Interval:** This is the amount of time, in minutes, that the POA will wait before rechecking the amount of disk space available. The disk check interval is directly tied to any disk check scheduled event configured for this POA. (Scheduled events are discussed a little later in this chapter.) These events have *thresholds* of remaining disk space, and if the POA disk check determines that the GroupWise volume has dropped below that threshold, it spawns that disk check event's actions.
- **Disk Check Delay:** Should a disk check event be triggered by a disk check, it might take some time for that event to free up some space. The disk check delay is the amount of time the POA will wait, regardless of thresholds that have been tripped, before spawning another disk check event.

You should keep all of the settings on this page enabled. The only thing that needs fine-tuning is when you perform these tasks. The maintenance settings should be configured to happen during nonpeak hours. The Perform User Upkeep should happen sometime after midnight.

The Log Settings Property Page

This page allows you to control the amount of information captured in the POA log, as well as the amount of disk space that old logs will take up.

Here is an explanation of the settings on this page, and a couple of recommendations:

- **Log File Path:** By default, this field is blank. POA logs are placed in the `WPCSOUT\OFS` directory under the post office directory. If you choose to keep logs elsewhere, enter the path here. I don't recommend that you put logs on a separate server—performance might suffer, and if that server goes down, the POA will not function.
- **Logging Level:** There are three menu items in this list:
  - **Off:** No logging.
  - **Normal:** The POA tracks "major" events in the log, but most of the detail will be gone.
  - **Verbose:** The log contains useful detail and is the recommended setting.
- **Max Log File Age:** This is the oldest that any log file on disk can be before the POA deletes it. The default is seven days, and this is typically sufficient.
- **Max Log Disk Space:** This is the maximum amount of disk space that all of the log files together can consume. If the logs reach this limit, the oldest log file is deleted. The Max Log Disk Space overrides the Max Log File Age setting in that, if the Max Log Disk Space threshold is met, it doesn't matter how young a log file is, it's going to be deleted if the Max Log Disk Space threshold is met. If you choose to set the Max Log File Age beyond seven days, you will want to raise this limit to make sure that you actually keep your oldest logs for the time that you specify. Unfortunately, this can be very difficult to estimate. The POA will generate a new log file when the old one reaches 1025KB (1 megabyte) in size.

POA logs are an important troubleshooting tool. I recommend configuring the POA so that you can take the best advantage of this tool.

The Scheduled Events Property Page

You will use the Scheduled Events tab to automate message store maintenance. You can use this page to configure the POA to run mailbox/library maintenance (GWCHECK) on a post office at some kind of a time interval. One of the best things about scheduled events is that they can be configured to happen when the system is being used the least. Chapter 17, "Maintaining the GroupWise System," discusses scheduled events in even more detail.

The SSL Settings Property Page

From this page you configure your POA to use SSL. Chapter 27 tells how to utilize SSL on the POA. The capability to use SSL to encrypt communication is overhead for many customers, but it helps the security folks sleep better at night!

Monitoring and Configuring the POA at the Console Screen

Once the GroupWise POA has successfully loaded, the screen shown in Figure 8.4 will be available from the server console or from a remote console session.

TIP

Remember, to load the POA, type `LOAD GWPOA @`*`STARTUPFILENAME`*`.POA`**. (By default, the startup filename is the name of the post office.)**

You can control the POA, to some extent, with keyboard commands you issue. The commands available from the main screen are the following:

- **F4:** Configuration
- **F7:** Exit
- **F9:** View Log File
- **F10:** Options

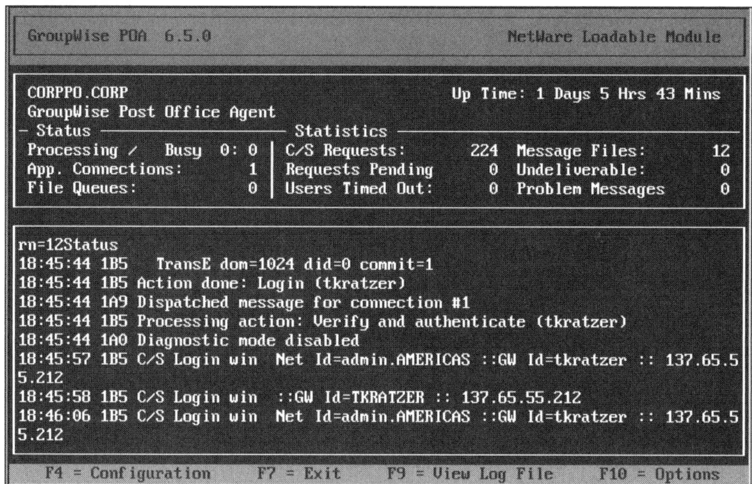

FIGURE 8.4
The POA console on a NetWare 6 server.

The F7 and F9 keystrokes need little explanation. Pressing the F7 key unloads the POA. If client/server connections are active, or if the QuickFinder indexing process is running, you will be prompted to confirm your decision to exit.

Pressing the F9 key allows you to browse through the currently active log file.

The Configuration Menu

When you select the F4 key, the menu shown in Figure 8.5 appears.

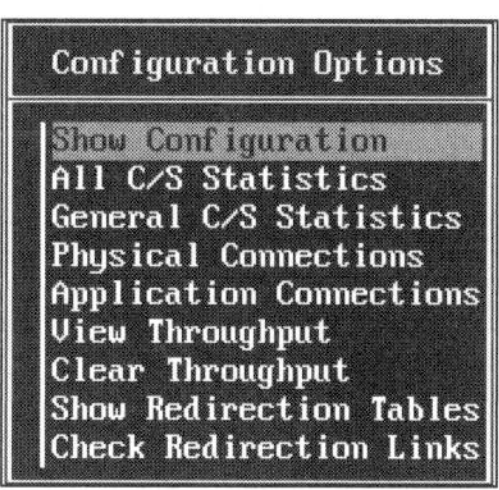

FIGURE 8.5
The POA Configuration Options menu.

Each of the menu items here is going to pump information into the active log file when executed.

- **Show Configuration:** This option lists the configuration values and settings currently in memory. The settings you learned about in the section of this chapter titled "Configuring the POA" are listed here. This list is identical in nature to the list of settings that the POA displays when it is first loaded. This list is not displayed in its own static window; rather it is dumped into the current active log of the POA. To review the configuration, press F9 to view the log file.

- **All C/S Statistics:** As the name suggests, this option dumps a list of all of the client/server statistics into the current log file. Each of the options that follow in the rest of this bulleted list is a subset of this option, and those individual statistics are covered in their respective sections.
- **General C/S Statistics:** This option creates a section in the log file titled *TCP Configuration*. Beneath this section, you will find values for the configured limits of application and physical connections (*Max*), as well as the current number of active connections (*Cur*) and the highest the current value has reached (*High*).
- **Physical Connections:** This option lists the IP address and GroupWise user ID for each user who has a physical connection to the POA. A physical connection is a memory address for the transmission and receipt of TCP packets and will correspond to a port number. The port number used by the client and the POA for each connection is unfortunately not displayed. The numbers range from 1024 to 2048 or higher, depending on the number of users currently logged in.
- **Application Connections:** This lists the IP address and GroupWise user ID for each user who has an application connection to the POA. Most users will have more than one application connection, because these connections represent the windows or applications within the GroupWise client that are sharing the user's current physical connection. For example, a user with only the Inbox window open can have only one or two application connections. A user reading a mail message, running Notify, and browsing a shared folder will have at least three, and perhaps as many as six, application connections.
- **View Throughput:** This displays the client/server TCP/IP throughput for the POA. It does not include message transfer throughput or files processed from the WPCSOUT queues.
- **Clear Throughput:** Use this option to clear the throughput count. When view throughput is executed, the throughput calculations will be based on the last time the throughput was cleared, or the last time the agent was loaded.
- **Show Redirection Tables:** This option shows each of the POAs on the system, and their configured IP addresses and ports. The redirection table is used by the POA to connect users to other post offices for

proxy purposes, for connections to libraries, or for redirected logins. The list shown here is from the perspective of this post office. Discrepancies between addresses shown on this list and addresses configured from ConsoleOne indicate a synchronization problem.

- **Check Redirection Links:** This option is the same as the Show Redirection Tables option, except that after each entry is listed, the POA attempts to connect to the POA at that address and shows the results of that attempt.

  This tool is especially valuable—with one keystroke, you can determine which POAs on your system are responding, and which are not.

You will use these options and statistics on rare occasions, generally when troubleshooting communication problems.

The Options Menu

Selecting the F10 key pulls up the menu shown in Figure 8.6.

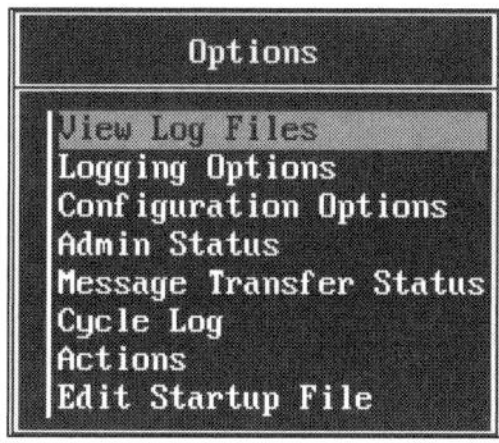

FIGURE 8.6
The POA Options menu.

- **View Log Files:** This option is similar to the main screen's F9 keystroke, but it offers more options. It brings up a list from which you can choose to browse not only the current log file (marked with an asterisk) but also any of the POA logs that reside on-disk.
- **Logging Options:** This option brings up the screen shown in Figure 8.7.

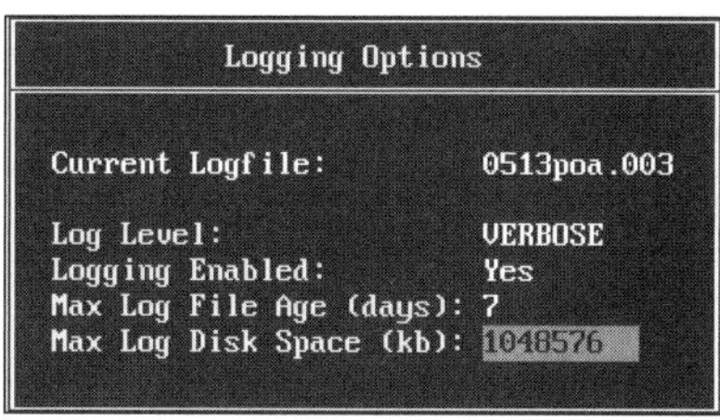

FIGURE 8.7
The POA Logging Options menu.

Use the up- and down-arrow keys to navigate and the Enter key to edit the selected logging option. The Esc key takes you back to the main screen.

TIP

It is better to configure the POA logging from ConsoleOne. This way, the POA always starts with the settings you have selected. Reserve making changes from the POA's console screen for temporary situations and when troubleshooting. When you make changes from the POA's console screen, those changes aren't retained after the POA has been unloaded and reloaded. The option for diagnostic logging is not available from ConsoleOne. Generally you do not want your POA to perform diagnostic logging except for short periods of time. If by chance, though, you do want your POA to start with diagnostic logging, just add the `/debug` **startup switch to the startup file of the POA.**

- **Configuration Options:** This menu option is identical to the main screen's F4 keystroke.
- **Admin Status:** Selecting this option brings up the submenu shown in Figure 8.8.

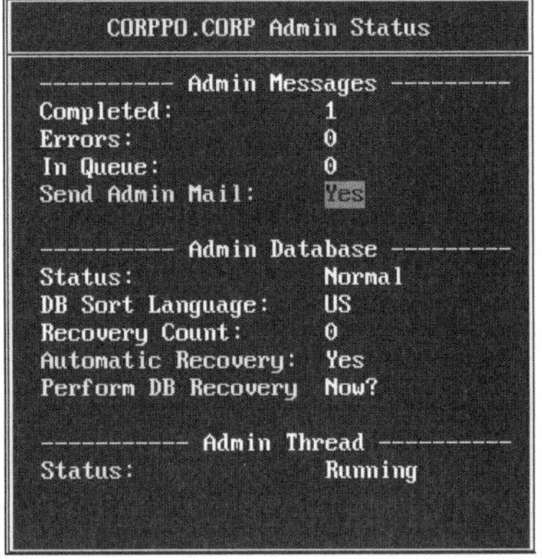

FIGURE 8.8
The POA Admin Status screen.

There are four available actions or configuration options in this dialog box. Again, use the up- and down-arrow keys to navigate, and press Enter to edit. These options are especially useful:

- **Perform DB Recovery:** Executes an immediate recovery of WPHOST.DB. A recover is a structural database rebuild of the WPHOST.DB file.
- **Status:** Allows you to suspend processing of administration tasks (very useful if you are currently rebuilding this database offline and want to keep things in sync). Selecting the Esc key takes you back to the Options menu.

- **Message Transfer Status:** This menu item calls up the Message Transfer Status screen shown in Figure 8.9.
- **Outbound TCP/IP:** Displays the IP address and message transfer port (MTP Port) of domain's MTA that the POA talks to in order to transfer messages out of the post office.
- **Inbound TCP/IP:** The IP address and message transfer port (MTP Port) of this POA. This reflects the IP address and port that the MTA is expecting the POA to be listening on for incoming traffic to the post office.
- **Hold:** This is the directory where this POA queues up messages if the connection to the MTA is blocked for some reason.
- **Last Closure Reason:** Shows why the POA cannot connect to the MTA. It might not tell you exactly what's wrong, but it can give you a good idea where the problem is. As with the Admin Status dialog box, selecting the Esc key takes you back to the Options menu.
- **Cycle Log:** Cycling the log dumps the current log into a file and begins a new log file. This is useful when you are getting ready to use the Configuration Options menu to list some TCP information, and you want it to be at the top of the log file for easy access later.
- **Actions:** This option calls up the Actions menu shown in Figure 8.9.

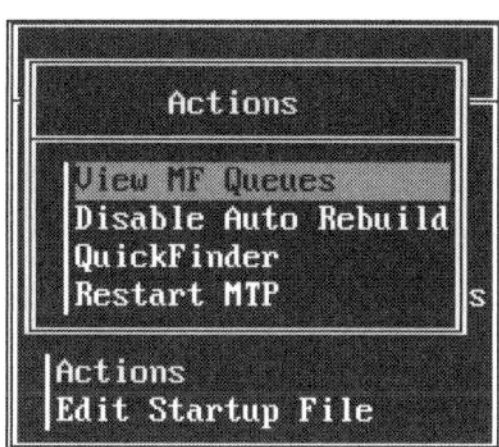

FIGURE 8.9
The POA Actions menu.

- **View MF Queues:** Allows you to see, at a glance, how many files are waiting in the WPCSOUT directory structure. These files are waiting for processing by the POA. The list is dumped into the current log file.
- **Disable Auto Rebuild:** This tells the POA not to attempt to rebuild damaged databases that it encounters in the course of message delivery or client/server processing.
- **QuickFinder:** This calls up the four-option dialog box shown in Figure 8.10.

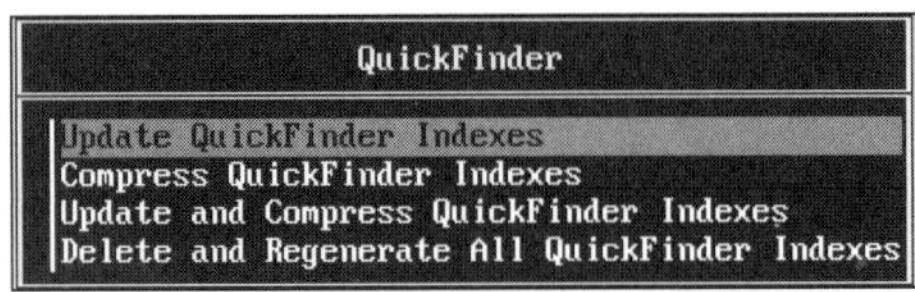

FIGURE 8.10
The POA QuickFinder menu.

- **Update QuickFinder Indexes:** This option launches the indexing process. All indices served by this POA, including the mailbox index and all library indexes, will be updated.
- **Compress QuickFinder Indexes:** This merges all incremental indexes with the permanent index. The permanent index files will be renamed to reflect the time the operation was performed.
- **Update and Compress QuickFinder Indexes:** This performs both of the preceding operations, beginning with the update.
- **Delete and Regenerate All QuickFinder Indexes:** This deletes all the *.INC and *.IDX files in the post `office\ofuser\index` directory, and launches the indexing process to re-index all databases in the post office.

WARNING **Kick off the Delete and Regenerate All QuickFinder Indexes option only when the POA has a lot of time to spare; for example, on a Friday night. Depending upon the amount of data you have, it can take more than a day to re-index all of your data.**

- **Restart MTP:** The MTP process is the process on the POA that sends and receives messages from the MTA. When troubleshooting connectivity problems between a POA and the MTA on the domain above the post office, it's often helpful to restart the MTP process.

Undocumented POA Commands and Switches

There are a few things that you can make the POA do that are not listed in the menu items. These commands are typically used by Novell's technical support personnel to resolve sticky problems, or for troubleshooting. There are other undocumented POA commands; however, the two listed here are the ones you are most likely to need for troubleshooting.

Let's take a look at the undocumented POA commands and switches, as follows:

- **Ctrl+Z (diagnostic logging keystroke):** This keystroke toggles *diagnostic* logging on and off. Diagnostic log files are much larger than *verbose* log files, but can contain information that is critical to correctly diagnosing a problem (hence the name). Running the POA in diagnostic mode for extended periods is not recommended. Performance degrades slightly in this mode.

- **`/IPLL-DIAG` startup switch:** This switch launches the POA with very detailed IP transaction logging, useful in conjunction with sniffer traces to isolate network problems.

TIP

The GroupWise POA has several other startup switches. Use the `/?` switch to view a listing of other common switches that the POA supports.

Understanding the Agent Log

The GroupWise POA is a multithreaded server application that performs large numbers of operations each second. The log files can be confusing. An entry indicating that something was received for processing might not be immediately followed by an entry indicating that the spawned process was completed.

Log Line Format

To help make sense of the log, each line in the agent log is divided into four main parts.

The first of these is the timestamp. Anyone who can read a 24-hour digital clock can make sense of this—it is in HH:MM:SS format. This is the hour, minute, and second of the day that the event in this log entry occurred.

The second part is the process number. This is more complex. The process number is typically a three-digit number identifying the process or *thread* that performed the operation described in this log entry. If you are trying to follow a thread in the log, you must do so by finding the next occurrence of this number. If process 118 attempts to deliver a message, and the next line indicates that process 244 encountered an error, the error was not with the message in the previous line. Look for the next occurrence of process 118 to determine whether the message was delivered.

The third part, which is not always present, is the process type. This is a three-letter string that identifies the admin engine or the message transfer engine. When the POA processes updates to the post office database (administration messages), the string is *ADM*. Message transfer events (connections to the MTA for transmitting or receiving messages of any type) use the string *MTP*.

The fourth part of the log entry is the event description. This might be short and cryptic, but after you have seen a few of them, you can easily make sense of them. It might be an error message, or it could announce the user ID of the user who just logged in.

Common Log Entries and Explanations

This section offers a look at some examples of log entries. In all of these examples, the log level was set to *verbose*, so that the maximum amount of useful information was captured without overburdening the POA.

Message Delivery

The following sequence tracks delivery of a mail message from `tkratzer` to `gbrown`.

```
20:44:20 1EC Distribute message from: tkratzer
20:44:20 1EC Begin distribution to 1 users
20:44:20 1EC Distributed: GBROWN
```

Notice that all three entries have the same process number, `1EC`. That's how you know that the transactions are related.

Administration Update

This next sequence is the result of the administrator changing the telephone number for user `ecornish`.

```
21:02:40 237 MTP: Receiver thread started: 1 running
21:02:40 262 MTP: Received file:
WWWFS1\SYS:/CORP/CORPPO\wpcsout\ofs\2\aec15d70.001, Size: 1010
21:02:40 251 Processing aec15d70.001
21:02:40 251 Processed OK
21:02:40 255 ADM: Completed: Update object in post office -

User MFG.MFGPO.ECORNISH (Administrator: (WWW_TREE_1)

TKRATZER.AMERICAS, Domain: MFG)
```

It looks confusing, but only because so much information has been packed into the event description. POA server process 237, which was running the MTP subprocess of the POA, received a message from the domain MTA, and placed the message in the *<post office>*\WPCSOUT\OFS\2 directory. A POA routing process, numbered 251, looked at the header of the message, and determined that the message was an administrative message. The POA routing process then moved the message from the wpcsout\ofs\2 directory to the wpcsout\ads\2 directory (this is not logged in the log file, but is mentioned to help you understand the flow of administration messages). The routing process then tickled the POA's administration thread called "ADM" running as POA server process 255. The ADM process committed the phone number change to the WPHOST.DB file. The log shows that the object updated was user ECORNISH in the MFGPO post office of the MFG domain.

The code in parentheses is especially useful. With this information, you can audit your administrators, ensuring that they are accountable for the changes they make to your system. The administrator who made the change was authenticated to the WWW_TREE_1 eDirectory tree, and used the TKRATZER account in the AMERICAS context. You can also see that the operation was performed while ConsoleOne was connected to the MFG domain's WPDOMAIN.DB database.

TIP

Although you can determine who makes administrative changes, you might find that sometimes the information recorded is incorrect. What will happen is the administrative update will actually reflect the person who made changes to this object, just prior to the person who made the latest administrative change. For example if last week Glenn Brown modified Eva's object, and then Tay Kratzer modified Eva's object, it may show that GBROWN **modified Eva's object.**

Best Practices

Post office agent performance is important to your users. If the agent does not have the resources it needs to quickly process client/server requests, your users will notice. The client will be sluggish, nonresponsive, and users might think their workstations have locked up. It is, therefore, critical that the system be built and configured so that the POA is always performing well for your users.

Carefully Consider Settings that Impact POA Performance

There are several settings that can affect the POA's performance. Many of the settings will not affect the POA's performance, if just one or two of them are poorly configured. However, the cumulative effect of several settings incorrectly configured can degrade performance. Here are several settings or conditions to watch for, and some brief detail about each of them:

POA—Settings

- Generally, you want one TCP handler thread allocated for every 25 users.
- Generally, you want one message handler thread allocated for every 50 users.
- For my customers, I set the CPU Utilization on the Agents Settings page of the POA to 95.
- If your post office is composed of caching users, set the Max Thread Usage for Priming and Moves on the Agent Settings page to 50%.
- Turn off SNMP on the POA if you are not using an SNMP monitoring solution.
- Make sure that QuickFinder Indexing happens after business hours.
- Always enable Perform User Upkeep to happen sometime after midnight. If you do it before midnight, the task items will not advance, nor will the trash items be emptied, until users log in the next day. Make sure that your QuickFinder Indexing and your Perform User Upkeep do not run at the same time. You probably should space them out by about four hours.
- Run scheduled events at a different time than when the QuickFinder indexing and the Perform User Upkeep run.

Post Office—Client Options

- Determine whether you are going to allow junk mail handling. You do not want to make the junk mail handling feature your only anti-spam solution. This is inefficient for a couple of reasons. First, the spam makes it all the way through your network, just to be rejected prior to the user getting it. Second, the POA will have to chug through all of the users on the junk mail list to determine whether the message should be rejected.
- Turn off wildcard addressing, unless you really intend for users to use this setting.
- Consider setting user limits on mailbox size, and maximum sent message size.

- In the Send options, consider which kind of status tracking you need. Some customers have set their status tracking to All Information. This level of status tracking can be a drag on a GroupWise system. For optimal performance, set the Send Options status tracking to Delivered and Opened.

Limit the Size of the Post Office

The first mistake made by many administrators is overloading the post office. Unfortunately, it is very difficult to determine exactly how many users can belong to a single post office. Performance depends more on what the users are doing than on how many of them there are. In practice, GroupWise administrators have seen that having more than about 700 users in client/server (online mode on the client) on a GroupWise post office often results in poor performance.

Creating post offices with thousands of users that are in both online and caching mode is not generally feasible. If you intend to grow to a larger post office, all of the users on the post office should be in caching mode.

Limit the Size of the Message Store

Post office agent performance degrades, and memory requirements increase, as the size of the message store grows. Performance problems are intensified if users keep too much mail in their master mailboxes. For a 700-user post office, I recommend purging mail older than 180 days. This should ensure good performance. If you do not have an email retention and expiration policy in place, you might consider using a third-party archiving solution, such as GWArchive, available at `www.gwtools.com`.

One Post Office Per Server

If you have a choice between putting two 350-user post offices on a single server, and putting one 700-user post office on that same server, I recommend the 700-user option. The POA will load-balance in favor of client/server threads, but if there are two POAs running on one CPU, they cannot "talk" to each other to determine the best allocation of the limited resources. Placing more than one post office (and, therefore, more than one POA) on a single file server is not recommended. That said, putting a few 100-user post offices on the same server will generally not cause problems, and is in fact a common practice. It's the larger post offices that have problems with two on a server.

As with the size of the post office, the number of post offices per server is an area where you might be able to ignore my advice and get away with it—especially on heavy-hitting hardware. Just be sure to consider my recommendations.

Dedicate the Server to GroupWise

If you have more than 200 users in the post office, don't use this server for other applications. User home directories, eDirectory authentication, APPS volumes, and Web servers should be on separate hardware. Your users will grow to depend on GroupWise more than almost any other application they run. They will demand good performance out of it, so GroupWise deserves to be treated as a mission-critical application. If another application can steal CPU slices out from under your POA, your users might eventually rise in revolt.

Monitoring Your POA Through a Web Browser

The GroupWise POA can be monitored through a Web browser. In fact, you can even suspend and restart some processes on the GroupWise POA. You can find lots of information about how your POA is functioning that you cannot find out in any other manner. For example, with the Web-browser monitoring interface of the POA, you can determine exactly which users are logged into the post office. You'll still find it useful to use the POA's console interface on your NetWare or Windows server, but as for monitoring the POA, nothing beats the Web-browser interface of the POA.

Simple Configuration

The GroupWise POA needs three settings tweaked in order to support HTTP monitoring of the POA. They are the following:

- An HTTP port specified
- An HTTP monitoring username specified
- An HTTP monitoring password for the username specified

You can configure all of these settings in ConsoleOne.

HTTP Port

To specify your HTTP port, go to the Network Address property pages of your POA object in ConsoleOne. Fill in the HTTP Port field. Fill in the

HTTP port with a value that you know is unique. Don't use the same port as the client/server port or message transfer port.

HTTP Username/Password

To specify the HTTP username and password settings, go to the Agent Settings property page of the GroupWise POA object.

At the bottom of the GroupWise Agent Settings property page, fill in the HTTP username field and the HTTP password field.

The HTTP username and password are not required to enable HTTP monitoring of the POA. It is highly recommended to enable the HTTP username and password feature, however, in order to secure access to the HTTP port of the POA.

Monitoring the POA with a Web Browser

Fill in the IP address or DNS name of the server running the POA, along with a colon and a port name. For example

```
http://192.168.95.101:8100
```

You will be prompted for the username and password; use the username and password you specified in ConsoleOne. Figure 8.11 shows the HTTP monitoring screen of a GroupWise POA.

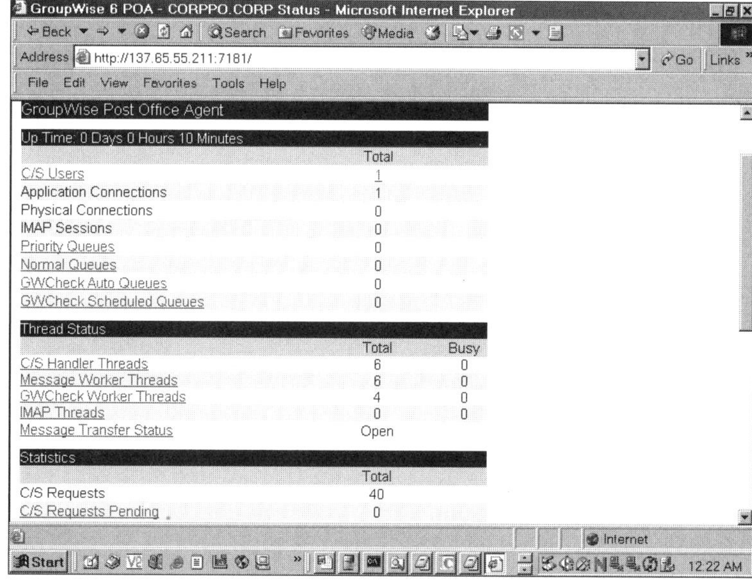

FIGURE 8.11 The GroupWise POA HTTP monitoring screen.

As shown in Figure 8.11, once you are in the GroupWise POA HTTP monitoring screen, you'll see a bevy of information. Figure 8.11 shows only a small part of the information you can get on the POA and the server running the POA.

TIP **When monitoring the GroupWise POA through a browser, if you do not remember the HTTP port number, you can also enter through the client/server port. This is usually 1677. The client/server port will redirect the browser to the correct HTTP port for monitoring.**

Advanced Configuration

The HTTP monitoring piece of the GroupWise POA has some powerful features that can be enabled if you want, including the following:

- HTTP refresh interval control
- GroupWise client version/release date flagging

HTTP Refresh Interval Control

To take advantage of this feature, you need to edit the startup file for the POA. This setting cannot be made from ConsoleOne.

To enable the switch, type the following:

```
/httprefresh
```

If you want to have the refresh take place every 20 seconds, the line would read as follows:

```
/httprefresh-20
```

Summary

This chapter discussed loading, configuring, tuning, and monitoring the GroupWise POA. This chapter also took a close look at the POA object in ConsoleOne and examined the options available from the POA's server console.

CHAPTER 9

Configuring the Message Transfer Agent (MTA)

Every GroupWise domain must have a message transfer agent defined for it. The message transfer agent (MTA) has three major responsibilities in the GroupWise system, as follows:

- Transferring messages between post offices and domains
- Writing administrative changes to the domain database (WPDOMAIN.DB)
- Transferring messages to or from gateways for transport to or from other mail systems

This chapter discusses operation and configuration of the MTA and explores link configuration for the GroupWise system. At the end of the chapter, you can find some best practices to help you design and configure your system correctly.

Loading the MTA

The GroupWise MTA requires certain information before it loads properly. Simply typing **GWMTA.NLM** from the server console results in an error message stating that required parameters are missing. There are two ways to provide the required parameters.

When the agent installation program ran on this server, you were prompted for some information. The installer used this information to create a startup file with all the information the MTA needs. The name of this file is the name of the domain, truncated to eight characters, followed by the .MTA extension (for example, CORP.MTA). If the installer ran more than once, the extension of the existing startup file was changed to .MT1, .MT2, and so on (depending on how many times you installed), and the new startup file retains the *.MTA extension. This is helpful if you need to review the original startup file for the MTA; note that it is not overwritten.

To use the startup file, load the MTA with the @ switch as follows:

```
LOAD GWMTA @<filename.MTA>
```

For the CORP domain, the command would be the following:

```
LOAD GWMTA @CORP.MTA
```

Loading the MTA with Command-Line Switches

Another way to provide the MTA with the information it needs is to use command-line switches. As was explained about the Post Office Agent (POA) in Chapter 8, "Configuring the Post Office Agent (POA)," these switches take the general format of /<parameter>=<value>. Neither the parameter nor the value strings are case sensitive. Any number of switches can be placed on the command line used to load the MTA, and they can even be used in conjunction with the @ switch described earlier.

The only required switch for the MTA is the Home switch, which gives the agent the path to the domain to be served. The syntax is as follows:

```
LOAD GWMTA /HOME=<volume>:\<path>
```

For a domain residing in the CORP directory on the MAIL volume of this server, the command line would look like this:

```
LOAD GWMTA /HOME=mail:\corp
```

Learning the Switches

Almost all of the switches the MTA will recognize are listed in the startup file. There is an unconfigured startup file on your GroupWise 6.5 Administration CD, AGENTS\STARTUPS \LANGUAGE\ STRTUPUS.MTA. Any switch found in this file can be entered on the command line used to load the agent.

The section, "Notable MTA Commands and Switches," found later in this chapter, includes a switch to turn off the Message Logging feature.

As indicated in Chapter 8, startup switches and startup files should be used only when a particular setting cannot be made in ConsoleOne. Administer the MTA through ConsoleOne.

Configuring the MTA

Each domain object has a child object representing its MTA. Double-clicking this object from the GroupWise view (or selecting Properties when right-clicking the MTA object) opens the window shown in Figure 9.1.

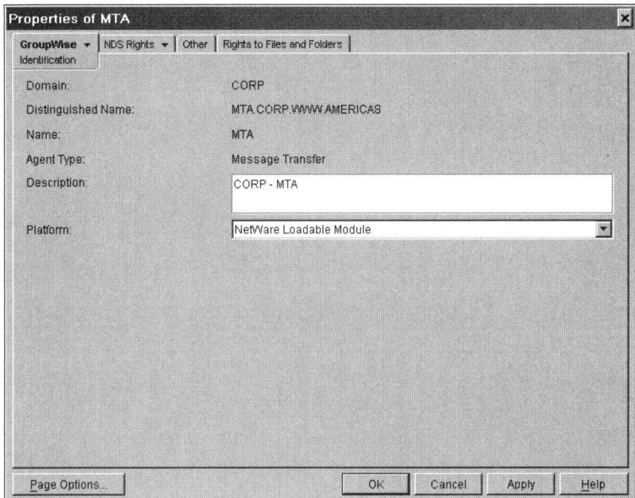

FIGURE 9.1
The MTA object details property page in ConsoleOne.

The rest of this section explores each of the eight property pages available from the GroupWise tab.

The Identification Property Page

The MTA Identification property page is shown in Figure 9.1, and as you can see, there is not much critical and configurable data here.

- **Description:** The text entered in this field is visible at the top of the agent screen on the server console. It might be useful to enter the phone number or pager number of the administrator responsible for configuring the MTA in this field.
- **Platform:** This window allows you to select the server platform on which the MTA will run. You will most likely want to select either the option for NLM (NetWare loadable module) or Windows. GroupWise 6.5 does not have Unix agents. In April of 2003, Novell announced that there would be Linux-based agents some time in the future.

The Agent Settings Property Page

As opposed to the available agent settings for the POA, there is little to configure for the MTA (see Figure 9.2).

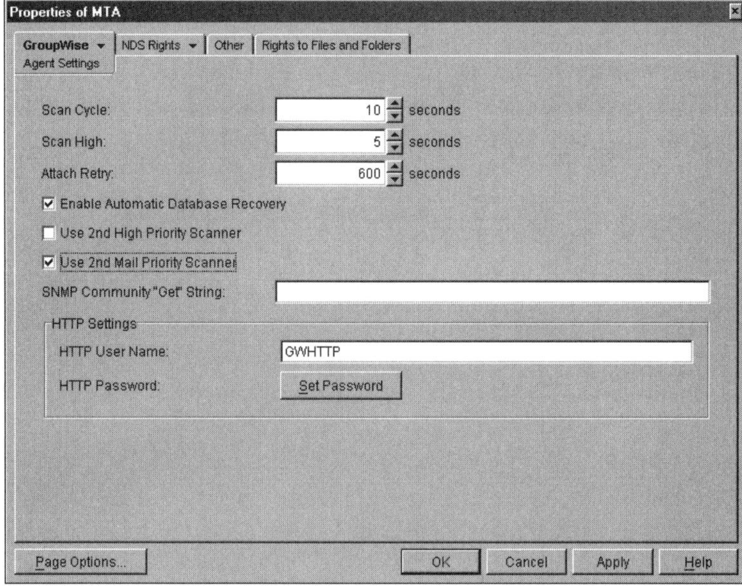

FIGURE 9.2 The MTA object Agent Settings property page.

From the property page, you control four aspects of MTA operation: scan cycles, database recovery, additional threads, and HTTP monitoring. Explanations of these settings are listed as follows:

- **Scan Cycle:** This is the interval, in seconds, that each normal-priority thread waits before scanning its assigned queues. The queues that the MTA scans are the WPCSIN\2 through WPCSIN\7 subdirectories of the domain directory. Also, if the MTA is linking to a post office via a UNC path, this is the interval between scans of the WPCSIN\2 through WPCSIN\7 subdirectories of the post office directory.

TIP

As you can imagine, an MTA with UNC links to multiple post offices could become seriously burdened just with polling directories if this value is set too low. Novell recommends that all post offices be linked with IP addresses to avoid this potential problem.

- **Scan High:** This is the interval, in seconds, that each high-priority thread waits before scanning its assigned queues. The high-priority queues are WPSCIN\0 and WPCSIN\1. Again, if this number is too low and there are lots of post offices linked via UNC, the MTA could be overtaxed just with file-polling.

- **Attach Retry:** If for some reason the MTA is unable to connect to another server, whether via TCP/IP links or UNC mappings, it will wait for the attach retry interval to expire before attempting another connection. The default value of 600 seconds (5 minutes) is good, because mail won't wait too long in the hold directories between attempts, and the MTA shouldn't bog down with consecutive reconnect attempts.
- **Enable Automatic Database Recovery:** This is the second aspect of MTA operation you'll control from this tab. If checked, this setting allows the MTA to perform a *recover* operation on a damaged domain database. If this is not enabled, damage to the domain database will result in the MTA shutting down.

  If your domain databases are getting damaged regularly (probably through unstable workstations being used for GroupWise administration), you should disable this feature and resolve the problem. This will help prevent certain kinds of record loss.
- **Use 2nd High Priority Scanner:** Each link the MTA must service is assigned its own threads. There are two—a high-priority routing thread and a normal, or mail, priority routing thread. If there are 10 links to be serviced, there will be 20 threads. Checking this box will spawn a second thread for high-priority routing for each link, which means you'll now have 30 threads (10 mail priority and 20 high priority). This should be used only if you have a significant amount of users using the busy search feature and scheduling users off of their post office.

  If you find bottlenecks at an MTA, consider using the queue assignment or link scheduling features described later in this chapter.
- **Use 2nd Mail Priority Scanner:** Like the preceding setting, this option spawns an additional thread for every link. The additional threads service queues 2-7. This option allows the MTA to process the 2-3 queues separately from the 4-7 queues. The end result is that messages in the 2-3 directories move more quickly through your MTA. Checking this option is particularly helpful for larger GroupWise systems, which have a lot of administrative changes.
- **SNMP Community "Get" String:** This field is for Simple Network Management Protocol (SNMP) community strings and is not required, unless you are using a third-party SNMP product.

- **HTTP User Name/Password:** This is the username password you intend to use when monitoring your MTA through a Web browser.

Most of the settings on this page are fine-tuning settings. The HTTP username and password are very helpful when monitoring your MTA with a Web browser.

The Network Address Property Page

The information found on the MTA Network Address property page is absolutely critical to proper communication across your GroupWise system. When creating a new domain (and hence a new MTA object), you will want to immediately specify the TCP/IP address and port of the MTA. The SSL portions of this screen are not discussed in this chapter. Chapter 27, "Securing Your GroupWise System via SSL," gives detailed information on how to enable SSL on the MTA.

WARNING

If the IP address of the domain file server must be changed, it is critical that the change also be reflected in the MTA object's network address panel. All other domain databases have a copy of this object record and use this information when communicating with this MTA. If the information is inaccurate, other MTAs will be unable to connect with this MTA to transfer messages.

This chapter discusses the best way to make changes to IP addresses and ports on a live system in the section called "Best Practices."

Utilizing the Network Address page, you can adjust various available settings.

To modify the TCP/IP address, follow these steps:

1. Click the button to the right of the field labeled TCP/IP Address.
2. Enter the IP address or DNS name of the server upon which this MTA runs.

The IPX/SPX address setting is relevant only if you use SNMP software that can access an IPX address.

Enter the message transfer port for this MTA in the Message Transfer Port field. If you are unsure of this value, use the default port, 7100. If there are multiple domains on a single server, each of the MTAs will need a unique port. Perhaps you could use sequential numbering in this case (such as 7100, 7200, 7300, and so on). It's helpful to have the MTAs end in 00 on the port. This way, if the POAs are sequential on the MTP port, it will not conflict with the MTAs. You might also need to renumber ports if there are POAs on this server that are communicating with their MTA via IP.

TIP

If you fill in the DNS address for the MTA, make sure that all of the servers that house MTAs in your GroupWise system are configured to query the DNS server. On a NetWare server this means there is a RESOLV.CFG file in the `SYS:ETC` directory. The RESOLV.CFG file would be configured with at least two lines, for example:

```
domain worldwidewidgets.com
nameserver 138.67.86.51
```

The HTTP port is used by the MTA and the GroupWise monitor utility. This port tells the MTA which port to listen to for Web-browser monitoring. This GroupWise Monitor utility reads the HTTP port value from the domain database in order to monitor the MTA.

Important

If you enable HTTP monitoring, you will also want to enable the HTTP username and the HTTP password. To do this, go to the Agent Settings property page and fill in the HTTP User Name and HTTP Password fields. Without defining the HTTP username and password, anyone can access the MTA's HTTP port without being prompted for authentication. Not a good thing to have wide open.

Not much on this page, but it is essential, particularly for domain-to-domain links that the information on this page is accurate.

The Log Settings Property Page

This property page allows you to control the amount of information captured in the MTA log, as well as the amount of disk space that old logs consume. Let's take a look at the settings on the Log Settings property page:

- **Log File Path:** By default, this field is blank. MTA logs are put in the `MSLOCAL` directory under the domain directory. If you choose to keep logs elsewhere, enter the path here. I do not recommend that you put logs on a separate server—performance might suffer, and if that server goes down, the MTA will not function.
- **Logging Level:** There are three menu items in this drop-down list, as follows:
  - **Off:** No logging.
  - **Normal:** The MTA tracks major events in the log, but most of the detail is gone.

  - **Verbose:** The log contains useful detail. This option is recommended.
- **Max Log File Age:** This is the oldest that any log file on disk can be before the MTA deletes it. The default is seven days, which is typically sufficient.
- **Max Log Disk Space:** This is the maximum amount of disk space that all of the log files can consume. If the logs reach this limit, the oldest log file is deleted. If you choose to set the Max Log File Age option beyond seven days, you will want to raise this limit to make sure that you actually get to keep your oldest logs for the time you specify. Unfortunately, this can be very difficult to estimate.

NOTE

The MTA automatically cycles to the next log file when the current log file reaches 1024KB (1MB), just as the POA log does.

The log settings of your MTA are not a critical function of the MTA, but having log settings configured correctly sure can help when it comes to troubleshooting.

The Message Log Settings Properties Page

Message logging is an integral part of the search feature of the HTTP monitoring piece on the GroupWise MTA. With message logging enabled, you can search for messages that passed through the MTA. In GroupWise 5x, customers were discouraged from turning on message logging; however, this is no longer the case. The MTA no longer uses a proprietary database, but the message log files are simple text files. The filename is in the format of MMDDMSG.00X, and message log files are located by default in the `DOMAIN\MSLOCAL\MSGLOG` directory. For example the first log file on December 14th would be named `1214MSG.001`. The MTA will cycle to a new MMDDMSG.00X just as it does with the traditional log files.

One advantage to enabling message logging is that you can hook into a couple of report-gathering features that are available in the GroupWise 6.5 monitor utility. For example, you can generate reports that will tell you how much data has been transmitted and received between two domains. This is very useful when a company has WAN links involved between the GroupWise agents. GroupWise 6.5 message logging is not the terrible performance degrader that it was in previous versions of GroupWise.

Figure 9.3 shows the GroupWise Message Log Settings property page.

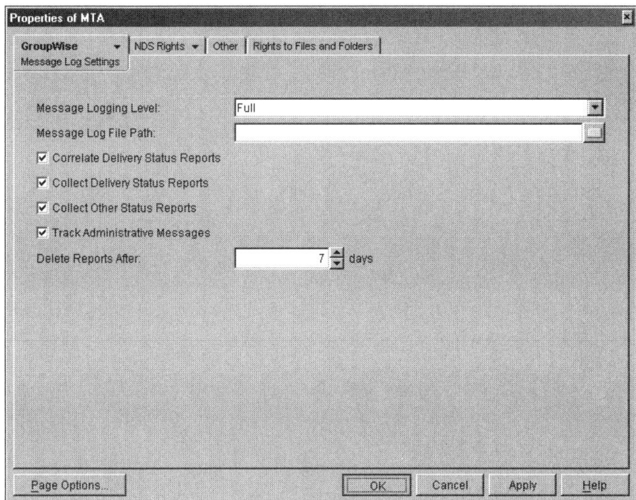

FIGURE 9.3 The MTA Message Log Settings property page.

The Scheduled Events Property Page

There is only one kind of scheduled event that a GroupWise 6.5 MTA can run, and that is an eDirectory user synchronization event. The MTA can scan eDirectory for *deltas,* which are changes to eDirectory user objects that are not correctly reflected in the domain database.

Here's a plausible situation in which eDirectory synchronization is very useful. At WorldWide Widgets, users can change their phone numbers in eDirectory via a Web portal. The administrator wants those changes to be pushed down to the GroupWise address book automatically. With eDirectory User Synchronization enabled on the GroupWise MTA, the MTA dredges eDirectory for changes to the user objects. Changes to the telephone number are then pushed down from eDirectory to the GroupWise directory store (WPDOMAIN.DBs and WPHOST.DBs).

A GroupWise MTA can be configured to dredge for eDirectory changes to users who are members of the domain that the MTA is servicing. A GroupWise MTA can also be configured to dredge for eDirectory changes to users who are not members of the domain that the MTA is servicing. In order for the GroupWise MTA to log into eDirectory, its object must have rights to read the attributes of the eDirectory objects you want it to dredge. Let's imagine that at the WorldWide Widgets, the administrator wants the following scenario:

- The GroupWise MTA for the `CORP` domain will run eDirectory synchronization for both the `CORP` domain and the `MFG` domain.
- The eDirectory synchronization will run once a day.

Here are the configuration steps needed to enable this setup:

1. Connect to the CORP domain in ConsoleOne.
2. In ConsoleOne, select Tools, GroupWise System Operations, eDirectory User Synchronization.
3. Press the Configure Agents button.
4. Highlight the MTA for the CORP domain and make sure that eDirectory access is enabled, as shown in Figure 9.4. Press the OK button to get back to the eDirectory User Synchronization Configuration window.

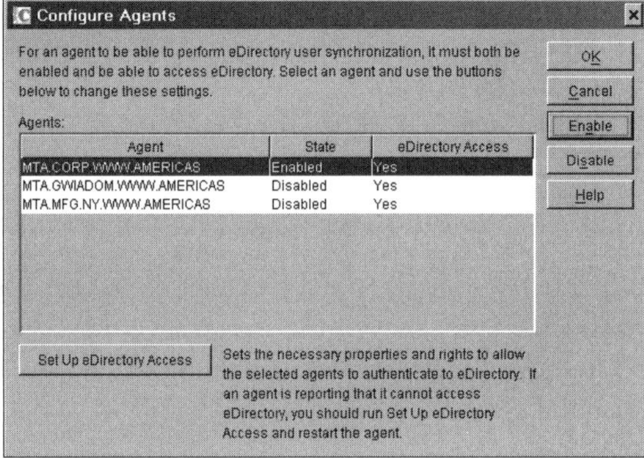

FIGURE 9.4
MTA eDirectory access is now enabled.

5. Highlight the row representing the MFG domain, and press the Change Assignment button.
6. Select the CORP domain's MTA as the MTA that will perform eDirectory user synchronization on the CORP domain's users. Press OK. Now, the eDirectory User Synchronization Configuration window should look similar to the one shown in Figure 9.5. Notice that the CORP domain's MTA is configured to perform eDirectory user synchronization for both the CORP and MFG domains, as shown in Figure 9.5.

TIP

In order for the GroupWise MTA to be able to access eDirectory, you must make sure that in the startup file of the MTA, you have enabled the /USER and /PASSWORD switches. The user must be someone with the eDirectory rights of Browse, Read, and Compare.

7. Now go to the MTA object for the CORP domain. Edit the properties of the CORP domain's MTA.
8. Select the Scheduled Events property page. Edit the existing eDirectory User Synchronization event, or create a new one.

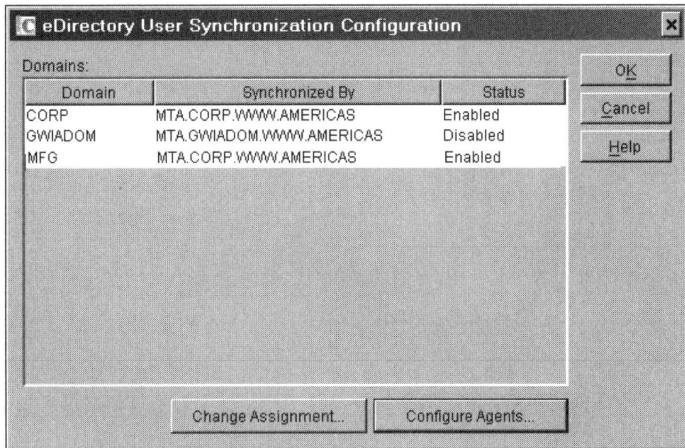

FIGURE 9.5
The eDirectory User Synchronization Configuration window.

9. Give the event a name, and then select the Daily trigger. Have the event execute at a time that is outside of business hours. The event is now fully configured, as shown in Figure 9.6. Each day, the `CORP` MTA will dredge the eDirectory for changes to user objects that reside on both the `CORP` and the `MFG` domains.

FIGURE 9.6
The MTA eDirectory User Synchronization event.

If ever you want to kick off the eDirectory User Synchronization event manually, there's a hidden keystroke on the GroupWise MTA on the NetWare platform for doing so. Select the F4 function key, and you will be asked if you want to perform eDirectory User Synchronization.

This scheduled event is enabled by default on the MTA. If you're running the MTA on an NT server, you might need to disable this event if the NT server does not have access to eDirectory to log in to the tree. Leaving this enabled in this situation can cause problems with the MTA.

The eDirectory Synchronization feature is not necessary for some GroupWise systems, but it can be helpful for systems in which data, such as user's phone numbers, is altered without the use of the GroupWise snap-ins to ConsoleOne.

The Routing Options Property Page

This property page enables you to override certain Internet addressing and default routing settings made at the system level. On large systems, this tool is critical to the proper administration of GroupWise Internet addressing, as well as configuration of MTA-to-MTA direct connectivity with other GroupWise systems. Chapter 16, "Internet Addressing," discusses when to use the settings shown on this page.

The SSL Settings Property Page

Configuring the SSL property page is not discussed in this chapter. Chapter 27 gives detailed information on how to enable SSL on the MTA.

Link Configuration and the MTA

On large GroupWise systems, you will likely have to spend some time with the Link Configuration Tool, shown in Figure 9.7, by optimizing or otherwise tweaking the connections between different domains, and between domains and post offices.

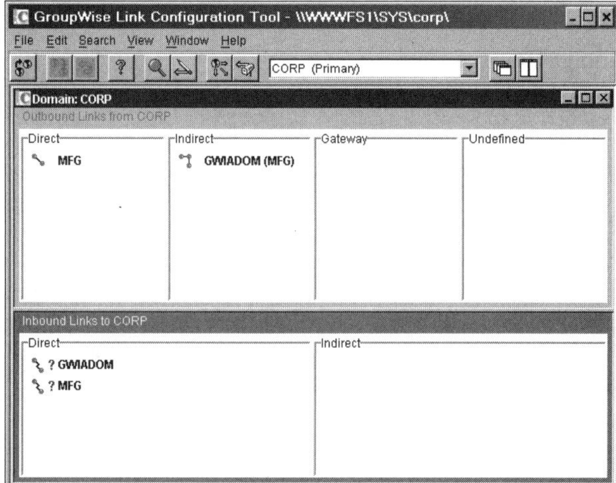

FIGURE 9.7 The link configuration tool is accessed via Tools, GroupWise Utilities.

In the example in Figure 9.7, there are two domains. The `MFG` domain's link is listed under direct links, and the `GWIADOM` domain is an indirect link. The domain to which ConsoleOne is currently connected and from which it reads the link configuration information is `CORP` (*Primary*). How do these domains communicate with one another? Are messages routed directly between all of them?

As Figure 9.7 shows, the **CORP** domain has a direct connection to the **MFG** domain. However, the **CORP** domain does not have a direct connection to the **GWIADOM** domain. Therefore, any messages that are destined from the **CORP** domain to the **GWIADOM** domain are routed to the **MFG** domain first.

In some customer environments, setting up indirect links between domains has some very practical purposes. For example, imagine a global firm with domains in many regions of the world. The Americas region has four domains: New York, Chicago, Los Angeles, and San Francisco. The Asian region has four domains: Japan, Taiwan, Hong Kong, and Singapore. The link speed between the Asian domains is somewhat fast. Only Japan has a somewhat fast network link to the New York office. So it is logical to have Taiwan, Hong Kong, and Singapore all connect to New York, Chicago, Los Angeles, and San Francisco through the Japan domain. The Chicago, Los Angeles, and San Francisco domains should all connect to the Asian region domains through the New York domain.

This link architecture has the following benefits:

- The fastest network links are being used, so messages will move more quickly.
- Slow network links are not being used, freeing up those links for traffic that's not as easily configurable, such as eDirectory synchronization traffic.

As this example illustrates, it is best to configure your link configuration records to follow your WAN network infrastructure.

Creating an Indirect Connection

Imagine you want to route messages from **CORP** to **GWIADOM** through **MFG**. Consider the following scenario:

- **CORP** connects directly to **GWIADOM**.
- The **CORP** MTA gets 8912 or 8913 errors (TCP timeouts), sometimes during business hours. These errors occur only when **CORP** is connected directly to **GWIADOM**.
- **MFG** has no problem communicating with **GWIADOM** because it is in close network proximity to **GWIADOM**, and **CORP** has no problem communicating with MFG. Therefore, **CORP** should connect to **GWIADOM** through **MFG**.

The following steps create an indirect connection between CORP and GWIADOM:

1. Connect to the domain whose MTA you want to affect.

   In this scenario, it's the CORP domain, which is done from GroupWise system operations, under Select Domain.

2. Select the appropriate domain object (GWIADOM, in this case). From the Tools menu, choose GroupWise Utilities, Link Configuration.

3. Double-click the link you want to edit. In this scenario, it is the GWIADOM domain link (see Figure 9.8).

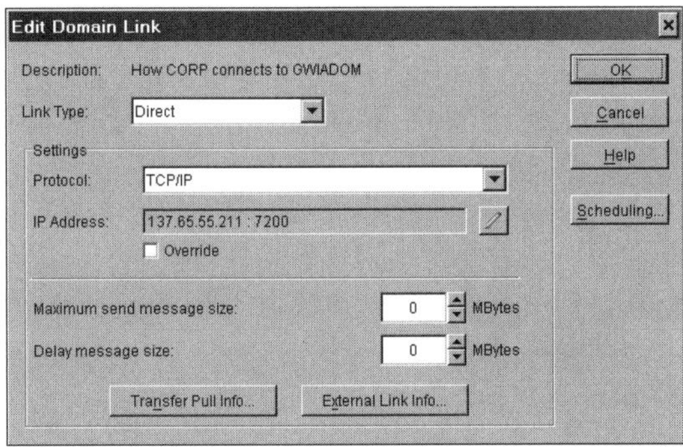

FIGURE 9.8
Direct link from CORP to GWIADOM.

   Here the link type is direct. Because this is what needs to be changed, grab that drop-down menu.

4. If you select indirect, as in Figure 9.9, everything changes.

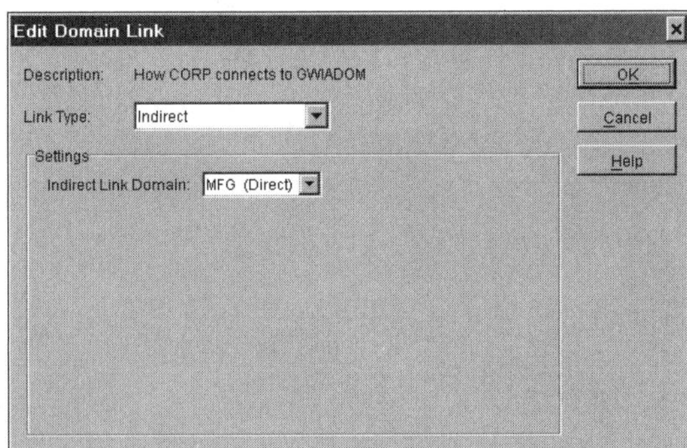

FIGURE 9.9
Indirect link from CORP to GWIADOM.

   No longer are there IP addresses and ports. With an indirect or gateway connection, the only aspect to specify is the domain or gateway, respectively, through which to connect. In this scenario, the MFG domain has been used.

5. Click OK and exit the link configuration tool.
6. When prompted to save changes to links, answer Yes.

Indirect connections are generally most useful in larger GroupWise systems.

Overriding Links with the Link Configuration Tool

In some circumstances, it might be necessary to use the link configuration tool to override the IP address that has been specified for an MTA or POA object.

Consider the following scenario:

- The MFG domain's MTA object is on a different IP address than the one listed in ConsoleOne.
- For some reason, the IP address on the MTA won't change correctly. The change does not propagate, and the link is now down between the domains CORP and MFG.

With the following steps, you can override the address:

1. Connect to the domain whose MTA needs to be affected, which in this scenario is CORP.
2. Select that domain object. From the Tools menu, choose GroupWise Utilities, Link Configuration.
3. Double-click the problem link that needs to be edited; in this scenario, it's the MFG domain link.
4. Check the box labeled Override.
5. Notice that there are now new fields for the IP address and port for this link. Enter the correct IP address and port here. Figure 9.10 shows a configured override link.

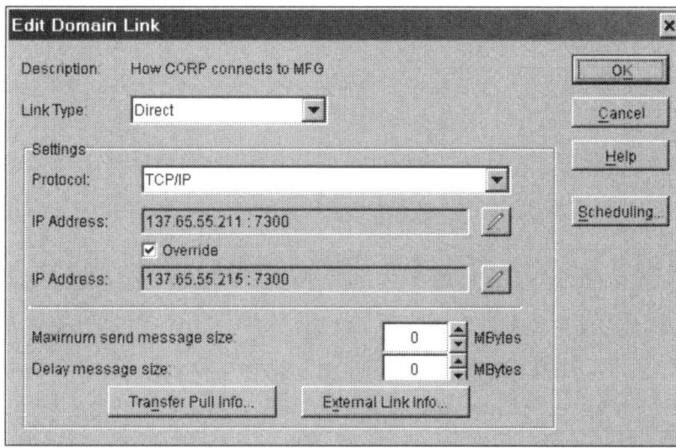

FIGURE 9.10
Override link configuration.

6. Click OK.
7. Exit the link configuration tool, responding Yes to the prompt to save changes.

You will rarely need to use the override feature. I have used it in situations in which Network Address Translation (NAT) is being used, and must be overridden for the sake of some domain's MTAs that cannot use the NATted address.

Configuring a Transfer Pull Link

Transfer pull assumes that two domains connect via UNC paths, but that one MTA is not going to be given any file system rights to the other MTA's domain directory. In this situation, the MTA that does have rights has to "pull" messages from the nontrusted MTA's domain directory.

To configure this, both MTAs must have their links changed. You must give the nontrusted MTA an override link to a new UNC path. This path will be on the nontrusted MTA's server. You will give the trusted MTA a transfer pull path to this new UNC path.

Consider the following scenario:

- `MFG` is the nontrusted MTA. The path it will use is `\\WIDGET_MFG1\DATA\XFERPULL` (on the `MFG` MTA's server).
- `CORP` is the trusted MTA. It will use the transfer pull path of `\\WIDGET_MFG1\DATA\XFERPULL`.
- The `CORP` MTA has already been assigned a login ID and password for the `MFG` server. This was done by adding the `/USER` and `/PASSWORD` switches to the startup file of the MTA.

The following steps configure the links:

1. Make a directory under the `WIDGET_CORP1` server on the `DATA` volume called `XFERPULL`.
2. Under the `XFERPULL` directory, make a directory called `WPCSIN`.
3. Under the `WPCSIN` directory, make individual directories 0 through 7.
4. Connect to the `MFG` domain and highlight that domain object.
5. From the Tools menu, choose GroupWise Utilities, Link Configuration.

6. Double-click the link to the CORP domain.

   Make sure the link type is direct and the link protocol is UNC.

7. Check the Override box.

8. Enter the new UNC path (\\WIDGET_MFG1\DATA\XFERPULL) in the UNC Override field.

9. Exit the link configuration tool and save all changes.

10. Connect to the CORP domain and highlight that domain object.

11. From the Tools menu, choose GroupWise Utilities, Link Configuration.

12. Double-click the link to the MFG domain.

    Make sure the link type is direct and the link protocol is UNC.

13. Click the Transfer Pull Info button.

14. Enter the new UNC path (\\WIDGET_MFG1\DATA\XFERPULL) in the Transfer Pull Directory field.

15. Enter a polling interval, in seconds.

    Remember that polling across a slow or untrusted link can be a performance hit for the MTA. Sixty seconds is usually fast enough to satisfy users whose mail traverses the link.

16. Click OK to dismiss the Transfer Pull Info dialog box, and click OK again to finish editing the link.

17. Exit the link configuration tool and save your changes.

The MFG MTA really has no idea what is going on. The MTA is simply redirecting any messages for CORP into a directory on its own file server.

The CORP MTA, however, is doing double duty. When the CORP MTA sends to the MFG domain, the MTA sends as it normally does, by dropping files in the directory specified as the MFG UNC path. But every 60 seconds, the CORP MTA polls the new UNC path (\\WIDGET_ MFG1\DATA\XFERPULL), the transfer pull directory, to see whether MFG has anything to send.

In this example when the MFG domain needs to send mail to the CORP domain, the domain simply places the files in the XFERPULL directory on the local server. Then every 60 seconds, the CORP domain will come along and scan this directory for mail that is destined for the CORP domain. This allows the MFG domain to send mail to CORP without needing rights to the server where CORP resides.

NOTE **The transfer pull method is rarely used today because of the availability of TCP/IP links. With TCP/IP links, no file system rights are granted. Transfer pull is used when there is no IP communication between two domains.**

Scheduling Links with the Link Configuration Tool

Suppose you have a TCP/IP WAN link to a particular domain, and during the day there is heavy traffic on that link. You have decided that GroupWise traffic should not be sent over this connection during the day, unless there are high-priority messages, or lots of files have queued up. Here's a walk through on this scenario:

- The MFG domain lies across a WAN link that is exceptionally busy from 8 a.m. to 5 p.m., Monday through Friday, because of a mainframe inventory program.
- The CORP MTA, which connects to MFG, is not to connect during the day, unless there are high-priority messages, a large volume of messages, or messages that have been waiting a long time.

The following steps help you work through this scenario:

1. Connect to the domain for which the link schedule will apply. In this scenario, it's the CORP domain.
2. Select that domain object. From the Tools menu, choose GroupWise Utilities, Link Configuration.
3. Double-click the link you want to edit.

   In this case, it's the MFG domain link.
4. Click the Scheduling button to get to the Link Schedule window (see Figure 9.11).

   You need to create two profiles. One is the default profile, which will be in force after hours. The other is the day time profile, which will be in force during business hours.
5. Click the Default button and click OK to dismiss the Default profile.
6. Click the Create button to get to the window shown in Figure 9.12.

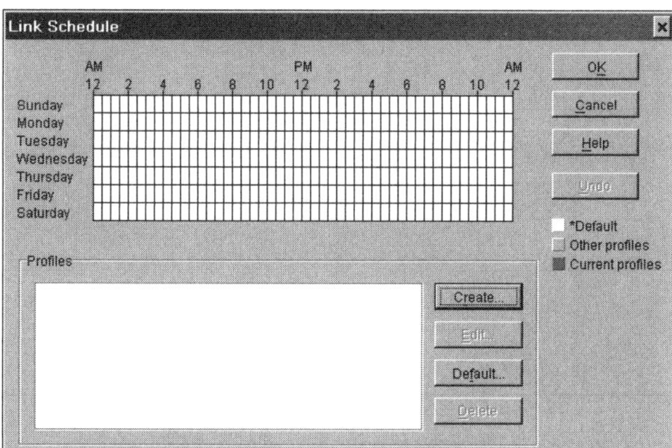

FIGURE 9.11 The Link Schedule window allows you to create a link schedule for your domain.

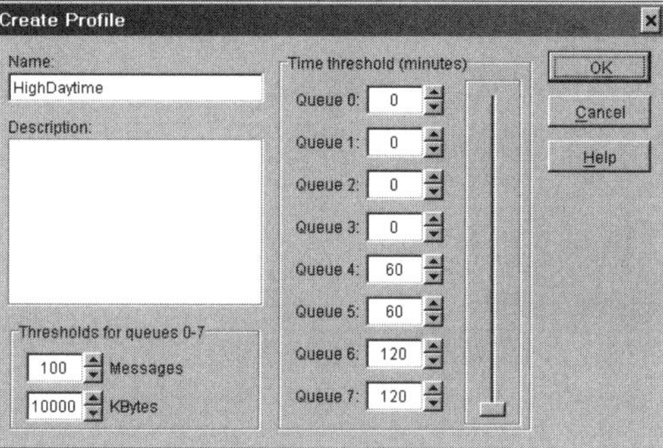

FIGURE 9.12 The Create Profile window, with changes made for link scheduling.

7. Name this profile.

   Now you are creating the profile for link scheduling during the day.

   In this example, the profile is set so that high-priority queues (0-3) are processed immediately. Normal-priority queues (4-5) are processed only after the oldest item in them has waited 60 minutes. Low priority queues (6-7) are processed only after the oldest item has waited two hours.

   This example has also been set up so that if a total of 100 messages exist across all queues, regardless of their age, the MTA will open the link. Also, if there are 10,000KB (10MB) of files across all queues, the MTA will open the link.

8. Click OK.

9. With this new profile selected, drag the mouse across the schedule pane to create a rectangle.

   The one in the example runs across the 8 to 5 block, Monday through Friday (see Figure 9.13). This is the schedule for which the selected profile will be active. During all other hours (the white space), the default profile will be active.

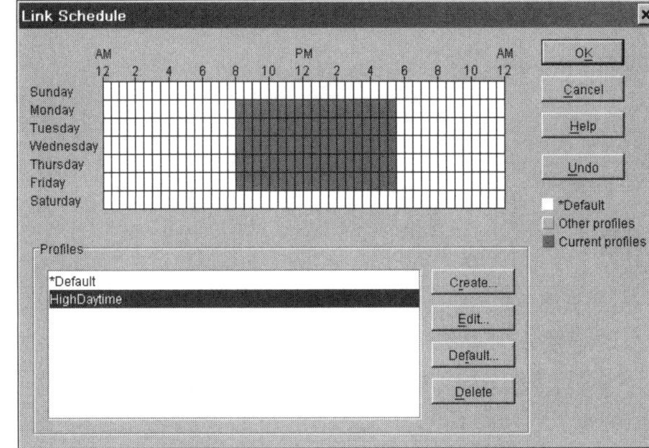

FIGURE 9.13 The Link Schedule window with the profiles created and scheduled.

10. Click OK to dismiss the Link Schedule window, and click OK again to close the Edit Link window.
11. Exit the link configuration tool and save your changes.

This is a great feature, but it's relevant only to specialized environments.

Message Transfer Agent Console Commands

The MTA typically runs on a NetWare or Windows NT file server. It has its own interface, and this section discusses that interface. When the MTA has been successfully loaded, you see the screen shown in Figure 9.14.

```
GroupWise MTA  6.5.0                                NetWare Loadable Module

 CORP                                     Up Time: 0 Days 23 Hrs 20 Mins
 CORP - MTA
 Status                              Statistics
 -             Total  Closed  |                        Total    10 Minutes
 Domains         3      0     | Routed                   31          8
 Post Offices    1      0     | Undeliverable             0          0
 Gateways        0      0     | Errors                    0          0

05-20 22:22:24 DIS: MTA restart request ignored
05-20 22:29:31 DIS: MTA restart in progress
05-20 22:29:32 DIS: No configuration changes detected
05-20 22:29:32 DIS: MTA restart request ignored
05-20 22:32:06 DIS: MTA restart in progress
05-20 22:32:06 DIS: No configuration changes detected
05-20 22:32:06 DIS: MTA restart request ignored
05-20 22:32:16 DIS: MTA restart in progress
05-20 22:32:17 DIS: No configuration changes detected
05-20 22:32:17 DIS: MTA restart request ignored

   F6 = Restart    F7 = Exit    F9 = View Log File    F10 = Options
```

FIGURE 9.14 The GroupWise MTA console on a NetWare 6 server.

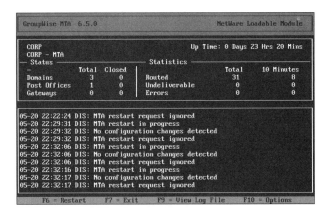

You can control the MTA from this screen with keyboard commands. Commands available from the main screen are the following:

- **F6:** Restart
- **F7:** Exit
- **F9:** View Log File
- **F10:** Options

You will be using these options often when troubleshooting the MTA.

Restarting and Exiting

This section offers a brief discussion about the difference between F6 (the Restart option) and F7 (the Exit option). When you press F6, you are prompted to confirm the restart. After confirmation, the agent closes its connections to other servers, stops all processing of transfer files on this server, and rereads configuration information from the domain database. The MTA does not, however, reread the MTA startup file. The MTA startup file is the ASCII file with configuration switches in it.

When selecting F7, you are prompted to confirm the exit command. After confirmation, the agent closes all connections, stops processing messages, and GWMTA.NLM (GWMTA.EXE on NT servers) unloads. If you then reload the agent from the server console, the MTA will reread the startup file and the configuration information from the domain database.

The F7 keystroke does exactly the same thing that the `UNLOAD` GWMTA.NLM command does on a NetWare server. If you made changes to the MTA startup file, and you want them to be applied, you must use F7 to exit (or the `UNLOAD` command), and then reload the MTA manually.

TIP

When running the MTA as a service on a Windows server, and it has been set to interact with the desktop, the F7 option will be grayed out. This is because it is running as a service. To shut down the MTA when it is running as a service, you need to stop that service from running. Open the Services option from the Windows server control panel. From there, you can start and stop the MTA that is running as a Windows service.

The Options Menu

Pressing F10 from the main screen presents you with the Options menu, shown in Figure 9.15.

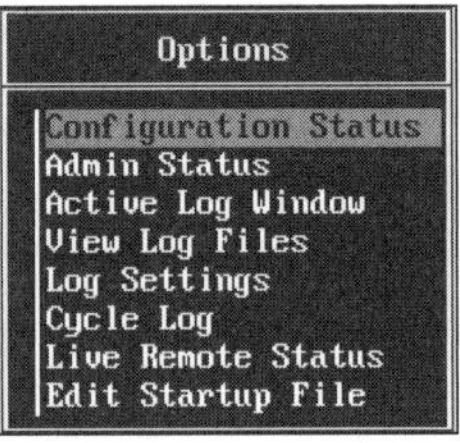

FIGURE 9.15
The MTA options menu enables you to look at almost all of the functions the MTA performs.

The following sections offer an explanation of each of these options in turn.

Configuration Status

The Configuration Status tool, shown in Figure 9.16, is one of the most powerful troubleshooting tools you have. It allows you to look at the status of the MTA's connections with other GroupWise domains, post offices, and gateways, and it tells you why those connections are down if there are problems. It even allows you to suspend connections should you want to prevent communication with another domain, post office, or gateway for some reason.

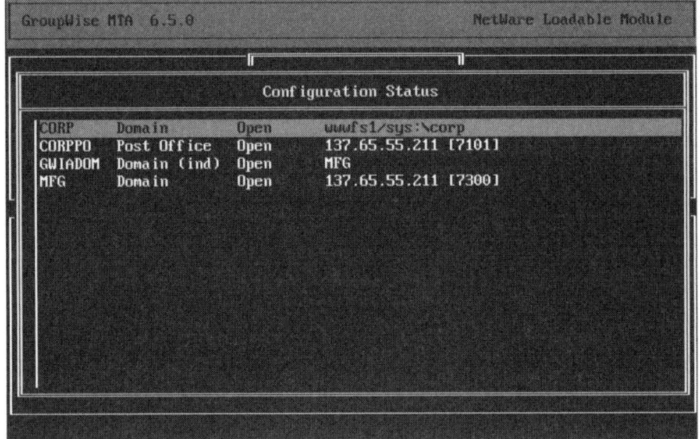

FIGURE 9.16
The MTA Configuration status screen.

In Figure 9.16, you find four columns of information, but the interface provides no column headers. From left to right, the column headers would be the following:

- Link Name
- Link Class
- Link Status
- Link Connection or UNC path

Consider the first line of text. The link name here is `CORP`, and the link class is `Domain`. This means that this line represents this MTA's link to the `CORP` domain. The link status is `Open`, and the link path is `wwwfs1/sys:\corp`. This means that this MTA can successfully write to this path on the `wwwfs1` file server.

In this example, this first line of text is a special one. It defines this MTA's link to its home directory. This MTA is running against the `CORP` domain database, servicing the `CORP` domain, so the `Corp` link shows up as the UNC path to the WPDOMAIN.DB file.

In Figure 9.17, the `MFG` link is highlighted, and I pressed the Enter key.

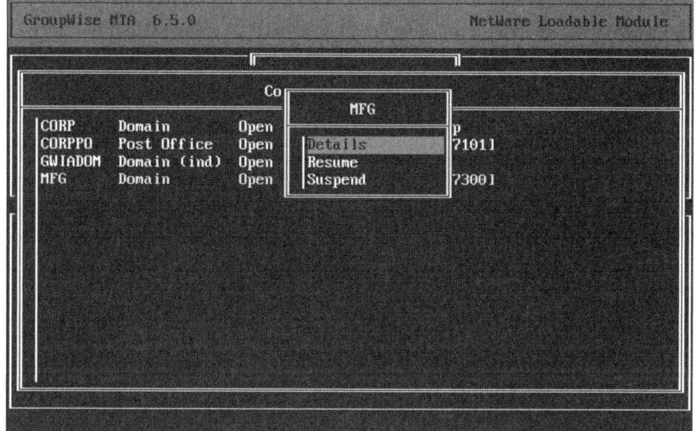

FIGURE 9.17
The MTA Link options menu.

There are three options presented on this menu:

- **Details:** This option brings up a window showing the details for the selected link.
- **Resume:** This option resumes service for this link, if someone previously suspended it, or the link was closed because of communication problems of some sort.
- **Suspend:** This option discontinues service for this link. Service will not be resumed until Resume is selected or until the MTA is restarted.

Figure 9.18 shows that the link status for domain `MFG` is open. Here's how to check out a link. Selecting Details for the MFG link presents the screen shown in Figure 9.18.

Here's a look at each of the fields available in this window:

- **MTP/HOME:** This field shows the IP address of the MTA or it shows the home directory, or link path, for this link. This can be a server path, or it can be an IP address and port. If it is a UNC path, the line that reads MTP in Figure 9.18 will say `HOME` instead.

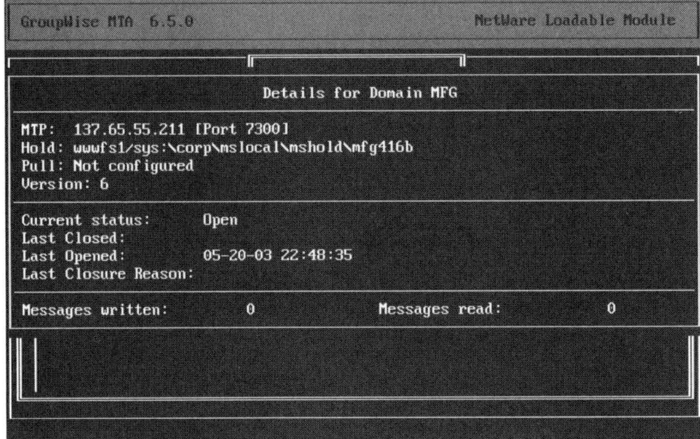

FIGURE 9.18 The MTA Link Details window.

- **Hold:** This field displays the directory that the MTA uses to queue up files destined for this domain if the home path is not accessible (that is, the link is down). Large numbers of files can queue up in this hold directory if the link stays down for an extended period of time.

TIP **You can easily see whether there are messages in an MTA's hold queue from the HTTP interface of the MTA under Links.**

- **Pull:** If you have configured the MTA for transfer pull, as described earlier in this chapter, the transfer pull path is listed here.
- **Version:** This field shows the version of the domain, post office, or gateway that the MTA is connecting to. This information is required so that the MTA can properly format transfer files for older versions of GroupWise.

NOTE **GroupWise 6.5 domains show up as "Version 6" in the Version screen.**

- **Current status:** This line indicates whether the link is open or closed.
- **Last Closed:** This field displays the date that this link was closed last. If the link has not been closed since the MTA was last restarted, this field is blank.
- **Last Opened:** This field is the date that this link was last opened. Again, it is only tracked since this MTA was last restarted.
- **Last Closure Reason:** Here is a big reason for visiting this screen in the first place. The MTA will indicate why a link is closed. For example, an MTA could complain that it cannot create files, which means it

has insufficient rights to the directory in question, or perhaps the directory in question does not exist.

- **Messages written:** This field shows the number of messages transferred to this link.
- **Messages read:** This field is the number of messages received on this link. If the link is TCP/IP, it will typically be 0 unless the connection is via UNC. Messages delivered to this MTA via UNC paths are not tracked on this screen.

From the information presented, you should be able to quickly determine the nature of a link problem. You will still need to perform some troubleshooting, but this screen will narrow your field of possibilities quite nicely.

Admin Status

When Admin Status is selected from the options menu, a window similar to the one shown in Figure 9.19 appears. Some of the lines in this window allow user interaction, whereas some are purely informative.

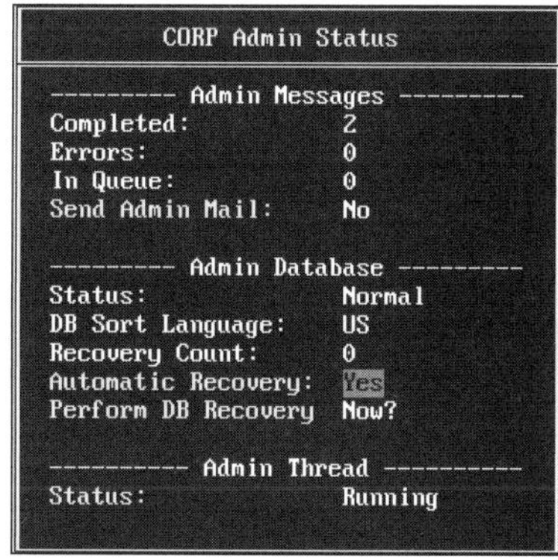

FIGURE 9.19
The MTA Admin status window.

Following are descriptions of the fields in the Admin status window:

- **Completed:** This first line, listed under the Admin Messages heading, indicates how many admin messages have been successfully written to the domain database since the MTA was loaded.
- **Errors:** This entry indicates how many errors have occurred when attempting to perform administrative transactions on the domain database. Errors in this column are not typically associated with domain database damage, though. They usually occur when domains are out of sync, and this domain receives a transaction that it cannot perform, such as adding a user who already exists or deleting a nonexistent user.

TIP **If you upgrade a GroupWise domain to a new version, after the MTA has recovered the MTA, it will report one error. This is normal, and there is no need to be concerned about this error.**

- **In Queue:** This line is a count of the admin messages awaiting processing. If lots of administration traffic is taking place (say, you just imported 2,000 users), you can expect a positive number here for a while. Usually it should be 0.
- **Send Admin Mail:** This line is interactive. Pressing Enter allows you to toggle between No and Yes. This option governs whether the MTA sends e-mail to the administrator of this domain when there are errors.
- **Status:** There are two status lines. This one, under the Admin Database heading, tells the status of the domain database. During an automatic recovery, the database can be locked against changes. This status should always read Normal.
- **DB Sort Language:** This is the language used to sort the address book.
- **Recovery Count:** This is the number of times since the MTA has been loaded that the MTA has run a recovery against the domain database. This number should always be 0. If it is not, you have had domain database damage at some point (or perhaps you have manually triggered a recovery, described later in this section).
- **Automatic Recovery:** This line is interactive. Pressing Enter allows you to toggle between Yes and No. In most cases, you will want to leave this set to Yes, thus allowing the MTA to recover the domain database if it encounters a structural error during transactions. If the MTA is restarted, this setting is not remembered; it is reread from the domain database. Permanent changes to this setting should be made to the MTA object from ConsoleOne.
- **Perform DB Recovery Now?:** Another interactive line; pressing Enter here allows you to spawn a database recovery. This option can be useful when you suspect the database is damaged.
- **Status:** This second status line indicates the status of the admin thread of the MTA. This line is interactive; press Enter to toggle between Running and Suspended. One common reason to suspend the admin thread is to prevent updates from taking place during an offline rebuild of the domain database. While the fresh database is being created, you want administrative changes to be queued up. Otherwise, they will be written to the current database, which is going to be replaced.

You will most likely use the information in the Admin Status screen when troubleshooting problems with directory synchronization in your GroupWise system.

Active Log Window

The main screen for the MTA shows what appears to be an active log, but all that is logged to the main screen are global sorts of messages. To see the blow-by-blow log, you need to select Active Log Window from the Options menu.

This is the active log for the MTA. Log entries here indicate the time of the operation, the thread name that performed the operation, and a description of the operation. This chapter discusses the interpretation of the MTA logs in the section titled "Understanding the MTA Log."

View Log Files

If the information you are looking for in the MTA log is not in the currently active log, you need to select View Log Files.

Selecting one of the log files listed and pressing Enter brings up a viewing window so you can browse that log file.

TIP

It is much easier to view the log files from the HTTP interface to the GroupWise agents, rather than from the MTA console screen. You will find it more readable and interactive. You can also use the browsers "Find" functionality to find specific information that you might be looking for when you use the HTTP option to view the log files.

Log Settings

You can use the Log Settings dialog box to change the logging level, the age of log files, and the space taken up by log files on the fly.

These settings are not retained after a restart, however. If you want to change the logging options permanently, make your changes from ConsoleOne, and then execute a restart (F6) on the MTA to force it to reread configuration information in the domain database.

Cycle Log

This command forces the MTA to begin writing to a new log file. This option is useful when the current log file needs to be moved or edited by another application (that is, opened in WordPad so that a Find operation can be performed).

Live Remote Status

This option lists GroupWise remote or cache client users who are connected to the MTA, along with the post offices and domains that the MTA communicates with in order to service the remote or cache client users. If you have more interest in live remote, read the section later in this chapter called "Configuring the MTA to Support Live Remote."

Edit Startup File

This option brings up the startup file for the MTA. You can enable and configure switches from the MTA's startup file. It is best to configure the MTA through ConsoleOne rather than through switches in the MTA. The only switches you might want to add are the "undocumented" switches mentioned in the next section.

Notable MTA Commands and Switches

There are several console command-line options that offer functionality that is not documented in the GroupWise MTA interface.

The commands and switches are as follows:

- **/NOMSGLOG:** This switch prevents the MTA from accessing or creating the message log files in the `<domain>\MSLOCAL\MSGLOG` directory. If the `MSGLOG` directory is renamed and MTA is reloaded with this switch, it re-creates the `MSGLOG` directory, but not the message log files.
- **F4 or Ctrl+D keystrokes:** These keystrokes execute an immediate eDirectory user synchronization operation. If you use these keystrokes while MTA is running, you will be presented with a confirmation prompt.
- **/TCPINBOUND-X:** The default number of inbound connections that the MTA can have is 40. With the `TCPINBOUND` switch, you can increase this setting. One customer I have that has a very busy MTA has this setting set to 150. An MTA that has been configured to communicate with a lot of other MTAs, or an MTA that communicates with other MTAs over a slow WAN link, is most likely to need this setting increased beyond the default of 40, which is just hard-coded in the MTA.

- **/TCPWAITDATA-X:** This setting is for the default time in seconds that an MTA will wait for data transmission from an established connection with another MTA. The hard-coded default for this setting is 20 seconds. An MTA that has been configured to communicate with other MTAs over a slow WAN link is most likely to need this setting increased beyond the default of 20 seconds.
- **/TCPWAITCONNECT-X:** The MTA attempts a connection four times consecutively. If it fails all four times, it reports an error, and then waits for 10 minutes before it tries again. During each attempt, the MTA will pass the `/tcpwaitconnect` value (or the default of 5 seconds if no value was provided) to the TCP/IP stack. This is how long each attempt will try to establish the connection. Therefore, if the `/tcpwaitconnect` switch is set to 10 seconds, the MTA will attempt the connection four times in a row, each time instructing the TCP/IP stack to wait for 10 seconds before timing out. If all four attempts fail, an error is reported. This means that in this setting, it would be as much as 40 seconds before the MTA reported that it was unable to successfully connect to another MTA. It will then wait for 10 minutes before it tries again. It will do this indefinitely.
- **/TCPTRUNKWIDTH-X:** By default a GroupWise MTA can only open four connections to another MTA. Each connection is used to send a message file with. If you were to increase this setting to 10 for example, and if a GroupWise MTA suddenly has 10 messages to send to another MTA, it might open 10 connections to that MTA.

The `/TCP...` switches are fine-tuning features that you are most likely to use in larger GroupWise systems.

Understanding the MTA Log

The MTA keeps two kinds of logs. I'll refer to them as the MTA Log and the Message Logging system. This section focuses on the MTA log, which keeps track of the actions performed by the MTA, including error messages, administration updates, and connections to other GroupWise agents.

Message Logging is a system whereby messages are tracked in a series of text files that are updated by the MTA. The tool for utilizing this information is the message-tracking feature of the HTTP monitoring piece on the GroupWise MTA.

You can browse the MTA logs from the MTA console using the View Logs tool under the Options menu. This tool does not allow for searching, however, and might be less convenient for you than using the HTTP interface of the MTA, which allows for detailed searches, or your favorite word processor.

MTA logs for a given domain's MTA are found at the root of the domain `MSLOCAL` directory. The log files have names such as **0125mta.003**, which indicates the month and day that the log file was created. The **003** in this example indicates that this was the third log file created, and of course, the file name shows that it was created on January 25th.

If a log file is a 0-byte file, the MTA is probably currently working with it, and you will not be able to open it without using the Cycle Log command from the Options menu.

The Top of the Log File

At the top of each log file, the MTA writes the settings that it is running with. These settings, as discussed at the beginning of this chapter, could have been passed to the MTA through the command line, the MTA startup file, or the domain database.

Following is a look at a sample log file. Following are log entries from the MTA for the `CORP` domain.

General Settings

These first few blocks of text tell which domain the MTA is running against, what the Internet addressing and routing settings are, and some of the other general settings.

```
23:00:17 0D7 CORPPO: Post office now open
23:00:17 0D7 MFG: Domain now open
23:00:17 0D7 GWIADOM: Domain now open
23:00:17 0CA LOG: Opening new log file: 0520mta.004
23:00:17 0CA General Settings:
23:00:17 0CA  Domain Directory:       wwwfs1/sys:\corp
23:00:17 0CA  Work Directory:        wwwfs1/sys:\corp\mslocal
23:00:17 0CA  Preferred GWIA:        GWIADOM.WWWGWIA
23:00:17 0CA  Default Route:
23:00:17 0CA  Known IDomains:        *wwidgets.com
23:00:17 0CA  Allow Direct Send to Other Systems:  No
23:00:17 0CA  Force Route:                 No
```

The last few settings deal with Internet addressing (covered in Chapter 16). Internet addressing has been enabled on this system. The preferred GWIA and default routing domain are listed, and then each of the IDOMAINs defined on this system is listed with a preceding asterisk.

```
23:00:17 0CA  Error Mail to Administrator:        No
23:00:17 0CA  Display the Active Log Window Initially:  No
23:00:17 0CA  eDirectory Authenticated:      Yes
➥MTA.CORP.WWW.AMERICAS
23:00:17 0CA  eDirectory User Synchronization:      Yes
23:00:17 0CA  Admin Task Processing:             Yes
23:00:17 0CA  Database Recovery:                Yes
```

The preceding are some of the operational settings for the MTA. This MTA has been authenticated to the directory, and eDirectory user synchronization is on. The admin thread is running, and if the MTA encounters domain databases damage, it will attempt to repair it.

TCP/IP Settings

An important part of your troubleshooting, should you have problems getting the MTA to "talk" to other GroupWise agents, is found here in the TCP/IP settings portion of the MTA log:

```
23:00:17 0CA TCP/IP Settings:
23:00:17 0CA  Maximum Inbound TCP/IP Connections:    40
23:00:17 0CA  TCP Port for Incoming Connections:     7100
23:00:17 0CA  TCP Port for HTTP Connections:       0
23:00:17 0CA  HTTP Refresh Rate:                60 secs
23:00:17 0CA  TCP/IP Connection Timeout:          5
23:00:17 0CA  TCP/IP Data Timeout:              20
```

The IP address of the MTA is not given here, because this parameter is defined at the server level. The inbound port is reported here, however. Also significant are the connection timeout and data timeout settings. These settings tell how many seconds the MTA will wait on an attempted connection or transmission. The values here are the defaults and can be changed with the `/tcpwaitconnect` and `/tcpwaitdata` switches in the MTA startup file.

Logging and Performance Settings

Here are the performance and logging settings for this MTA.

```
23:00:17 0CA Performance Settings:
23:00:17 0CA  Additional High Priority Routing Thread:  No
23:00:17 0CA  Additional Mail Priority Routing Thread:  No -
23:00:17 0CA  Low Priority Scanning Cycle:        10 Seconds
23:00:17 0CA  High Priority Scanning Cycle:       5 Seconds
```

```
23:00:17 0CA Message Log Settings:
23:00:17 0CA  Message Log Directory:   wwwfs1/sys:\corp\
➥mslocal\msglog
23:00:17 0CA  Track Messages:                On
23:00:17 0CA  Track Delivery Reports:          On
23:00:17 0CA  Track Status Reports:           On
23:00:17 0CA  Track Admin Traffic:            On
23:00:17 0CA  Correlate Delivery Reports:        On
23:00:17 0CA  Collect Extended Information:       On
23:00:17 0CA  Expire Records after How Many Day:     7
23:00:17 0CA  Message Log Database Size:         23552 bytes
23:00:17 0CA  Message Logging Enabled:          Yes
23:00:17 0CA Scheduled Event Settings:
```

In the performance settings section, it shows that there are no additional threads that have been spawned, and the scanning cycles for the MTA queues (`WPCSIN\<0-7>`) are every 5 seconds for the high-priority queues and 10 seconds for low-priority queues.

Finally, the log says that message logging is enabled, and indicates what the message log settings are set to.

The Body of the Log

Each line in the body of the MTA log is divided into three major sections: the timestamp, the process, and the statement. For example

```
16:13:56 MTP: MFG-ipS0: Connection established. 137.65.55.211
```

In this example, the timestamp reads `16:13:56` (56 seconds after 4:13 p.m.), the process is `MTP`, and the statement is `MFG-ips0: Connection established. 137.65.55.211`.

The Process Column

If you are to make sense of the MTA log, you must first understand the acronyms and abbreviations in the process column. This section defines them:

- **DIS:** The dispatch process is responsible for dispatching other processes. You will see the DIS process when the MTA receives a restart command.
- **RTR:** The router process is responsible for moving files from one directory to another, as part of the whole message transfer operation.

It is also the receive process when another MTA or POA transmits a file to this MTA via TCP/IP. If you have UNC links, RTR acts as both the send and receive process, because RTR handles movement between directories.

- **MTP:** The message transfer process is responsible for connecting to another GroupWise MTA or POA and transmitting a message file to it via TCP/IP. This is the send process for the MTA.
- **MLG:** The message logging process is responsible for writing to the message log database. Even with message logging disabled, you will see the MLG process announcing the results of RTR and MTP operations.
- **SCA:** The scanner process is responsible for polling gateway directories under the domain directory, as well as any post office directories where TCP/IP connectivity has not been set up.
- **ADM:** The administration process is responsible for updating the domain database with any GDS (GroupWise directory services) information that is being propagated around the system. Add a user while connected to one domain, and you should see the ADM process on every other domain's MTA add that user there. (You'll also see the ADM process in the POA logs as the user is added to the post office database.) On occasion, you might see the Administration thread report itself as ADA or ADS.
- **SNMP:** The Simple Network Management Protocol process shows up when SNMP is enabled. It periodically announces that it has obtained the necessary parameters to publish MTA operational information to any SNMP-aware query agent on the system.

The MTA log files are very helpful when troubleshooting, particularly when determining whether administrative messages are being processed.

Configuring the MTA to Support Live Remote

Prior to the GroupWise 5.5 Enhancement Pack, the MTA never "talked" directly with the GroupWise client. Now, however, the GroupWise MTA can communicate with the client, if the client is a GroupWise 5.5 Enhancement Pack (5.5E for short) or GroupWise 6.5 client running in remote mode. This might sound like a funny thing for an MTA to do, but it has an application in some environments. This feature was added to allow GroupWise systems to better support remote-user connections over the Internet.

End-users increasingly have their own connections to the Internet. It is natural for GroupWise users to want to connect to their organization's GroupWise system in order to download their GroupWise mail to their GroupWise remote mailbox. Prior to GroupWise 5.5E, the only way administrators could enable this functionality was to allow Internet hosts to contact each post office's POA and speak with the POA at any port. This raised all sorts of security issues. Because of this, most organizations opted not to allow users to access their POA from outside their organization's firewall. Now the GroupWise 6.5 POA supports connectivity via proxy server. For more information on configuring the POA to support proxy server connectivity, read Chapter 8.

The GroupWise MTA can accept a connection from a GroupWise client at the live remote port configured for the MTA. The GroupWise MTA can then open a virtual live remote session with the POA that supports the user's post office. The effect then is that system administrators can tell users that if they have a connection to the Internet they can configure GroupWise to connect to **MTA.WORLDWIDEWIDGETS.COM** using port **8100**.

The MTA must have two lines enabled in the startup file of the MTA. They are the following:

```
/liveremote-<port number>
/lrconn-<# of connections>
```

The first line specifies the port that the MTA will use to listen for live remote connections. The second line specifies the maximum number of simultaneous live remote connections that the MTA will allow. Each remote user will require one connection for the duration of their upload and download sequence.

For the MTA to be able to support live remote, every link between this MTA and the rest of the system must be a TCP/IP link. There can be indirect links, but the entire path must be TCP/IP, all the way down to the POA. This applies even if your POA and MTA are on the same file server.

Take the following scenario:

- **USERA** is the live remote user
- **POSTOFFICEA** is **USERA**'s post office
- **DOMAIN1** is **USERA**'s domain
- **DOMAIN2** is another domain in the GroupWise system whose MTA is configured to receive live remote connections

The message flow will run as follows:

1. USERA establishes a live remote connection with the DOMAIN2 MTA.
2. The DOMAIN2 MTA establishes a live remote connection with DOMAIN1 on behalf of USERA.
3. The DOMAIN1 MTA establishes a live remote connection with the POSTOFFICEA POA.
4. The POSTOFFICEA POA accesses the information store on behalf of USERA and passes responses back along the live remote chain to the user.

Live remote connections can be monitored on the MTA. The DOMAIN2 MTA will register USER1 **as a live remote user. The MTA will also show a Domain link to** DOMAIN1 **under F-10, live remote status. The DOMAIN1 MTA will register DOMAIN2-MTA and** POSTOFFICEA **as live remote connections under F-10, live remote status. The** POSTOFFICEA **POA will register** USER1 **in the log as the live remote user.**

The GroupWise remote client does not need a special kind of live remote connection type. GroupWise remote client simply specifies another TCP/IP connection as though the MTA that is listening for live remote connections is a POA.

Best Practices

Following are some practices that have been observed to improve the performance and stability of the GroupWise MTA. They are not hard-and-fast rules, however, and anything published by Novell should likely take precedence.

System Design

Keep in mind that you can have an MTA only where you have a domain. This means that if your system has some natural transfer points (such as on the segment with an edge-router, or at the firewall), you might want to consider putting a domain there so that there will be an MTA at that point.

Assume that you will be building a large system and will be using occasional indirect connections. Here are a couple of rules of thumb:

- Avoid putting any post offices under the primary domain, and don't use the primary domain as a hub for indirectly connected domains.

- If you have more than one domain on a LAN, those domains should all connect directly via IP. The MTAs can handle this easily. Thus, LAN connections should be mesh style.
- If you have multiple LANs as part of a wide area network, consider having one domain at the edge of each LAN acting as a hub for indirect connections between that LAN's domains and others.
- If you have busy gateways (such as the GWIA, which will be covered in the next chapter), you might want to consider devoting a domain (and, therefore, an MTA) to those gateways.

Remember, even though MTAs can communicate directly with any other MTA with a valid IP address, this is not always the best way to connect, especially where there are many router hops between them. Because packets are going to be stored and forwarded on these long routes, you should consider having the MTA store and forward the messages (by using indirect connections). This way you will be less likely to have problems with TCP connection timeouts, and your message transfers will be more efficient.

TCP/IP vs. UNC Links

TCP/IP links between MTAs or between the MTA and the POA are always preferred. This is true even when the MTA and the POA are on the same server. Here's why: When a link between the MTA and the POA is UNC, messages are queued, and then discovered via a polling cycle. The queuing and polling process causes messages to flow at a slower rate than when messages are sent via TCP/IP.

Moving MTAs to New IP Addresses or Ports

First of all, if you are moving an MTA to a new IP address, it is probably because you are moving the entire domain directory to a new server. If that is the case, review Chapter 20, "Troubleshooting Message Flow," for the complete procedure.

Perhaps, though, all you are doing is moving the file server to a new LAN segment and assigning it a new IP address. Here is the procedure you should follow:

1. Connect to the domain that is being moved.
2. Change the MTA object's network address to reflect the new address or port.

Connections between other domains and this one will now start to drop off. Other domains, and this domain's post office, will show this domain as closed.

3. Unload the MTA.
4. Move the server to the new address and/or port, making the appropriate address or port changes at the server level.
5. Reload the MTA.

   Check the connection to this MTA from other MTAs on the system, and from this domain's post office's POAs. The connections should begin opening, now that they "see" this MTA at the new address and/or port.

These are just a few simple steps, but they are essential for connectivity.

Tuning the MTA

Typically, a busy MTA needs little tuning to keep up with its queues. If TCP/IP links are used exclusively, the MTA will not need to waste CPU cycles polling or maintaining idle connections and will have the resources it needs.

You might find, however, that some types of messages need to be moved faster than others. Remote users and users making busy searches both use the high-priority queues. To weigh these queues a little more heavily, check the Use 2nd High Priority Router box found on the Agent Settings tab of the MTA detail window. This will spawn an additional thread for the 0 and 1 subdirectories. The more connections the MTA services, the more threads will be spawned. If the server is having trouble keeping up with queues, this will mean that the mail priority queues (2 through 7) will back up even further, whereas the 0 and 1 are processed more quickly.

On large systems, an MTA on a Pentium II-class server should be able to process at least 100,000 messages each day without noticeable backups in any of the queues. Some administrators have seen MTAs that process three times that many messages in a day.

Monitoring Your MTA Through a Web Browser

Just like the GroupWise POA, the GroupWise MTA can be monitored through a Web browser. Using the HTTP interface of the MTA can greatly enhance your capability to troubleshoot and maintain your GroupWise system. It will be to your advantage to become very familiar with all the various components you can review and monitor via the HTTP port of the MTA.

Simple Configuration

The GroupWise MTA needs three settings tweaked in order to support HTTP monitoring of the MTA. They are the following:

- An HTTP port specified
- An HTTP monitoring username specified
- An HTTP monitoring password for the username specified

All of these settings can be configured in ConsoleOne.

HTTP Port

To specify your HTTP port, edit the MTA object in ConsoleOne and go to the Network Address property page. Fill in the HTTP port as shown in Figure 9.20.

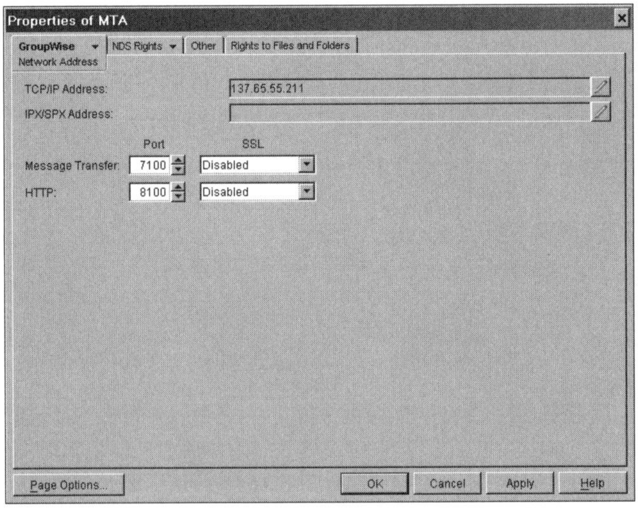

FIGURE 9.20 Specifying the HTTP port—it must be unique.

Fill in the HTTP port with a value that you know is unique. Don't use the same port as the message transfer port or your MTA will not be able to listen on the MTP port, and all inbound connections will fail to this MTA.

HTTP Username/Password

To specify your HTTP username and password settings, go to the Agent Settings property page of the GroupWise MTA object. At the bottom of the GroupWise Agent Settings property page, fill in the HTTP User Name and HTTP Password fields.

Monitoring the MTA with a Web Browser

Fill in the IP address or DNS name of the server running the MTA, along with a colon and a port name. For example

```
http://137.65.55.211:8100
```

You will be prompted for the username and password with a dialog box.

Once you are in the GroupWise MTA HTTP monitoring screen, you'll see a bevy of information. Figure 9.21 shows just one of the screens in the GroupWise MTA HTTP monitoring screen. Once again, the HTTP interface of the MTA offers a wealth of information that can help you better maintain and troubleshoot your GroupWise system. It is to your advantage to become familiar will all of the options on the MTA's HTTP interface.

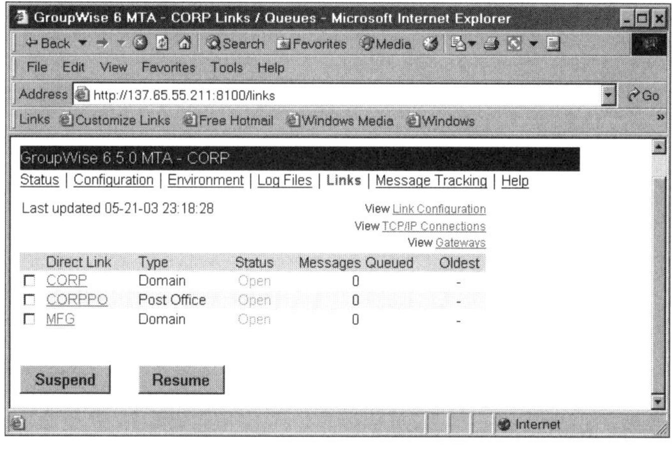

FIGURE 9.21
MTA HTTP monitoring.

Summary

This chapter covered all aspects of the GroupWise message transfer agent, from the details window found in ConsoleOne to the understanding of troubleshooting features at the MTA's server console screen. This chapter also discussed the link configuration tool and walked you through its use.

CHAPTER 10

Installing and Configuring the GroupWise Internet Agent

The GroupWise mail format is a proprietary format; although GroupWise supports many open standards, it is not an open system. Due to its proprietary format, translation is required in order to communicate with other systems.

The GroupWise Internet Agent is the most popular translator for GroupWise, because it allows GroupWise users to send e-mail messages to recipients via the Internet. It does much more than that, however. It also provides access to the GroupWise system from five different open-standard protocols.

This chapter looks at the architecture of the GroupWise Internet Agent and the protocols it supports. It also explores the installation, configuration, and operation of the GroupWise Internet Agent, otherwise known as the GWIA.

GWIA Architecture

GWIA architecture—the way in which the GWIA works with the rest of the GroupWise system—is best understood in terms of general gateway architecture. All GroupWise gateways perform one or more of the following functions:

- Translation
- Transport
- Mailbox access

The functions performed by the gateway determine the way in which the gateway connects to the rest of the system. The GWIA performs all three of these functions. The following sections look at each of the functions in turn.

Translation

The GWIA translates messages from Simple Mail Transfer Protocol (SMTP) format or Multipurpose Internet Mail Extensions (MIME) format into GroupWise format. It also translates GroupWise messages from the proprietary GroupWise format into SMTP or MIME format. This allows messages sent by GroupWise users to be read by users of e-mail systems that can receive SMTP or MIME e-mail messages.

NOTE **Other gateways that perform translation include the GroupWise API gateway and the GroupWise gateways for Exchange, Notes, and the Messaging Architect's GWFax software.**

The translation function requires that the GWIA receive messages from the GroupWise system. The Message Transfer Agent (MTA) handles this by dropping Internet-bound messages into the GWIA's input queues. When messages are sent to the GroupWise system from the Internet, the MTA transfers those messages once the GWIA has translated them into GroupWise format.

Transport

Translated messages originating in the GroupWise system must be transported to the correct mail host on the Internet. The GWIA performs this function independently of the GroupWise MTA. The GWIA functions as a sendmail host, which means it can communicate with any other sendmail host on the Internet (assuming a connection is established).

This transport is performed in TCP/IP through port 25, the industry-standard sendmail TCP port. The GWIA performs the appropriate Domain Name System/Services (DNS) lookup to locate the recipient's mail host, and then connects and transfers the translated message. For inbound messages, the GWIA is always "listening" for similar connections from other sendmail hosts.

Mailbox Access

The GWIA can give users access to their mailboxes from alternate clients, such as Eudora, Netscape Messenger, or Microsoft Outlook Express, as well as other POP3 clients on handheld computers. The GWIA supports two forms of mailbox access: Post Office Protocol (POP3) and Internet Message Access Protocol (IMAP4). The GWIA also allows users to access the GroupWise address book via the Lightweight Directory Access Protocol (LDAP).

In order to do this, the GWIA must be able to connect directly to the users' post offices. This can be accomplished by the GWIA talking directly to the post office, or by using TCP/IP to the Post Office Agent (POA) for every user who needs POP3 or IMAP4 access. Typically, the GWIA connects to the POA in client/server mode and thus acts as an intermediary between the POA and the third-party mail client.

LDAP address-book access is provided a little differently. The GWIA reads the necessary address-book information directly from the domain database. The GWIA is hard-coded to look to its parent domain directory for the necessary domain database file.

Architectural Summary

When the GWIA is functioning in its capacity as a sendmail host (translation and transport), it connects with the GroupWise system via the MTA and standard file-polling. When the GWIA functions as a POP3 or IMAP4 host (mailbox access), it connects with the GroupWise system via the POA in client/server or direct access mode. When the GWIA functions as an LDAP host, it connects with the GroupWise system via a UNC mapping to the domain database.

Installing the GWIA

The GWIA is not installed, by default, when you create your GroupWise system. It is not required for users to be able to send messages to each other. Of course, because it is required for users to send Internet e-mail, a GroupWise system without a GWIA is a little bit like a Harley that you only use to walk your dog. That's an interesting picture!

This section walks through the process of installing the GWIA, so users can send e-mail to their biker friends in Sturgis, South Dakota, or anywhere else in the world. First though, let's lay down some prerequisites for the server that will run the GWIA:

- The GWIA server should have access to the Internet, unless the GWIA will relay to another SMTP host.
- The GWIA must have a way to resolve Internet domain names to Internet addresses. The server that houses the GWIA needs to be configured to point at a DNS server. On a NetWare server that means there is a RESOLV.CFG file in the `SYS:ETC` directory. The RESOLV.CFG would looking something like this:

```
domain wwwidgets.com
nameserver 137.65.55.200
nameserver 137.65.55.201
```

- The GWIA should be configured as an Internet host, accessible from the Internet. On a NetWare server, this means that the `SYS:ETC\HOSTS` file has a listing of the server's IP address and its fully qualified Internet domain name. The Internet domain mentioned in the Internet domain name should match the Internet domain mentioned in the RESOLV.CFG file mentioned earlier. For example

  ```
  137.65.55.211 SMTP.WWWIDGETS.COM
  ```

- The GWIA should be running on a server with plenty of horsepower; it's good to have plenty of disk space, but not like a post office. The GWIA keeps messages in a holding queue only for a short time.
- Your DNS administrator will want to make an `A` record and an `MX` record for the server that is running the GWIA. An `A` record is an Address Record pointing to the server running the GWIA. This helps to establish the server on the Internet as a member of the Internet domain that the server is a member of. In our example, the Internet domain is `wwwidgets.com`. An `MX` record indicates to other SMTP hosts which host in the `wwwidgets.com` Internet domain to try to send SMTP messages through. So, for example, if the Internet domain name is `WWWIDGETS.COM` and the aforementioned server had a name of `SMTP.WWWIDGETS.COM`, the `MX` record would point to `SMTP.WWWIDGETS.COM` as being the Internet host that has the capacity to receive SMTP messages from the Internet for the Internet domain `WWWIDGETS.COM`.

Following are the steps to install a GWIA:

1. First, locate the GWIA installation program.

   It is found in the `GWIA` directory, under the `INTERNET` directory at the root of your GroupWise 6.5 Software Distribution Directory (SDD) or the GroupWise 6.5 Administration CD.
2. Run INSTALL.EXE under the `<SDD>\INTERNET\GWIA` directory.

   The License agreement screen comes up, followed by the welcome screen, which explains what this installation program is going to do.
3. Click Next.

Next comes the prompt for the software platform screen. These instructions will be for installing the GWIA on the NetWare/NLM platform.

4. After making the platform selection, click Next.

   The installation needs the paths for the NLMs and the NetWare load script (it's talking about an *.NCF file) that the GWIA will use. This will generally be the system directory on the SYS volume of the server where the GroupWise domain that owns this GWIA resides. However, if you are using Novell Clustering Services, you might want to install this software to a different path of your choosing, on a clustered volume. You can also update the Autoexec.ncf file, or cluster-enable the GWIA install.

5. After making the code location selection, click Next.
6. The GWIA, like all GroupWise agents, can be monitored from a Web browser. In the next installation step, you will be prompted for the port that the GWIA should listen to for Web-browser monitoring requests, as well as the username and password to use. I recommend skipping this step (or not checking the option to enable the Web Console), and entering this information from ConsoleOne instead.

   At this point, the installation asks whether the GWIA is going to send directly to the Internet or if it is going to use a relay host (see Figure 10.1). Relay hosts are commonly used on large, heterogeneous systems where Internet access must be tightly controlled at the firewall.

7. If a relay host is needed, provide the installation program with the IP address of the relay host machine and click Next.

   When you click Next, the install wizard will check for Internet connectivity either to the Internet or to the relay server you specified. If the server where you are installing the GWIA agents does not have connectivity, you will receive a warning about this. You can continue the install by selecting the option to "I will fix this problem later". Just remember to come back and fix the problem.

   You might also be prompted about no DNS name resolution if the server is not properly configured to talk to a DNS Server to resolve Internet names. Once again, you can continue the install by selecting the option to fix this problem later.

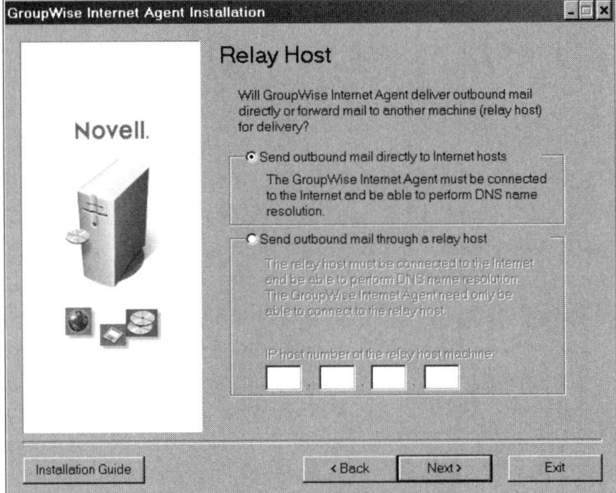

FIGURE 10.1 Choosing between direct connection to the Internet and connection via a relay host.

8. In the next window, you need to indicate which GroupWise domain to connect the GWIA to.

   You should have made this decision well in advance of this step, because in step 4 you selected the server to which you are installing the software. The GWIA will be most efficient if it runs on the same server on which the GroupWise domain resides. This server should also be running the GroupWise MTA for that domain. The installation also prompts for a name of the subdirectory for the GWIA. The default is `GWIA`. Because that name is pretty intuitive, it's a good default.

9. In yet another case of intuitive naming, the installation asks for the name of the object that will represent the GWIA in the GroupWise system and in eDirectory (see Figure 10.2). This object will appear as a child object of the domain selected in an earlier step. You can name it GWIA or some other name that works for you, such as SMTP.

10. After clicking Next, you are prompted for the Internet domain name that the GWIA should listen as. For example, `wwwigets.com`. The value you enter here is added to the Foreign ID field on the GroupWise property page of the GWIA. If your GWIA will listen for several Internet domain names, just enter the most popular one in this field, and later you can add the others. Figure 10.3 shows this installation screen.

    When you click Next, the install routine will check for DNS entries for this domain name. If none are found you will be warned about the problem. Once again, you can continue the installation by choosing to fix the problem later.

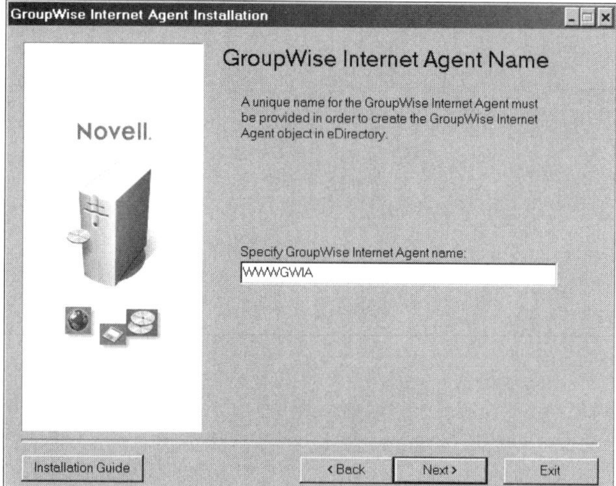

FIGURE 10.2 Naming the GWIA object.

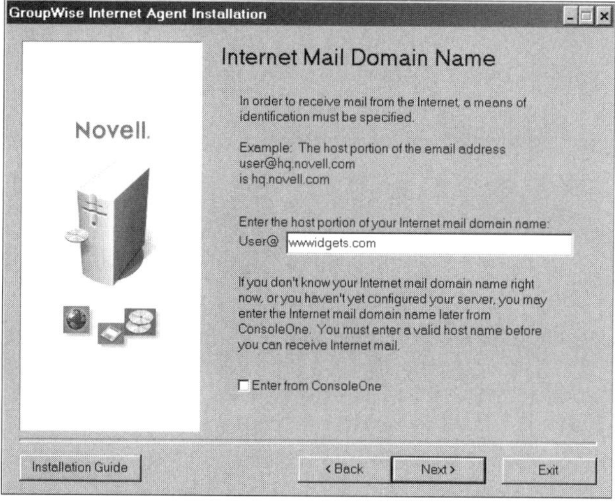

FIGURE 10.3 Here, you enter the host portion of your Internet domain name.

11. Armed with all the information provided during the installation, the wizard is now ready to actually install something. If you reach this point and decide you want to change something, you can use the Back button as many times as you want. When you are ready, click Install.

WARNING

While the GWIA software is being installed, a fairly standard installation bar comes up. Using the Stop button at this point will result in an incomplete (and therefore broken) installation.

When the installation is done, you have the option to launch the GWIA. However, consider waiting on launching the GWIA until you have it completely configured. It might not be able to correctly send Internet e-mail, but it is up and running. If during the installation, problems came up that you decided to fix later, now might be a good time to unload the GWIA so that it does not begin generating undeliverable messages.

Loading the GWIA

The previous two chapters discussed how the MTA and POA must be provided with certain startup parameters in order to load correctly. The GWIA needs the same sorts of parameters, but they are not provided to the GWIA the same way they are to the MTA or POA. For the GroupWise MTA and POA, most of the settings dealing with how the MTA or POA is configured are housed in the `WPDOMAIN` or `WPHOST` databases. The startup file for most MTAs and POAs has only one switch activated, the `/home=` switch. The GWIA is very different. Most of the GWIA's settings are not contained in the WPDOMAIN.DB file; they are contained in a file called GWIA.CFG. The following sections explain how the GWIA is configured.

If you have not finished configuring your GWIA, you might want to wait to load it a little later. Many of the configuration changes you make to the GWIA will just cause the GWIA to automatically reload and reread its configuration information. Some settings do not cause the GWIA to reload, and so the GWIA must be brought down (press F7 on the GWIA's console screen to do so), and then loaded again.

To load the GWIA once it has been installed and configured, enter the following at the server console:

```
GWIA
```

Novell has very thoughtfully provided an NCF file for the GWIA, called GWIA.NCF.

No startup parameters needed to be passed to the GWIA manually, because it is hard-coded to look in its startup directory (typically `SYS:\SYSTEM`) for a file named GWIA.CFG. In the case of the NCF file, the GWIA was passed a parameter telling it where to look for the configuration file, but it wasn't necessary.

This assumes, however, that you are using the default installation directory for the GWIA (`SYS:\SYSTEM` on the server where the domain resides). If you need to move the GWIA to another directory or to another server, you might have some extra work to do before it will load correctly.

Understanding GWIA Configuration Files

The GWIA.CFG file should be in the same directory as the GWIA.NLM file (or GWIA.EXE, for NT servers). This is just a regular text file that you can view with any editor.

When you make changes to the GWIA from ConsoleOne, the GWIA configuration snap-ins must find the GWIA.CFG file in order to allow you to make configuration changes to the GWIA. The GWIA configuration snap-in finds the GWIA.CFG using the following architecture. When you installed the GWIA, a little text file called EXEPATH.CFG was created. This file is found in the `<DOMAIN>\WPGATE\<GWIA GATEWAY DIRECTORY>`. The EXEPATH.CFG file's sole purpose is to point the ConsoleOne snap-ins to the path of the GWIA.CFG file, which typically resides in the `SYS:SYSTEM` directory on a NetWare server.

Configuring the GWIA

Just like the MTA and POA, the GWIA should be configured using ConsoleOne. The GWIA object is found under the domain object under the Gateways drop-down list in ConsoleOne. After right-clicking the GWIA object, selecting properties, and then selecting the GroupWise tab, you should see the Identification property page as shown in Figure 10.4.

Along the top are a series of property pages. The GWIA does quite a bit, so more configuration information might be required. Fortunately, each property page (and most of the dialog boxes that can be spawned from those property pages) have Help buttons. The online help for the GWIA is very informative and should keep you on track if you find yourself editing your GWIA without this book at your side.

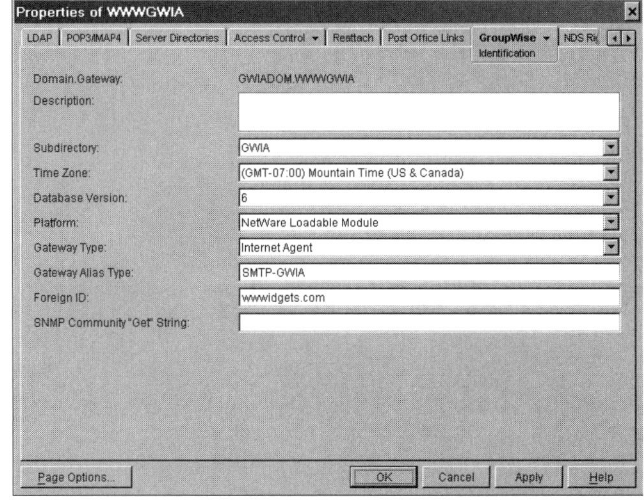

FIGURE 10.4
The GWIA Object identification property page is where you configure general information about the GWIA.

NOTE **Almost all of the settings changes you make on the GWIA are held in the GWIA.CFG file, and not in the WPDOMAIN.DB or eDirectory.**

Understanding the GroupWise Identification Property Page

This page is most likely over to the right, and it's labeled GroupWise. This section starts here, because this is the most basic information on the GWIA.

This page, shown in Figure 10.4, is where general information about the GWIA is configurable. These fields are common to all GroupWise gateways, which is why some of them might seem a little out of place for the GWIA.

- **Domain.Gateway:** This is the GroupWise name of the gateway. In the example in Figure 10.4, the value `GWIADOM.WWWGWIA` means that the agent belongs to the `GWIADOM` domain and is named `WWWGWIA`.
- **Description:** This is free text; you can use this for the pager number of the GWIA administrator, or perhaps to warn viewers not change the GWIA object without permission from the administrator.
- **Subdirectory:** This field is populated by a drop-down list. It shows where the queue directories for this gateway reside. In the case of the GWIA, you should pick GWIA (or whatever you named your GWIA subdirectory during installation). This is a subdirectory under the `<DOMAIN>\WPGATE` directory.

- **Time Zone:** By default, the GWIA has the same timezone as its parent domain. This setting is used to timestamp inbound and outbound SMTP/MIME messages.
- **Database Version:** For the GroupWise 6.5 GWIA, this should be set to 6. This setting indicates to the MTA whether it needs to convert messages back to 4.x or 5.0 format (for compatibility with older gateways).
- **Platform:** In the example for this chapter, the NLM version of the GWIA was installed, so NetWare Loadable Module is selected.
- **Gateway Type:** For the GWIA, the only valid value here is Internet Agent. Obviously, with other gateways, other values would be appropriate.
- **Gateway Alias Type:** This field is used to associate this GWIA with user or post office aliases. If you have more than one GWIA, you will need to have more than one gateway alias type, because each GWIA (and each GroupWise gateway) must have its own unique gateway alias type.

  Gateway aliases can be useful and sometimes very common, particularly for customers who have used GroupWise for a long time. However, there might be some more effective strategies for giving a person an Internet address than using aliases. For example, by using a free-form Internet address for the user, and then defining nicknames to the user to allow for multiple incoming Internet addresses for one user. See Chapter 16, "Internet Addressing," for more details.
- **Foreign ID:** This is the name by which your GroupWise system will be known on the Internet. It is critical that this value match the domain portion of the To line for all messages that are destined to your users. If the GWIA receives a message that is addressed to a domain that does not match one of its foreign domains, the message will be rejected.

  The Foreign ID field can have several domains on it. The names simply need to be separated by spaces. For example

  ```
  wwwidgets.com worldwidewidgets.com
  ```

  The default Internet domain name should be listed first. All others should be listed afterward.

TIP

The Foreign ID field can hold only 124 characters. To accommodate more domain names, the GWIA is hard-coded to look in the `<DOMAIN>\WPGATE\<GWIA>` directory for a file called FRGNAMES.CFG. This is an ASCII text file that contains a listing of all the Internet domain names. Each name should be on a line by itself, and the last line of the file should be blank. Here's an example:

```
wwwidgets.com
worldwidewidgets.com
sales.worldwidewidgets.com
newyork.worldwidewidgets.com
widgetsoftheworld.com
```

NOTE

You can also define which Internet domains the GWIA will receive Internet mail as by using Internet addressing. Chapter 16 discusses Internet addressing; you can use IDOMAINs in the place of multiple domain names on the Foreign ID field or in the FRGNAMES.CFG file. Each Internet domain name you define should have a corresponding `MX` record in your DNS.

- **SNMP Community "Get" String:** Enter the SNMP community string that the gateway should use for all SNMP `GET` commands. The community name is case sensitive.

Configuring the Network Address Property Page

Figure 10.5 shows an example Network Address property page.

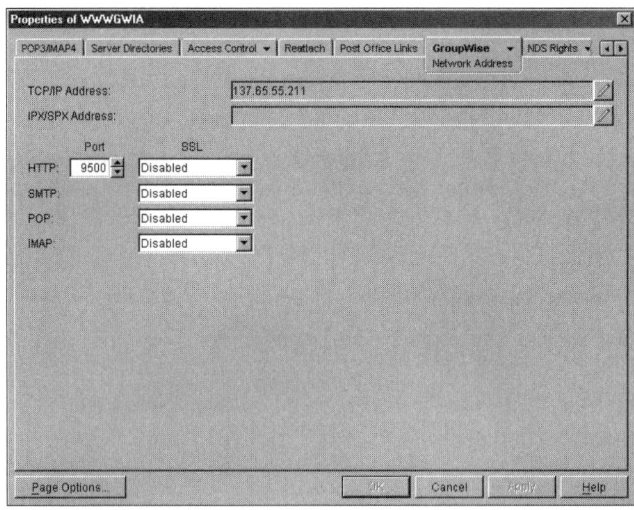

FIGURE 10.5
The GWIA Network Address property page allows you to configure the network address.

The fields on this page are as follows:

- **TCP/IP Address:** Enter the TCP/IP address of the server where the GWIA executes.

  The GWIA uses the standardized ports for SMTP, POP3, IMAP4, and LDAP services. For example, SMTP uses port 25, POP3 services uses port 110, IMAP services use 143, and so on. These ports are not configurable.

- **HTTP Port:** Enter the HTTP port that the GWIA should use to listen for HTTP monitoring of the GWIA. You should also have a HTTP username and an HTTP password assigned in order to secure the use of HTTP monitoring on the GroupWise GWIA. You can configure these from the Optional Gateway Settings property page on the GroupWise tab.

  The SSL portions of this screen are not discussed in this chapter. Chapter 27, "Securing Your GroupWise System via SSL," gives detailed information on how to enable SSL on the GWIA.

TIP

Do not fill in the IPX/SPX Address field; it's of no use.

The TCP/IP address and HTTP port on any agent are not only used by the agent itself, they're also used by the GroupWise Monitor Agent. The GroupWise Monitor Agent reads this information in order to monitor the GWIA.

Configuring the GroupWise Gateway Time Settings Property Page

The Gateway Time Settings property page shown in Figure 10.6 is used to configure the polling intervals and operational cycles for the GWIA. This page is available on the drop-down list of the GroupWise page.

The fields on this page are as follows:

- **Send/Receive Cycle:** This is the number of seconds that will be split between the GWIA's send and receive cycles. In the example in Figure 10.6, the 120 seconds specified will give the send and receive cycles each 60 seconds to complete processing. If a message file is being processed when the time expires for that process, the process will complete before swapping out.

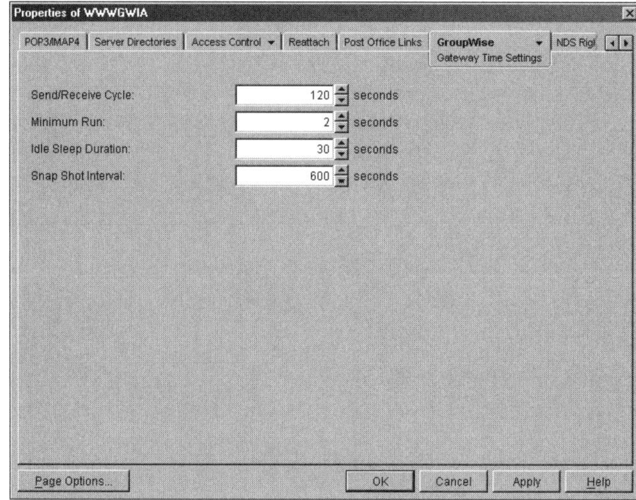

FIGURE 10.6 The GWIA Gateway Time Settings Property Page enables you to configure the GWIA's polling intervals and operational cycles.

- **Minimum Run:** This is the minimum amount of time, in seconds, that the gateway will be "awake" once the idle sleep duration has passed. Typically, this is best set at 0, but if you pay more to open a connection than to maintain the connection, you might choose to raise this value. This might catch some additional messages and send them on the current connection, rather than opening a new one for them later.

TIP

A minimum run of more than *XX* seconds is probably only going to be meaningful in conjunction with dial-up connectivity.

- **Idle Sleep Duration:** This is the amount of time, in seconds, that the GWIA will "sleep." During this time, messages can be accumulating in the <DOMAIN>\WPGATE\<GWIA>\WPCSOUT\<GWIA-FID>\0-7 directories. This setting allows you to reduce the amount of CPU time spent supporting polling.

NOTE

The GWIA is actually two separate processes in one—the gateway and the daemon. The gateway translates messages from GroupWise format to ASCII and vice versa. The daemon listens on port 25 to receive messages and sends the ASCII files generated for it by the gateway as SMTP messages on the Internet. Although the gateway has an idle sleep duration, the daemon never sleeps.

- **Snap Shot Interval:** This is a sliding window for statistical purposes. The default, 600 seconds, results in 10 minutes of GWIA statistics being shown on the GWIA console. Regardless of the size of this window, it slides forward every 60 seconds.

For most customers, the default gateway time settings are sufficient.

Configuring the GroupWise Log Settings Property Page

The GroupWise Log Settings Property page looks just like the Log Settings pages for the POA and MTA. The fields on this page are as follows:

- **Log File Path:** By default, this field is blank. GWIA logs are placed in the `<DOMAIN>\WPGATE\<GWIA>\000.PRC` directory. If you choose to keep logs elsewhere, enter the path here. It's not recommended that you configure the GWIA to put logs on a separate server. Performance will suffer, and if the server containing the logs goes down, the GWIA will not function.
- **Logging Level:** There are four menu items in this drop-down list, as follows:
    - **Off:** No logging.
    - **Normal:** The GWIA will track "major" events in the log, but most of the detail will be gone.
    - **Verbose:** The log will contain useful detail. Although this is not the default, it is the recommended logging level.
    - **Diagnostic:** This is typically used when troubleshooting the GWIA. It's very detailed and should be run only for troubleshooting purposes.
- **Max Log File Age:** This is the oldest that any log file on disk can be before being automatically deleted by the GWIA. The default is seven days, and this is typically sufficient.
- **Max Log Disk Space:** This is the maximum amount of disk space that the log files can consume. If the logs reach this limit, the oldest log file is deleted. If you choose to set the maximum log file age beyond seven days, you will want to raise this limit as well to ensure that you actually get to keep your oldest logs for the time you specify.

Logging is your friend on the GWIA. Particularly if you enable real-time blacklists, as explained in the section titled "Configuring the GWIA Access Control Property Pages."

Configuring the GroupWise Optional Gateway Settings Property Page

Figure 10.7 shows the Optional Gateway Settings page. This page is the same for all GroupWise gateways; there are options here that do not apply to the GWIA. The Directory Sync/Exchange field, for instance, is not supported by the GWIA.

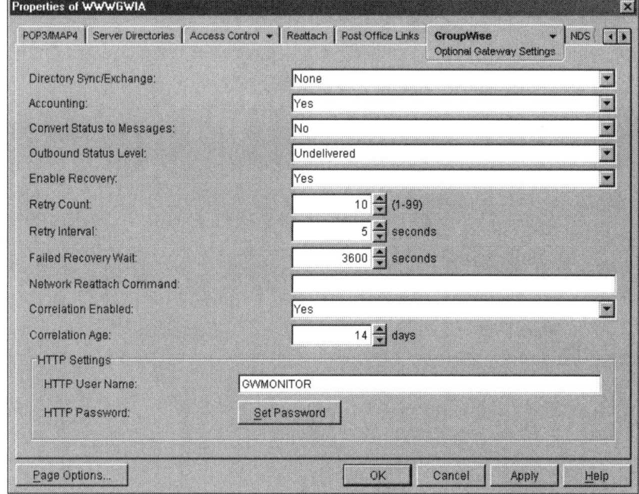

FIGURE 10.7 The GWIA Optional Gateway Settings property page.

The other fields on this page are as follows:

- **Accounting:** If set to Yes, the GWIA creates an accounting file, ACCT, in the `000.PRC` directory, which describes all traffic it processes. This file is e-mailed each day to the user specified as the Accountant under the Gateway Administrators property page.
- **Convert Status to Messages:** This setting does not apply to the GWIA.
- **Outbound Status Level:** Set this to Undeliverable so that users get a message if they send mail to an invalid address. You can customize the status messages that users get by configuring the STATUSxx.XML file in the GWIA's root directory under the `<DOMAIN>\WPGATE` directory.
- **Enable Recovery:** This setting allows the GWIA to restart itself or attempt to reconnect to a foreign host if a connection is interrupted.
- **Retry Count:** The GWIA does not read this value; it has hard-coded values it complies with for retries.
- **Retry Interval:** The GWIA does not read this value; it has hard-coded values it complies with for retries.

- **Failed Recovery Wait:** The GWIA does not read this value; it has hard-coded values it complies with for retries.
- **Network Reattach Command:** Populate this field with a command line or with the filename of a batch file for mapping drives to reattach the GWIA to a domain file server. It only applies to the GWIA running on an NT server. If the GWIA is running on a NetWare server, use the Reattach Settings property page.
- **Correlation Enabled:** Set this to Yes. Correlation is needed for the GWIA to send back undeliverable messages if needed.
- **Correlation Age:** Keep the default of 14 days.
- **HTTP Settings:** This area has two options:
  - **HTTP User Name:** Enter the username that you will use to monitor the GWIA through a Web browser.
  - **HTTP Password:** Enter the password you will use when monitoring the GWIA.

TIP

The HTTP information on any agent is not only used by the agent but also by the GroupWise Monitor Agent. The Monitor Agent reads this information in order to monitor the particular agent.

Your GWIA will work just fine without configuring this screen, but I recommend that you do fine-tune the settings mentioned in this section.

Configuring the GroupWise Gateway Administrators Property Page

In order to make your GWIA *RFC-compliant* with established SMTP protocols, you must specify a postmaster for the GWIA. From the GroupWise Gateway Administrator's property page, you can specify the postmaster of your GroupWise system.

Here is an explanation of the various administrator roles:

- **Operator:** Administrators specified as operators will receive certain kinds of GWIA errors in their mailboxes.
- **Accountant:** Administrators with this role will receive gateway accounting and statistical logs each day.
- **Postmaster:** Administrators with this role will receive any message that comes in to the GWIA addressed to `postmaster@`<*GWIA Foreign ID*>. For example, `postmaster@wwwidgets.com`.

- **Foreign Operator:** This role has no GWIA-related functionality. With other gateways, it allows you to specify a user on a foreign mail system who can e-mail certain commands to the gateway. This field is very useful for gateways that provide direct connectivity between GroupWise and third-party mail systems.

Defining a postmaster is good Internet protocol. Defining an operator is also a good practice.

GroupWise Gateway Aliases Property Page

This page, shown in Figure 10.8, provides a listing of the users who have a gateway alias associated with this GWIA. This is a great feature for determining which user has which gateway alias.

There is nothing to configure on this property page; it's strictly an informational page. Chapter 16 talks more about using gateway aliases for the GWIA. Consult Chapter 16 before using aliases widely, as most customers will want to avoid gateway aliases for reasons explained there.

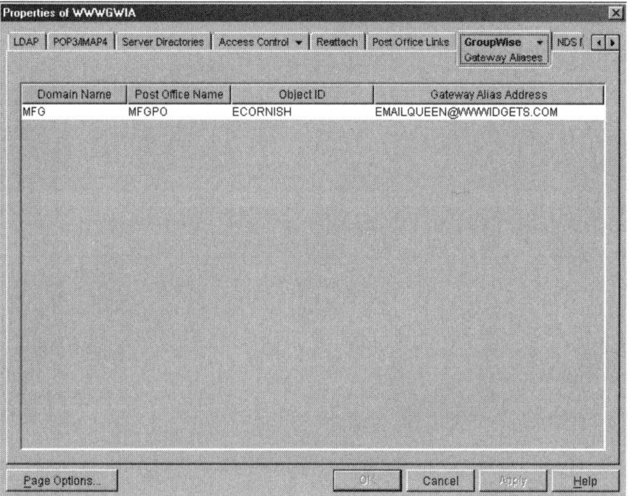

FIGURE 10.8 The GWIA Gateway Aliases property page.

Configuring the SMTP/MIME Settings Property Page

There is a whole lot of configuration control offered through the SMTP/MIME Settings property pages. This is where you govern address handling, message formatting, SMTP dial-up, and other assorted SMTP/MIME-related communications settings. First we will look at the SMTP/MIME Settings property page, as shown in Figure 10.9.

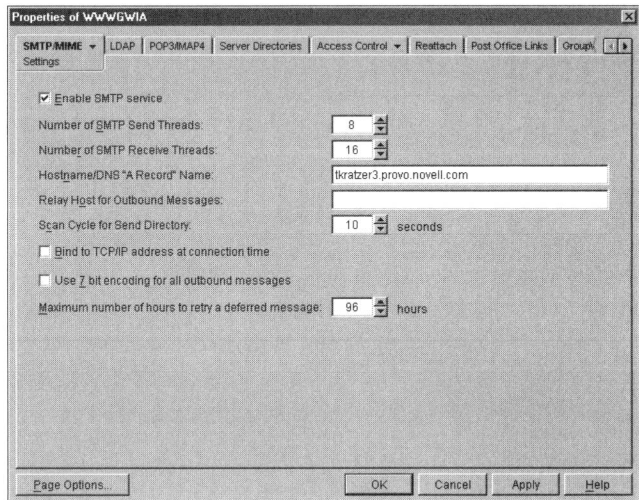

FIGURE 10.9 The GWIA SMTP/MIME Settings property page.

This GWIA SMTP/MIME Settings page, shown in Figure 10.9, has nine fields that govern some global settings:

- **Enable SMTP Service:** This box must be checked before users can send or receive Internet e-mail messages through this GWIA. If you unchecked this box, the GWIA would no longer listen for SMTP sessions on TCP port 25.
- **Number of SMTP Send Threads:** This is the number of server processes, or threads, that will be devoted to SMTP send operations. This setting affects the GWIA's daemon process. If the GWIA runs out of threads (that is, all of them are busy), messages waiting to be sent to Internet recipients will have to wait until a thread is freed up. My customers have this value set to 100.
- **Number of SMTP Receive Threads:** This is the number of server processes that will be devoted to SMTP receive operations. When a sendmail host on the Internet tries to communicate with the GWIA, one receive thread will be dedicated to managing that communication. If there are no threads available, the sendmail host will determine that the GWIA is busy or not responding and will retry the transmission according to its own configured preferences. My customers have this value set to 100.

  Because receiving messages is considered to be a higher priority than sending messages, the GWIA will "steal" threads from the Send Threads option, rather than rejecting connections just because it does not have enough receive threads.

- **Hostname/DNS "A Record" Name:** This is the name of the GWIA, as it is known on the Internet. Populate this field with a valid DNS name only. This is the name that will be returned to any SMTP service that connects into port 25 on the GWIA. If this name does not match a valid DNS name, you might have problems receiving mail if other SMTP sendmail hosts do reverse-DNS lookups on your GWIA's IP address.
- **Relay Host for Outbound Messages:** Some administrators can expose only a very few machines to the Internet through their firewalls. In cases like this, you can configure the GWIA to relay all outbound SMTP/MIME messages through another machine. Populate this field with the IP address or DNS name of the relay host (for example, `unixmailer.wwwidgets.com`).
- **Scan Cycle for Send Directory:** This is the interval, in seconds, at which the SMTP send threads will poll the SMTP send directory for messages to be transmitted to Internet hosts.
- **Bind to TCP/IP Address at Connection Time:** The TCP/IP address noted here is the one on the Network Address property page discussed earlier in this chapter. If a server has multiple IP addresses, the GWIA will send messages using the address defined in the Network Address field. When hosts on the Internet do a reverse-DNS lookup, it is important that the GWIA is sending messages using the IP address that matches its publicly defined DNS `A` record.

  The GWIA listens for inbound messages on all IP addresses.
- **Use 7-Bit Encoding for All Outbound Messages:** When the GWIA sends messages, by default it uses an encoding format called 8-bit MIME. Many older hosts on the Internet cannot understand 8-bit MIME. The GWIA should be able to determine this, and the GWIA will automatically change to sending the message in 7-bit MIME format. If your GWIA is not doing this well, recipients of messages from your GWIA might complain of garbled messages from your GWIA. If this is the case, checking this option will generally resolve this problem.
- **Maximum Number of Hours to Retry a Deferred Message:** When the GWIA gets a `4XX` level SMTP error, this setting determines how long the GWIA will retry sending the message before giving up, and sending an undeliverable status message to the original recipient. The default is 96 hours. If you set the maximum to 0, senders will immediately get a message from the GWIA reporting that the GWIA cannot send to the Internet host, if the GWIA has a `4XX` type error.

  The GWIA is hard-coded as to how it manages retries. Here's how it works. Imagine that the GWIA tries to send to another Internet mailer on the Internet. But the GWIA reports a `450 Host Down` error in its log file. The GWIA will move the message to the `<DOMAIN>\WPGATE\<GWIA>\DEFER` directory, and then requeue the message to the DAEMON process on the GWIA after 20 minutes has passed. If the message fails, the GWIA waits another 20 minutes and tries again. If after another 20 minutes the GWIA cannot send the message, it will try to send the message again in four hours, and then every four hours after that, up to 96 hours (four days). The only piece of this algorithm you can change is for how long the GWIA will continue retrying. You can change the default of 96 hours to 10 if you want. You do this from the SMTP/MIME—Settings property page of the GWIA. Change the value under the setting Maximum Number of Hours to Retry a Deferred Message.

If you set the maximum to 0, senders will immediately get a message back from the GWIA reporting that the GWIA cannot send to the Internet host, if the GWIA has a `4XX` type error. For example, if the GWIA reports a `450 Host Down` error, the GWIA will send a message to the sender indicating that the Internet host is down.

The default settings for the GWIA might not be the best for your environment. Perhaps you will want to increase threads, or you might not want the GWIA to retry a message for four days.

Configuring the SMTP/MIME Address Handling Property Page

The Address Handling property page (see Figure 10.10) is generally a place where you make settings and then leave them as they are.

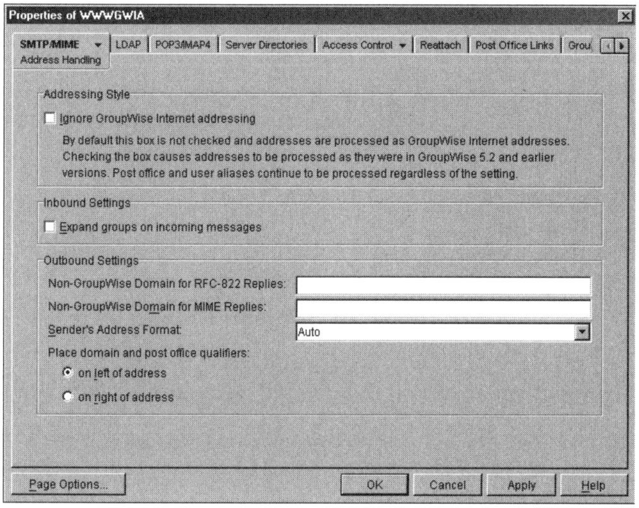

FIGURE 10.10
The SMTP/MIME Address Handling property page.

The settings on this page are as follows:

- **Addressing Style: Ignore GroupWise Internet Addressing:** This setting allows the administrator to revert to old-style GroupWise address parsing at the GWIA level only. When you use this option, all replies to Internet mail must go back out the same GWIA they came in. Also if you use this option, the GWIA will receive mail only to domains defined in the Foreign ID field. It will *not* read the `IDOMAIN` list of domain names from the domain database. Also, the GWIA will not try to resolve recipient addresses to the newer formats Internet addressing provides, such as `First.Last`, `Last.First`, and the free-form Internet address you can define on the GroupWise user ID. Leave this box unchecked unless you have been told to check it by Novell technical support. By default, this setting is unchecked.

NOTE

Checking the Ignore GroupWise Internet Addressing option enables the `/DIA` switch in the GWIA.CFG file. For a complete discussion of Internet addressing, refer to Chapter 16.

- **Inbound Settings:** The Expand groups on Incoming Messages check box allows for some very powerful functionality. If Expand Groups on Incoming Messages is checked, Internet users can send to distribution lists on your GroupWise system. They will need to know the name of the list, and would simply address it as *`<groupname>@<host>`*. For example, to send to the `CorpUsers` distribution list on our example system, an Internet e-mail user would address the message to `corpusers@wwwidgets.com`. The GWIA would then expand the address of the message, adding each of the mailboxes listed under the `CorpUsers` distribution list.
- **Outbound Settings:** The address format settings under the Outbound Settings options become obsolete when GroupWise Internet addressing is enabled. For more information on Internet addressing, see Chapter 16. The settings you can choose from here are as follows:
  - **Non-GroupWise Domain for RFC-822 Replies:** This field builds the TO line when a GroupWise user replies to an RFC-822 (SMTP) message that came in through the GWIA.
  - **Non-GroupWise Domain for MIME Replies:** This field builds the TO line when a GroupWise user replies to a MIME message that came in through the GWIA.

- **Sender's Address Format:** This setting is enabled only if Ignore GroupWise Internet Addressing has been checked. It allows you to choose how the GroupWise user's reply-to address is built from the various components of his or her GroupWise address.
- **Place Domain and Post Office Qualifiers:** These radio buttons allow you to choose where domain and post office components go if they are included in the Sender's Address Format field you selected. If they are on the left, the address is `user.po.domain@host`. If they are on the right, the address reads as `user@po.domain.host`.

You should consult Chapter 16 before making changes on most of the settings of this page.

Configuring the SMTP/MIME Dial-Up Settings Property Page

Later in this chapter, there's a section called "Configuring Dial-Up Internet Access" that talks about how to use the Dial-Up Settings page.

Configuring the SMTP/MIME ESMTP Settings Property Page

ESMTP stands for *extended SMTP.* The ESMTP protocol is a special, new, protocol through which enhancements to the SMTP protocol, called *service extensions,* can be created. The GroupWise 6.5 GWIA supports ESMTP service extensions. Some of the ESMTP extensions that the GWIA supports are the following:

- DSN
- STARTTLS (secure SMTP, POP, or IMAP over TLS/SSL)
- AUTH

DSN

DSN is short for Delivery Status Notification. This protocol is described in the Internet RFC 1894. By enabling this protocol, the GWIA can confirm to the sender that their message was delivered to the intended recipient. Before the DSN protocol, the GWIA would report only problems getting a message to its recipient's host. The sender had to assume that the recipient got the message, because they never got a response back saying that it was or wasn't received.

With the DSN Hold Age option, you select the number of days that you want the Internet Agent to retain information about the external sender so that status updates can be delivered to the sender. The default hold age of four days causes the sender information to be retained for four days. If the Internet Agent does not receive delivery status notification from the GroupWise recipient's POA within that time period, it deletes the sender information and the sender does not receive any delivery status notification.

NOTE

A DSN Hold Age of four days is plenty generous. Generally, you will not want to increase the DSN Hold Age over four days. The Delivery Status Notification pointer messages are kept in the `...\WPGATE<GWIA >\DSNHOLD` **directory. If you ever go out to this directory and see a bunch of files, don't let this alarm you. You should not see files older than the DSN Hold Age you specified. If you do, you can delete those files.**

STARTTLS

The GWIA supports sending messages over the Internet via SSL. This is a rather new protocol, and the GWIA will send SSL encrypted messages only to SMTP hosts that will receive via the STARTTLS protocol. The STARTTLS protocol is described in RFC 2487. Chapter 27 talks about how to enable STARTTLS on the GWIA.

AUTH

Allows other SMTP gateways to authenticate before sending mail. This is useful if you have relaying disabled. Anyone that authenticates is allowed to relay off the GWIA.

Configuring the SMTP/MIME Message Formatting Property Page

From this page, you set the inbound and outbound for conversion of messages to and from GroupWise format. The Inbound Settings portion has two available fields for you to edit:

- **Number of Inbound Conversion Threads:** This is the maximum number of server processes the GWIA will devote to converting messages from SMTP/MIME format to GroupWise format. This setting affects the GWIA's gateway process, and not its daemon process.
- **GroupWise View Name for Incoming Messages:** This is the name of the view (the embedded name, not the actual filename) that the GroupWise client will be told to use when displaying a message that was received from the Internet. This field should not be edited unless you are designing your own views with the GroupWise SDK. GroupWise views are the *.VEW files in a post office `OFVIEWS\WIN`

directory. Use this feature if you want all inbound Internet mail to be displayed using a custom view file from the GroupWise client. You can add a note to the view that says this file was received from the Internet as an SMTP message or something to this effect, if you want.

TIP

If you change the name of the view from Internet to something else, users cannot use the Anti-SPAM capabilities in the GroupWise 6.5 client. This is because the GroupWise 6.5 client identifies mail that came from the Internet by looking for the view type of Internet.

Under Outbound Settings, you have a few more fields to focus on. These settings are more likely to have an effect on your users' Internet e-mail experience:

- **Number of Outbound Conversion Threads:** This is the maximum number of server processes the GWIA will devote to converting messages from GroupWise format to SMTP/MIME format. This setting affects the GWIA's gateway process, and not its daemon process.
- **Default Message Encoding:** There are two options here. Basic RFC-822 is the older message format. MIME is the newer standard, and it is generally more efficient when binary files (executables, images, and so on) need to be transmitted. When RFC-822 encoding is selected, binary attachments must be encoded in the 7-bit UUEncode format. The UUEncode All Text Attachments option will force text attachments to also be encoded.

NOTE

If your users complain that people that they send Internet e-mail to cannot read the messages they send, you might investigate whether enabling RFC-822 encoding on all messages resolves this issue.

- **Enable Quoted Printable Text Line Wrapping:** This check box allows you to select the quoted printable MIME standard for text line wrapping. If this is not checked, outbound messages will wrap text according to the Line Wrap Length setting that follows this one.
- **Line Wrap Length for Message Text on Outbound Mail:** This is the number of characters after which the GWIA inserts a soft return. This prevents messages entered with no returns from appearing all on the same line. Of course, the recipient's mailer might need to be "told" to respect the soft return character.

Configuring the SMTP/MIME Scheduling Property Page

The GWIA SMTP/MIME Scheduling property page is used to define the times of the day and days of the week that the GWIA will process SMTP/MIME messages. Scheduling cannot be employed for POP3, IMAP4, or LDAP services. If those services are enabled, the GWIA will attempt to provide them all the time, regardless of the settings made on the Scheduling property page.

The Scheduling property page is especially useful when configuring the GWIA for dial-up access to the Internet, using the SMTP/MIME Dial-up Settings property page.

Configuring the SMTP/MIME Security Settings Property Page

Security is an important part of any Internet strategy. Because the GWIA is normally exposed to the Internet when receiving messages, it is critical that it be protected against certain kinds of attacks. The SMTP Security Settings dialog box in Figure 10.11 allows you to defend the GWIA from two kinds of common e-mail attacks: identity spoofing and mailbombs.

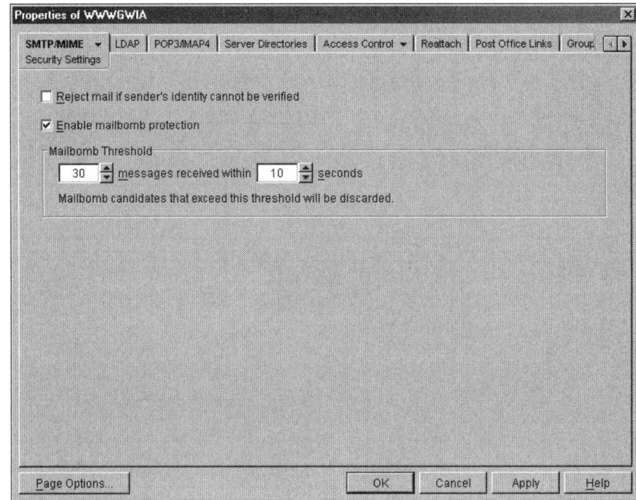

FIGURE 10.11 The GWIA SMTP/MIME Security Settings property page allows you to protect against SPAM and mailbombs.

The settings on this page are as follows:

- **Reject Mail if Sender's Identity Cannot Be Verified:** This setting prevents the GWIA from accepting e-mail from anonymous sendmail hosts. Although some legitimate e-mail is routed in this manner, spammers often use anonymous mailers. The GWIA will perform a reverse-DNS lookup on the name of the sendmail host to verify that its given name is in the DNS tables on the Internet. If it cannot find the name, it will not accept mail from this host.

Although it might seem logical to enable the Reject Mail if Sender's Identity Cannot Be Verified, enabling this feature might cause your system to reject e-mail from legitimate hosts. The reason for this is that the site sending to your GWIA might not have defined the A record of their SMTP mailing host. This problem is evidence of a lack of correct DNS configuration, but alas, the world isn't perfect.

- **Enable Mailbomb Protection:** If checked, the GWIA will use the mailbomb thresholds to prevent a single host from tying up the GWIA inbound threads with a mass mailing. Some mass mailings are actually designed not to deliver large numbers of messages, but to tie up the receiving host. The default mailbomb threshold of 30 messages received in 10 seconds is typically sufficient to identify a mailbomb attack before any harm is done.

If you need to enable a SPAM solution for the GWIA, make sure to see Chapter 25, "Configuring a SPAM/Junk Mail Control Solution."

Configuring the SMTP/MIME Timeouts Property Page

Each of the fields is populated with the number of minutes (not seconds) that the GWIA will wait before timing out on a particular operation. This timeout can be due to a noisy line, an unresponsive host, or some other loss of connectivity.

Configuring the SMTP/MIME Undeliverables Property Page

This page is where you instruct the GWIA how to handle inbound messages that cannot be delivered.

NOTE

Undeliverable messages that are outbound are handled by the destination mail host. That host can choose to reply, can forward the message to the configured postmaster, or can simply discard the message. As a GroupWise administrator, you have no control over how other e-mail administrators choose to handle undeliverable e-mail.

The settings on this page are as follows:

- **Amount of Original Message to Return to Sender When Message Is Undeliverable:** This is the amount of the original message, in kilobytes, that will be returned to the sender if the message cannot be delivered. Typically, it is not necessary for a sender to have more than a few lines of his or her message to identify it. This allows you to save a little bit of bandwidth.

- **Forward Undeliverable Inbound Messages to Host:** If you are operating a heterogeneous mail system, you might have a single DNS name but multiple mail hosts. If the GWIA is the default inbound mail host, you can configure it to forward any undeliverable messages to another mail host on your system. This other mail host might then find the desired recipient of the e-mail message. This option is useful when you are using Novell's NetMail mail system with the same domain name as your GroupWise users.
- **Move to Problem Directory:** If this option is checked, undeliverable messages are placed in the `GWPROB` directory of the GWIA subdirectory.

NOTE **The `GWPROB` directory is not purged automatically. You will have to purge it manually on occasion.**

- **Send to Postmaster:** If this option is checked, the user who has been configured as the postmaster will receive the full text (and attachments) of any undeliverable messages. This allows the postmaster to straighten out addressing problems, as well as to manually forward messages to the correct recipients.

  If neither of the previous two options is checked, problematic messages are simply discarded.

It is important that you create an undeliverable mail strategy, and configure it using the settings on the SMTP/MIME Undeliverables Property Page.

Configuring the LDAP Settings Property Page

The property page in Figure 10.12 allows you to configure the LDAP service provided by the GWIA. In order to complete configuration of the LDAP service, however, you must also choose Allow Access from the LDAP Public Settings property page, which is on the Access Control tab. From the LDAP Public Settings page, you can also limit which fields on a user's address information are visible to a client's LDAP address lookup query against your GWIA.

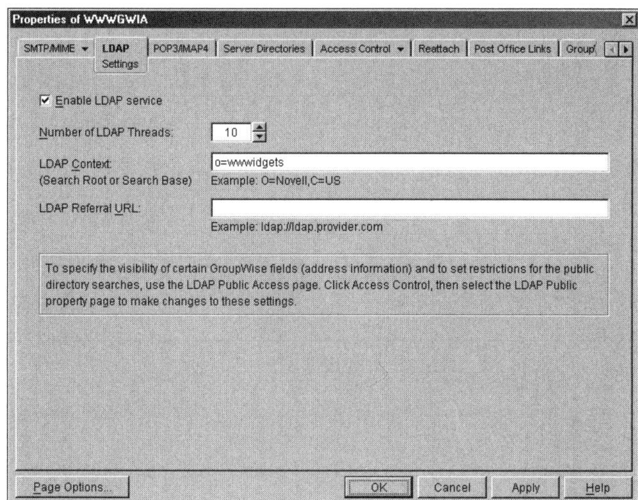

FIGURE 10.12
The GWIA LDAP Settings property page.

The settings that you can configure on this page are as follows:

- **Enable LDAP Service:** This must be checked for the GWIA to be able to provide LDAP service to browsers and e-mail clients.
- **Number of LDAP Threads:** This is the maximum number of server processes that will be devoted to handling LDAP requests.
- **LDAP Context:** Set a Search Root, which for the GroupWise LDAP directory doesn't really do anything. This setting is required for LDAP clients to be able to speak in LDAP to the GWIA. For example, `o=wwwidgets`.

  For users, the Search Root entry in your users' browsers' or e-mail clients' LDAP setup information must match the string you have in the LDAP Context field. (*Search Root* is the term used by Netscape Communicator. *Search Base* is the term used by MS Outlook Express.)
- **LDAP Referral URL:** This setting allows you to define a secondary LDAP server to which you can refer queries that the GWIA was unable to resolve. Obviously, the secondary LDAP server would be configured and managed separately from the GWIA. For this feature to work, the client performing the LDAP lookup to the GWIA must support the tracking of referral URLs.

The LDAP feature of the GWIA isn't very robust, so you might want to consider a different LDAP directory solution, such as eDirectory.

Configuring the POP3/IMAP4 Settings Property Page

If you want your users to be able to use a POP3 or IMAP4 e-mail client to access their GroupWise messages, you will need to begin by enabling POP3 and IMAP4. In order to complete configuration of the POP3 and IMAP4 service, however, you must allow POP3 and/or IMAP4 access from the Access Control property page, described a little later in this chapter. From this page, you can configure the following:

- **Enable POP3 Service:** This must be checked before the GWIA will respond to POP3 requests from e-mail clients.
- **Number of Threads for POP3 Connections:** This is the maximum number of server processes that the GWIA will devote to servicing POP3 mailbox connections. Each connection will tie up one thread, but connections are usually cleared fairly quickly. A small number of threads can support a large user community, depending on how often users download e-mail via POP3.
- **Enable IMAP4 Service:** This must be checked before the GWIA will respond to IMAP4 requests from e-mail clients.
- **Number of Threads for IMAP4 Connections:** This is the maximum number of server processes that the GWIA will devote to servicing IMAP4 mailbox connections. Each connection will take up one thread, and connections are more latent than POP3 connections are. This is due to the fact that with IMAP4, the user mailbox always exists on the server, and the client must rerequest items that the user wants to reread.

For more information about setting up POP3 or IMAP4 access for your users, refer to the section titled "Configuring Access Control," later in this chapter.

Configuring the Server Directories Settings Property Page

Some third-party software requires that you configure the Server Directories Settings property page that the GWIA uses to process SMTP/MIME messages. Otherwise, the defaults work fine. The settings that you can configure on this page are as follows:

- **Conversion Directory:** This path becomes the GWIA's "work" directory. By default, this is found at `<domain>\WPGATE\<GWIA>\000.PRC\GWWORK`. The GWIA uses this directory to store temporary files used during message conversion.

- **SMTP Queues Directory:** This path becomes the parent directory for the SMTP `SEND`, `RECEIVE`, and `RESULT` directories, which are the input and output queues for the SMTP inbound and outbound threads.
- **Advanced:** Clicking this button brings up the SMTP Service Queues Directory dialog box. This dialog box is used for trapping messages between the SMTP daemon and the gateway. If you populate this field with a path, all inbound and outbound messages will be dropped in subdirectories of this directory. They will remain there until another process moves them to the appropriate SMTP queue directory. An example of third-party software that will require that you use this field is GWAVASig (`www.beginfinite.com`) or Guinevere (`www.openhandhome.com`). Typically, these directories are located under the domain directory, in the GWIA structure under WPGATE.

Generally, you should keep the default settings on this property page unless you are implementing third-party software.

Configuring the GWIA Access Control Property Pages

The GWIA Access Control property pages are used to configure *blacklists* (SPAM blocking) POP3, LDAP, IMAP4, and SMTP relay access for the GWIA. These property pages (except the Blacklist feature) allow for the creation of classes of service and memberships. Each membership can be assigned to one or more classes of service.

This property page is explained and utilized in the section titled, "Configuring Access Control," later in this chapter.

Using the Access Control Settings "Test" Page

The GWIA Access Control Test property page allows you to test the memberships and classes of service created with the Access Control property page. The display can be changed to include domains, post offices, distribution lists, or users.

Clicking View Access displays a dialog box that shows the GWIA access allowed for the selected object. The Access Control Test property page is used in an example later in this chapter.

Using Access Control Blacklists Property Page

Chapter 25 talks about how to configure the Blacklist (RBL) feature of the GWIA. Read this chapter for instructions on how to configure the settings on this page.

Using the Access Control SMTP Relay Settings Property Page

This page allows you to define whether your GWIA is an open relay. It also lets you define exceptions to allow specific hosts to relay or not relay off your GWIA. You can also use the Access Control settings to define relay exceptions. An example of this is given later in this chapter.

Using the Access Control LDAP Public Settings Property Page

See the section "Configuring the LDAP Settings Property Page," earlier in this chapter for how you should use this page.

Using Access Control Database Management Property Page

The GWIA does not use the domain database for access control. The access control database is called GWAC.DB, and it's in the `<DOMAIN>\WPGATE\<GWIA>` directory. Thus, a separate tool has been provided for maintaining and repairing the GWIA access control database. You can configure the following options from this page:

- **Validate Now:** This button checks the physical structure of the database, essentially making sure that all records can be read correctly. Clicking Validate Now displays a live validation window that shows the validation process's progress.
- **Recover Now:** The recover option should be used only after the validation report has been generated and reviewed. Recovery is not a perfect process. If records have been damaged and cannot be read, they cannot be regenerated. They will be removed, and the new, recovered access database will not re-create the removed records.

  Any addresses you define in the blacklist section of the GWIA are not written to the GWAC.DB file. These setting are contained in BLOCKED.TXT. This is a new feature of the GroupWise 6.5 GWIA. Because of this, you should never edit a GroupWise 6 or newer GWIA's blocklist with the GroupWise 6.5 snap-ins, as the 6.5 snap-ins will use the BLOCKED.TXT file, and the older GWIA does not read the BLOCKED.TXT file for its blocklist.

The Access Control features of the GWIA make the GWIA very flexible. Make sure to utilize these features of the GWIA to control the maximum message size that users can send on the Internet, or the maximum size of Internet messages your GWIA will receive.

Understanding the Reattach Settings Property Page

When the GroupWise GWIA acts as a POP3 or IMAP4 server, it must access the POP3/IMAP4 user's mailbox. In the Post Office Links property page, the links to post offices can be UNC or TCP/IP. The TCP/IP link is generally preferred, but if UNC is chosen, the GWIA must log in to the server using a user ID and password in the fields in this property page.

The settings on this page are as follows:

- **Tree:** This is the name of the eDirectory tree that the GWIA is logging into.
- **Context:** This is the eDirectory context for the user who the GWIA will attempt to connect as.
- **User ID:** This is the eDirectory user object that the GWIA will attempt to connect as.
- **Password:** This is the password that the GWIA will use when logging in.

  I highly recommend that if you do enable POP3/IMAP4 on the GWIA, you allow the GWIA to connect to post offices only via TCP/IP connection, and not via a UNC path connection.

Most customers will not have to use the settings on this page.

Using the Post Office Links Property Page

The Post Office Links property page is used to define the connection between the GWIA and each of the post offices to which it must connect to provide users with POP3 or IMAP4 access. As recommended in the preceding paragraph, you should configure your GWIA to talk to your POAs via a TCP/IP, client/server link to the POA.

TIP

If you do not intend to enable POP3 or IMAP4 features on your GWIA, don't worry about configuring the link to the post offices.

Configuring Access Control

By default, everyone in your organization has full access to all features you enable on the GWIA. This includes the capability to collect their e-mail via POP3 or IMAP4 service, as well as to send and receive messages of unlimited size via SMTP/MIME.

For many customers though, the following are common settings under Access Control:

- No POP3 or IMAP4 mailbox access
- SMTP relay access is turned off
- No rule-generated messages can be sent through the GWIA
- Users are limited to a certain message size that they can send through the Internet

You can administer all of these controls on the GWIA via Access Control. Generally, when you want your Access Control to apply to all users, you configure the Default Class of Service. Imagine though, that you want to be able to make exceptions to the settings you defined from Default Class of Service. For example, a couple of users will eventually need POP3 access. Here are the steps to accomplish such exceptions:

1. Open the GWIA object's properties window and go to the Access Control, Settings property page.
2. To the right of the Class of Service pane, click Create.

   You should be presented with the dialog box shown in Figure 10.13.

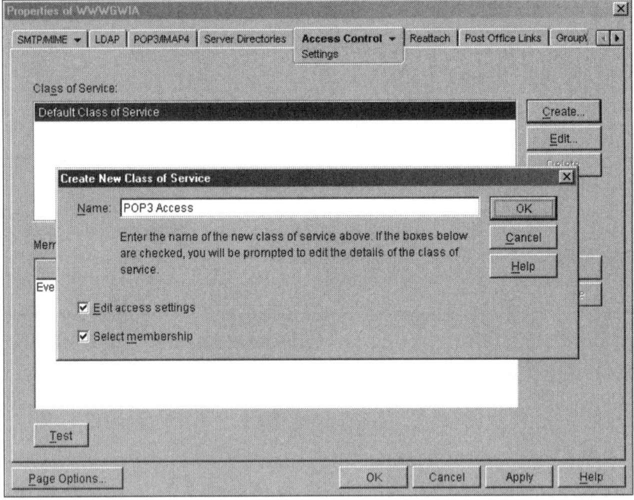

FIGURE 10.13
Creating a new class of service.

3. Enter a name for this class of service, such as POP3 Access.

   After clicking OK and selecting the POP3 tab, you get the screen shown in Figure 10.14.

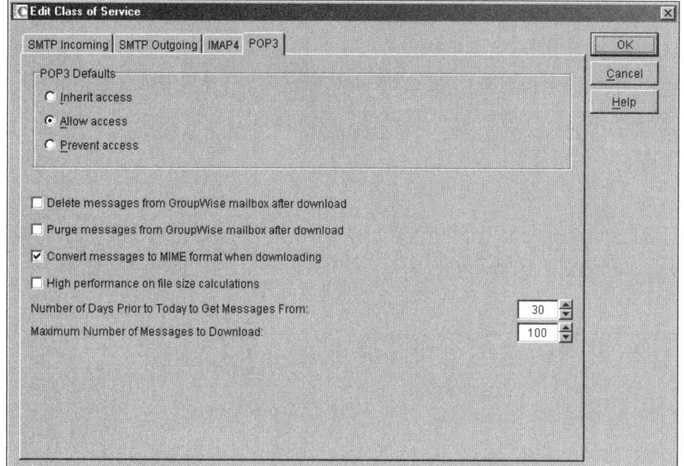

FIGURE 10.14
The Edit Class of Service dialog box allows you to define how the service is configured.

4. Beneath the defaults, select Allow Access and leave all other settings at their defaults. Click OK.
5. You will be presented with a user list, as shown in Figure 10.15. Select the users who can use the GWIA as a POP3 server, and click OK.

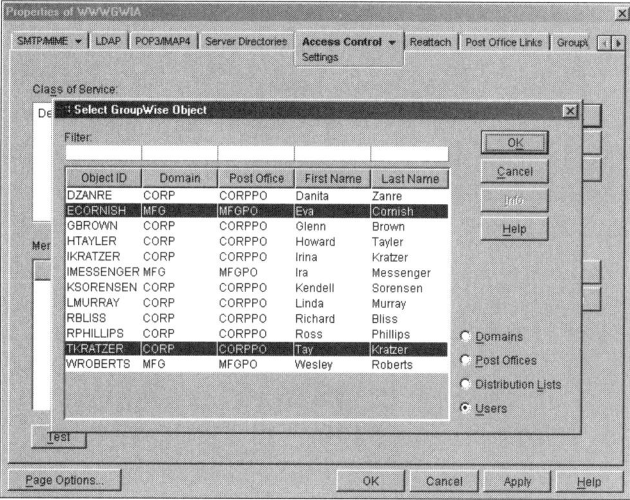

FIGURE 10.15
Adding users to a class of service.

The users defined under the POP3 Access Class of Service will be able to retrieve their e-mail via POP3, and relay off of the GWIA.

It is important to note that you did not configure any type of SMTP relay on the GWIA, and yet these POP3 users are able to relay off of the GWIA. The reason for this is that the GWIA will allow a user who has authenticated via a POP3 session to relay through the GWIA. Because the POP3 session required the user to authenticate as a valid user, the GWIA assumes the user should be able to use the GWIA as an SMTP relay server.

In order for your users to be able to use SMTP relay, their POP3 client must be configured to allow authenticate to the SMTP server (which is the POP3 server also) before sending SMTP messages to be relayed. Some newer POP3 clients just assume that this is the case, so this option of whether to do it is not even presented to the users.

Configuring an SMTP Relay Class of Service

Let's imagine another scenario. You have deployed Novell's ZENWorks server management product. The ZENWorks server management product has an alerting mechanism that requires an SMTP relay host. You want your GWIA to allow relaying, but only from the server running the ZENWorks server management.

Following are the steps for setting up the GWIA to act as a relay host:

1. In the GWIA's property pages, select Access Control, SMTP Relay Settings. Confirm that the radio button labeled Prevent Message Relaying is selected.
2. Under Exceptions, and to the right of the Allow pane, click Create.
3. In the From field, enter the IP addresses that will be allowed to relay through the GWIA. You do not need to specify a To address.
4. Click OK, and you will see the new exception as shown in Figure 10.16. Click OK again to save all changes.

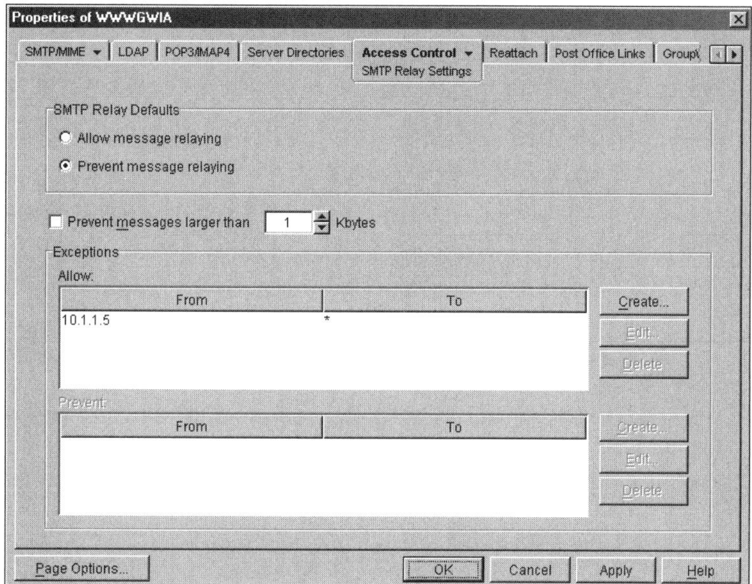

FIGURE 10.16 Adding an exception to the SMTP relay access.

Understanding the GWIA Console

The GWIA console is particularly helpful when troubleshooting the GWIA.

Figure 10.17 shows the GWIA console on a NetWare 6 server. From the GWIA console, there are only five keystroke commands:

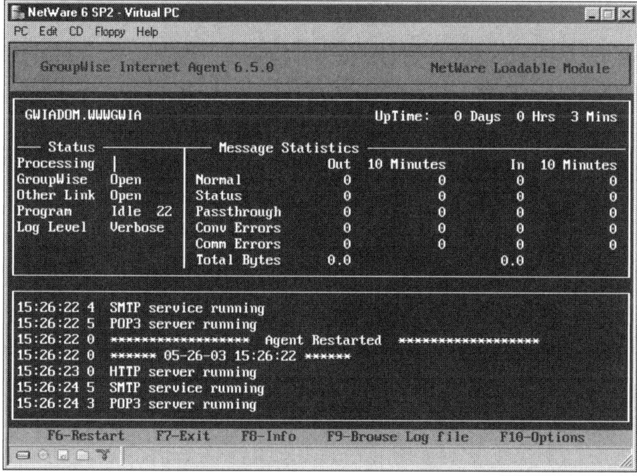

FIGURE 10.17 The GWIA console allows you to view and troubleshoot the GWIA.

- **F6—Restart:** This feature causes the GWIA to reload, and reread its GWIA.CFG and BLOCKED.TXT files. It's a great new feature added to the GroupWise 6.5 GWIA.
- **F7—Exit:** This option presents you with the following prompt: Terminate Agent (Yes/No). Pressing Y unloads the GWIA module.
- **F8—Info:** This option reports the settings from GWIA.CFG, the GWIA configuration file, into the current log file. This is helpful for determining which settings the GWIA is currently observing.
- **F9—Browse Log file:** This option allows you to search the current log file that the GWIA is logging to.
- **F10—Options:** This option brings you into the GWIA Options menu, where you have the following choices:
    - **F1—Exit Options:** This option exits the Options menu, taking you back to the main screen.
    - **F2—Log Level:** This option toggles the log level through the various settings: Low, Normal, Verbose, and Diagnostic.
    - **F6—Colors:** This option changes the color scheme of the GWIA console. None of the color schemes is especially attractive, but if you get tired of the white-on-blue, this at least gives you some options.
    - **F8—Zero Stats:** This option resets to zero all the statistics that the GWIA has been keeping. This is useful if you want to note current traffic levels.

      This command clears the statistics only from the Message Statistics screen. It does not reset the SMTP, POP, IMAP, or LDAP statistics.
    - **F9—Stats:** This option cycles the upper-right pane of the GWIA console between each of the five statistical panes: Message Statistics, SMTP Service Statistics, POP3 Service Statistics, LDAP Service Statistics, and IMAP4 Service Statistics.

The balance of this section looks at these statistics a little more closely.

- **Message Statistics:** These are general statistics that have to do with mail messages that are converted by the gateway process. Each statistic is reported in two ways: the total time that the GWIA has been loaded and the total messages processed for the preceding 10 minutes. Possibilities are as follows:

- **Normal:** The number of mail messages that the gateway has processed.
- **Status:** The number of status messages that the gateway has processed. These are typically transferred statuses sent back to users on this GroupWise system.
- **Passthrough:** This feature is no longer valid. Pass-through messaging happens at the MTA level now, and is explained in Chapter 16 in the section called "Allowing MTAs to Send Directly to Other GroupWise Systems."
- **Conv Errors:** The number of errors the gateway has encountered while attempting to convert messages from GroupWise format to other formats, and vice versa.
- **Comm Errors:** The number of communication errors the gateway has encountered while attempting to communicate with other hosts.
- **Total Bytes:** The number of bytes transferred through the GWIA.

- **SMTP Service Statistics:** These statistics pertain to the SMTP services provided by the GWIA. Some of these statistics are incorporated into the general message statistics described earlier, but for the real story, you want to be looking at this screen. Values here are as follows:
  - **Messages Sent:** The number of messages sent to sendmail (SMTP or MIME) hosts on the Internet.
  - **Send Threads:** The number of server processes actively processing SMTP/MIME send operations. The number to the left of the colon is the number of threads currently being used. The number to the right of the colon is the maximum number of threads allocated for sending messages. The maximum number of Send Threads correlates to the Number of SMTP Send Threads setting on the GWIA's SMTP/MIME Settings page.
  - **MX Lookup Errs:** The number of errors the GWIA has encountered when looking up DNS mail exchange (`MX`) records. Before the GWIA can send to an Internet host, it must first find that host's `MX` record in DNS. An example of an MX Lookup Error is `450 MX lookup failure`.
  - **TCP/IP Read Errs:** The number of errors the GWIA has encountered attempting to read from a TCP socket. Errors here can indicate problems with internetworking segments that carry

Internet traffic, or they can be indicative of network problems within your organization.

- **Hosts Down:** If the GWIA finds a hosts `MX` record, but cannot contact the host, that host is down, and this number will be incremented by one.
- **Message Size Denied:** This number indicates the number of messages, to be sent or to be received, that were discarded because they exceeded size limitations set on your GWIA. Message sizes are configured under Access Control, and most likely configured under any one of the Classes of Server, most likely the Default Class of service.
- **Messages Received:** The number of SMTP/MIME messages received by the GWIA from hosts on the Internet.
- **Receive Threads:** The number of server processes actively processing SMTP/MIME receive operations. The number to the left of the colon is the number of threads being used. The number to the right of the colon is the maximum number of threads allocated for receiving messages. The maximum number of receive threads correlates to the Number of SMTP Receive Threads setting on the GWIA's SMTP/MIME Settings page.
- **Unknown Hosts:** The number of SMTP hosts the GWIA cannot resolve to a DNS address in order to send to the host.
- **TCP/IP Write Errs:** The number of errors that the GWIA has encountered attempting to write data to a TCP socket. Errors here can indicate a problem local to you, or a problem somewhere out on the Internet.
- **Connections Denied:** When a sendmail host sends to the GWIA, but that host does not identify itself correctly or its identity cannot be determined via a reverse-DNS lookup, this number is incremented. Mail from unknown hosts will be rejected if you configure the GWIA to do so. This setting is found on the SMTP/MIME Settings property page, using the Security button. The setting is Reject Mail if Sender's Identity Cannot Be Verified. Connections that have been denied because the host has been added to a blacklist are also listed here. Finally, if you have defined a host under Access Control that you do not want to receive mail from, that will also increment this number.
- **Relaying Denied:** If your GWIA is configured to not allow message relaying, and someone attempts to relay a message off of

your GWIA, this number will increment each time. Relaying is a common practice for POP3 and IMAP4 clients that need to send mail.

- **POP3 Service Statistics:** These statistics pertain to the GWIA's POP3 service and can help you gauge the amount of traffic your organization is generating by accessing user mailboxes via POP3. The values shown here are as follows:
  - **Total Sessions:** The number of POP3 mailbox sessions since the GWIA was loaded. A POP3 session is defined as a *download* of POP3 mail. If a user keeps his or her POP3 mailer open all day, and downloads GroupWise e-mail three times, that user will increment this count by three.
  - **Active Sessions:** The number of POP3 currently active mailbox sessions.
  - **Sessions Avail:** The number of server processes available to service POP3 mailbox connections. The active and avail numbers should add up to the number of POP3 threads you specified under the GWIA POP3/IMAP4 Settings property page.
  - **Store Login Errs:** The number of errors that the GWIA has encountered attempting to connect to post office information stores. If you see this number incrementing, it's time to look at the GWIA's Post Office Links property page. From there, make sure that the links to your post offices are correct and that the POA is available.
  - **Unknown Users:** The number of errors in which the username furnished was invalid. A high number here might be indicative of a hacker attempting to guess mailbox IDs.
  - **TCP/IP Read Errs:** The number of errors that the GWIA has encountered attempting to read data from a TCP socket.
  - **Messages Sent:** The number of messages downloaded to users' POP3 mailers and uploaded to their master mailboxes.
  - **Retrieval Errs:** The number of errors encountered retrieving messages from post office information stores.
  - **Conversion Errs:** The number of errors encountered converting messages from GroupWise format to clear text format for POP3 download.
  - **Pass Auth Errors:** The number of errors that the GWIA has encountered due to users entering invalid passwords. A high

number here can be indicative of a hacker with a correct username attempting to guess at the mailbox password.

- **Denied Access Cnt:** The number of times that the GWIA has denied mailbox access to a user attempting to authenticate. A high number here can indicate hackers guessing at mailbox IDs and passwords.
- **TCP/IP Write Errs:** The number of errors that the GWIA has encountered attempting to write data to a TCP socket.

- **LDAP Service Statistics:** The statistics here pertain to the GWIA's LDAP service, as follows:
  - **Public Sessions:** The number of LDAP sessions that the GWIA has opened for users who were not authenticated.
  - **Auth Sessions:** The number of LDAP sessions that the GWIA has performed for authenticated users.
  - **Sessions Active:** The number of LDAP sessions currently active. Each active session requires its own LDAP thread.
  - **Sessions Avail:** The number of LDAP threads available to service LDAP sessions. The active and avail numbers should add up to the number of LDAP threads that you specified from the GWIA's LDAP Settings property page.
  - **Search Requests:** The number of search requests that the GWIA has processed.
  - **Entries Returned:** The number of address entries that the GWIA has provided via LDAP.
- **IMAP4 Service Statistics:** The statistics here are very similar to those seen under the POP3 Service Statistics screen, but of course these are specific to IMAP4 service, which has much higher overhead than POP3. The statistics beneath this section are as follows:
  - **Total Sessions:** The number of IMAP4 mailbox sessions since the GWIA was loaded. If a user keeps his or her IMAP4 mailer open and connected all day, this number will only increment by one. (Remember that these stats are reset to zero with the F8 key; the IMAP4 stats are not reset, however.)
  - **Active Sessions:** The number of IMAP4 currently active mailbox sessions.
  - **Sessions Avail:** The number of server processes available to service IMAP4 mailbox connections. The active and avail

numbers should add up to the number of IMAP4 threads that you specified on the GWIA POP3/IMAP4 Settings property page.

- **Store Login Errs:** The number of errors that the GWIA has encountered attempting to connect to post office information stores. If you see this number incrementing, it's time to look at the GWIA's Post Office Links property page. From there, make sure that the links to your post offices are correct.
- **Unknown Users:** The number of errors in which the username furnished was invalid. A high number here can be indicative of a hacker attempting to guess mailbox IDs.
- **TCP/IP Read Errs:** The number of errors that the GWIA has encountered attempting to read data from a TCP socket.
- **Messages Sent:** The number of messages downloaded to users' IMAP4 mailers and uploaded to their master mailboxes.
- **Retrieval Errs:** The number of errors encountered retrieving messages from post office information stores.
- **Conversion Errs:** The number of errors encountered converting messages from GroupWise format to clear text format for IMAP4 download.
- **Pass Auth Errors:** The number of errors that the GWIA has encountered due to users entering invalid passwords. A high number here can be indicative of a hacker with a correct username attempting to guess at the mailbox password.
- **Denied Access Cnt:** The number of times that the GWIA has denied mailbox access to a user attempting to authenticate. A high number here can indicate hackers guessing at mailbox IDs and passwords.
- **TCP/IP Write Errs:** The number of errors that the GWIA has encountered attempting to write data to a TCP socket.

The next tool that you will use to troubleshoot the GWIA is the GWIA's log file.

Understanding the GWIA Log

This section shows some sample sections of the GWIA log files, and explains how to interpret them. The goal is to help you understand what you see in your own GWIA logs, so that you can more effectively administer your system.

Log Line Format

Each line in the agent log is divided into four main parts. The first of these is the date and timestamp, that is, the date, hour, minute, and second that the event in this log entry occurred.

The second part is the process number. This number identifies the server process or thread that performed the operation described in this log entry. If you are trying to follow a thread in the log, you must do so by finding the next occurrence of this number. If process 12 claims to be processing an outbound message, and then process 17 reports an MX lookup error, the error was not with the message in the previous line. Look for the next occurrence of process 12 to see if the outbound message was processed correctly. Look for the previous occurrence of process 17 to see what it was doing before it got the MX lookup error.

The third part, which is not always present, is the process type. This string identifies the service engine that is currently active. When the GWIA is servicing POP3, IMAP4, or LDAP connections, this string will be POP3, IMAP4, or LDAP, respectively. SMTP processing is defined as the DMN process.

The fourth part of the log entry is the event description. This might seem a little bit cryptic, but after you have seen a few of them, you will be making sense of them easily. Events you'll see here include error messages, login IDs for POP3 or IMAP users, or descriptions of the conversion and transfer of SMTP/MIME messages.

Configuration Information in the GWIA Log

Here's the first block of text you will see in the GWIA log, the GWIA configuration:

```
11-23-03 13:14:41 1 Begin Configuration Information
11-23-03 13:14:41 1  Platform= NLM
11-23-03 13:14:41 1  Domain and Agent= CORP.GWIA
11-23-03 13:14:41 1  Foreign Name= wwwidgets.com
11-23-03 13:14:41 1  Description= GWIA
11-23-03 13:14:41 1  Alias Type= SMTP-GWIA
11-23-03 13:14:41 1  Root Directory= MAIL:\GWIADOM\WPGATE\GWIA
11-23-03 13:14:41 1  Work Directory=
➥MAIL:\GWIADOM\WPGATE\GWIA\000.prc\gwwork
11-23-03 13:14:41 1  Log File= MAIL:\GWIADOM
➥\WPGATE\GWIA\000.prc\1123log.00e
11-23-03 13:14:41 1  Directory ID= www4d5c
```

These first 10 lines show that process 1, at 1:14 p.m. on November 23, 2003, began reading configuration information. These lines correspond to information you might recall entering from the GWIA's Information property page. The GWIA indicates which directory it is working from. The log also includes the name of the current log file, as well as the directory ID of the GWIA. This directory ID is a directory within the `DOMAIN\WPGATE\GWIA\WPCSOUT` directory that the MTA will use to queue messages for the GWIA to send out.

```
11-23-03 13:14:41 1  Directory Synchronization= NO
11-23-03 13:14:41 1  Directory Exchange=    NO
11-23-03 13:14:41 1  Accounting=         YES
11-23-03 13:14:41 1  Convert GroupWise Status to Messages= NO
11-23-03 13:14:41 1  Outbound Status Level= UNDELIVERED
```

The preceding five lines come from the GWIA's Optional Gateway Settings property page under the GroupWise drop-down tab. You can see that accounting has been enabled, and users whose outbound messages cannot be transferred will get an `Undeliverable` status back.

```
11-23-03 13:14:41 1  Log Level=   Verbose
11-23-03 13:14:41 1  Log Max Age=  7 days
11-23-03 13:14:41 1  Log Max Space= 65536 kb
11-23-03 13:14:41 1  Enable Recovery=   YES
11-23-03 13:14:41 1  Retry Count=     10
11-23-03 13:14:41 1  Retry Interval=    60  seconds
11-23-03 13:14:41 1  Failed Recovery Wait= 3600 seconds
11-23-03 13:14:41 1  Network Reattach Command= <none specified>
11-23-03 13:14:41 1  Correlation DB Enabled= YES
11-23-03 13:14:41 1  Correlation DB Age=   14 days
11-23-03 13:14:41 1  Correlation DB Directory=
➥MAIL:\GWIADOM\WPGATE\GWIA
11-23-03 13:14:41 1  Send/Receive Cycle= 2  minutes
11-23-03 13:14:41 1  Minimum Run=      0  minutes
11-23-03 13:14:41 1  Idle Sleep Duration= 30 seconds
11-23-03 13:14:41 1  Snap Shot Interval= 10 minutes
11-23-03 13:14:41 1  Time Zone= MST
11-23-03 13:14:41 1  GMT Offset= -7 hours, 0 minutes
11-23-03 13:14:41 1  Hemisphere= NORTH
11-23-03 13:14:41 1  Daylight Saving Change= 1 hours, 0 minutes
11-23-03 13:14:41 1  Daylight Saving Begin= 4/4 (month/day)
11-23-03 13:14:41 1  Daylight Saving End=  10/31 (month/day)
```

The preceding set of lines show the logging level, recovery and retry settings, gateway correlation settings, polling intervals, and timezone information in effect for the GWIA. Some of these settings come from the Optional

Gateway Settings property page, some come from the Log Settings property page, and the timezone information is read from the appropriate timezone definition in the domain database.

```
11-23-03 13:14:41 1   SMP Off
11-23-03 13:14:41 1   SNMP On
11-23-03 13:14:41 1   Startup Switches= /Home-
➥\\WWWFS1\MAIL\GWIADOM\WPGATE\GWI
11-23-03 13:14:41 1    A /DHome-\\WWWFS1\MAIL\GWIADOM
➥\WPGATE\GWIA /SMTP /LDAP
11-23-03 13:14:41 1     /MIME /MUDAS=2 /MailView-Internet /SD-16
➥/RD-8 /P-10
11-23-03 13:14:41 1     /TE-2 /TG-5 /TC-5 /TR-5 /TD-3 /TT-10
➥/PT-30 /IT-30 /
11-23-03 13:14:41 1    LdapThrd-10 /ST-4 /RT-4 /IRFOUID /SMP
➥/LDAPcntxt=WWWIDGETS
11-23-03 13:14:41 1    S /POP3 /IMAP4
11-23-03 13:14:41 1 End Configuration Information
```

In this last set of configuration entries, the log says that the GWIA will not use a second processor (`SMP Off`), and that it will publish simple network management protocol (SNMP) information. The log also shows all the start-up switches that have been written to the GWIA.CFG file. These switches govern the number of threads for the various services, among other things.

Message Processing Log Entries

When the GWIA processes a message that was sent from a GroupWise user to a recipient on the Internet, the log entries look a lot like this:

```
1: 06-25-03 08:01:30 7 MSG 6 Processing outbound message...
2: 06-25-03 08:01:30 7 MSG 6 File:
   ➥ERAFF1/MAIL:\GW6\DO1\WPGATE\GWIA\wpcsout\gwif
      i. 94a\4\4EF956D2.M80 Message Id:
         ➥(3EF9AB2B.B51:8:40818) Size:
     ii. 455
3: 06-25-03 08:01:30 7 MSG 6 Sender: ecornish@wwwidgets.com
4: 06-25-03 08:01:30 7 MSG 6 Converting message to MIME:
   ➥ERAFF1/MAIL:\GW6\DO1\WP
      i. GATE\GWIA\send\xef956d8.001
5: 06-25-03 08:01:30 7 MSG 6 Recipient: glenn@brown.com
6: 06-25-03 08:01:30 7 Switching link state to
   ➥SENDING_ALLOWED.
7: 06-25-03 08:01:30 7 MSG 6 Queuing message to daemon:
   ➥ERAFF1/MAIL:\GW6\DO1\WPG
      i. ATE\GWIA\send\sef956d8.001
8: 06-25-03 08:01:30 7 DMN: MSG 7 Sending file:
   ➥ERAFF1/MAIL:\GW6\DO1\WPGATE\GWIA
```

```
        i. \send\pef956d8.001
 9: 06-25-03 08:01:30 7 DMN: MSG 7 Connected to
    ➥mail-mx.brown.com
10: 06-25-03 08:01:30 7 DMN: MSG 7 Transferred
```

The GroupWise 6.5 GWIA has much more logging information than any pervious GWIA. It is much easier to troubleshoot your GWIA when you are running version 6.5. Let's break down the 10 log lines from one piece of mail being sent from `ecornish@wwwidgets.com` to `glenn@brown.com`.

Line 1—GWIA reports that it is processing an outbound message. Notice that the GWIA assigns a MSG ID of 6 to this message.

Line 2—Displays that the GWIA is picking up a message from its input queue. The MTA placed the message here. One very helpful piece of information is the Message ID: (`3EF9AB2B.B51:8:40818`). This value will exactly match the user's sent items. If you were to look at the user's sent item properties, this is the identifying Message ID that will never change as the message flows through the GroupWise system.

Line 3—Identifies who the sender of the message is.

Line 4—Shows the GWIA converting the message into SMTP MIME format and placing it in the GWIA SEND directory. Notice that the file begins with an X. This means the GWIA SMTP daemon is "hands off" as the conversion process is happening.

Line 5—Identifies who the recipient is. In this example, it is `glenn@brown.com`.

Line 6—GWIA switches into sending state.

Line 7—The X locked message that is in the SEND directory is unlocked. The filename now begins with an S, which signifies that the SMTP daemon can grab it and send it to the destination SMTP daemon.

Line 8—The GWIA begins sending the SMTP message to the destination SMTP gateway. At this point the filename begins with a P for "processing". This means the GWIA is in the process of sending it out, and has its hands on it.

Line 9—Shows the GWIA has done a DNS lookup for `brown.com` and identified the destination SMTP server as `mail-mx.brown.com`, and is connecting to it.

Line 10—Shows the message as being transferred to the destination SMTP gateway.

That is easily double the amount of logging about a sent message that the GroupWise 6 GWIA reported. You can easily identify that this message was successfully transferred to the destination SMTP gateway.

As you can see, from the GWIA log you can see exactly which users on your system are sending mail to Internet users, and you can capture every address. You can also see which Internet users are sending e-mail to which users on your system. I know of at least one case in which information from a GWIA log has been used to expose users who were selling company secrets to the competition. Your users might consider this to be an infringement on their privacy, so you should be sure to word your organization's e-mail policy in such a way as to allow you to scan GWIA logs freely.

Here's a look at what happens with an SMTP error:

```
11-23-03 13:54:13 0 Analyzing result file: r83a9c7e.084
11-23-03 13:54:41 0 Analyzing result file: r83a9c5d.083
11-23-03 13:54:41 0   Command: stribling.com
11-23-03 13:54:41 0   Response: 250 ok
11-23-03 13:54:41 0   Command: HELO mail.wwwidgets.com
11-23-03 13:54:41 0   Response:
250 Hello mail.wwwidgets.com [137.65.55.211], pleased to meet
➥you
11-23-03 13:54:41 0   Command: MAIL FROM:<DZanre@wwwidgets.com>
11-23-03 13:54:41 0   Response: 250 <DZanre@wwwidgets.com>..
➥Sender ok
11-23-03 13:54:41 0  Detected error on SMTP command
11-23-03 13:54:41 0   Command: RCPT TO:<darren@stribling.com>
11-23-03 13:54:41 0   Response: 420 TCP read error
```

This file shows that process 0 analyzed a result file named r83a9c7e.084. This result file corresponds to an SMTP communication. Because there's no more information about this result file, you know that the communication was error-free.

In the second line, process 0 picks up another result file to analyze, and this one has an error in it. Scanning through the available information, you can see that user `DZanre@wwwidgets.com` sent a message to `darren@stribling.com`. The GWIA looked up and then opened a connection with the `stribling.com` mail host. You can see this from the successful `HELO` commands and the success of the first `MAIL` command. Unfortunately, the GWIA got a TCP read error trying to transmit the recipient address. This indicates that the connection between `wwwidgets.com` and `stribling.com` is too noisy, was dropped, or timed out.

Unfortunately, the result file does not indicate what time these events occurred. What is visible is the GWIA's analysis of the SMTP daemons actions after the fact.

POP3 Connection Log Entries

Each time a user initiates a POP3 connection with the GWIA, that action is logged. Here is a sample of such a connection:

```
11-23-03 13:53:59 8 Accepted POP3 connection with: 10.10.40.232
11-23-03 13:53:59 8 POP3 Command: USER ksorensen
  11-23-03 13:53:59 8
   Successful login with
   client/server access:
   wwwfs1.wwwidgets.com:1677

11-23-03 13:53:59 8 POP3 Command: PASS
11-23-03 13:53:59 8 POP3 Command: STAT
11-23-03 13:53:59 8 POP3 Command: QUIT
11-23-03 13:53:59 8 POP3 Session ended: 10.10.40.232
```

Process 8 handled the entire connection, as to be expected, because the GWIA can have only as many simultaneous POP3 sessions as it has POP3 threads. The log shows the IP address of the user workstation that is running the POP3 mailer, and then the log indicates which POP3 commands were issued. The entire POP3 connection lasted only a second, and then process 8 was free to service another connection or return to the pool of idle threads.

Configuring Dial-Up Internet Access

Some organizations might not have the luxury of a permanent connection to the Internet. In these cases, you can configure the GWIA to dial an Internet service provider (ISP) for temporary connectivity. The requirements for such a connection are as follows:

- The ISP must provide ETRN service, as per RFC-1985.
- The ETRN hostname provided by the ISP must have a static address.
- The IP stack on the GWIA server must be able to dial the ETRN host. This can be accomplished with BorderManager on NetWare servers.

If these requirements have been met, the procedure for configuring dial-up SMTP access for the GWIA is as follows:

1. Open the SMTP/MIME Settings property page on the GWIA and click the Dial-up Settings page. The dialog box shown in Figure 10.18 appears.

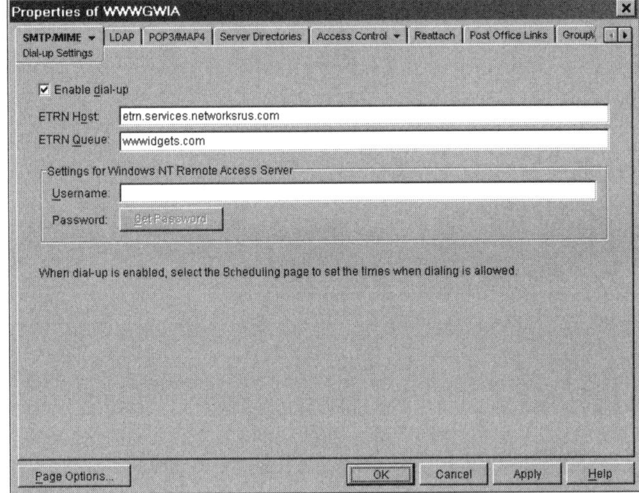

FIGURE 10.18 Enabling dial-up access from the SMTP/MIME Dial-up Settings property page.

2. Check the box labeled Enable Dial-up.
3. Under ETRN Host, enter the name of the ISP's ETRN host.

   This is the name of the host that will be receiving e-mail for your GWIA when your GWIA is not connected.
4. Under ETRN Queue, enter the foreign name of the GWIA.

   This must be the same as the domain name that your ISP has assigned you. This is the queue the ETRN host will use to identify the GWIA when the GWIA connects to collect messages.
5. Click OK.
6. Go to the Scheduling property page under the SMTP/MIME tab.
7. Highlight Default and select the Edit button.
8. Enter the appropriate thresholds. For example, you could configure the GWIA to dial the ETRN host if there are 10 messages queued, if there is at least 500KB of mail queued, or if the oldest item queued has been waiting at least 30 minutes.
9. Set the polling interval, under Dial parameters, to the minimum amount of time you want the GWIA to wait before checking the ETRN host for inbound mail. Seeing that the longest you want an outgoing message to be waiting is 30 minutes, set this number to 30 minutes also. This is just an example though; do what is best for your system.

10. Click OK.

11. With the new profile selected, block out the hours of the day that you want this profile to be in force.

    You should probably select all hours of the day, on all days of the week. You can also create additional profiles for lower frequency dial-up after hours or on weekends.

Monitoring the GWIA Through a Web Browser

The GWIA allows you to monitor it though a Web browser. The GWIA must be configured for HTTP monitoring, as discussed earlier in this chapter.

When the GWIA is configured for HTTP monitoring, you can monitor it using the following syntax:

```
http://<gwia IP Address or DNS Name>:<HTTPPORT defined in
➥ConsoleOne>
```

For example, here is one sample string:

```
http://137.65.55.211:9500
```

You are asked to authenticate to the GWIA using the user ID and password specified in the ConsoleOne. Then you will see a screen such as the one in Figure 10.19.

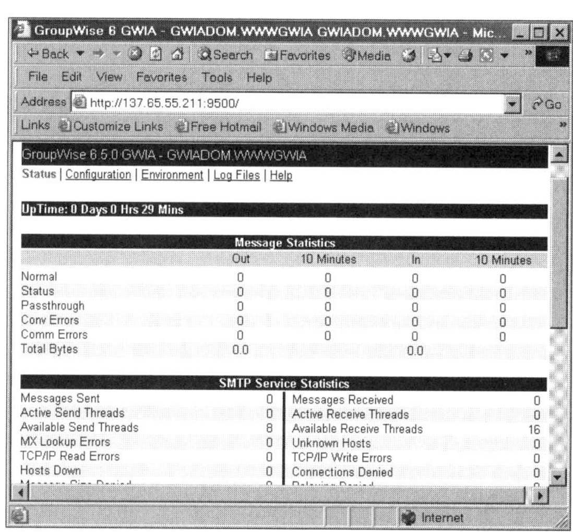

FIGURE 10.19
Monitoring the GWIA through a Web browser can be easier due to the layout of the screen.

The monitoring shows statistical information, but what's really neat is that the entire configuration of your GWIA is all laid out on the Configuration page. It's easier to see how your GWIA is configured in the HTTP monitoring screen than it is through ConsoleOne.

Best Practices

It is difficult to make recommendations for GWIA implementation without first discussing GroupWise Internet addressing. Because Chapter 16 covers Internet addressing in detail, I suggest that you review the best practices there before installing or configuring the GWIA. Here are a few recommendations, however:

- **Dedicate a domain to the GWIA.** I discuss default GWIAs and routing domains more in Chapter 16. For now, it is enough to say that if you have heavy Internet traffic (more than 30,000 messages per day), you might want to offload that traffic from your other production domains. Create a domain with no post offices, and dedicate a machine to running just that domain's MTA and the GWIA.
- **If POP3 access is strategic for your organization, install a GWIA on the same box as the post office for speedier POP3 access.** This GWIA need not support SMTP/MIME traffic. The GWIA can be devoted to providing POP3 mailbox access to users on this post office. Although it might not be feasible for large organizations to put a GWIA on every post office, if POP3 mailbox access is being used heavily, this configuration will improve performance.
- **Monitor GWIA statistics and adjust threads accordingly.** If you see more than 80 percent of the total threads for a given service active at any given time (such as the Send threads), you should increase the number of threads for that service by 25 percent. This will ensure that the GWIA can request additional server resources to meet the demands of your user community. Of course, if server utilization regularly climbs over 70 percent, you should consider upgrading your server hardware, or perhaps using more than one GWIA. (See Chapter 16 for a discussion about configuring multiple default GWIAs.)
- **Strongly consider Access Control features.** There are some great features under Access Control. For example, under the Default Class of Service, you should control the maximum mail message size that users can transmit via the GWIA. If you do not do this, users might end up using the GWIA as an FTP utility (effectively), which isn't an

efficient use of the server. You can also create a special profile and add a few key users (such as yourself <grin>) who are able to send larger files than the users under the Default Class of Service.

Summary

The GWIA is a critical piece of any GroupWise system. Without the GWIA, your GroupWise users don't have Internet e-mail, and they don't have the capability to use their POP3 or IMAP4 mail programs. This chapter showed you how to install and configure the GWIA. This chapter also explained the meaning behind the entries you will find in the GWIA log files.

CHAPTER 11

Configuring GroupWise WebAccess

This chapter explores the aspects of WebAccess in relation to a GroupWise system. GroupWise provides several options for users to access their mailboxes via the Internet. Having a good understanding of WebAccess will prepare you to set up and maintain a reliable implementation of WebAccess in your GroupWise environment.

Understanding WebAccess Architecture

To understand the WebAccess component of your GroupWise system, it is important to understand the WebAccess architecture. This will help with installing, configuring, and troubleshooting the WebAccess components.

Understanding the WebAccess Agent

WebAccess is composed of two main pieces. The first piece is referred to as the *WebAccess Agent* and is responsible for requesting and receiving data from a user's mailbox. This GroupWise Agent can run on NetWare as an NLM (GWINTER.NLM) or on NT as an executable (GWINTER.EXE) or a Windows NT service. You can think of the WebAccess Agent as a client that communicates directly via TCP/IP with a Post Office Agent (POA) via its client/server port such as `1677`, or via a UNC path where it would touch the user and message databases directly.

Understanding the WebAccess Application

The second piece is referred to as the *WebAccess Application* and is responsible for taking the data received by the WebAccess Agent and delivering it to the Web browser that is being used to access WebAccess. The WebAccess Application runs on a Web server as a Java servlet. It runs on any of the following supported Web server platforms:

- NetWare Enterprise (Novonyx) Web Server on NetWare 5.x and NetWare 6.x
- Apache Web Server for NetWare 6 (or higher)
- Netscape Enterprise Server 3.6 (or higher) for Windows NT
- Microsoft Internet Information Server 4.0 (or higher) for Windows NT
- Microsoft Internet Information Server 5 (or higher) for Windows 2000
- Apache Web Server 1.3.3 (or higher) for UNIX Solaris

The WebAccess Application communicates with the WebAccess Agent via TCP/IP. By default, the WebAccess Agent listens on port 7205 for information coming from the WebAccess Application. The data that is exchanged between the Agent and the Application is encrypted using an encryption key. This is not your standard SSL type of encryption, but simply an encryption key that each piece (Agent and Application) uses to encrypt data between them. The encryption key is discussed later in this chapter in the section titled "Configuring the GroupWise WebAccess Gateway."

Let's quickly see how a request coming in from a Web browser in order to log into a GroupWise mailbox would act. This will help you to understand the flow of information through a WebAccess system, as well as help you see the relationship between the WebAccess Application and Agent:

1. A user enters the URL to GroupWise WebAccess into their browser. For example, the URL might be `http://groupwise.wwwidgets.com`.
2. The browser is directed to the Web server that DNS resolves them to. Once here, the user sees the GroupWise WebAccess login screen. (There are lots of options as to what you will have your users doing; for simplicity, the Web server at `http://groupwise.wwwidgets.com` goes directly to the WebAccess login screen.) This screen is a standard HTML document that the Web server is displaying. Figure 11.1 shows this screen.

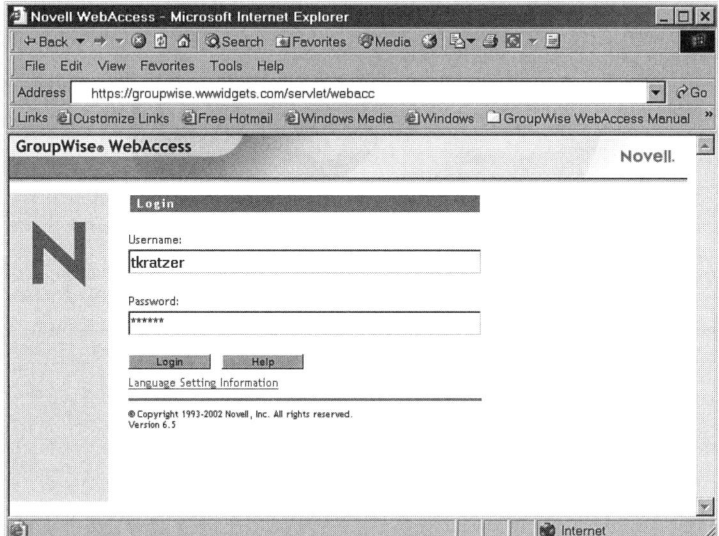

FIGURE 11.1
The GroupWise WebAccess login screen.

3. The user enters a user ID and password and clicks Login.
4. The Web server hands this information over to the WebAccess Application that is running as a Java servlet on the Web server. The servlet also detects the platform and manufacturer of the browser, and creates a session for this user, using the correct template types based on the browser type.
5. The WebAccess Application takes the user ID and password and determines which WebAccess Agent it should route the request to. It discovers that it needs to send the request to an IP address of `X.X.X.X` on port `7205`.
6. The WebAccess Application encrypts the data using the encryption key found on the local Web server and sends the username and password to the WebAccess Agent running on a NetWare or NT server via port `7205`.
7. The WebAccess Agent receives the data, decrypts it using the same encryption key that was used to encrypt the data, and then does a lookup in the WPDOMAIN.DB to identify the domain and post office where the user is.
8. Once the user's domain and post office are located, the WebAccess Agent determines how it will communicate with this particular post office. It discovers that it must communicate via TCP/IP.

9. The WebAccess Agent sends the user ID and password down to the POA object for the user's post office, and acts like a traditional GroupWise client, in that it connects to the POA via client/server port 1677. The POA picks up the request and authenticates the user into the mailbox.

This represents a quick and simple outline of how a user's request flows from an actual browser into a GroupWise mailbox. At this point, I don't discuss the return path of the data from the post office to the Web browser. Basically, the return path for the data coming from the post office is in reverse order, minus a few of the lookups, because a session ID is in place to route the data back from the Agent to the Application.

This should give you a basic understanding of how the WebAccess Application and the Agent work together to access the user's mail via WebAccess. Now that you have an understanding of GroupWise WebAccess architecture, you're ready to install GroupWise WebAccess.

Installing the GroupWise WebAccess Gateway

This section offers a walkthrough of a simple GroupWise WebAccess installation to get you a little more familiar with the basic install of WebAccess. This section includes some behind-the-scenes information that you might find beneficial.

NOTE

Before you can install WebAccess, you need a functional Web server. The supported Web servers are listed in the previous section.

In this example, you see a simple installation of the WebAccess Agent and Application being installed onto a single NetWare server. In the section titled "Advanced Installation Options for WebAccess," you can find additional information about installing the Agent and Application on different servers. For now, this section provides a good understanding of the install options for the Agent and Application. Follow these steps:

1. Map a drive to the server that runs the WebAccess Agent. Map a drive also to the server that is running the Web server. If your Web server is Microsoft IIS, you need to run the install from the same computer running the IIS Web server.

2. To begin, launch the SETUP.EXE from the `INTERNET\WEBACCES` directory located in your GroupWise software distribution directory or GroupWise 6.5 CD.

   Proceed past the license screen. Choose the Install the WebAccess Agent and Application option, as shown in Figure 11.2. If you are using GroupWise Document Management (GroupWise Libraries) and are either currently using WebPublisher or want to add WebPublisher to your installation, choose that option as well.

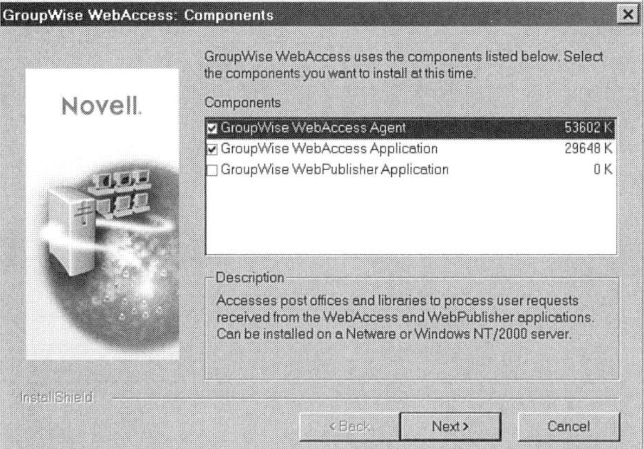

FIGURE 11.2
Choosing which GroupWise WebAccess components to install.

3. The WebAccess Agent and Application were discussed earlier. The WebPublisher Application is used to access documents stored in GroupWise document management libraries. If you are using GroupWise document management, you might want to enable the WebPublisher Application. This example does not include installing the WebPublisher Application.

4. Choose the platform and file location for your WebAccess Agent. For the installation software, make sure to indicate a drive letter mapping. A UNC path doesn't work well. Click Next.

   This is the path to the server the WebAccess Agent will be installed on, as well as the path to place the install files. The Agent can run either on a NetWare or a NT/2000 server. This step determines what code the install script will install. If you select NetWare as the platform, GWINTER.NLM is installed for the Agent. If you select Windows NT, GWINTER.EXE is installed. (There are, of course, additional files that are installed, but the GWINTER is the main workhorse for the Agent piece.) The path that you define here will be where the Agent files are installed. You can make this path anything you choose. The directory specified here can be eight characters or fewer.

5. Choose the IP address or DNS name for the WebAccess Agent.

   Now you are prompted to enter the IP address or DNS name of the server on which you are installing the Agent. The install script tries to auto-detect this information for you and displays it, as seen in Figure 11.3. Before this screen though, the first thing the script does is query the server that you defined to verify whether any GroupWise modules are loaded. If they are, you are prompted to unload the GroupWise modules.

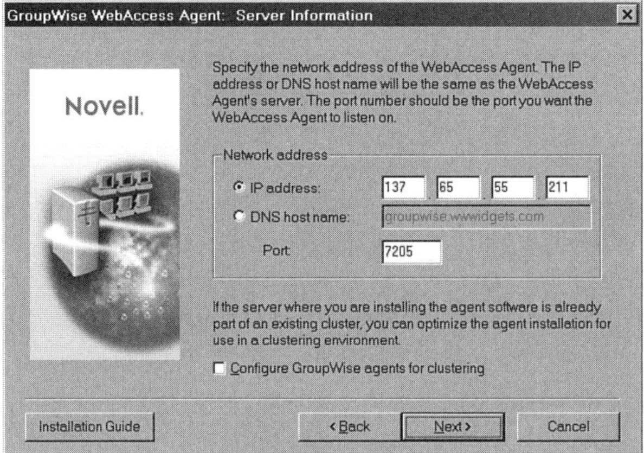

FIGURE 11.3
GroupWise WebAccess Agent server information includes supplying an IP address and related information.

> **TIP**
>
> **On NetWare, the DNS hostname comes from the `HOSTS` file found in the `SYS:\ETC` directory. Before proceeding, make sure that the local `HOSTS` file on the Web server contains the local IP address and a Web server name. This information can appear anywhere in the `HOSTS` file.**
>
> ```
> 137.65.55.211 groupwise.wwwidgets.com
> ```
>
> **If the DNS name is incorrect, the `HOSTS` file is where this information is coming from.**

The information about the DNS name and IP address of the server is used to help create a binary file on the Web server called COMMGR.CFG, which the WebAccess Application reads in order to determine on which server and port the WebAccess Agent is installed. This information is also placed into the GroupWise WPDOMAIN.DB to notify the WebAccess Agent which port it should listen on for connections coming from the WebAccess Application.

Note the option to cluster-enable the WebAccess Agent. Checking this box simply changes the definition of the path to the WebAccess Agent when the Agent loads. You will see an example of what checking this cluster option does in the next section, which talks about how to load the WebAccess Agent. If you are installing this WebAccess Agent into a Novell cluster, you will want to check this box. If you do check the option to configure the GroupWise Agent for clustering, and you are *not* running in a cluster environment, don't worry. The Agent will load just fine on a nonclustered server.

6. After confirming the server information for the server that will run WebAccess Agent, click Next. You will see the screen shown in Figure 11.4.

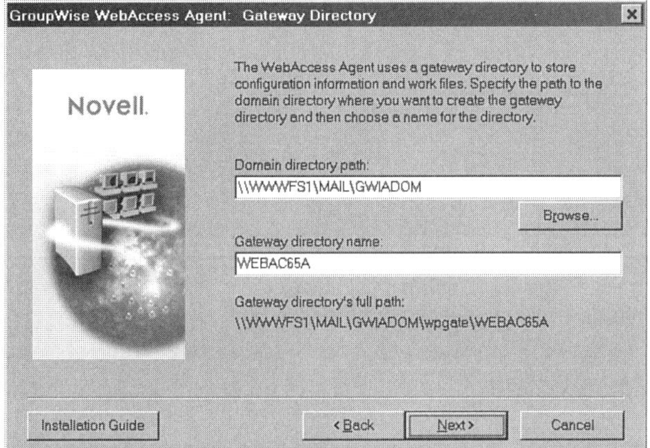

FIGURE 11.4
GroupWise WebAccess Agent gateway directory configuration.

You are now prompted for the path to the domain. Once again, the install script tries to provide this information for you; however, it might not be correct. The path to the domain that you see here comes from the workstation's Registry that you are running the install from. Notice that it gives you the full path of where the gateway directory will be. GroupWise stores all the gateway directory structures in `<DOMAIN>\WPGATE\`. Hence, you will see this in the gateway directory, full path information.

Keep this directory within eight characters or fewer. The install script will check to make sure that the directory exists; if it does not, it will prompt you to create it. If it does exist, you might be asked whether you are sure you want to use this directory.

7. After specifying the gateway directory, click Next.

 You are now asked what you would like the WebAccess Agent gateway object to be called. This is the object that you will see from ConsoleOne under the GroupWise domain defined earlier. For simplicity, it is best to keep these names the same.

 The next step, shown in Figure 11.5, might have you wondering why this is necessary. You're queried for a username and password so that it can access the WPDOMAIN.DB of the WebAccess Agent's domain. It's a good idea to place the domain and WebAccess Agent on the same server. Hence, a username and password are not necessarily required. However, the install requires you to enter a username and password here. The main reason for this is that if your domain is on `FS1`, and you are installing the WebAccess Agent on `FS2`, the Agent *must* be able to directly access the WPDOMAIN.DB to read some of its configuration information. Because of this, the Agent must log into the `FS1` server in order to access the domain database. Also, if the Agent must communicate to post offices via a direct link, it will use this username and password to authenticate to the post office server.

NOTE

Beginning with GroupWise 6.5 support pack 1 the user and password switches are written to the WebAccess Agent startup file that is referenced by the STRTWEB.NCF file. More information about this is mentioned in this section under loading the WebAccess Agent.

FIGURE 11.5
Username and password are required for the GroupWise WebAccess Agent.

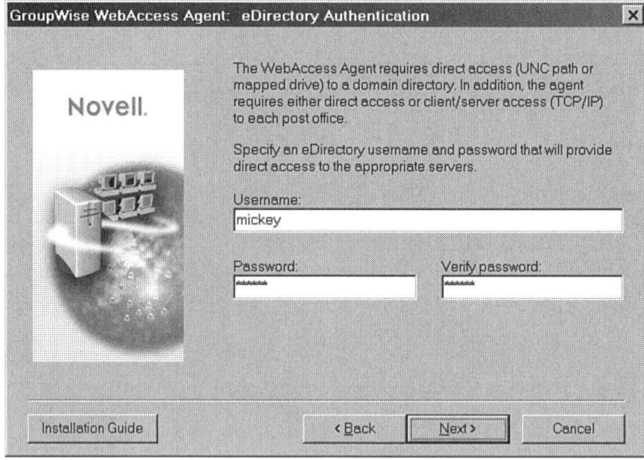

8. After entering the username and password, click Next.

 The next screen gives you the option to monitor the WebAccess Agent through a standard HTTP browser. This allows you to check in with your WebAccess Agent to see how it is running without having to actually look at the Agent console screen. Although this is a great feature, I recommend not enabling the feature through the installation wizard. Doing so inserts command-line switches in the startup file of the WebAccess Agent. It is best to edit the WebAccess Agent after the installation and enter this information from ConsoleOne. This way the information is also available to the GroupWise Monitor Agent to read from the WPDOMAIN.DB.

9. Do not check the Enable Web Console option. Simply click Next to proceed to the WebAccess Agent installation summary screen.

   You will get one additional prompt about the WebAccess Agent supporting the WebPublisher. This example doesn't install WebPublisher. If you are installing WebPublisher, you would want to enable this check box.

10. You now see a summary of the WebAccess Agent setup information. Verify that all information is entered correctly, and click the Next button.

This concludes the WebAccess Agent portion of the install. The wizard now takes you directly into the WebAccess Application wizard install, shown in Figure 11.6.

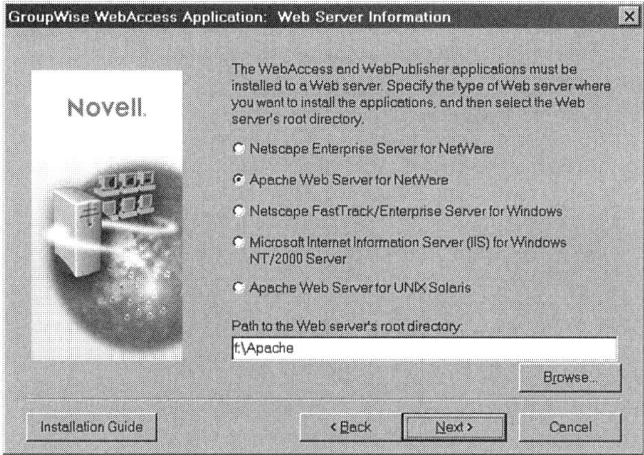

FIGURE 11.6
The first choice of the WebAccess Application install asks which Web server to install the application to.

NOTE

The WebAccess Application is the piece that runs as a servlet on a Web server and communicates to the WebAccess Agent via TCP/IP.

The first thing you are prompted for in the WebAccess Application install process is what type of Web server you will be installing the Application on. Follow these steps to complete the WebAccess Application install process:

1. Select the Web server platform, verify that the path to the root of the Web server is correct, and then click Next.

   Now you are prompted for the IP address or DNS name for the server that will run the WebAccess Application. This information is required so the installation software can make a *.PQA (Palm Query Application) for Palm OS devices that use Web clipping.

TIP

If you need to re-create the *.PQA file to reflect something different, you can run the WebAccess installation with a `/PQA` **switch (for example,** `SETUP.EXE /PQA`**). With this installation option, you are prompted only for information relevant to generating a new *.PQA file.**

2. Configure the IP address or DNS server name, and then choose Next.

   The next screen asks whether you want to replace your Web server's default Web page. If you do decide to replace your Web server's default Web page, the default Web page will be renamed so that you will not lose it.

TIP

If you do keep the existing default Web page for your Web server, you might want to add a link on it that points to `http://<your Web server DNS name>/servlet/webacc`**. This will allow users to click and be sent directly to WebAccess login page.**

3. Select the Web server default Web page option you prefer, and click Next.

   You are then prompted as to where you want the configuration files for the WebAccess Application to be located. This defaults to the `<\\<SERVER NAME>\SYS\NOVELL` directory for NetWare. The install creates a WebAccess directory under the specified directory where the configuration files are actually placed. These configuration files should exist on the same server as the Web server.

NOTE

If this directory does not exist, you will be prompted to create it.

4. Enter the path for the configuration files and click Next.

   You will then be prompted as to which Java servlet gateway you will be using (see Figure 11.7). Take the default, unless you must use a different Java servlet gateway.

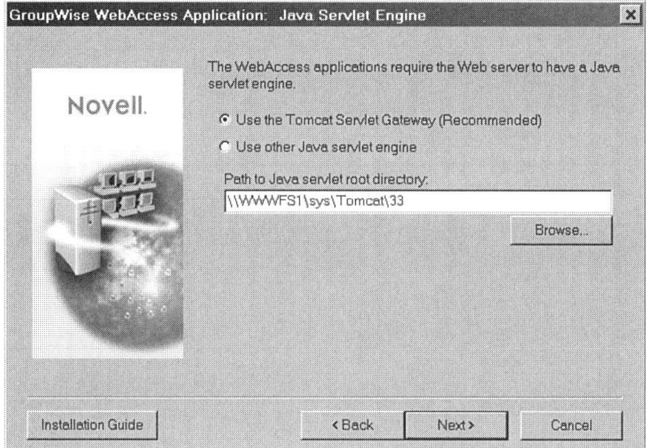

FIGURE 11.7
The Java servlet gateway runs the WebAccess Application.

5. Select the servlet gateway and then click Next.

   The installation asks for the default language selection. The default is English. This is the language that users see when they visit the http://*<your Web server DNS name>*/servlet/webacc link.

6. Select the default language and click Next.

   This next option (see Figure 11.8) asks in what context of your eDirectory tree should the application objects be created. These application objects consist of the GroupWise WebAccess object, the `GroupWiseProvider` object, the `LDAPProvider` object, and the `NovellSpeller` object. These objects, and the services they perform, are discussed more in the section titled "Configuring the GroupWise WebAccess Gateway." The default context is the context of the domain object. This is usually sufficient, as these objects should exist close to the domain for administration purposes.

It might be a bit confusing to see the name of the GroupWise domain listed at the beginning of the context. Even though a GroupWise domain object is not considered an eDirectory organization or organization unit, which are your traditional container objects that would contain eDirectory leaf objects, the domain's eDirectory object has an attribute that defines it as a container object. Because of this, you can actually create *some* objects under the domain—you can create GroupWise gateways, service providers, and application objects. Therefore, it makes sense to have the context listed as the domain object. This makes it nice because in eDirectory you can then simply click the domain eDirectory object to view all the associated objects.

FIGURE 11.8 Choosing an eDirectory context for WebAccess Application's objects.

7. Verify that the context is correct and click Next.
8. You will see a summary of the WebAccess Application information that you entered. Verify this information and click Next.
9. If prompted to unload Java, do so manually rather than allowing the installation to do so.

   To unload Java manually from the NetWare console prompt, enter the following commands:

   ```
   java -killall
   java -exit
   ```

10. The install will then proceed to install the WebAccess Agent and Application. You might be prompted to overwrite older files. If so, you will want to keep the newest file.

    The last thing that you see is a summary screen with information on how to load the components that were just installed.

In the next section, you learn how to put on the final touches to the WebAccess Agent installation. If you leave the last options checked, the Install wizard launches the WebAccess Agent and restarts the Web server for you. This gives you a functioning WebAccess system.

Important GroupWise WebAccess Agent Configuration Steps

There are just a couple of settings you should make on the WebAccess Agent so it will function correctly from the get go. Here are the steps for configuring the last few essential WebAccess Agent settings:

1. In ConsoleOne, edit the properties of the WebAccess Agent.
2. Select the Post Office Links property page. Make sure that all links are *client/server only* and all of the IP addresses of the POAs are filled in.
3. Next, go to the GroupWise tab, and select the Log Settings property page.
4. Change the logging level to verbose.
5. Specify a log file path on the server that houses the WebAccess Agent. The default path is the `<DOMAIN>\WPGATE\<WEBACCESS>\000.PRC`.
6. Increase the max log disk space; for example, to **`50000`**.

The reason you must specify a log file path is that the WebAccess Agent will not create a log file on the disk, unless you specifically indicate the path to create log files. This is a quirk with the WebAccess Agent that other GroupWise Agents do not have.

See Figure 11.9 for example of a configured Log Settings page.

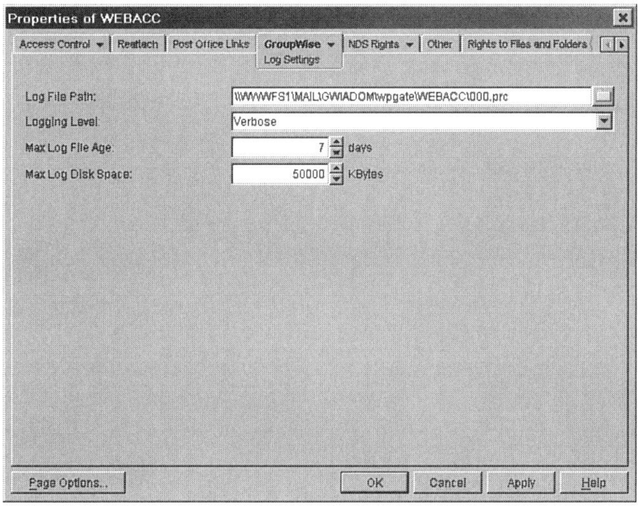

FIGURE 11.9 WebAccess Agent log settings are important if you need to troubleshoot your GroupWise WebAccess Agent.

Loading the GroupWise WebAccess Agent and Application

This section discusses how to start the WebAccess Agent and WebAccess Application. The WebAccess Agent is one process and the WebAccess Application is two processes.

Loading the GroupWise WebAccess Agent

For NetWare 5.x and NetWare 6.x, load the GroupWise WebAccess Agent by typing **STRTWEB**, which calls the STRTWEB.NCF file. You should also consider adding load commands to the server's AUTOEXEC.NCF file.

For NetWare 4.2, follow these steps:

1. At the NetWare System Console or from an *.NCF file, enter the following commands:

   ```
   load clibaux
   load clib
   load fpsm
   load nlmlib
   load nwsnut
   load requestr
   load threads
   STRTWEB
   ```

2. The STRTWEB command calls the STRTWEB.NCF file. You should consider adding load commands to the STRWEB.NCF file and creating a reference to the STRTWEB.NCF file in the server's AUTOEXEC.NCF file.

TIP

If you installed your WebAccess Agent files to a directory other than SYS:\SYSTEM, the STRTWEB.NCF file does not pick up this path when it loads GWINTER. You will need to modify the STRTWEB.NCF file to include the correct path to the GWINTER.NLM file.

For Windows servers, follow these steps: For NT/Windows 2000, a shortcut called GroupWise WebAccess has been created for you, or the Agent has been configured as a service if you choose that installation option. Generally the shortcut is available under Start, Programs, Novell GroupWise WebAccess. A batch file called STRTWEB.BAT is created, and is installed in the `C:\WEBACC` directory by default. If the Agent has been installed as a service, you must start and stop the WebAccess Agent via the Windows Services found in Control Panel, Administrative Tools, Services.

Here's an explanation of what's in the STRTWEB.NCF file on a NetWare server. Following is a sample STRTWEB.NCF file:

```
Load SYS:system\gwinter/ph=wwwfs1\mail:GWIADOM

\WPGATE\WEBAC65A /user=mickey /password=minnie
```

The first command-line parameter in the STRTWEB.NCF file is the `/ph` switch, which contains the path to the gateway directory. Next are the `/user` and `/password` switches. Remember you entered these during the installation.

When you load the WebAccess Agent, take notice that the GWINTER.NLM auto-loads several other NLMs, starting with VS*.NLM or SC*.NLM. These NLMs are used when a user views an attachment that might be some sort of document type from the WebAccess client. These VS*.NLMs take very little server memory because only a small piece of them loads when you load the Agent. When a user needs to actually view a document, the entire viewer NLM loads at that point.

The install also creates a STOPWEB.NCF file, which will shut down the WebAccess Agent. It simply contains the line `UNLOAD GWINTER`, which will unload the WebAccess Agent.

Following are some useful switches that can be used in the strtweb.ncf or strtweb.bat (if you're loading the Agent on an NT box):

- `@filename`: This switch allows you to place all startup switches in a particular file. This is similar to when a domain or post office agent is loaded. This switch is not used by default.
- `/help`: If the GWINTER.NLM or GWINTER.EXE files are loaded with the `/help` switch, all startup switches are displayed with brief descriptions.
- `/maxusers-`: Enter the maximum number of concurrent users that the Agent will support. The default is 250 users.
- `/user-`: This switch is used only with the NLM version of the Agent. Enter an eDirectory username that has rights to the domain directory here. The `/user-` switch is also used when the NLM version of the Agent is configured to link to a post office via a UNC connection.

- `/password-`: This switch is used only with the NLM version of the Agent. Enter the password for the eDirectory user defined in the `/user-` switch.
- `/ip-`: Enter the IP address that the Agent will bind to. The Agent will bind to the first bound IP address of the server by default.

NOTE

Beginning with GroupWise 6.5 support pack 1 (6.5.1) when you install the WebAccess Agent, it will create a startup file that it will use to replace the startup switches in the STRTWEB.NCF file. This startup file is the name of the WebAccess Agent that you defined during the install (by default, WEBAC65A.WAA).

An example of a 6.5.1 STRTWEB.NCF file is `load sys:system\gwinter @WEBAC65A.waa`**.**

The WEBAC65A.waa file contains most of the startup switches that you might use on the WebAccess Agent, just like the Message Transfer Agent (MTA) and POA startup files do. A sample WebAccess Agent startup file can be found at the following location: `GroupWise 6.5.1 SDD\INTERNET\WEBACCES\config\AgentConfig.waa`**.**

Loading the GroupWise WebAccess Application

With just the WebAccess Agent running, you have only one piece of the entire WebAccess system running. You need to get the WebAccess Application up and running as well.

To do so, load the Web server and the servlet gateway. The instructions for loading the Web server or servlet gateway are different based upon the platform you are using. The WebAccess Application needs two components in order to work: a Java servlet gateway and a Web server.

TIP

Generally it's a good measure to reboot the server with the Web server on it after the installation. Sometimes the WebAccess Application will not seem to behave as it should. Look at the following Web server tips for instructions on the steps you might need to take to load the components that support the GroupWise WebAccess Application.

Following are the steps for loading the GroupWise WebAccess Application. Choose the OS you are running the WebAccess Application on, and follow the instructions associated with that OS.

NetWare 5.x

To install on the NetWare 5.x server platform, you need to use the command NVXWEBUP or NSWEB when you load the Netscape Enterprise Web Server for NetWare (Novonyx). You do not need to do anything special to load the Novell servlet gateway; it is configured to load automatically when the Netscape Enterprise server loads. The Novell servlet gateway also unloads when Netscape Enterprise server is unloaded. On occasion the Novell servlet gateway does not register itself with the Novonyx Web server, and so it does not load automatically. These two NetWare console commands might be of help to you if you are having problems with the Novell servlet gateway:

- **NSGCFG**—Registers the Novell servlet gateway with the Novonyx Web server.
- **SGJINIT**—Starts the Novell servlet gateway, but it will keep running only if the Novell Enterprise Web Server is running.

NetWare 6 Web Servers—NetWare Server Platform

The command to load your Netscape Enterprise (Novonyx) Web server for NetWare is normally NVXWEBUP or NSWEB. The command to unload is NVXWEBDN or NSWEBDN.

When you choose Apache as your Web server, the GroupWise WebAccess Application install creates an *.NCF file to create a customized instance of the Apache Web server. The command to start the instance of Apache for GroupWise WebAccess is with the *.NCF file called GWWEBUP. The command to unload this instance of Apache is GWWEBDN.NCF. These files are in the SYS:APACHE directory. The *.CONF file for the GroupWise instance of Apache is called GWApache.conf.

The GWWEBUP.NCF file is not loaded from the AUTOEXEC.NCF by default. You should consider adding the following two lines to the AUTOEXEC.NCF, so Apache will load when the server boots.

```
SEARCH ADD SYS:APACHE
GWWEBUP.NCF
```

Java Servlet Gateway—NetWare 6 Server Platform

Both NetWare Enterprise (Novonyx) and Apache Web servers use the Tomcat servlet engine. The command to load Tomcat is TOMCAT33.

The Tomcat servlet engine might not be loaded automatically with your Apache or NetWare Enterprise (Novonyx) Web server on the NetWare platform. You can load Tomcat from the AUTOEXEC.NCF file. Also, the Tomcat servlet gateway can be loaded before or after the Web server loads. To load the Tomcat servlet gateway use the following two separate commands:

```
SEARCH ADD SYS:TOMCAT\33\BIN
TOMCAT33.NCF
```

If ever you want to unload the Tomcat servlet gateway we have found this generally to be the best method. At the NetWare system console prompt use the following command:

```
JAVA -KILLALL
JAVA -EXIT
```

Or if you need to be a little more careful because your server is using `JAVA` for other things than the Tomcat servlet gateway, you need to just kill the Tomcat process. To show and then kill the Tomcat process, use this command:

```
JAVA -SHOW
```

The `JAVA -SHOW` command reports the process ID. You can then issue this command:

```
JAVA -KILL<PROCESS ID>
```

So if the process ID for my Tomcat servlet gateway was `176` as reported by the `JAVA -SHOW` command, my command line would read as follows:

```
JAVA -KILL176
```

The speller is no longer a separate process you must start up. The speller component is now a servlet called the Speller Application. This also means that you can use the Speller Application securely (via SSL), without needing to open another port through the firewall.

Microsoft IIS—Web Server

The GroupWise WebAccess Application is designed to start when the Microsoft IIS Service and Web Server is started. The Microsoft IIS Web server is designed to start when the Microsoft Internet Information Server service is started. You can start these services from the Control Panel. Choose Administrative Tools, Services.

Java Servlet Gateway—Microsoft IIS Server

The Novell servlet gateway is designed to automatically load when you start the IIS service.

The spell checker is a separate process you must start. The batch file to start the speller is called SPELLSRV.BAT.

Troubleshooting the Novell Servlet Gateway on Microsoft IIS Servers

In my experience, installing the Novell servlet gateway on Microsoft IIS Servers can be problematic. Use these tips if you have problems with the GroupWise WebAccess Application on IIS:

- To see whether the Novell servlet gateway is working after you have started IIS, query the SnoopServlet Java servlet that the Novell servlet gateway makes available. The syntax to access SnoopServlet is as follows: `http://`*`<server ip or dns name>`*`/servlet/SnoopServlet`.
- The Novell servlet gateway, which is part of the install of the WebAccess Application on an IIS Web server, sometimes does not integrate properly with IIS. You won't necessarily get errors in the installation, but when you try to use your Web server to access *`<web server address>`*`/servlet/webacc` or *`<web server address>`*`/servlet/SnoopServlet`, you might find that the servlet engine is not responding. There is a really good document on the Novell servlet gateway, and instructions on how to configure it to run with the IIS platform. This document is called SERVGATE.PDF and it is located in the `<GroupWise 6.5 SDD>\COMMON\ServletGateway\shared\java\servlets\doc` directory.

Logging In to the GroupWise WebAccess Client

Now that the Application and the Agent are up and running, you are ready to read mail. This section doesn't spend a lot of time on the actual WebAccess interface and all the options that are available.

To begin, you must launch your Web browser and point it to the Web server on which you installed the WebAccess Application. If you replaced the default home page, you can simply enter **`http://`*`<yourWeb server DNS name>`***, and the language page for WebAccess should be displayed. If you did not replace your default Web page, you can enter **http://<*yourWeb server DNS name*>/servlet/webacc**, and the login page will be displayed. You can then enter a GroupWise user ID and password and click Login.

TIP

WebAccess users are required to have passwords on their GroupWise accounts in order to log in via the WebAccess client. If your POA is configured to query eDirectory via LDAP, users can also use their eDirectory passwords if they have not assigned a password to their GroupWise mailboxes.

You should now be viewing your GroupWise master mailbox from the WebAccess client. Figure 11.10 displays a GroupWise 6.5 user's mailbox as viewed from the WebAccess client.

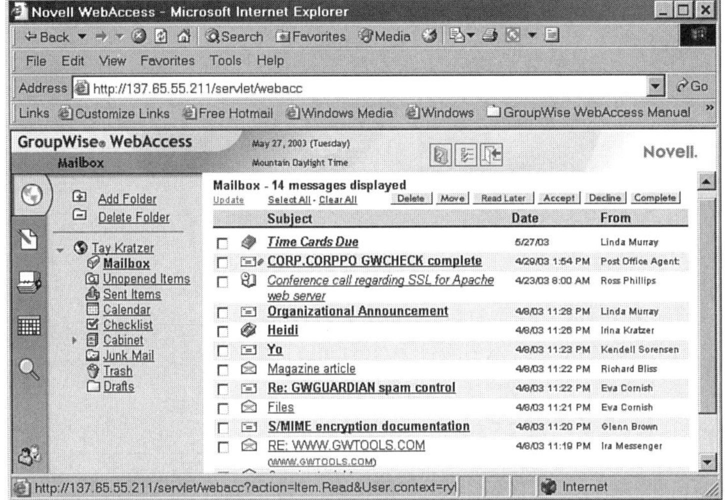

FIGURE 11.10
The GroupWise WebAccess client.

Configuring the GroupWise WebAccess Gateway

In this section, you learn about some of the eDirectory objects that are associated with the WebAccess gateway, what functions they perform, as well as how to configure all aspects of the WebAccess gateway. This section goes through each configuration screen, discussing most of the options and how they affect the overall performance or functionality of the WebAccess gateway. This section does not discuss every option, because some of the options are self-explanatory and make minor changes to the functionality of WebAccess. Also, there are a few generic gateway options that are of minimal consequence that will not be discussed.

The WebAccess Agent

This is the object that you can see associated with a domain when you select to view gateways. It is the only object associated with a WebAccess gateway that is directly associated with a domain. When you edit the properties of the WebAccess Agent, you can configure the settings associated with this agent.

GroupWise Identification Property Page

Following is an explanation of the Identification property page of the GroupWise WebAccess Agent:

- **Subdirectory:** This is the directory of the owning domain for the agent. It's located under the WPGATE directory. If you select the drop-down button, you will see all the gateway directories under this gateway. This should be the directory that the WebAccess Agent uses for some of its configuration files.
- **Time Zone:** This allows you to enter the agent's default time zone.

Users can adjust the time zone from the WebAccess client so that appointments will show up in their local time zone.

- **Platform:** You should specify on which platform this WebAccess Agent will be running. If you are running the agent on an NT platform, you will need to change this to reflect Windows.
- **Gateway Alias Type:** For the WebAccess gateway, you should not need an alias type. This field is active on any of the GroupWise gateways.
- **Foreign ID:** For the WebAccess gateway, you should not need a foreign ID. Again, this field is active on any of the GroupWise gateways and is primarily used with a GWIA.
- **SNMP Community "Get" String:** If you are using SNMP-monitoring software to monitor the WebAccess gateway, this field allows you to set the `get` string to match your monitoring software. Blank is the default.

Network Address Property Page

Following is an explanation of the Network Address property page of the GroupWise WebAccess Agent:

- **TCP/IP Address:** This should be the TCP/IP or DNS address for the WebAccess Agent.
- **HTTP Port:** The HTTP port is used by the WebAccess Agent and the GroupWise Monitor utility. This port tells the WebAccess Agent which port to listen on for Web-browser monitoring. This GroupWise Monitor utility reads the HTTP port value from the domain database in order to monitor the WebAccess Agent.

TIP **To enable HTTP monitoring, you should also enable the HTTP username and password. To do this, go to the Optional Gateway Settings property page and fill in the HTTP username and password fields.**

The SSL portions of this screen are not discussed in this chapter. Chapter 27 "Securing Your GroupWise System via SSL," provides detailed information about how to enable SSL for WebAccess.

- **TCP Port:** This is the port that the WebAccess Application running on the Web server will use to communicate data to the WebAccess Agent. In other words, the agent will listen on this port for data coming from the application.

Configuring the GroupWise Optional Gateway Settings Property Page

Most optional gateway settings are generic gateway settings that do not apply to the WebAccess gateway. The help file regarding them should suffice. Be sure to fill in the HTTP username and password fields.

Understanding the GroupWise Gateway Administrators Property Page

Here you can define a GroupWise user or group as the administrator for the GroupWise agent. The roles are generic roles for all gateways. The one role that you might be interested in setting is the operator.

The operator role allows the defined user(s) or group(s) to receive mail messages when errors occur at the GroupWise agent. This helps alert you to problems with the gateway.

The user who you add as an administrator must be a GroupWise user. Also, if you add a group or distribution list, its visibility must be set to `system`.

Configuring the WebAccess Settings Property Page

Shown in Figure 11.11, this page is important to enabling the application and agent to communicate properly. Both settings are stored in the domain database and the COMMGR.CFG file, which is located in two places. It is located in the `DOMAIN\WPGATE\<WEBACCESS>` directory for the WebAccess Agent, and a copy of this file is made available to the WebAccess Application on the Web server, the default of which is `\NOVELL\WebAccess`. On a NetWare server, the `NOVELL\WebAccess` directory is generally in the root of the `SYS:volume`. On a Windows 2000/NT server, it's usually off the in the `C:\` drive. The COMMGR.CFG file is encrypted and cannot be manually manipulated.

The COMINT.CFG file located in the *<DOMAIN>*\WPGATE\<WEBACCESS> directory is basically a live backup of the COMMGR.CFG file. If your COMMGR.CFG file becomes damaged or corrupt, you can copy the COMINT.CFG file to COMMGR.CFG.

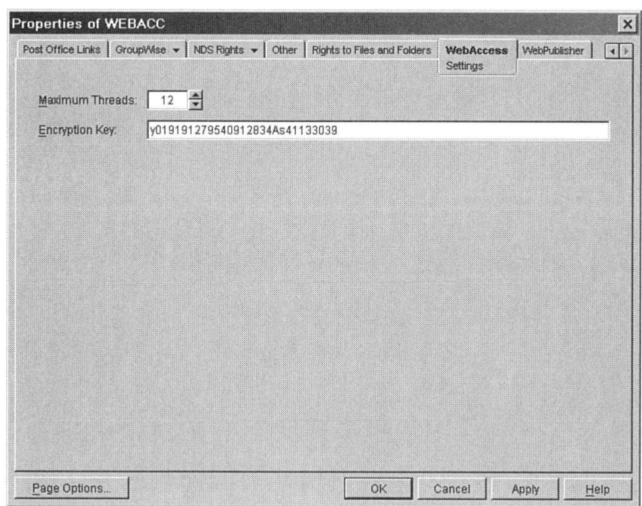

FIGURE 11.11
The WebAccess Settings property page.

When you make changes to the maximum threads or encryption key settings, it will update three files. They are the COMINT.CFG and COMMGR.CFG files located at the `<DOMAIN>\WPGATE\<WEBACCESS>` directory, as well as the COMMGR.CFG file, which is located on the Web server in the `\NOVELL\WebAccess` directory.

NOTE **When you make changes to the maximum threads of encryption key settings, the COMMGR.CFG file in the `\NOVELL\WebAccess` directory is first backed up to COMMGR.CFG.1 and a new COMMGR.CFG file is placed here. For this reason, you might see several COMMGR.CFG.X file in your `\NOVELL\WebAccess` directory. This indicates whenever a change was made to the threads of encryption key.**

Following is an explanation of the Settings property page of the GroupWise WebAccess Agent:

- **Maximum Threads:** This setting allows you to increase or decrease the maximum number of threads that the WebAccess Agent will use for communication. If you find that your users are receiving slow responses when using WebAccess, you might need to increase this number. You can monitor your agent to see whether it's reached the maximum number of threads. You will learn how to identify how many threads the WebAccess Agent is using in the upcoming section titled "Understanding the GroupWise WebAccess Console."
- **Encryption Key:** The encryption key value defined here is used to encrypt data that is sent between the WebAccess Agent and the WebAccess Application provider. This ensures that communication between these two WebAccess components is encrypted and secure. As mentioned earlier in this section, this encryption key is stored in the COMMGR.CFG file. Because both the WebAccess Agent and Application provider must use the same encryption key, the COMMGR.CFG file is accessible to them both.

  You can accept the default encryption key that the install generates, or you can use your own encryption key, if desired. If the Application cannot talk to the Agent, it is good to double-check the COMMGR.CFG file on the Web server running the Application and the server running the Agent. You can manually copy the COMMGR.CFG file from the `<DOMAIN>\WPGATE\<WEBACCESS>` directory to the `\NOVELL\WEBACCESS` directory if you do have a communication problem between these two agents.

Configuring the Access Control Settings Property Page

This configuration page allows you to determine who can use the WebAccess gateway to access the GroupWise mailbox. You can define multiple classes of service with corresponding members. The default class of service contains everyone and allows everyone access to the WebAccess Agent.

One of the most important settings under Access Control is the Timeout After setting. The default of 20 minutes (as shown in Figure 11.12) is generally a good setting to keep. If you increase this setting, users may needlessly tie up resources on the WebAccess Agent, when they have already closed their browser.

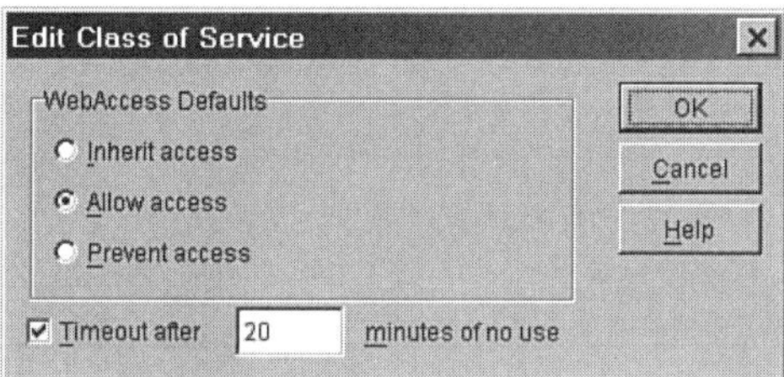

FIGURE 11.12 Configuring the WebAccess client timeout value requires some consideration as to what the users need.

To edit the Timeout After value, do the following:

1. Go to the Access Control page.
2. Highlight the class of service you want to affect, which is typically the Default Class of Service.
3. Click the Edit button.
4. Modify the Timeout After *X* Minutes of No Use field to reflect your desired timeout length.

Understanding the Access Control Database Management Properties Page

All of the access control settings regarding classes of service and membership are stored in a database called GWAC.DB. This database is located in the `<DOMAIN>\WPGATE\<WEBACCESS>` directory. This database management tab allows you to validate and recover this database.

Following is an explanation of the Access Control Database Management property page of the GroupWise WebAccess Agent:

- **Validate Now:** Clicking this option will basically run a structure check on the GWAC.DB file which reports any inconsistencies found in the database. It also tells you how many bytes, fields, and indexes it validated. If inconsistencies are found, you should perform a recover now on the database.
- **Recover Now:** Clicking this option will basically run a structural rebuild of the GWAC.DB that will repair any structural damage in the database. The GWAC.DC file is used as a template file on how to structurally build the new GWAC.DB file.

This section spoke of how to fix the GWAC.DB. However, you will rarely get issues with the GWAC.DB file.

Configuring the Reattach Settings Property Page

This tab is used when you are running the WebAccess Agent on an NT platform *and* when the links to the post office are direct (or UNC) (post office links are discussed in the next section). If you are running the WebAccess Agent on a NetWare platform or if the post office links are TCP/IP, you do not need this information. Remember that the WebAccess Agent acts like a client when it accesses the user's user and message databases. If the agent is running on NT, and you have defined direct links to post offices, the NT server running the agent must log into the post office's server in order to access the message store. This facilitates the need to supply the following information.

Following is an explanation of the Reattach Settings property page of the GroupWise WebAccess Agent:

- **Tree:** Enter the name of the eDirectory tree where the server that houses the post offices is located.
- **Context:** Enter the full context of the eDirectory user who will be used to log in to the post office server.
- **User ID:** Enter the ID of the eDirectory user who has rights to the post office directory. (This user must have read, write, create, erase, modify, and file scan rights to the post office directory.)
- **Password:** Enter the password for the eDirectory user.

Customers who use NetWare will most likely not have to use this settings on this property page.

Understanding the Post Office Links Settings Property Page

This tab is very important. It defines exactly how the WebAccess Agent will communicate to the post offices in the GroupWise system. Remember that the agent acts like a client in that it must access the post office message store to retrieve a user's mail.

Following is an explanation of the Post Office Links Settings property page of the GroupWise WebAccess Agent:

- **Domain Column:** This defines the domain that the post office is under.
- **Post Office Column:** This identifies the name of the post office.
- **Access Mode:** This defines how the WebAccess Agent will access the post office. You have four options here, as follows:
    - Client/server and direct
    - Client/server only
    - Direct only
    - Follow P.O. (use current post office access)

If the access mode is set to Use Current Post Office Access (also known as "Follow P.O."), it depends on what the post office object access mode is set to. If it is set to client/server only, you will see an IP address or DNS name in the Link column. If it is set to direct only, you will see the UNC path to the post office in the Link column. If it is set to client/server and direct, you might see either an IP address or UNC path. You need client/server access from the WebAccess Agent to each post office.

WARNING

It's not possible to have a post office set to allow client/server only on the access mode, but have the WebAccess Agent set to a direct connection. If this were the case, users of the WebAccess client would not be able to log in to their post offices, because the post office would reject direct connections coming from the WebAccess Agent.

You can edit any of the post office links from this interface if they are not configured correctly. Simply highlight the post office you would like to edit and click the Edit Link button.

Notice that the Post Office Links Settings window defines what the access mode for the post office is currently set to so that you don't have to pull up the details of each post office object to find this. Also, when you have Follow P.O. selected, you cannot modify the links; they are grayed out. This is because it will read the UNC path and IP address from the POA object record in the WPDOMAIN.DB and use it. If you select any of the other three options, you will be able to modify either the UNC path or the IP address and port.

TIP

When troubleshooting WebAccess to POA connectivity problems, go to the Post Office Links property page first. Quite often, WebAccess will have the incorrect IP address or port for the POA. Somehow, when a POA's IP information, or a post office's access method is updated, it is not always communicated well enough to WebAccess. Making the change from the Post Office Links property page is often the solution.

Configuring the WebPublisher Settings Property Page

These settings are used only if you installed the WebPublisher piece of WebAccess during the initial gateway install. Here's an explanation of these options so that if you are running GroupWise document management, you can configure this piece of the WebAccess gateway.

Following is an explanation of the WebPublisher Settings property page of the GroupWise WebAccess Agent:

- **WebPublisher Proxy User Mailbox ID:** This is the GroupWise mailbox ID of a GroupWise user who will actually be retrieving documents in the GroupWise system. Document management users must share their documents with this particular proxy user in order for them to view these documents from WebPublisher. The proxy user is just a GroupWise user created in your system, for the express purpose of supporting WebPublisher.

- **WebPublisher Proxy User Mailbox Password:** Enter the Proxy user's GroupWise password here.
- **Library Access:** Here is where you define what libraries will be visible from WebPublisher. If you have multiple libraries in your GroupWise system, you can allow or restrict access to these libraries for the WebPublisher agent.
- **Assign General User Access to WebPublisher Users:** If you enable this option, documents in the available libraries that are accessible to general users are available through WebAccess. In other words, if a user creates a document and this particular document type is accessible by all users, the WebPublisher proxy user would be able to see it, so the document would be available through WebPublisher. The owner of the document would not need to explicitly share it with the WebPublisher proxy user.
- **Disk Cache Size:** This setting determines the size of the disk cache where cached documents will reside. When a user retrieves a document from a GroupWise document management library from within WebPublisher, the document will be cached. This setting determines how large this cache can grow to.
- **Cache Synchronization Interval:** This value in seconds determines how often the WebPublisher Application will synchronize the document(s) in the cache with the real document sitting in the GroupWise library.
- **Disk Cache Path:** This defines the location of the cache for documents that are retrieved via WebPublisher. It is recommended to have this directory located on the same server as the one where the WebAccess Agent is running. The default location for this cache on a NetWare server is `SYS\SYSTEM\CACHE`; for NT, it is `C:\GROUPWISE\CACHE`.

You should now be comfortable configuring the WebAccess Agent and should understand how these settings can affect the performance and functionality of your WebAccess Agent.

The next section discusses the eDirectory objects that are created with the WebAccess Application installation. It is through these eDirectory objects that you administer the remaining components of the WebAccess gateway.

Configuring the WebAccess Agent Sub-Components

As already explained, there are two main components of WebAccess: the Agent and the Application. To be technically correct, the WebAccess Application refers to several sub-components that work together to make up the WebAccess Application. One of these components is referred to sometimes as the *servlet component*, and the others are referred to as the *service provider components*. These two sets of components work together in regards to the WebAccess Application. You might have noticed that there was an option called the WebPublisher Application. Think of the WebPublisher Application as a mirror piece to the WebAccess Application with minor differences. They both perform the same functions, and they both talk to the same WebAccess Agent(s). The WebPublisher Application is used strictly for GroupWise document management access through a Web interface. It does *not* retrieve user's mail, appointments, tasks, and so on.

Before discussing the next few components of the WebAccess gateway, let's take a look at what these additional objects are actually called:

- GroupWise WebAccess object
- GroupWise `WebPublisher` object
- `NovellSpeller` object
- GroupWise document provider object
- `GroupWiseProvider` object
- `LDAPProvider` object

These six objects exist exclusively in the eDirectory tree and are located in the context specified during the install of the WebAccess Application or WebPublisher Application. (Remember that this context might be under the GroupWise eDirectory domain object. They are not necessarily associated with a domain and do not exist in the WPDOMAIN.DB databases.) These objects are used to configure and administer the GroupWise Application pieces of WebAccess. Because GroupWise 6.5 offers many more features in WebAccess than previous versions, these objects are used as a better way to manage these functions. Also, because GroupWise 6.5 WebAccess allows you to service multiple WebAccess Agents from a single WebAccess Application install, there has to be a way to manage just the WebAccess Application pieces of the picture. Having said that, the following discussion of the GroupWise WebAccess objects will help you understand how these all relate to the big picture of WebAccess.

GroupWise WebAccess Object

The GroupWise WebAccess object is the main component of the WebAccess Application. You can think of this object as being the WebAccess Application object that loads as a servlet on the Web server. Through this object, you configure many of the settings that will affect the user's connection to WebAccess. This is the object that allows you to configure how a users interact with the WebAccess gateway. Feel free to pull up the properties of your own GroupWise WebAccess object in your eDirectory tree and follow along.

To find the GroupWise WebAccess object, go into your eDirectory tree and highlight the GroupWise domain that you installed GroupWise WebAccess to. Figure 11.13 shows the location of the GroupWise WebAccess object in the `wwwidgets` system. The GroupWise WebAccess sub-components discussed in this section are not available from the GroupWise view in ConsoleOne.

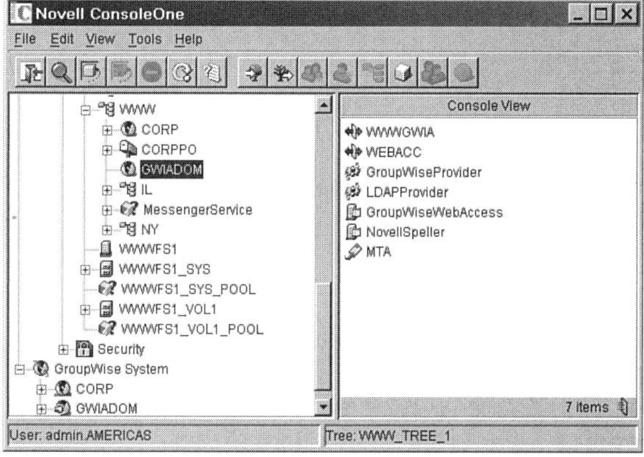

FIGURE 11.13 Locating the WebAccess Application objects.

When you edit the GroupWiseWebAccess object, you can configure the following options.

Application/Environment Property Page

From this page it is possible to define some of the basic environment settings for the WebAccess Application object. The settings beneath this page are

- **Configuration File:** This is the path to the WEBACC.CFG file. The WEBACC.CFG file contains all the configuration information regarding the GroupWise WebAccess object. This is a text file and can be viewed from any text editor. You can manually edit this file; however, it's kind of an all or nothing prospect. If you do edit the WEBACC.CFG manually, the changes you make are not written to eDirectory. But then when you try to edit the WebAccess Application from the ConsoleOne snap-ins, sometimes the snap-ins get confused and the WEBACC.CFG is configured incorrectly.

- **File Upload Path:** This is the path to which attachments are uploaded to the Web server when a user attaches a file to a newly composed email from WebAccess. As soon as the user presses OK to attach a file, WebAccess begins uploading it to this directory. This allows the upload to be taking place in the background, so the user can continue to compose the mail message. After the message is sent or cancelled, the uploaded file is deleted from this upload directory.
- **Logout URL:** Here you can enter an URL that a user will be sent to when logging out of the WebAccess client. You can enter any URL here, and the user's browser will be directed there upon logging out. This is very handy if you want to send the user to a particular Web site upon exiting.

Together, these three settings allow you to configure the paths employed by the WebAccess Application object.

Application/Log Settings Property Page

This is where you can configure the log settings for the WebAccess Application. Rarely will you need to access the Application's log files. It's the WebAccess Agent's log files that are generally of interest.

Application/Services Property Page

Here is where you can define which services are available through the WebAccess Application by listing what are called GroupWise *providers*. These providers are discussed in just a bit. For now, think of this tab as providing the ability to configure whether or not the WebAccess Application can access either a WebAccess Agent or an LDAP server. The reason for the LDAP server portion is because, from the WebAccess address book, you can query other LDAP servers to look up names and addresses in their directories. Without the LDAP provider defined as an active service on the GroupWise WebAccess object, LDAP lookups from the WebAccess client address book would fail. Similarly, if you did not have the GroupWise provider listed here as an active service, the application could not physically talk to a GroupWise agent.

You cannot have multiple instances of the same provider listed here. If you choose to edit a listed provider, it takes you to the properties of that particular provider, which you will read about shortly. Deleting a listed provider does not actually delete the provider from the system, but simply deletes it from the GroupWise WebAccess object, so that this service is not active from the GroupWise WebAccess object's point of view.

Application/Templates Property Page

Here is where you can define the type of interface users see when accessing WebAccess. It might be helpful for you to understand what *templates* are, first. Figure 11.14 shows the Application/Templates Property Page.

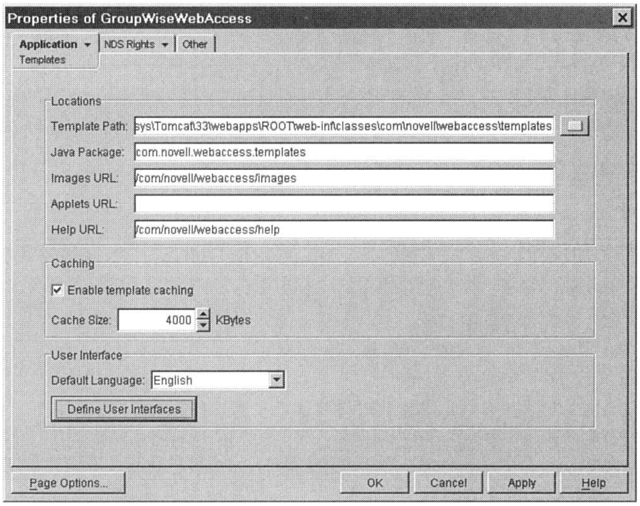

FIGURE 11.14
Application/Templates property page.

You can think of templates as being containers that hold or display the data that is retrieved from a user's mailbox located at the post office. Templates are associated with the type of browser or device being used to access WebAccess. For example, if you were to access your GroupWise mailbox from a standard PC-based Web browser such as Internet Explorer or Netscape, you would be using the standard HTML templates to view the contents of your mailbox. If you were to access your mailbox from a Pocket PC device running a browser, you would probably want to use a different set of templates, called *simple HTML* templates. Or if you were to access your mailbox from a wireless cellular phone, you would need to view your mail by using a different set of templates called *WML (wireless markup language)* templates. Templates are explained much more in Chapter 24, "Using Wireless and Handheld Devices with GroupWise 6.5 WebAccess." Just remember that templates are the key to how flexible the GroupWise WebAccess system is as far as supporting and displaying the contents of a user's mailbox across many types of devices. For now, this chapter discusses some of the basic configuration options that are available for the WebAccess Application.

- **Template Path:** This defines where all the template directories exist. If you were to look in the directory defined here, you would see several subdirectories beneath these, one representing each set of templates that WebAccess supports.
- **Java Package:** A Java package name is a directory path that uses the period (.) instead of a slash (\) to separate components of the path. This path identifies the location of the template string tables. Unless you are an HTML developer and creating your own custom templates, you will not need to modify this path.
- **Images URL:** This is the path under the Web server's document root directory where the images that you see from the WebAccess client are located. These images are *.GIF files; they make up the icons and buttons that you see from the browser.
- **Applets URL:** This identifies the path to the WebAccess applets. This should be blank unless you have moved the applets to a different server. You would then enter the path to another root directory. The default location of applets is beneath the Web server's document root directory.
- **Help URL:** This is the path under the Web server's document root directory where the help HTML files are located. If WebAccess users want to pull up the online help, they are directed to the INDEX.HTM file.

TIP

Under this help directory, there is a subdirectory that represents the language that the user is using. For example, if the language is English, you will see an EN **directory under the** HELP **directory, which would contain the INDEX.HTM. You could then create your own help files, if desired.**

- **Enable Template Caching:** This option allows the WebAccess Application to cache the templates in RAM the first time they are used. This increases performance. Keep these settings intact.
- **Cache Size:** This value determines how much RAM the Web server will use to cache the templates. You can increase the template caching to 4,000KB, which is my preference. Setting the cache beyond that is probably just a waste of memory.

- **Default Language:** This identifies the default language that will be presented to users when they reach your Web server's home page and you have selected to use the default WebAccess home page.
- **Define User Interfaces:** Clicking this button allows you to set up custom user interfaces. This is useful when your users are using different types of devices to access their mailboxes. More about this in Chapter 24.

Application/Security Property Page

- **Timeout for inactive sessions:** This setting allows you to configure how many minutes of inactivity must pass before a user's connection becomes disconnected from the application. The WebAccess Application does not tie up too many resources maintaining a WebAccess client session. I suggest changing the timeout to 60 minutes.
- **Path for inactive sessions:** Imagine that you were in the middle of composing an email from the WebAccess client and were interrupted for several minutes. The inactive session timeout value kicks in, and you get disconnected. The WebAccess Application saves your session before disconnecting. When you come back and reauthenticate to WebAccess, you can resume your email.
- **Use client IP in securing sessions:** If this option is checked, the WebAccess Application uses the client's IP address to help construct the hash value used to identify the user's browser session within the WebAccess Application. Be aware, however, that if a user's browser is configured to use a proxy server, there is a chance that the proxy server can use different IP addresses during the same session. This would cause *invalid hash errors* to appear on the WebAccess Application. If you see this type of problem, you will want to disable this option. The GroupWise 6.5 WebAccess Application handles session security through the use of cookies. The only reason you would need to check this option is if users access GroupWise WebAccess through a browser that does not accept cookies.

WARNING

AOL users usually have difficulties using GroupWise WebAccess if you enabled Use Client IP in Securing Sessions. The AOL client relies heavily upon proxy servers, and so a user's session with the WebAccess Application can change often as their proxy server's IP address changes.

Application/Settings Property Page

This page, shown in Figure 11.15, is where you enable or disable options that users will see from the WebAccess client. If you disable them, that particular option's interface will be missing for all WebAccess users accessing this particular WebAccess Application.

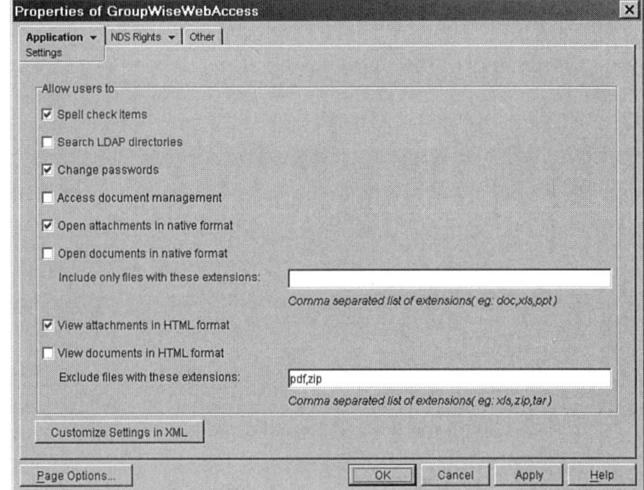

FIGURE 11.15 Application/Templates property page, where options such as the LDAP directory search has been disabled.

- **Spell check items:** Here you can either enable or disable the user's ability to spell check newly composed email messages before sending them.
- **Search LDAP directories:** If this is disabled, users will not be able to search the admin-defined LDAP servers for email addresses. If you do not have an LDAP address book for your users to search (most people don't), there's really no reason to have the LDAP address book capability show up in the WebAccess client address book. In the example shown in Figure 11.15, the LDAP directory search has been disabled. More about setting up LDAP servers in the upcoming section "Configuring an LDAP Address Book for WebAccess."
- **Change passwords:** This allows users to change their GroupWise master mailbox password from WebAccess. Be aware that if LDAP is enabled, and you are using Novell's eDirectory as your LDAP server, when users change their password here, they are changing their eDirectory password also. This is really slick when you think of it. Conceivably, your users can change their eDirectory authentication from their WAP-enabled cell phones.

- **Access document management:** This option controls user access to documents from within GroupWise libraries. Some organizations want users to access document management only from a GroupWise 32-bit client. This is the case at WorldWide Widgets. In the example Settings page shown in Figure 11.15, the capability to view documents from WebAccess is disabled.
- **Open attachments in native format:** This setting governs whether users can open attachments from their browsers. Their Web browser needs to be able to determine the file type, and then launch the document into the associated application. Some browsers do a better job of this than other browsers. I recommend checking this option.
- **Open documents in native format:** This has to do with GroupWise document management. Most customers, even those using document management, will want to disable this check box. Opening a document from document management in the WebAccess client can cause version-control issues.
- **Include only these file extensions:** By filling in this field you can specify just what kinds of files users have an option to open. The users can always save the file to their own computer and try and open it there.
- **View attachments in HTML format:** This option is useful if you do not want to give users the ability to view attachments from within WebAccess. It removes the view option from mail with attachments when they read them. You can allow users to open the attachments in their native applications, though. Personally I think it is a good thing to allow users to view attachments in HTML format, but not all attachment types. Fortunately, there's a place where you can exclude certain document types; read on!
- **View documents in HTML format:** This option performs the same functionality as the preceding function. If you disable this option, yet document management is enabled, users can view the document in HTML format.
- **Exclude files with these extensions:** This setting allows you to exclude files such as *.PDF files (which are better viewed from Acrobat reader) from HTML viewing.

TIP

The WebAccess Agent gets really bogged down when trying to render complex, large files into HTML. By excluding certain file types—PDF, ZIP, and XLS—your WebAccess Agent will have less work to do, which is helpful if your WebAccess Agent is already busy.

- **Customize Settings in XML:** This button launches an XML editor that can be used to modify the settings on the WebAccess Application. There are several settings that you can enable or disable through this interface. For example, if you want to disable the calendar functions from a WebAccess Application, you can do so from this interface. Or you might want to set a limit on the size of attachments that are viewable through the WebAccess Application. This can be done by changing the <Novell><WebAccess><Application><Attribute Name><Document.View.maxSize> setting. The default value is 1MB. I like this setting; however if you want to increase this setting beyond 1MB you can. If a file exceeds the View.maxSize setting, the users cannot view the document, but they can save the file and then launch it in the native application.

NovellSpeller Object

The `NovellSpeller` object basically represents the GroupWise speller servlet object. It is created when you install the WebAccess Application object. The speller servlet object automatically starts when the Web server loads the WebAccess Application.

Application/Log Settings Property Page

From here, you can configure the log settings for the speller. Rarely will you need to look at the speller's log files.

Application/Environment Property Page

This is really the only thing that you can configure on the speller object, other than the logging.

- **Configuration File:** This is the path to the spell checker's configuration file. It is a text file and contains all of the configuration information regarding the spell checker.
- **Dictionary Path:** This is the path to the dictionary files that contain the word lists and suggestions when spell checking.

- **Maximum Suggestions:** Here you can enter the maximum number of suggestions to give when a misspelled word is encountered during a spell check.
- **Customize Settings in XML:** Here you can also modify these settings from the included XML configuration editor.

That's all the settings available for the speller object. Most customers will not need to make any changes to the speller object.

GroupWiseProvider Object

The `GroupWiseProvider` object works in conjunction with the GroupWise WebAccess object or the WebAccess Application. Think of it as the actual transport provider that is responsible for carrying the data between the WebAccess Agent and the WebAccess Application. This might sound a bit confusing because the entire chapter notes that the GroupWise WebAccess Application talks directly to the WebAccess Agent. Basically it does, but for administration purposes and future support for additional features in WebAccess, it has been broken into providers.

A user's Web browser talks to a servlet running on the Web server. This servlet functions as the default WebAccess Application. The Application then looks up which providers it has access to and hands the request over to the appropriate provider. This all happens on the same server. There is not an actual separate program that acts as the provider; it is all bundled into the WebAccess Application but it acts as a separate, configurable subprocess of the WebAccess Application. The provider then communicates directly to the agent. If you think of it this way, it will be much easier to understand how the provider objects relate to the WebAccess Application or servlets.

GroupWiseProvider/Environment Property Page

Configuring the GroupWise provider object is really quite simple and straightforward. The following properties of the GroupWise provider object can be configured:

- **Timeout for Busy Search:** This value sets the number of minutes that the provider waits when performing a busy search to the WebAccess Agent. This allows the administrator to control how soon busy searches are cancelled through the WebAccess client.

NOTE

A busy search is a feature that allows you to check when other GroupWise users are available so you can schedule an appointment with them through the GroupWise calendar.

- **Configuration File:** This simply points to the COMMGR.CFG file that the provider uses to determine where the WebAccess Agent is (the IP address and port) and how to encrypt the data in transit using the encryption key embedded in the COMMGR.CFG file.
- **GroupWise WebAccess Agents:** This is where you list all of the WebAccess Agents that the provider will be able to communicate with. You must have at least one agent defined here, but you can have multiple agents. This gives you a level of fault tolerance in regards to the WebAccess Agent. More information regarding fault tolerance with WebAccess is discussed in the section titled "Configuring GroupWise WebAccess for More Scalability and Stability."

The GroupWise Provider object is most useful when used for the fault-tolerance capabilities of WebAccess.

LDAPProvider Object

The `LDAPProvider` object basically serves the same function as the `GroupWiseProvider` object; the WebAccess Application sends requests for LDAP lookups to it, and then the LDAP provider looks up and hands the results back to the GroupWise WebAccess object. The `LDAPProvider` object does *not* communicate with the WebAccess Agent like the `GroupWiseProvider` object does. Instead, it queries whatever LDAP servers have been configured for lookups directly.

Following is an explanation of the settings you can configure on the LDAPProverider object:

- **Configuration File:** This points to the path of the LDAP configuration file. This is a text file that contains all the configuration information for the LDAP provider. This file contains the settings for the LDAP servers, for example.
- **LDAP Servers:** This lists the configured LDAP servers that would be available to search from the WebAccess client. In the upcoming section, "Configuring an LDAP Address Book for WebAccess," you learn how to set up additional LDAP services.
- **Customize Settings in XML:** Once again, you can configure these settings from the XML configuration editor, if desired.

You should now be comfortable configuring most of the aspects of the WebAccess gateway, including the WebAccess Agent and Application. In future sections, you'll learn how to leverage these settings to create a highly reliable, and scalable, GroupWise WebAccess gateway for your environment.

Understanding the GroupWise WebAccess Console

This section discusses the options seen when you view the WebAccess console. This section goes through each statistic; they help you understand the status of the WebAccess Agent. Figure 11.16 shows the WebAccess Agent console for a WebAccess Agent running on the NetWare platform.

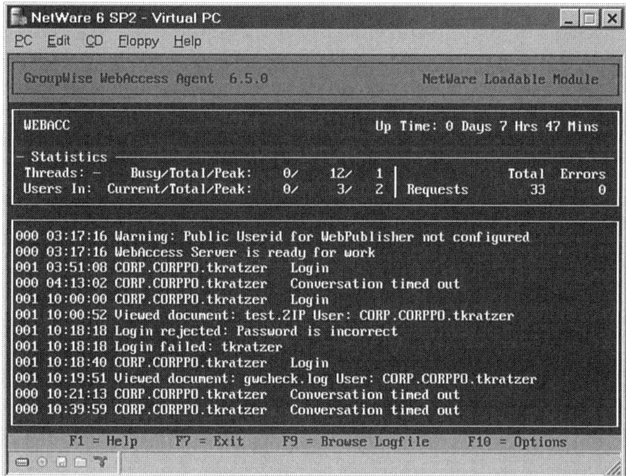

FIGURE 11.16
The WebAccess Agent console screen on NetWare is a great place to look when troubleshooting the WebAccess Agent.

Following is an explanation of the interface of the GroupWise WebAccess Agent running on the NetWare platform:

- **Threads:** Here are some of the most valuable statistics you can gather from the WebAccess Agent. There are three thread values here. The *Busy* value represents how many WebAccess threads are currently in use. The *Total* value represents how many total threads are available to service requests. This is the maximum number of threads available. The *Peak* value represents the maximum number of concurrent threads that have been active at the same time.
- **Users In:** There are three values here as well. The *Current* value lists the number of currently logged in users at this moment in time. The

Total value is the total number of users who have logged in since the agent has been up. (Up time is indicated in the upper-right corner of the WebAccess Agent.) The *Peak* value represents the maximum number of users logged in at the same time.

- **Requests:** There are two statistics here. The *Total Requests* value represents how many requests have come into the WebAccess Agent since it has been up. The *Errors* value shows how many errors have occurred since the agent has been up. You can view the log files to determine which errors occurred. In the upcoming section, "Monitoring GroupWise WebAccess Through a Web Browser," you will learn how to search these log files.
- **Logging Box**: This is the window directly under the Statistics window, and it displays the activity on the WebAccess Agent. The far left value represents the thread number that is performing the task. Next is the time that the event occurred, and last is the information associated with the particular request being logged. The logging level determines how much information is displayed here.
- **F9 = Browse Logfile**: Pressing F9 from the agent console screen brings up a static copy of the current log file. Notice that at the beginning of each log file is the basic configuration information of the agent. It might be helpful information to verify which settings the agent is using.
- **F10 = Options**: Pressing F10 brings up a dialog box with two options: View Log files and Logging Options. If you select to view log files here, you are given a list of all the log files that the WebAccess Agent has created over a period of time. You can select any of the log files and view their contents. If you select the Logging Options option, you can change the current log settings that the agent is using. These log settings will be discussed further in the upcoming section, "Understanding the GroupWise WebAccess Log Files."

TIP

When you change these log settings here, they are active only during the timeframe that the WebAccess Agent is up and running. When the WebAccess Agent is restarted, it will pick up the log settings from either the startup file or the setting defined through the properties of the WebAccess Agent object in ConsoleOne.

If you are running the WebAccess Agent on Windows NT, the console screen is different. You do have some function keys that help to control the console screen from within Windows. Here are the commands you can issue from the console when running on Windows NT/2000. Note that these commands are not available when running the agent as a service:

- **F1 or F7:** Pressing F1 or F7 from the agent screen will exit the WebAccess Agent.
- **F2:** Pressing F2 will cycle the log level on the WebAccess Agent. The available levels are normal (default), verbose, and diagnostic. Normal is usually adequate unless you are troubleshooting a particular problem with the agent and need additional logging information.

TIP

Using F2 to set the log level is active only as long as the WebAccess Agent is up. If it is restarted, the log level is set to the option defined in either the startup file or in the WPDOMAIN.DB file through ConsoleOne.

- **F12:** Pressing F12 will display the statistics and thread activity of the agent. This is the same thread information that you get from the agent when it is running on NetWare as an NLM. The values mean the same thing. It also gives you the current log level, whether disk logging is enabled, and the name of the current log file.

As you can see, there are not a lot of different statistics or configuration pieces to the WebAccess Agent compared to some of the other agents or gateways.

Understanding the GroupWise WebAccess Log Files

This section explains how to access and understand the different log files that are generated by the components that make up the WebAccess gateway. Generated log files can be invaluable in troubleshooting and resolving problems with any GroupWise component, not just WebAccess. The log files are generated by the following pieces of the GroupWise WebAccess gateway:

- WebAccess Agent
- WebAccess Application
- WebAccess speller application
- WebPublisher application

To begin with, here's a definition of some of the standard logging settings that most of the components in WebAccess share:

- **Log File Path:** This defines the path where the log files will be located for a particular Agent or Application. For the WebAccess Agent it is important that you specify a location for the log file in ConsoleOne. If you do not do so, the WebAccess Agent will write to a log file.
- **Logging Level:** This setting defines the logging level for the Agent or Application. The valid settings are generally normal (default), verbose, diagnostics, and off. The higher the level of logging, the more detailed the log files will be. Diagnostic logging should be used only when you're troubleshooting a problem and you need very detailed information as to what is happening at the particular agent or application level. You should not run diagnostic logging as a standard practice. Normal or verbose will suffice. I prefer verbose logging on the WebAccess Agent.
- **Max Log File Age:** This setting allows you to set the number of days that log files will be kept. If, say, this is set to seven days (the default), when a log file reaches an age of seven days, the Agent or Application will automatically delete this log file. I like to increase this setting to around 30 days if possible, because you never know when you might need to dig back through a few weeks' worth of log files to help track down and troubleshoot problems.
- **Max Log Disk Space:** This setting determines how much disk space all the log files for a particular Agent or Application can consume. It is *not* how large a single log file can be. All the individual log files will be 256KB in size, and then the Agent or Application will cycle into another log file. As mentioned, this setting allows you to control how much disk space is used by the log files. I like to increase this setting. It depends on your environment as to how large you set this value. I have seen systems where 10MB worth of logs would keep only a couple of days' worth because of the volume of information that was being generated. You will want to take a baseline of your system to see which value works best for your environment.

Therefore, whatever setting is reached first—be it the max log file age or the max log disk space setting—will take precedence over the other. Having these two settings together allows you to completely control how many and how long the log files stick around for your WebAccess processes. Now that you understand some of the shared characteristics of logging on the WebAccess processes, the following discussion points out the differences between the different processes.

WebAccess Agent Log Settings

By default, the WebAccess Agent does not generate a log file to disk. You must enable this option by adding the `/logdiskon` switch to the STRTWEB.NCF file, or by defining a path to the log files on the WebAccess Agent object. This will enable disk logging for the WebAccess Agent. Without this switch or a defined path to the log files, the WebAccess Agent will not log to disk any events. The default location of the WebAccess Agent log files is the `<DOMAIN>\WPGATE\<WEBACCESS>\000.PRC` directory, but you can change this with the log file path setting on the agent.

There are also startup switches that allow you to set all the logging options from the command line when the agent is loaded. These switches are contained in the Agent startup file if you are running 6.5.1 or later code or in the STRTWEB.NCF file if you are running 6.5.0 code. You can modify the following switches:

- `/log=`: The path to the log files.
- `/logdiskon`: Enables disk logging.
- `/loglevel=`: Sets the log level. Values are normal, verbose, and diagnostic.
- `/logdays=`: Sets the number of days to keep logs. Enter a number that represents days.
- `/logmax=`: Sets the size of log files. Enter a size in kilobytes.

Even with all the possibilities, I still recommend that you configure these settings from ConsoleOne, and not from the startup file of the WebAccess Agent.

GroupWise WebAccess Object Log Settings

The GroupWise WebAccess object log settings, or in other words, the WebAccess Application settings, are configured by going to the properties of the GroupWise WebAccess object and selecting Application/Log Settings.

Notice that here you have a few additional options besides the standard settings:

- **Log Language:** This allows you to define the language that the log files are written in.
- **Log Time Format:** This allows you to change the format of the time value displayed in the log file. The default is H:mm:ss for

Hour:Minute:Second. If desired, you can change this order. You have the option of adding MM/dd or dd/MM for Month/Day or Day/Month to the logging, which might be useful.

TIP **The name of each WebAccess Application log file will be in the format of MMDDWAS.*XXX*, where *XXX* is an incremented number throughout a 24-hour time period. The agent always cycles to a new log at 24:00 hours.**

WebAccess Speller Application

Configuring the speller log settings is similar to configuring the agent and application log settings. This can be done by going to the properties of the `NovellSpeller` object in eDirectory. For this agent, you do not have the options of setting the max log disk space and max log file age, however.

WebAccess WebPublisher Application

The WebAccess WebPublisher log settings are exactly the same as the GroupWise WebAccess object settings.

Configuring GroupWise WebAccess for More Scalability and Stability

For this section, the topic centers on shoring up and making the WebAccess system more scalable and fault tolerant. With only one WebAccess Application and Agent running, users would be unable to access their mailboxes through WebAccess if either of these components fails. With multiple agents set up and being serviced by multiple applications, the overall WebAccess availability will be greatly enhanced. It also allows you to bring down pieces of the WebAccess system, without interrupting all access to user's mailboxes. This is useful for upgrades, or for maintenance on anything from the GroupWise system to servers to applications running on the servers. This section begins by discussing what is involved in getting multiple agents and application services working together.

Configuring Multiple Agents and Application Servers for a Fault-Tolerant WebAccess System

With the introduction of GroupWise 6.X WebAccess, administrators can set up multiple agents and applications that all work together. This section explores how to configure a single application to talk to multiple agents. It also discusses how configuring multiple agents can provide a fault-tolerant WebAccess system. With a simple install of WebAccess, you have only one WebAccess Application talking to a single WebAccess Agent. There is very little that changes when you consider setting up multiple applications talking to multiple agents. Consider the following example scenario that discusses how to make it all work together.

You want to have the WebAccess Application on your Web server communicate with two WebAccess Agents. These agents are installed in close proximity to the two major sections of your WAN. In this scenario, you will see how to configure and set this up.

Before explaining exactly how to configure and set up this scenario, it is very important that you understand how a WebAccess Application determines which agent or agents it should communicate with. When there is more than one WebAccess Agent installed in your GroupWise system, the application must check to see which agent the user should be directed to. Chapter 5, "Working with GroupWise Objects," mentioned that you can configure a default WebAccess object for a domain or post office. Configuring a default WebAccess setting on users' domains or post offices is critical to setting up multiple agents in a GroupWise system. Here is the order that the application will check in order to determine which WebAccess Agent to log a particular user to:

1. If there is an agent specified in the URL field that is entered when a request reaches the Web server where the WebAccess Application is running, the Application performs no lookups and sends the user request directly to the agent that was defined in the URL. An example of how this URL might look like is the following:

   ```
   http://groupwise.wwwidgets.com/servlet/webacc?GWAP.ip=137.
   65.55.211&GWAP.port=7205
   ```

   The IP address would reflect the IP address of the server where the WebAccess Agent is running, and the port is the port the WebAccess Agent is listening on.

2. If there was no agent defined in the URL, the application performs a lookup to determine if there is a default WebAccess defined at this user's post office. If so, the user is routed to this agent.
3. If there was no default WebAccess defined at the user's post office, a lookup is performed on the user's domain for a defined default WebAccess object. If one is found here, the user is routed to this agent.
4. If there was no default WebAccess Agent defined at the domain, the application will look at the service provider that it is associated with and route the user to the first agent defined in the GroupWiseProvider's "GroupWise WebAccess Agents" list.
5. If there are no defined agents for the service provider, the application will read the COMMGR.CFG file located in the `SYS:\NOVELL\WEBACCESS` directory and route the request to this agent.

This list not only supplies the application with the information about which agent to send the user to but also which agents to fail over to if any agents are down. For example, if there were a default WebAccess Agent defined at the domain level, but it was unavailable, the application would then roll over to the next lookup method, which would be the agents defined at the service provider level, and send the request to the first agent there. If this agent were down, it would cycle to the next defined agent for the service provider, if there were one. If none of the defined agents for the service provider is accessible, the last resort is to check the agent listed inside the COMMGR.CFG file. If this agent is down, the user cannot log in.

Phew, that is quite a process! The next section breaks all this process down into a few scenarios to make sure you understand how the lookup/failover model works.

Lookup/Failover List: Scenario 1

Presume that you have three agents installed in your GroupWise system, all being serviced by one application:

DEFINITION	WEBACCESS AGENT
Entered URL	No agent defined in URL `groupwise.wwwidgets.com`
Post office	Agent 1 defined as the default agent for this post office
Domain	No agent defined

DEFINITION	WEBACCESS AGENT
Agents defined at GroupWiseProvider object on the Environment property page:	Agent 1 & 2COMMGR.CFG file has a reference to Agent 3

With this configuration, when a user logs in, the application builds a list of WebAccess Agents that it uses to send the user's request to. If any of these agents are down, the application cycles to the next agent in the list. The following table shows what the application builds in regards to which agent this user should be sent/failed over to:

APPLICATION LIST VALUE	GENERATED FROM
Agent 1	Post office definition
Agent 2	Service provider list
Agent 3	COMMGR.CFG file

Because there is an agent defined for the user's post office (Agent 1), this is the first agent that the application tries to access. If this agent is down, it sends the user to the first agent listed in the service provider's list (Agent 2). If both of these agents are down, it sends the request to the agent listed in the COMMGR.CFG file.

NOTE

Technically there are two agents listed at the service provider list in this example (Agent 1 and Agent 2). Because the Application finds the same Agent twice (Agent 1) from the post office override and the service provider list, it removes the entry to Agent 1 found at the service provider level. The Application does not list or use the same agent multiple times in this situation.

Lookup/Failover List: Scenario 2

Assume that you have four agents installed in your GroupWise system, all being serviced by one application:

DEFINITION	WEBACCESS AGENT
Entered URL	No agent defined in URL `webmail.worldwidewidgets.com`
Post office	No default agent defined for the post office
Domain	Agent 2 is defined as the default agent for this domain
Agents defined at GroupWiseProvider object on the Environment property page:	Agent 1 & 3COMMGR.CFG file has a reference to Agent 4

Using the preceding table, the following table shows what the application builds in regards to which agent this user should be sent/failed over to.

APPLICATION LIST VALUE	GENERATED FROM
Agent 2	Domain agent definition
Agent 1	Service provider list
Agent 3	Service provider list
Agent 4	COMMGR.CFG file

In this scenario, the user does not experience any interruption of service unless all four agents go down. If Agent 2 fails, the application automatically rolls the user over to Agent 1 and so on. With this information, you should carefully plan how you define the agents that the users are directed to. With the understanding you now have, you should be able to design a very reliable WebAccess system.

There's one more additional little piece that is important. How does the application know whether there is a default WebAccess Agent defined at the domain or post office level? This information is not stored on the Web server, and the application was never designed to talk directly to a GroupWise domain database to discover this information. Here is what happens.

In order to build the list of agents when a user logs in, the application must determine whether there is a default WebAccess gateway defined at the domain or post office level for the user. When the user ID and password are entered at the login page for WebAccess, the application sends this information to the service provider, and the service provider contacts any one of the agents listed in the "GroupWise WebAccess Agents" list. The WebAccess Application tries these agents in a round-robin fashion. It then queries the agent to look in the domain database for a default WebAccess Agent defined at either the post office or domain level. This agent then returns the results to the application through the service provider. Now that the application knows whether the user has a default WebAccess Agent defined, it can build the correct list of agents to route the user to.

Now that you understand the lookup and failover model, the following section explains how to configure this type of setup.

Matching Encryption Keys

In order for a single WebAccess Application to be able to talk to multiple agents, the encryption key between the application and all agents it communicates with *must* be the same. The WebAccess Application will read the COMMGR.CFG file located by default in the `\NOVELL\WEBACCESS` directory of the Web server. Remember that this COMMGR.CFG file contains the encryption key that must match the encryption key stored in the COMMGR.CFG file located in the `<DOMAIN>\WPGATE\<WEBACCESS>` directory for *each* of the WebAccess Agents. The easiest way to facilitate seamless communication from the application to each agent is to make the encryption key the same for all agents that a single WebAccess Application will be configured to talk to. (A simple copy-and-paste procedure works great.) This is done by editing the WebAccess Agent that is directly associated with a particular GroupWise domain and accessing the WebAccess settings. Figure 11.17 shows this screen.

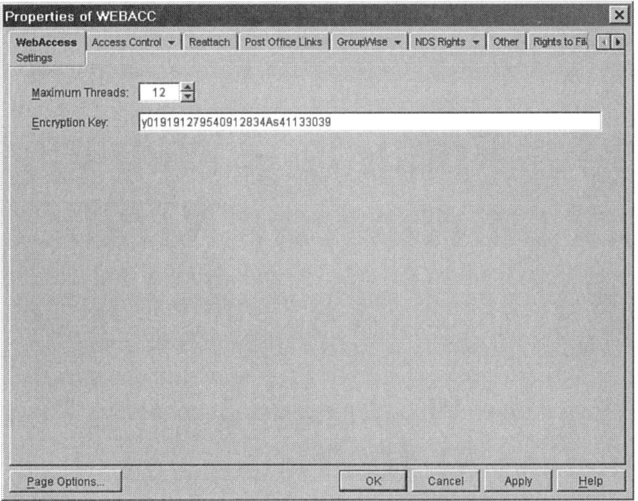

FIGURE 11.17
Editing the WebAccess encryption key.

From here, you should enter the same encryption key on all agents. This will update the COMMGR.CFG file on both the Web Access Application and Agent directories.

Configuring the Default WebAccess Agents for a Domain or Post Office

To configure a default WebAccess Agent at the domain or post office level, you need to access the properties of the respective domain or post office object. From the respective property pages, choose the GroupWise, Default WebAccess properties page. From here, you click the override box in order to browse through the eDirectory tree and select the appropriate WebAccess Agent object.

To configure the agents known by the service provider, you need to access the GroupWise provider object's property page. From here, you can add, edit, or delete any WebAccess Agents from the list. You can also move any agent up or down on the list to change the order that they are accessed from the application. Remember that the application will start at the top of this list and work down when it builds its login/failover table for use when a user logs in.

You need to double-check that the WebAccess Application object has the correct WebAccess provider so that it knows which provider to use to look up the agents. This provider is configured by going to the details of the GroupWise WebAccess object and selecting the services option under the Application tab. From there, you can add, edit, or delete providers that are defined in your tree.

Tips for Running a WebAccess Agent on Windows NT/2000

The following sections offer several tips for running the GroupWise WebAccess Agent on the Windows server platform.

Installing the WebAccess Agent to Run on Windows NT/2000

This procedure assumes that you are installing the WebAccess Agent on a Windows server platform.

The Novell client for Windows NT/2000 must be installed to the Windows NT/2000 server in order to be successful. After installing and configuring the new GroupWise domain and WebAccess Agent components, you can remove the Novell client for Windows 2000/NT. If you do not establish a GroupWise domain on the Windows 2000/NT server, you must keep the Novell client installed.

I recommend that before installing the GroupWise WebAccess Agent for Windows NT/2000, when possible, the WPDOMAIN.DB file should be on the hard drive of the Windows NT server that will be running the Windows NT WebAccess Agent. To do this, you must first install a GroupWise domain to the Windows NT/2000 server.

Installing a GroupWise Domain on a Windows NT/2000 Server

Follow these steps to install a GroupWise domain on an NT/2000 server:

1. Log in to your Novell eDirectory tree where your GroupWise system is installed using the Novell client, as well as at the Windows NT/2000 server that you will be configuring to run the GroupWise WebAccess Agent for Windows NT/2000. Also, install ConsoleOne with the GroupWise 6.5 snap-ins to ConsoleOne to the local C: drive of the Windows server.
2. Connect to the primary domain for your GroupWise system.
3. Create a new directory that will hold the WPDOMAIN.DB file on the Windows server. Next you should share this directory. By doing this, you can define a UNC path to the new WPDOMAIN.DB file that you will be creating on this server. For example, if my server name is `WIN2K1` and I wanted the new domain to be placed in the `C:\NTDOM1` directory on the Windows server, I would have a UNC path of `\\WIN2K1\NTDOM1`, which I would use in step 4 to define the path to the domain database.
4. Create a new GroupWise domain by highlighting the GroupWise system object, right-clicking, and choosing New, Domain. Establish the domain on the hard drive of the Windows NT server, located in the share you created in step 3.
5. When the domain is created, choose Tools, GroupWise System Operations, Select Domain from ConsoleOne. Make sure that you are connected to the WPDOMAIN.DB file on the hard drive of the Windows NT server.
6. Install the GroupWise MTA software for the Windows NT/2000 platform.

This software is located in the `<GroupWise 6.5 software distribution directory>\AGENTS` folder.

7. Load the GroupWise MTA for your newly created GroupWise domain on the Windows NT/2000 server.

   Make sure that the MTA is communicating with the rest of the GroupWise system.

TIP **If you are installing the agent as a service on Windows 2000, the WPDOMAIN.DB file is *not* located on the hard drive of the Windows 2000 server, but on a NetWare server, so you must have service pack 2 for Windows 2000 installed.**

This section explained how to create a GroupWise domain on a Windows server. You do this in order to fulfill the ideal that the GroupWise WebAccess Agent have local access to the WPDOMAIN.DB file for the domain it is configured under.

Installing a GroupWise WebAccess Agent on a Windows NT/2000 Server

This section walks you through installing a WebAccess Agent on an NT/2000 server:

1. Run SETUP.EXE from the `INTERNET\WEBACCES` directory on the GroupWise 6.5 CD or the GroupWise 6.5 SDD, and accept the license agreement.
2. Install just the WebAccess Agent and click Next.
3. Now select the platform, which will be Windows NT.

   If you need to modify that path for the agent files, you can do so here and then click Next. When you click Next, you will be prompted to create the directory if it does not exist. You will also be prompted to shut down any agents running on this Windows NT box.

TIP **The NT install does not attempt to stop any GroupWise agents that are running on the NT server. You must manually perform this operation to shut down all GroupWise agents on the NT server.**

You are then prompted to enter the IP address or DNS name of the NT server. The install will try to discover this information for you. It's the static IP address that is assigned to the NT server. If you are installing the agent to a Windows NT workstation, you must obtain a static IP address for the workstation.

4. Enter or verify the IP address or DNS name, as well as the port, and click Next.

   You then are prompted to enter the path to the domain database and define a gateway directory. If you created a domain on the local hard drive as explained earlier in this chapter, you will want to specify the path on the local NT server. You can accept the default gateway directory of WEBAC65A or enter a different gateway directory here.

NOTE

The gateway directory name must not be longer than eight characters.

5. Enter the correct path and gateway directory and click Next.
6. Next you will define the name of the WebAccess Agent object. This is the object that represents the gateway in eDirectory. It defaults to the same name as was entered in step 5 for the WebAccess directory name. It is recommended that this name be the same as the directory name. Verify or enter the object name and click Next.
7. This next step is the first big difference between a NetWare install and a Windows install. You are asked whether you want to install and configure SNMP support for the WebAccess Agent, as well as whether you want to run the agent as a Windows service. If you enable the option to install SNMP support, the install allows the agent to be monitored via SNMP. If you want to run the agent as a service, you must select how the service will be configured for startup. The default is to automatically start the WebAccess Agent service. The advantages of running the agent as a service is that it will load automatically when the Windows NT box is booted up.

   Select the appropriate options and click next.
8. If installing as a service, you are then asked to enter a username and password. This username and password allow the service to log into the Windows NT box in order to load. The install script does not allow you to use the system account for the service. If you are not installing as a service, this question is not asked.

TIP

If you get the error stating that the username you're using does not have service logon rights, this indicates a bug in the original shipping GroupWise 6.5 software. Upgrade to the latest support pack to resolve this problem.

   If you get this prompt, enter a username and password of a user who has rights to this particular NT server.

If the WPDOMAIN.DB file is located on a different server than the NT box, for example on a NetWare server, this username and password must be the same on the Windows and eDirectory accounts.

9. You now get the option to enable the WebConsole for the WebAccess Agent. I recommend skipping this screen, and entering the information from ConsoleOne instead.
10. Install the WebPublisher support if you desire, and then click Next.
11. At the summary screen, review the information about how the agent will be installed, and click Next.

The agent will begin copying the necessary agent files. The last thing that the install will do is create the eDirectory object for the WebAccess Agent under the domain object. You must have access to the eDirectory tree from the workstation you are running the install from. If you do not, you will be prompted with an eDirectory login screen during this portion of the install. You will need to log in to complete the install.

Starting the GroupWise WebAccess Agent Service for Windows NT/2000

There are two approaches to starting the agent when it is running on Windows NT. If you installed the agent as a service, you must start and stop the agent using the services manager. To access Windows NT services, open the control panel and select the services option. This displays all available services on the local NT box. You should see a service called WebAccess *<name of your agent>*. Just highlight this service, and you will be able to start or stop it. You can also configure how this service will start by default. Your options are Manual (you must manually load the agent), Automatically (the service will start with the Windows NT box is booted), or Disabled (the service will be disabled and cannot be started until enabled).

When you run the WebAccess Agent as a service, elements such as the home path are stored in the Windows Registry, so there is no STRTWEB.BAT file as there is if you did not install the WebAccess Agent as a service. Windows simply reads the appropriate information regarding the WebAccess Agent service in order to load the agent.

NOTE

Beginning with GroupWise 6.5 service pack 1 (6.5.1), the WebAccess Agent on NT uses a startup file. This is where all the settings for WebAccess are stored. They are no longer stored in the Windows Registry. The name of the startup file is the name of the WebAccess Agent with a .waa extension.

Starting the GroupWise WebAccess Agent from a Batch File

If when you installed your WebAccess Agent, you did not install it as a service, the WebAccess Agent is started with a batch file. This file is found in the `C:\WEBACC` directory (or the directory specified during the install of the agent). You will find a file called STRTWEB.BAT. Following is a sample of a default STRTWEB.BAT file:

```
title Novell GroupWise WebAccess
@echo off
cls
GWINTER.EXE /ph=D:\WINDOM\WPGATE\GW65NT
```

Starting the agent when running on Windows NT is as simple as running this batch file. You can modify this batch file to include additional switches, if desired. You might also want to add this batch file to the startup folder on the Windows NT server. This will cause the agent to start automatically *after* a user is logged into the NT server.

TIP

Even if you installed the WebAccess Agent as a Windows service, this STRTWEB.BAT file still exists in the `C:\WEBACC` directory. If you shut down the service, you can manually load the WebAccess Agent with this batch file. Doing so will let you see the WebAccess Agent console.

You should now be familiar with how to start both the NetWare and NT versions of the WebAccess Agent.

Configuring an LDAP Address Book for WebAccess

This section explains how to configure an LDAP address book. From the address book, the user can perform LDAP lookups on predefined LDAP servers. As an administrator, you have the flexibility of defining additional LDAP servers, thus allowing users to query LDAP compliant servers for addresses. The GroupWise Windows 32-bit client gives users the ability to define LDAP address books, and so this functionality has also been added to the GroupWise WebAccess client. By default, there are two LDAP servers created when the WebAccess Application is installed. They are the popular public LDAP servers *BigFoot* and *SwitchBoard*.

You configure additional LDAP servers through the LDAP provider object. This object was created when the WebAccess Application was installed. Figure 11.18 shows the details of the LDAP provider object.

FIGURE 11.18
The GroupWise WebAccess LDAP provider object details.

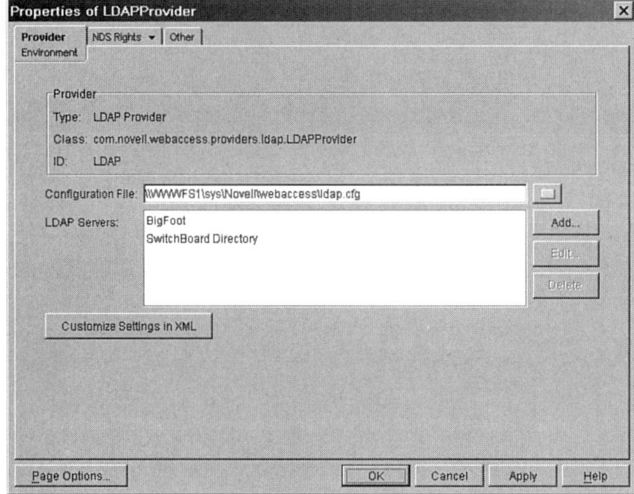

Here you will see the two default LDAP servers. You are presented with a configuration screen that allows you to set up the new LDAP server. When you select the Edit or Add buttons, you'll see the following options:

- **Name:** Enter the name of the LDAP server. This is the name that the user will see when selecting an LDAP server to search from the WebAccess client.
- **Server:** Enter the DNS name or IP address of the server that is servicing LDAP requests from clients.
- **Port:** The standard LDAP port is `389`. If the LDAP server that you are defining has been configured to use a different port, you should modify this field. If not, keep the default port.
- **Maximum Results:** Enter the maximum number of results that can be returned to the WebAccess client from the LDAP server. The default is `100`.
- **Timeout:** The timeout value here represents how long the LDAP provider will wait on the configured LDAP server for a reply. The default is 30 seconds
- **Search Base:** Enter the search base value here. LDAP servers allow you to configure a search base that sets limits on how many objects can be searched. When the LDAP server was set up, there should have

been a search base defined. This search base should match the search base defined on the LDAP server.

- **Image URL:** This is the path to the image file that you would like displayed to represent the particular LDAP server you are defining. This path must be defined off the root of the Web server's `DOCS` directory. For the NetScape Enterprise Web server, this would be the `SYS:\NOVONYX\SUITESPOT\DOCS` directory. If using the NetScape Enterprise Web server and your GIF representing the LDAP server is physically located at `SYS:\NOVONYX\SUITESPOT\DOCS\COM\NOVELL\WEBACCESS\IMAGES\YOURPIC.GIF`, the image URL would be `/COM/NOVELL/WEBACCESS/IMAGES/YOUPIC.GIF`.
- **Web URL:** This is where users are sent if they click on the image defined in the Image URL: value. This is a nice way to link a Web site to the LDAP server graphic.
- **Username:** Enter the LDAP username that must be used to authenticate to the LDAP server you are defining. Some LDAP servers do not require authentication.
- **Password:** Enter the LDAP username's password here. This allows the LDAP provider object to authenticate to the LDAP server and perform the query, if necessary.
- **Define Field Mappings:** Click this option to set up field mappings. If your LDAP server is configured to return additional values for each user, you can map these fields to fields that will be displayed in the WebAccess client.

  If you need to add additional field mappings, click Add. This will add a row where you can then type in the LDAP and local fields.

This section spoke of how to create additional LDAP address books that are then available within the GroupWise WebAccess address book.

Monitoring GroupWise WebAccess Through a Web Browser

This section discusses the options for monitoring your WebAccess system through any standard PC-based Web browser. You have been able to monitor the WebAccess Agent since GroupWise 5.5. Enhancement Pack was released. However, you have not been able to monitor the GroupWise WebAccess Application from a Web browser until GroupWise 6.5 support pack 1 (6.5.1). This section discusses how to monitor both the WebAccess Agent and the WebAccess Application.

Monitoring the Agent from a Web Browser

In order to have this functionality, the WebAccess Agent must be enabled to allow HTTP monitoring. This can be done during the install, with startup switches, or by modifying the WebAccess Agent object from ConsoleOne (which is my preference).

Once you have the HTTP monitoring enabled for a WebAccess Agent, you can browse to the agent using a Web browser and the following syntax: `http://<server IP or DNS address>:<http port>`. For example, `http://groupwise.wwwidgets.com:7211`.

You will be prompted with the HTTP username and password that you configured for the GroupWise WebAccess Agent. Figure 11.19 shows a WebAccess Agent that is being monitored from a Web browser.

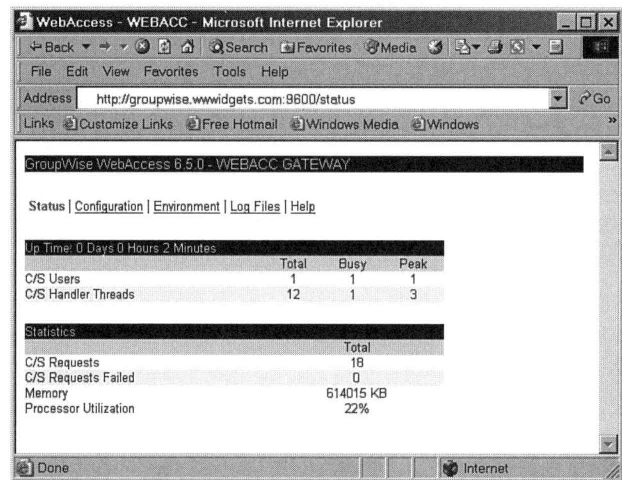

FIGURE 11.19 Monitoring GroupWise WebAccess through a Web browser.

Here's an explanation of some of the information shown in Figure 11.19:

- **Status:** The status page shows you the current status of the WebAccess Agent. Here you can get a good idea of how the WebAccess Agent is performing. Notice under the Statistics section that you can view how much memory the server has as well as the current processor utilization of the server.

If the agent is running on an NT server, you do not get the processor utilization reading.

- **Configuration:** The configuration tab shows you the current configuration of the WebAccess Agent. This is helpful if you need to check how the WebAccess Agent is configured. You can quickly check all configuration settings here.
- **Environment:** The Environment tab shows you different options depending on which platform your agent is running on—NetWare versus Windows. The NetWare Environment tab shows you the following information in regards to the server configuration:

Server	WWWFS1
Company	Novell
O.S. Revision	NetWare 5.60.02
O.S. Date	July 10, 2002
Memory	614015
Processor utilization	5%
Supported connections	31
Connections in use	1
Clib version	5.6
Receive buffer max	5000

It also shows all loaded modules on the NetWare server.

If you look at the Environment tab when the agent is running on Windows NT, you get the following server configuration information:

Company	Microsoft
O.S. Revision	Windows NT 5.0 Build 2195 Service Pack 2
Memory	523744KB

Also, you get just the WebAccess components that are loaded on the Windows server.

- **Log Files:** The Log Files tab allows you to view the contents of the WebAccess log files. You will see a list of all agent log files. You can highlight any one and select View Log to see the entire contents of that particular log file. If disk logging is not enabled, you cannot view any logs, because there are not any.

This section spoke of how to configure HTTP monitoring of the GroupWise WebAccess Agent. The next section explains how to configure HTTP monitoring of the WebAccess Application.

Monitoring the Application from a Web Browser

As previously mentioned, you could not monitor the WebAccess Application prior to GroupWise 6.5.1 code. However, with the introduction of GroupWise 6.5.1, you can now monitor the WebAccess Application from a Web browser. This is extremely helpful in identifying who is using your WebAccess system, and there is a wealth of information that you can obtain from monitoring the WebAccess Application through a Web browser. If you are not running GroupWise 6.5.1 or later on your Application, this section is not an option for your environment.

By default, the Application does not have HTTP monitoring enabled, so you must manually enable this service. This is accomplished by performing the following steps:

1. Edit the WEBACC.CFG file found in the `SYS:\NOVELL\WEBACCESS` directory with any text editor.

NOTE

You might see several WEBACC.CFG.X files in this directory as well. These are backup copies of the WEBACC.CFG file. You are interested in the WEBACC.CFG file, as this is the file that the Application reads for its configuration information.

2. Identify the following section of this file:

```
#Application Administration Tool
# Invoked on the URL
# (e.g. http://<server>/servlet/webacc?action=Admin.Open)
############################################################
Admin.WebConsole.enable=false
Admin.WebConsole.username=admin
Admin.WebConsole.password=admin
```

3. Change the line that reads `Admin.WebConsole.enable=false` to `Admin.WebConsole.enable=True`.
4. Change the username from `admin` to a username of your choosing in the `Admin.WebConsole.username=` field. This is not an eDirectory or a GroupWise userID, and is strictly used for monitoring the WebAccess Application.

5. Change the password from `admin` to a unique password in the `Admin.WebConsole.password=` field. This password should be very secure. Make it at least eight characters long and include numbers, punctuation marks, and letters. The reason for using such a hard-to-guess password is that there is no intruder detection here, and anyone can access the `/servlet/webacc` page of your WebAccess system if they guess the username and password. So in the interest of security, please change the default user and password values from `admin` to something that you are comfortable with.
6. Shut down the WebAccess Application and restart it.

TIP

If you are running the Application on NetWare 6 or newer with the Tomcat33 servlet engine, you can simply issue the following commands on the NetWare server console:

```
Java -killall
Java -exit
Tomcat33
```

This will shut down just the servlet engine and then restart it.

7. Now you are ready to access the HTTP interface of your Application. You do this by using the following URL:

   ```
   /servlet/webacc?action=Admin.Open
   ```

   Notice that all you need to do is access the signin page of your WebAccess server, which places you at the *`yourserversDNSName/`* `servlet/webacc`. You then add the `?action=Admin.Open` to the end of your URL.
8. You are then prompted for the user and password that you defined in the WEBACC.CFG file in steps 4 and 5. Enter this information, and you will then access the HTTP monitoring of the WebAccess Application. Figure 11.20 shows what you might see.

Here's an explanation of some of the information shown in Figure 11.20.

- **Status:** The status page will display information about all users who have logged into WebAccess from this particular Application. You can see the date and time that the user logged in, as well as the last time they communicated with the Application. This can be helpful to identify users who use WebAccess the most, and stay connected for long periods of time. You can also see their client IP address of their browser, their `UserID.PostOffice.Domain`, and the WebAccess Agent version that is currently servicing this user. You can also see which browser the user is using to access WebAccess. This can be great to identify users who are using PDAs or WAP devices. It can also be used to identify any new browsers. You can also sort on any of these columns. This is great if you want to see all the users who are accessing a particular agent, or to see who has logged in the most.

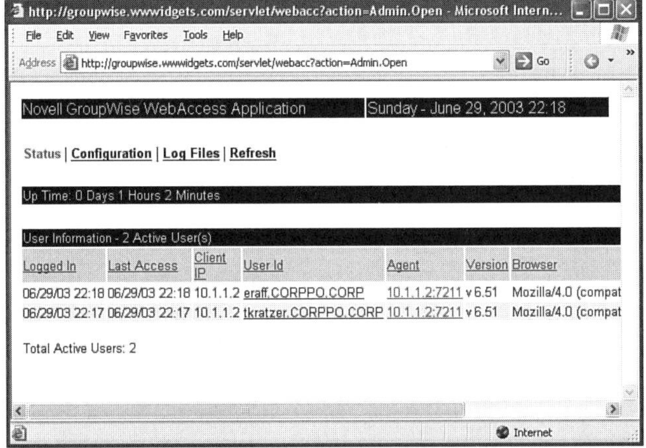

FIGURE 11.20 Monitoring GroupWise WebAccess Application through a Web browser.

If you click on a user who is logged in, you will be taken to a page that will display detailed information about this user. You can see which templates the user is using, the language they are running in, as well as the list of WebAccess Agents that the Application can fail over to for this particular user. You can easily see exactly which agent the user is currently talking to, and which agent they will fail over to in case the current agent has a problem. The * in the Using column indicates which Agent the user is currently communicating with. Figure 11.21 shows an example of this.

- **Configuration:** The Configuration tab displays information about the version of Application you are running, and how the Application is currently configured. You get Java vendor information on your Java servlet as well. You can also view all of the Applications configuration files in a read-only mode. This is great if you need to quickly see how something is configured.
- **Log Files:** The Log Files link allows you to view the logs of the WebAccess Application. This is very useful to see which agents the

Application could not communicate with, or other errors that occurred at the Application.

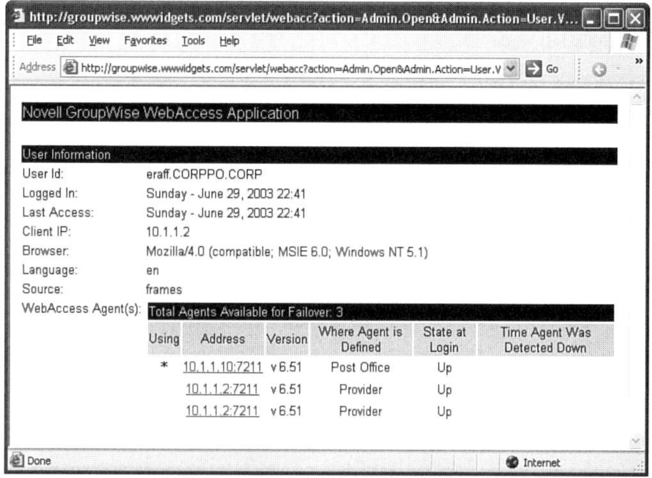

FIGURE 11.21
Viewing a user through the WebAccess Application monitor.

There you have it; you now have several excellent tools to monitor the current state of your WebAccess system. The ability to monitor the Application is well worth the upgrade to 6.5.1 code. There are so many useful applications in this upgrade.

Advanced Installation Options for WebAccess

This section discusses some of the more complex and advanced installation options in WebAccess. These might not apply to your environment, but should be useful for many of the GroupWise administrators out there.

Distributed Installation Concepts

To begin with, it is important to review a few of the concepts to a distributed install for WebAccess. Distributed installation entails having the WebAccess Application installed on one server and the agent(s) installed on different servers. It can also mean having multiple WebAccess Applications throughout an organization. In a nutshell, think of this as having options about how to set up a large enterprise WebAccess solution.

Also, keep in mind that GroupWise 6.5 gives you the capability to have one entry point via a WebAccess Application that will talk to multiple agents. You can also configure GroupWise domains and post offices to have a preferred WebAccess Agent. This will come into play when you configure which agents will service which users.

Installing Additional WebAccess Agents

The procedure to install additional WebAccess Agents is the same as the one used to install the WebAccess gateway—see the section "Installing the GroupWise WebAccess Gateway," earlier in this chapter. You only need to follow the part of the section that talks about installing the WebAccess Agent. Also, make sure the encryption key on the newly installed WebAccess Agent matches the encryption key on all the other WebAccess Agents. When you run the GroupWise WebAccess installation, do not install the GroupWise WebAccess Application. You will need to manually start the GroupWise WebAccess Agent, which you learned how to do in the section titled "Loading the GroupWise WebAccess Agent and Application." The installation summary shows you a text file that contains all the settings that you entered during the install wizard. If you leave the option Start the GroupWise WebAccess Agent selected, the install script will load the WebAccess Agent for you if desired.

Changing the GroupWise WebAccess Login Experience

This section talks about what the user sees and experiences before actually seeing the mailbox from the WebAccess client. This section also covers the options for accessing WebAccess by entering additional information on WebAccess' URL line.

To begin with, there are many ways that you can design access into a user's mailbox through WebAccess. Here is a list of the more common approaches I've seen:

- You can have the user simply enter a URL into a browser in order to access the language page for WebAccess. Once here, the user selects the language and then is prompted for a GroupWise username and password.

- You can skip the language page altogether and send the user directly to the username and password page.
- You can configure your WebAccess system so that users must enter a generic username and password in order to get to the username and password screen of WebAccess. This might help to deter would-be hackers from trying to guess GroupWise usernames and passwords.
- You can send users to a company welcome page with FAQs and information about WebAccess on it. From here, users would click some sort of link to get to the WebAccess username and password screen.

As you can imagine, there are many ways to determine what users see before they actually get to their mailboxes. The important thing to remember is that the last thing users must see in order to access their mailboxes from WebAccess is the login page. This is where they will enter their GroupWise usernames and passwords. In order to get to this login page, the user must get to the following type of URL:

```
http(s)://<your Web server DNS Name>/servlet/webacc
```

Once users get here, they enter their user IDs and passwords and are logged into their GroupWise accounts.

The following URL provides some additional information to help determine how to set up access into users' mailboxes through WebAccess:

```
http://yourserverhere/servlet/webacc?GWAP.ip=10.1.1.1&GWAP.port=
7205&User.lang=en
```

This URL directs the browser to use a specific agent located at the IP address `10.1.1.1` using port `7205`, and to specify English as the language.

```
http://yourserverhere/servlet/webacc?User.interface=Simple
```

This URL forces the WebAccess Application to use the simple HTML templates to deliver the content to the browser. This can be helpful for testing purposes. If users were using a very slow link, you might want to add this as a link from a main page. WebAccess is a bit quicker when the simple templates are used compared to the default frames.

You will see that after the `/servlet/webacc` you must begin the operands with a `?` (question mark). Then you separate each operand with an `&`

(ampersand). Knowing this, you can string together something like the following:

```
http://yourserverhere/servlet/webacc?GWAP.ip=10.1.1.1&GWAP.
➥port=7205&User.lang=en&User.interface=Simple
```

NOTE

These URL examples are case sensitive. You cannot enter `user.lang` **or** `user.interface=simple` **and have it work.**

Skipping the GroupWise WebAccess Language Page

When you install the WebAccess Application and replace the existing default Web page, you are prompted to select your language when you log in to WebAccess. In many cases, you might want to simply skip this language page and send users directly to the login page.

If you are planning on setting up a Web page that gives users a jumping-off point before they get to the login page, it is very simple to skip the language page. For example, say you want the users to get a welcome HTML page that includes company information or information about how to use the WebAccess system. You simply add a link to the default HTML page that points to the WebAccess Application running on your Web server. When you define the link into WebAccess, it would look something like this:

```
http://<your Web server's DNS name>/servlet/webacc
```

Because you specified the actual servlet that WebAccess is using, you skip the language page. The users enter their usernames and passwords and are directed to the correct or default WebAccess Agent.

Tuning Apache and Tomcat on NetWare 6.x

There are two issues I have run into using Apache and the Tomcat servlet gateway. Following are my notes on functions that you can tweak.

Increasing Java Memory

I've noticed the following issue for customers that install GroupWise WebAccess to a NetWare 6.x server. The Tomcat servlet gateway uses a lot of Java's resources, and Java gets tapped out on memory. You might find that users get an error `Error 500 java.lang.OutOfMemoryError`. This happens when there are many users using GroupWise WebAccess. By default, Java can use a maximum of 64MB. This is often too small. The maximum amount of memory that Java can use on the NetWare 6.0x platform, in comparison, is 450MB.

Assume your WebAccess Application is running on a server with 750MB of memory and the server is dedicated to just running the WebAccess Application on top of the Tomcat servlet gateway and the Apache Web server. Allow Java to take 128MB of RAM by default, and allow the Java memory to increase to 350MB when needed. Here is what must be done:

1. Bring down any Java processes with the following commands:

```
JAVA -KILLALL
       Wait about 10 seconds
JAVA -EXIT
```

2. Edit the *.NCF file that loads Java. In most cases, this will be the TOMCAT33.NCF file. This file is typically located in the `SYS:TOMCAT\33\BIN` directory. Find the line that loads Java; it might look something like this:

```
java -envCWD=$TOMCAT_HOME -classpath $TOMCAT_CLASSPATH -
➥Dtomcat.home=SYS:\tomcat\33 org.apache.tomcat.startup.Main -f
➥sys:/tomcat/33/conf/nwserver.xml %1
```

Add the `-Xms<NNN>m -Xmx<NNN>m` arguments just after the `java` statement. For example `-Xms128m -Xmx350m`. Here's an example:

```
java -Xms128m -Xmx350m -envCWD=$TOMCAT_HOME -classpath
➥$TOMCAT_CLASSPATH -Dtomcat.home=SYS:\tomcat\33 org.apache.
➥tomcat.startup.Main -f sys:/tomcat/33/conf/nwserver.xml %1
```

4. Load TOMCAT again. You typically type **TOMCAT33** at the NetWare system console prompt to load it.

Now Java is loaded with 128MB allocated, and 350MB available.

Resolving Page Cannot Be Displayed Errors with Microsoft Internet Explorer

It is likely that your WebAccess Microsoft IE users will experience "Page Cannot Be Displayed" errors. Typically, the users will get this error when sending a large attachment, or when viewing a large attachment. Your MSIE users will only experience this problem when your WebAccess runs from an Apache Web server.

To resolve this issue, do the following:

1. Edit the *.CONF file for your Apache Web server.
2. Add the following three lines to the *.CONF file, either at the beginning or the end of the *.CONF file.

```
BrowserMatch "MSIE 6\." nokeepalive downgrade-1.0 force-
response-1.0
BrowserMatch "MSIE 5\." nokeepalive downgrade-1.0 force-
response-1.0
BrowserMatch "MSIE 4\." nokeepalive downgrade-1.0 force-
response-1.0
```

3. Bring the Apache Web server down. Then bring the Web server back up. This is necessary to get Apache to reread its *.CONF file.

Best Practices

In this section, I share some tips that I have learned through trial and error that will help you to better design or set up and maintain the WebAccess system:

- **Keep WebAccess Agents as close to users as possible.** In other words, if you have a domain across a WAN link, it's best to install a WebAccess Agent under this domain, and then define this WebAccess Agent as the preferred agent for this domain.
- **Keep the agent on the same server as the GroupWise domain.**
- **Configure your Web server to support SSL.** Chapter 27 explains how to do this for an Apache Web server on the NetWare 6 platform.
- **Monitor closely how heavily the WebAccess Agent is being used.** You might need to increase the thread count to provide suitable performance for users.

I wrote an Novell Appnote in December of 2002 called "Implementing a High Availability WebAccess Solution with GroupWise 6". This article has even more tips for making the GroupWise WebAccess solution stable. The solution is compatible with GroupWise 6.5.

Novell Appnotes are available on the Internet at `http://www.novell.com/appnotes`.

Summary

This chapter discussed many of the aspects of the WebAccess system. By reading and studying this chapter, you should be able to successfully implement a robust and scalable WebAccess system. You will also be able to successfully monitor and identify how your WebAccess system is being used, and by whom. By understanding some of the underlying concepts related to how the WebAccess system works, you will also have the knowledge to provide solutions in your environment for users needing access to their GroupWise mailboxes from any Web browser. Chapter 24 closely ties to this chapter, because GroupWise wireless piggybacks GroupWise WebAccess.

CHAPTER 12

Administering the GroupWise Client

The GroupWise client is the user piece of the GroupWise system. It provides access to the user mailbox, documents in libraries, and archive and remote mailboxes. It offers the user tools for creating rules, sharing folders and address books, and of course doing all of those things normally associated with e-mail.

The GroupWise client also offers some tools that can be considered administrative, especially when document libraries are concerned. These include mass-change operations on documents. For that matter, any operation that makes use of a user's administrator-assigned *manage right* to a library is going to be performed from the GroupWise client.

This chapter covers administration of the GroupWise 32-bit Windows client. Specifically, this chapter looks at deploying and updating the client, and administering logins and client options.

Understanding the GroupWise Windows Client Installation Process

The GroupWise 6.5 client is installed from the GroupWise 6.5 Client CD or from the `CLIENT\WIN32` directory of the GroupWise 6.5 Software Distribution Directory (SDD). With some configuration the GroupWise client can be installed from a Web server. The user runs SETUP.EXE, and the familiar InstallShield setup program interface appears, walking the user through the process of installing the client. By default, the installation process prompts the user for several kinds of installation decisions the user might not be prepared to make. This chapter discusses how to remove the prompts that require users to make installation decisions.

NOTE **The GroupWise 6.5 32-bit Windows client runs on the following platforms: Windows 98, Windows Me, Windows NT/2000, and Windows XP. GroupWise WebAccess is also a GroupWise client. The GroupWise WebAccess and wireless client solutions help GroupWise to support practically any major platform.**

Here are five ways that you can have the GroupWise client installed:

- Distribute the GroupWise client via ZENWorks.
- Install the GroupWise client by running SETUP.EXE from the GroupWise 6.5 Client CD.
- Install the GroupWise client by running SETUP.EXE from a GroupWise SDD.
- Distribute one small executable called SETUPIP.EXE to users and have them run it from their workstations.
- Upgrade the GroupWise client either via SETUP.EXE when users have rights to the Software Distribution Directory (SDD) or via SETUPIP.EXE when users do not have rights to the SDD.

NOTE **There is a way to distribute the GroupWise Messenger client along with the GroupWise 6.5 Windows client. You'll learn about GroupWise Messenger in Chapter 29, "Configuring a GroupWise Messenger (Instant Messaging) System," which provides instructions on how to roll out the GroupWise Messenger client along with the GroupWise Windows client.**

Distributing the GroupWise Client via ZENWorks

If your organization has implemented ZENWorks, distributing the GroupWise 6.5 client can be pretty sweet. With ZENWorks, you can just push down an image of GroupWise 6.5, configured in just the manner you want.

The *.AOT files needed to roll out the GroupWise client are located in the following locations:

- The GroupWise 6.5 Client CD in the `CLIENT\ZEN` directory
- The GroupWise 6.5 SDD in the `CLIENT\ZEN` directory

Installing the GroupWise Client from CD

You can create a GroupWise 6.5 Client CD that practically mirrors the GroupWise 6.5 Client CD. However, it is recommended that you make some changes. With these changes you can accomplish the following desired effects:

- The users will place the CD in their CD-ROM drives.
- The GroupWise Installation will kick off automatically (as long as the users have not disabled auto-run). Otherwise, users must run the SETUP.EXE at the root of the CD. Users will not be prompted with any installation questions.

The next section discusses a scenario regarding the installation requirements, and then will show you how to configure the SETUP.CFG based upon those goals.

Installation Requirements Scenario

Following are the requirements of this GroupWise client installation scenario:

- The default IP address and port for a Post Office Agent (POA) in the system will be indicated.
- Users should not be prompted to answer any installation questions.
- GroupWise Notify will be placed in the Windows startup group.
- Document integration will be disabled.
- Users will not be prompted for the language to install; the only language supported by this company is US English.
- All other factory defaults are accepted.

Follow these steps to make a GroupWise 6.5 Client CD:

1. Copy the entire contents of a GroupWise 6.5 Client CD to a location on your local hard drive called `CLIENTCD`.
2. Go to the `CLIENTCD\CLIENT` directory. Locate the SETUP.CFG file and copy it to the `CLIENTCD\CLIENT\WIN32` directory.

3. Locate the SETUP.CFG file that you copied to the `CLIENTCD\CLIENT\WIN32` directory. Edit the properties of the file in Windows Explorer, and remove the read-only attribute.
4. Use Windows Notepad to edit the SETUP.CFG file; you should configure the SETUP.CFG and the SETUP.INI files as explained in the next section.

SETUP.CFG and SETUP.INI Changes

In the SETUP.CFG and SETUP.INI files, make the following changes according to the scenario outlined earlier:

1. To specify the default IP address and port, remove the semicolon from the following arguments in the SETUP.CFG file: `DefaultIPAddress=x.x.x.x` and `DefaultIPPort=xxxx`. Configure them with the IP address and port of a GroupWise POA in the GroupWise System. For example

```
DefaultIPAddress=155.123.178.16
DefaultIPPort=1677
```

TIP

It might be desirable to define a DNS name for the `DefaultIPAddress` that is publicly resolvable and accessible. When doing this, you will be assured that no matter where the GroupWise client is installed from, the client can find a POA in your organization and log in. You must also configure the public IP address to point to a POA. This can easily be done using Network Address Translation (NAT) from the public address to an internal private address. This concept ties back to the proxy server option discussed in Chapter 8, "Configuring the Post Office Agent (POA)."

2. To ensure that users will not be prompted with installation questions, change the line that reads `HideAllDialogs=No` to `HideAllDialogs=Yes`.
3. To place Notify in the Windows startup group, find the line that reads `Notify=No` and change it to `Notify=Yes`.
4. To turn off Document Integration, find the section that reads `[IntegrationApps]`. After the name of each application containing a `=Yes`, change it to `=No`. For example

```
Lotus WordPro=No
Microsoft Binder=No
Microsoft Excel=No
```

And so on.

5. By default, the GroupWise Client CD has GroupWise configured to install the English client. However, users are still prompted as to which language to install. In order to remove this prompt, locate the SETUP.INI file, found in the `C:\CLIENTCD\CLIENT\WIN32` directory. Edit the properties of the file in Windows Explorer, and remove the read-only attribute. Edit the SETUP.INI file, and find the line that reads `EnableLangDlg=Y`. Change it to read `EnableLangDlg=N`.

Test this installation by running the SETUP.EXE file in the `C:\CLIENTCD` directory. If the installation behaves in the manner you expect, burn the CD as described next. If it does not behave in the manner you expect, tweak the SETUP.CFG file as needed.

Burn a CD with the contents of the `CLIENTCD` directory at the root of the CD-ROM. At the root of the CD-ROM directory there will not be a `GWCLIENT` directory; there instead will be two files—AUTORUN.INF and SETUP.EXE. There will also be a folder called `CLIENT`.

Installing the GroupWise Client by Running SETUP.EXE from a Network Drive

Your users can run the SETUP.EXE file from a GroupWise 6.5 SDD, but when they do so, they are confronted with a lot of questions that they might not know how to answer. It is best to design your GroupWise client installation in such a manner that users do not need to answer any questions regarding what to install and where to install it.

The following section discusses a scenario regarding the installation requirements, and then shows you how to configure the SETUP.CFG and SETUP.INI files based upon those goals.

Installation Requirements Scenario

Following are the requirements of this GroupWise client installation scenario:

- The default IP address and port for a POA in the system will be indicated.
- Users should not be prompted to answer any installation questions.
- Notify will be placed in the Windows startup group.
- Document integration will be disabled.

- Users will not be prompted for the language to install; the only language supported by this company is US English.
- All other factory defaults are accepted.

Following are the steps to configuring the GroupWise client installation according to the example scenario:

1. Go to the `<SDD>\CLIENT` directory. Locate the SETUP.CFG file and copy it to the `<SDD>\CLIENT\WIN32` directory.
2. Locate the SETUP.CFG file that you copied to the `<SDD>\CLIENT\WIN32` directory. Edit the properties of the file in Windows Explorer, and remove the read-only attribute, if necessary.
3. Use Windows Notepad to edit the SETUP.CFG file.
4. In the SETUP.CFG and SETUP.INI files, make the following changes according to the scenario outlined earlier:
   - To specify the default IP address and port, remove the semicolon from the following arguments in the SETUP.CFG file: `DefaultIPAddress=x.x.x.x` and `DefaultIPPort=xxxx`. Configure them with the IP address and port of a GroupWise POA in the GroupWise system. For example

```
DefaultIPAddress=155.123.178.16
DefaultIPPort=1677
```

TIP

It might be desirable to define a DNS name for the `DefaultIPAddress` that is publicly resolvable and accessible. This way, you can be assured that no matter where the GroupWise client is installed from, the client will be able to find a POA in your organization, and log in. If doing this, you must also configure the public IP address to point to a POA. This can easily be done using Network Address Translation (NAT) from the public address to an internal private address. This concept ties back to the proxy server option discussed in Chapter 8.

   - To ensure that users will not be prompted with installation questions, change the line that reads `HideAllDialogs=No` to `HideAllDialogs=Yes`.
   - To place Notify in the Windows startup group, find the line that reads `Notify=No` and change it to `Notify=Yes`.
   - To turn off Document Integration, find the section that reads `[IntegrationApps]`. After the name of each application that contains a `=Yes`, change this to `=No`. For example

```
Lotus WordPro=No
Microsoft Binder=No
Microsoft Excel=No
```

And so on.

- By default, the GroupWise Client CD has GroupWise configured to install the English language. However, users are still prompted as to which language to install. In order to remove this prompt, find the SETUP.INI file, which is in the `<SDD>\CLIENT\WIN32` directory. Edit the properties of the file in Windows Explorer, and remove the read-only attribute, if necessary. Edit the SETUP.INI file by finding the line that reads `EnableLangDlg=Y` and changing it to `EnableLangDlg=N`.

5. Test this installation by running the SETUP.EXE file in the `<SDD>\CLIENT\WIN32` directory. If the installation behaves in the manner you expect, proceed to the next step. If it does not behave in the manner you expect it to, tweak the SETUP.CFG file as needed.
6. Allow your users network rights to the `<SDD>\CLIENT` directory and subdirectories. Do not allow your users to have rights to the `<SDD>` directory or any of its (well, other subdirectories other than the `\CLIENT` directory and its subdirectories).
7. Have your users run the SETUP.EXE file from the `<SDD>\CLIENT\WIN32` directory. You can also tell the SETUP.EXE file to execute from a Novell Client login script.

Distribute one small executable called SETUPIP.EXE to users and have them run it from their workstations. (The WRITEIP.EXE utility mentioned in this section is located on the GroupWise client CD-ROM in the \SETUPIP directory.)

Distributing the GroupWise Client via SETUPIP

This section assumes you are using GroupWise 6.5 Support Pack 1 or better.

Installing the GroupWise client by distributing the SETUPIP.EXE utility has distinct advantages. One of the advantages is that users do not need access rights to a network drive in order to install their GroupWise clients. This is particularly helpful for customers that are no longer deploying the Novell

Windows client. Another advantage to SETUPIP is that software to be installed is compressed, and so installation runs faster over WAN links.

NOTE **You must have a Web server of some sort. The Web server must allow connections on port 80, the standard HTTP port.**

Your users can run the SETUPIP.EXE file, but when they do so, they are confronted with a lot of questions that they might not know how to answer. It is best to design your GroupWise client installation in such a manner that users do not need to answer any questions regarding what to install and where to install it.

Here is a scenario with a set of installation requirements, and the way in which you should configure the SETUP.CFG and SETUP.INI files based upon these goals:

The following are requirements of this scenario:

- The default IP address and port for a POA in the system will be indicated.
- Users should not be prompted to answer any installation questions.
- Notify will be placed in the Windows startup group.
- Document integration will be disabled.
- Users will not be prompted for the language to install; the only language supported by this company is US English.
- All other factory defaults for the installation are accepted.

1. Go to the `<SDD>\CLIENT` directory. Locate the SETUP.CFG file and copy it to the `<SDD>\CLIENT\WIN32` directory.
2. Locate the SETUP.CFG file that you copied to the `<SDD>\CLIENT\WIN32` directory. Edit the properties of the file in Windows Explorer, and remove the read-only attribute if necessary.
3. Use Windows Notepad to edit the SETUP.CFG file.
4. In the SETUP.CFG and SETUP.INI files, make the following changes according to the scenario outlined earlier:
   - To specify the default IP address and port, remove the semicolon from the following arguments in the SETUP.CFG file: `DefaultIPAddress=x.x.x.x` and `DefaultIPPort=xxxx`. Configure them with the IP address and port of a GroupWise POA in the GroupWise system. For example

```
DefaultIPAddress=155.123.178.16
DefaultIPPort=1677
```

TIP

It might be desirable to define a DNS name for the `DefaultIPAddress` that is publicly resolvable and accessible. You will then be assured that no matter where the GroupWise client is installed from, the client will be able to find a POA in your organization, and log in. You must also configure the public IP address to point to a POA. This can easily be done using Network Address Translation (NAT) from the public address to an internal private address. This concept ties back to the proxy server option discussed in Chapter 8.

- To ensure that your users are not prompted with installation questions, change the line that reads `HideAllDialogs=No` to `HideAllDialogs=Yes`.
- To place Notify in the Windows startup group, find the line that reads `Notify=No` and change it to `Notify=Yes`.
- To turn off Document Integration, find the section that reads `[IntegrationApps]`. After the name of each application that contains a `=Yes`, change them to `=No`. For example

  ```
  Lotus WordPro=No
  Microsoft Binder=No
  Microsoft Excel=No
  ```

  And so on.
- By default, the GroupWise Client CD has GroupWise configured to install the English language. However, users are still prompted as to which language to install. In order to remove this prompt, locate the SETUP.INI file, found in the `<SDD>\CLIENT\WIN32` directory. Edit the properties of the file in Windows Explorer, and remove the read-only attribute, if necessary. Edit the SETUP.INI file. Find the line that reads `EnableLangDlg=Y` and change it to `EnableLangDlg=N`.

You still have a little ways to go, but to confirm that your SETUP.CFG and SETUP.INI files are configured correctly, run the SETUP.EXE file in the `<SDD>\CLIENT\WIN32` directory. If the installation behaves in the manner you expect, proceed to the next section. If it does not behave in the manner you expect, tweak the SETUP.CFG file as needed.

Configuring the NetWare Enterprise (Novonyx) Web Server

The next step is to configure your Web server to support SETUPIP. The following are instructions for NetWare Enterprise, Apache on NetWare, and then generic instructions for configuring all other Web servers:

1. Create an empty GroupWise client directory structure under the document root directory of the Novonyx Web server.
2. Locate the document root directory called `SYS:NOVONYX\SUITESPOT\DOCS`.
3. Create a GroupWise Client Distribution Directory by the name of `GWCLIENT` within the document root directory. The path to this directory is `SYS:NOVONYX\SUITESPOT\DOCS\GWCLIENT`. This directory must match the directory you defined in the WRITEIP.EXE utility.

NOTE **The case of the directory name does not matter (`gwclient` vs. `GWCLIENT`).**

4. Create a directory within the `GWCLIENT` directory called `WIN32`. The entire path to this directory is `SYS:NOVONYX\SUITESPOT\DOCS\GWCLIENT\WIN32`.

Now it is time to add the compressed GroupWise client (SETUPIP.FIL) and the GroupWise English language file (SETUPIP.US). You also need to implement the configuration files (SETUP.CFG and SETUP.INI) in the GroupWise Client directory structure on the NetWare Enterprise (Novonyx) Web server.

1. In your SDD, locate the `ADMIN\UTILITY\SETUPIP` directory.
2. Copy the SETUPIP.FIL and SETUPIP.US files from `ADMIN\UTILITY\SETUPIP` to the `SYS:NOVONYX\SUITESPOT\DOCS\GWCLIENT` directory.
3. In your post office-specific SDD, locate the file called SETUP.CFG. This file is generally in the `CLIENT` directory or the `CLIENT\WIN32` directory. In this example post office, it's in the `GW65SDD\CLIENT\WIN32` directory.
4. Copy the SETUP.CFG file to the `SYS:NOVONYX\SUITESPOT\DOCS\GWCLIENT\WIN32` directory.
5. Make sure this SETUP.CFG file is configured correctly according to the technical directives explained earlier.
6. From the post office-specific SDD, copy the `<SDD>\CLIENT\WIN32\SETUP.INI` file to `SYS:NOVONYX\SUITESPOT\DOCS\GWCLIENT\WIN32`.

7. Make sure this SETUP.INI file is configured correctly to not prompt for the language, as explained earlier in this section.

Now that you've configured your NetWare Enterprise (Novonyx) Web server, skip through the rest of the Web server configuration information, and go to the section in this chapter titled "Creating a SETUPIP.EXE File."

Configuring the Apache Web Server for NetWare

The instructions for this procedure are based upon using an Apache Web server on a NetWare 6 server. You should configure your Apache Web server to support Fancy Indexing by following these steps:

> **NOTE**
> **Even if Fancy Indexing is already enabled, taking the following steps will not cause problems if you already have it enabled.**

1. With Windows Notepad or a similar text editor, edit the *.CONF file of your Apache Web server. The default *.CONF file for Apache is called ADMINSERV.CONF. These instructions assume that your *.CONF file is called ADMINSERV.CONF. Just substitute your own *.CONF name any time the ADMINSERV.CONF file is mentioned.

> **NOTE**
> **The *.CONF file for your Apache Web server could have a different name. For example, if you have installed the GroupWise WebAccess Application to this Web server, Apache might be using the file GWAPACHE.CONF as its configuration file. To determine the *.CONF configuration file that your Apache Web server is using, look at the *.NCF file that you use to load Apache Web server.**

2. At either the very beginning or the very end of the ADMINSERV.CONF file, add the following three lines (syntax and case are important).

```
<IfModule mod_autoindex.c>
IndexOptions FancyIndexing
</IfModule>
```

3. Restart your Apache Web server so that it reads the `FancyIndexing` parameter.

The next step is to create an empty GroupWise client directory structure under the document root directory of the Apache Web server. Follow these steps:

1. Determine the document root directory of your Apache server. By default, with NetWare 6 Apache Web server it is `SYS:APACHE\NWDOCS`. It can also be `SYS:APACHE\HTDOCS` or possibly even something else. When Apache is loaded into protected memory, the document root directory by default is `HTDOCS` unless specified otherwise. If you are not sure which directory is your document root directory, just search in your Apache Web server's *.CONF file for the string `"DocumentRoot"`. If no `DocumentRoot` value is specified, and Apache is loaded into a protected memory space, the document root directory is the `SYS:APACHE\HTDOCS` directory. If Apache is not loaded into protected memory, and the `DocumentRoot` is not specified, the document root folder is `SYS:APACHE\NWDOCS`.
2. Create a GroupWise Client Distribution Directory by the name of `GWCLIENT` within the document root directory. For example, if the document root directory is `NWDOCS`, the path to this directory is `SYS:APACHE\NWDOCS\GWCLIENT`.

NOTE **The case of the directory name does not matter (`gwclient` vs. `GWCLIENT`).**

3. Create a directory within the `GWCLIENT` directory called `WIN32`. For example, if the document root directory is `NWDOCS`, the path to this directory is `SYS:APACHE\NWDOCS\GWCLIENT\WIN32`.

Next, you must add the compressed GroupWise client (SETUPIP.FIL and SETUPIP.US) and setup configuration files (SETUP.CFG and SETUP.INI) to the GroupWise Client directory structure on the Apache Web server. The following steps detail how to do this:

1. In your SDD, locate the `ADMIN\UTILITY\SETUPIP` directory.
2. Copy the SETUPIP.FIL and SETUPIP.US files from `ADMIN\UTILITY\SETUPIP` to `SYS:APACHE\NWDOCS\GWCLIENT`.
3. In the post office's SDD, locate the file called SETUP.CFG. This file is generally in the `CLIENT` directory or the `CLIENT\WIN32` directory.
4. Copy the SETUP.CFG file to the `SYS:APACHE\NWDOCS\GWCLIENT\WIN32` directory.
5. Make sure this SETUP.CFG file is configured correctly with technical directives explained earlier.
6. Copy the `<SDD>\CLIENT\WIN32\SETUP.INI` file from the SDD you are using for this post office to the `SYS:APACHE\NWDOCS\GWCLIENT\WIN32` directory.

7. Make sure the SETUP.INI file is configured correctly to not prompt for the language, as explained earlier in this section.

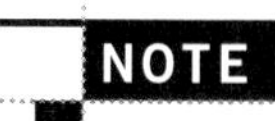

Remember in the Apache section, we assumed the Apache root document directory was `NWDOCS`. We also assumed that the *.CONF file was ADMINSERV.CONF. Neither of these assumptions is necessarily correct; it is quite possible that you are using the `HTDOCS` directory as your root document directory, and another *.CONF file as the configuration file for your Apache Web server.

Now that you've configured your Apache Web server, skip through the rest of the Web server configuration information, and go to the section in this chapter titled "Creating a SETUPIP.EXE File."

Configuring a Generic Web Server

You now need to configure your Web server, or at least confirm that the Web server supports file downloading into directories created within the document root folder. You must first create an empty GroupWise client directory structure under the document root directory of the Web server, as outlined here:

1. Locate the document root directory.
2. Create a GroupWise Client Distribution Directory by the name of `GWCLIENT` within the document root directory.
3. Create a directory within the `GWCLIENT` directory called `WIN32`.

Next, add the compressed GroupWise client file (SETUPIP.FIL and SETUPIP.US) and setup configuration file (SETUP.CFG) to the GroupWise Client directory structure on the Web server. The steps to do this are as follows:

1. In your SDD, locate the `ADMIN\UTILITY\SETUPIP` directory.
2. Copy the SETUPIP.FIL and SETUPIP.US files from `ADMIN\UTILITY\SETUPIP` to the `GWCLIENT` directory you made on your Web server.
3. In your SDD, locate the file called SETUP.CFG. This file is generally in the `CLIENT` or `CLIENT\WIN32` directory.
4. Copy the SETUP.CFG file to the `GWCLIENT\WIN32` directory you created on the Web server.
5. Make sure this SETUP.CFG file is configured correctly according to the technical directives explained earlier.

6. Copy the `<SDD>\CLIENT\WIN32\SETUP.INI` file to the `GWCLIENT\WIN32` directory on your Web server.
7. Make sure this SETUP.INI file is configured correctly to not prompt for the language, as explained earlier in this section.

Creating a SETUPIP.EXE File

Now that you have configured the GWCLIENT directory on the Web server, you must configure the SETUPIP.EXE utility. Follow these steps to do so:

1. Locate the `<SDD>\ADMIN\UTILITY\SETUPIP` directory.
2. Run the utility called WRITEIP.EXE.
3. In the WRITEIP utility, enter the DNS name or IP address of the Web server with the appropriate location to the GroupWise client directory on the Web server. You haven't actually created the GroupWise client directory yet, but you will soon. In this case, the GroupWise client directory is called `GWCLIENT`. So configure the location to be *`<Your web server's DNS name or IP address>`*`/gwclient`, as shown in the example in Figure 12.1. You can make other configuration changes in the WRITEIP utility as needed.

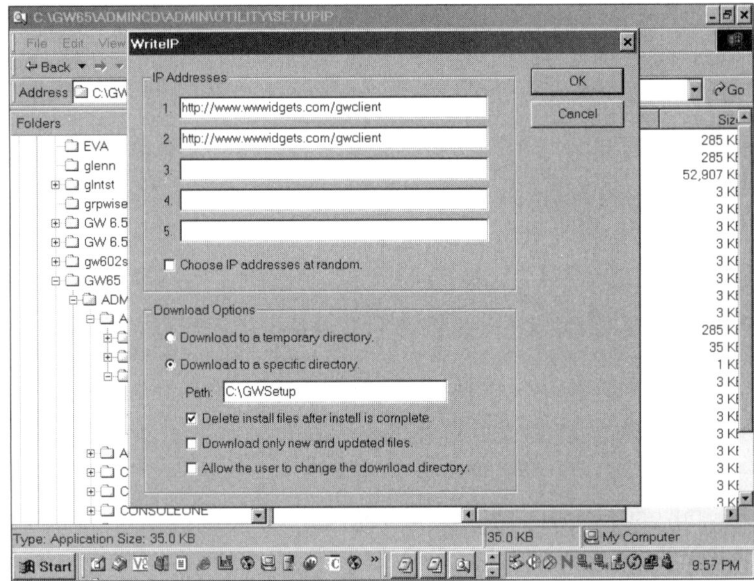

FIGURE 12.1
The WRITEIP utility.

NOTE

You cannot download the GroupWise client via an SSL connection; you cannot use the syntax `https://......`

You can define multiple Web servers that users can download the GroupWise client from. This allows the client to be downloaded from random sites. If the first Web server is down, the client will be downloaded from the next Web server on the list.

4. After entering the information in the WRITEIP utility, select the OK button, which will generate a new executable in the `ADMIN\UTILITY\SETUPIP` directory called SETUPIP.EXE.
5. After configuring the Web server (as explained in the next section), distribute the SETUPIP.EXE file to users using a drive letter mapping, an e-mail message, or using a Web server. From a Web server, all you need to do is place the SETUPIP.EXE in the document root directory and then place a hypertext link on a Web page to *<webserver's DNS name>*`\SETUPIP.EXE`.

You have now created the SETUPIP.EXE executable. It's a good idea to test it before rolling it into a production environment. Just run the SETUPIP.EXE in order to test it. The next section talks about troubleshooting SETUPIP.

Troubleshooting SETUPIP

The SETUPIP utility creates a SETUPIP.ERR file when it fails to work correctly. You can find this file in the Windows root directory. On a Windows 2000 workstation, for example, this would typically be the `C:\WINNT` directory.

In my own testing, I have found that when SETUPIP downloads files from the Web server, the SETUPIP.EXE software doesn't like it when you flip screens to something else while SETUPIP is running.

Upgrading the GroupWise Client via a Network Drive

The following section assumes that the GroupWise client is already installed on the user's desktop, and you are upgrading to a newer version of the GroupWise client.

In order for you to understand how to upgrade a GroupWise client, it's advantageous for you to consider several issues first. These are discussed in the following sections.

The Auto-Update Algorithm

The auto-update algorithm is how the GroupWise client, installed in the users' computers, knows it should upgrade itself to a newer version of the GroupWise client. By using the auto-update algorithm, you can automate the process of upgrading the GroupWise client to the GroupWise 6.5 client without the users having to initiate the setup process. Here's how it works.

GroupWise has SDD, which house the GroupWise software after it has been installed or copied from the Novell GroupWise CD. When patches are released, they are applied to a GroupWise SDD. A GroupWise SDD is not only a location for software, but it can be defined in GroupWise Administration and assigned to post offices. In GroupWise 6.5 using ConsoleOne, the GroupWise SDD are defined under Tools, GroupWise System Operations, Software Directory Management. See Figure 12.2.

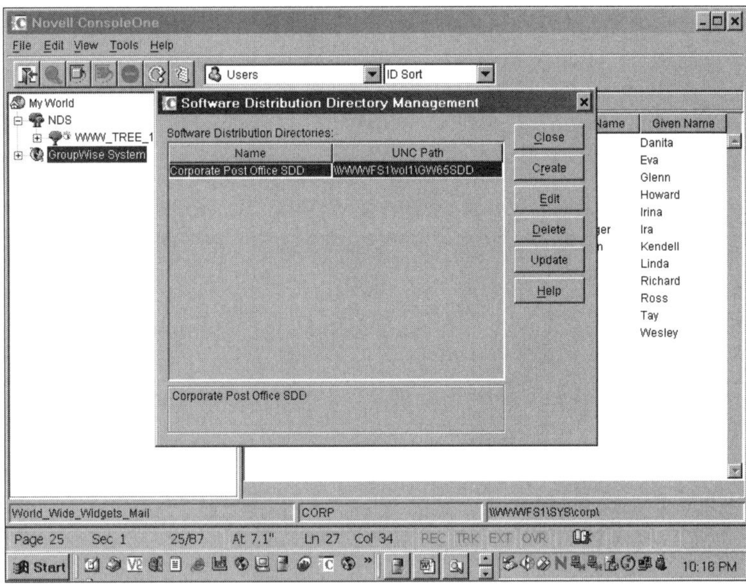

FIGURE 12.2
SDD Management.

A GroupWise SDD has a value called a *bump* number associated with it. The bump number starts at 0 and can be incremented to 1, and then 2, and then 3, and so on. Controlling the bump number is essential to controlling the GroupWise client upgrade process.

Every GroupWise post office should have an SDD associated with it. In fact, when you create a GroupWise post office, one of the required fields is the SDD that will be associated with the post office. You can configure an SDD that can be used by several post offices. For upgrade purposes, creating post office-specific SDDs is often the best practice. An SDD is used primarily so that the GroupWise client knows where to look in order to upgrade itself to a newer version of GroupWise. Even if you intend to use a solution such as ZENWorks, GroupWise requires you to define which SDD is to be used by each post office. To see or change the SDD associated with a GroupWise post office, view the properties of that post office and select the Post Office Settings property page from the GroupWise tab. See Figure 12.3.

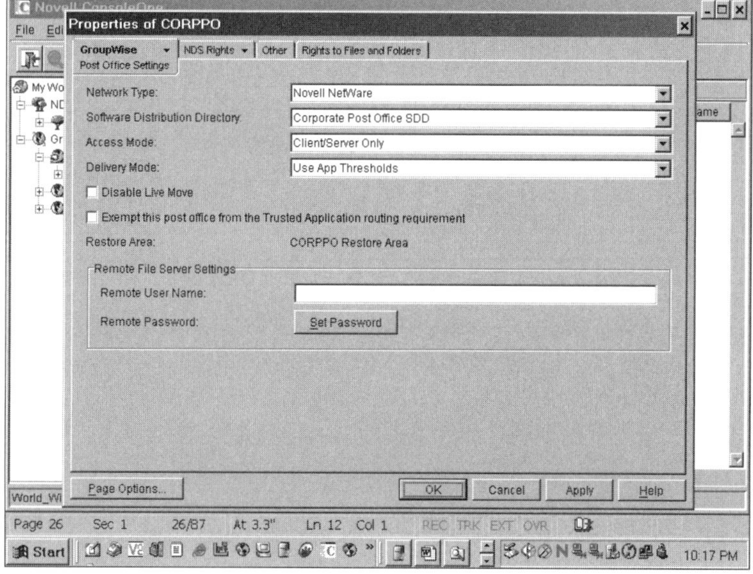

FIGURE 12.3
The SDD associated with a post office.

The GroupWise SDD should, and typically will, have the GroupWise 32-bit client installed. The GroupWise client is located in the <SDD>\CLIENT folder. Sites that intend to use the GroupWise SDD for GroupWise client software distribution must grant users Read and File Scan rights to the <SDD>\CLIENT folder and its subfolders. Users should not have rights in any other location of the SDD. If you are using ZENWorks or a similar solution, or if you use SETUPIP, explained later in this chapter, your users should not have any rights to the SDD.

To construct a SDD for a post office, make a directory called GW65SDD under the post office directory. Copy the CLIENT directory and its contents from the master GroupWise 6.5 SDD to GW65SDD directory under the post office.

WARNING

When you define an SDD, the path to the SDD should not include `CLIENT`**. The** `CLIENT` **portion is assumed, so the directory that is the parent to the** `CLIENT` **directory is where the SDD should point.**

In the `<SDD>\CLIENT` folder are two files that are an essential part of the GroupWise upgrade, as well as the auto-update algorithm. These files are SOFTWARE.INF and SETUP.CFG. In addition to these files from the SDD, a value in the WPDOMAIN.DB and the WPHOST.DB files, known as the *bump* number, is an essential part of the auto-update algorithm. All of these factors are detailed here:

- The SETUP.CFG file resides in the `<SDD>\CLIENT` directory. This is a "template" file that allows the administrator to customize the way in which the GroupWise client is installed at the user's workstation. The SETUP.CFG file should be copied to the `CLIENT\WIN32` directory and modified according to the administrator's preferences for the install of the GroupWise client. The important settings for the SETUP.CFG file as pertains to the auto-update algorithm are under the `[AutoUpdate]` section. The `Enabled` value must be set to `Yes` in order for the automatic update to occur.
- The SOFTWARE.INF file is an ASCII file containing a small amount of information. In fact, here are the entire contents of the SOFTWARE.INF file from the GroupWise 6.5 SDD.

```
[General]
BuildNumber=2085
```

The `BuildNumber` is really the version number in development terms. But to you and me, GroupWise releases versions of the GroupWise software in versions that you and I typically know as 5.5, 5.5.4.1, 6.5.0, and 6.5.1. The `BuildNumber` of `2085` is the GroupWise 6.5 original shipping client. The `BuildNumber` version of the GroupWise 6.5 Support Pack #1 client is `2517` (`2092`, for example).

Now here's what the `BuildNumber` means to the auto-update algorithm. Whenever the GroupWise client is installed, the `BuildNumber` of the GroupWise client is placed into the Windows Registry, as shown in Figure 12.4. The `BuildNumber` string value is kept in the following location:

```
HKEY_LOCAL_MACHINE\SOFTWARE\Novell\GroupWise
```

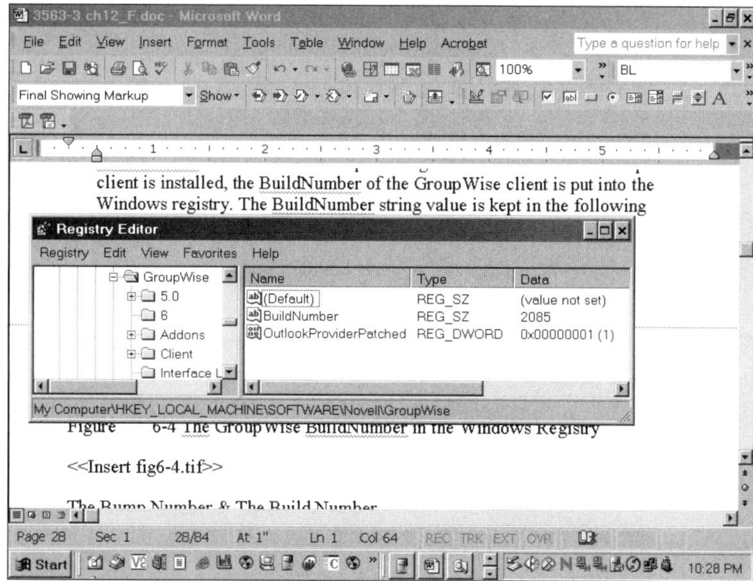

FIGURE 12.4
The GroupWise BuildNumber in the Windows Registry.

The Bump and Build Numbers

It is important to understand the relevance of the `BuildNumber` value. You might remember that every GroupWise post office has an SDD associated with it. The SDD has a bump number associated with it. Each time the GroupWise client loads, it asks for the bump number associated with the SDD for the user's post office. This bump number is obtained for the GroupWise client from the WPHOST.DB file. When the GroupWise client loads and contacts the POA, the conversation goes something like this:

CLIENT: Hi Post Office Agent (POA) at IP address 192.168.100.237, port 1677. I need a client/server session with you. Here are my authentication credentials.

POA: Here's a client/server session, and here's the port we will use to speak.

CLIENT: Hey POA, before I load the user interface of this client, what is the bump number for the SDD associated with my post office?

POA: It's 5.

CLIENT: Okay, let's see, the last time I installed the GroupWise client, the bump number was 4. This is held in the Windows Registry at the following location:

```
HKEY_LOCAL_MACHINE\SOFTWARE\Novell\GroupWise\Client\5.0
```

The value is called NewSoftwareBump. In this example, you see that the bump number for the SDD is different than the bump number in the Windows Registry. Thus, the GroupWise client must look further to see whether it is essential to upgrade the GroupWise client. Let's keep going.

CLIENT: Hey POA, what's the location of my SDD?

POA: It's in the WWWFS1\VOL1\CORPPO\GW65SDD directory.

CLIENT: Okay, let me look at the SOFTWARE.INF file from the ..DENPO\GW65SDD\CLIENT directory. The BuildNumber is 2517 in the SOFTWARE.INF file, and the BuildNumber in the Windows Registry on my machine is 1807. It seems like it's time to upgrade. Now let me the SETUP.CFG file from the <SDD>\CLIENT directory to see whether the [AutoUpdate] section of this file has a line that reads Enabled=Yes. Yes it does! It's upgrade time!

Here is a quick synopsis of what has transpired:

- If the bump number for the SDD associated with a post office is different (not higher per se, just different) than the bump number in the Windows Registry, the client compares the build number in the SOFTWARE.INF file with the build number in the Windows Registry.
- If the build number in the SOFTWARE.INF file is greater than the build in the Windows Registry, the GroupWise client looks at the SETUP.CFG file.
- If the [AutoUpdate] section in the SETUP.CFG files contains Enabled=Yes, the GroupWise client will attempt to upgrade itself.
- The GroupWise client can then upgrade itself by launching SETUP.EXE from the <SDD>\CLIENT\WIN32 directory, or by launching SETUPIP.EXE that the POA sends to the GroupWise client that it retrieved for the client from the <SDD>\CLIENT\WIN32 directory.

This section explained the auto-update algorithm, which is essential to understand if you want the GroupWise client to update automatically.

Upgrading All Users on a Post Office with a Mapped Drive to the GroupWise SDD

The GroupWise administrator can fully configure what users will see during the GroupWise client upgrade, and just what will be installed. Before covering the upgrade steps, let's walk through an example. The following looks at WorldWide Widget Corporation's technical directives with regard to the upgrade of the GroupWise client:

- Users will be forced to upgrade/update their GroupWise clients.
- The default IP address and port for a POA in the system will be indicated.
- Users should not be prompted to answer any installation questions.
- Notify will be placed in the Windows startup group.
- Document integration will be disabled.
- Users will not be prompted for the language to install; the only language support by this company is US English.
- All other factory defaults for the installation are accepted.

The following steps are example procedures for upgrading a post office. After reading this section, you should be able to modify this scenario to match the needs of your organization:

1. Physically create and configure a slimmed-down GroupWise 6.5 SDD. To do this, create a directory within the post office directory called `GW65SDD` and copy the `<GroupWise 6.5 SDD>\CLIENT` folder structure to the `<post office>\GW65` directory. In the end, you will have a folder structure that looks like `<Post Office Directory>\GW65SDD\CLIENT`.

   The SDD that you create needs a full copy of the `CLIENT` folder and subfolders from a GroupWise 6.5 SDD.

NOTE

You are welcome to place the SDD in some other location than the post office directory. As long as the users have rights to the location and no other folders or files in the post office directory structure, you can place it in the post office directory.

2. Go to the `<SDD>\CLIENT` directory. Locate the SETUP.CFG file and copy it to the `<SDD>\CLIENT\WIN32` directory.
3. Locate the SETUP.CFG file that you copied to the `<SDD>\CLIENT\WIN32` directory. Edit the properties of the file in Windows Explorer, and remove the read-only attribute, if necessary.
4. Use Windows Notepad to edit the SETUP.CFG file.

The next order of business is to make changes to the files. In the SETUP.CFG and SETUP.INI files, make the following changes according to the scenario outlined earlier:

1. To force users to update, change the line that reads `ForceUpdate=No` to `ForceUpdate=Yes`.
2. To specify the default IP address and port, remove the semicolon from the following arguments in the SETUP.CFG file: `DefaultIPAddress=x.x.x.x` and `DefaultIPPort=xxxx`. Configure them with the IP address and port of a GroupWise POA in the GroupWise system. For example:

   ```
   DefaultIPAddress=155.123.178.16
   DefaultIPPort=1677
   ```

3. To ensure that users are not prompted with installation questions, change the line that reads `HideAllDialogs=No` to `HideAllDialogs=Yes`.
4. To place Notify in the Windows startup group, find the line that reads `Notify=No` and change it to `Notify=Yes`.
5. To turn off Document Integration, find the section that reads `[IntegrationApps]`. After the name of each of the applications, there's a `=Yes`; change this to `=No`. For example

   ```
   Lotus WordPro=No
   Microsoft Binder=No
   Microsoft Excel=No
   ```

   And so on.
6. By default, the GroupWise Client CD has GroupWise configured to install the English language. However, users are still prompted as to which language to install. In order to remove this prompt, do the following:
   a. Locate the SETUP. file, found in the `<SDD>\CLIENT\WIN32` directory.
   b. Edit the properties of the file in Windows Explorer. Remove the read-only attribute, if necessary.
   c. Edit the SETUP.INI file. Find the line that reads `EnableLangDlg=Y` and change it to `EnableLangDlg=N`.

You still have a little ways to go, but to confirm that your SETUP.CFG and SETUP.INI files are configured correctly, run the SETUP.EXE file in the `<SDD>\CLIENT\WIN32` directory. If the installation behaves in the manner you expect, proceed to the next section. If it does not behave in the manner you expect, tweak the SETUP.CFG file as needed.

Defining a GroupWise SDD

To logically define the newly created GroupWise 6.5 SDD:

1. Go into ConsoleOne. Make sure to connect to the primary domain.

Whenever you are going to make a change or an addition through System Operations, it is best to be connected to the primary domain.

2. In ConsoleOne, select Tools, GroupWise System Operations, Software Directory Management.
3. Click the Create button. Give the SDD a name and a description—for example, Corporate Post Office SDD. Define the UNC path to the SDD, which in these examples is the `<post office directory>\GW65` directory. The UNC path should not point all the way to the `<post office directory>\GW65\CLIENT` directory, because the `CLIENT` portion is assumed. See Figure 12.5.

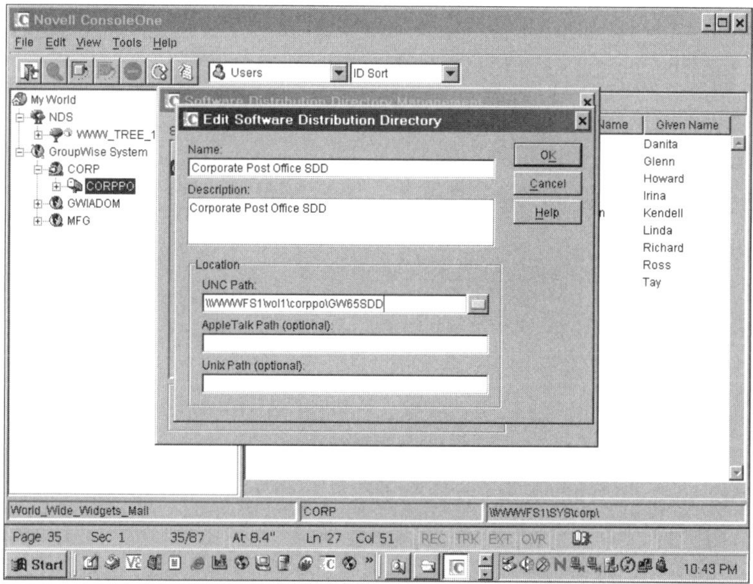

FIGURE 12.5
A newly defined GroupWise 6.5 SDD.

4. Select OK and Close to get to the main ConsoleOne screen.

This section described how to create an SDD. Now you need to select an SDD to associate with the post office.

Selecting a SDD for a Post Office

The steps to assign the new GroupWise 6.5 SDD to the post office are as follows:

1. Edit the properties of the post office and select the Post Office Settings property page from the GroupWise tab.
2. In the SDD field, select the appropriate SDD for this post office, and then select OK.

This might be enough to kick off the auto-update process. But there's also a chance that it isn't. If the original GroupWise 5.x SDD for the post office you are upgrading had the same bump number as the SDD for the GroupWise 6.5 SDD you just created, the GroupWise client doesn't pick up on a bump number change. A change in the bump number is the first part of the auto-update algorithm, so the bump number must change before GroupWise will discover the new GroupWise client it should upgrade to. If the upgrade process does not seem to be happening, and you want it to, you can proceed to the steps outlined under the next task.

This section simply talked about how to associate an SDD with a post office. This might have been enough to kick off the upgrade, and it might not have. Make sure to take the steps explained in the next section.

Updating the Bump Number of a GroupWise SDD

To initiate the GroupWise client upgrade with the Update feature, follow these steps:

1. Go into ConsoleOne and make sure to connect to the primary domain.
2. In the GroupWise view in ConsoleOne, select Tools, GroupWise System Operations, Software Directory Management.
3. Highlight the new GroupWise 6.5 SDD that you recently created and select the Update button.
4. In the next dialog box that comes up, select the check box next to the words that read "Force auto-update check by GroupWise components". Click the OK button.
5. If needed, repeat steps 1-4 if users are not being prompted to upgrade their GroupWise clients. Remember that users will be prompted to upgrade only if the `BuildNumber` in their local Registry is lower than the `BuildNumber` in the `<SDD>\CLIENT\SOFTWARE.INF` file.

Upgrading the GroupWise Client with SETUPIP

Just so you can envision what SETUPIP will do, here's a quick outline of what users will see when their GroupWise clients are upgraded by SETUPIP.

1. Users are prompted to upgrade, and they will be presented with two buttons: OK and Cancel.
2. After the user has selected OK, SETUPIP downloads the GroupWise client software from the Web server.
3. After the GroupWise client is downloaded and expanded, the familiar Windows InstallShield screen shows when the SETUP.EXE program is launched. The GroupWise client installs.

By using the SETUPIP client installation method, you eliminate the need for users to have rights to a network drive. Also, the installation process creates less network traffic when SETUPIP is used.

Here's how you configure GroupWise so that when users are prompted to upgrade, they will launch SETUPIP.EXE:

1. Follow all of the steps of the section of this chapter titled "Distributing the GroupWise Client via SETUPIP."
2. Follow all of the steps in the section of this chapter titled: "Upgrading the GroupWise Client via a Network Drive." Make sure the POA has rights to access the SDD for the post office to be upgraded. The GroupWise POA will scoop up the SETUPIP.EXE and some other files on behalf of the GroupWise client running at the desktop, and send them down to the GroupWise client to execute SETUPIP.EXE locally. If the POA needs to scoop up files from the SDD, the POA must have rights to the SDD. You can assign these rights by adding the `/user` and `/password` switches in the startup file of the POA, or you can place the SDD on the same server where the post office is located, and where the POA is executing.
3. Make sure users do not have rights to the SDD for the post office, or their clients will not be prompted to install via SETUPIP. Instead, their clients will execute SETUP.EXE.
4. Place the SETUPIP.EXE in the `<Post Office SDD>\CLIENT\WIN32` directory.
5. Edit the SETUP.CFG file in the `<Post Office SDD>\CLIENT\WIN32` directory. Make this additional change to the SETUP.CFG—find the argument that reads `SetupIPEnabled=No` and change it to `SetupIPEnabled=Yes`.

This section explained how to get the SETUPIP.EXE utility to launch automatically without users taking any action.

Configuring Non-English Clients via SETUPIP

The steps for installing the non-English clients are practically as simple as the steps for installing the English client. First, follow the steps in the sections prior to this one regarding SETUPIP. You must then do two things differently in order to allow configuration of non-English clients:

- Replace the SETUPIP.US file mentioned in the SETUPIP sections before this one with the correct SETUPIP.XX language file for the client that you need to support. If you want your installation to support more than one language, place more than one SETUPIP.XX language file in the GWCLIENT directory. When SETUPIP runs, it will prompt the users as to which language to install.
- In your `<`*`WEB SERVER'S DIRECTORY STRUCTURE`*`>GWCLIENT\WIN32` directory on the Web server, locate the file called SETUP.INI. Make sure that the line `EnableLangDlg=Y` is enabled (in other words it shouldn't say `EnableLandDlg=N`).

Adding Grace Logins Before a Forced Upgrade

You might want to allow your users some *grace logins* before they are forced to upgrade their GroupWise clients. This allows users the flexibility to install the GroupWise client at a more convenient time.

In order to do this, you need to edit the SETUP.CFG in the GroupWise 6.5 SDD assigned to the post office. In addition to the changes to the SETUP.CFG explained earlier in this chapter, you should put a value in the `GraceLoginCount=` argument. For example, if you wanted the users to have five grace logins before upgrading, the setting would look as follows:

```
GraceLoginCount=5
```

The `GraceLoginCount=` argument, when combined with the `ForceUpdate=Yes`, causes the GroupWise client installation to allow for grace logins before users are forced to upgrade their clients.

Forcing a Windows Registry Change Through SETUP.CFG

This section is only for those of you who are very savvy with the Windows Registry. You can define Windows Registry settings and changes that you might want to make. If there's a Registry setting that you know the GroupWise client installation makes, yet you want to specify a different setting, follow these steps:

1. Edit the SETUP.CFG file, either in the SDD or on the Web server if you are using SETUPIP.
2. Add the following syntax to SETUP.CFG for the Registry setting you want to define or change:

```
[Registry Setting x]
Action=Add or Delete
Type=String or DWORD
Key=Key Name
Name=Value Name
Value=Value to set
```

Here are a few examples:

This change will add a value named `BuildNumber` under the GroupWise key set to `2085`:

```
[Registry Setting 1]
Action=Add
Type=DWORD
Key=HKEY_LOCAL_MACHINE\SOFTWARE\Novell\GroupWise
Name=BuildNumber
Value=2085
```

This change will delete a value named `BuildNumber` under the GroupWise key:

```
[Registry Setting 2]
Action=Delete
```

```
Key=HKEY_LOCAL_MACHINE\SOFTWARE\Novell\GroupWise
Name=BuildNumber
```

This change will delete the GroupWise key and all subkeys (use this one with caution):

```
[Registry Setting 3]
Action=Delete
Key=HKEY_LOCAL_MACHINE\SOFTWARE\Novell\GroupWise
```

This section explained how the GroupWise installation can also roll out or delete Registry settings.

Auditing the GroupWise Client Upgrade

Following are steps you can take to determine who has upgraded/updated their GroupWise client:

1. The GroupWise 6.5 POA has a feature that can give you a quick look at who has upgraded the GroupWise client to GroupWise 6.5. In order to see this feature, your GroupWise 6.5 POA should support HTTP monitoring and your post office should support some other features. You can enable HTTP monitoring in ConsoleOne or in the startup file of the POA; using ConsoleOne is recommended. The other GWClient settings mentioned in this section should be defined on the post office object, so you can easily edit them and they will take effect without using startup switches in the POA.
2. Open the properties of the GroupWise Post office object, Client Access Settings .
3. From there, you will see two sections that allow you to define the minimum client release version and date. From the Minimum Client Release Version (x.x.x), you can choose a version of the GroupWise client from a drop-down list, or if the version of the client you are interested in is not listed, you can type the version number of the GroupWise client you are interested in monitoring. In the Minimum Client Release Date field, you can check the calendar icon to specify a date of the GroupWise client release. Notice that when you select a predefined version, the date field is entered automatically for this particular version of the GroupWise client. You should verify that this

information is correct by checking the GroupWise client from Help, About GroupWise. This will tell you the release date and version of this particular client.

4. After enabling these settings on the post office, click OK to apply them.
5. Go to the POA's HTTP port in this manner from your Web browser at `http://207.40.197.201:718`.

If you are not sure what HTTP port your POA is using, you can access the C/S port (1677) and it will redirect you to the HTTP port.

6. You might be prompted for a username and password. Once you've accessed the POA via HTTP, go to the C/S Users link. From there, you can view the version of GroupWise client that your various users are using. Any user who is using an older GroupWise client than you specified will appear in red. Any user who is using a newer GroupWise client will appear in blue. See Figure 12.6 for an example of the screen.

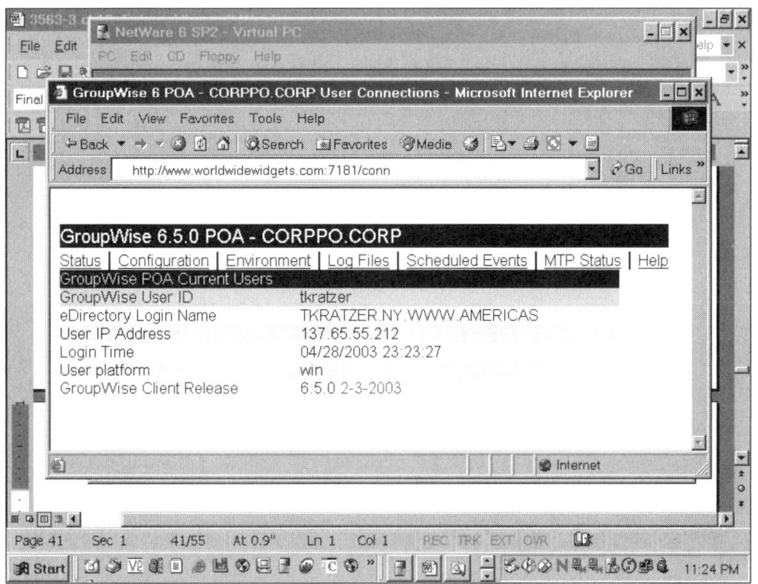

FIGURE 12.6
Using the POA's HTTP monitoring screen.

This section explained how to monitor a GroupWise client upgrade with help from the GroupWise POA HTTP monitoring screen.

Understanding the GroupWise Login Process

Understanding the login process is helpful when configuring your GroupWise system to support the GroupWise client login process. It's also helpful to understand the login process when troubleshooting login difficulties.

When you double-click the GroupWise application, the client must successfully connect you to your mailbox. To do this, it consults several sources of information for "clues" to connecting:

- Other GroupWise code in memory
- Command-line options on the shortcut
- Login parameters in the Windows Registry
- The registered network provider
- Novell Directory Services
- Domain Name Services
- User data entered in a login dialog box

The preceding list includes the order in which the client consults them. The following section walks through the login process.

Is GroupWise in Memory?

If a GroupWise component, such as Notify or the address book, is currently running, that component has already connected with your mailbox. The GroupWise client will use that same connection. Sometimes you might quit GroupWise, and then try specifying a command-line option, only to get connected the same way you connected last time. This occurs because GroupWise was still unloading when you launched it again. Some code portions were still in memory, so it used the old connection.

Command-Line Options

There are several command-line options you can enter on the GroupWise shortcut. These should be used as troubleshooting tools rather than administrative purposes, because they are not easy to globally administer. Figure 12.7 shows a command-line parameter that will force the GroupWise client to bring up the Login dialog box.

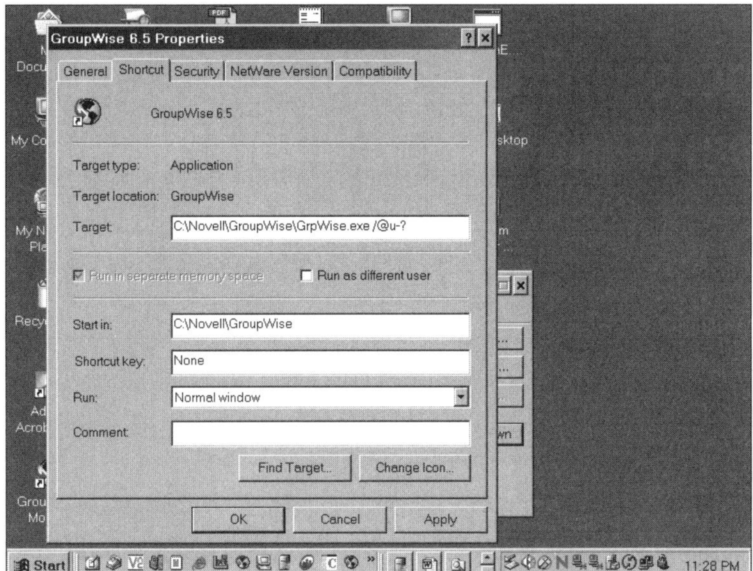

FIGURE 12.7
Using the /@U-? switch to force the GroupWise client to bring up the Login dialog box.

Here are the other command-line switches that concern logging into GroupWise:

- /@U-*<GroupWise user ID>*
- /IPA-*<IP address for GroupWise POA>*
- /IPP-*<IP port for GroupWise POA>*
- /PR-*<Path to GroupWise remote data on local drive>*
- /PH-*<Drive letter path to post office>* (this switch works only if the post office supports Direct mode; most do not)
- /PC-<Path to GroupWise cache data on local drive>

During the GroupWise login process, two critical pieces of information are required. The GroupWise client needs answers to the following two questions:

- Whose mailbox do I connect to?
- How do I get to it?

This information can be provided via command-line options. Consider the following string:

```
C:\NOVELL\GroupWise\Grpwise.exe /@u-tkratzer /ipa-10.0.0.1 /
➥ipp-1677
```

This string tells the GroupWise client to log in as user `tkratzer`, and that the POA can be found on port `1677`, at address `10.0.0.1`.

If the `/@U-` switch has been set to a question mark, the client will prompt the user with the Login dialog box. This can be a useful tool for an administrator who routinely checks multiple mailboxes and wants to be prompted each time. Here's the command line switch to use this option: `/@U-?`.

The Network Provider

The GroupWise client is going to make a call to the network provider. This call, `WnetGetUser`, will return the login name that this individual used to gain access to the network.

When the GroupWise client finally connects to the POA, it will check the security level of the post office. If the PO is set to high security, the client will compare the network ID obtained through `WnetGetUser` with the network ID associated with the GroupWise mailbox (usually the eDirectory user ID). If these values do not match, the user will be prompted for a password.

If the security is set to high–eDirectory authentication or high—LDAP authentication, the client will allow matches only with values it knows it obtained through Novell eDirectory or LDAP. This prevents users from setting up a private network to spoof the `WnetGetUser` security and hack into a GroupWise mailbox.

eDirectory

The GroupWise client already consulted with Windows to see who the user was logged in as. With the `WnetGetUser` information in hand, the GroupWise client knows what kind of a network the user logged into. If it detects eDirectory, the GroupWise client will attempt to discover GroupWise post office information from the eDirectory user object for this user.

This is the power of the directory at work. The eDirectory user object is associated with a post office object (from the GroupWise Account property page of the user object). That post office object has two attributes for the GroupWise client to check:

- Access mode
- Location

If the access mode is set to direct access, the client will connect directly to the location (UNC path) specified.

If the access mode is set to client/server only or client/server and direct, the GroupWise client will browse to the POA object, which is a child object of the PO object. That object will have one attribute for the GroupWise client to check, the network address, which will provide the GroupWise client with the IP address and port of the POA so that a client/server connection can be established.

This might seem very involved, but it is extremely fast. The Novell client for the Windows 32-bit platforms will have already pulled down most of the required information regarding the user object. If the PO object exists in the same physical partition as the user, or if the partition it is in is on the same server the user authenticated to, the discovery will take place in a fraction of a second.

The Windows Registry

Suppose that nothing is on the command line, and either the NetWare client is not logged in or is not even installed on the Windows machine. The client will now check the Windows Registry at the following key:

```
[HKEY_CURRENT_USER\Software\Novell\GroupWise\Login Parameters]
```

There are several possible parameters to be found underneath this key. If you were to export the entire key for a particular user, you would see something like the following:

```
[HKEY_CURRENT_USER\Software\Novell\GroupWise\Login
➥Parameters\Account Name]
@="tkratzer"

[HKEY_CURRENT_USER\Software\Novell\GroupWise\Login
➥Parameters\Mode]
@="Master"

[HKEY_CURRENT_USER\Software\Novell\GroupWise
➥\Login Parameters\Path To Remote Database]
@="c:\\gwremote"

[HKEY_CURRENT_USER\Software\Novell\GroupWise\Login
➥Parameters\PostOfficePath]
@=""
```

```
[HKEY_CURRENT_USER\Software\Novell\GroupWise\Login
➥Parameters\TCP/IP Address]
@="10.0.0.1"

[HKEY_CURRENT_USER\Software\Novell\GroupWise\Login
➥Parameters\TCP/IP Port]
@="1677"
```

In each of these lines, the value in quotation marks after the `@` sign is the parameter value. In the preceding example, user `tkratzer` will be connected to the POA at `10.0.0.1:1677`. If this address and port are not accessible, the GroupWise client will look for an IP address and port defined at this location in the Windows Registry:

```
[HKEY_LOCAL_MACHINE\Software\Novell\GroupWise
\Client\5.0\DefaultIPAddress] @=151.155.1.2
[HKEY_LOCAL_MACHINE\Software\Novell\GroupWise\Client\5.0\Default
➥IPPort] @=1677
```

These two keys are created if the following has been defined in the SETUP.CFG file:

```
DefaultIPAddress=x.x.x.x
DefaultIPPort=xxxx
```

So, using the previous example, if the GroupWise client is not able to connect to `10.0.0.1:1677`, because the `DefaultIPAddress` and `DefaultIPPort` are defined in the Registry, the client will go to `151.155.1.1:1677` and try to connect. This allows you to specify where you would like the GroupWise client to go to in order to connect. Also remember that the `151.155.1.2` class address does not necessarily have to be this user's particular POA. When a POA gets a login request for a user, if this user is not owned by the POA, it will redirect the client to the user's owning post office.

TIP

The `DefaultIPAddress` can be a DNS entry as well; the client will read either an IP address or DNS entered here.

If neither of these network connections are available, tkratzer will be connected to his remote database at `c:\gwremote`. The `PostOfficePath` parameter is blank because tkratzer's post office allows only client/server connections. A UNC path or drive mapping here is impossible.

These Registry entries were written the last time that the GroupWise client connected to a mailbox. The implication here should be obvious: If you can get the client to connect once, it will "remember" how it did it when the time comes to connect again.

As previously mentioned, you can use the SETUP.CFG file to define two IP addresses in the Windows Registry that the GroupWise client will also read. These keys are

```
IPAddress=x.x.x.x
IPPort=xxxx
DefaultIPAddress=x.x.x.x
DefaultIPPort=xxx
```

TIP

If the Windows Registry already contains the `IPAddress` and `IPPort` values, the values in the SETUP.CFG file will not overwrite these settings.

Domain Name Services

Now suppose that there are no command-line switches, network information, or Windows Registry information for the GroupWise client to use. In this case, the client will still not have discovered which post office to connect to.

At this point, the client falls back on DNS. The GroupWise client will perform a DNS lookup for a server named NGWNAMESERVER first and then on the NGWNAMESERVER2 server. If the administrator has assigned that domain name to a valid GroupWise POA (any POA on the system), the GroupWise client will connect to that POA at the port 1677.

TIP

The POA that the DNS server points to as NGWNAMESERVER must be configured to listen at port 1677.

NOTE

The GroupWise client will not try to resolve NGWNAMESERVER if the `DefaultIPAddress` and `DefaultIPPort` Registry keys are present and contain an IP or DNS address and port. As stated, NGWNAMESERVER is queried only if there is no information in the Registry about where the client should go to connect.

NGWNAMESERVER Redirection

Now, suppose that this POA is not the right one for this user. On a large system, the odds are good that it will not be. In this case, the POA will ask the client who it is logging in as (information that the client got from

WnetGetUser) and then will look in the address book. The POA will then check the redirection table to find the IP address for the user's correct POA.

The user will be automatically redirected to the correct POA. Assuming reasonable network performance, this will happen in just a few seconds.

TIP **The same redirection concept is true for the `DefaultIPAddress` and `DefaultIPPort` values that you can specify in the Registry. In reality, the purpose of using the `DefaultIPAddress` and `DefaultIPPort` Registry settings is so that an administrator can tell the GroupWise client where to go in order to find one POA object in the GroupWise system. This, in essence, replaces the need for `NGWNAMESERVER`. This is why `NGWNAMESERVER` is not queried when the `DefaultIPAddress` and `DefaultIPPort` values are present.**

Prompting the User

Suppose, though, that the administrator has been lax in his/her responsibilities. Not only are eDirectory and LDAP authentication not available, but the Domain Name Services has not been configured either. The NGWNAMESERVER lookup will time out (after a minute or so, which will be very long and painful for an impatient user), and then the user will see the screen in Figure 12.8.

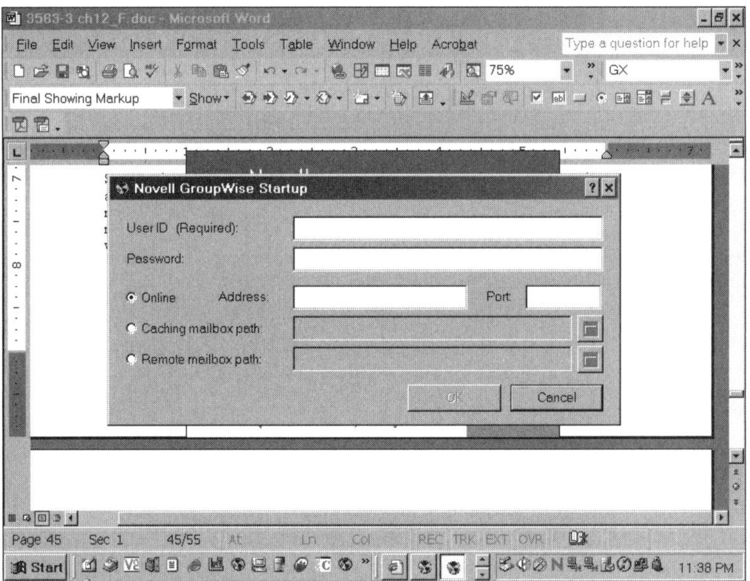

FIGURE 12.8 The GroupWise Client Login dialog box.

This is a disaster. Have a look at the number of fields the lucky user gets to populate. Do you suppose this user will populate these correctly? Not likely. The user will pick up the phone and call you.

You can provide the user with this information automatically in at least four ways before it came to this, and this chapter covered each of those. The next section walks you through the process of covering all of your bases, ensuring that users with new machines or toasted Registries do not need to make that phone call.

Administering the Login Process

This section teaches you how to ensure that the GroupWise client can get the necessary login parameters through Novell Directory Services or the DNS. This section also discusses Registry entries to "push" to workstations, should you happen to be using a tool such as Novell ZENWorks.

Configuring eDirectory

All users of a GroupWise post office should have browse, read, and compare rights to the post office object itself, as well as to the POA associated to that post office. (However if you are using LDAP authentication, you users do not need these rights.) For simplicity, assign the rights to the post office object, and the POA object to the OU or OUs in which the users for the post office reside.

The following steps provide you with the tools to verify access modes and IP addresses when configuring eDirectory:

1. Open the Post Office Settings page for the post office object associated with the users whose GroupWise login you are administering. The Post Office Settings property page for a post office object allows you to check on the access mode, among other things.
2. Verify that the Access Mode field reads Client/Server and Direct or (preferably) Client/Server Only. Client/server access to mailboxes is much preferred over direct access.
3. Verify that the UNC path to this post office is correct on the Identification property page. This is not a big issue if you are running in client/server mode, but it is still good to be accurate here.
4. Make sure that Disable Logins is not checked. This option should be checked only if, for some reason, you want to keep users out of their mailboxes temporarily.

5. Close the details for the PO.
6. Open the Identification property page for the POA associated with this PO.
7. Go to the TCP/IP Address field and verify that the TCP/IP address and port are accurate.

TIP **For NetWare, you might need to go to the server console and type `CONFIG` to view the actual IP address of the server. From NT/2000, you can open a DOS window and type `IPCONFIG` to get the IP address of the NT/2000 server.**

8. Close the POA object.

In these eight steps, you have accomplished two tasks:

- You ensured that the GroupWise client can get login parameters from eDirectory
- You ensured that those parameters are accurate

TIP **You can easily display the IP address and port for each POA object in the system by adding these columns to the POA view. Simply highlight a POA object, and then go to Tools, Edit Columns. From there, you can add columns that apply to the POA object. Select the IP address and port and you will see every IP address and port for all your POA objects in the GroupWise system. You can also do the same thing for the UNC path. You must have the post office object highlighted when adding columns for the UNC path.**

Configuring DNS

Now you need to choose a POA, preferably one that is centrally located on the LAN, to serve as the NGWNAMESERVER agent. On very large systems, it might be advisable to create a dummy post office (no users) with a POA dedicated to NGWNAMESERVER redirection.

1. Make sure that this POA is listening on port 1677. This is done from the Network Address field of the POA's Agent Settings property page.
2. Create a DNS record on your domain name server. This server is not part of the GroupWise system and can be on almost any server platform, including NetWare 4, 5, or 6, Windows server platforms, or any flavor of UNIX or Linux.
3. In your DNS server, enter the hostname as NGWNAMESERVER.
4. Enter the IP address of the POA that you chose to act as NGWNAMESERVER.

In these four steps, you have ensured that any GroupWise client that looks for **NGWNAMESERVER** on your system will find a POA at the IP address specified. That POA will then redirect the client to the correct POA for connection to the user's mailbox.

Administering GroupWise Client Options

The GroupWise administrator snap-ins for ConsoleOne provide you with a powerful tool for controlling the way the GroupWise client works. If while selecting a domain, post office, or user, you choose Tools, GroupWise Utilities, Client Options, you will see the dialog box in Figure 12.9.

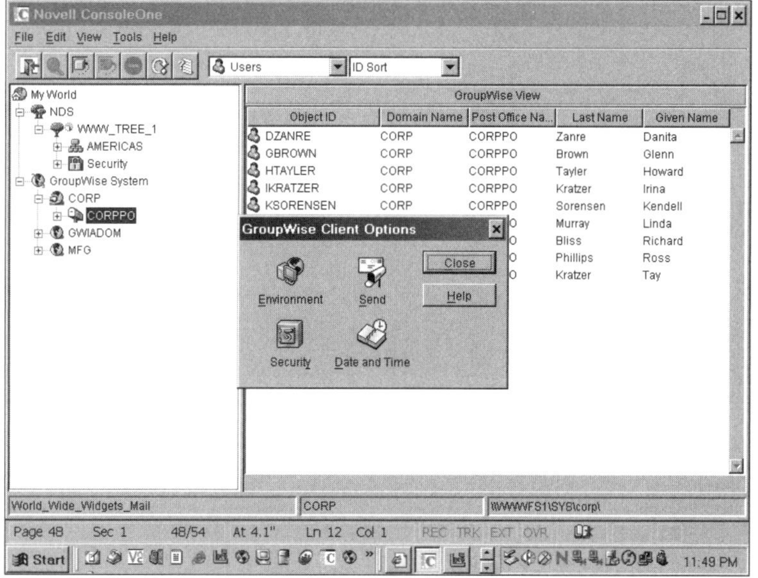

FIGURE 12.9
The GroupWise Client Options dialog box in ConsoleOne.

After selecting Environment, you see the dialog box shown in Figure 12.10.

Some of the options in this window are also available in the GroupWise client. Take note, however, of the set of padlock buttons on the right side, as well as several other options.

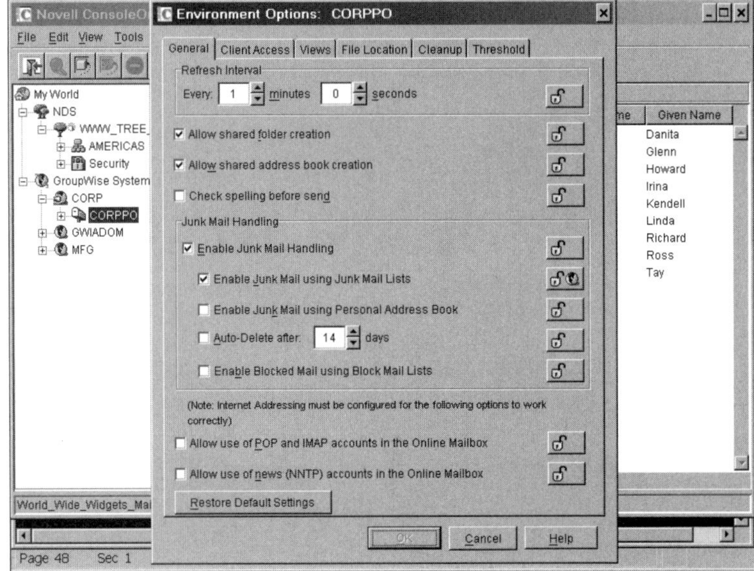

FIGURE 12.10 Administering GroupWise client environment options in ConsoleOne.

You can change any setting listed in this dialog box, which will effectively change the default options for users who have not changed their defaults. By clicking the adjacent padlock, you can also lock a setting in place. This will prevent users from changing individual defaults, and it will also force the setting on users who might have already changed it.

As noted in Chapter 3, "Understanding the GroupWise Directory," GroupWise administration writes changes directly to the GroupWise domain database to which it is connected. For client options to take effect, however, the changes must propagate all the way down to the GroupWise user database, USERxxx.DB. The following numbered list examines the architecture that makes this happen:

1. The administrator makes a change to client options.

   For example, imagine that you have unchecked the box labeled Allow Shared Folder Creation and then locked that setting. In this scenario, a post office object was selected when going into Tools, GroupWise Utilities, Client Options. This means that the setting will apply to the entire post office.

2. The GroupWise administration snap-ins write the change to the GroupWise domain database and create an administration update file to propagate this change to the post office.

3. The Message Transfer Agenet (MTA) transmits this file to the POA.

4. The POA administration thread writes this change to the post office database. The POA then writes the preference changes to the preferences capsule of all USERxxx.DB files in the post office.

This section explained how GroupWise client options set from ConsoleOne get to the GroupWise message store.

Using Clients for Non-Windows Platforms

This chapter focused exclusively on the GroupWise 6.5 32-bit client. Some organizations will require other client platforms, however. This section briefly evaluates each of these platforms in terms of feature parity, strengths, and weaknesses.

GroupWise 6.5 32-Bit Windows Client

This is the flagship client for GroupWise. All of the functionality available to any GroupWise user is typically available within this client. It requires a 32-bit Windows platform.

Strengths

The primary strengths of this client lie in the fact that it is the flagship client for Novell GroupWise. When new features or functionality are coded for GroupWise, they are coded for this platform first. The following list is hardly complete, but it does illustrate some of what is present (so that you can judge the other clients against this one):

- Notification of new messages
- Document administration features (see Chapter 14, "Library and Document Administration")
- Remote-access capabilities (via GroupWise remote; requires a standard installation)
- Archive access
- Full-featured toolbars, menus, and quick menus
- Full collaboration features, including folder sharing, GroupWise library access, item tracking, calendar viewing, and more

Weaknesses

The primary weakness of this client lies in the fact that it must be installed to every workstation that needs to run it. The GroupWise client also takes over 50MB of disk space.

GroupWise 5.2 32-Bit Macintosh Client

For Macintosh users, the GroupWise 6.5 system will support connections from the older GroupWise 5.2 Macintosh client. The primary weakness of this client lies in the fact that it is no longer receiving active development attention at Novell.

For customers who purchase GroupWise 5.2, the Macintosh 5.2 client can be used against a GroupWise 6.5 post office. You must obtain the *.VEW files so that the Macintosh client can utilize a GroupWise 6.5 post office. Obtain the file GWMACVEW.EXE from Novell's support site for these *.VEW files.

NOTE **In April 2003, at Novell's BrainShare, Novell announced that a new GroupWise client is being developed using Java, and so MAC OS 10 or better MACs will soon have a GroupWise client.**

Strengths

Here are some of the 5.2 Macintosh client's strong points:

- Native PowerPC support
- Notification of new messages
- Robust collaboration support, including shared folders, access to GroupWise libraries, calendar viewing, and full status tracking
- Remote mailbox support allows you to work offline

Weaknesses

The Macintosh client's primary weakness is that several features available in the GroupWise 6.5 Windows client are not available in the GroupWise Macintosh client.

GroupWise 5.2 16-Bit Windows Client

The GroupWise 5.2 16-bit Windows client is technically unsupported, but it works against a GroupWise 6.5 post office, in client/server mode. Some organizations still support a few legacy 486- or even 386-class machines, which lack the horsepower to support a 32-bit version of Windows. These machines, running Windows 3.1, will support the GroupWise 5.2 16-bit client. This client is no longer receiving development attention from Novell and does not support the full suite of features found in the 32-bit client. This client is available only to customers who have upgraded from previous versions of GroupWise.

Strengths

Here are the strengths for maintaining a 16-bit Windows client:

- Support for Windows 3.1 or Windows NT 3.5
- Out-of-the-box macro support (This is not available in any other GroupWise client. Some organizations choose to run the 16-bit client on a 32-bit platform for support of macros they created under earlier versions of GroupWise.)
- Collaboration support includes full status tracking and full calendar support

Weaknesses

The 16-bit Windows client's primary weakness is that several features that are in the GroupWise 6.5 Windows 32-bit client are not available in the GroupWise 16-bit client.

GroupWise 6.5 WebAccess Full-Featured Browser Support

Novell has long been touting the standards-based platform as the future alternative platform for GroupWise. If the 32-bit Windows client won't work for you, any machine that can run a Web browser can access a GroupWise mailbox through the WebAccess gateway.

Strengths

WebAccess with full-featured browser support has several strong features:

- No installation required. Any Java-compliant Web browser can serve as the GroupWise client.
- Low bandwidth. This client will perform acceptably over a dial-up connection.

- Wide cross-platform support. This client performs the same on Windows, Macintosh, UNIX, and Linux workstations.
- Support for SSL connections ensures security for mailbox access across the Internet.

Weaknesses

This platform also has its weaknesses:

- No notification of new messages
- No offline support
- No archive access

GroupWise 6.5 WebAccess/Wireless Simple HTML Browser Support

The advent of handheld computers has brought back the need for simple HTML support, the stuff GroupWise WebAccess was made of, long ago. So, for example, a Pocket PC platform device can access GroupWise 6.5 WebAccess. The interface is simpler and leaner, specifically for the popular handheld computer platforms. Figure 12.11 shows the GroupWise 6.5 WebAccess simple HTML browser support interface.

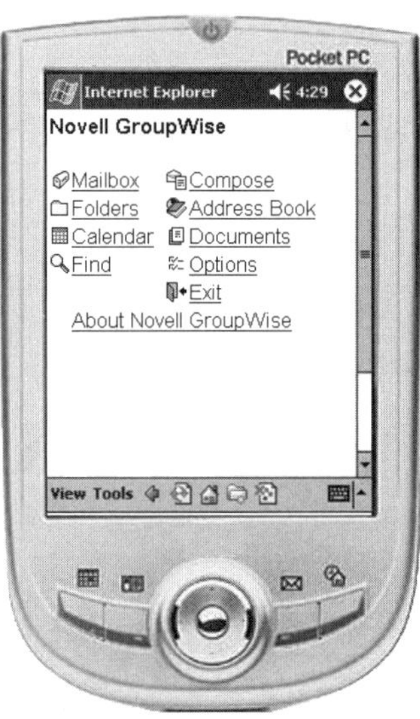

FIGURE 12.11 GroupWise 6.5 WebAccess with simple HTML support.

Strengths

WebAccess with simple HTML browser support has several strong features:

- No installation required. Any Mozilla 4.x compatible browser or better can support this version of WebAccess.
- Low bandwidth. This client will perform acceptably over a dial-up connection.
- Wide cross-platform support.
- Support for SSL connections ensures security for mailbox access across the Internet.

Weaknesses

This platform also has its weaknesses:

- No notification of new messages
- No offline support
- No archive access

Strengths

This platform's primary strength is its very broad device support.

Weaknesses

Most wireless clients can read messages, but not attachments, and you can compose simple messages. The weaknesses are not really in GroupWise wireless, but in the devices themselves.

GroupWise Internet Agent POP3/IMAP4

Some of your users might want to access their GroupWise e-mail from home, using their Eudora, Netscape Mail, or Outlook Express mailers. Any mail application that supports POP3 or IMAP4 mail access can collect GroupWise e-mail through a correctly configured GroupWise Internet agent. There are POP3 clients for almost any platform, including the very popular Palm OS devices.

NOTE

Chapter 10, "Installing and Configuring the GroupWise Internet Agent," talks more about where to configure POP3 and IMAP4 functionality on the GroupWise Internet agent.

Strengths

Following are the strengths for this support:

- Low user-education costs; they use the tool that they are familiar with
- Low bandwidth
- Mailbox can be used offline (POP3 only)
- Wide cross-platform support

Weaknesses

This configuration has some weaknesses:

- Limited collaboration support; all items show up only as e-mail items on the POP3 or IMAP4 mail application
- No archive access
- No GroupWise library access

Summary

This chapter explained the process of deploying the GroupWise client and administering it. This chapter also introduced the wide variety of platforms and formats that a GroupWise mailbox can access. If you need even more information on upgrading the GroupWise client, see the GroupWise 6.5 Upgrade Guide available at `http://www.caledonia.net`.

PART IV

Practical Administration

CHAPTER 13

Moving Users

CHAPTER 13

A casual survey of GroupWise administrators will reveal that moving users is one of the more problematic tasks they perform. This chapter exposes the architecture behind user moves and presents ways to avoid problems when moving users. This chapter also walks you through the process and explores ways to troubleshoot user moves that have gone wrong.

The superstitious reader might associate ill omens with the fact that the move-user process is discussed in Chapter 13. Although I cannot refute such superstitions, I can assure you that it was not some sort of evil coincidence that this topic ended up on Chapter 13. I did it deliberately…

TIP

Moving a user or a resource involves mainly the same process. The only thing you must do differently in a resource move process is assign a new owner to the resource that already resides on the destination post office.

Understanding the Directory Level Move of a GroupWise User Object

A GroupWise move-user operation is both a GroupWise directory operation and a message-store operation. This section explores what happens in the GroupWise directory when a user object is moved from one post office to the next.

Moving a user is actually called a *rename* by the GroupWise directory processes. The following POA log shows when a user named `BSmith` is moved from one post office to the next:

```
ADM: Completed: Rename object in Post Office
 - User DOMAIN2.PO2.BSMITH (Administrator: (WWW_TREE)
tkratzer.www.americas, Domain: DOMAIN1)
```

The directory-level move of a GroupWise object rarely fails. If you make sure you connect to the destination domain when you perform the move, you will further reduce the likelihood of problems.

In a move-user operation, the *owning domain,* as explained in Chapter 3, "Understanding the GroupWise Directory," isn't readily apparent as in most operations. In a move-user operation in which a user is moved from `DOMAIN1.PO1` to `DOMAIN2.PO2`, the destination domain immediately becomes the owning domain. This means that the destination domain must approve the move/rename operation before anything else will happen. The most important directory processes in a move-user operation are the ones at the destination domain *and* the post office. To ensure a smooth move-user operation at the GroupWise directory level, an administrator should be connected to the destination domain's WPDOMAIN.DB database before issuing the move of the user.

Determining When a Move Is Pending

When you move a user, eDirectory is updated with the object's post office change, but the GroupWise directory might still be propagating the change. If eDirectory reports that the user's post office is `PO2`, but the GroupWise directory reports that the user's post office is `PO1`, the GroupWise snap-in will know that a move is pending. Or if eDirectory reports that a user's post office is still `PO1`, but the GroupWise directory reports that it's `PO2`, the GroupWise snap-in will think that a move is pending.

This condition will exist until the GroupWise directory has successfully broadcast the user move to all other domains. This condition can exist also when the eDirectory replica that you made changes to when moving the user is not the same replica that NetWare administrator is talking to at a certain moment in time. Until this condition no longer exists, the GroupWise directory is in a freeze state regarding the user's object. If you attempt to view the details or edit this user's object while in this freeze state, you will see the message shown in Figure 13.1.

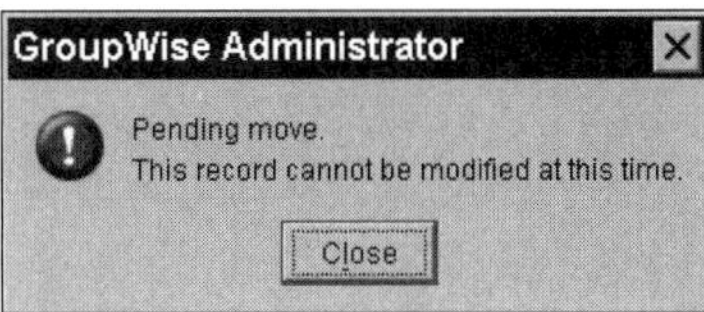

FIGURE 13.1
The pending move warning.

This freeze state can be a two-edged sword at times. It sometimes means that the GroupWise directory is waiting to catch up to the eDirectory. Generally, however, it means that eDirectory is behind the GroupWise directory. Follow this fictitious scenario with the following players for an explanation of how this happens:

- USERA a user on DOMAINA
- DOMAINA
- DOMAINB
- eDirectory called PARTITION-A-REPLICA-1
- eDirectory called PARTITION-A-REPLICA-2

Following is an explanation of how GroupWise and eDirectory can get out of sync during a GroupWise user move:

1. The state of the system at the directory level is as follows:
    - GroupWise administrator is connected to DOMAINB.
    - The NetWare client is communicating with the eDirectory PARTITION-A-REPLICA-1.
2. The GroupWise administrator moves USERA to DOMAINB.
3. The immediate state of the system at the directory level becomes
    - DOMAINB is the destination domain on the move operation, so DOMAINB approves the move operation.
    - eDirectory PARTITION-A-REPLICA-1 knows about the change to USERA's post office.
    - DOMAINA doesn't know about the change to USERA yet; it's still replicating.
    - eDirectory PARTITION-A-REPLICA-2 is not aware of the change to USERA; it hasn't synched with eDirectory PARTITION-A-REPLICA-1 yet.
4. The error state is as follows:
    - Another administrator, authenticated to eDirectory PARTITION-A-REPLICA-2, launches GroupWise administrator.

- GroupWise administrator is connected to **DOMAINB**.
- The NetWare client is communicating with eDirectory **PARTITION-A-REPLICA-2**.
- eDirectory **PARTITION-A-REPLICA-2** hasn't received the change from eDirectory **PARTITION-A-REPLICA-1**.

Now a condition exists in which there is a post office mismatch between GroupWise and eDirectory. The result is that the administrator will continue to get the pending move message shown in Figure 13.1.

Generally, this condition will rectify itself with time. Sometimes it doesn't, though. In this case, you will have to do something to clean up the directory. For example, you could delete the user's eDirectory account when you are not snapped into GroupWise. You could also try removing the link between GroupWise and eDirectory, which is called *disassociating* GroupWise attributes. This option is in ConsoleOne under Tools, GroupWise Utilities, GW/eDirectory Association.

Understanding the Chronology of the Move-User Process

The following is an investigation into how a user is moved. The user, **USERA**, is being moved from the **SOURCE** post office to the **DESTINATION** post office. The entire move-user process at both the directory level and the message-store level is mapped out in this section.

The GroupWise 6.5 Post Office Agents (POAs) support a much faster move-user method than previous versions of GroupWise. The method of using a user's message store is called a *live move*. The traditional, slower move method is called a *message-file move* or a *batch move*. This chapter first explains the message-file move process, and then the live-move process.

GroupWise message-file move is the old standby architecture for a move-user operation. GroupWise 6.5 POAs prefer to use live move, and will attempt to use the live move architecture first. POAs use the message-file move method only when one of the following conditions exist:

- Either post office object has the Disable Live Move check box checked under the Post Office Settings property page.
- One POA cannot contact the other via its TCP/IP address.
- Either POA is version 5.5.x or older.

Moving a GroupWise User via Message-File Move

When performing this move, you are connected to the destination domain, DOMAIN2.

Following is a step-by-step explanation of a user move via a message-file move:

SOURCE

POST OFFICE	DOMAIN
PO1	DOMAIN1

DESTINATION

POST OFFICE	DOMAIN
PO2	DOMAIN2

TIP

If the user will be moving to a new domain, make sure to be connected to the new domain when issuing the move-user operation.

TIP

In order to show the detail in the GroupWise POA logs as shown in this example scenario, your POAs must have their logging level set to verbose.

Following is an explanation of a user move scenario in which a file based/batch move mechanism is used:

1. In ConsoleOne, the GroupWise administrator is connected to DOMAIN2 and moves USERA to DOMAIN2.PO2.

   The MTA for DOMAIN2 broadcasts the USERA move to PO2. PO2's POA must approve the rename of USERA.PO1.DOMAIN1 to USERA.PO2.DOMAIN2.

NOTE

DOMAIN2 **does not broadcast the** USERA **move operation to the rest of the GroupWise system yet.**

2. PO2 receives the USERA rename and the ADMIN thread of the POA updates its WPHOST.DB file with the USERA "rename" operation. Also note that POA reports that the user ADMIN.AMERICAS is the person who performed the rename operation.

The ADMIN thread of the POA creates a message to be sent back to its domain, DOMAIN2, indicating that PO2 received and approved the rename of USERA.

```
20:10:36 275 MTP: Received file: WWWFS1\SYS:
/DOMAIN2/PO2\wpcsout\ofs\2\af09d3bc.005, Size: 590
20:10:36 25C Processing af09d3bc.003
20:10:36 25C Processed OK
20:10:36 25C Processing af09d3bc.005
20:10:36 25C Processed OK
20:10:36 25E ADM: Completed: Rename object in
post office - User DOMAIN1.PO2.USERA (Administrator:
(WWW_TREE_2) admin.AMERICAS, Domain: DOMAIN2)
20:10:36 25E ADM: Completed: Update object in
post office - Misc DOMAIN2.PO2 (Administrator:
(WWW_TREE_1) admin.AMERICAS, Domain: DOMAIN1)
20:10:36 25E ADM: Completed: Update object in
post office - Misc DOMAIN2.PO2 (Administrator:
(WWW_TREE_1) admin.AMERICAS, Domain: DOMAIN1)
20:10:38 1E9 MTP: File sent: AF09D3BC.001 Queue: 2
➥Size: 1442
20:10:38 184 MTP: File sent: AF09D3BC.003 Queue: 2
➥Size: 654
20:10:39 1E9 MTP: File sent: AF09D3BC.005 Queue: 2
➥Size: 434
20:10:39 149 MTP: File sent: AF09D3BC.007 Queue: 2
➥Size: 434
```

3. DOMAIN2 receives the message from PO2 indicating an all-systems-go on the move-user operation.

   DOMAIN2 broadcasts the rename of USERA to the entire GroupWise system by sending the rename operation to the primary domain and to all of the post offices in DOMAIN2. DOMAIN2 also sends a few messages down to the destination post office that contains the client option settings for the user, which are merged into the user database. At this point the USER*xxx*.db exists on the destination post office.

4. DOMAIN1 receives the message from the primary domain indicating the rename of USERA.

   DOMAIN1's MTA-ADMIN thread updates the WPDOMAIN.DB file with the rename of USERA. DOMAIN1's MTA transmits the rename of USERA to PO1.

5. PO1 receives the USERA rename operation.

   PO1's POA updates the WPHOST.DB file with the rename of USERA.

6. **P01** sends an inventory list of **USERA**'s mailbox to **P02**.

   P01's POA creates a message containing the inventory list of all the records in **USERA**'s mailbox. **P01**'s POA reads as follows:

```
20:10:51 269 MTP: Received file: WWWFS1/sys:
\DOMAIN1\PO2\wpcsout\ofs\2\af09d3cb.001, Size: 1494
20:10:51 17C Processing af09d3cb.001
20:10:51 17C Processed OK
20:10:51 176 ADM: Completed: Rename object in post
➥office -
User DOMAIN1.PO2.USERA (Administrator: (WWW_TREE_2)
admin.AMERICAS, Domain: DOMAIN2)
20:10:51 170 MTP: Sender thread started for link
➥DOMAIN1: 5 running
20:10:51 189 MTP: File sent: 2F09D3CB.001 Queue: 2
➥Size: 1414
20:10:51 150 MTP: File sent: AF09D3CB.003 Queue: 2
➥Size: 658
20:10:56 269 MTP: Received file: WWWFS1/sys:
\DOMAIN1\PO2\wpcsout\ofs\2\2f09d3d0.001, Size: 1498
20:10:56 17C Processing 2f09d3d0.001
20:10:56 17C Processing admin task: Rename
20:10:56 17C (TRACKMOVE) BEGIN PHASE -
'SendInventoryList_Begin': USERA (3xq)
20:10:56 17C (TRACKMOVE) (.Move) Initiating: USERA (3xq)
20:10:56 17C User USERA moved, terminating current
➥session
20:10:56 17C (TRACKMOVE) (.Move)
Queue First Deferred Retry Message: USERA (3xq)
20:10:56 17C (TRACKMOVE) Attempting
➥'SendInventoryList': USERA (3xq)
20:10:56 17C (TRACKMOVE) (.Move) Sending Inventory
➥List (43): USERA (3xq)
20:10:56 17C (TRACKMOVE) END PHASE -
'SendInventoryList_Begin' (0 0x00000000): USERA (3xq)
20:10:56 17C Admin task completed: OK
```

7. **P02**'s POA receives the inventory list and requests the inventory items. The POA reports the following in its log:

```
20:11:03 25C (TRACKMOVE) BEGIN PHASE -
'SendRetrievalList_Begin_Batch': USERA (3xq)
20:11:03 25C (TRACKMOVE) (Move.) Receiving Inventory
➥List: USERA (3xq)
20:11:03 25C (TRACKMOVE) Receiving and storing
INVENTORY list - should only happen once: USERA (3xq)
20:11:03 25C Purge record 02CC
```

```
20:11:03 25C (TRACKMOVE) (Move.) Inventory List
➥Received  (43): USERA (3xq)
20:11:03 25C (TRACKMOVE) (Move.)
Queue First Deferred Retry Message: USERA (3xq)
20:11:03 25C (TRACKMOVE) (Move.) Requesting User
➥Data: USERA (3xq)
20:11:03 25C (TRACKMOVE) Attempting
➥'SendRetrievalList': USERA (3xq)
20:11:03 25C (TRACKMOVE) Establish Transfer
➥BATCH: USERA (3xq)
20:11:03 25C (TRACKMOVE) (Move.)
Remaining Inventory Count (43): USERA (3xq)
20:11:03 25C (TRACKMOVE) END PHASE -

'SendRetrievalList_Begin_Batch' (0 0x00000000):
➥USERA (3xq)
```

8. The source post office sends the user's entire inventory, one record at a time.

   PO1's POA receives the message requesting the inventory items from PO2's POA; the log reads as follows:

```
20:11:11 269 MTP: Received file: WWWFS1/sys:
\DOMAIN1\PO1\wpcsout\ofs\6\ef09d3df.7t1, Size: 1192
20:11:11 17C Processing ef09d3df.7t1
20:11:11 17C Replication Request: USERA
20:11:11 17C (TRACKMOVE) BEGIN BATCH
➥'NgwrepReqBoxNeed': USERA (3xq)
20:11:11 17C (TRACKMOVE) (.Move)
Request for User Data Received: USERA (3xq)
20:11:11 17C (TRACKMOVE) (.Move) Folders
➥Sent (13): USERA (3xq)
20:11:11 17C (TRACKMOVE) (.Move) Bag Records
➥Sent (13): USERA (3xq)
20:11:11 17C (TRACKMOVE) (.Move) Category Records
➥Sent (4): USERA (3xq)
20:11:11 150 MTP: File sent: EF09D3DF.7T3 Queue: 6
➥Size: 944
20:11:11 189 MTP: File sent: EF09D3DF.7T1 Queue: 6
➥Size: 792
20:11:11 150 MTP: File sent: EF09D3DF.7T5 Queue: 6
➥Size: 844
20:11:11 189 MTP: File sent: EF09D3DF.7T7 Queue: 6
➥Size: 972
20:11:11 150 MTP: File sent: EF09D3DF.7T9 Queue: 6
➥Size: 836
20:11:11 189 MTP: File sent: EF09D3DF.7TB Queue: 6
➥Size: 848
```

```
20:11:11 150 MTP: File sent: EF09D3DF.7TD Queue: 6
➥Size: 836
20:11:11 189 MTP: File sent: EF09D3DF.7TF Queue: 6
➥Size: 844
20:11:11 150 MTP: File sent: EF09D3DF.7TH Queue: 6
➥Size: 836
20:11:11 189 MTP: File sent: EF09D3DF.7TJ Queue: 6
➥Size: 840
20:11:12 150 MTP: File sent: EF09D3DF.7TL Queue: 6
➥Size: 840
20:11:12 189 MTP: File sent: EF09D3DF.7TN Queue: 6
➥Size: 1008
20:11:12 150 MTP: File sent: EF09D3DF.7TP Queue: 6
➥Size: 1032
20:11:12 189 MTP: File sent: EF09D3DF.7TR Queue: 6
➥Size: 860
20:11:12 17C (TRACKMOVE) (.Move) Items Sent (6):
➥USERA (3xq)
20:11:12 17C (TRACKMOVE) (.Move)
AddressBook Components Sent (3): USERA (3xq)
20:11:12 17C (TRACKMOVE) (.Move) User Settings
➥Sent (4): USERA (3xq)
20:11:12 17C (TRACKMOVE) END BATCH
'NgwrepReqBoxNeed' (0 0x00000000): USERA (3xq)
20:11:12 17C Processed OK
```

The log reports that USERA's inventory items were sent to PO2. The log file also indicates that when a user's mailbox is moved, every record is extracted and moved individually as its own file.

9. PO2 receives USERA's inventory.

   PO2's POA receives each record and reports the following in its log:

```
20:11:18 275 MTP: Received file: WWWFS1\SYS:
\DOMAIN2\PO2\wpcsout\ofs\6\ef09d3e6.7t1, Size: 1028
20:11:18 25C Processing ef09d3e6.7t1
20:11:18 25C (TRACKMOVE) (Move.) Folder Received:
➥USERA (3xq)
20:11:18 25C Processed OK
20:11:18 275 MTP: Received file: WWWFS1\SYS:
\DOMAIN2\PO2\wpcsout\ofs\6\ef09d3e6.7t3, Size: 876
20:11:18 25C Processing ef09d3e6.7t3
20:11:18 25C (TRACKMOVE) (Move.) Folder Received:
➥USERA (3xq)
20:11:18 25C Processed OK
20:11:18 275 MTP: Received file: WWWFS1\SYS:
/DOMAIN2/PO2\wpcsout\ofs\6\ef09d3e6.7t5, Size: 928
```

```
20:11:19 25C Processing ef09d3e6.7t5
20:11:19 25C (TRACKMOVE) (Move.) Folder Received:
➥USERA (3xq)
20:11:19 25C Processed OK
20:11:19 275 MTP: Received file: WWWFS1\SYS:
/DOMAIN2/PO2\wpcsout\ofs\6\ef09d3e7.7t1, Size: 1056
20:11:19 25C Processing ef09d3e7.7t1
20:11:19 25C (TRACKMOVE) (Move.) Folder Received:
➥USERA (3xq)
20:11:19 25C Processed OK
20:11:19 275 MTP: Received file: WWWFS1\SYS:
/DOMAIN2/PO2\wpcsout\ofs\6\ef09d3e7.7t3, Size: 920
20:11:19 25C Processing ef09d3e7.7t3
20:11:19 25C (TRACKMOVE) (Move.) Folder Received:
➥USERA (3xq)
20:11:19 25C Processed OK
20:11:19 275 MTP: Received file: WWWFS1\SYS:
/DOMAIN2/PO2\wpcsout\ofs\6\ef09d3e7.7t5, Size: 932
20:11:20 25C Processing ef09d3e7.7t5
20:11:20 25C (TRACKMOVE) (Move.) Folder Received:
➥USERA (3xq)
20:11:20 25C Processed OK
20:11:20 275 MTP: Received file: WWWFS1\SYS:
/DOMAIN2/PO2\wpcsout\ofs\6\ef09d3e8.7t1, Size: 920
20:11:20 25C Processing ef09d3e8.7t1
20:11:20 25C (TRACKMOVE) (Move.) Folder Received:
➥USERA (3xq)
20:11:20 25C Processed OK
20:11:20 275 MTP: Received file: WWWFS1\SYS:
/DOMAIN2/PO2\wpcsout\ofs\6\ef09d3e8.7t3, Size: 928
20:11:20 25C Processing ef09d3e8.7t3
20:11:20 25C (TRACKMOVE) (Move.) Folder Received:
➥USERA (3xq)
20:11:20 25C Processed OK
20:11:20 275 MTP: Received file: WWWFS1\SYS:
/DOMAIN2/PO2\wpcsout\ofs\6\ef09d3e8.7t5, Size: 920
20:11:22 25C (TRACKMOVE) (Move.) Bag Record
➥Received: USERA (3xq)
20:11:22 25C Processed OK
20:11:22 275 MTP: Received file: WWWFS1\SYS:
/DOMAIN2/PO2\wpcsout\ofs\6\ef09d3ea.7t5, Size: 952
20:11:23 25C Processing ef09d3ea.7t5
20:11:23 25C (TRACKMOVE) (Move.) Bag Record
➥Received: USERA (3xq)
20:11:23 25C Processed OK
20:11:23 275 MTP: Received file: WWWFS1\SYS:
```

```
/DOMAIN2/PO2\wpcsout\ofs\6\ef09d3eb.7t1, Size: 984
20:11:23 25C Processing ef09d3eb.7t1
20:11:23 25C (TRACKMOVE) (Move.) Bag Record
➥Received: USERA (3xq)
20:11:23 25C Processed OK
20:11:23 275 MTP: Received file: WWWFS1\SYS:
/DOMAIN2/PO2\wpcsout\ofs\6\ef09d3eb.7t3, Size: 968
20:11:23 25C Processing ef09d3eb.7t3
20:11:23 25C (TRACKMOVE) (Move.) Bag Record
➥Received: USERA (3xq)
20:11:23 25C Processed OK
20:11:23 275 MTP: Received file: WWWFS1\SYS:
/DOMAIN2/PO2\wpcsout\ofs\6\ef09d3eb.7t5, Size: 972
20:11:24 25C Processing ef09d3eb.7t5
20:11:24 25C (TRACKMOVE) (Move.) Bag Record
➥Received: USERA (3xq)
20:11:24 25C Processed OK
20:11:24 275 MTP: Received file: WWWFS1\SYS:
/DOMAIN2/PO2\wpcsout\ofs\6\ef09d3ec.7t1, Size: 964
20:11:24 25C Processing ef09d3ec.7t1
20:11:24 25C (TRACKMOVE) (Move.) Bag Record
➥Received: USERA (3xq)
20:11:25 25C Processed OK
20:11:26 275 MTP: Received file: WWWFS1\SYS:
/DOMAIN2/PO2\wpcsout\ofs\6\ef09d3ee.7t1, Size: 836
20:11:26 25C Processing ef09d3ee.7t1
20:11:26 25C (TRACKMOVE) (Move.) Category Record
➥Received: USERA (3xq)
20:11:26 25C Processed OK
20:11:26 275 MTP: Received file: WWWFS1\SYS:
/DOMAIN2/PO2\wpcsout\ofs\6\ef09d3ee.7t3, Size: 840
20:11:26 25C Processing ef09d3ee.7t3
20:11:27 25C (TRACKMOVE) (Move.) Item Received:
➥USERA (3xq)
20:11:27 275 MTP: Received file: WWWFS1\SYS:
/DOMAIN2/PO2\wpcsout\ofs\6\ef09d3ef.7t3, Size: 1800
20:11:27 25C Processed OK
20:11:27 25C Processing ef09d3ef.7t3
20:11:27 25C (TRACKMOVE) (Move.) Item Received:
➥USERA (3xq)
20:11:27 25C Processed OK
20:11:27 275 MTP: Received file: WWWFS1\SYS:
/DOMAIN2/PO2\wpcsout\ofs\6\ef09d3ef.7t5, Size: 936
20:11:27 25C Processing ef09d3ef.7t5
20:11:27 25C (TRACKMOVE) (Move.) Bag Record Received:
➥USERA (3xq)
```

```
20:11:27 25C Processed OK
20:11:27 275 MTP: Received file: WWWFS1\SYS:
/DOMAIN2/PO2\wpcsout\ofs\6\ef09d3ef.7t7, Size: 836
20:11:28 25C Processing ef09d3ef.7t7
20:11:28 25C (TRACKMOVE) (Move.) Category Record
➥Received: USERA (3xq)
20:11:29 25C (TRACKMOVE) (Move.) AddressBook
Component Received: USERA (3xq)
20:11:29 25C Processed OK
20:11:29 275 MTP: Received file: WWWFS1\SYS:
/DOMAIN2/PO2\wpcsout\ofs\6\ef09d3f1.7t4, Size: 956
20:11:29 25C Processing ef09d3f1.7t4
20:11:29 25C (TRACKMOVE) (Move.) AddressBook
➥Component Received: USERA (3xq)
20:11:29 25C Processed OK
20:11:30 275 MTP: Received file: WWWFS1\SYS:
/DOMAIN2/PO2\wpcsout\ofs\6\ef09d3f2.7t0, Size: 872
20:11:30 25C Processing ef09d3f2.7t0
20:11:30 25C (TRACKMOVE) (Move.)
AddressBook Component Received: USERA (3xq)
20:11:30 25C Processed OK
20:11:30 275 MTP: Received file: WWWFS1\SYS:
/DOMAIN2/PO2\wpcsout\ofs\6\ef09d3f2.7t2, Size: 952
20:11:30 25C Processing ef09d3f2.7t2
20:11:30 25C (TRACKMOVE) (Move.) User Setting
➥Received: USERA (3xq)
20:11:30 25C Processed OK
20:11:30 275 MTP: Received file: WWWFS1\SYS:
/DOMAIN2/PO2\wpcsout\ofs\6\ef09d3f2.7t4, Size: 924
20:11:30 25C Processing ef09d3f2.7t4
20:11:30 25C (TRACKMOVE) (Move.) User Setting
➥Received: USERA (3xq)
20:11:30 25C Processed OK
20:11:31 275 MTP: Received file: WWWFS1\SYS:
/DOMAIN2/PO2\wpcsout\ofs\6\ef09d3f3.7t0, Size: 1152
20:11:31 25C Processing ef09d3f3.7t0
20:11:31 25C (TRACKMOVE) (Move.) User Setting
➥Received: USERA (3xq)
20:11:31 25C Processed OK
20:11:31 275 MTP: Received file: WWWFS1\SYS:
/DOMAIN2/PO2\wpcsout\ofs\6\ef09d3f3.7t2, Size: 884
20:11:31 25C Processing ef09d3f3.7t2
20:11:31 25C (TRACKMOVE) (Move.) User Setting
➥Received: USERA (3xq)
20:11:31 25C (TRACKMOVE) The INVENTORY list is now
➥EMPTY: USERA (3xq)
```

```
20:11:31 25C (TRACKMOVE) (Move.)

Transfer Complete. All Items Received: USERA (3xq)
```

Several other lines with this same syntax are reported in the POA log file. You should note that the line in the log file that reads: `The INVENTORY list is now EMPTY` means that all of `USERA`'s data was received by `PO2`.

10. `PO2` received all the records indicated on the original inventory list, so it tells `PO1` to purge `USERA`'s mailbox. The log file for `PO2` reads as follows:

```
20:11:31 25C (TRACKMOVE) (Move.) Sending Purge
➥Notification: USERA (3xq)
20:11:31 25C (TRACKMOVE) Sending ACTION_DELETE_USER:
➥USERA (3xq)
20:11:31 25C (TRACKMOVE) Deleting INVENTORY list
```

11. `PO1` purges `USERA`'s messages.

`PO1` receives the request to purge `USERA` and reports the following in its log:

```
0:11:36 17C (TRACKMOVE) BEGIN PHASE -
➥'DeleteMovedUser_Batch': USERA (3xq)
20:11:36 17C (TRACKMOVE) (.Move) Purging User Data:
➥USERA (3xq)
20:11:36 17C (TRACKMOVE) Attempting 'WpeDeleteUserExt':
➥USERA (3xq)
20:11:36 17C Delete user/resource: USERA
20:11:36 17C Purge item record
20:11:36 17C Purge item record
20:11:36 17C Purge message record
20:11:36 17C Purge item record
20:11:36 17C Purge message record
20:11:36 17C Purge item record
20:11:36 17C Purge message record
20:11:36 17C Purge item record
20:11:36 17C Purge message record
20:11:36 17C Purge item record
20:11:36 17C Purge message record
20:11:36 17C (TRACKMOVE) Moved user deleted
'WpeDeleteUserExt' (0 0x00000000): USERA (3xq)
20:11:36 17C (TRACKMOVE) Completed
'WpeDeleteUserExt' (0 0x00000000): USERA (3xq)
20:11:36 17C (TRACKMOVE)
Sending status MOVE_USER_FINISHED: USERA (3xq)
```

```
20:11:36 17C (TRACKMOVE) END PHASE -
'DeleteMovedUser_Batch' (0 0x00000000): USERA (3xq)
20:11:36 17C Processed OK
```

Several other lines in the log indicate that the POA purged the user's records one by one.

NOTE **When a user's mailbox is purged, you should see the messages** `Purge item record`**, but you will not see a message that says something like** `USERA deleted`**.**

Key Technical Factors in the Message-File Move

Remember that a user move is a move of both a user's directory object and his or her messages. Moving the GroupWise user's message store tends to be much more problematic than moving the object in the GroupWise directory. An understanding of the move-user architecture can really help you out of a bind. The discussion in this next section still refers to USERA and other terms introduced in the previous section.

The Twelve-Hour, Seven-Day Clock

When the destination PO receives the inventory list, it puts the inventory list in the USERxxx.DB file for USERA.

NOTE **The** xxx **is replaced with** USERA**'s file ID, or FID, as explained in Chapter 4, "Understanding the GroupWise Information Store."**

The USERxxx.DB file should already exist because of the client options that were sent down by the destination domain at the beginning of the move. The POA will place the inventory list within the USERxxx.DB file. The pointer to the inventory list is also placed in the PO\OFMSG\NGWDFR.DB file (the deferred delivery database) on the destination post office. The inventory list in the deferred delivery database serves as a reminder to the destination PO to query the source PO for the items on the inventory list for USERA every 12 hours for seven days. Items remaining on the inventory list indicate that the destination PO has not received all the items from the source PO. Once all of a user's message items have moved across, and the purge notification is sent, the POA on the source PO deletes the pointer to the inventory list.

The reminder mechanism was designed to create a fail-safe message-store move operation. This fail-safe mechanism is good, but it can create problems. Here are the contributing factors for potential problems:

- Message-store items are moved one item at a time
- The message-store items are sent through the "6" queue directories
- The POA is hard-coded to use only one thread to service the WPCSOUT\OFS\6 directory

Now consider this scenario:

- An administrator moves 50 users from PO1 to PO2
- The users have an average of 3,000 message items each, with many attachments
- PO1 and PO2 are across the WAN from each other
- The WAN link speeds are slow

In this scenario, it is unlikely that PO1 and PO2, or the MTAs between them, will each be able to process 150,000 messages in 12 hours.

The 12-hour clock will pass, and PO2 will assess that PO1 has not sent all of the inventory items. The items might be in transit to PO2, or might even be waiting in PO2's WPCSOUT\OFS\6 directory. Because PO2 has not processed the items, though, PO2 has not acknowledged that the items have arrived. PO2 requests the items from PO1 again. Another 150,000 items begin their journey across your WAN. Now you've got a real mess, and it is possible that neither post office will recover from the situation.

What cardinal rule should be used to prevent this scenario? *Don't move a large amount of users at one time!*

Some administrators ask, "How many can I safely move?" If the move is across a WAN link, and your users have a large amount of messages, move them one at a time. If your users have a small amount of e-mail, or you are moving them in a fast, LAN-type environment, you can usually get away with moving 10 users at a time. If you move 10 users at once, and the WPCSIN and WPCSOUT/OFS "6" directories don't back up, your agents and your network are up to the challenge, and you can consider moving more than 10 users. If the queues back up for more than an hour or so, you are probably moving more users at once than you should be.

Integrity of the Message Store

When a user moves from PO1 to PO2, the integrity of the message store on both post offices is important. The integrity of the message store on PO1 is critical. If a customer is implementing message-store maintenance routines on their GroupWise post offices, then there is generally little concern about the message store. The move-user task list (in the upcoming section "Moving a GroupWise User") talks about which Mailbox/Library Maintenance/GWCHECK routines to run on a user to be moved.

Now that you are familiar with the "old" way of moving users, let's see what the new live user-move technology consists of, so you can see the major differences between a batch move and a live user move. You will see the advantage of the live user move over the batch user move.

Moving a GroupWise User via Live Move

When performing this move, you are connected to the destination domain, DOMAIN2. Table 13.1 lays out the scenario details for this example user move.

TABLE 13.1 **Live User Move Scenario Details**

SOURCE		
POST OFFICE	**POA IP ADDRESS & PORT**	**DOMAIN**
PO1	137.65.55.211:1677	DOMAIN1
DESTINATION		
POST OFFICE	**POA IP ADDRESS & PORT**	**DOMAIN**
PO2	137.65.55.211:1678	DOMAIN2

TIP **When moving a user from one post office to another, if the user will be moving to a new domain, make sure to be connected to the new domain when issuing the move-user operation.**

Following are the details regarding an example of a live user move:

1. In ConsoleOne, the GroupWise administrator is connected to DOMAIN2 and moves USERA to DOMAIN2.PO2.

   The MTA for DOMAIN2 broadcasts the USERA move to PO2 so that PO2's POA can approve the rename of USERA.PO1.DOMAIN1 to USERA.PO2.DOMAIN2.

DOMAIN2 does not broadcast the USERA move operation to the rest of the GroupWise system yet.

2. PO2 receives the USERA rename. The ADMIN thread of the POA updates its WPHOST.DB file with the USERA "rename" operation.

   The ADMIN thread of the POA creates a message to be sent back to its domain, DOMAIN2, indicating that PO2 has received and approved the rename of USERA.

```
20:10:36 275 MTP: Received file: WWWFS1\SYS:
/DOMAIN2/PO2\wpcsout\ofs\2\af09d3bc.005, Size: 590
20:10:36 25C Processing af09d3bc.003
20:10:36 25C Processed OK
20:10:36 25C Processing af09d3bc.005
20:10:36 25C Processed OK
20:10:36 25E ADM: Completed: Rename object in
post office - User DOMAIN1.PO2.USERA (Administrator:
(WWW_TREE_1) admin.AMERICAS, Domain: DOMAIN2)
20:10:36 25E ADM: Completed: Update object in
post office - Misc DOMAIN2.PO2 (Administrator:
(WWW_TREE_1) admin.AMERICAS, Domain: DOMAIN1)
20:10:36 25E ADM: Completed: Update object in
post office - Misc DOMAIN2.PO2 (Administrator:
(WWW_TREE_1) admin.AMERICAS, Domain: DOMAIN1)
20:10:38 1E9 MTP: File sent: AF09D3BC.001 Queue: 2
➥Size: 1442
20:10:38 184 MTP: File sent: AF09D3BC.003 Queue: 2
➥Size: 654
20:10:39 1E9 MTP: File sent: AF09D3BC.005 Queue: 2
➥Size: 434
20:10:39 149 MTP: File sent: AF09D3BC.007 Queue: 2
➥Size: 434
```

3. DOMAIN2 receives the message from PO2 indicating an all-systems-go on the move-user.

   DOMAIN2 broadcasts the rename of USERA to the entire GroupWise system by sending the rename operation to the primary domain and to all of the post offices in DOMAIN2. DOMAIN2 also sends a few messages down to the destination post office that contain the client option settings for the user, which are merged into the user database. At this point, the USERxxx.db now exists on the destination post office.

4. DOMAIN1 receives the message from the primary domain indicating the rename of USERA.

DOMAIN1's MTA-ADMIN thread updates the WPDOMAIN.DB file with the rename of USERA. DOMAIN1's MTA transmits the rename of USERA to PO1.

5. PO1 receives the USERA rename operation.

   PO1's POA updates the WPHOST.DB file with the rename of USERA.

6. PO1's POA logs into the PO2's POA as USERA and gives it an inventory list of all the records in USERA's mailbox. PO1's POA log reads as follows:

```
20:53:08 17C (TRACKMOVE) BEGIN PHASE -
'SendInventoryList_Begin': USERA (5nw)
20:53:08 17C (TRACKMOVE) (.Move) Initiating: USERA (5nw)
20:53:08 17C User USERA moved, terminating current
➥session
20:53:08 17C (TRACKMOVE) (.Move)
Queue First Deferred Retry Message: USERA (5nw)
20:53:08 17C (TRACKMOVE) Attempting 'SendInventoryList':
➥USERA (5nw)
20:53:08 17C (TRACKMOVE) Beginning 'LiveMoveLogin':
➥USERA (5nw)
20:53:08 17C (TRACKMOVE) Attempting connection
'LiveMoveLogin' to 137.65.55.211:1678: USERA (5nw)
20:53:08 170 MTP: Sender thread started for link
➥CORP: 5 running
20:53:09 1C5 MTP: Received file:
WWWFS1/sys:\corp\corppo\wpcsout\ofs\2\af09cfa5.001,
➥Size: 830
20:53:09 17C (TRACKMOVE) (.Move) Sending Inventory
➥List (56): USERA (5nw)
20:53:10 19F MTP: File sent: AF09CFA4.003 Queue: 2
➥Size: 842
20:53:10 203 MTP: File sent: AF09CFA4.001 Queue: 2
➥Size: 842
20:53:10 17C (TRACKMOVE) END PHASE -
'SendInventoryList_Begin' (0 0x00000000): USERA (5nw)
```

7. PO2's POA reports that PO1's POA has logged in and PO2's POA receives the inventory list. The POA reports the following in its log:

```
20:54:47 27A C/S Login dos ::GW Id=USERA :: 0.0.0.0
20:54:47 27A Remote Request From: USERA
20:54:47 27A (TRACKMOVE) BEGIN PHASE -
'SendRetrievalList_Begin_Live': USERA (5nw)
20:54:47 27A (TRACKMOVE) (Move.) Receiving Inventory
➥List: USERA (5nw)
20:54:48 27A (TRACKMOVE) Receiving and storing
```

```
INVENTORY list - should only happen once: USERA (5nw)
20:54:48 27A Purge record 02CC
20:54:48 27A (TRACKMOVE) (Move.) Inventory List
➥Received (58): USERA (5nw)
20:54:48 27A (TRACKMOVE) (Move.)
Transferred Item from Prime User: USERA (5nw)
20:54:48 27A (TRACKMOVE) (Move.)
Transferred Item from Prime User: USERA (5nw)
20:54:48 27A (TRACKMOVE) (Move.)
Queue First Deferred Retry Message: USERA (5nw)
20:54:48 27A (TRACKMOVE) END PHASE -

'SendRetrievalList_Begin_Live' (0 0x00000000):
➥USERA (5nw)
```

8. P02's POA looks at the inventory list and determines whether it has any of the items in the inventory list within its message store already. The POA for P02 then logs into the POA for P01 as USERA. It requests the inventory items it doesn't already have. This step shows what happens on P02's POA. The POA reports the following in its log:

```
20:55:00 252 (TRACKMOVE) BEGIN PHASE -
'SendRetrievalList_LiveRetry': USERA (5nw)
20:55:00 252 (TRACKMOVE) (Move.) Requesting User
➥Data: USERA (5nw)
20:55:00 252 (TRACKMOVE) Attempting 'SendRetrievalList':
➥USERA (5nw)
20:55:00 252 (TRACKMOVE) Beginning 'LiveMoveLogin':
➥USERA (5nw)
20:55:00 252 (TRACKMOVE) Attempting connection
'LiveMoveLogin' to 137.65.55.211:1677: USERA (5nw)
20:55:00 252 (TRACKMOVE) Establish Transfer LIVE:
➥USERA (5nw)
20:55:00 252 (TRACKMOVE) (Move.)
Remaining Inventory Count (58): USERA (5nw)
20:55:00 252 (TRACKMOVE) BEGIN LIVE 'Dispatch':
➥USERA (5nw)
20:55:00 252 (TRACKMOVE)
Continue LIVE 'Dispatch' (1 0x00000001): USERA (5nw)
20:55:00 252 (TRACKMOVE) (Move.) Folder Received:
➥USERA (5nw)
SEVERAL SIMILAR LINES OMITTED
20:55:01 252 (TRACKMOVE) (Move.) Bag Record Received:
➥USERA (5nw)
SEVERAL SIMILAR LINES OMITTED
20:55:01 252 (TRACKMOVE) (Move.) Category Record
➥Received: USERA (5nw)
```

```
20:55:01 252 (TRACKMOVE) (Move.) Item Received:
➥USERA (5nw)
SEVERAL SIMILAR LINES OMITTED 20:55:01 252 (TRACKMOVE)
➥(Move.)
AddressBook Component Received: USERA (5nw)
SEVERAL SIMILAR LINES OMITTED
20:55:01 252 (TRACKMOVE) (Move.) User Setting
➥Received: USERA (5nw)
SEVERAL SIMILAR LINES OMITTED 20:55:01 252 (TRACKMOVE)
➥(Move.) Remaining Inventory Count: USERA (5nw)
20:55:01 252 (TRACKMOVE) END LIVE 'Dispatch'
➥(0 0x00000000): USERA (5nw)
20:55:01 252 (TRACKMOVE) The INVENTORY list is now
➥EMPTY: USERA (5nw)
20:55:01 252 (TRACKMOVE) Finished retrieval
LIVE - will be purging SOURCE database: USERA (5nw)
20:55:01 252 (TRACKMOVE) (Move.)
Transfer Complete. All Items Received: USERA (5nw)
20:55:01 252 (TRACKMOVE) (Move.)
Sending Purge Notification: USERA (5nw)
20:55:01 252 (TRACKMOVE) Deleting INVENTORY list
20:55:01 252 (TRACKMOVE) END PHASE -
'SendRetrievalList_LiveRetry' (0 0x00000000):
➥USERA (5nw)
```

9. This step shows what was happening simultaneous to step 8 in which `P02`'s POA is logged into `P01`'s POA and is asking for the inventory items from `P01`'s POA. `P01`'s log file reads as follows:

```
20:55:00 264 C/S Login dos ::GW Id=USERA :: 0.0.0.0
20:55:00 264 Remote Request From: USERA
20:55:00 264 (TRACKMOVE) BEGIN PHASE - 'GetMoveBoxLive':
➥USERA (5nw)
20:55:00 264 (TRACKMOVE) (.Move)
Request for User Data Received: USERA (5nw)
20:55:00 264 (TRACKMOVE) BEGIN LIVE
'GetMoveBoxLive' (1 0x00000001): USERA (5nw)
20:55:00 264 (TRACKMOVE) (.Move) Folders Sent
➥(14): USERA (5nw)
20:55:00 264 (TRACKMOVE) (.Move) Bag Records Sent
➥(19): USERA (5nw)
20:55:00 264 (TRACKMOVE) (.Move) Category Records
➥Sent (4): USERA (5nw)
20:55:00 264 (TRACKMOVE) (.Move) Items Sent (5):
➥USERA (5nw)
20:55:00 264 (TRACKMOVE) (.Move)
AddressBook Components Sent (10): USERA (5nw)
```

```
20:55:00 264 (TRACKMOVE) (.Move) User Settings Sent (6):
➥USERA (5nw)
20:55:00 264 (TRACKMOVE) (.Move) Remaining Inventory
➥Count: USERA (5nw)
20:55:00 264 (TRACKMOVE) END LIVE
'GetMoveBoxLive' (1 0x00000001): USERA (5nw)
20:55:00 264 (TRACKMOVE) END PHASE -
'GetMoveBoxLive' (0 0x00000000): USERA (5nw)
20:55:01 264 Remote Request From: USERA
20:55:01 264 (TRACKMOVE) BEGIN PHASE -
➥'DeleteMovedUser_Live': USERA (5nw)
20:55:01 264 (TRACKMOVE) Sending LIVE
➥'PurgeUser_AsSource': USERA (5nw)
20:55:01 264 (TRACKMOVE) (.Move)
Sending LOCAL Purge Notification: USERA (5nw)
20:55:01 264 (TRACKMOVE) Sending ACTION_DELETE_USER:
➥USERA (5nw)
20:55:01 264 (TRACKMOVE) END PHASE -

'DeleteMovedUser_Live' (0 0x00000000): USERA (5nw)
```

10. In step 8, P02's POA requested that P01 delete all of USERA's inventory items. It did so via the message file though, rather than via a request that it makes while logged into P01's POA. P01's POA reports the following in its log file.

```
20:55:07 29B MTP: Received file:
WWWFS1/sys:\corp\corppo\wpcsout\ofs\2\2f09e713.001,
➥Size: 936
20:55:07 17C Processing 2f09e713.001
20:55:07 17C Processing update:
20:55:07 17C (TRACKMOVE) BEGIN PHASE -
'DeleteMovedUser_Batch': USERA (5nw)
20:55:07 17C (TRACKMOVE) (.Move) Purging User Data:
➥USERA (5nw)
20:55:07 17C (TRACKMOVE) Attempting 'WpeDeleteUserExt':
➥USERA (5nw)
20:55:07 17C Delete user/resource: USERA
20:55:07 17C Purge item record
20:55:07 17C Purge item record
20:55:07 17C Purge item record
20:55:07 17C Purge item record
20:55:07 17C Purge item record
<<Several other "Purge item record" messages
20:55:08 17C (TRACKMOVE) Moved user deleted
'WpeDeleteUserExt' (0 0x00000000): USERA (5nw)
```

```
20:55:08 17C (TRACKMOVE) Completed
'WpeDeleteUserExt' (0 0x00000000): USERA (5nw)
20:55:08 17C (TRACKMOVE) Sending status
➥MOVE_USER_FINISHED: USERA (5nw)
20:55:08 17C (TRACKMOVE) END PHASE -
'DeleteMovedUser_Batch' (0 0x00000000): USERA (5nw)
20:55:08 17C Processed OK
```

It's important to note that several other lines in the log indicate that the POA purged the user's records one by one.

TIP

When a user's mailbox is purged, you should see the messages `Purge item record`, but you will not see a message that says something like `USERA deleted`.

Moving users from one post office to another has been enhanced to increase performance and reliability. At Novell, a benchmark test was done that involved moving an account with 47,000 items. The live move took 45 minutes, whereas the message-file move took more than four hours.

Both source and destination post offices must have at least one new POA with an IP address and port defined for client/server processing in order for a live move to work.

In live-move mode, individual files containing each message in a user's mailbox are no longer transferred. Instead, a client/server thread is used to transfer information between the post offices. If a connection cannot be made by PO1's POA to PO2's POA, there will be a timeout of 15 minutes. The connection will be retried two more times, after which the message-file move method will be attempted. If a connection is made but the other POA does not support the live-move method, the old message-file move method will be used without any retries.

After the inventory list is pushed to PO2's POA, PO2's POA will attempt to connect to PO1's POA using an IP connection to retrieve the data. If a connection cannot be made, there will be a timeout of 15 minutes. The connection will be retried four more times, after which the message-file move method will be attempted. If a connection is made, but the other POA does not support the new method (because it is older, or because live move has been disabled), the old retrieve data method will be used without any retries.

With live moves, the recommendation is still to move one user at a time. Multiple simultaneous moves can be successful, but if all client/server threads on the target POA are being used, the previously mentioned time-outs could occur, and the old method will be used.

All GroupWise 6.5 POAs attempt a live move first, before falling back to a message-store move. When you move a user, you cannot request a live move over a message-store move. The POA is hard-coded to attempt a live move if everything is in place. If for some reason, you want to disable live move, do the following:

1. Go to the destination's post office object in ConsoleOne.
2. Go to the Properties of the post office object.
3. Go to the GroupWise Post Office Settings property page.
4. Check the Disable Live Move check box.
5. Follow steps 1–4 on the source post office object as well.

Moving a GroupWise User

The following is an exhaustive task list for moving a user. If you are moving several users, most steps in the list can be done simultaneously for all users.

TIP

Do not proceed from one item to the next unless you have achieved success with the current task!

Here are some terms to keep in mind as you review the task list:

- **Destination domain:** The domain that owns the post office the user is being moved to
- **Destination PO:** The post office that the user is being moved to
- **Source PO:** The post office that the user is currently a member of
- **USERA:** The user being moved

Following are the minimum recommended steps for moving a user:

1. In ConsoleOne, connect to the destination domain.

   To do this, select Tools, GroupWise System Operations, Select Domain. Browse to the UNC path for the destination domain and select the WPDOMAIN.DB file.

TIP **Throughout the remainder of this checklist, always stay connected to the *destination* domain.**

2. Check and clean USERA's message store with Mailbox/Library Maintenance routines.

NOTE **Avoid using the stand-alone GWCHECK (GWCHECK.EXE). It is slower compared to the POA routines spawned from Mailbox/Library Maintenance.**

   Highlight USERA and select Tools, GroupWise Utilities, Mailbox/Library Maintenance. Then select the Structural Rebuild option, make sure that only the User check box is checked under the Databases tab, and then click Run.

   Issue an Analyze/Fix Databases command on the contents of USERA's user database (don't bother with the message database). You can issue this Mailbox/Library Maintenance job immediately after issuing the structural rebuild.

   Confirm that both of these maintenance routines happened, and that there are no major problems with USERA's message store. Make sure—if you are not set up as the GroupWise domain's administrator in ConsoleOne—that you CC yourself via the CC option on the Results tab.

3. Make sure that USERA's object will synchronize to the source and destination POs.

   Temporarily change USERA's phone number.

   Log in as a test user on the destination PO and confirm that USERA's phone number changed, and that the user shows up as a member of the source PO.

   Log in as a test user on the source PO. Confirm that USERA's phone number changed, and that the user shows up as a member of the source PO.

   Change USERA's phone number back.

TIP **When moving a large amount of users in a short period of time, it won't be feasible to take this step. Try to synchronize all of the users though. When moving multiple users, simply highlight the users to be moved by Shift-Click or Ctrl-Click and select Tools, GroupWise Utilities, Synchronize.**

If you are going to move USERA to another eDirectory OU, go to step 4. If not, skip to step 5.

4. Disassociate USERA's eDirectory object from the user's GroupWise object.

   Highlight USERA. Select Tools, GroupWise Utilities, GW/eDirectory Association, Disassociate GroupWise Attributes. Move USERA to his/her new eDirectory OU.

5. View the details on USERA and make note of the FID.

   Highlight USERA and edit the properties. Select the GroupWise Account property page to take note of the file ID.

6. Move USERA.

   Highlight USERA in the GroupWise view. Right-click the USERA object, and select Move. Select the world icon in the GroupWise Move dialog box and browse to and select the destination post office. Follow the remaining prompts to allow the user to move.

7. If you disassociated USERA's eDirectory object from USERA's GroupWise object, re-associate them.

   Highlight USERA in the eDirectory view, not the GroupWise view. Edit USERA, and go to the GroupWise Account property page. Click the world icon to the right of the Post Office field. Select the post office that USERA is now a member of. When you press OK as though you want to finish the operation on USERA, a message should come up that asks if you want to associate USERA's eDirectory object with its GroupWise object. Click the Yes button, if everything is correct.

8. Assess the success of your move. Do so using the User Move Status utility explained in the next section. Make sure to use the Clear Status feature when you have determined that the user did move successfully.

When you have confirmed that USERA has moved successfully, make sure to reassociate the user's GroupWise object with his or her eDirectory object. Do this by highlighting USERA in the GroupWise view and selecting Tools, GroupWise Utilities, GW/eDirectory Association, Associate Objects. Then associate USERA's GroupWise object with his or her eDirectory object.

Assessing the Success of a User Move

You moved a user and everything seems to be quiet on the POAs. You might now be asking, "Did everything get moved?"

Now I'll introduce a utility new to GroupWise 6.5 called User Move Status. The User Move Status utility is one of the best ways to assess the status of a user move. Here's how you assess whether a user move is successful. Please note that this utility requires that you have GroupWise 6.5 Support Pack 1 snap-ins to ConsoleOne. The source and destination domains and post offices must also be version 6.5 to report this information properly. If you are in a mixed system, you will not get all the information from this utility like you would with a pure 6.5 system. Follow these steps to use the User Move Status utility:

1. Connect to the destination domain (the domain the user is now a member of) in ConsoleOne.
2. Highlight the user who moved, and select Tools, GroupWise Utilities, User Move Status.
3. When the User Move Status utility comes up, verify that the user's move status is "Move completed", as shown in Figure 13.2.

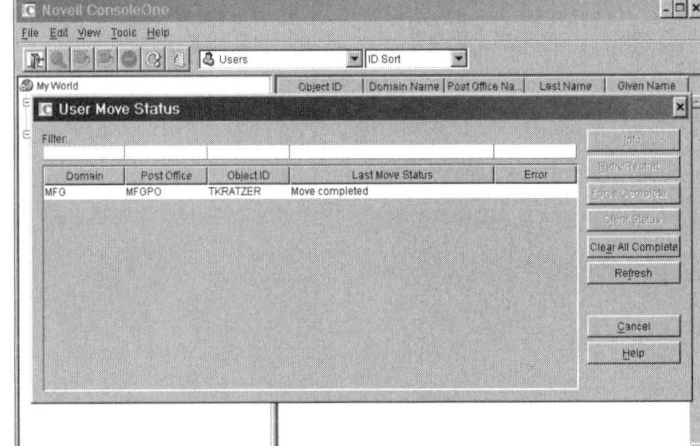

FIGURE 13.2 The User Move Status utility showing a successful user move.

The User Move Status utility shows several status reports for a standard successful move. I've listed most of them, in chronological order. Here they are:

```
Destination domain updated
Destination post office updated
```

```
Primary domain updated
Source domain updated
Source post office updated
Build item request
Fixing proxy lists
Retrieve mailbox items
Build item list
Mailbox inventory list received
Mailbox inventory transfer completed
Send item request
Completed retrieving items
Purge mailbox request received
```

The POAs for the source and destination post offices actually create these statuses at different stages during a user move. These statuses are sent as administrative messages. These administrative messages are sent up from the GroupWise POAs to the MTAs to commit to the GroupWise WPDOMAIN.DBs. You can read these statues through ConsoleOne via the User Move Status utility.

If your user move happens quickly, it might be difficult to catch each of these statuses. The final status of "Move Completed" (assuming the move was successful) will always remain until you actually remove the status via the Clear Status option from the User Move Status utility. I strongly recommend that you do select the Clear Status button. If you do not, and then later need to move the user again, you might have difficulty doing so.

Using the User Move Status Utility When Something Goes Wrong Moving a User

There are a several kinds of move-user failures. Don't panic—you can generally dig your way out. This section looks at the most common kinds of failure, and how to solve those problems with the User Move Status utility. This discussion assumes that both the source and destination post offices are running GroupWise 6.5 POAs.

The User Moved, but None or Only a Part of the User's Messages Moved

This is a common scenario. You could wait for 12 hours, and let the POA try again. But why, when you've got the User Move Status utility. Consider the following scenario.

TKRATZER is being moved from MFGPO to CORPPO. He can log into CORPPO, but none of his mail is in his mailbox at CORPPO. You can use the User Move Status utility to help kick off the move again:

1. In ConsoleOne, highlight TKRATZER's user object in the GroupWise view.
2. Select Tools, GroupWise Utilities, User Move Status.
3. As long as the Last Move Status does not read "Move Completed" the Retry/Restart button should be available, as shown in Figure 13.3.

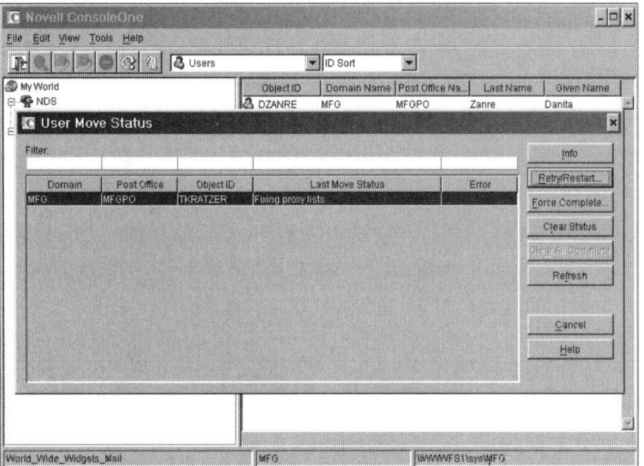

FIGURE 13.3
The User Move Status utility with the Retry/Restart button.

4. This is a great feature, not just because you can kick-start the move, but also because you can look at the POAs or the POA logs and watch for what happens after you use Retry/Restart. There's another set of choices to make after starting the Retry/Restart option. Figure 13.4 shows you the choices you can make from this screen.
5. The most conservative action to take is to retry the last step of the mailbox move. It's important to note though, that you really should observe the destination and source POAs to see what errors might appear after taking this action. Very often there's a good chance that this option won't advance the mailbox move process.

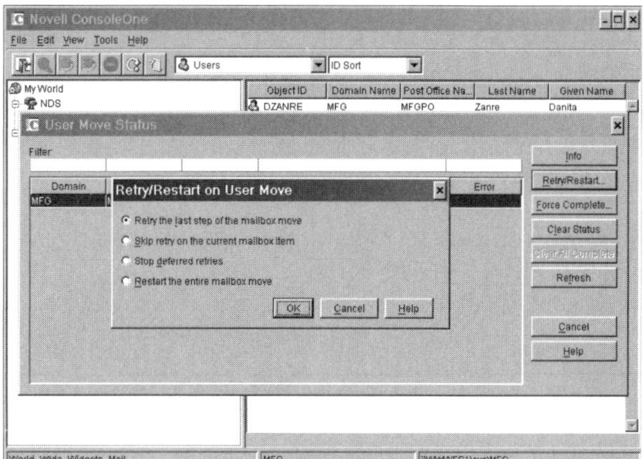

FIGURE 13.4
Choose from the Retry/Restart options.

6. If the "Retry the last step of the mailbox move" option does not resolve the problem, and you have confirmed that your POA's aren't having a problem connecting to one another, generally the next best thing to do is choose "Skip retry on the current mailbox item". This tells the POAs to skip the action they are currently trying to take, and move to the next action.

You then proceed to use the other options available to you in the Retry/Restart dialog box shown in Figure 13.4 if you determine the appropriate option to use. None of the options has the potential to be very harmful. You should feel comfortable using any of them.

The User Moved, but the User's Password Was Lost

If you have LDAP authentication enabled, this section does not apply to you.

This problem is similar to the previous problem. A user's password is just another record in the User Settings section of the user database. The user settings are the last things to be moved in a mailbox move. It is possible that nothing was moved to the user's mailbox on the new post office. The best thing to do is reset the user's GroupWise password from ConsoleOne. The user can then access his/her mailbox and tell you the status of the move.

Other Features of the User Move Status Utility

There are some other options/buttons available to you in the User Move Status utility, as follows:

- **Info**—When you highlight a user in the status section and click the user's Info button, you will see all the info on that user. This can be particularly helpful when there is a long error message associated with the user move. You'll have difficulty seeing the error unless you use the Info button. Scroll down until you see the Move Error or Move Status field.
- **Force Complete**—If users are satisfied that they have everything they want, but the POAs still are being held up by something, you can use Force Complete. It tells the POAs to stop trying to move anything else, and to purge the user's mailbox from the source post office. You should always determine whether a user move was successful. If the status in ConsoleOne does not indicate "Move completed" but your user is satisfied with the move, make sure to use the Force Complete option. If you do not, it's possible that the source post office won't thoroughly purge messages that should be purged from the source post office.
- **Clear Status**—This option just clears the current status you are highlighting. If the status is anything other than "Move completed", when the POAs send up their next move status message, that new status message will appear. You should use the Clear Status button after a user's move is successful (Move completed), or after you've forced it to complete with the Force Complete button.
- **Clear All Complete**—This is kind of like a bulk "Clear Status" option for clearing the "Move completed" status on user objects that have successfully moved.

The User Move Status utility also tracks resource moves.

Resources are just like user moves (except a new owner has to be assigned to the resource). The move behavior, including the troubleshooting process, is the same when moving a resource.

Tips for Moving Many Users

Many GroupWise customers are consolidating GroupWise post offices. There are a few actions you should take to ensure that the move-user process goes successfully, as follows:

- Make sure that QuickFinder Indexing is not scheduled to run during the time that the user moves are happening. If needed, disable QuickFinder Indexing. Make sure to re-enable it when the job is done.
- Make sure that every POA has at least six TCP handler threads and three message handler threads configured, at minimum! When moving a big load of users, you might consider doubling both the TCP handler threads and the message handler threads on both POAs during the period you are moving users.
- On the POA's Agent Settings screen, there's a Max Thread Usage or Priming and Moves option. The default is set to 20%, which is generally sufficient. But during the time that you are moving users, you should consider changing this value—perhaps to around 70%. Move this setting back down after the moves have completed.
- Because you will likely be sending Mailbox/Library Maintenance/GWCHECK jobs to the source POA, you should consider increasing the maintenance handler threads. By doing so, the Mailbox/Library Maintenance/GWCHECK jobs will happen faster; unless your server's CPU is too slow and it cannot handle so many GWCHECK threads at once. You can do this by going to the Maintenance property page of the destination POA. The default is four maintenance handler threads; the maximum is eight. Increase this number when performing maintenance on the users to be moved, and then lower the setting as needed after the user moves.

Follow these tips, and your user moves should go faster. They real keys to successful user moves include following the directions in the section titled "Moving a GroupWise User," and ensuring that the destination and source post offices have been maintained with schedule maintenance events all along.

Summary

This chapter discussed moving users safely and troubleshooting user moves that have gone awry. To ensure safe user moves, do the following:

- Clean the user's message store before initiating the move. It is also assumed that the source and destination post offices have regular Mailbox/Library Maintenance scheduled event routines enabled.
- Don't move more than 10 users at a time (unless you've carefully benchmarked the move process on your system).
- Be connected to the *destination* domain when initiating the move.

When troubleshooting moves that have not gone well, remember these tips:

- Don't panic; read the sections of this chapter that talk about the move-user architecture.
- Determine the extent of the failure of the move (messages missing, directory entries incorrect, and so on) before taking any action.
- Use the user move status and the POA logs to determine the problem.

CHAPTER 14

Library and Document Administration

This chapter introduces some basic document-management concepts, and illustrates how document management is implemented in the GroupWise system. This chapter also walks through some common library and document-administration tasks. Finally, this chapter presents field-tested best practices and recommendations.

GroupWise provides powerful document-management functionality right out of the box. This allows users to work with documents in the same way they work with e-mail messages, appointments, tasks, and reminder notes. Documents become just another item type in the GroupWise information store.

Understanding the Role of Document Management

Document management can be defined as a storage system that utilizes indexing to retrieve documents. This includes managing the creation, revision, review, storage, and ultimate disposition of documents.

Imagine for a moment all of the documents in an organization are stored on workstation hard drives and as hard copy in file cabinets. Ask yourself how accessible these documents are to users who need to view, revise, or copy these documents. What if the hard drives become inaccessible, or if the key to the file cabinet is misplaced? What if the user who owns the document is out on sick leave? What if users forget the path to the documents? How many times have you had to stop and think about which "folder" contains a certain document on your hard drive?

In this situation, documents are likely to be accessible only to the user(s) who created them. Other users are dependent upon the creator for access to the documents. If the user who owns the document is not accessible, the process of accessing the document might break down.

Good document-management points to consider include the following:

- Which process will ensure the latest copy of the document is the copy that's updated?
- What process will ensure that the history of the document is preserved so all versions of the document are maintained?
- What process will create an activity log of users who have accessed the document?
- What process will be used to enforce security of the document so that only authorized users can access the document?

Without a centralized electronic document-management system, these questions are difficult to answer. Many of these document processes require manual attention and thus are subject to manual rates of completion.

In a document-management system, all of these manual processes are handled automatically by document-management software. In a document-management system, documents reside in a centralized place where they are managed and backed up by the system. Version control, accessibility, security, and document lifecycles are all handled by the document-management system.

Electronic documents stored in a document-management system are indexed and can be found by searching using full text, which looks at the contents of the document, or by properties, which are the user-defined attributes of the document. Properties and their related property pages or sheets categorize the document based upon the needs of the company.

Electronic document management first started in the legal and governmental industries and has been steadily spreading to other industries. Many organizations have recognized the value of document management. Today, many law firms use document-management systems to store and organize their documents.

A large law firm can create tens of thousands of documents a year and depends on a document-management system to organize and manage all of its documents. Another example is a research and development department that would like to keep track of their design documents. Another might be pharmaceutical company that wants to centrally manage their product formulas.

To determine whether your organization will benefit from document management, ask yourself these questions:

- Are word processors, spreadsheet applications, or other document-creation applications used in the organization?
- Do users e-mail text documents, presentations, spreadsheets, or other documents to each other as part of their day-to-day jobs?
- Does important information exist in text documents, spreadsheets, or other document files?

If you answered yes to any of these questions, your organization will benefit from document management. You might not need a million-document library, but you will definitely see productivity rewards when you implement a document-management system.

Working with GroupWise Documents

As eluded to, GroupWise documents contain electronic data that needs to be managed. They can be drafts of presentations, briefs, sales reports, pictures, or corporate policies. Even executables can be stored as documents in a GroupWise library.

End-users will access documents through their GroupWise mailbox or through WebAccess or WebPublisher. There are four ways to access documents from the GroupWise client:

- Document references in the Documents folder
- The Find feature in GroupWise
- Query folders
- Document references in shared folders

Most document-management features are available only in the GroupWise Windows 32-bit client. Limited document-management functionality is available in the GroupWise Web client.

Document References

By default, when a user creates or accesses a document, a special pointer to that document is created in the Documents folder of the user's mailbox. This pointer is called a *document reference*. The Documents folder, with its collection of document references, can be considered a user's work list. Figure 14.1 shows a user's Documents folder.

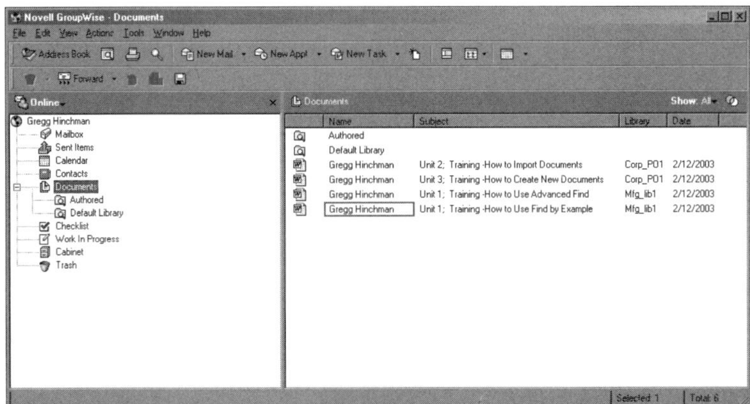

FIGURE 14.1
Document references in a user's Documents folder.

A document reference is a pointer to a document stored in the library. Many users think a document reference is necessary to access a document, but in truth a document reference is nothing more than a handy shortcut to a document.

To open a document in a GroupWise library, simply double-click the appropriate document reference.

Document References and Deleted Documents

A document reference that points to a document that has been deleted from the library is not very handy, because it points at something that no longer exists. It does have some use, however. The document reference still contains a link to the document activity log found in the appropriate DMDLppnn.DB file. This file has some very useful information about what happened to the document and where it was last located. For example, a dialog box like the one shown in Figure 14.2 will appear when you're trying to open a document reference to a document that no longer exists.

FIGURE 14.2 E811 error on a document reference.

Notice the path information given in this dialog box (the line beginning with `\\DEMO2SVR`). This is the last known path of the document Binary Large Object (BLOB) file. To retrieve the actual document, the document BLOB can be restored from tape, provided the backup system has been working properly. This BLOB file can be re-imported as a new GroupWise document by a user who previously accessed the original document, or by a user with the Manage right to this library. The document will then be uncompressed, unencrypted, and placed into the library as new document with a new document number.

The Find Feature

Users can use the Find feature to locate documents. The Find Results window will display a list of pointers, also known as document references, which users can double-click to access documents. Any document that matches the criteria in the Find dialog box will show up in the Find Results window. Users can then save the results as a query folder if the query will be needed again.

The Find feature can search the contents of a document for an occurrence of a word or it can search the properties of a document properties page for said properties.

NOTE

A *document property page* is an electronic form that contains specific information (called properties) about the specific document to which it belongs. A property page contains the following properties: the creator's name, the author's name, the date the document was created, the document type, and other customizable information fields. Properties are specifically designed to assist in describing the document's purpose.

Query Folder

A query folder can be created with predefined search criteria to locate documents. Each time the folder is accessed, the search is dynamically performed. This means the user will always access the newest documents that meet the search criteria as long as indexing is current.

For example, user Gregg in the IS department creates a query folder that searches for any document in any library. Each time he opens this folder, all documents in all libraries are displayed assuming that Gregg has been given at least View rights to the document, and that Gregg has rights to the libraries. Gregg can also have Manage rights on these libraries, and must apply that right in his search criteria.

Shared Folder

A shared folder can be used to hold document references. This creates a rather unique situation. Any user who has rights to the shared folder will have View rights, at least, to any documents with references in the shared folder. The folder's sharing list takes precedence over the document's sharing list.

The documents in the shared folder shown in Figure 14.3 is viewable to any GroupWise user who has access to the shared folder, whether or not that user was included in the sharing list for the document itself. When a document is added to the shared folder, you will receive a message detailing the rights given, as in Figure 14.4.

NOTE

The use of shared folders is not recommended with GroupWise document management. Aside from the potential document security hole, a large amount of shared folders places an unnecessary strain on the GroupWise system. Use query folders whenever possible.

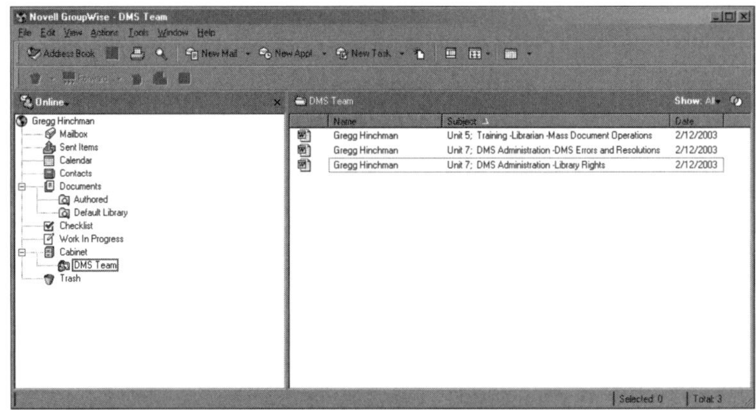

FIGURE 14.3
Documents in a shared folder.

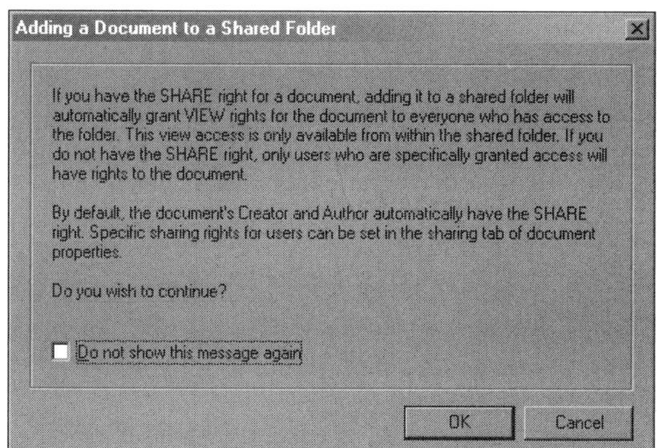

FIGURE 14.4 Message for adding a document to a shared folder.

Document Management and Application Integrations

As mentioned, when a user double-clicks a document reference (a shortcut to the document stored in the library), that document opens. This means GroupWise must communicate with the application into which the document is opened.

The most common and effective means of integrating your document applications with GroupWise is via the Open Document Management API (ODMA). ODMA integrations occur when the integrated application calls the ODMA library on the workstation to determine whether an ODMA service provider is present. When the GroupWise client is installed and the application integrations are enabled, GroupWise shows up as an ODMA service provider.

ODMA integrations allow the GroupWise interface to be used in place of the application's usual Save or Open dialog boxes.

Document Management Security

Security is a key feature of GroupWise document management, and it is administered through a three-tier system. The three types of rights are:

- *Library rights:* Granted by the administrator; these apply to an entire library
- *Document rights:* Granted by document creators; these apply to individual documents
- *Document version rights:* Granted by document creators; these apply to individual versions of individual documents

In order for users to access a document, they must have all three types of rights in some form. If a user is given document rights, but not library rights, the user cannot access the document. This is due to the fact that the user will not be able to access the library in which the document is stored. Also, if a user is given library rights, but has no rights to an individual document or a document version, the user cannot access the document or version. Nor will the user see a document reference when doing a search for the document using either a query folder or the Find feature. This is a common incident when GroupWise document manage is first implemented. Training on document rights and their uses will resolve such incidents. Training is discussed later in the chapter.

Library Rights

Library rights include Add, Change, Delete, View, Set Official Version, Reset In-Use Flag, and the Manage right (for users to serve as GroupWise librarians). These rights are granted through ConsoleOne via the Library object's rights property page (see Figure 14.5). They can be given per library to all users, to a few privileged users, or to a combination of the two. Library rights can further be divided into the following rights:

- *Public rights:* Grant all users in the GroupWise system rights to the library
- *Individual/Distribution List rights:* Grant specific users and/or distribution list members' rights to the library

NOTE

By default, when GroupWise is first installed, a library is created and all public rights are enabled. This means all users in the GroupWise system have rights to place documents into the library, whether they intended to or not. Many GroupWise administrators have been surprised to find out that users are using document management.

TIP

It is recommended you disable document management until users have been trained and your company is prepared to implement and support it. To disable GroupWise document management, deselect the public rights.

The Add right allows a user to add a document to the library. A user with the Add right can import and create a new document or new version (if he or she has Add rights to the library).

The Change right allows users to edit documents they create, or that they have been given the Edit document right to. If users have not been given the Change library right, they cannot exercise the Edit document right.

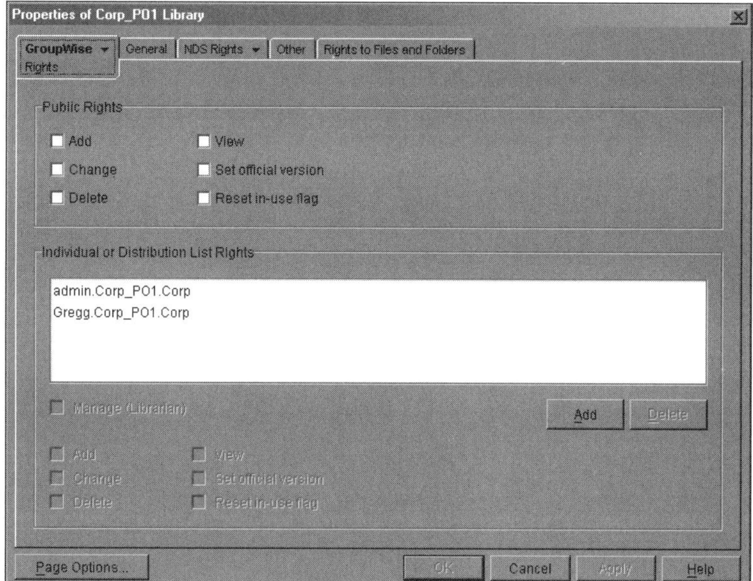

FIGURE 14.5 The Rights property page on a GroupWise library object.

The Delete right allows a user to delete a document or version from the library. This right should be used sparingly, because once a document version is deleted from the library, the only way to bring it back is to get a copy of the document BLOB from a backup tape and import the document BLOB. If you want to allow users to delete documents, but want to closely control the actual deletion process, here's a solution for you. Make a document type of Delete in the Document Properties Maintenance tool. Then tell the users to set the document type to delete when they have a document or version number they want to delete. A little later in this chapter, you will learn how to use the Document Properties Maintenance tool.

Figure 14.6 shows a document that has been changed. In this case the Delete document type has been created with criteria allowing documents that have not been accessed in 30 days or more to be deleted.

When a user changes the document type to delete, the document will not be deleted immediately. The document will not be deleted until it meets the criteria to be deleted as configured in the Document Properties Maintenance tool, and an Archive/Delete Documents maintenance action is run. This gives the administrator much more control over the deletion of documents.

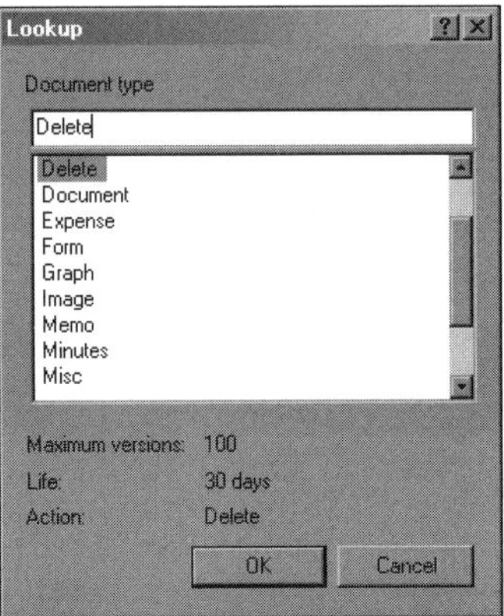

FIGURE 14.6 Changing a document's document type to delete.

TIP

It is recommended you do not delete any documents. This can cause more work for the GroupWise administrator than it's worth. Instead, have a librarian or GroupWise administrator with Manage rights to the library remove all document rights to the document for all users. In a sense, they will be deleted from the users' view. If, at a later time, the documents need to be restored, the same person can simply give the rights back.

The Set Official Version right allows a user to designate a particular version of a document as the official version of that document. There are three possible version types for a document:

- *Official:* The version considered the official copy of the document
- *Current:* The version with the highest version number
- *Other:* Any version other than the current or official versions

Official versions and current versions will be returned on all searches for the official version of a document.

The Reset In_Use Flag right allows a user to change the In_Use flag to "available" without checking the document back into the library. If there is a copy of the document checked out, it will no longer be managed by GroupWise.

For this reason, the Reset In_Use Flag right should be given out sparingly unless you know your users will not abuse the right. If a user does not have rights to Reset In_Use Flag they will see error shown in Figure 14.7 when they try to access this feature. In the GroupWise client, Reset In_Use Flag corresponds to the action of highlighting a document and selecting Actions, Reset Document Status.

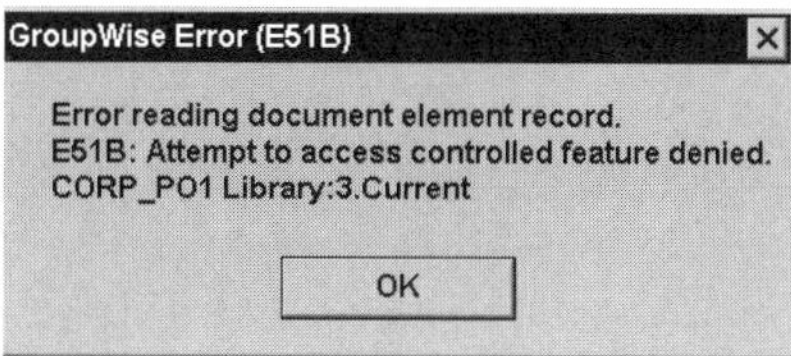
GroupWise Error (E51B)

Error reading document element record.
E51B: Attempt to access controlled feature denied.
CORP_PO1 Library:3.Current

OK

FIGURE 14.7
The E51B error dialog box.

The Manage right cannot be granted for all users; Figure 14.5 illustrates this. It only appears in the lower portion of the Library Rights tab, and can only be checked when a specific user has been added to the library Individual/Distribution List rights access list.

The Manage right allows a user to find any document in the library, even though the author or creator of the document might not have shared the document with anyone. Users with the Manage right can alter the sharing list of any document in the library, granting themselves or anyone else full rights to documents. For this reason, the Manage right should be reserved for system administrators or users who are serving in a capacity as GroupWise librarian.

NOTE

The library Manage right is applied by the librarian user via the GroupWise client, and allows the librarian user more control over document rights than other users.

This chapter discussed the rights that can be set at the Library level. The system administrator sets these rights from the Library object's details window in ConsoleOne. Document rights, however, are set by the users who create documents, and they are set from the document properties page. They can also be set as defaults from the Documents page, by choosing Tools, Options, Documents, Properties, Sharing Defaults.

TIP

Do not give individual user accounts the Manage right. Instead, create an external entity as a librarian. Then assign a user, such as an administrative assistant, the librarian GroupWise account. Use the `/@U-` switch in a GroupWise icon on their desktop. This helps ensure that the librarian will not accidentally perform manage operations. They will have to think about which GroupWise account they need to use to manage a library. Also, this account can be assigned to another person, if the original person is on vacation or leaves the company. And finally, this allows for further security and tracking via the Activity log.

The rights that can be set at the document level are

- Not Shared
- View

- Edit
- Delete
- Share
- Modify Security

Document rights are specific to a document. By default, only the author or creator of a document will have document rights. Document authors or creators can choose to grant document rights to other users, and can even set a default so that other users have document rights to all new documents he or she creates. Remember, though, that a user without Library rights (granted by the administrator) cannot exercise document rights. Also remember that the librarian user (the user or users with the Manage right to this library) can change document rights independently of the Author or Creator of the document.

NOTE

The Creator is the person physically placing the document into the library. The Author might be the person who wrote the document and was assigned Author status for the document by the Creator. The Author has the same rights as the Creator. This means the Author can remove the Creators' rights. If the Creator or the Author want to exclude the other, they will need to explicitly list the user (Creator or Author) and deny them rights.

The Not Shared feature allows the Creator the absolute highest level of security. When this feature is used, no other users can see the document in the library, except the Author. Again, the Author has the same rights as the Creator. The Author's rights must be explicitly denied. Also, remember those with manage rights can see all documents, even if "Not Shared" is used.

The View right allows a user to view the document. The document cannot be edited, but the user can create a new document by copying the original. This right is also required for the user to find the document when doing a search.

If users have the View right, they can forward the document to anyone inside or outside of the GroupWise system. GroupWise logs this in the activity log of the document as a save function. If the users receiving the document have access to the library where the document is stored, they will access the document directly from the library. If they do not have access to the library, they will access a "snapshot" of the document. GroupWise calls the document a *static copy*, which denotes that it cannot be returned to the library and that all document-management features and functions do not apply to this copy of the document.

If users have only the View right to a document, they cannot check out the document. Logically, GroupWise realizes the Creator/Author does not want the user to be able to change the documents' contents. Therefore, it does not allow the document to be checked out, and consequently changed.

Users cannot create a new version of an existing document if they have the View right. However, they can create a new document using the File, Save As, New Document feature. This creates a new document with a new document number using the old document.

The Edit right allows the document version to be opened in Edit mode. With the Edit right, a user can delete the contents of a document, and save it again. Thus, the Edit right gives users' full power over the content of a document. The Edit right also allows a user to change the properties of a document, or property sheets. When users have the Edit right, they also receive the View right. A user must be able to see the document in order to change its contents.

In order for users to check out a document, they must have the Edit right.

A user cannot create a new version of an existing document if they have the Edit right. However, they can create a new document using the File, Save As, New Document feature. This creates a new document with a new document number using the old document.

TIP

The Edit right cannot be exercised without the Change right at the library level.

The Delete right allows a user to delete the document version. This will remove the associated property sheets and BLOB files from the GroupWise library. This means a user can permanently remove a document from the library. The document can be restored, provided a backup of the library was performed. When the Delete right is given, the user also receives the View right.

Some organizations choose to not allow users to delete documents from a library. They allow only librarians to delete documents from a library. The ability to delete a document from a library is given at the library rights level. The effect is that when users try to delete a document, they receive a message that they do not have sufficient rights.

TIP

The Delete right cannot be exercised without the Delete right at the library level.

The Share right allows a user to place a document into a shared folder. Once the document is in the shared folder, any user who has been given access to the shared folder can view the document. However, when the user searches for the same document in the library explicitly, they will not see it. When the Share right is given, the user also receives the View right. The Share right has no effect on versioning, check out, or e-mail.

The Modify Security right allows a user to change the security settings on a document. This is like an admin equivalent right on the document. This right is necessary if a user needs to create a new version of the document (unless a new version of the document is created indirectly through a GroupWise remote session). Figure 14.8 shows the dialog box that will appear if a user attempts to create a new version of a document, but does not have the Modify Security right. When the Modify Security right is given, the user also receives the View and Edit rights.

A user must have Modify Security rights in order to create a new version of a document. Logically, when users create a new version of a document, they are adding to the documents' "family." This is effectively a change in the document's security structure.

In order for users to have the ability to mark a document as the official version, the users must have the Modify Security right. If they do not have this right, they will get an **E816** error, as shown in Figure 14.8. Logically, marking a version as official changes the security structure of the document.

FIGURE 14.8
The E816 error trying to modify the security on a document.

The Version Specific rights granted at the document level can also be granted more granularly, at the document-version level. To show how this would be useful, consider the following scenario:

> Gregg has created a spreadsheet for the WorldWide Widget Fiscal 2003 budget. He needs to be able to make changes to the document, and needs to allow other users to make changes. At the same time he needs to be able to maintain a static, official copy of the document.

This is where version-specific rights come to play. Gregg creates a new version of the document, and designates the old version as the "Official" version. He then grants all users version-specific rights. Other users can view and edit the "Current" version, but will only be given the View rights to the "Official" version. Gregg will reserve Edit rights to the Official version to himself. This also means if Gregg, the Creator/Author of the document, marks a different version (such as the Current version) as Official, the users will now see the new Official version only. All rights to the "Official" version transfer from the "old" Official version to the "new" Official version.

Version-specific rights are basically the same as document rights, but they are granted on each of the three version types: Official, Current, and Other.

If a user has View and Edit rights to a specific version of a document, the user can check out the document. If the users only have View rights to a specific version of a document, they cannot check out the document.

A user cannot be given the right to create a new version from another version in version level security. As stated previously, a user must have Modify Security rights to create new versions. There is not a Modify Security right at the version level.

A user cannot be given the right to Mark versions as official in version level security. A user must have Modify Security right to mark documents as official, and there is not a Modify Security right at the version level.

A user can be given the right to place a version into a shared folder. This is the Share right and can be given on the official, current, or other version at the version level.

A user can be given the right to delete a version. This is the Delete right and can be given on the official, current, or other version at the version level.

TIP

Give document rights using distribution lists. This will ease the administration of libraries and documents for all users and librarians. If an employee leaves the company, his or her name can simply be removed from the distribution list, and all rights to all libraries and documents are removed. The opposite is true as well. A new employee added to a distribution list will receive all rights to all libraries and documents where the distribution list is named.

A document storage area is a location on disk where document BLOB files are stored. By default, all documents are stored under the post office directory structure in `GWDMS\<LIBRARY>\DOCS`. Additional document storage areas are administered from the Storage Areas tab of the Library object's details window. The storage area can be changed at any time to any path that the Post Office Agent (POA) can access. Administrators can create document storage areas, as shown in Figure 14.9, on separate servers or separate volumes from the post office, and separate directories on the same volume as the post office, in order to be able to manage the disk space. By default, GroupWise creates a storage area under the post office directory structure.

NOTE

If the path of a Library Storage Area changes, existing document BLOBs in the old storage area will stay in the old storage area until they are accessed again. When an existing document in the old storage area is checked out and back in, a new BLOB file is created in the new storage area.

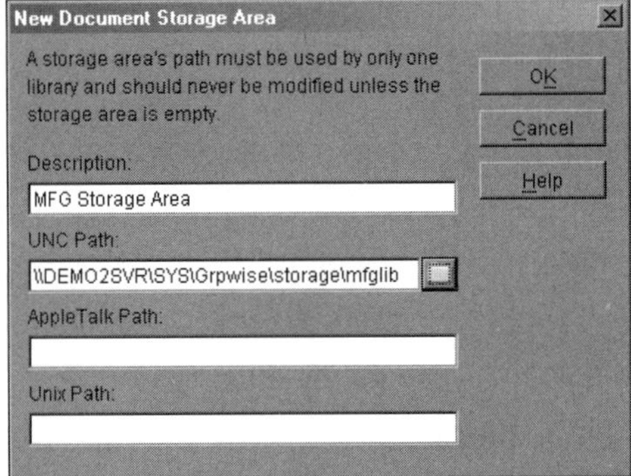

FIGURE 14.9
Creating a new document storage area.

The document storage area object exists in the domain and post office databases. It also exists in the guardian database, and the DMSH and DMSD databases specific to the GroupWise library. Once a document storage area is added to a library, the POA for the post office will not load unless the document storage area is accessible. Therefore document storage areas located remotely from the post office server should only be placed on servers that are guaranteed to be accessible.

TIP

You can force a POA to load even if the library storage area is inaccessible by using the `/noconfig` switch in the POA load statement or startup file. The `/noconfig` switch tells the POA to disregard any POA configuration information in the post office database. Any settings that the POA requires will therefore not be available from WPHOST.DB, and will need to be specified in the POA startup file.

The QuickFinder indexing process is a low-priority POA process that indexes user mailboxes (including attachments and document references) as well as all documents in libraries on the post office. Chapter 8, "Configuring the Post Office Agent (POA)," showed a POA log file that included some QuickFinder indexing.

QuickFinder does not index images or .EXE files. The property sheets of image or EXE document objects are indexed, but any text contained in the actual binary file (such as image comments windows, for example) are not included in the full-text index.

Understanding the QuickFinder Indexing Process

This section explains the function that the QuickFinder Indexing process plays with GroupWise document management.

The QuickFinder indexing process proceeds as follows:

1. The POA begins the indexing run with the library found in the `LIB0001` directory (this is the first library created on this post office). Processing will continue through `LIB00FF`.
2. The POA checks the indexing queue found in the document property databases (DMDD*.DB). This queue indicates which documents have been added or updated since the last indexing run, thus telling the POA which documents need to be indexed or re-indexed.
3. The POA opens each document BLOB file for each document that must be indexed. From this BLOB file, it reads each unique word, and adds that word to a word-list BLOB file unique to this document. Thus, for every document in the library, there are two BLOB files—a document BLOB and a word-list BLOB.
4. If the users have created a document reference, the DMDD files will contain pointers to those document references. For each document reference, a copy of the word-list BLOB will be "hooked" to the mailbox indexing queue. If the mailbox is on a remote post office, the word-list BLOB will be sent to that PO's POA, for inclusion in the mailbox index.

TIP

It is strongly recommended that users create query folders, because each document reference on a remote post office generates BLOB traffic.

5. After all of the queued documents have word-list BLOB files, the word-list files are used to generate the incremental library index database. This database is found in the *.INC files in the `GWDMS\<LIBRARY>\INDEX` directory.

6. With the libraries indexed (remember, you began with `LIB0001` and ran through `LIB00FF`), it is time to begin indexing mailboxes. The POA indexes user databases in alphabetical order, beginning with any prime user databases (PUxxxxxx.DB) in the `OFUSER` directory, and moving through the user databases (USERxxx.DB) in alphanumerical order.

> **TIP**
>
> **When I say the POA indexes user databases in alphanumeric order, it is actually reversed alphabetical order, based off the user's FID. For example, if there are three user databases of userxvc.db, useryub.db, and userzta.db, these user databases would be indexed in this order: userzta.db, useryub.db, and finally userxvc.db.**
>
> **Notice that the POA takes the three-digit FID, reverses it, and then starts the alphabetical indexing.**

7. The POA checks the indexing queue found within each PU or USER database. This queue tells the POA which items were added to the mailbox or to the shared folder since the last time the mailbox was indexed.
8. The POA opens each item found in the PU or USER database it is indexing. The item content can be found in the PU or USER database, or it can be found in a message database (MSGn.DB) or in a BLOB file in the `OFFILES` directory. The item data is indexed from the appropriate master record, wherever that record is located.
9. If the item being indexed is a document reference, the POA should now have a word-list BLOB file hooked to that document reference. This word-list file is used to generate the full-text index of the document reference. This prevents the POA from having to go back to the library and re-index the document (or, worse yet, index a document residing in a library in a remote post office).
10. All index data is written to the incremental index files (*.INC) found in the `OFUSER\INDEX` directory.
11. At the end of the last indexing run of the day, all *.INC file content is combined with the permanent index content found in the *.IDX files. This goes for both the library index and the mailbox index. The *.INC files are deleted, and the *.IDX files are renamed to reflect the fact that they have been updated with new content. All changes to the index databases are reflected in the database catalog in the guardian database (NGWGUARD.DB).

NOTE

Items only need to be indexed once, unless their content changes. Once an item has been indexed, the appropriate indexing queue is updated to reflect the fact that the item need not be indexed again. If the item is updated, even if no changes were made, the item will be added to the indexing queue again. For instance, if a document is checked out and checked back in with no changes, it will still be re-indexed on the next run.

Intervening in the Indexing Process

Once the indexing process begins, the only way to stop it from running is to unload the POA. Fortunately, cases in which it's necessary to call an immediate halt to the indexing process are rare.

Sometimes administrators want to trigger indexing manually. This must be done from the POA console. From the F10, Actions, QuickFinder menu there are four options pertaining to QuickFinder indexing:

- *Update QuickFinder Indexes:* Launches the indexing process. All indexes served by this POA, including the mailbox index and all library indexes, are updated.
- *Compress QuickFinder Indexes:* Merges all incremental indexes with the permanent index. The permanent index files will be renamed to reflect the time the operation was performed.
- *Update and Compress QuickFinder Indexes:* Performs both of the previous operations, beginning with the update.
- *Delete & Regenerate All QuickFinder Indexes:* Deletes the entire index *.IDC and *.IDX files in the `OFUSER\INDEX` directory and the `LIBNNNN\INDEX` directories. It then re-creates the *.IDX files. This option can also be activated by a hidden keystroke. You must be at the initial load screen of the POA. Hold down the Ctrl and Q keys at the same time.

WARNING

Delete & Regenerate All QuickFinder Indexes can take a very, very long time. Perhaps days, if you have a large post office and lots of documents. The index rebuild process will immediately delete all of the indexes for this post office and start to regenerate them. Depending on CPU speed, the POA can index between 10,000 and 30,000 documents an hour. If your post office supports a library with 500,000 documents, and has 500 users each with 2,000 items in their mailbox, you are looking at indexing 1,500,000 documents. At 10,000 per hour, this could take up to 150 hours, or a little over six days.

Non-Dedicated POA for QuickFinder Indexing

By default, the GroupWise POA is set to run the QuickFinder Index. This index runs against both the e-mail and document-management libraries of its respective post office. It is non-dedicated. This works fine for small GroupWise post offices with light document management use. But if the post office is large, has several hundred users or more, and/or document management is used heavily, other options must be implemented. This is especially true if user's expectations are to find documents immediately after inputting them into a library. This requires the QuickFinder Index interval be set to "continuous", or 0 in the details of the POA object, or in the POA configuration file.

WARNING

Setting the QuickFinder Interval to index continuously can severely disrupt e-mail service when using a non-dedicated POA. Also, with a setting of continuous indexing, mass document imports might fail, because the POA is too busy indexing.

TIP

GroupWise 6.5 has a new feature that allows you to set the QuickFinder Interval in minutes. This new feature can be implemented from the details of the POA object under the Quick Finder option.

Dedicated POA for QuickFinder Indexing

If the GroupWise post office(s) are large and document management is being used, you might have a need for a dedicated POA for QuickFinder indexing. A dedicated POA performs only indexing, nothing else. There are two ways to implement a dedicated indexing POA.

The first way assumes a separate server, with a POA running on it, which points back to the library housed on the post office server. This means two POAs are servicing one post office.

The QuickFinder server does not need to be a top-of-the-line server, however. In many cases, a workstation-class machine will suffice. The indexing process is a background process that users do not interact with directly. As long as the CPU speed is reasonably fast (300MHz or better), the POA on this machine should be able to keep up with your indexing needs. Of course, if you have 500,000 documents in your library, and the documents are changing frequently, you might want to consider using a powerful server to perform the Quick Finder process.

The second way to implement a dedicated indexing POA utilizes a separate server and a separate post office for DMS libraries. This means you will have a post office for all your users and their e-mail. The second post office houses all DMS libraries, and no users or e-mail. This option also introduces a design concept called the dedicated post office. A further discussion of this concept occurs later in this chapter.

Planning the Document-Management System

Even if you already have an established GroupWise e-mail system, you will want to take care in the way you implement document management. Consider this: In 1994, most companies that used GroupWise considered e-mail a convenience. By 1998, those same companies considered e-mail "mission-critical." It is not too much of a stretch to imagine the same sort of shift in the document-management arena. You might look at document management as a convenience today, but the odds are good that what you will really be building is a mission-critical system.

This section discusses the areas in which you need to do some research. This section is designed to require you to ask, and answer, some questions about your own organization, so that you can effectively plan your document-management system.

Planning Considerations

There are several factors to consider before implementing GroupWise document management. The list presented here is not inclusive, but it will get you started.

Cost

How much does it cost to implement GroupWise document management? Some of the larger, well-known document-management systems cost hundreds of thousands of dollars and require a whole staff of consultants to implement. Not to mention the staff needed to support it. If the company owns GroupWise, they own document management. There is not an additional software purchase. That is a large savings to start.

How much will it save the company? A good question to be sure. Measuring the savings can be as simple as measuring the time it takes a user to locate a document, whether it's in paper or stored in a directory structure on a server. It can be as complex as measuring how many times users have to re-create documents because they misplaced them or were unaware that someone else had already created them. When does return on investment (ROI) show up? This depends upon the acceptance of document management by the users. ROI can be immediate, if users are accepting and have been well trained. Or it can take months.

Solution

Is document management the right solution? If the company suffers from "knowledge loss," or "knowledge hording," or "misplacement of knowledge," any document-management system will resolve these issues and more. More and more companies are placing SANs (Storage Area Networks) into their environment. This increases the amount of potential disk space available for company files, and makes managing that disk space easier. However, it makes locating a single file among millions more difficult.

Do you have a company-wide need or do just a few departments like the idea? This is a very important point. In order to successfully implement any new system, you must have "buy in" and support from the top, down. This means CEOs must recognize the business problem document management solves. Furthermore, they must agree to enforce the use of document management.

Health

Is your GroupWise system healthy? Is it designed correctly? Does it have any current issues or quirks? Before document management can be implemented, GroupWise must be running well. All links should be IP, for users, POAs and Message Transfer Agents (MTAs). All pending operations should be cleared. Communication throughout the GroupWise system must be tested.

Does the current GroupWise design work? Or do you need to redesign first? How are you going to design GroupWise document management? You must choose among dedicated indexing, non-dedicated indexing, dedicated post offices, or non-dedicated post offices. Is the current GroupWise design capable of growth? Or, are you limited to the servers/design you have? These are all valid design questions.

Is GroupWise optimized and running well? All the servers should be optimally configured for GroupWise. There are several documents at Novell's support Web site that address optimizing GroupWise servers, as does this book. The GroupWise system should have the latest service pack installed on the back end.

Resources

Do you have the physical and technological resources to build and maintain a DMS system? This is an extremely important question. Is there money? If you are implementing document management company-wide, you need servers and staff dedicated to the project. If you are just doing a single department as a pilot, you will still need a small staff and some hardware to support it.

Expertise

Does your company have the technical knowledge to design, build, and maintain a DMS system? If your technical support staff is already overworked and is in "reactive" mode, they will not have time to learn how to successfully implement document management. You might need to hire a consultant. The consultant can lead the project or just provide knowledge transfer. Knowledge can come from this book, Novell's Web site, Novell Library forums, or other books.

Users

Are you going to roll out a pilot document manage library and have just one department try it out? Or, is DMS going to be rolled out to all users at once? The first question you need to ask yourself is how many users are going to use the document-management system.

What about training? How will you train the users? Training is one of the most important factors to a successful implementation of GroupWise document management. Users need to understand that DMS is a paradigm shift, a complete shift in thinking. Users need to learn how to input documents, how to search for documents, and how to revise and set security, to name a few. One focused eight-hour, hands-on training class can be the difference between users accepting or rejecting document management.

TIP

A recommended way to start a roll out of GroupWise document management is to set up a pilot. Pick a department within the company, say HR, containing a small amount of users—no more than 20. Demonstrate GroupWise document management to them, and explain the benefits. If needed, you might spend several days teaching them how to use document management. Build a library around the department, customizing it for them. Then sit back and see what happens. After weeks or months of use, have the users evaluate the system. If the pilot is successful, you can use the library to demonstrate DMS to other departments. Remember, even if you do not expand DMS after the pilot, you will still have to support it. It's far easier to support a small group of users, than the entire company.

Library Design

Planning your document-management system is crucial. How and where you place the libraries can have a huge impact upon your GroupWise system and ultimately the success of document management. There are two design principles to consider. They are

- Centralized versus decentralized libraries
- Dedicated versus non-dedicated post office

How is the GroupWise system administered? Is it centralized or decentralized administration? Centralized administration means GroupWise administrators exist in one location and manage the entire system from that one location. There might be GroupWise servers and post offices at remote sites, but they are administered from the central (corporate) site.

Decentralized has many administrators placed at various sites, managing various parts of the GroupWise system. There are almost always GroupWise servers and post offices in remote sites. The deciding factor as to library placement is how your GroupWise system is currently administered.

The second principle is how to implement libraries. Will you use a dedicated post office just for GroupWise document management libraries or use a non-dedicated post office? A dedicated post office requires a post office that will house only libraries and will only service document management. No e-mail and no users will in the post office.

A non-dedicated post office will have libraries, e-mail, and users in a post office. In the case of the non-dedicated post office, you also have to decide if you will use a dedicated or non-dedicated POA for indexing, as discussed previously.

Centralized vs. Decentralized Libraries

Centralized libraries have the following characteristics:

- Users at remote offices can access GroupWise across Wide Area Network (WAN) links
- Users at remote offices can access libraries across WAN links
- All libraries are physically located in the corporate offices; no libraries are stored in remote offices
- GroupWise servers and post offices can be physically located at either the corporate office or remote offices

Here are a few pro and cons of centralized libraries. The pros are as follows:

- Cost to maintain is lower than decentralized
- Less administration
- Central storage and retrieval of documents for the entire company

The cons are as follows:

- DMS use is slower for remote office users due to WAN links
- Increased demand on WAN bandwidth
- WAN outages cause decrease in remote user productivity

Decentralized libraries have the following characteristics:

- Users at remote offices access GroupWise locally
- Users at remote offices access libraries locally and potentially across WAN links, for corporate libraries
- GroupWise servers and post offices are physically located in remote offices
- Corporate office users access GroupWise locally and potentially across WAN links to remote libraries

Here are a few pro and cons of decentralized libraries. The pros are as follows:

- Faster document access—users primarily access documents locally
- Demand on WAN links is potentially decreased
- This design mirrors GroupWise best practice design principles, with MTA and POA at each remote office

The cons include

- More expensive to implement and maintain
- Increased administration
- Increased implementation time

If ever there is a time to call a design meeting, this is it. The success of your DSM system will largely depend upon design.

Dedicated vs. Non-Dedicated Post Office

The second design principle in question is whether you will implement a separate post office for housing DMS libraries or use a current user's post office. Document management is most efficiently maintained when users reside on the same post office as the libraries they use the most. This eliminates the need for users to pull their documents across WAN links, and makes the indexing process more efficient, because document references for local libraries need not be sent across the wire. It also speeds up the query process for documents. Local libraries are queried directly by the same POA that services the GroupWise client in client/server mode. Remote libraries are queried via a store-and-forward system, guaranteeing at least a few seconds of additional lag before search results are returned to users.

NOTE

The downsides to implementing libraries on the post containing the users are limited scalability, less fault tolerance, maintenance events take longer, and it's less flexible.

Dedicated DMS Post Office

The following are characteristics of setting up a dedicated DMS post office, as represented in Figure 14.10.

1. Set up a separate post office.
2. Set up DMS post office POA for "continuous" mode indexing (`/gfinterval-0`).

   All libraries are in the DMS post office.

Advantages to the dedicated post office include

- *High fault tolerance.* If the messaging post office is down, document access is still available.
- *Highly scalable.* If needed, several DMS post offices can be set up.
- *Very flexible with design changes.* Libraries are not affected by post office moves or redesigns. Maintenance and rebuilds are manageable for both messaging and DMS post offices.

Disadvantages to the dedicated post office include

- Requires separate server(s) for DMS
- Increased administration
- More complex GroupWise system due to more post office(s)

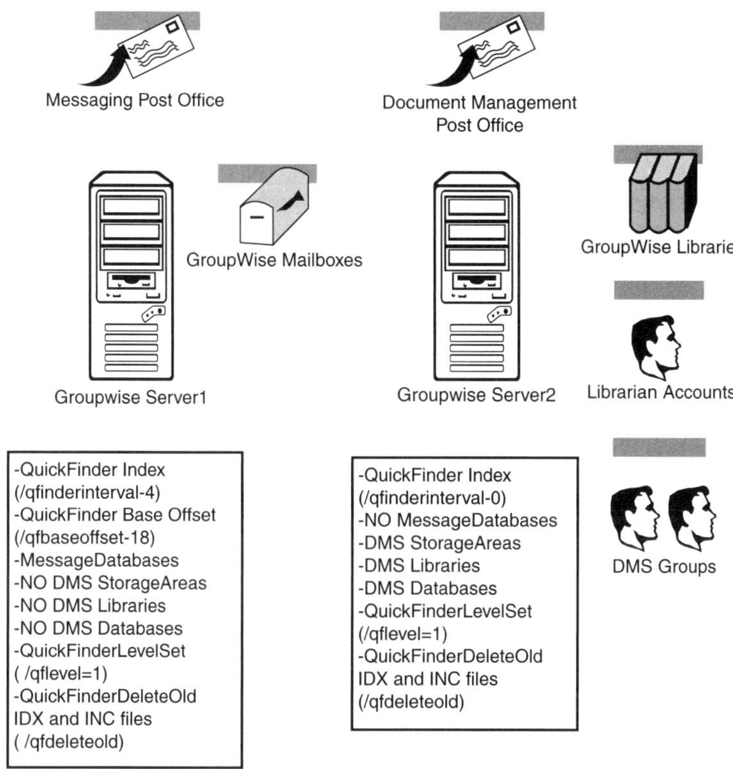

FIGURE 14.10 Dedicated DMS post office.

Non-Dedicated DMS Post Office

The following are characteristics of a non-dedicated DMS post office, as represented in Figure 14.11. The set-up process is as follows:

1. One post office houses users, resources, and libraries, and so on.
2. All library databases are held in the same post office as the e-mail databases.

Advantages of the non-dedicated post office include

- Least expensive
- Less administration

Disadvantages of the non-dedicated post office include

- Not very scalable
- Not fault tolerant—if the e-mail post office fails, document access fails
- Less flexibility for design changes
- Maintenance and rebuilds will take a very long time

The dedicated post office model is the preferred method of document-management design. Even in small companies, it has great merit. Remember, documents are currently stored on one to many servers, and by the time DMS is fully implemented, the documents will be merged to one location.

A post office can have a maximum of 255 libraries per post office. Each library can hold up to four billion documents. Try to keep the number of documents per library around 500,000 or fewer. It's easier to manage smaller pieces, and indexing and schedule events will take less time.

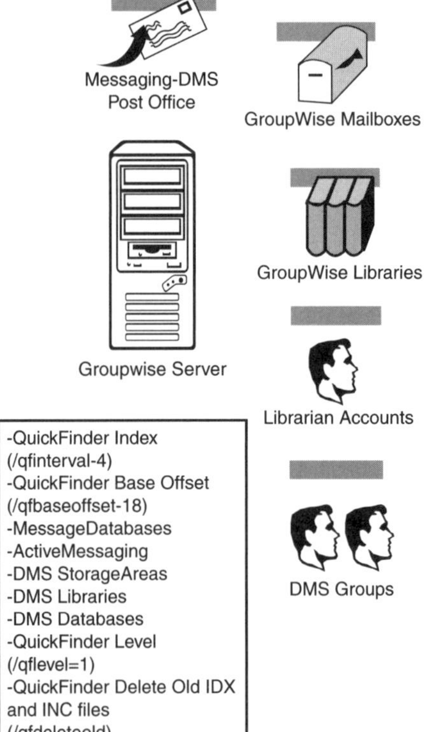

FIGURE 14.11
Non-dedicated DMS post office.

Disk Space for Document Management

Once a design is in place, it's time to determine the amount of disk space required. Perhaps the most difficult challenge you will face as a GroupWise document-management administrator is determining the amount of disk space your users will require for their libraries.

Space Needed Today

Begin by determining how much space is required to import all of the documents system-wide into GroupWise libraries, assuming a full implementation of DMS. Add up the disk space taken up by all of the document directories on servers and individual workstations. The space required for these documents in GroupWise will be about 70% of their space on disk.

Remember, documents are compressed and encrypted. A pure text document might be a mere 20% of its original size. A compressed image file, however, will probably be right around 100% of its original size. If you assume that most of your documents will be compressed by about 50%, the BLOB files for your existing documents will require about 50% of the space the documents currently require.

There are also the document property sheets, activity logs, and word-list BLOB files to consider. Typically, these files add about 40% to the space taken up by the document BLOB files (or 20% of the space taken up by uncompressed documents). So, add 20% to the 50%, and you have 70%.

If your documents are currently taking 20GB, spread across several servers and a few hundred workstations, importing all of those documents into GroupWise libraries will require around 14GB. This can be spread across multiple libraries and storage areas, of course.

Space Needed in the Next Three Years

Now that you know how much space you need today, you need to plan for the future. Check how many of your current collection of documents were created in the last year. Use this number to formulate a growth curve to estimate the amount of space needed for documents in the next two to three years.

If 30% of your 20GB of documents were created in the last 12 months, you should assume that your users are going to create at least 6GB worth of documents per year. Taking 70 percent of that gives you 4.2GB per year for growth of the GroupWise libraries.

Keep in mind that these numbers are rough estimates. Your organization might have done business modeling that more accurately predicts document creation, or you might have access to benchmarks from organizations like yours that have implemented GroupWise document management. If this is the case, use your more accurate data rather than these kinds of ballpark figures.

Keep in mind, also, that with document management in place, you will see a much higher re-use of existing documents. Users will be better able to share the documents they create, so you might see a significant decrease in the growth of these libraries (coupled with an increase in productivity).

Plan for Additional Hardware

Aside from the disk-space considerations previously discussed, you might need additional server hardware to support your DMS design. If you are putting in a pilot document management library, a small class server will work. If, however, you know the DMS installation will be a full implementation company-wide, you will want a powerful box. This is especially true if you are designing a dedicated post office for the libraries. Remember, all of the knowledge your company has will be held on these servers; do not skimp on hardware and fault tolerance.

User Training

As mentioned, user training is critical to the successful implementation of GroupWise document management. Most users are reluctant to change the way they work. Document management represents a significant change, so steps should be taken to make things as easy as possible on your users. It has also been my experience that once users become accustomed to using document management, they wonder how they ever got along without it. The trick is getting your users to that point without upsetting them.

Formal instruction is a must for all users who will use DMS. There are four categories users must learn—searching, importing, creating new documents, and security. Other categories to consider are check in/check out processes and versioning. With the right effort and an effectively designed training course, users can be trained the basics in an eight-hour session. Realize that as humans, we tend to forget what we do not use repetitively. Therefore, it's better to space out the training into four separate two-hour classes and enforce the learning with "homework."

TIP

Set up a Training library. This can be part of the current GroupWise system or a new training GroupWise system. Either way, you can deliver "homework" to the users via GroupWise Tasks. You can also use the activity logs to determine whether users completed the homework.

Selecting the DMS staff

Fully implementing and supporting GroupWise document management will require a staff of people. A hierarchical structure of staff might be required. The following are some ideas for supporting DMS.

Librarian

One of the most important aspects of your document-management system is choosing someone to work as a librarian. A user with the Manage library right has the capability to find all documents in the library regardless of security, and change the document security of any document in the library. The librarian user should generally be a person who is always in the office and who is a member of the department that will use the library(s). An administrative assistant usually fits this description, and he has the best skill set for the job. Now, you might be thinking, why not a system administrator? Simple, the system administrator is responsible for the GroupWise system or the network; they do not have time to "change the rights" of a document. They also do not know the inner workings of the department(s) and might make changes that are not departmentally approved.

TIP

Any time the Manage right is used to provide a user with access to a document, the system notifies the owner of the document of the security change message, as shown in Figures 14.12 and 14.13. So, although your librarian can read any document in the library, he or she cannot be sneaky about it.

Also, as mentioned in the previous tip box, create an external entity and give it the Manage right. Then assign that GroupWise account to a user. This has several benefits. First, the security benefit that was previously discussed. The librarian account can be e-mailed instead of the user account. So, if you name the librarian account `HR-Librarian`, when a user wants changes made, they can e-mail them to the external entity account. Also, this one librarian account can service multiple libraries; there is no limitation.

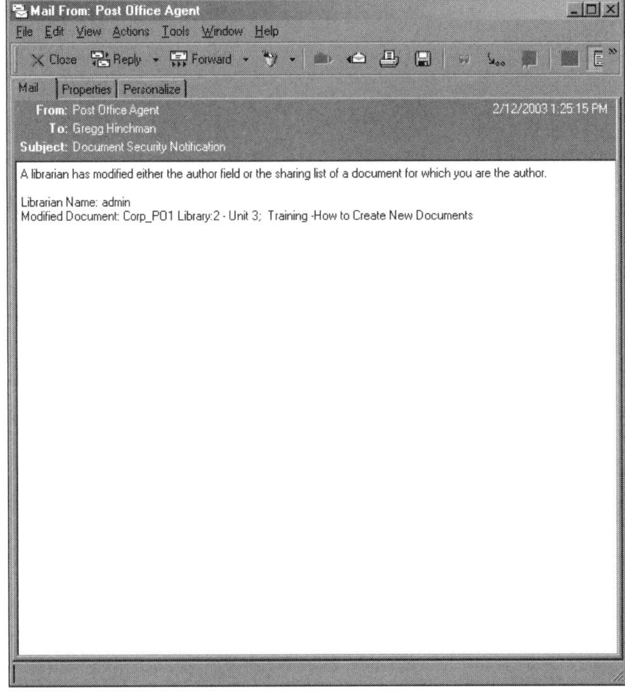

FIGURE 14.12 Mail notification that the librarian made a change in the security to a document.

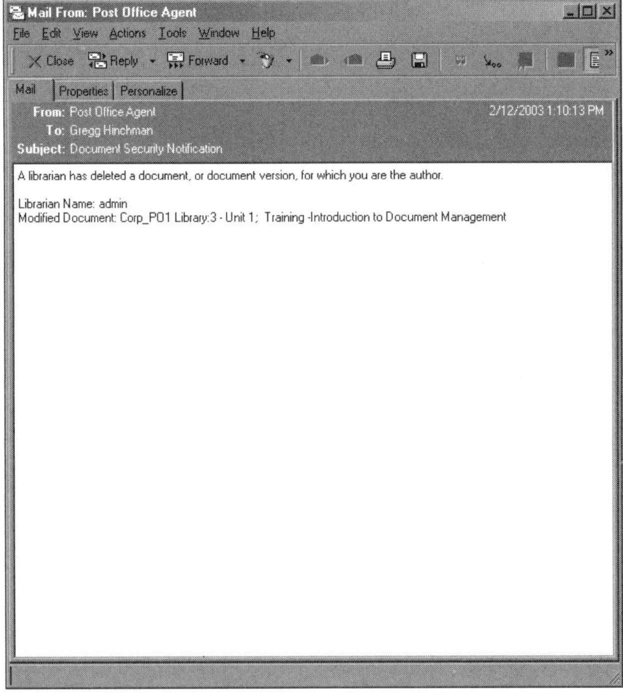

FIGURE 14.13 Mail notification that the librarian deleted a document.

The librarian will have the following set of responsibilities:

- Teach advanced DMS tips and tricks
- Keep DMS libraries clean
- Ensure the integrity of the libraries by making sure improperly filled out document property pages are corrected
- Handle orphaned documents
- Perform mass document operations
- Assist in any redesigns of the departmental library(s)

***Orphaned documents* are documents that do not have an author. Either the author has left the company or the GroupWise account was deleted. The librarian will perform a mass document operation to add a new author.**

The librarian will be responsible for reporting to the departmental manager concerning policies and guidance that pertain to the library(s). The librarian will also report to the DMS administrator when it pertains to improving or making changes to the departmental library(s).

DMS Administrator

The DMS administrator will coordinate all document-management facets. An office manager is a perfect person for this position. This position is especially important in a company-wide implementation of GroupWise DMS. Again, this requires an external entity with a separate GroupWise account for security and library integrity. The DMS administrator has the following responsibilities:

- Support departmental librarians
- Fill in for librarians on leave
- Build new libraries
- Train users
- Maintain DMS distribution lists
- Write company-wide DMS policies and provide guidance
- Oversee company-wide DMS implementation
- Assist network administrators in preventative maintenance for DMS libraries

The DMS administrator will report to management, such as the CIO or CEO. They will also report to the network/GroupWise administrator with maintenance or technical issues. The librarians will come to the DMS administrator with any DMS issues.

Network Administrator/GroupWise Administrator

The network or GroupWise administrator is solely responsible for the GroupWise system, as a whole. They will not be involved in the day-to-day operations of DMS. However, they do have DMS responsibilities. They are

- Support DMS administrators
- Back up and restore DMS libraries
- Resolve GroupWise system-level technical issues
- Support GroupWise servers

The network or GroupWise administrator will report to someone like the director of IT. Any DMS design changes will come to the administrator from the DMS administrator. Figure 14.14 shows an example DMS administration hierarchy.

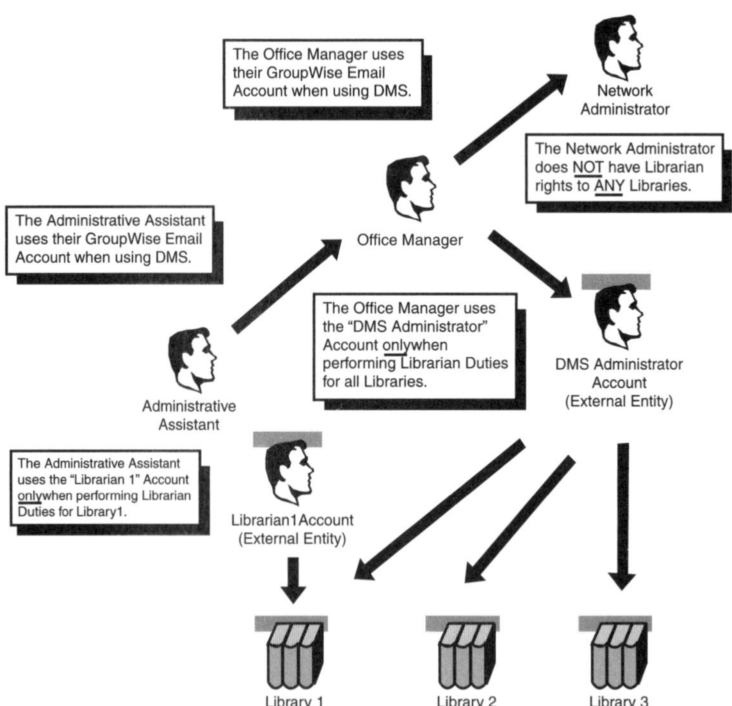
Document Management Administration Hiearchy
The Office Manager uses their GroupWise Email Account when using DMS.
Network Administrator
The Network Administrator does NOT have Librarian rights to ANY Libraries.
Office Manager
The Administrative Assistant uses their GroupWise Email Account when using DMS.
The Office Manager uses the "DMS Administrator" Account onlywhen performing Librarian Duties for all Libraries.
DMS Administrator Account (External Entity)
Administrative Assistant
The Administrative Assistant uses the "Librarian 1" Account onlywhen performing Librarian Duties for Library1.
Librarian1Account (External Entity)
Library 1
Library 2
Library 3

FIGURE 14.14
A DMS administration hierarchy.

Help Desk Personnel

Finally, we have help desk. Even if you are rolling out a pilot document-management system, you need help desk support. It's advisable to train at least 25 percent of your help desk in GroupWise document management. This way, they can take the first line calls and solve client issues and training issues immediately. Remember any issue that a user has with DMS is one more nail in the coffin. Too many nails and the DMS system will not survive.

The next several sections walk you through some of the most common tasks required for building and customizing accessories of GroupWise libraries.

Creating a Library

This section walks you through the creation of a new GroupWise library. Before doing this, here are some points to remember:

- At least one library is created by default when installing a new GroupWise 6.5 system.
- After a new GroupWise system has been created, or an existing system migrated to GroupWise 6.5, library options will appear anytime a new post office is created.
- Existing post offices can have new libraries added at any time.
- A post office can hold a maximum of 255 libraries.

Before you create a library, you should verify that all agents are up and running and no connections are closed. You should also verify that administration changes are being propagated down to the post office. This can be done by changing a user's phone number from ConsoleOne, and then checking the address book from the GroupWise client to verify that the change made it.

1. Create the library object in your system by highlighting the GroupWise post office that will host the library. With the post office highlighted, right-click and select New, Library.
2. Enter the details of the Library in the resulting dialog box shown in Figure 14.15. Give the library a name, an NDS context, and check the Define Additional Properties box.

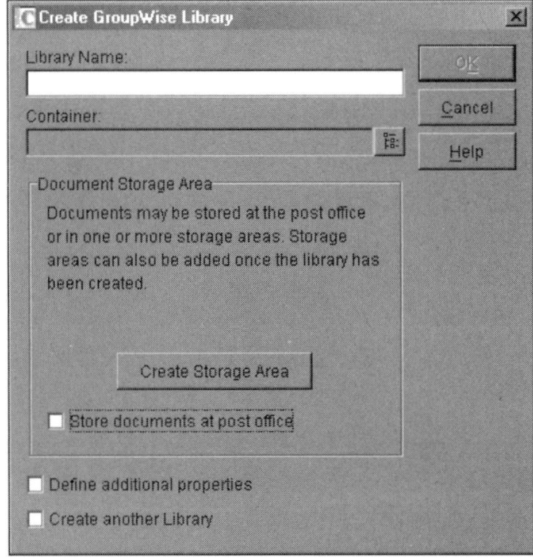

FIGURE 14.15 The Create GroupWise Library dialog box.

NOTE **External document storage does not need to be created unless you expect production documents will take up more space than is available on the post office volume. For scalability, it is recommended that an external document storage area be created. The downside to external storage areas comes into play when you're moving a post office and trying to keep it linked to the external storage area. (There are plenty of TIDs covering this issue on the Novell's support site.) If you need to create an external document storage location, start the process when you get to step 8.**

3. Click Create. You will now be presented with the Library object's Identification property page, as seen in Figure 14.16, so that you can define additional library properties.
4. Fill in the Description field with the purpose of the library, or the pager number of the library administrator, or some other useful information.
5. The Start Version Number can be left as 1 or changed to 0. This value determines whether the first version of a document is version 0 or version 1. Most people think in terms of ordinal numbers (we count to 10 starting with one, not zero), so it makes more sense to use 1.
6. Maximum archive size in bytes is the number of bytes allowed for archive sets. The size should be smaller than the size of your backup media. For example, if your backup media is 6GB you might want the maximum archive size to be 1.5GB. Each archive set would be 1.5GB so you would only need to wait for 1.5GB of archived documents before you would have a complete archive set to move to backup tape. If you set the size to 6GB, you would have to wait for 6GB of archived documents before an archive set would be complete.

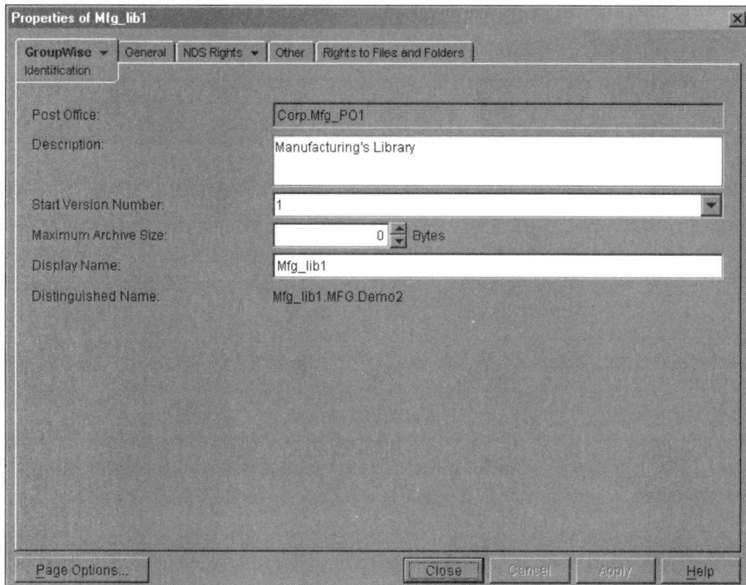

FIGURE 14.16 The Library object's "information" property page.

Avoid archiving if possible. Disk space is so cheap these days; it does not make sense to add more work to a network administrator's job.

7. The display name can be left at the default (the name of the library object) or changed to a longer name. The display name is the name that users will see in their library configuration list, so it should be something intuitive.
8. If you are going to create an external storage area, click the Storage Areas property page on the GroupWise tab, and uncheck the Store Documents at Post Office check box. If you do not need an external document storage area, skip to step 13.

TIP

By default, GroupWise stores all documents under the post office. When first setting up a GroupWise system it is recommended that you deselect the Store Documents at Post Office box, and add a small external storage area. This will ensure that the post office directory or volume is not filled to capacity by accident.

9. Click the Add button (it can only be clicked after Store Documents at Post Office has been unchecked).
10. Fill in an appropriate description of the storage area.
11. Fill in the appropriate UNC path. A Browse button is available, which will populate the UNC path field.

12. Click OK.

NOTE

The library path used here must be unique. If multiple libraries use the same path, document BLOB file maintenance cannot be run safely. Do not share storage areas among multiple libraries.

13. Click the Rights property page below the GroupWise tab and choose to disable the public rights for Delete and Reset In-Use Flag. You might want to disable all public rights, and assign rights using a distribution list. This will give you greater control of who has access to the library.

NOTE

See the "Library Rights" section earlier in this chapter for a full discussion of these settings.

14. Use the Add button to add at least one user. Assign that user the Manage right. It is critical that every library have at least one librarian user assigned.

Now that you have created the library, you need to customize it.

Customizing the Library

Once a library has been created, you will likely want to begin customizing the way the document properties page appears for documents in the library(s). This section walks you through the use of the Document Properties Maintenance tool.

Document Properties Maintenance is used to add or remove fields from libraries, to edit lookup tables, and to edit document types.

NOTE

A *document type* is a category of documents. It's the format in which specific information is presented. An Expense Report can be created in a spreadsheet, but its true type is REPORT. A Rental agency will have agreements with their renters. They call the agreement a "lease" or maybe a "Rental Agreement." This is a type of document. Even though it is an Equipment Rental Lease, the type of document is "Lease." A memo is a type of document. E-mail is also a type of document.

To open the tool, follow these steps:

1. From ConsoleOne, select the post office object for which Document Properties Maintenance needs to be run (the post office that owns the library you just created).
2. Select Tools, GroupWise Utilities, Document Properties Maintenance. You will be presented with the window shown in Figure 14.17.

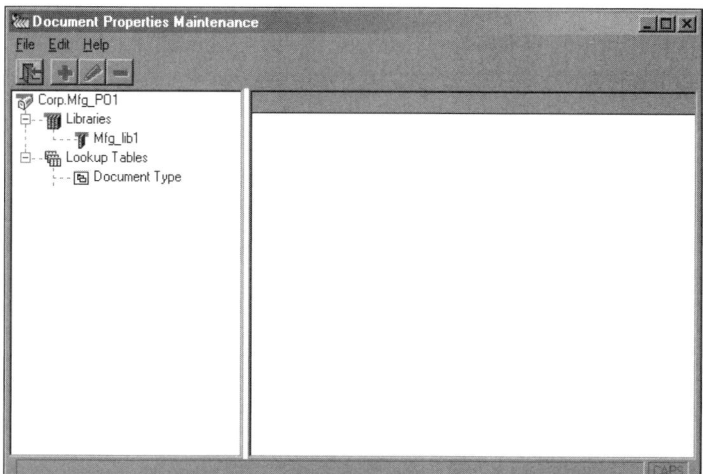

FIGURE 14.17
The Document Properties Maintenance interface.

In this section, you will create related fields for your document property page. This scenario will show how to create and populate lookup tables for Make and Model. This scenario also adds the Make and Model property fields to the Mfg_lib1 document property page.

NOTE

A *lookup table* is list of informational items that can be accessed to fill in a specific property field of a document. Informational items provide details about the document and provide continuity within the library. This preserves the integrity of the library. For example, the Make is the parent property field. Its lookup table can have Chevrolet, Dodge, or Ford listed as choices.

1. Expand the Lookup Tables list, and then select the root Lookup Tables icon.
2. Click the + button on the toolbar to begin adding a lookup table. You will be presented with the dialog box shown in Figure 14.18.

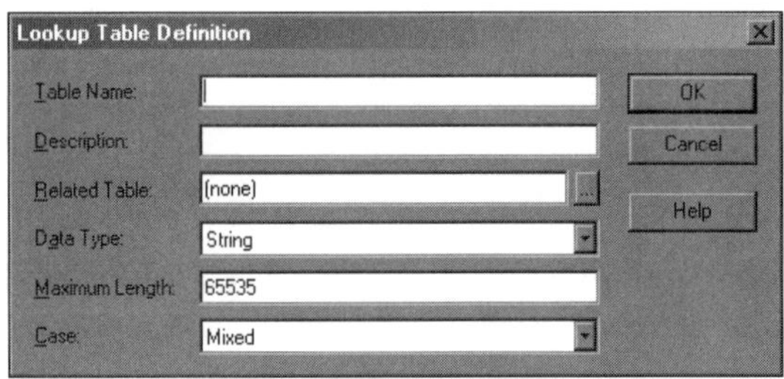

FIGURE 14.18
The Lookup Table Definition dialog box.

3. Type the Table Name as MAKE Lookup Table and the description as Lookup Table for MAKE.
4. Leave the Related Table definition as (none). This is because Make is going to be the parent field for Model.
5. Leave the Data Type as String, the Maximum Length as `65535`, and Case as Mixed.
6. Click OK. The Make table has now been created.
7. Now highlight Make Lookup Table and click the + button to add values, as shown in Figure 14.19.

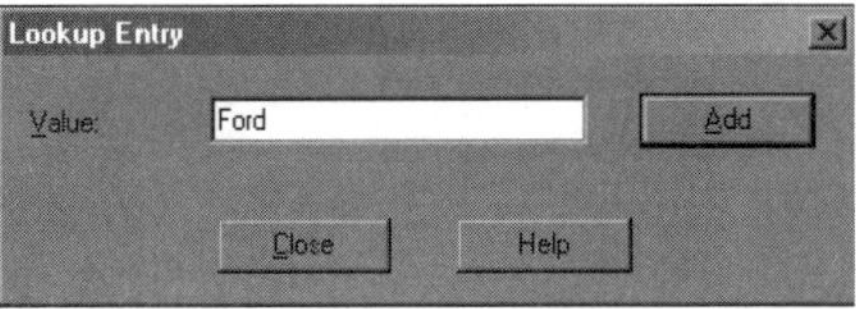

FIGURE 14.19
Adding the value Ford to the Make Lookup Table.

8. Add the lookup entries of Dodge, Chevrolet, and Ford by entering the value in the field and then clicking the Add button.
9. Click the Close button to dismiss the Lookup Entry dialog box.
10. Highlight the Lookup Tables icon again and click the Add button.
11. Enter the table name as MODEL Lookup Table and the description as Lookup Table for MODEL.
12. Select MAKE Lookup Table from the Browse button on the Related Table field.
13. Leave the Data Type String and the maximum length at `65535` and the Case as Mixed.
14. Click OK. The Model table is now created, and is considered a child of the Make Lookup Table.

Parent lookup tables can have many child lookup tables. Lookup tables can be used in multiple properties on a document property page. Unfortunately, the Document Type lookup table can be neither a parent nor a child. Also, the Document Type lookup table is directly related to all libraries of a post office. Therefore, if you have multiple libraries in a post office, they will share the same Document Type lookup table. You can overcome this design weakness by making each department define a Document Type, based upon their usage.

15. Now highlight Model Lookup Table and click the + button to add values. The dialog box shown in Figure 14.20 appears.

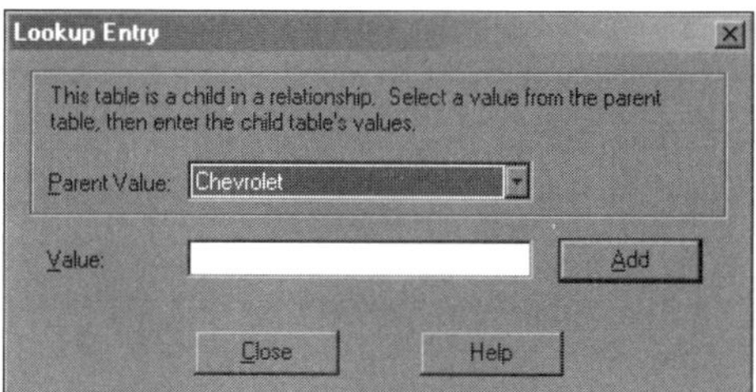

FIGURE 14.20
Adding a Model value that will relate to the Chevrolet Make value.

16. The first value of the Make Lookup Table will appear as the Parent Value. In this example, the first Parent Value is Chevrolet. At this point, add values to the Parent Value Chevrolet by entering the values into the value field and clicking the Add button.
17. Add the values Corsica and Impala to the Parent Value Chevrolet.
18. Now change the Parent Value to Dodge and add the value Durango to the Parent Value Dodge.
19. Now change the Parent Value to Ford and add the value F150 to the Parent Value Ford.
20. Click the Close button.
21. Expand the Libraries icon and select the library to which you want to add the fields Make and Model. Click the + button to begin Add Mode. You'll see the dialog box in Figure 14.21.
22. Enter the Property Label as MAKE and the Description as MAKE of Automobile.

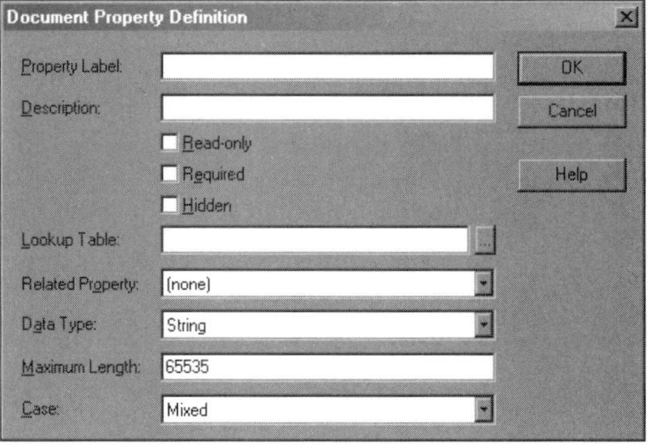

FIGURE 14.21 Assigning the Make field to document property sheets for all documents in a library.

TIP

Be careful here. If the display description is too long, it will get cut off on the document property page when the user views it. Also, any Property Label listed will be permanent to the GroupWise system. This means it will show up during an Advanced Find, or when choosing a column. Novell Technical Support cannot remove these from the GroupWise databases; they can only rename them. So be careful with spelling and word usage.

23. Check the Required check box. The Read-only check box should be used only if you need a field stamped on every document property sheet, for example "Property of WorldWide Widgets—Internal Use only". The hidden value should be used only if you need to have a value that is placed in the field, but is hidden from the users.
24. Click the Lookup Table browse button, select MAKE Lookup Table from the list, and then close the dialog box by clicking OK.
25. Again, expand the Libraries icon and select the same library to which the Make field was added. Click the + button to begin Add Mode.
26. Enter the Property Label as MODEL and the description as MODEL of Automobile.
27. Make the property required and assign it to the Model Lookup Table.
28. Leave the Related Property as Make and click the OK button.

Here is what you have accomplished so far:

- The Make Lookup Table has makes of cars in it.
- The Model Lookup Table has models of cars in it, and the make that is selected determines which models are available.
- Both Make and Model are available fields on document property pages.

- When a user creates a document, that document can now be related to a specific automobile with just a couple of clicks. This might be useful for a library at an auto dealership, but how can it be applied to your organization?
- Related fields like Client and Matter Number or Customer and Contact can be used to organize documents based on attributes in their document property pages. If all documents at a law firm have the Client and Matter Number fields populated, it becomes a simple matter to locate all documents by querying the library based on the Client field. For involved cases, a query for both the Client and Matter Number fields can be used to call up all documents specific to that particular case.

TIP

Try to keep lookup tables relatively short. One hundred entries are easy to look through, but 10,000 would shake up even the best user. It's not a limitation of GroupWise, but rather eases the use for the user. Imagine opening up a lookup table with 1,000 entries in it. Now try to find what you are looking for in that table. Hint: Start typing, and name completion will assist.

More Library Customization

As shown in the example scenario, the Document Property Maintenance tool can be used to create related fields. It is also the tool you will need to use to create or edit document types.

The document type lookup table is just another lookup table, similar to the Make lookup table. It is populated with descriptive names for document types, as well as criteria for the expiration of these documents.

You will also use the Document Property Maintenance tool to add fields to document property pages. In the scenario you added the Make and Model fields to the document property pages. You linked them to lookup tables, but not all fields need to be linked to a static table. You can create a custom field called Customer, for instance, and allow users to populate it with the name of the customer or client for whom the document was created. But keep in mind spelling. If a user misspells a customer name in the field, and another user tries to search for the customer using the correct spelling, no documents will be found.

TIP

When you add property fields to a library using the Document Properties Maintenance utility (these fields will always exist in the GroupWise post office and will be visible when performing an advanced find) display all fields from the GroupWise client. They can only be removed by Novell Technical support. Because of this, be wise about the names you use when creating additional property fields in a GroupWise post office.

Maintaining GroupWise Libraries

Library maintenance is necessary to fix inconsistencies created by hardware, software, or user errors. Obviously, hard drive corruption can cause database inconsistencies. To keep your libraries functioning properly, scheduled events must be configured to routinely run library checks to keep your libraries in good working order and to alert you of potential problems.

Here is a discussion of the tools available to you for library maintenance. When a GroupWise library is selected, and Mailbox/Library Maintenance is activated from the Tools, GroupWise Utilities menu, there will be an option for Analyze/Fix Library, as shown in Figure 14.22.

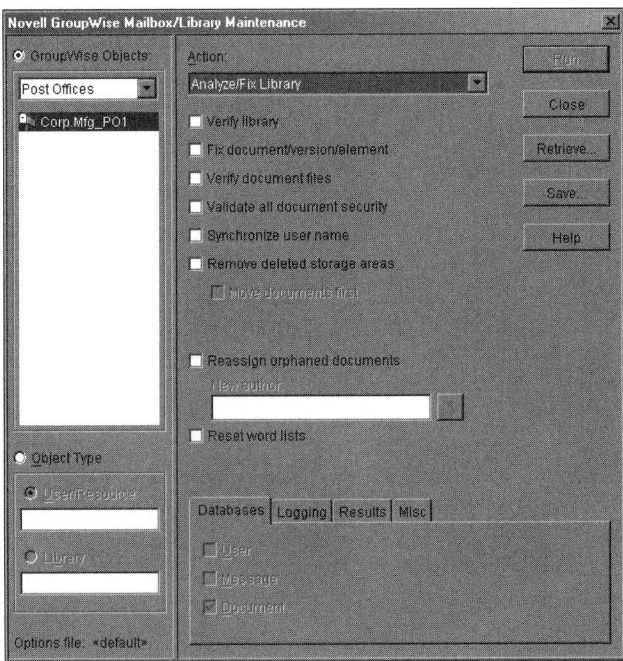

FIGURE 14.22 The Mailbox/ Library Maintenance tool with Analyze/Fix Library selected.

There are several check boxes available with this option selected:

- Verify library
- Fix document/version/element
- Verify document files
- Validate all document security
- Synchronize user name
- Remove deleted storage areas
- Reassign orphaned documents
- Reset word lists

This section discusses each of these options in turn.

Verify Library

The Verify Library operation will clear up inconsistencies between a post office database and the DMSH.DB file. These two files are responsible for telling the POA and the clients which libraries are available on this post office.

In cases where DMSH.DB does not "know about" a library, but the post office database does, `Problem 70` messages will start to appear anytime library maintenance is performed. The problem could also manifest itself in GroupWise clients by not showing the correct list of libraries under Tools, Options, Documents.

Verify Library fixes the cause of these `Problem 70` messages. It also checks to make sure the Document Class schema is correct. The schema is re-applied if it is found to be invalid.

Fix Document/Version/Element

This check makes sure that every document, version, and element record has a match. This is similar to a Contents check on a user mailbox (covered in Chapter 17, "Maintaining the GroupWise System"). When pointers do not line up correctly, this tool will attempt to resolve the problem. In cases where the problem cannot be resolved, the tool will report the document number of the document that is problematic.

This tool will also report the document number of every document BLOB file that was referenced in a properties sheet but not found on disk. It will provide the administrator with the last known path to the document, which allows the administrator to find the document BLOB file on a tape backup system.

Verify Document Files

Like Fix Document/Version/Element, Verify Document Files will report the document number and last known path to every document BLOB file referenced in the library but not present on disk. It does not verify or fix the assorted document pointers in the library, however. If all you are looking for is a list of missing BLOB files, this option will run more quickly than Fix Document/Version/Element.

Validate All Document Security

Validate All Document Security matches the listings for document authors, creators, and any user who is on the sharing list for the document against the listings for these users' mailboxes. It does this by comparing the Globally Unique IDs (GUIDs) in all three of these listings. If the GUIDs don't match, the routine will capture the mailbox GUID and apply it to the GUID fields for author, creator, or user who has the document being shared to them via the security access field.

This type of problem typically occurs when a user is deleted from the system, and then re-imported later with the original FID. The problem stems from the fact that mailbox access can be granted based on the three-character FID, which can be specified in the import file, but document access is granted based on the 32-digit GUID. Security problems based on invalid GUID information can also occur when information store files are damaged, but this is rare.

NOTE

A GUID is a system-level unique identifier of a GroupWise object. This 128-bit code is represented as a 32-digit hexadecimal number, and can have 3.4*1038 possible values (that's 34 followed by about 38 zeros, or over 340 times a billion times a billion times a billion times a billion). The GUID is created when a user object is created and never changes because it's guaranteed to be unique throughout the system.

Synchronize User Name

Synchronize User Name goes through the Author and Creator fields and verifies that the display name is correct. This type of check should be run if the first or last name of a user changes, and that user is either the author or creator of documents in the library.

Remove Deleted Storage Areas

If a document storage area needs to be removed, the Remove Deleted Storage Areas operation must be used.

1. Delete the storage area from the Library Storage Areas tab on the Library object.
2. Select the post office to which this library belongs. From the Tools menu, select GroupWise Utilities, Mailbox/Library Maintenance.
3. Select Analyze/Fix Library and check the Remove Deleted Storage Areas and Move Documents First boxes.
4. Click Run.

This operation will move all document BLOB files from the deleted storage area to the currently active storage area, and will update all property sheets and activity logs with the new path. It will also allow you to remove the physical directory structure of the old storage area that you deleted.

If you delete a storage area, but do not run this operation, and then delete the physical directory structure (or otherwise make the deleted storage area unavailable to the POA), the next time the POA attempts to load it will fail. It is therefore critical that the POA be up and running throughout steps 1 through 4. If you must delete a storage area, do not wait very long between deleting it from the library object and running this operation.

NOTE

If you need to move a storage area from one physical location to another, refer to "Moving a Document Storage Area" later in this chapter.

Reassign Orphaned Documents

If a user has been deleted from the GroupWise system, and that user is the creator of documents in GroupWise libraries, those documents become orphaned. The Reassign Orphaned Documents operation allows you to specify a new creator for all orphaned documents in the library.

If you plan to delete a user from the system, you should also plan to reassign that user's documents to someone else using this feature.

Reset Word Lists

Selecting this option allows the QuickFinder Indexing process of the POA to regenerate the document library word list the next time an index operation is performed. This word list allows users to search for a document by keywords as well as by any word contained within a document.

Creating Library Maintenance Schedule Events

The previous section discussed each of the Analyze/Fix Library options found when you are running Mailbox/Library Maintenance. These options can be run manually for troubleshooting purposes, but it is recommended that they be scheduled to run automatically. This will ensure that database problems are caught quickly, and will help prevent the loss of document data.

The following are steps for creating scheduled events specific to document management:

1. Open the details window for the POA object. If there are multiple POAs for this post office (a dedicated indexing POA), select the POA that performs message file processing. Select the Schedule Events property page.
2. Click the Create button. You will be presented with the dialog box shown in Figure 14.23.

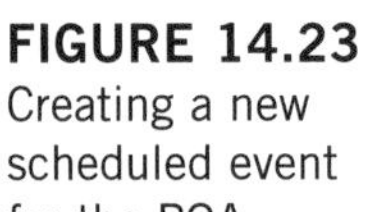

FIGURE 14.23
Creating a new scheduled event for the POA.

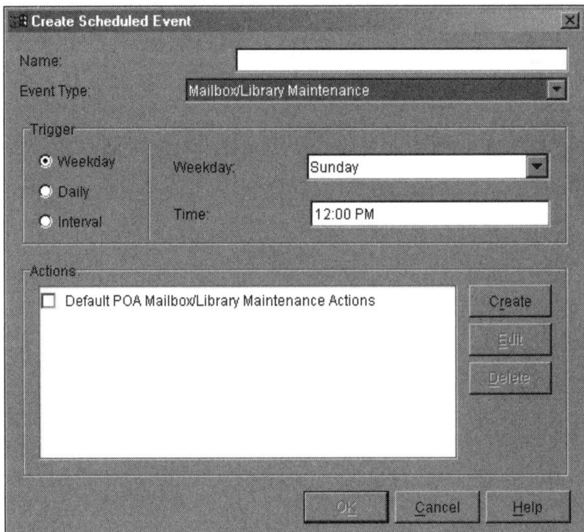

3. Name the event Default Library Maintenance Event.
4. Change the type from Disk Check to Mailbox/Library Maintenance.
5. Leave the Trigger at Weekday and the weekday setting at Sunday.
6. Change the time to 3:00 a.m. (This example scenario shows a time when no other scheduled events are running and backup jobs will be finished. Of course, this time might differ for you.)
7. Click the Create button; you will get the dialog box shown in Figure 14.24.

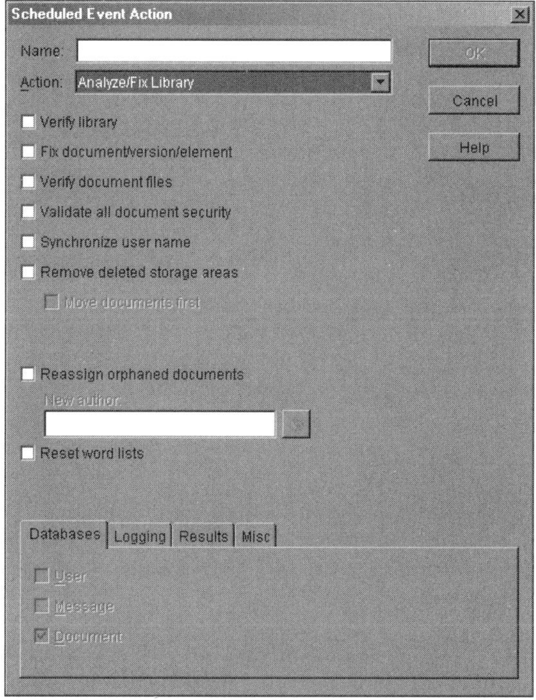

FIGURE 14.24
Assigning actions to the new scheduled event.

8. Enter the name <Library Name> Library Maintenance. Change the action to Analyze/Fix Library.
9. Check the Verify Library, Fix Document/Version/Element, Verify Document Files, Validate All Document Security, and Synchronize User Name options.
10. Click the OK button.
11. Finally, enable the Default POA Mailbox/Library Maintenance Actions action and then click the OK button of the dialog box.

12. Click the OK button of the Edit Scheduled Event dialog box to save the new event. By default the new event will already be enabled.

Next Sunday at 3:00 a.m., the POA will launch a thread to perform maintenance on all libraries owned by this post office. Monday morning, the administrator will have a log file from this operation waiting in his or her mailbox. The log file should be carefully reviewed to ascertain the current health of the libraries.

Mass Document Operation: Change Authors

One of the more common document-administration tasks involves making changes to the property sheets for large numbers of documents. In this scenario, Gregg is now taking over the responsibilities for Ed, so the librarian (or DMS administrator) will need to change all documents authored by Ed to be authored by Gregg. Before beginning, keep these issues in mind:

- All Mass Change operations are initiated through the GroupWise client.
- Mass Change operations should be performed by users with the Manage right. These users are the only ones who can be confident all documents that need to be changed have been selected. This is because users with the Manage right can find documents in the library that have not been shared. This is a function of the departmental librarian or DMS administrator.

The following are the steps you take to perform a mass change on the Author field of documents:

1. Log into the mailbox of a librarian user for the post office to which you will be making changes.
2. From the Tools menu, select Mass Document Operations. You will be presented with the dialog box shown in Figure 14.25.
3. Leave the Operation selection as change properties.
4. Leave the selection method set to Use Find/Advanced Find. This is the method used to select documents.
5. Click Next. You will be presented with the dialog box shown in Figure 14.26.

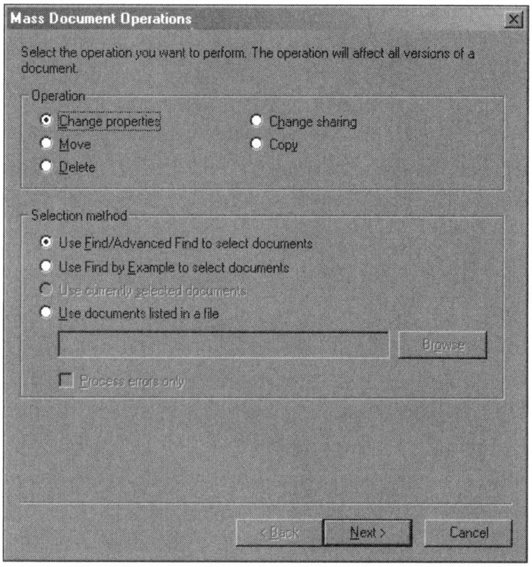

FIGURE 14.25 The Mass Document Operations dialog box.

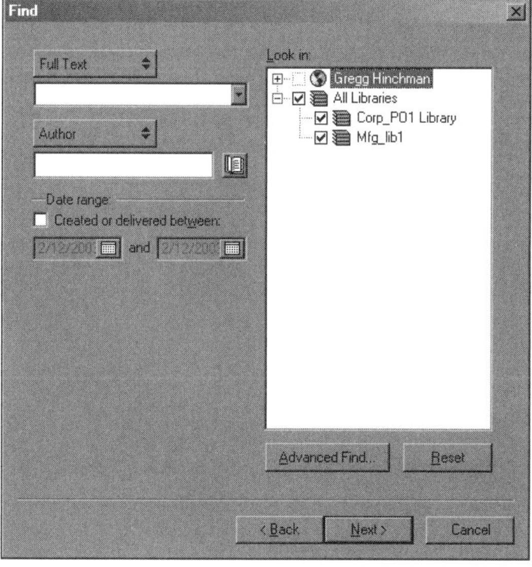

FIGURE 14.26 Property sheets used to find mass document operations.

6. In the Author field, use the Browse button to enter the name of the Author who needs to be updated. In the example scenario, the name is Ed.

7. If you prefer to change documents only within a certain date range (perhaps you only need to change documents that Ed created after he transferred to the corporate office on 1/1/2001), select the Created or Delivered Between field and enter the appropriate date range.

8. In the Look in pane, you will need to specify which libraries to search for documents that meet your criteria. By default, only the library this user has specified as their default library (under Tools, Options, Documents) will be checked.
9. Check the box labeled Apply Librarian Rights. This ensures that you will be able to find and change all of the documents in the selected libraries.

NOTE

To do this properly, you must have the Manage right for all of the libraries that are selected in the Look In pane. If you don't see the Apply Librarian Rights check box, you definitely do not have the manage right for all of the libraries in the system. More specifically, you do not have the Manage right to the default library of the mail account to which you are logged in.

10. Uncheck Find Only Official Document Versions. Otherwise, documents with multiple versions will only be partially processed.
11. Click Next. You will be presented with the dialog box shown in Figure 14.27.

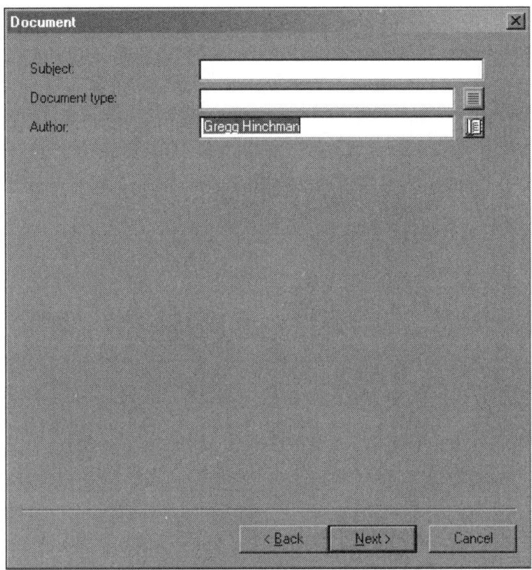

FIGURE 14.27
Entering target values for the mass change operation.

12. Use the Browse button to pick the new author value. In the example case, the new author value is `Gregg Hinchman`.
13. Click Next. You will be presented with the dialog box shown in Figure 14.28.

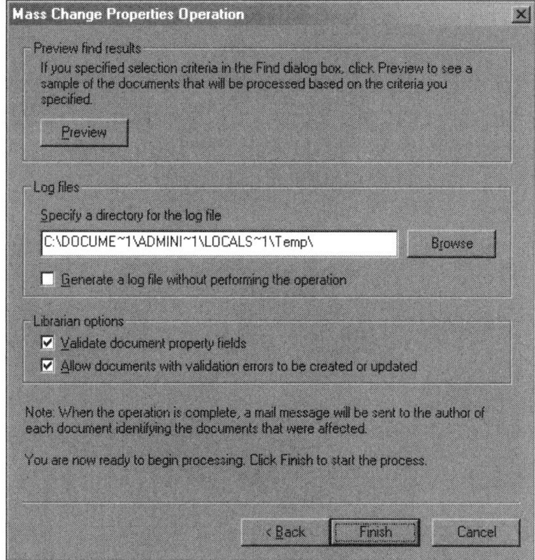

FIGURE 14.28
Setting the operational parameters for the mass change operation.

14. Click the Preview button so that you can see exactly which documents will be changed by this operation.
15. If you want to make sure that all parties (authors) affected are okay with the changes, check the Generate a Log File Without Performing the Operation check box. If you click Next with this option enabled, the utility will generate Mass0000.err and Mass0000.logs in your Windows TEMP directory as well as send you a copy of the logs. The logs can then be sent to others to verify the changes are correct and approved. If this option is enabled, the mass change operations must be repeated to actually complete the operation when the change is approved.

NOTE

If you decided to generate a log file without performing the operation, every document shown in the log file will show a `Not Processed` error. This is normal, and tells you that the criteria were met, but the operation was not actually performed.

16. If you check Validate Document Property Fields, you will be informed of documents that have invalid document property fields (property sheets that are missing a value for a required property field). If you do decide to do this and you want the change to go through even if the document property page has an invalid value, you must also check Allow Documents with Validation Errors to be Created or Updated. Otherwise documents with invalid property values will not be updated in the operation.

17. Click Next. A Mass Change Progress window will then summarize the operation. If you checked Validate Document Property Fields, you might see a Validation Error dialog box after the operation is complete.

There you have it, all the steps needed to change the author field. It's a task, but with the step-by-step approach I've shown you it's not hard.

Mass Document Operation: Author Name Change

In this scenario, Ed now wants to be known as Edward. To accommodate this the administrator changed the First Name field of Ed's eDirectory user object to Edward. Now Ed's name on his GroupWise mailbox has been updated to Edward but all of the documents for which Edward is the author still show "Ed" as the first name of the author. Figure 14.29 shows this situation; notice that his mailbox name is Edward.

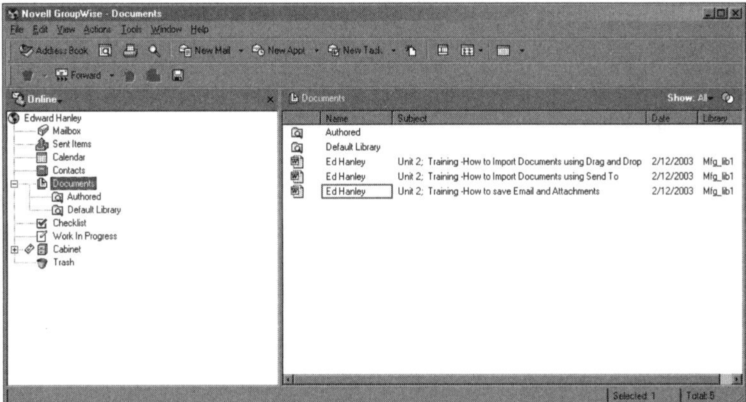

FIGURE 14.29
Documents showing "Ed" as the author.

This operation can be performed from the GroupWise client as a true mass document operation, but in this case there is an administrative tool that is much easier to use. In order to synchronize the document properties sheets with the address book regarding Ed, you can run a Synchronize User Name library check. Here are the steps for doing this:

1. Launch ConsoleOne.
2. Highlight the library or libraries in which Edward's documents are kept.

If you want to select all of the libraries at once, select the GroupWise System icon. Click the libraries filter. All of the libraries in the system will appear. You can now select these libraries with a Ctrl-click mouse routine.

3. With the libraries highlighted, select Tools, GroupWise Utilities, Mailbox/Library Maintenance. You will be presented with the window shown in Figure 14.30.

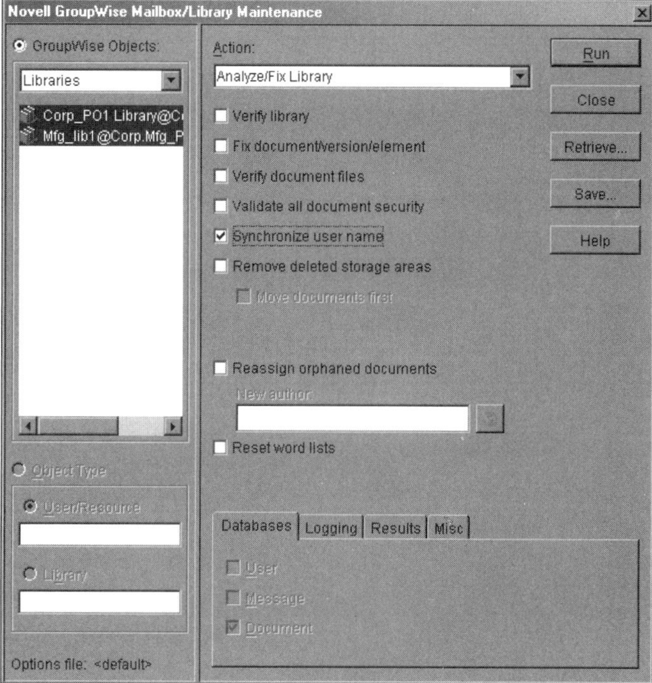

FIGURE 14.30 The Mailbox/Library Maintenance tool, with multiple library objects selected.

4. Change the action to Analyze/Fix Library.
5. Check Synchronize User Name. You are not required to select a user to synchronize. The operation will synchronize all usernames.
6. Click Run.

Each POA that services a library in the list will then synchronize first and last names in document property fields with the first and last names in the address book. Even if a username has completely changed, the POA will be able to synchronize the change. This is because the user GUID remains the same through any number of name changes or post office moves.

Figure 14.31 now shows that "Edward" is the author of the documents that were originally created when the author's name was "Ed".

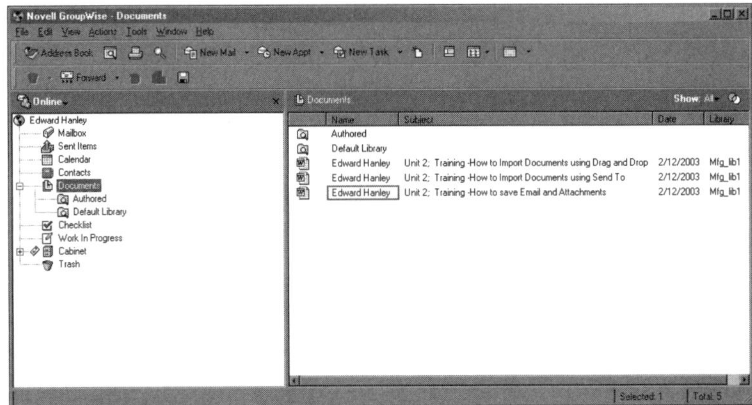

FIGURE 14.31 Documents now show "Edward" as the author.

Archiving and Deleting Documents

If you begin to run out of disk space on a server volume housing a GroupWise library, it might be time to run an Archive/Delete Documents operation. This operation uses the criteria specified under document types to determine which documents are to be archived, which are deleted, and which documents remain in the library. As stated, these functions can be handy, but can create more work for GroupWise administrators in the long run. It's best to avoid these features if possible.

Document Types and the Archive/Delete Operation

Before beginning, this section discusses how document type information is applied. In Figure 14.6 earlier in this chapter, the Delete document type was presented. The following is an explanation of how to make the Delete document type. These concepts can be applied to any document types. The following are the steps for making a Delete document type:

1. Launch ConsoleOne.
2. Highlight a GroupWise post office where you want to create the Delete document type.
3. Click Tools, GroupWise Utilities.

   Click the + sign next to the Lookup Tables to expand the lookup tables.
4. Highlight the Document Type icon.

5. Click the Add button (+ sign) on the menu to add a new document type.
6. Fill in the Value field. This is the name of the document type. When users create documents, they assign document types to them by selecting this value from a list on the Property sheet.
7. Indicate the maximum versions. This is the maximum number of versions allowed for this document type. It has no bearing on the Archive/Delete operation.
8. Choose the expiration action. This is action that is going to be taken on this document by the Archive/Delete operation. Possible values are Archive, Delete, and Retain. Document types with an expiration action of Retain will always remain in the library. For the Delete document type you are creating, the action is Delete.
9. Choose the document life (in days). This value is used to determine whether the expiration action is performed. If the value is 30, this document will be eligible for the expiration action after it has been untouched for 30 days. This means that an actively viewed or edited document with a document type of Delete could remain in the library indefinitely. For the Delete document type you are creating, the document life is 30 days.

In the example scenario for the Delete document type, when the Archive/Delete operation is run, all documents that have not been accessed within 30 days will be deleted.

Moving a Document Storage Area

Moving a document storage area can be tedious, because the document storage area object is stored in multiple databases. Information about document storage areas appears in all domain databases, the post office database, NGWGUARD.DB, DMSH.DB, and DMSD000n.DB. Because the information is contained in several places, care must be taken to ensure that the change correctly propagates. Remember, if the POA finds a document storage area object record, but cannot connect to the document storage area at the defined path, the POA will not load.

NOTE

Hopefully, good planning of the GroupWise document management system will help you avoid a storage area move. It's important to accommodate your DMS system by providing enough disk space, as mentioned earlier.

Guidelines

Before beginning, here are some issues to consider when contemplating moving a document storage area:

- If you are going to move a document storage area to a new server, this should be done before the old server is decommissioned.
- Make sure the new document path conforms to an 8.3 naming convention.
- If you are moving an entire post office and documents are stored at the post office, there is no need to worry about the update. It will occur automatically.
- If you are moving an entire post office and documents are stored in document storage areas, you should move the document storage areas before you move the post office.

Now that you have taken these guidelines in account, read the best-practice procedures for moving document storage areas.

Procedure

Follow these procedures for moving a document storage area:

1. Create a test document in the library to verify that the current document storage area and library are working properly. Check the activity log on the property sheet of the document to be sure the document is being written to the path defined in the document storage area.

> **TIP**
> **When you go to the activity log of a document, by default you do not see the path to where the BLOB file of this document is stored. Simply right-click any of the column names (Date, Name, Action, Version) and the filename will appear off the right-click. Select it to add the Filename column. Now you can see the exact path of this document.**

2. Disable logins on the post office by checking the Disable Logins check box on the post office's information screen. If users attempt to log in to that post office, they will see the dialog box shown in Figure 14.32.
3. Unload the POA.
4. Ensure that the POA has the necessary `/user-` and `/password-` switches to connect with full rights to the new document storage area and to the old document storage area. If the two locations are on servers in different eDirectory trees, you will need to create identically

named accounts, and then provide appropriate bindery contexts so that the username (without context) is all that is required for connection.

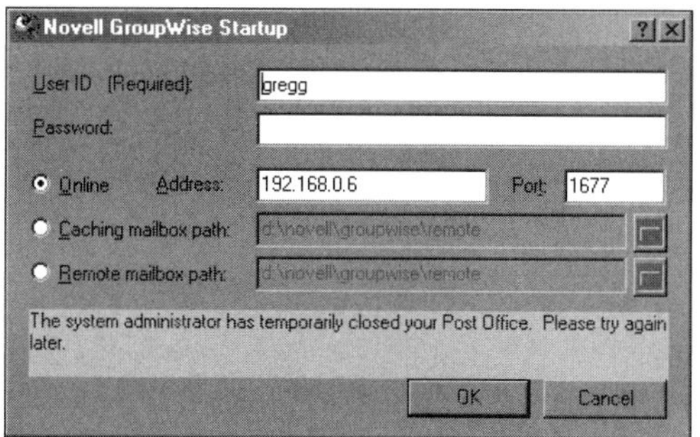

FIGURE 14.32
Can't log into the post office.

5. Reload the POA.
6. Verify that no users are connected to the POA by looking at the POA screen. The POA screen should show "0" user connections. Attempt to log in to this post office to be sure that the POA is not allowing connections.
7. Copy the document storage area to the new location, and verify that all of the directories and files were copied.
8. Launch ConsoleOne and open the Identification property page for the GroupWise library.
9. Select the Storage Areas property page. Edit the document storage area entry of the library object to reflect the new path on the new server. Click OK to save your changes, and then cancel to close out of the Storage Areas property page.
10. Wait for the POA to process the change of the document storage area.
11. From the post office object's, Client Access Settings property page, uncheck the Disable logins box.
12. Make sure that the test document you created in step 1 is still accessible (try opening or viewing it).
13. Create a new document in the library and look at the activity log of the property sheet to verify the document is being stored in the new path of the document storage area.

As long as your system is fully communicating, this set of procedures should make the move successful. If it does not, you might need to contact Novell

Technical Support for more help. I have personally had Document Storage Area moves that required special tools at Novell in order to resolve problems related to the move. The troubleshooting steps in the next section might also help.

Troubleshooting Document Storage Area Move Problems

If you follow the preceding procedures carefully, you should not run into problems moving document storage areas. If you have managed to get yourself into trouble, however, the following troubleshooting tips might help:

- Make sure the `/user-` and `/password-` switches are correct. Ensure that the same user account can be used to access the old and the new storage location.
- If the POA will not load, apply the `/noconfig` switch to the `load` statement or to the POA startup file. This should be treated as a temporary fix that lets you get the POA up and running so that it can process the change.
- Rebuild the post office database using the System Maintenance tool (choose Tools, GroupWise Utilities).
- Try toggling the UNC path for the storage area back to its original value. Once that change has propagated, test to make sure the old path actually works by creating a new document and viewing its activity log. If the old path works, try the walkthrough procedure again to move the storage area to the new location.
- Try running the Remove Deleted Storage Area operation.

If these troubleshooting tips fail, contact Novell Support to get the problem resolved.

NOTE

There have been situations where WPDOMAIN.DB and WPHOST.DB are correctly updated, but NGWGUARD.DB, DMSH.DB, and DMSD0001.DB are not. In these cases, Novell Technical Services must manually edit the databases with secure Novell tools. Until the problem is resolved, the POA has to be loaded with the `/noconfig` switch.

Backing Up the GroupWise Document Management System

System backups are critical to the timely restoration of a mission-critical system, and this is especially true when you are using document management. If documents make up a large part of your business, you should spare no expense ensuring that the document-management system is backed up regularly.

The best solution currently is to use backup software that can handle backing up open files. This will ensure that all document-management databases and BLOB files are backed up, even if there is some activity on the system during the backup run.

Potential Problems

As stated earlier, documents are stored in BLOB files. Every time a document opened and subsequently brought back into the library, a new document BLOB is created and the old document BLOB is deleted. This architecture can interfere in the backup process.

Consider what would happen if a user opened and closed a document between the time that the backup agent had backed up the Property sheet information and backed up the document BLOB. In this situation, the document BLOB that the backed up property sheet points to is not the BLOB file that's backed up. For this reason, all of the users should be out of the post office to get a good backup of a library. You might want to consider unloading the POA for the DMS post office and then reloading after the backup is finished. This will ensure users are not into the system.

Fortunately, if the BLOB file has become orphaned in this manner, there is a solution. I'll cover this in the next section.

Exporting Orphaned Document Blobs

If document BLOB files are restored from tape without their accompanying property sheets (the DMDD*.DB files), some of these BLOB files might not be referenced by any property sheet. These document BLOBs are now orphaned. The trick is finding them. After all, there are huge scores of BLOB files, and there are only likely to be a few orphans.

Fortunately, the stand-alone GWCheck tool, GWCHECK.EXE, can be used to export all orphaned document BLOB files.

Here are the procedures for exporting orphaned document BLOB files:

1. Run GWCHECK.EXE.
2. Select Library for the object type, and enter the name of the library.
3. Select Analyze/Fix for the action, and check the options for Contents and Documents.
4. Click Run.

GWCHECK.EXE will look in each document storage area for document BLOB files that do not have a corresponding entry in the DMDD*.DB files. Any document BLOB files thus determined to be orphaned will be moved to an FDxx directory structure underneath the root of the directory from which GWCHECK.EXE was run.

The log file will list the pertinent information about each of the orphaned documents, including library name, original document number, version, original path to document BLOB, and author name. You can then use this information to return the document BLOB files to their author. The author of the document can then import the BLOB file as a new document by simply dragging and dropping the file onto the GroupWise client window.

Document-Management Tools from Third Parties

This section briefly touches on three products that increase the functionality of GroupWise document management.

The first product, ViewWise by CompuThink, expands the functionality of document management using imaging technology. This allows companies to take that old file room and all those old documents in file cabinets, and make them available via GroupWise document management. They become searchable and can be manipulated. Security can even be increased to secure portions of a single document. ViewWise can be found at `www.computhink.com`.

A second third-party product is eWorks by MetaStorm. This product links to GroupWise and provides a Business Process Management (BPM) solution to your company. eWorks allows you to build a workflow around a business process, essentially automating a routine. The resulting "paperwork" can be stored within GroupWise document management. eWorks can be found at `www.metastorm.com`.

The final third-party product discussed here is DocuWise by 2ND C. DocuWise extends the functionality of GroupWise by integrating the best with GroupWise. From the image database in GroupWise and the relational- and table-based information in the SQL database. DocuWise can be found at `www.2ndc.com`.

Best Practices

There are many ways to implement GroupWise document management. This section contains recommendations that have proven themselves in the field. These recommendations make the assumption that DMS will be a critical system and it will require high availability and scalability, just like the e-mail side of GroupWise. Furthermore, these recommendations have been proven to improve the stability and/or performance of GroupWise document-management systems. They are considered "best practices" of a successful GroupWise document-management implementation. Please remember that no two GroupWise systems are alike; your GroupWise system might require a different DMS setup. So, without further delay, here are the ideal DMS best practices:

- Plan your document-management system.
- Consider the factors and set key objectives.
- Ensure the GroupWise system is healthy before you start setting up DMS.
- Decide on centralized or decentralized libraries. Decentralized libraries are normally the better choice.
- Decide on dedicated or non-dedicated DMS post offices. The dedicated post office is normally the better choice.
- Use a dedicated POA for indexing. Do not, however, use a dedicated POA for indexing on a separate server in a non-dedicated DMS post office environment.
- Allow enough disk space for GroupWise DMS to grow.
- Use enterprise servers for a full implementation of GroupWise DMS company-wide.
- Use external storage areas and avoid storing data under the post office.
- Do not share external storage areas among multiple libraries.

- Disable all public rights to the library(s) until users are trained. Use distribution lists to add users until DMS is completely rolled out company-wide.
- Start with a pilot group or department of users and get feedback.
- Customize the library(s) around the users who will use them. For example, an HR library should be customized for the HR department, not for the company.
- Avoid creating company-wide libraries, unless you're dealing with a small company.
- Set a document limit of 500,000 or fewer for each library. Remember, it's easier to work with smaller pieces; 100,000 documents is a good small number. Even though GroupWise architecture can handle over 1,000,000 documents in a library, performance begins to degrade with libraries of that size. Running a Fix Document/Version/Element on a very large library might take over a week.
- Keep lookup table lists short when possible. Try to design better document property pages using parent and child property fields and tables.
- Provide a DMS staff to support a company-wide implementation of DMS.
- Use external entities accounts to manage DMS, and assign them to users.
- Institute company-wide and departmental DMS policies and guidance. DMS usage, document deletion, and proper implementation of document property pages should be covered.
- Train users about the basics of GroupWise document management. This includes searching, importing, and creating new documents, as well as security and check in/out procedures. This is a *must*!
- Train librarians in the management of libraries. Include mass document operations.
- Users should give rights to documents based upon distribution lists.
- Users should use query folders for locating documents. Avoid the use of document references.
- Set up proper scheduled events to maintain the integrity of GroupWise document management.
- Avoid moving storage areas whenever possible.

- Avoid archiving and deleting documents. Remove the rights from all users, including Creator/Author, to simulate the appearance of deleting the document.
- Back up the GroupWise document-management system.

What a list! GroupWise document management is really its own collaboration system. That's why this chapter is so long and there are so many best practices in this list.

Summary

This chapter discussed GroupWise document management, including its planning and design aspects. It then walked through some key library and administration tasks, and explained how to best maintain a mission-critical document-management system.

GroupWise document management is the most cost-effective document-management solution on the market today. The integration of document management with the user mailbox makes the tool as easy to use as e-mail, and reduces the cost of ownership by centralizing and simplifying administration. Remember, users will perceive the GroupWise system has failed if document management fails. So, use good judgment and this chapter to implement document management correctly.

CHAPTER 15

Administering Multiple GroupWise Systems

It is not uncommon, in this age of mergers, acquisitions, and outsourcing, for an administrator to be confronted with the task of administering more than one GroupWise system. This chapter covers the tasks that are common to multiple-system administration—merging systems, releasing systems, and synchronizing address books between systems.

Multiple-System Concepts

Before discussing the tasks that are common to multiple-system administration, there are several concepts you need to understand. The following sections walk through those concepts.

The Primary Domain Defines the System

If you are working with more than one GroupWise system, you are also working with more than one primary domain. The primary domain database, WPDOMAIN.DB, contains complete information about all objects contained in its GroupWise system.

In order to administer multiple systems, you need to know which primary domain owns which objects. You also need to know which system you are connecting to when you make changes.

External Domains Are Placeholders

A primary domain can contain a special kind of record—an external domain record. This is essentially a placeholder that allows the primary domain to be aware of the existence of another GroupWise system. Note, however, that this placeholder does not give the primary domain any control over objects that exist in the other system.

External domains allow you to manage the connectivity between two or more GroupWise systems as if they were a single system—almost. You will use external domain records as you merge systems into a single system, or release domains into their own systems. You will also use external domain records to set up address-book synchronization between two systems that are external to each other.

Releasing Domains

When a GroupWise secondary domain needs to become its own system (as part of an outsourcing contract, perhaps), the administrator must tell the primary domain to *release* the secondary domain that must be let go.

The secondary domain then becomes the primary domain in its own, single-domain system.

Merging Systems

When two GroupWise systems need to be combined, the primary domain for one system will release all of its secondary domains. This, in effect, creates several GroupWise systems, each with its own primary domain. The primary domain for the destination system must adopt each of these domains in turn. Thus, when merging two systems, you must first go through the process of releasing all the secondary domains on one of the systems.

When the merges are complete, all domains will belong to a single system, and there will be only one primary domain. Of course, partial merges are not uncommon—one department or division might be sold to another company. In this case, that division's domain would be released from the original system and merged with a new one.

Synchronizing Systems

When two GroupWise systems need to remain separate, but also need to share their address books, the administrator can enable *external system synchronization*. This can be a great boon to productivity.

The downside to external system synchronization is that it can potentially bloat the GroupWise directory, making rebuild times on WPDOMAIN.DB and WPHOST.DB files longer. This is typically the case when two very large organizations (5,000 or more users) decide to synchronize their address books. Some customers choose to use an LDAP solution, to create address-book solutions that do not bloat the GroupWise directory.

Releasing a Secondary Domain to Create a New GroupWise System

Now that the concepts are covered, this section provides a walkthrough of the first of the multiple-system scenarios discussed in this chapter.

The WorldWide Widgets Corporation has decided to outsource its manufacturing division. The manufacturing division is its own separate company called ACME. They will have their own eDirectory tree, named ACME. The following is a discussion of how ACME and WorldWide Widgets pull this off.

ACME'S Pre-Domain Release Preparation

First of all, ACME is going to be getting new file servers as part of the outsourcing. Take the following steps before releasing the secondary domain to become a new system:

1. Install a new GroupWise software distribution directory to ACME's NetWare server.
2. Install the latest patches to the GroupWise software distribution directory.
3. Install the GroupWise agents so that they are ready to run on the ACME server.
4. Create an eDirectory OU, named `APPS`, to house the GroupWise system for manufacturing.
5. Create an eDirectory OU, named `STAFF`, to house the manufacturing staff.

   Figure 15.1 shows the ACME tree.

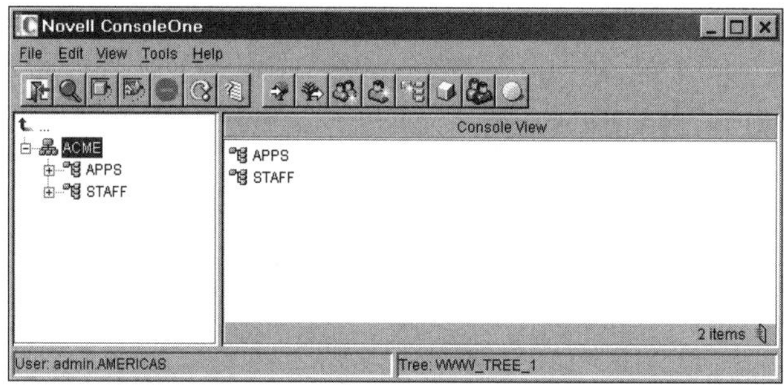

FIGURE 15.1 The ACME location shown in ConsoleOne.

Figure 15.2 shows how the manufacturing division currently looks in the WorldWide Widgets system.

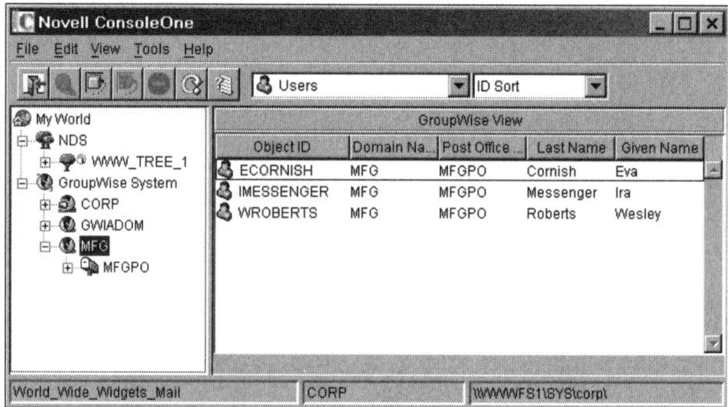

FIGURE 15.2 The manufacturing division at WorldWide Widgets.

6. Move the MFG domain and the MFGPO post office to the ACME server so that they physically reside on the ACME server.

   This operation is covered in Chapter 21, "Moving Domains and Post Offices."

7. Check that the MFG domain has no pending operations. To do this, choose Tools, GroupWise System Operations, Pending Operations.

The preparation steps are finished. Now the domain can be released.

WorldWide Widgets: The Release

The WorldWide Widgets administrator is now all set to release the MFG domain. Follow these steps to release a secondary domain:

1. Connect to the primary domain named CORP.
2. Select the MFG domain.
3. Choose Tools, GroupWise Utilities, System Maintenance.

4. In the System Maintenance screen, select the Release Secondary option, as shown in Figure 15.3, and click Run.

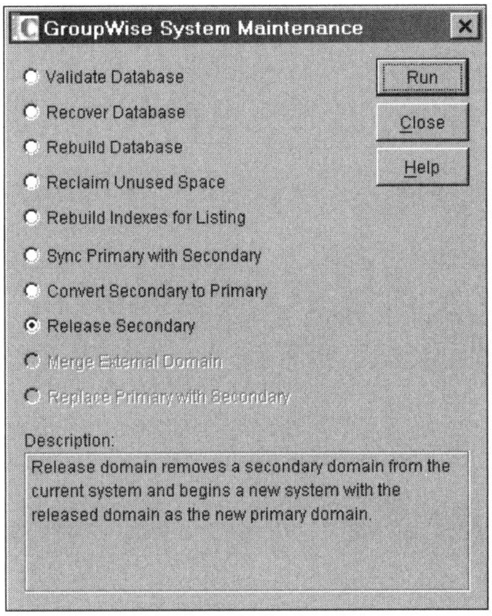

FIGURE 15.3 The Release Secondary Option appears on the GroupWise System Maintenance dialog box.

5. When the Release Domain from System wizard comes up, click the Next button. You'll advance to the screen, where you specify a path to the MFG domain. Click the Next button again.
6. Now you see a window that allows you to name the ACME GroupWise system. In this example the name of the new GroupWise system is `ACME_Mail`.

TIP

The name of the new system must not be the same as the old WorldWide Widgets GroupWise system. If you ever need to determine the system name of a GroupWise system, highlight any object in the left pane of the GroupWise view. At the bottom of the status tray in ConsoleOne, you will see the system name. In Figure 15.2, you can see that the name of the existing system is `World_Wide_Widgets_Mail`.

7. The Release Domain wizard prompts you to update eDirectory objects.

   You will want to do this. This option takes the MFG and MFGPO1 objects out of the WorldWide Widgets eDirectory tree.
8. Follow the Release Domain wizard's prompts to unload the Message Transfer Agent (MTA) on the Primary domain, as well as on the MFG domain that is being released.
9. The final dialog box says that you are ready to release the domain. Click the Release button.

The domain is released and becomes an external GroupWise domain to the `World_Widc_Widgets_Mail` GroupWisc systcm. Thc MFG domain becomes its own primary domain over the `ACME_Mail` system. The domains in the `World_Wide_Widgets_Mail` GroupWise all show up as external to the `ACME_Mail` system. Figure 15.4 shows how the GroupWise view looks when connected to the `CORP` domain.

FIGURE 15.4
The newly revised GroupWise system.

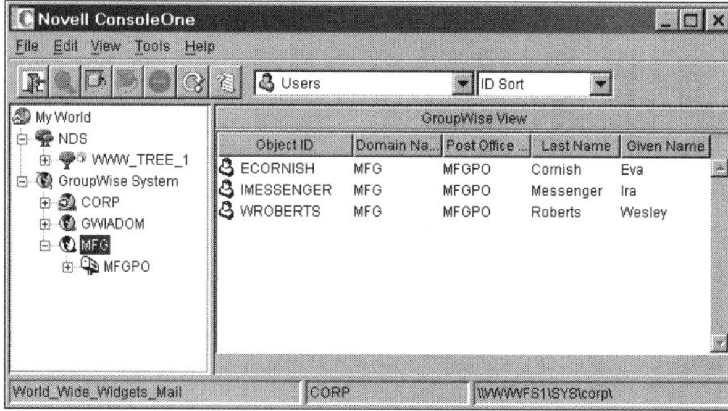

TIP

When writing this section and following the steps outlined in this section, I received errors when I tried to release a secondary domain. The errors seem to have been related to removing the Update eDirectory Objects selection that I made. The MFG domain was released, despite the error that I got, but I didn't know that until I actually connected to the domain that I released. When I did connect, I saw that the old primary domain was a white earth icon, rather than a blue earth icon, which told me that the domain had in fact been released. Also when I edited the MFG domain, I could see that the domain type was primary.

The domain is now released, but that's not the end of the story. The MFG domain and the MFGPO1 post office still need to be grafted into the ACME tree. And three users—`ECORNISH`, `IMESSENGER`, and `WROBERTS`—still need to be created in the ACME tree. Here's the process to follow:

1. Log into the ACME tree.
2. Connect to the MFG domain, which is now a primary domain. To do this select Tools, GroupWise System Operations, Select Domain.
3. Go into the eDirectory browser portion of ConsoleOne. Highlight the `APPS` organizational unit.
4. Choose Tools, GroupWise Utilities, GW/eDirectory Association, Graft GroupWise Objects. The Graft GroupWise Objects wizard appears.
5. Select the domains, post offices, and gateways option, and proceed through the wizard. Do not attempt to graft users until you read the

next step. In the `ACME_INC` tree, the MFG domain (and the MFGPO post office) will be grafted into the `APPS.ACME` eDirectory context, as shown in Figure 15.5.

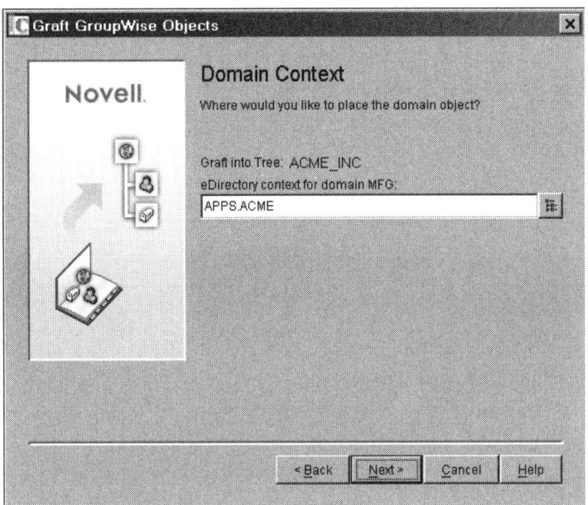

FIGURE 15.5
Grafting the MFG domain.

Now the MFG Domain and MFGPO post office are in the eDirectory tree. You can now try to graft the users into the new `ACME_INC` tree. This process isn't quite as straightforward as grafting the domain and post office. The great thing about this procedure is that you do not have to manually re-create your users into eDirectory.

Following are example procedures for grafting the users from the MFG domain into a new eDirectory tree:

1. From the eDirectory browser view, highlight the `STAFF` context and then choose Tools, GroupWise Utilities, GW/eDirectory Association, Graft GroupWise Objects.
2. Select the option to graft users, resources, distribution lists, and libraries.

   Follow the prompts of this wizard, making sure to specify the right eDirectory contexts, as well as the eDirectory contexts in which the users who moved with MFG have been created. See Figure 15.6.
3. Proceed to the Unmatched Users screen as shown in Figure 15.7. Choose the option to create the users as GroupWise external entities.

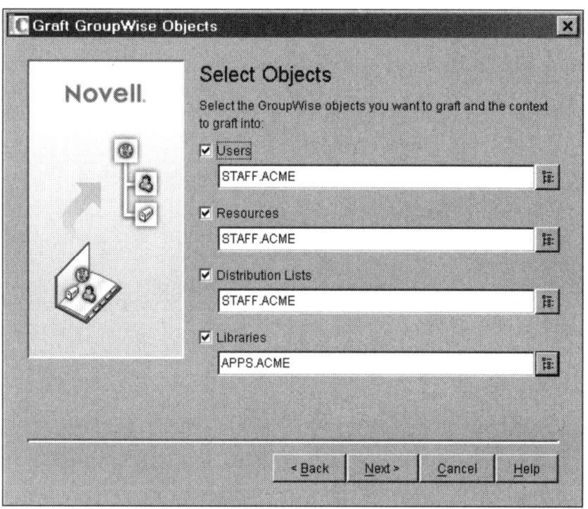

FIGURE 15.6 Grafting users and other objects is possible using the Select Objects dialog box.

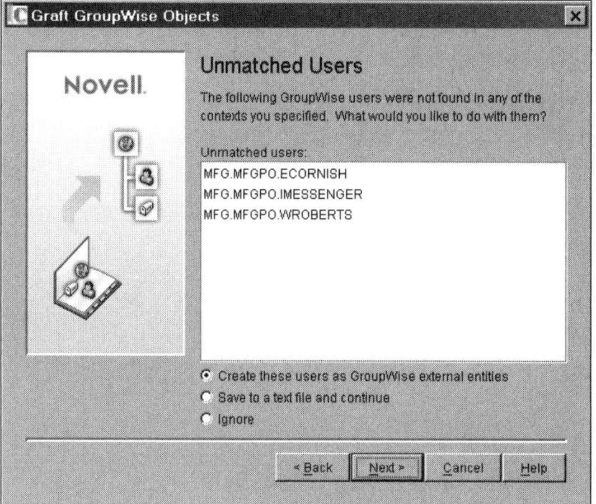

FIGURE 15.7 Unmatched users will become GroupWise external entities.

4. Proceed through the rest of the grafting wizard.

   Now the users are GroupWise external entities; they are not full eDirectory users as shown in Figure 15.8. The next few steps describe how to convert these GroupWise external entities into full eDirectory users.

5. Highlight all of the GroupWise external entities in the eDirectory browser view. Then select Tools, GroupWise Utilities, GW/eDirectory Association, Convert External Entity to User.

6. In the Convert External Entity to User dialog that appears, select Yes All. The users become full eDirectory user objects, as shown in Figure 15.9.

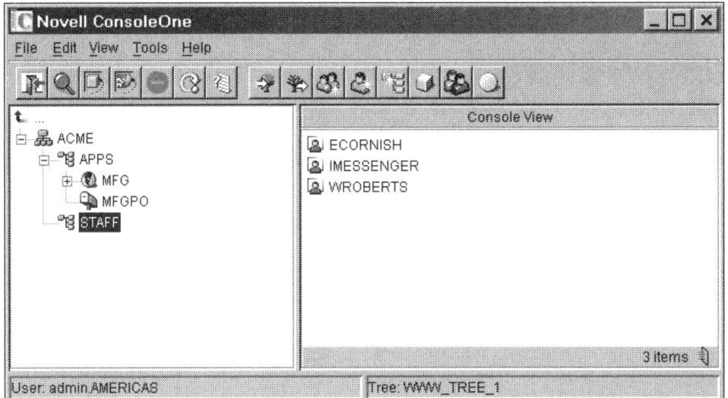

FIGURE 15.8
GroupWise external entity users are users without an eDirectory account.

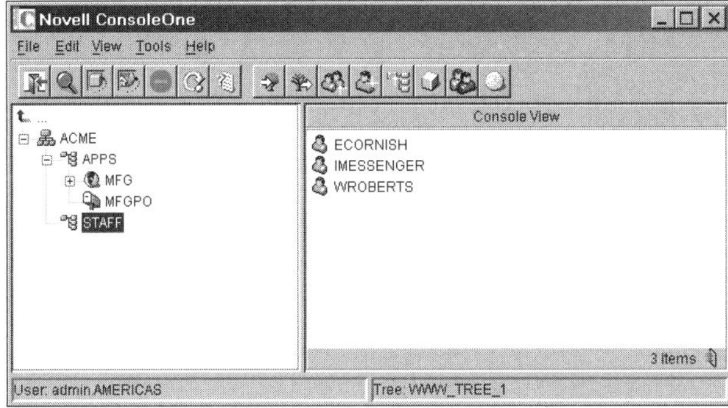

FIGURE 15.9
Full eDirectory user objects.

Now you have created your user objects in eDirectory. You should now give the users rights throughout your eDirectory as needed.

Final Steps and Cleanup

The new GroupWise system needs to have a software distribution directory definition pointing to the newly installed GroupWise software distribution directory. You define a software distribution directory under Tools, GroupWise System Operations, Software Directory Management, as outlined in Chapter 6, "Using GroupWise System Operations."

The MFGPO1 post office needs to have its "software directory" pointing to the new ACME software distribution directory.

The users in the ACME tree should be given browse, read, and compare rights to the MFG post office, as well as the POA below that post office object. This will allow users' GroupWise clients to dynamically discover their new POA IP address.

In this example, WorldWide Widgets and ACME do not need to reference each other anymore. Both sides will delete any reference to one another.

This means that the WorldWide Widgets administrator will delete the external domain for manufacturing, and the administrator of the `ACME_Mail` system will delete all external domains left over from the WorldWide Widgets system. First though, in each system they must go to Tools, GroupWise System Operations, External System Synchronization and delete the reference they have to one another. Then they should be able to delete the external domain reference to one another.

The manufacturing division's eDirectory user objects should also be deleted from the WorldWide Widgets eDirectory tree.

Synchronizing External Systems

Continuing the World Wide Widgets and ACME Manufacturing scenario, imagine that WorldWide Widgets acted a little hastily. They deleted all user objects and external references to manufacturing, but now they discover their users need to exchange address books.

For the balance of this chapter, the GroupWise system for WorldWide Widgets is called System 1; ACME's system is called System 2.

Creating System Definitions for Synchronizing

First, from System 1, you need to create a definition for System 2.

Following are the steps for creating a reference to an external system:

1. Highlight the GroupWise system object. Then select File, New, External Domain.
2. Fill out the appropriate System 2 information in the Create External GroupWise Domain dialog box (see Figure 15.10). In order to do external system synchronization, you must define the primary domain for the other system as the new external domain.

At this point, the MFG domain again exists in the WorldWide Widgets system, but only as an external domain. The post office below the MFG domain and the users on that post office are not currently represented.

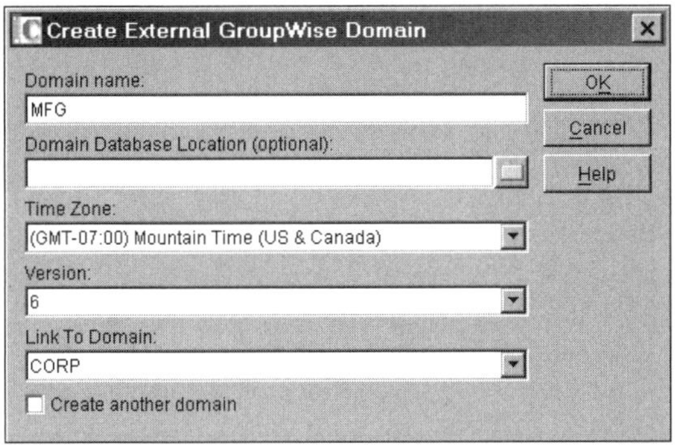

FIGURE 15.10 Creating a new external domain in another GroupWise system.

TIP

External domains appear as a white earth icon, rather than a blue earth icon.

TIP

When defining an external GroupWise system for synchronization purposes, you must define the primary domain for that system. Defining a secondary domain in another system, rather than the primary domain, is fine, but a secondary domain does not support external system synchronization.

To create a definition for System 1 from System 2, you need to repeat the procedure in the previous section, but from System 2's perspective. Follow these steps to create a reference to an external system:

1. Connect to System 2 and highlight the GroupWise system object in the GroupWise view.
2. Click the right mouse button, select New, and then select External Domain.
3. Fill out the information in the next dialog box that's appropriate for System 1.

At this point, the CORP domain exists in the `ACME_Mail` system, but only as an external domain.

Creating MTA Connectivity

To create MTA connectivity between System 1 and System 2, you need to define how System 1's MTAs deliver messages to System 2's MTAs, and vice-versa. Follow these steps to create MTA level connectivity between two GroupWise systems:

1. While connected to System 1, choose Tools, GroupWise Utilities, Link Configuration.
2. Edit the link from the primary domain to System 2's external domain.

   Fill in the correct information so that the MTA on System 1 can contact the MTA on System 2, as shown in Figure 15.11.

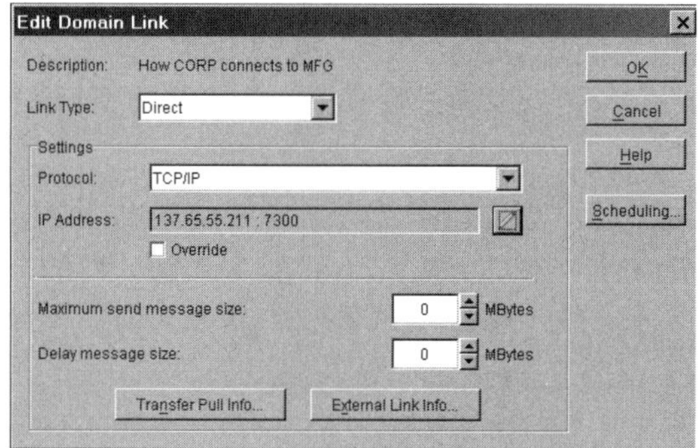

FIGURE 15.11 Link configuration for MTA connectivity to an external GroupWise domain.

3. While connected to System 2, choose Tools, GroupWise Utilities, Link Configuration.
4. Edit the link from the primary domain to System 1's external domain.

   Fill in the correct information so that the MTA on System 2 can contact the MTA on System 1.

Now the MTAs of both systems know how to transfer messages between systems.

Testing System Connectivity

Before enabling external system synchronization, you need to test the connection. Otherwise, you might end up with thousands of address-sync messages queued up in `<DOMAIN>\MSLOCAL\MSHOLD` directories.

Following are steps to test system connectivity between two external GroupWise systems:

1. Send an email from a user on System 2 to a user on System 1.

   To do this, compose a message in this manner: On the To line, type the name of the external domain followed by the post office and username, all separated with dots.

For example, you want to send to the user TKRATZER on the post office CORPPO off of the CORP domain in System 1. The To line of the message should read `CORP:corppo.tkratzer`. Figure 15.12 shows this syntax.

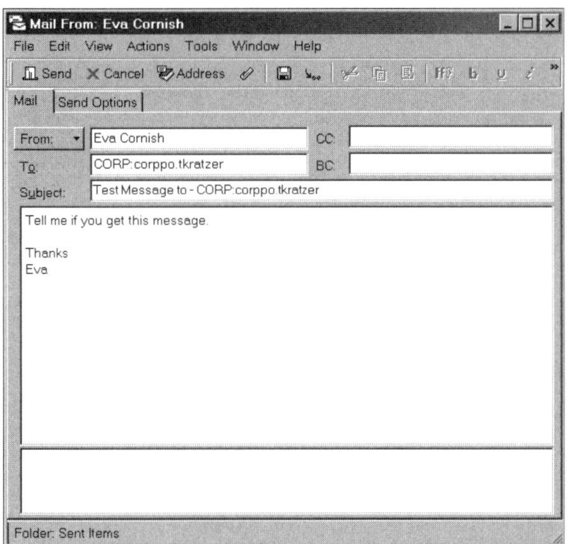

FIGURE 15.12
Sending email to an external system via the connection to an external domain.

Suppose that the `CORP` primary domain did not have a post office under it. There is a post office under the `Sales` domain though. You can still send from System 2 to System 1. You can utilize the connection to `CORP` to route a message to the `Sales` domain. Here's how the To line would appear: `CORP:SALES.SALESPO.TKRATZER`.

2. Confirm that the email went through.

   Check the properties of the original sent item. Does it say that it was delivered? If so, the connection in both directions is okay. You know this because the original message was delivered (System 2 to System 1), and the delivered status message came back (System 1 to System 2).

Now that you have confirmed that both sides can send one another messages, you are ready to enable external system synchronization.

Configuring External System Synchronization

Now you know that communication works between the two systems, so you are ready to synchronize their address books. This operation requires that you make changes on both systems.

Following are the steps for configuring external system synchronization:

1. Connect to System 1's primary domain.
2. Choose Tools, GroupWise System Operations, External System Synchronization.
3. Click the Add button and fill in the GroupWise system name for the external system.

   In the example scenario, it is `ACME_Mail`. Pay attention to the spelling and case—this field is case sensitive. The name `acme_mail` would not be correct.
4. In the External Domain field, browse to the external domain's primary domain that represents System 2's connectivity point.
5. Select the options to send and receive the domains, post offices, and users from the external domain.

   Figure 15.13 shows a configured external domain link from System 1 to System 2.

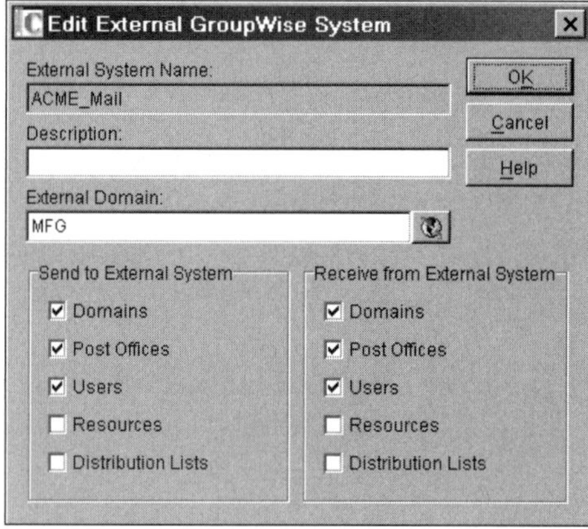

FIGURE 15.13
Setting up external system synchronization for System 1.

6. Click OK.
7. Connect to the primary domain on System 2.

8. Choose Tools, GroupWise System Operations, External System Synchronization.
9. Click the Add button and fill in the GroupWise system name for the external system.

   In the example scenario, it is `World_Wide_Widgets_Mail`.
10. In the External Domain field, browse to the external domain that represents System 1's connectivity point.
11. Select the options to send and receive from the external domain the domain, post offices, and users.

All systems are go, but you still have not kicked off the initial synchronization between both GroupWise systems. These steps are covered in the next section.

Synchronizing Systems

Now that both sides are prepared to send changes to each other, you must kick off the synchronization by having each side request all the objects it needs from the other side.

Following are the steps to initiate external system synchronization:

1. While connected to the System 1's primary domain, choose Tools, GroupWise System Operations, External System Synchronization.
2. Highlight System 2's external system and click the Request button.

   Be aware that this step does generate a lot of traffic—at least one mail message per user on System 2.
3. While connected to System 2's primary domain, choose Tools, GroupWise System Operations, External System Synchronization.
4. Highlight System 1's external system and select the Request button.

   Again, be ready for lots of traffic.

If all goes well, both sides should synchronize, and the post offices and users from the external system will be visible.

TIP **I have worked with external system synchronization problems several times. Based on the experience I have had, it's quite possible that you will need to request the objects a few times. If it appears as if the request operation just does not get all the objects from the other GroupWise system, you can synchronize the users manually from System 1. This information will automatically replicate to System 2 as well. This might help to get all objects synchronized between both systems the first time.**

Merging Two External GroupWise Systems

This walkthrough takes you through the process of merging two GroupWise systems. The primary domain in System 2 will become subordinate to the primary domain in System 1, which means it will eventually be converted to a secondary domain.

NOTE **Only primary domains can be merged with an existing system, and they can be merged only if they do not own any secondary domains. If you need to merge a multi-domain system with yours, you must first have that system release all of its domains. Refer to the section, "Releasing a Secondary Domain to Create a New GroupWise System," earlier in this chapter.**

The Merge Scenario

The WorldWide Widgets Corporation wants to acquire the ACME Corporation. (Forget, for just a moment, that you released the ACME system in an earlier walkthrough. Or perhaps you could assume that this is a real-life example of a confused corporate reorganization.)

They both have GroupWise systems. It is natural for them to merge their two GroupWise systems. This will cause the MFG domain to be a GroupWise secondary domain to the CORP Primary domain. WorldWide Widgets and ACME will still keep separate trees, however. Remember that System 1 is WorldWide Widgets' system, and System 2 is ACME's system.

Creating System Definitions for Merged Systems

From System 1, follow the steps to create a definition for System 2. From System 2, follow the steps to create a definition for System 1. All of the steps are in previous sections of this chapter. Follow all of the steps in the sections titled "Creating System Definitions for Synchronizing," "Creating MTA Connectivity," and "Testing System Connectivity."

On System 2 (the system that will be merged), follow all the steps necessary to release its secondary domains. The steps for doing this are described in the section titled "Releasing a Secondary Domain to Create a New GroupWise System."

TIP

The reason for releasing domains is that you cannot merge another GroupWise system when it contains multiple domains. You must pare it down to a single primary domain to merge it into a different GroupWise system.

Now, connect to System 1's primary domain (the domain that will assimilate System 2). Log into the eDirectory tree that houses the primary domain for System 2. In this scenario it's the `ACME_INC` tree, and the domain is the MFG domain.

Highlight the external domain that represents the primary domain that you are assimilating to become a new secondary domain. Select Tools, GroupWise Utilities, System Maintenance. Choose the option Merge External Domain and then click the Run button. Follow the prompts of the Merge External Domain wizard. When you get the prompt to Update eDirectory Objects, choose No at least in this scenario where the MFG domain will still be contained in the `ACME_INC` tree.

When prompted to do so, bring down the MTA for both of the primary domains. Proceed through the wizard, and merge the two systems.

TIP

If you get the "Merge Domain Error", there is an MTA or a gateway still up that is accessing the WPDOMAIN.DB, or ConsoleOne is tripping over its own shoelaces (this is often the case in scenarios such as this). The solution is simple. Make sure that you are connected to System 1's primary domain, and then exit ConsoleOne. Load ConsoleOne, and then attempt the merge again. If the problem persists, someone else is accessing the WPDOMAIN.DB for the primary domain for either System 1 or System 2. You can use Monitor on NetWare and check for File, Open Lock activity, and then browse to the WPDOMAIN.DB file to determine who is accessing the database.

Synchronizing Objects

Merging two systems is rather easy. However, the merge does not broadcast the new objects brought in from System 2 to the rest of System 1. Also, the domains and post offices originally associated with System 2 don't have a clue about the objects in their new system.

In order to get all domains and post offices acquainted with the new, larger system, you must perform a top-down rebuild. This can be a big task. A top-down rebuild requires that all GroupWise domains and post offices be rebuilt. Here are some important pointers to top-down rebuilds:

- Before rebuilding a secondary domain, synchronize it with the primary domain. See the beginning of this walkthrough for instructions on how to do this.
- Rebuilding a GroupWise domain or GroupWise post office database requires exclusive access to that database.
- For more information about rebuilding domain and post office databases, refer to Chapter 22, "Troubleshooting the GroupWise Directory."

After the top-down rebuild, all GroupWise domains and post offices should be aware of the new domains and post offices.

Defining IDOMAINs for an External Domain

This is kind of an obscure feature, but you might find it handy. First off, Chapter 16, "Internet Addressing," talks in more depth about IDOMAINs. Just in case you wanted to know, there is a way to define the Internet domain for an external GroupWise system. Here's an example of how this feature might be applied. Users at WWWIDGETS.COM are accustomed to sending messages to users at ACMEWIDGETS.COM. Now though, these two systems are connected to one another and they do external system synchronization. There is no longer a reason for users at ACMEWIDGETS.COM to send to users via the syntax: USERID@WWWIDGETS.COM.

There's no reason for users at WWWIDGETS.COM to send to USERID@ACMEWIDGETS.COM.

The users should just select one another from the address book. Alas, old habits are hard to break. The impact is that messages are not being kept in their native GroupWise format, and they are being sent out the GWIA. Here's the solution. We will explain this solution from the perspective of the system with the WWWIDGETS.COM IDOMAIN—in this scenario, this is the system that has the CORP domain as the primary domain.

1. Connect to System 1's primary (called CORP).
2. Highlight the external GroupWise domain. In this scenario the name of the domain is MFG.
3. Edit the properties of the MFG domain.
4. Select the Internet Addressing property page under the GroupWise tab.
5. Place a check mark next to the Internet Domain Name field.
6. Fill in the Domain Name field with the Internet domain name of the external domain. See Figure 15.14.
7. Repeat these steps for all domains in the external system.

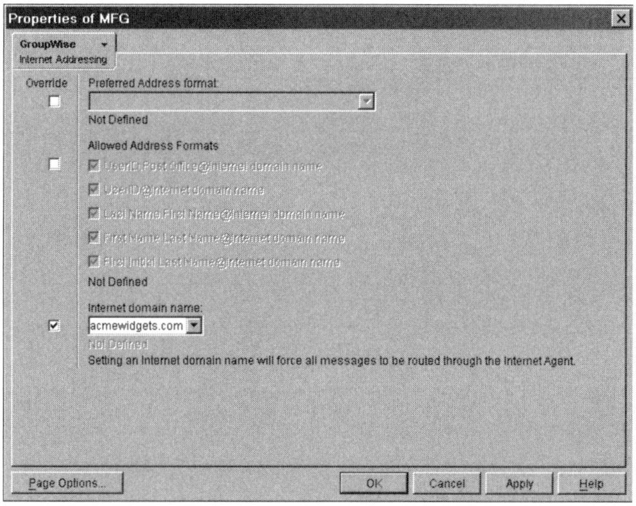

FIGURE 15.14 Defining an IDOMAIN for an external domain.

Now, since you have defined the IDOMAIN for your external GroupWise system, messages sent to the external domain's Internet domain will not pass through the GWIA. This will allow the messages to contain more formatting and features, such as status tracking.

Summary

The GroupWise directory is fairly flexible in allowing you to work with multiple GroupWise systems. The decision to merge systems rather than simply synchronizing them is one for you to make. There are advantages and disadvantages to each.

Chapter 16 talks about Internet addressing, which enables another means for communicating effortlessly with other email systems on the Internet.

The advantages to merging systems are as follows: They include synchronization between domains automatically and require no additional configuration. They include a single primary domain database, which allows for central administration. Distributed administration is possible.

Merging systems does, however, has its disadvantages. These include adding the necessity for some degree of central administration. This might not be appropriate for some organizations. Additionally, the larger the system is, the more crowded the address book becomes.

CHAPTER 16

Internet Addressing

As mentioned in previous chapters, GroupWise features an option for Internet addressing. By default, when you install GroupWise, Internet addressing is not enabled, so you should take steps to enable it as soon as possible. As GroupWise evolves, certain features rely upon you having Internet addressing enabled. This chapter examines the Internet addressing standard and explores the changes that take place when Internet addressing is enabled on a GroupWise 6 system.

Overview of GroupWise Internet Addressing

To begin with, it is important to provide a high-level overview of what GroupWise Internet addressing is and the background as to why Internet addressing was added to GroupWise. More detail will follow on the basics of Internet addresses and how GroupWise addressed messages using the old-style addressing scheme before GroupWise supported Internet addressing.

GroupWise was designed and engineered before the Internet was widely in use for sending SMTP messages via e-mail. As a result, GroupWise uses a proprietary addressing scheme that is made up of the domain, post office, and user ID in a GroupWise system. Because of this if you were to create a new GroupWise system, and then install the GroupWise Internet agent (GWIA) to send SMTP messages via the Internet, your users would not be able to simply type an address in the format of `user@internetdomain.com` and expect the GroupWise system to know what to do with this address. Before GroupWise supported native Internet style addresses, the administrator got around this issue by having to set up a slew of system addressing rules that allowed users to send mail in the format of `user@internetdomain.com`.

Novell, knowing that GroupWise must be able to natively understand Internet style addresses, came up with a solution that was first introduced in GroupWise 5.5. This is where the term *Internet addressing* was introduced to GroupWise.

When an administrator enables Internet addressing, all GroupWise agents—including the GroupWise client—become aware of this fact, and are able to resolve Internet style addresses natively. This gives the administrator a lot of flexibility in regards to the way that GroupWise can address and resolve Internet style addresses.

The following sections explore the details of Internet addressing.

Defining an Internet Address

Internet addressing is the standard addressing format that is used to route and resolve Internet mail to appropriate mail hosts and user mailboxes. The format of an Internet address is *`<username>@<Internet DNS domain name>`*. Any e-mail message routed across the Internet must adhere to this format.

Following is an explanation of the portions of an Internet e-mail address:

- **Internet username:** The username (or user ID) portion is an identifier for a mailbox in a mail system. For example, `eraff` is the username for Eric Raff. The username portion of an Internet address is typically controlled at the company or Internet service provider (ISP) level. Usually, companies or organizations specify a standard method for creating usernames, often using portions of users' full names. In this book's example company, WorldWide Widgets, the naming standard for creating usernames is to use the first letter of the first name and follow it with the last name.
- **Internet domain name:** The domain name portion of an Internet address is the string on the right side of the address following the `@` sign. This string identifies the mail host that Internet users must reach when sending to a particular organization. For example, the username `eraff` belongs to the domain name `wwwidgets.com`, so Eric Raff's fully qualified Internet address is `eraff@wwwidgets.com`.

Usually, domain names are based on the actual company or organization name. In the example of this book, WorldWide Widgets is the company name, and the domain name that refers to WorldWide Widgets on the Internet is `wwwidgets.com`. When selecting a domain name, an organization has to pick a unique name and register that name so that no other organization will use it.

- **Domain name registration:** All registered domain names can be resolved through a domain name server (DNS). Domain names are registered through an organization called *Internic*. A DNS resolves domain names to show the actual Internet protocol (IP) address of the mail hosts that an organization uses to send and receive Internet mail. The DNS takes a domain name, which is like a ZIP code in the postal system, and translates it into an IP address of a mail host, which is like a local post office that handles mail for that domain.

TIP

Information regarding Internic as well as information about how to register a domain name can be found at `www.internic.org`.

- **Guaranteed uniqueness:** The great value of having a central body such as the Internic in charge of domain names is that all domain names are guaranteed to be unique. Because the domain names are guaranteed to be unique, fully qualified Internet addresses are also guaranteed to be unique. For example, two users who have a common username will still be uniquely identified on the Internet, as long as the domain portion of the Internet address makes the entire Internet addresses unique. There are countless postmaster mailboxes on the Internet, but they are uniquely defined by the fact that their domain names are different.

All valid Internet e-mail addresses will have the elements explained, no matter which e-mail system is being used.

Understanding Old-Style GroupWise Addressing Format

A basic characteristic of Internet addresses is that the address is ordered from general to specific, as the address is resolved from right to left. The most specific part of the address is the username, on the far left. The most general part is the upper-level domain name (for example, `.com` or `.net`) on the far right. Processes that read and resolve Internet addresses read backward compared to the way you are reading the text of this book. They start on the right side and work their way to the left.

In contrast, old-style GroupWise addresses (prior to GroupWise 5.5 with Internet addressing) are resolved from left to right. They are still resolved from general to specific, though. This GroupWise address format is `Domain.PostOffice.User` (DPU). Note that a GroupWise domain is not quite the same as an Internet domain. GroupWise domains are named by GroupWise administrators, and they do not need to be unique worldwide. There is no central naming authority for GroupWise domains.

The fact that GroupWise domains are not unique didn't matter until companies that had common domain names began to connect to each other. To make the mail between their systems routable, each company would have to alter the name of the external domain definitions they created so that their address books would not show two `CORP` domains, for example.

As Internet connectivity became more and more common (almost as common as television!), GroupWise users realized that they had to know two addressing formats, one for users on their GroupWise systems and a different one for users elsewhere on the Internet.

True Internet addresses, where every name is guaranteed to be unique, leave no question as to what domain a piece of mail should be routed to, regardless of where the piece of mail originated. To communicate through the Internet, GroupWise had to conform to the standards of Internet addressing to allow GroupWise mail hosts to communicate with other Internet mail hosts.

Old-Style GroupWise Internet Address Resolution

By *old-style,* I am talking about any GroupWise system that does not have GroupWise Internet addressing enabled. This means all versions of GroupWise prior to GroupWise 5.5 (where the option was not available), as well as any GroupWise 5.5x to GroupWise 6.5 system where Internet addressing is not yet turned on.

As discussed in Chapter 10, "Installing and Configuring the GroupWise Internet Agent," GroupWise systems connect with the Internet through the GroupWise Internet agent (GWIA). This gateway allows GroupWise users to send e-mail to Internet users by acting as a mail host and as an address resolver. The GWIA converts GroupWise addressing formats to Internet addressing formats, and resolves Internet addresses to GroupWise addresses.

The gateway also acts as a mail host to physically send and receive mail from the Internet. The GWIA stamps the outgoing mail with an Internet-style return address. Incoming mail is converted to a GroupWise address format. For example, a message sent from `Corp.Corp_po1.eraff` to an Internet recipient will have its reply-to address changed to `eraff@wwwidgets.com`. An incoming mail message from the Internet will have its delivery address converted from `eraff@wwwidgets.com` to a GroupWise address of `Corp.Corp_po1.eraff`.

Old-Style GWIA Creation of Reply-To Addresses

When mail is passing from the GroupWise system to the Internet, the GWIA has to create an Internet-standard reply-to address from the GroupWise information so that Internet recipients of GroupWise mail can reply. The gateway formulates the reply-to Internet address by using the rules shown in Figure 16.1.

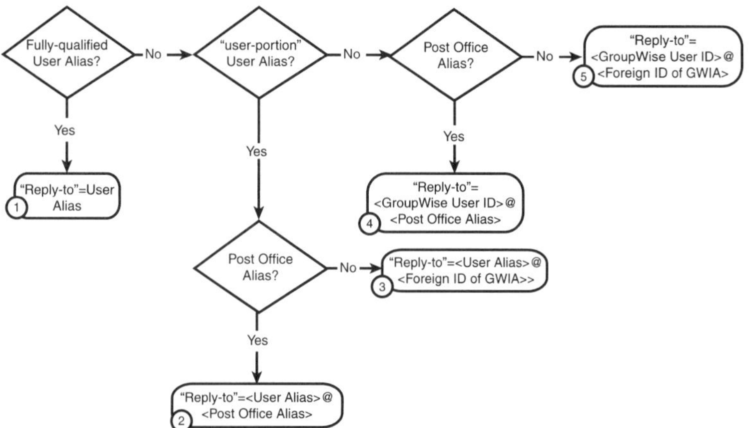

FIGURE 16.1
Old-style GroupWise process for stamping reply-to on outbound messages, without Internet addressing enabled.

Here is a look at each of these reply-to addresses in turn, with each numeral in the following list corresponding to the number in Figure 16.1:

1. If there is a fully qualified user alias for the GWIA, (that is, the user alias has both a user portion and a domain portion), the reply-to address will be set to the user's alias. If Bob Snow's user alias is set to `BobSnow@bob.wwwidgets.com`, that will be his reply-to address.

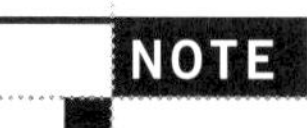
NOTE

If a user has more than one alias for the GWIA, the first listed alias will always be used for constructing the reply-to address.

2. If there is a user alias and a post office alias, the reply-to address will be set to *<User Alias>@<Post Office Alias>*. For example, if BSnow's user alias is `BobSnow`, and the post office alias for his post office is `sales.worldwidewidgets.com`, the e-mail he sends will be

stamped with `BobSnow@sales.worldwidewidgets.com` in the reply-to field.

3. If there is a user alias, but no post office alias, the reply-to address will be set to *<User Alias>@<Gateway Foreign ID>*. If the GWIA has more than one gateway foreign ID set, the first one on the list will be used.

The GWIA's gateway foreign ID is defined under the properties of the GWIA. Figure 16.2 shows the Foreign ID field on the WorldWide Widgets GWIA.
A GWIA can have multiple foreign IDs. The first foreign ID is the default foreign ID for the GWIA. Foreign IDs are separated (delimited) with a single space.
The Foreign ID field on the GWIA cannot exceed 124 characters. If you have several foreign IDs, create an ASCII file in the `<DOMAIN>\WPGATE\<GWIA>` **directory called FRGNAMES.CFG. List the main domain name, such as** `worldwidewidgets.com`**, on the first line. List each of the other domain names, such as** `sales.worldwidewidgets.com`**, on a line by themselves. Put a blank line at the end of the file. Restart your GWIA so that it reads this file.**

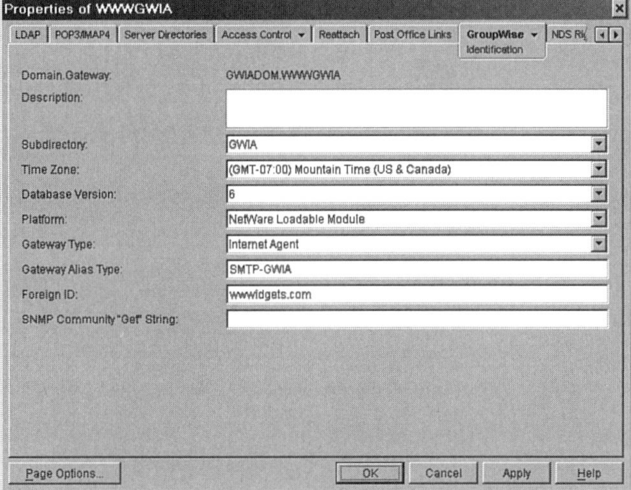

FIGURE 16.2
The Foreign ID field for the GWIA must be filled in.

4. If there is no user alias, but there is a post office alias, the reply-to field will be set to *<GroupWise UserID>@<Post Office Alias>*.

5. If there is no user alias, and there is no post office alias, the reply-to address will simply be *<GroupWise UserID>@<Gateway Foreign ID>*. This is the default case. A GWIA must have a foreign ID specified, and users must have a user ID, but aliases are not required.

Old-Style GWIA Resolution of Inbound Internet Addresses

Figure 16.3 shows what happens when a message is coming inbound to the GWIA.

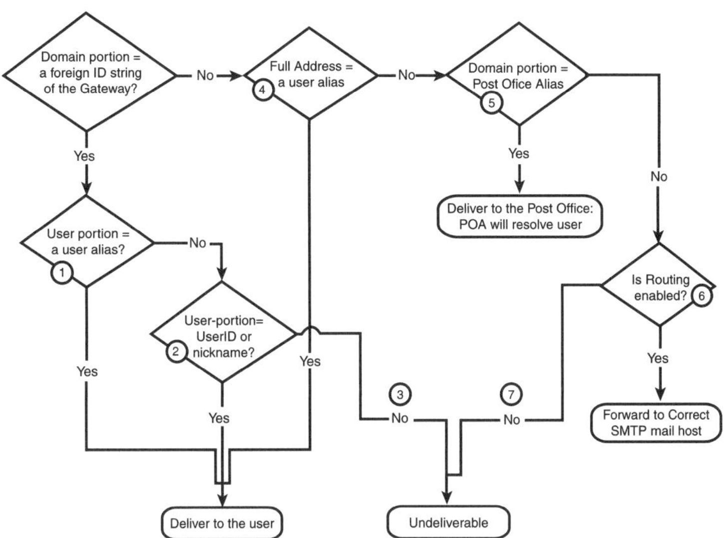

FIGURE 16.3
Old-style GWIA inbound message resolution.

Inbound Internet mail arrives at the GWIA when a foreign mail host connects to the GWIA and sends something in on port 25. Typically, this happens because the foreign host found an MX record (DNS mail exchange) matching the GWIA up to the domain portion of an address. If DNS says that `worldwidewidgets.com` resolves to the IP address of the GWIA, any message to any user at `worldwidewidgets.com` will get sent to that GWIA.

This means that your GWIA could receive mail that is *not* destined for your GroupWise system. The GWIA needs to be able to deal with this. The rest of this section describes how mail coming through a GWIA is resolved to a GroupWise user address.

First, the gateway compares the domain name of the message recipient with all of the foreign IDs of the gateway. This is where the GWIA is checking to see if the mail is actually destined for your system. If there is a match, begin with step 1; otherwise begin with step 4:

1. If a match is found, the GWIA checks to see if the user portion of the recipient address matches a user alias. If so, the message is delivered to that user.
2. If there is no user alias, the GWIA checks for matches with user IDs and nicknames. If a match is found, the message is delivered to that user.

3. If no match is found for user aliases, nor for user IDs and nicknames, the message is undeliverable.
4. If the foreign ID string of the gateway does *not* match the domain portion of the address, the GWIA determines whether there is a match with a fully qualified user alias (a user alias where both the user and domain portions of the address are specified). If the GWIA finds a match, the message is delivered to that user.

TIP

I have seen situations in which step 4 of this algorithm did not work. It is just best to define all Internet domain names in the Foreign ID field or the FRGNAMES.CFG file.

5. If there is no fully qualified user alias, but there is a match between a post office alias and the Internet domain portion of the address, the GWIA will not receive the message. By default, the GWIA does not allow relaying and the Daemon portion of the GWIA will not be able to fully resolve the address, hence it will drop it.
6. If there are no alias matches, and the foreign ID did not match, the message is not really destined for this GroupWise system. If message routing, or *relaying,* is enabled, the GWIA will attempt to pass the message on to the correct SMTP host.
7. If message relaying is not enabled, the message is undeliverable.

Pitfalls with Old-Style GroupWise Addressing

Before discussing native GroupWise Internet addressing, this section explores the limitations of the old-style addressing. Following are the pitfalls of the old-style GroupWise address:

- **User training issues:** With the prevalence of consumer Internet e-mail, most users know how to address a message Internet-style. These users will want to be able to send to the Internet from GroupWise the same way they do from other e-mail applications.

  Without GroupWise Internet addressing, these users must enter additional information in order to get their Internet messages out of the GroupWise system. Specifically, they must enter the domain and gateway name of the GWIA prior to the address, or they must enter the name of a foreign domain that has been associated with the GWIA.

Thus, outbound messages are typically addressed `internet:user@domain`. A message simply addressed to `user@domain` will not make it out of the GroupWise system.

GroupWise addressing rules can be used in place of true Internet addressing. This will alleviate the user training issues, but won't help in other areas.

- **GWIA limitations:** Another potential problem with this traditional handling of address conversion is that the gateway might only narrowly interpret incoming mail as being part of its GroupWise system. This limitation is primarily due to the way in which the GWIA looks at its Foreign ID field/FRGNAMES.CFG file. Addresses that don't match this field (or don't match user or post office aliases) might be marked undeliverable.
- **User alias limitations:** A third problem lies in limitations of GroupWise user aliases. Only two addresses per gateway can be used to identify a GroupWise user. For example, Eric Raff has a mailbox ID of `Raffe` and a user alias of `Eric.Raff@worldwidewidgets.com`. This means that his outgoing Internet mail will be sent to the Internet as being from `Eric.Raff@worldwidewidgets.com`, and he can receive e-mail bound for the address of either `Raffe@worldwidewidgets.com` or `Eric.Raff@worldwidewidgets.com`.

Hopefully by now I've convinced you that you need to enable Internet addressing, which is discussed in the next section.

Benefits of GroupWise Internet Addressing

GroupWise Internet addressing offers several advantages over the old-style GroupWise addressing format. Following are some of the advantages of Internet addressing:

- GroupWise addresses become true Internet addresses.
- GWIA gains flexibility as it resolves Internet addresses to GroupWise users.
- Client addressing rules might no longer be needed.
- GroupWise systems can connect to each other natively, without defining external domains.
- Certain features of GroupWise require Internet addressing.

Here is a discussion of each of these in turn.

- **GroupWise addresses become Internet addresses:** With native Internet addressing, GroupWise addresses no longer need to be converted to Internet addressing formats when GroupWise mail is being sent out to the Internet. Instead of users being known internally to the GroupWise system as `Domain.PostOffice.UserID`, users will be internally known as `UserID@Internet` *`domain name`*.
- **GWIA gains flexibility:** With Internet addressing enabled, the GWIA will work very hard to match an Internet address with a GroupWise user for incoming SMTP mail. The gateway will still look for the old-style matches with aliases and foreign IDs as well as the following Internet domain name formats:
  - **Full:** `UserID.PostOffice.Domain@Internet` *`domain name`*
  - **Post office unique:** `UserID.PostOffice@Internet` *`domain name`*
  - **User ID unique:** `UserID@Internet` *`domain name`*
  - **First/Last:** `Firstname.Lastname@Internet` *`domain name`*
  - **Last/First:** `Lastname.Firstname@Internet` *`domain name`*
  - **FirstInitial/LastName:** `Firstinitial.Lastname@Internet` *`domain name`*
  - **Free Form Address**: Any RFC-compliant `characters@Internet` *`domain name`*

TIP

The free-form address format is new to GroupWise 6.5. This is not enabled at the system level as the other formats are. It can be implemented as an override option at the user level. In order for the Free Form Address override to work, the user's post office and domain, and your GWIA must be at GroupWise 6.5. If any of these agents is not at version 6.5, the free-form address might not work properly. Also if the post office is not at version 6.5, the ConsoleOne snap-ins do not even display the free-form field for you to use.

The term *Internet domain name* is specific to GroupWise Internet addressing. The Internet domain name is an extra attribute attached to every address in GroupWise, and therefore makes GroupWise addresses comply with Internet address formats.

NOTE

Internet domain names are sometimes referred to as *IDOMAINS*. This term might help avoid confusion.

- **Client addressing rules are no longer needed:** When Internet addressing is enabled, client addressing rules are no longer needed to route mail messages to the Internet. Because GroupWise addresses are Internet addresses, mail addressed Internet-style will be correctly routed to the GWIA without the explicit address of the GWIA.

  Also, turning on Internet addressing will enable GroupWise users to send to other internal GroupWise users or external Internet users by simply typing the Internet address, such as `UserID@Internet` *`domain name`*. Internet addressing removes the need for addressing rules that search for an Internet-style address and replaces the address with a GroupWise `gateway:internet` address or with an external foreign `domain:internet` address.

- **Direct MTA-to-MTA connectivity between systems:** With Internet addressing enabled, you can allow any Message Transfer Agent (MTA) on your system to connect directly to another GroupWise system. The GroupWise message transfer protocol (GWMTP) allows GroupWise users to transparently communicate over the Internet with other GroupWise users in other systems.

  GWMTP sending effectively eliminates the need to convert messages bound to other GroupWise systems. No gateway or gateway conversions are needed for the two systems to communicate. Leaving the messages in their native format also allows for native GroupWise encryption, compression, and message formats to be retained. Keeping the native message type allows appointments to be sent to users in other GroupWise systems as appointments. These items will show up correctly on calendars, can be accepted or rejected, and full status tracking is available. The native format also allows for busy searches across the Internet GroupWise systems.

- **Future GroupWise enhancements will require Internet addressing:** Upcoming enhancements will require Internet addressing to be turned on. One current GroupWise feature that requires Internet Addressing is the capability for the GroupWise client to use `S/MIME` to encrypt messages. Without Internet addressing enabled, the GroupWise client cannot encrypt e-mail using `S/MIME`.

Although when you install GroupWise it does not require you to enable Internet addressing, you should enable it as soon as possible.

Potential Pitfalls When Enabling Internet Addressing

GroupWise functionality is becoming entrenched in Internet addressing. It is likely that you will eventually have to enable it for full functionality. Unfortunately, enabling Internet addressing is not without a few potential hazards, including

- Personal address books are converted to Internet address formats.
- Legacy clients still use the old addressing format.
- Client Internet addressing rules are no longer used.
- Turning off Internet addressing isn't really an option.

The following discussion will go over each of these in turn:

- **Address-book conversion to Internet address formats:** When Internet addressing is enabled, users' address books will be converted to Internet addressing format for the e-mail address column. This means that gateway names will be removed, as will foreign domain names.

  In some circumstances, I have seen the conversion process fail for some addresses. You might want to be alert to delivery problems for the first few weeks after Internet addressing has been enabled.

- **Legacy clients still use the old addressing format:** If your system contains a mix of 4.1, 5.2, 5.5x, and 6x post offices, your 4.1 and 5.2 users will still use the old addressing scheme. You might even have 16-bit clients, UNIX clients, or Macintosh clients on your 6.x post offices. These clients will also use the old addressing scheme.

  For these legacy clients, you will need to maintain your foreign domain names (for Internet-style addressing), as well as your addressing rules.

- **GroupWise 5.5x and GroupWise 6x clients ignore some addressing rules:** When Internet addressing is enabled, all GroupWise 5.5x and GroupWise 6x 32-bit clients will no longer use certain addressing rules. If a rule executes on address strings that contain an `@` sign followed by a dot (.) and replaces it with a string that includes a colon (:), that rule will be ignored.

  For example, an addressing rule that searches for `*@*.com` and replaces that string with `inet:%1@%2.com` will be ignored by the 5.5x and 6x clients when Internet addressing is enabled.

This should not be a problem, but it is possible on large systems that addressing rules meeting these criteria will still be needed for some reason or another.

- **Turning off Internet addressing can be painful:** The biggest disadvantage to enabling Internet addressing is that you cannot really back out of it.

If you do have problems enabling Internet addressing, seek technical support help rather than attempting to turn it off.

Enabling Internet Addressing

There are three things you are going to have to configure to enable Internet addressing:

- Default GWIA
- Default Internet domain name
- Preferred addressing format

All of these must be configured in the Internet Addressing window shown in Figure 16.4.

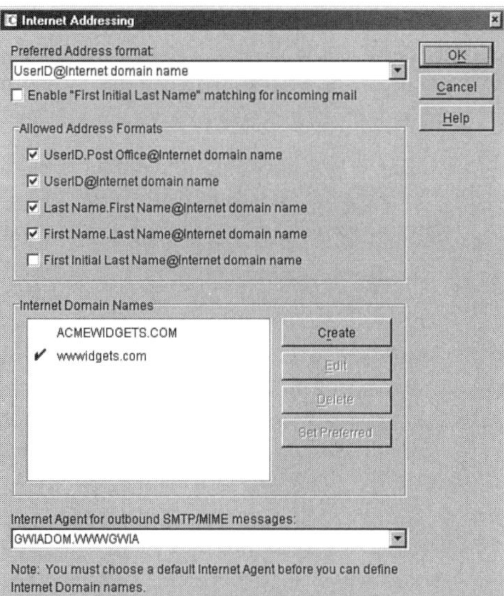

FIGURE 16.4
The Internet Addressing dialog box.

Selecting the Default GWIA

First, start with the default GWIA. Before you can select the default GWIA, you must have installed the GroupWise Internet agent somewhere on your system. See Chapter 10 if you do not yet have a GWIA installed on your system.

Following are the steps for selecting the default GWIA for a GroupWise system:

1. Choose Tools, GroupWise System Operations, Internet Addressing. The window shown in Figure 16.4 appears.
2. Populate the field labeled Internet Agent for outbound SMTP/MIME messages using the drop-down list.

   All GWIAs on your system should appear on this list.

A default GWIA must be assigned so that mail that is not deliverable locally, and that cannot be resolved through GWMTP, will be automatically routed to the GWIA. This automatic routing is what allows the client Internet addressing rules to become obsolete. You don't need to specify the GWIA in the message address, because it has been specified system-wide here.

Selecting a Default Internet Domain Name

Now enter a domain name. This must be the name that your organization uses on the Internet. It will probably be the first foreign name configured for your GWIA in the Foreign ID field/FRGNAMES.CFG. Following are the steps for selecting a default Internet domain name:

1. From the Internet Addressing window, click Create to call up the window shown in Figure 16.5.

TIP **Internet domain names cannot be created until a default GWIA has been selected.**

2. Enter your organization's Internet domain name, including upper-level domain names (that is, enter `company.com` rather than just company).
3. Enter a description for this domain name, if desired.

   This might be useful if you plan to have more than one Internet domain name.
4. Click OK.

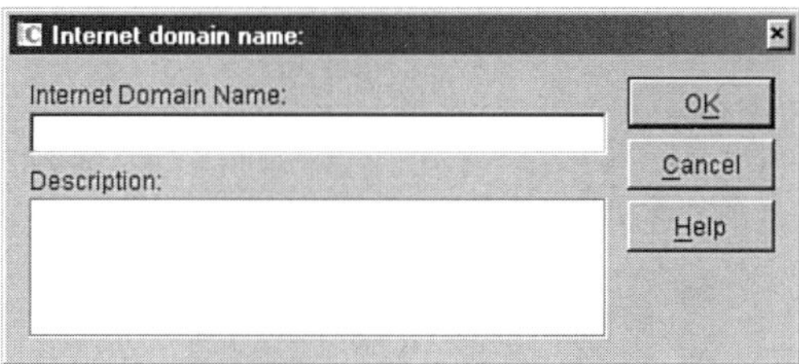

FIGURE 16.5
The Internet Domain Name dialog box is where you enter a new Internet domain.

You have now enabled Internet addressing and/or defined a new Internet domain that your GroupWise system recognizes.

Choosing a System-wide Preferred Internet Addressing Format

A preferred Internet address format can be specified after a default GWIA and Internet domain name have been set. The preferred addressing format defaults to `User ID@Internet domain name`, but can be configured to one of several settings.

The Internet addressing format will then be used as the default username format that the GWIA stamps on all outgoing mail. This format also determines how addresses appear in the GroupWise address book. This format will not be used for resolving routes on inbound e-mail. Users' Sent Items properties will also show the Created By field in this format instead of the legacy `User.PostOffice.Domain` format.

Following are the steps for setting the preferred system-wide default for Internet addressing format:

1. From the Internet Addressing window, pull down the Internet Addressing Format list shown in Figure 16.6.
2. Select the format that best suits your organization's needs.

Most organizations find that `UserID@Internet` *`domain name`* works best. The reasoning behind this addressing format is discussed in the section titled "Best Practices," later in this chapter.

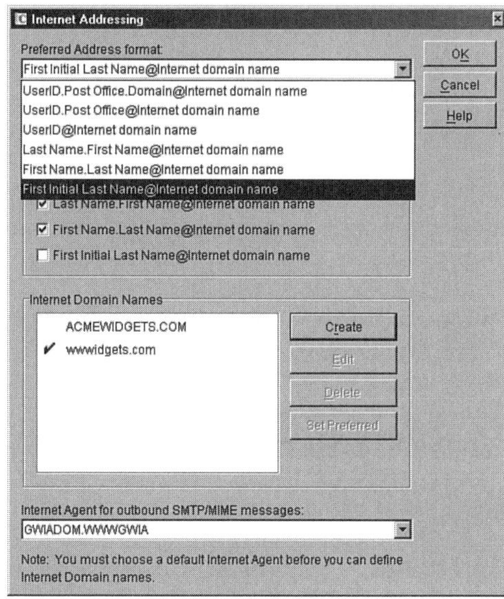

FIGURE 16.6 The Internet Addressing Formats selection pull-down menu allows you to set the system-wide Internet addressing format.

Identifying Acceptable Address Formats

You can also select which addressing formats are allowed in your GroupWise system. By default, when you enable Internet addressing, all address formats are enabled except the First Initial Last Name. These addressing formats allow users to receive mail in this format as well as the preferred address format you selected previously.

For example, if your preferred address format is `UserID@Internet` *`domain name`*, and you had the `first.last` format enabled, users could be addressed either as `userid@domain.com` or `first.last@domain.com`. The first and last names are defined on the eDirectory user object for each user, so it is important that this information be correct in eDirectory.

You will also notice that you can enable or disable the system from trying to resolve first-initial, last-name format in your system. Using first-initial, last-name format can be useful if your GroupWise UserID's are not user friendly. For example if your userID was `12345abc`, you probably don't want to have your users use this as the addressing format. You might want to choose first-initial, last-name format where a user of Eric Raff would be addressed as eraff. Once again the first-initial, last-name fields are pulled from the eDirectory user object's first and last name fields. Unless you have a need to resolve first-initial, last-name formats, it is not recommended to use this format. The chance of having duplicate userIDs increases with this format. This is why you can disable this format from being resolved in the GroupWise system.

Internet addressing is now enabled with these settings system-wide. You can override some of the settings you made here at the domain, post office, or even user level. These options are discussed in the section titled "Internet Addressing Overrides," later in this chapter.

Enabling MTA-Direct Connectivity (GWMTP)

With Internet addressing enabled, MTAs can now connect directly to other GroupWise systems. This type of connectivity, often called GWMTP, for GroupWise message transfer protocol, allows native message format and encryption to be maintained.

Retaining the GroupWise message format between GroupWise systems is not a new concept. The same functionality is available without GWMTP, but it requires a passthrough GWIA or Async gateway. To get the same functionality with these gateways, an external domain and post office would have to be configured and maintained for every other system to which your users will send e-mail. The maintenance of these external user entries and external domains could require a lot of an administrator's time.

The big advantage of GWMTP is that the setup only has to be done once. Once it has been enabled, ongoing maintenance should be minimal. The three basic requirements to enable GWMTP are the following:

- Both systems must enable Internet addressing.
- Both systems must configure MTAs to use GWMTP.
- Both systems must publish GWMTP records to the Internet via domain name services (DNS).

This chapter has already discussed enabling Internet addressing. This next section moves directly to a walkthrough of configuring the MTA.

Allowing MTAs to Send Directly to Other GroupWise Systems

Like the heading says, the first thing you need to do is allow MTAs to send directly to other GroupWise systems.

Following are the steps to enable an MTA in your GroupWise system in order to communicate on the Internet with other GroupWise MTAs:

1. Choose Tools, System Operations, System Preferences, Routing Options to get the window shown in Figure 16.7.

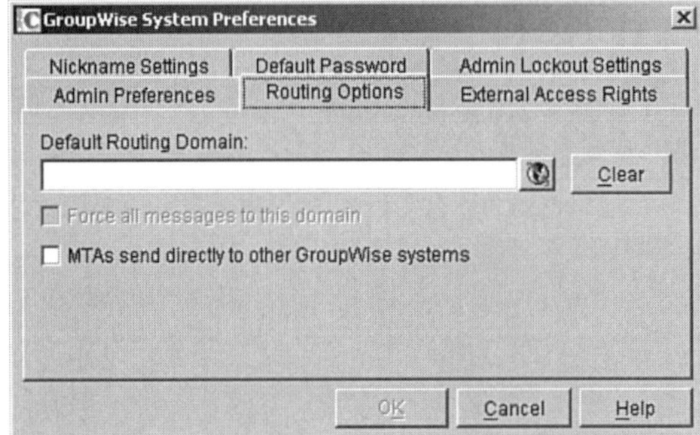

FIGURE 16.7 The System Preferences—Routing Options window is used to define which MTA will receive messages that should be sent on the Internet.

2. Make sure a default routing domain is specified.

   This is the domain that will be able to talk directly to other MTAs over the Internet. You do *not* want to check the option to force all messages to this domain. Doing so can potentially be catastrophic.

3. Check the box labeled MTAs send directly to other GroupWise systems.
4. Close the Preferences window.

You have told the entire GroupWise system that if users send a message to an Internet domain that is not in your GroupWise system, the message should first be sent to the default routing domain. If the MTA for the default routing domain determines that the destination domain does not support GroupWise MTP communication over the Internet, it should route the message to the GWIA.

Allowing MTAs to Browse DNS

Now every MTA in your system is going to attempt to look up other GroupWise systems via DNS. This means that every MTA must be able to see a valid domain name server. Typically, DNS requests are transmitted on port 53, so you should make sure that this port is not being filtered by your firewall. Most organizations won't have a problem with this, assuming that they allow end-users to browse the Web. Web browsing also requires DNS requests, so port 53 is probably already open.

Allowing MTAs to Connect on High-Numbered Ports

You might, however, have a problem with high-numbered ports. Once the MTA finds another system's MTA on the Internet (via DNS), it will try to open a connection there, and its source port will be a high-numbered port.

For security reasons, many administrators do not want to have all MTAs exposed to high-numbered ports on the Internet. If you have this same concern, read about default routing domains and overrides in the next section.

Default Routing Domains and Overrides

The best way to avoid exposing all the MTAs in your system is to tell the GroupWise system to send all mail not destined to a known IDOMAIN to a default route. This would basically be all Internet mail. You rarely will want to force *all* messages (even messages going to a known IDOMAIN) to the default route. A single system-wide default routing domain is usually advisable only for GroupWise systems that have a low volume of outbound Internet e-mail, however. On large, high-volume systems (more than 50,000 Internet messages per day), the burden on a single MTA can be too great, because all Internet-bound e-mail passes through this MTA. Each outbound message requires a DNS lookup to determine if it is bound for another GroupWise system.

The solution is to use overrides, as follows:

1. Choose Tools, GroupWise System Operations, System Preferences, Routing Options.
2. Check the box labeled Force All Messages to Default Routing Domain.
3. Close the window.
4. Choose a second domain for routing.

   This domain will be used as an override default routing domain.
5. Choose a domain or domains to use the override routing domain instead of the system default specified in system preferences.

   In most cases, you will make this decision based on your WAN topology. For instance, all domains in one city should use a routing domain in that city.
6. Perform steps 7 through 11 for each domain whose routing you want to override.

7. Browse to the domain's MTA object, right-click it, and select Properties.
8. Click the Routing Options tab shown in Figure 16.8.

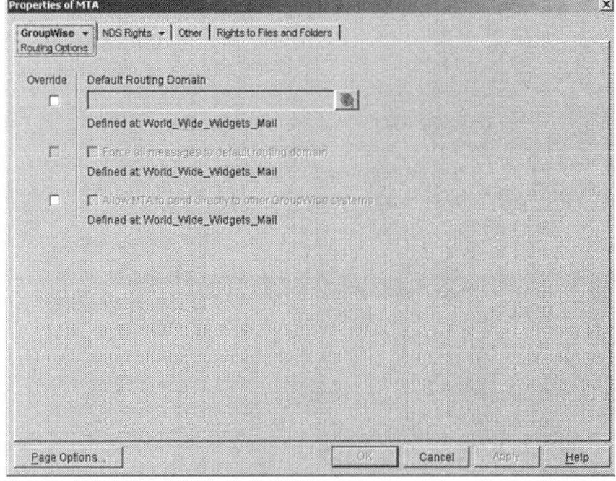

FIGURE 16.8 The MTA Routing Options tab enables you to override the default routing domain.

9. Click the topmost check box in the Override column.

   This will override the default routing domain specified at the system level.
10. In the field labeled Default Routing Domain, browse to the domain you have chosen as an override routing domain.
11. Click OK to close the window and save your changes.

To summarize how these default routing domains work, there are basically three options that you can set at the system level in this area:

- **MTAs send directly to another GroupWise system:** This option enables *all* MTAs system-wide to be able to perform DNS lookups. So if a user sends mail to `user@unknownIdomain.com`, the MTA will try to perform a DNS lookup on it. If it can, and it finds the appropriate DNS entries for `unknownIdomain.com`, it sends it directly over the Internet to this other MTA. If for any reason it cannot perform a DNS lookup or cannot find any DNS entries for `unknownIdomain.com`, it simply hands it off to the domain that owns the default GWIA. (Unless there are any overrides anywhere, and then it obeys the override.)
- **Default routing domain:** With this option, if the MTA gets a message to a *known* IDOMAIN, it resolves the domain (doesn't have to perform a DNS lookup) to the GroupWise domain that the user is in, reads the link configuration to see how to talk to this GroupWise

domain, and sends the message to it. If it gets a message to `user@unknownIdomain.com`, it once again tries to perform a DNS lookup. If it fails or cannot do this, it sends the message off to the default routing domain. It does *not* send all mail to this domain, only Internet mail that is destined for unknown IDOMAINs. The default routing domain gets the message, and then tries to resolve it via DNS; if this fails, it goes ahead and sends it to the default GWIA.

- **Force all messages to this domain (the default routing domain):** Finally, with this option, when an MTA gets *any* message, whether or not it is destined for a known IDOMAIN, it simply shoves it over to the forced default routing domain.

You can use the override options on any of these settings, which basically allows you to change what any particular domain is going to use that differs from what you set under System Preferences, System Operations, Routing Options.

There are basically two ways that I recommend for setting up default routing domains so that you do not need to have all MTAs doing DNS lookups. If the majority of the domains should be performing DNS lookups, follow this approach:

1. From System Operations, System Preferences, click the check box that allows MTAs to send directly to other GroupWise systems.
2. Next, define a default routing domain that all Internet mail will go to if a DNS lookup fails or if the MTA gets mail that is destined for unknown IDOMAINS.

   Do not check the option to force all messages through the default routing domain.
3. Go to the properties page of the MTA objects in the domains that you *do not* want to perform DNS lookups and select Routing Options from the drop-down list.
4. From here, click the last check box in the override column (Allow MTA to Send Directly to Other GroupWise systems), and then *uncheck* the option to perform this operation that this MTA inherited from the system level.

   Voila! This MTA is not allowed to perform DNS lookups. This works great if most of your MTAs *will* perform DNS lookups because you only have to do the override on the MTAs that you do *not* want to perform the DNS lookups.

If most of your domains should *not* perform DNS lookups, you take the reverse approach, as outlined in the next series of steps:

1. From System Operations, System Preferences, *do not* check the box to allow MTAs to send directly to other GroupWise systems.
2. Define a default routing domain that all Internet mail will go to if a DNS Lookup fails. Otherwise, the MTA is not allowed to perform DNS lookups and it gets mail destined for unknown IDOMAINs.

   Once again, *do not* check the option to force all messages through the default routing domain.
3. Go to the properties page of the MTA objects in the domains that you *do* want to perform DNS Lookups.

   (Obviously, you need to make sure that you do this on the default routing domain defined in step 2.)
4. Select Routing Options from the drop-down list. Click the last check box in the override column (Allow MTA to Send Directly to Other GroupWise systems), and then check the option next to it to actually turn this feature on.

The MTA can now perform DNS lookups. If it cannot find the DNS entry, it sends the message to the default routing domain.

Now a tip on how to determine what each MTA is really doing: The top of an MTA's log file contains the configuration information. Following is an example of the general settings at the beginning of the MTA log:

```
23:26:20 574 General Settings:
23:26:20 574  Domain Directory:                 d:\do3
23:26:20 574  Work Directory:                  d:\do3\mslocal
23:26:20 574  Preferred GWIA:                  Do1.GWIA6
23:26:20 574  Default Route:                   Do3
23:26:20 574  Known IDomains:                  *wwwidgets.com
23:26:20 574  Known IDomains:                  *eraff.com
23:26:20 574  Allow Direct Send to Other Systems:    No
23:26:20 574  Force Route:                    No
23:26:20 574  Error Mail to Administrator:          No
23:26:20 574  Display the active log window initially:  Yes
23:26:20 574  NDS Authenticated:                  Yes [Public]
23:26:20 574  NDS User Synchronization:              Yes
23:26:20 574  Admin Task Processing:                Yes
23:26:20 574  Database Recovery:                  Yes
23:26:20 574  Simple Network Management Protocol (SNMP):
➥Enabled (index 1)
```

What you are looking for are the Default Route, Known IDOMAINs, Allow Direct Send to Other Systems, and Force Route values. These will tell you exactly how this particular MTA will act.

Remember to think of this entire process from the perspective of the MTA when it receives a message in Internet addressing format. It will first determine whether the IDOMAIN is a known IDOMAIN. If it is, and the Force Route value is No, it will perform a lookup in its index to determine which GroupWise domain the user is in, because it should know about the user, and then look at its link configuration to determine how to route the message to the internal user.

If the message is destined for a user in an *unknown* IDOMAIN, the MTA will once again check the Force Route value. If the value is set to No, the MTA checks to see whether it can perform a DNS lookup. If it can, it tries to do so. If it finds a match, the MTA tries to connect to the destination MTA across the Internet. If no match is found, it checks the Default Route value, and if something is defined here, the MTA sends the message to this domain. If nothing is defined here, the MTA simply routes the message to the default GWIA.

Publish GWMTP Records to the Internet

Now your MTAs can route messages to other GroupWise systems on the Internet. This is half of the picture. The other half is allowing your MTAs to receive messages from other GroupWise systems. For this to happen, other systems must be able to find at least one of your MTAs using DNS.

GWMTP.TCP Record Information for the DNS Administrator

The following information will be useful to your DNS administrator when defining your GroupWise MTA as an entity that can be contacted on the Internet to transmit GroupWise messages to.

To resolve a foreign Internet domain name, a GWMTP-enabled MTA will perform a DNS lookup for an address record of a particular Internet domain name. If the address record is found, the MTA will look for either a service (SRV) or text (TXT) record for the GWMTP.TCP service.

A full explanation of domain name server configuration is beyond the scope of this text. What this book will try to do is provide you with enough information so that you can explain to your DNS administrator which records you need.

Each GWMTP.TCP record will have several values associated with it:

- **Name:** The service name must begin with GWMTP.TCP, for instance GWMTP.TCP.NOVELL.COM.
- **Class:** The record class can be SRV or TXT. Choose whichever of these is easiest for you to support using the DNS tools you have.
- **Priority:** This can be any number, but for a single-MTA system, it should be 0. If you have more than one MTA, you can set one to be 0, and another to be 1. In this case, the MTA with a priority of 1 will be used only if the MTA with a 0 priority is not responding.
- **Weight:** Weight can also be any number. This value is used for load balancing. If two MTAs have the same priority but different weights, the one with the lower weight is preferred. If that MTA is too busy, connections will be made to the MTA with the higher weight (and the same priority) next.
- **Time to live:** Typically listed in seconds, this is the amount of time this record will be valid before being refreshed. If you need to make a change to an MTA's IP address or port, the time to live can be the minimum amount of time it will take your changes to propagate across the Internet DNS system.
- **IP address:** This is the IP address of the MTA.
- **Port:** This is the GWMTP port for this MTA, typically 7100. If you choose another port value here, you must also choose that value under the Network Address tab of the MTA object properties.

Now your DNS has an entry for your MTA that allows other MTAs on the Internet to discover your MTA's capability to speak GWMTP.

Internet Addressing Overrides

After Internet addressing has been enabled, customizations or overrides can be used to increase the flexibility of Internet addressing within the GroupWise system. Overrides can be enabled at the Internet Addressing tab on the detail screen of domains, post offices, and users.

Internet Domain Name Overrides

Overrides at a domain, post office, or user level can be used to specify a certain Internet domain name. For example, the sales division in the Sales GroupWise domain might want to be known as `sales.worldwidewidgets.com` rather than just `worldwidewidgets.com`. An override can be set on each domain to allow all members of each domain to have the specific Internet domain name value. If the members of a post office wanted a specific Internet domain name for their post office, an override could be done for that post office through the Internet Addressing tab on that post office object's properties window.

NOTE

All Internet domains that your organization wants to use need to be defined in two places: first, the Internet Domain Names section under Tools, GroupWise System Operations, Internet Addressing. Secondly, your Internet domains should be defined for the sake of the GWIA, in the Foreign IDs field or the FRGNAMES.CFG file explained earlier in this chapter. Having all Internet domains defined in the Foreign ID field on the GWIA is not critical. If the `/dia` switch in the GWIA.CFG is *not* being used, the GWIA reads all IDOMAINs from the domain database to find out its identity, if you will. However, if the `/dia` switch is active on the GWIA, it *will not* read the domain to get the list of known IDOMAINs, and will strictly use the foreign ID names for building reply-to addresses, both inbound and outbound. It will not honor the overrides at the domain, post office, or user level also when the `/dia` switch is in use on the GWIA.

The last type of Internet domain name override happens at the user level. If a user or group of users wants a different Internet domain name than the one being used at the system, domain, or even post office level, you would use the Internet Addressing tab on their user objects. You can also override the actual e-mail address at the user level. You can use a free-form type of address that allows you to type the user's e-mail IDs that they want to use. This feature is designed to replace the need for gateway aliases on the GWIA. So if you have been using alias records, you can now replace these with the free-form Internet address override at the user level. Remember that the user's post office must be version 6.5 to see the override option in ConsoleOne.

Preferred Addressing Format Overrides

Domains, post office, and user objects can also have overrides to specify a specific preferred addressing format. This means that while the system default for preferred addressing format can be set to `UserID@Internet` domain name, any domain, post office, or user can have one of the other available preferred addressing formats (such as `First.Last@Internet` *`domain name`*).

TIP

Even though you select a preferred addressing format, users can receive mail at *any* of the allowed addressing formats that is defined at the system, domain, post office, or user level. This preferred format just determines what the reply-to address format is. Hence, Billy Bob could receive mail at `billy.bob@wwwidgets.com`, `bbob@wwwidgets.com`, `bob.billy@wwwidgets.com`, **and so on if these formats have not been disabled at the system, domain, post office, or user level. If you want to prevent Billy Bob from receiving mail using the other formats, you can simply disable a particular format at the system, domain, post office, or user level.**

Default GroupWise Internet Agent Overrides

On a large GroupWise system, there might be more than one point at which the system connects to the Internet. Novell's corporate network is an example of this. They maintain permanent Internet connections for their corporate offices in San Jose, California, and in Provo, Utah, as well as in many of their regional offices.

In these cases, it makes sense to allow regional domains to route Internet mail through a local GWIA, instead of forcing all messages through the default GWIA. Domain objects have an Internet agent for outbound SMTP/MIME messages override, allowing the system administrator to select from any GWIA defined on the system. Figure 16.9 shows the property page of a GroupWise domain object that allows you to override the system-level Internet addressing format.

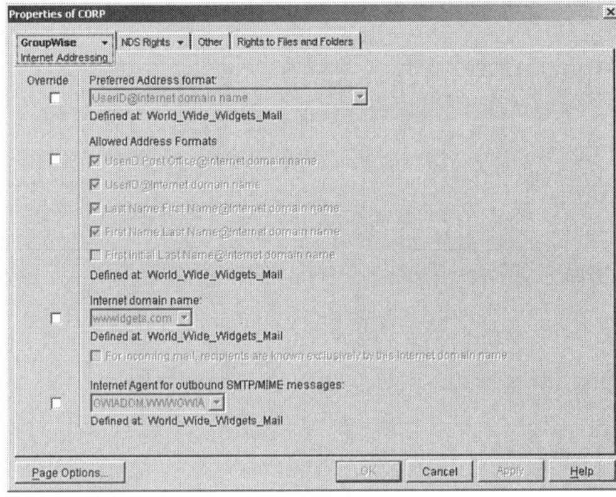

FIGURE 16.9 The Internet Addressing property page allows you to override the system-wide Internet addressing format.

If you have defined a default routing domain at the system level, you cannot override the Internet Agent for Outbound SMTP/MIME Messages option.

MTA Overrides

The last type of override is found in MTA objects. MTA overrides can be used to do the following:

- Specify default routing domains on a domain-by-domain basis (rather than at the system level)
- Force all mail to be routed to the routing domain
- Specify MTA to allow GWMTP communication

A routing option override can be used to route undeliverable local mail through a different domain that might have GWMTP enabled. Additionally, if a routing domain is defined and an override is selected to force all messages to a default routing domain, the domain's MTA will force all mail that is not deliverable in its local domain to be routed through the default routing domain. The last routing option, which allows MTA to send directly to other GroupWise systems, is used to specify whether the domain MTA is allowed to communicate via GWMTP.

TIP

Here is the difference between a default routing domain and a default GWIA. The default routing domain is for Internet-bound e-mail that can be sent via GWMTP. The default GWIA is for Internet-bound e-mail that cannot be sent via GWMTP. For routing purposes, it would therefore make sense to have the default GWIA reside on the default routing domain.

Mail Routing with Internet Addressing Enabled

Now that you understand the concepts behind GroupWise Internet addressing, this section discusses the flow of e-mail through an Internet addressing-enabled GroupWise system.

Outbound E-mail

Internet addressing-aware (or IA-aware) clients (GroupWise 5.5x and newer clients) allow mail with Internet addresses to be routed internally or to Internet users without the use of addressing rules or external domain definitions. Without Internet addressing enabled (and no addressing rules in use), messages sent to users with Internet-style addresses are flagged as undeliverable when mail is sent from the client.

With Internet addressing enabled, the client performs less lookup on recipient addresses. Messages with Internet-style addresses are pushed on by the client to be resolved by the POA, MTA, or GWIA. Note, though, that each component in an IA-aware GroupWise system is capable of parsing Internet address information to some extent, including the GroupWise client. Each component (client, POA, MTA, and GWIA) will do the best it can to resolve the address from its perspective.

If the POA cannot resolve an address, it pushes the message to the domain MTA. If the message is addressed to an Internet address, and the domain MTA cannot resolve the message to one of its post offices; or internal to the system, it will route the message to the default routing domain for a GWMTP lookup by the MTA there. If the recipient address cannot be resolved with a GWMTP DNS lookup, the message will be routed to the default GWIA for transfer to the Internet.

Inbound E-mail

When a message arrives at a GroupWise system from the outside world, it does so in one of two ways:

- Direct MTA-to-MTA transfer via GWMTP
- SMTP/MIME transfer via the GWIA

NOTE

Messages can also come in through another GroupWise gateway, but typically those are not going to be outside world messages. Most other gateways, such as the Exchange gateway or the Lotus Notes gateway, are handing explicitly addressed messages to the GroupWise MTA, so the messages can be treated as internal to the GroupWise system.

When a message comes in via GWMTP, the MTA receiving the message will process the message by sending it to the GroupWise domain within the GroupWise system of which the recipient is a member. The recipient's domain routes the message to the recipient's POA, which delivers the message to the recipient's mailbox.

When a message comes in through the GWIA, via SMTP/MIME, it is processed with the flow described in Figure 16.10. The GWIA checks the domain portion of the recipient address for user alias, post office alias, foreign ID, or Internet domain name matches. If GWIA does not find a match for the recipient domain address, it will route or relay the message to an appropriate Internet mail host for the specified domain or it will send an undeliverable message back to the sender.

Assuming a match was found (that is, the message must be delivered to this GroupWise system), the second level of resolutions involves checking the username portion of the recipient mail address to determine whether a unique match can be found.

The GWIA is fully backward compatible for resolving traditional GroupWise addressing, in addition to using the flexible rules of Internet addressing resolution.

This section and Figure 16.10 explore this address resolution process in more detail.

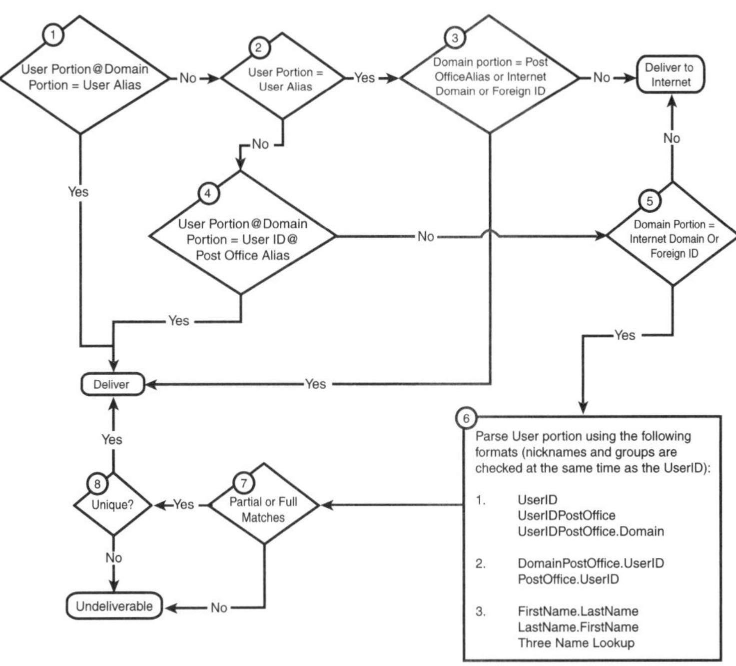

FIGURE 16.10
The GWIA inbound resolution process with Internet addressing enabled.

Following is the logic that the GWIA uses in routing in-bound Internet e-mail.

1. Compare `user@domain` (the entire string, not just the user portion) against user aliases defined at the GWIA. If there is a match, the message can be passed directly to the MTA to be routed to the user. If there is no match, move to step 2.

2. Compare the user portion of the address against user aliases defined at the GWIA. If there is a match, move to step 3. If not, move to step 4.

3. Compare the domain portion against post office aliases, Internet domain names, or foreign IDs defined for this system or assigned to the GWIA. If there is a match, the message is passed to the MTA to be delivered. If not, the message does not belong to this GroupWise system and will be passed to the Internet (or passed to another host if the GWIA is configured to allow the feature called Forward Undeliverable Inbound Message to Host). Otherwise, the message is discarded.

NOTE **If the message arrived at the GWIA from the MTA (that is, it came from inside the system), it will still be checked to determine whether it belongs on this system, using steps 1 through 3. This is how messages addressed by non-IA-aware components to recipients on this system are handled.**

4. Does `user@domain` match up with a `UserID@`*`Post office`* alias string? If so, the message is passed to the MTA for delivery. If not, go to step 5.
5. Compare the domain portion of the address against the Internet domain names defined on the system and against the foreign ID assigned to the GWIA. If there is a match, move to step 6. If not, the message is delivered to the Internet.

NOTE **Steps 1 through 5 checked out aliases, which are shortcuts to address resolution. Anything that makes it to step 6 is not going to match up to a user or post office alias, but does match up with this system's Internet name or names.**

6. Once the message is known to belong to the system, a parsing engine tries to uniquely resolve the user portion of the address with a GroupWise user. The parser engine compares the user portion of the recipient address (everything on the left side of the `@` symbol) with the following GroupWise information:
   - **Free Form/User Override set:** The contents on the left of the `@` sign are checked for any matches defined on the Internet Addressing properties page of a user object. The free-form override setting is one way to give a user an Internet address that does not comply with the system defaults. This setting is on the Internet Addressing properties page of any user object. The free-form field is the second field below the Preferred Address Format field. If a match is found here, the system has a unique match. See Figure 16.11.

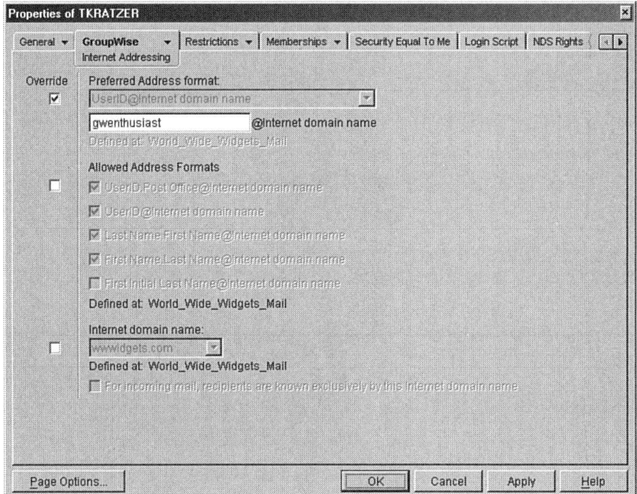

FIGURE 16.11
Free-form Internet addressing for a user object is used to override the system-, domain-, or post office-level Internet addressing format.

- **U.P.D. resolution:** The address is parsed and compared against the address book for matches in `UserID.PostOffice.Domain` format. If the user portion has less than three segments (that is, there aren't two dots in the user portion), it will be compared in `UserID.PostOffice`, or just `UserID`, format.
- **D.P.U. resolution:** The address is parsed and compared against the address book for matches in `Domain.PostOffice.UserID` format. Again, if the string is not long enough, it will be compared in `PostOffice.UserID` format.
- **Name-based resolution:** The address is parsed and compared against the address book for matches to `FirstName.LastName`, `LastName.FirstName`, and `FirstInitialLastname`.

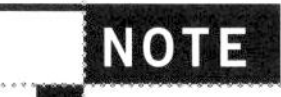

`FirstInitialLastname` format is not enabled by default in a GroupWise 6.5 system, and will not be looked up unless the administrator has enabled it.

7. If there are no matches for the parsed user portion of the address, the message becomes undeliverable. If there are matches, even partial matches, move to step 8.
8. A preference filter is applied, and if the parsed address is unique at any level of preference, it is delivered. Partial addresses are passed to the MTA for complete resolution at the MTA or POA level. If the parsed address is not unique, the message is undeliverable.

The process that the GWIA uses to get a message to a recipient is quite complex. The flexibility that GroupWise gives you for defining a user's address format is what makes the process so complex.

Understanding the Parsing and Lookup Process

In the flow in the preceding section, the GWIA reached a point in step 6 in the section just prior to this one, where it had to parse the user portion of an Internet-style address, and then perform a lookup to determine whether there were any matches. It is important that you understand the rules behind the parse and lookup, because they will affect the decisions you make when implementing Internet addressing on your GroupWise system.

Every component on an IA-aware GroupWise system can perform the parsing and lookup operations described next and outlined in Figure 16.12. When messages come in to the system through the GWIA, the GWIA parses and looks up. Messages coming in through the MTA via GWMTP will have their addresses parsed and looked up by the MTA.

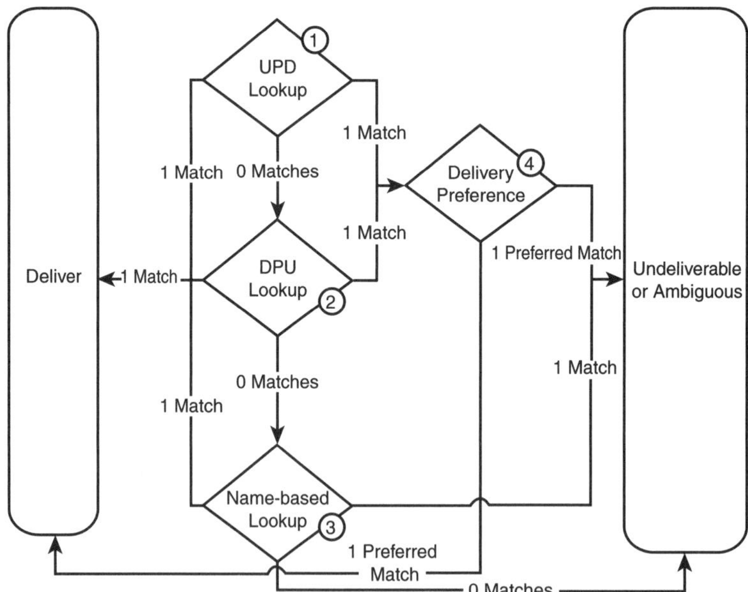

FIGURE 16.12
An example of the parsing and lookup process.

In the process shown in Figure 16.12, an Internet-style address has been handed to a GroupWise component, and that component has reached the point where it must parse the user portion of the address. The balance of this section explores the process.

Following is the parsing process that GroupWise uses to determine the correct recipient of a message:

1. GroupWise begins with a parse and lookup for matches in U.P.D. (`User.PostOffice.Domain`) format. If the user portion of the address has less than three components, GroupWise will perform a `User.PostOffice` or a user lookup. If there is one and only one match, GroupWise delivers the message. If there is more than one match, GroupWise goes to step 3. If there are no matches, GroupWise continues with step 2.
2. GroupWise now parses and looks for matches in D.P.U. (`Domain.PostOffice.User`) format. This is the legacy addressing format used by GroupWise. Again, if there are less than three components to the user portion of the address, GroupWise will perform a `PostOffice.User` lookup. There's no need to do a user lookup, though—GroupWise did that in step 1. If there is one and only one match, GroupWise delivers the message. If there are multiple matches, GroupWise goes to step 3. If there are no matches, GroupWise goes to step 4.
3. Messages will be delivered to the closest match. If one of the matches is on the same post office as the component doing the parsing and lookup, that match will be chosen above other matches. If there is only one preferred match, the message will be delivered. If there is more than one match (that is, no preferred matches), the message becomes undeliverable or ambiguous.

   If the GWIA, the POA, or the MTA reaches this point, the message is undeliverable. If the client reaches this point, however, the user might be prompted to resolve the ambiguity.
4. GroupWise now checks the usernames. GroupWise looks for matches in `First.Last`, `Last.First`, `FirstInitial.Last`, and three-part name format and will check all possibilities at once. If there is one, and only one, match, the message is delivered. If there is more than one match (for example, the message is addressed to `James.Howard`, and you have a Howard James and a James Howard on the system), the message is ambiguous or undeliverable. No delivery preferences are applied. If there are no matches, the message becomes undeliverable.

Parsing Usernames

It might be helpful at this point to look deeper at step 4 from the preceding section. Here is the logic followed when a GroupWise component parses the user portion of the address for matches with users' full names:

1. Replace all periods left of the `@` sign with spaces.
2. If there is more than one space, see step 7.
3. Assign the text left of the space to `Part_A`.
4. Assign the text right of the space to `Part_B`.
5. Search the given and last names for all users in the GroupWise system. Compare the following combinations, and select all matches:

   ```
   Given=Part_A
   Last=Part_B

   Given=Part_B
   Last=Part_A
   ```

6. Skip to step 11.
7. Assign the text left of the first space to `Part_A`.
8. Assign the text between the first space to the second space to `Part_B`.
9. Assign the rest of the text to `Part_C`.
10. Search the given and last names for all users in the GroupWise system. Compare the following combinations, and select all matches:

    ```
    Given=Part_A
    Last=Part_B Part_C

    Given=Part_A Part_B
    Last=Part_C

    Given=Part_C
    Last=Part_A Part_B

    Given=Part_B Part_C
    Last=Part_A
    ```

11. If no matches exist, skip to step 16.
12. If a unique match is found, skip to step 17.
13. External users who match are eliminated if internal matches exist.

14. Matches outside the local GroupWise domain are eliminated if matches exist in the local GroupWise domain.
15. If a unique match is found, skip to step 17.
16. The message is undeliverable because no match is found.
17. Deliver the message.

Understanding parsing scenarios is most likely to be important in larger GroupWise systems, and in GroupWise systems that do external system synchronization with one another.

Parsing Scenarios

Here are a couple of example scenarios to let you see how these pieces fit together, beginning with the following:

- Message is addressed to `mike.sales@wwwidgets.com`.
- User Mike Sales exists in the `CORP` post office.
- There is a post office called `Sales` on the system somewhere.
- No user or post office aliases exist.

Here's what will happen. The GWIA for WorldWide Widgets will decide the message belongs on this system and will attempt to resolve the user portion of the address. Now walk through the logic in the following steps:

1. The string `mike.sales` is compared against the address book for U.P.D. matches. Because there are only two parts to the string, it compares `mike` for user matches and `sales` for post office matches.
2. A partial match is found. There is a post office called `sales` on this system.
3. The message is routed to the `sales` POA for resolution of the remainder of the address.
4. The `sales` POA looks for a user ID `mike` on the local post office and finds none. The message is undeliverable.

   Note here that having post office names that match usernames can cause problems for messages addressed in `First.Last` or `Last.First` format.

And now for the second scenario, note the following:

- Message is addressed to `rip.van.winkle@wwwidgets.com.`
- A user with the first name Rip and a last name Van Winkle exists in the `CORP` post office.
- No user or post office aliases exist.

In this case, the GWIA for WorldWide Widgets will end up attempting to resolve the user portion of the address as a three-part name.

1. The GWIA looks for a user ID "`rip`" on the post office "`van`" in the domain "`winkle`". No matches are found. The names `van` and `winkle` do not match any post office or domain names on this system.
2. The GWIA looks for a user ID `winkle` on the post office `van` in the domain `rip`. No matches are found. The names `van` and `rip` do not match any post office or domain names on this system.
3. The GWIA looks for users with the following names:

   ```
   First=Rip, Last=Van Winkle
   First=Rip Van, Last=Winkle
   First=Winkle, Last=Rip Van
   First=Van Winkle, Last=Rip
   ```

4. One match is found, and the message is delivered to user Rip Van Winkle.

Best Practices

Internet addressing is going to be increasingly important to GroupWise administrators, so I encourage you to enable it. Before you do, however, you should be sure to carefully plan your Internet addressing implementation to avoid potential pitfalls. This section outlines some of the practices that administrators use successfully.

Naming Conventions

Following are a few tips to keep in mind as you plan your Internet addressing strategy:

- **Strive to make all user IDs unique throughout the GroupWise system.** GroupWise administrator will only require user IDs to be unique per post office, so you will need a separate tool to ensure that you are not duplicating a user ID.

- **Use `UserID@Internet` *`domain name`* as your preferred addressing format.** The preferred addressing format is used to build the reply-to address, and if user IDs are unique system-wide, this format allows you to move users to any post office on your system without their Internet address changing. This setting will prevent reply-to addresses that are ambiguous in cases where first- and last-name combinations are not unique.
- **If user IDs cannot be unique, avoid using Internet domain names to make an Internet address unique within the same GroupWise system.** If Internet domain names are making the user portion of a local Internet address unique, the exclusive flag must be set on users who do not have unique user portions for their Internet addresses. This will mean that the user might only be known by the particular addressing format and Internet domain name. It also means extra work for the administrator. If user IDs cannot be unique, it will likely be easier to use the override option at the user level to define a free-form Internet address.
- **User IDs, first names, and last names should not be the same as post office or domain names.** (See the first scenario in the section "Parsing Scenarios," earlier in this chapter.) One easy solution for this is to include numbers or underscores in post office and domain names.
- **Users should have no more than three names embedded in their complete name.** Rip Van Winkle is okay, but Sir Rip Van Winkle is not. Think of it this way: You can have a space in either the First name or the Last name field, but never in both fields. Only the first name or last name can have a space in the name, not the first name and last name.
- **Users cannot share the same first and last name or user ID unless each of the users has a unique Internet domain name, and the exclusive flag is specified on the Internet addressing tab for each of the users.** The exclusive flag will allow each user to be known only by the specified Internet domain name, thereby guaranteeing that the users' Internet addresses are unique.
- **When used, user aliases and nicknames should be unique throughout the system. I recommend eliminating aliases on all users within your GroupWise system. Aliases on users defined under external domains are fine.**

- **If you intend to send messages via `S/MIME` or `PGP/MIME`, do not use aliases. Rather, use free-form Internet addresses.** When `S/MIME` or `PGP/MIME` certificate has an e-mail address that differs from the From field of an SMTP message, the messages is considered invalid. Eliminating aliases resolves this potential problem.

The key here is to move toward unique Internet addresses. You should consider using the E-mail Address Lookup feature on the GroupWise Utilities menu in ConsoleOne to help you create unique addresses in your GroupWise system.

System Design

This section offers a few suggestions on effectively setting up GroupWise Internet addressing on your GroupWise system:

- **If direct MTA-to-MTA connectivity is enabled, the GroupWise domain that owns the default GWIA should be the default routing domain.** This will simplify firewall administration (only one machine needs to be outside the firewall) and reduce traffic.
- **On large systems that span wide area networks, use default GWIA and default routing domain overrides to ensure that traffic bound to the Internet takes the most efficient route.** (This assumes that your system has more than one connection to the Internet.)
- **If an external system (such as a UNIX mail host) shares your Internet domain name, enable the option Forward Undeliverable Inbound Messages to Host (found on the SMTP/Mime Undeliverable property page of the GWIA).** See Chapter 10 for more details.
- **Ensure that all GWMTP-enabled MTAs can receive packets from their assigned port from the Internet and that they can send packets out to the Internet on high-numbered ports.**

These system design suggestions are most relevant in large GroupWise systems (5,000 or more), of which there are many!

Summary

GroupWise Internet addressing is an essential piece of current and future GroupWise technology. Before implementing it, however, administrators must carefully consider their naming conventions and system design. You should also take message flow and parsing into consideration. An understanding of the way the system works will help the prudent administrator design or redesign a GroupWise system so that it is easily administered and maintained.

CHAPTER 17

Maintaining the GroupWise System

If you have implemented a good system design (discussed in Chapter 19, "Building Your GroupWise System Correctly"), regular maintenance of your GroupWise system can be automated. Through automation, it is possible to reduce the amount of time you spend functioning as an administrator.

If your users access the post office in client/server access mode, and you implement a few appropriately scheduled events, your chances of losing data due to information store damage are minimized. This chapter covers the maintenance of the GroupWise information store and the GroupWise directory and walks you through the creation of some appropriate events to schedule.

Information Store Maintenance Concepts

The GroupWise information store—the collection of databases and directory structures discussed in Chapter 4, "Understanding the GroupWise Information Store"—is susceptible to damage, just like any other file on a server. The information store is written to thousands of times each day, and although the odds of any individual transaction failing are astronomically low, after enough reads and writes the odds begin to add up in favor of an occasional problem.

For the purposes of this discussion, there are really only two kinds of damage or corruption possible:

- Structural damage
- Content damage

It is easiest to explain these categories using an analogy. Suppose that you have a filing cabinet, and each file in each drawer contains not only its own information but also references to other files. Then one day, a herd of rampaging elephants being chased by a swarm of mosquitoes charges through your office and dents the filing cabinet. One of the drawers will not open any more. This is structural damage.

Now, suppose that you fix the cabinet by transferring all the files you could get to from the dented cabinet into a new one. Unfortunately, you could not recover any of the files from the dented drawer. Later, when reading a file in one drawer, you see a cross-reference to a file in another drawer. You follow the cross-reference, but that referenced file is not there. This is content damage.

As you can see, structural damage can lead to content damage if not properly repaired. This is important to understand and remember when dealing with the GroupWise message store.

Structural Maintenance

Your greatest concern regarding the GroupWise information store should be the structural health of the GroupWise databases. If there is a herd of elephants running around denting your databases, you need to know about it. You should take steps to ensure that all user and message databases on a post office are structurally analyzed and fixed every day. This is done via the Scheduled Events tab on the POA (Post Office Agent) object.

Content Maintenance

The contents of the GroupWise information store need to be verified on a weekly basis. The contents analysis ensures that the pointers from one record to another record are valid. The contents check and fix also ensures that master records (as discussed in Chapter 20, "Troubleshooting Message Flow") have pointers to the other supporting records for a message.

The Relationship Between Structure and Contents

As was alluded to in the example of the filing cabinet and the herd of elephants, one common reason for content-related problems is structural damage. Consider this scenario, for example:

> USERA's USER123.DB file has a pointer to record #286 in MSG17.DB. Unfortunately, a large block of MSG17.DB is damaged (for example, the server abended while the file was being written to). The next time the

POA works with this file, it detects the damage, and the file is rebuilt. The damaged block could not be recovered, though, and record #286 is lost from MSG17.DB.

USERA's USER123.DB file now has a contents inconsistency. The contents analyze-and-fix routine will take the pointer in USERA's USER123.DB file and tie it off so that it points nowhere. This, in effect, makes the received item a posted item. USERA can still read the subject line and can see who sent the message, but the message contents and any attachments are lost. USERA can contact the sender, having him or her resend or recompose the message, if necessary.

Contents Analysis Is Time-Consuming

Contents analysis can take a long time, especially if your post office is a large one, or if your users retain their messages indefinitely. If your information store is large, you will want to run your contents analysis over a weekend. I have encountered organizations whose GroupWise information stores were so large that a contents analysis for a single post office took well over 24 hours to run.

E-mail Expiration

Based on what you just learned, you can see part of the logic behind not allowing your users to keep their e-mail forever. Thus, I strongly recommend that you implement an e-mail expiration policy. You might choose to expire all e-mail messages after they are 90 days old, but allow appointments to stay on the system for a full year. You might also decide to purge all deleted items (items in the trash) early each morning.

Justification for E-mail Expiration

The downsides to allowing a GroupWise information store to grow too large are the following:

- Backup operations might not complete overnight, due to the sheer volume of data to be backed up.
- Contents analysis takes a very long time.
- QuickFinder indexing might take longer, and a QuickFinder index rebuild operation (executed from the POA console) will take much, much longer than you might have time for.
- Larger information-store databases impede POA performance, which will in turn mean that your users will observe poorer performance from the GroupWise client.

These downsides are real! The time required to run a Mailbox/Library Maintenance on a post office with a large message store makes the operation so time consuming that you may find that maintenance cycles cannot complete before regular business hours have resumed.

Overcoming Hurdles to E-mail Expiration

There are really only three reasons to keep an e-mail message longer than 90 days:

- *Sentimental reasons:* If this is the case, invite your users to use the GroupWise archive. They will still have access to the items, but they will not be impacting performance on the master mailbox. GroupWise archives should not be allowed to grow too much either. Maintaining archives can become a big issue. You should consider a third-party archive solution such as those available from the following Web sites:

  `www.gwtools.com`

  `www.nexic.com`

  `www.intellireach.com`

- *Legal reasons:* If e-mail messages are considered legal documents in your company, consider writing your e-mail policy in such a way that your backup tapes can be considered the legal record of these documents.
- *As a reminder of important information:* Any e-mail message that is still being read regularly after 90 days should probably become a GroupWise document (in a GroupWise library) or should be on your company's internal Web page.

It is important to know why users want to keep their e-mail for a long time. Knowing this will help you suggest alternatives. In short, if you approach the problem from the right direction, you should be able to implement an e-mail expiration/archive policy—with the blessing of your user community.

GWCHECK/GroupWise Message Store Check

The software used to maintain and repair the GroupWise information store is commonly called *GWCHECK*. There are actually three places where this software resides:

- *The post office agent:* Each POA has the GWCHECK code built into it. The code is launched when one of the following occurs:

- Mailbox/library maintenance is run from ConsoleOne.
- A scheduled event runs.
- The POA detects a problem with a database it is trying to work with and kicks off a GWCHECK job.

- *GWCHECK.EXE:* Found in the software distribution directory `ADMIN\UTILITY\GWCHECK`, this is the stand-alone GWCHECK software. It runs as a Win32 application, so to run it you must have full file access to the information store from a computer with a Windows 32-bit operating system.
- *The GroupWise client:* The version of GWCHECK built into the client does not fix a user's master mailbox, but it can fix archive, caching mode, and GroupWise remote message store databases.

The post office-based GWCHECK can be automated to run GWCHECK jobs on a scheduled maintenance routine. The stand-alone and client-based GWCHECK cannot be automated.

Benefits of Running GWCHECK on the POA

I often encourage my customers to use the POA-executed GWCHECK. Here are some very good reasons to run mailbox/library maintenance, or to use scheduled events, instead of running the GWCHECK.EXE:

- *Speed:* Assuming that the POA runs on the same box where the information store is located, the POA can run the GWCHECK routines at least twice as fast as GWCHECK.EXE. It can run the operation right "on the bus" rather than across a network connection.
- *Stability:* GWCHECK.EXE runs on the Windows platform and must run "across the wire." If something goes wrong on the workstation (GPF, blue screen of death, and so on), or if the LAN connection goes down, GWCHECK.EXE might do more harm than good. The POA is not as vulnerable in this way.
- *Scheduling:* The scheduled events (which can be enabled on the POA) are automatic GWCHECK jobs that are performed by the POA. The stand-alone GWCHECK.EXE does not provide tools for automation. As an administrator, you need not manually launch regular maintenance operations if you enable scheduled events.

The benefits of running POA-based GWCHECK jobs far outweigh the fact that you cannot see the GWCHECK log as it is getting created as the stand-alone GWCHECK allows you to do. The stand-alone GWCHECK is best saved for one-off operations. For example, issuing a structural rebuild on a MSGXX.DB file.

Benefits of Running GWCHECK.EXE

If there were no circumstances under which you might need the stand-alone GWCHECK, Novell would not have written the tool. Here are a few cases in which GWCHECK.EXE is preferred over the POA's routines:

- *Low risk to the server:* In cases where you suspect that a corrupt database is causing the POA to abend a NetWare server, you should try GWCHECK.EXE. If this routine dies while doing a database repair, it will not take the whole server with it. Fortunately, these cases are getting fewer and farther between.
- *Watch it work:* Some administrators like to see what GWCHECK is doing. The POA does not log GWCHECK operations onscreen, but GWCHECK.EXE does. When troubleshooting is being done, or a one-user GWCHECK is being done, this is fine. For regular maintenance routines though, the server-based GWCHECK routine is always better.

There are many times the stand-alone GWCHECK is helpful, however if it's a decision of whether or not to use the stand-alone GWHCECK versus the POA-based GWCHECK, use the server-based GWCHECK if possible.

Getting GWCHECK Log Files

It is always a good idea to review GWCHECK logs, even if you don't want to watch the operation work. To receive a GWCHECK log from the POA, make sure that you are set up as the administrator of the domain that owns the post office against which you are running GWCHECK.

1. Highlight the domain object, right-click, and select Properties.
2. From the Identification property page, click the button to the right of the Administrator field.
3. Browse to your eDirectory user object and click OK.

NOTE **The eDirectory user object you select must be grafted to a GroupWise mailbox.**

The next time the POA runs a GWCHECK operation, the log file will be e-mailed to the user defined as the "Administrator" of the domain that owns this post office.

TIP

If you are not able to change the defined administrator of the domain that owns the user you want to run GWCHECK on, you can click the Results tab before running the GWCHECK operation, and then specify that the log file (or the results) be sent to your GroupWise mailbox. This way, you never have to change the domain administrator, but you can still get the GWCHECK log files. You can also send the results to the user if you want. Most of the time, the user has no idea what he or she just received, so I rarely use this option unless I am running a mailbox statistics type GWCHECK and I want the user to see these type of results.

Understanding Scheduled Events for Post Office Maintenance

Every POA object has a Scheduled Events property page. This page is used to create, schedule, and edit events for the POA.

Every scheduled event has two parts: the event and the associated action or actions. The *event* is the record that tells the POA what triggers to use. The *actions* are the operations that the POA will perform when the triggers have been set.

Triggers can include low disk space (for the disk check event type) or a particular day of the week and time of day (for the mailbox/library maintenance event type). Actions can include analyze/fix mailboxes or expire/reduce.

Events and actions created from one POA are visible by (and can be executed by) every other POA on the system.

Even though events and actions can be used by multiple post offices, I suggest making events and actions specific to each post office in your system. I've seen problems occur when an administrator of one post office modifies a scheduled event that has an action that is catastrophic for another post office.

Managing Scheduled Event Creation and Modification

It should be obvious (especially to administrators of large systems) that you will want to manage how administrators create and modify scheduled events.

The following are considerations to take into account when creating scheduled events:

- *Rights:* In order for a GroupWise 6.5 administrator to create or modify a scheduled event, or any of the listed actions, he or she must have supervisory rights to the primary domain object in eDirectory. If you need to control access to scheduled events, restrict administrators' access to the primary domain object.
- *Administrative procedures:* Although an administrator might be restricted from creating or modifying events or actions, even with object rights restricted, you will want to ensure that the right operations run on the right information stores. There are two ways to do this:
  - *Create different scheduled events for each post office:* Naming conventions are critical here. In this case, I recommend that administrators name their events using the name of the post office the event applies to.
  - *Create standard events that work for all post offices:* Again, naming conventions are important. Make sure that the name of the event describes the operation.

In the next section, "Creating Schedule Events for Maintenance," you are encouraged to create scheduled maintenance routines one post office at a time, naming the events appropriately.

Creating Scheduled Events for Maintenance

Here is the example scenario used in this section:

> WorldWide Widgets wants to implement scheduled events for information-store maintenance. They have established an e-mail retention policy stating that all GroupWise messages will be retained for only 90 days, excluding calendar appointments. Furthermore, all trash items will be deleted every morning. Those users who use GroupWise remote, or use the GroupWise client in caching mode, can retain items for as long as they would like. Archiving is encouraged if users want to retain messages beyond 90 days.

This section assumes the task of creating scheduled events for `CORPPO`.

Structural Maintenance

This example begins with the structural maintenance. This event will analyze and fix the structure of all information-store databases on a daily basis.

The following are the steps to creating a scheduled event to keep a post office's message store structurally consistent:

1. Edit the POA for CORPPO.
2. Go to the Scheduled Events property page shown in Figure 17.1.

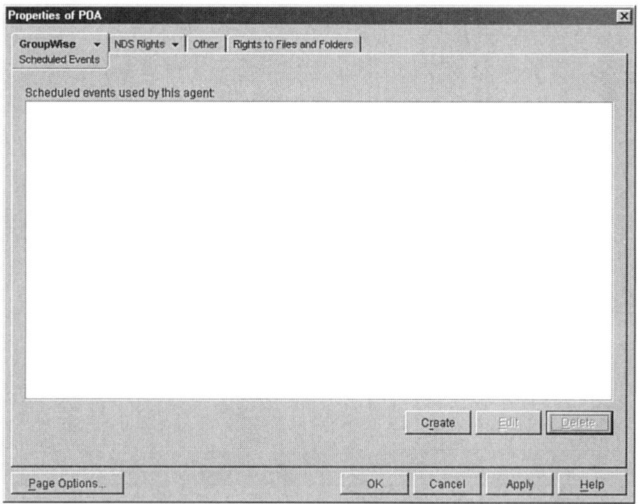

FIGURE 17.1
The Scheduled Events page for the CORPPO POA.

3. Click Create and enter **CORPPO-Structure-Event** as the name of the event.
4. Change the Type field to Mailbox/Library Maintenance.
5. Change the Trigger field to Daily and the Time field to 1:00 a.m. If you have problems changing the Trigger field, see the tip.

If the Trigger field does not change to show you the time intervals as shown in Figure 17.2, click the OK button, and then come back into the Scheduled Event. The Trigger field will then show the time intervals.

You now have the event name, type, time, and trigger. What hasn't been set up yet is what the event will do. You now need an action. Your scheduled event should look something like Figure 17.2.

6. Click Create.
7. Enter **CORPPO-Structure-Action** (the name of the action helps you associate it with the appropriate event).
8. Select the Action named Analyze/Fix Databases.

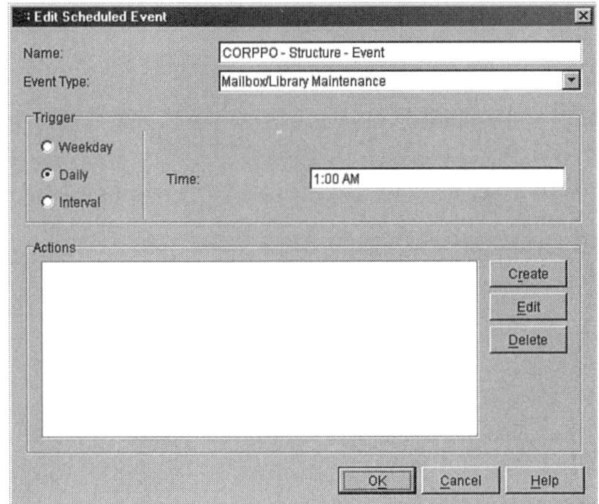

FIGURE 17.2
Defining the scheduled event.

9. Put check marks in the Structure, Fix problems, User, and Message check boxes.

   Figure 17.3 shows a configured action.

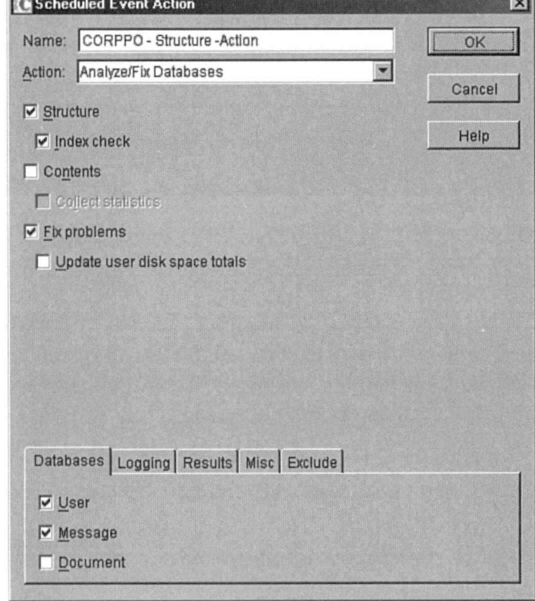

FIGURE 17.3
Defining the scheduled event action.

TIP

In my own testing I have found the "Index Check" of a user database to be a good thing, but potentially very time consuming. Only use the "Index check" option if you have plenty of time for this GWCHECK routine to run.

10. Click the Results tab at the bottom of the window and make sure that the results are sent to the administrator.
11. Click OK once to dismiss the action, and then make sure that a check mark is placed next to the action. Click the OK button again, and you now have the structure scheduled event defined.

That's the first event, now you have more to create. The structural maintenance of your post office is the most important. So it should be run regularly.

Contents Maintenance

Now you need to make sure that the content of the CORPPO information store is checked regularly.

The following are the steps to creating a scheduled event to keep a post office's message store's pointers from record to record consistent:

1. Edit the POA for CORPPO.
2. Go to the Scheduled Events property page.
3. Click Create and enter **CORPPO-Contents-Event** as the name of the event.
4. Change the Type field to Mailbox/Library Maintenance.
5. Change the Trigger field to Weekday, and change the day to Sunday and the time to 12:00 p.m., as shown in Figure 17.4.

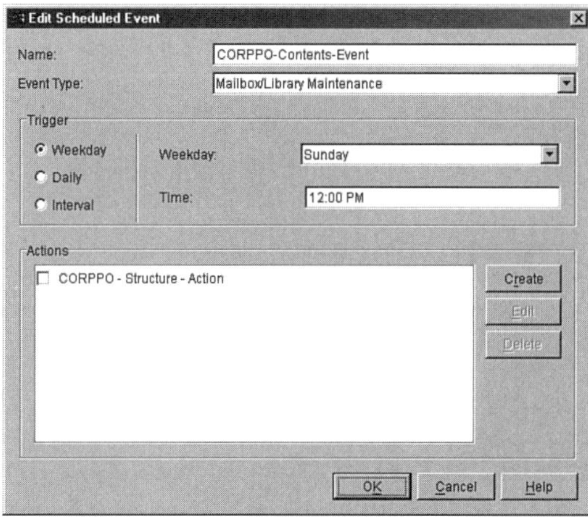

FIGURE 17.4 Defining the event.

TIP

You will always see the other actions created though the system; however, do not place a check mark next to these actions. These actions are specific to other scheduled events in the system.

6. Click Create to create an action.
7. Make the name **CORPPO-Contents-Action**.
8. Select the Action named Analyze/Fix Databases.
9. Select the Contents, Collect Statistics, Fix Problems, Update User Disk Space Totals, User, and Message check boxes.
10. Click the Results tab, and make sure that the results are sent to the administrator.
11. Click OK once to dismiss the action, and then make sure that a check mark is placed next to the action. Click the OK button again, and you now have the contents scheduled event defined.

NOTE

You might notice in step 9, that I checked several check boxes under the contents event action. A contents GWCHECK job takes so long as it is, why not do everything in the same pass? It's just more efficient.

Trash Deletion

Now you need to indicate when to delete regularly the contents of the CORPPO information store.

The following are the steps to creating a scheduled event for trash deletion:

1. Edit the POA for CORPPO.
2. Go to the Scheduled Events property page.
3. Click Create and enter **CORPPO-Trash-Event** as the name of the event.
4. Change the Type field to Mailbox/Library Maintenance.
5. Change the Trigger field to Daily and the time to 2:00 a.m.
6. Click Create.
7. Make the name of your action **CORPPO-Trash-Action**.
8. Select the Action named Expire/Reduce Messages.
9. Select the Expire and Reduce Messages radio button.

10. Put check marks in the Trash Older Than, Received Items, Sent Items, and Calendar Items check boxes and make sure that the Trash Older Than field is set to one day.

If you are using the smart purge features, you might want to check the Only Backed-Up Items option. If you are not using the smart purge features, do not check this box. If you do, and you have not fully implemented a backup solution that works with the GroupWise TSA, mail messages will not get purged, and your information store will continue to grow.

11. Make sure that the Items Older Than, Downloaded Items Older Than, Items Larger Than, and Reduce Mailbox To check boxes are not checked, as shown in Figure 17.5.

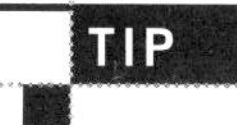

The Downloaded Items Older Than option is referencing messages that have been downloaded by GroupWise remote or the GroupWise client running in caching mode.

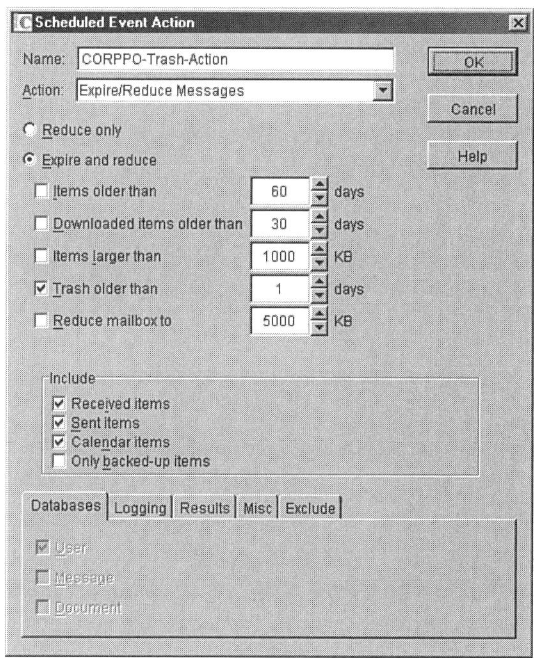

FIGURE 17.5
Deleting trash items with a scheduled event.

12. Click OK once to dismiss the action, and then make sure that a check mark is placed next to the action. Click the OK button again, and you now have the trash deletion scheduled event defined.

Now you need to create a fourth and final event—the one that expires old mail:

1. Edit the POA for `CORPPO`.
2. Go to the Scheduled Events property page.
3. Click Create and enter **CORPPO-Expire-Event** as the name of the event.
4. Change the Type field to Mailbox/Library Maintenance.
5. Change the Trigger field to Weekday. Change the day to Saturday and the time to 6:00 a.m.
6. Click Create to create the action to be taken.
7. Make the name **CORPPO-Expire-Action**.
8. Select the Action named Expire/Reduce Messages.
9. Select the Expire and Reduce radio button.
10. Select the following check boxes: Received Items, Sent Items, and Items Older Than (set this last one to 90 days).
11. Make sure that the following check boxes are not checked: Downloaded Items Older Than, Items Larger Than, Trash Older Than, Reduce Mailbox To, Reduce Mailbox to Limited Size, Calendar Items, and Only Backed-Up Items.

    Figure 17.6 shows the correct configuration.
12. Click OK once to dismiss the action, and then make sure that a check mark is placed next to the action. Click the OK button again, and you now have the mail expiration scheduled event defined.

There you have it. You have now implemented a scheduled event for keeping the message store more manageable. I highly recommend an expiration event. Combined with an third-party archiving solution such as "GWArchive" by `www.gwtools.com` you can create a solution that keeps the GroupWise message store manageable, while giving your users access to messages they must retain.

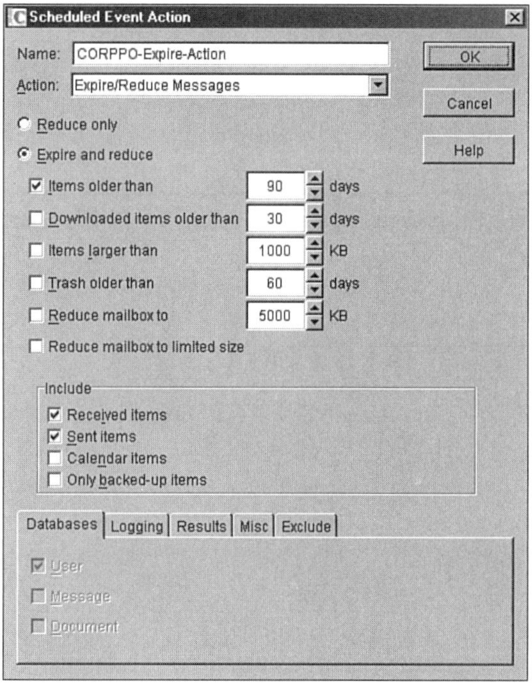

FIGURE 17.6
Defining the expire scheduled event action.

Order and Timing of Scheduled Events

Before you run a content analysis of a database, you should make sure that the structure is okay. In the preceding walkthrough, the scheduled contents analysis occurs after the structural analysis. The expire event in the example scenario was scheduled to come after the contents event.

In short, before you check contents, you should ensure that the structure is clean. Before you expire anything, you should ensure that the contents are consistent.

Seeing a POA's Scheduled Events from the Console Screen

You can see which scheduled events a POA intends to carry out by doing the following:

1. Go to the POA screen.
2. Select the F10 key, Configuration Options, Show Configuration.

   This dumps the POA's current configuration to the POA's log file.

3. Select the F9 key and view the end of the log file.

   You will see the configuration information for the POA, including the scheduled events you have created. If you do not find these scheduled events, you need to rebuild that post office's WPHOST.DB file.

TIP **You can also view the scheduled events by accessing the HTTP port of the POA, and clicking the Settings page.**

Editing Scheduled Events

Take care when modifying scheduled events. Sometimes modifications do not correctly propagate down to the post office. You can check this by looking at the POA log to see which events are enabled. If the events don't match changes you made in ConsoleOne, you either need to rebuild the post office database or delete and re-create the events in question.

Because of this possibility for problems, I typically recommend that if you need to edit a scheduled event, *don't*. Instead, delete the action for the event and then delete the event itself. Then you can re-create the scheduled event and the action associated with it.

GroupWise Archive Message Store Maintenance

Most users have no idea that the GroupWise 6.5 32-bit client has GWCHECK built into it. If a user is complaining of problems in an archive mailbox that seems like database damage, you can have the user run GWCHECK on his own archive. Here's how to do it:

1. Have the user open the GroupWise mailbox.
2. Have the user hold down the Ctrl and the Shift keys simultaneously, and then choose File, Open Archive while the Ctrl and Shift keys are still pressed.
3. The user should see the alert box shown in Figure 17.7.

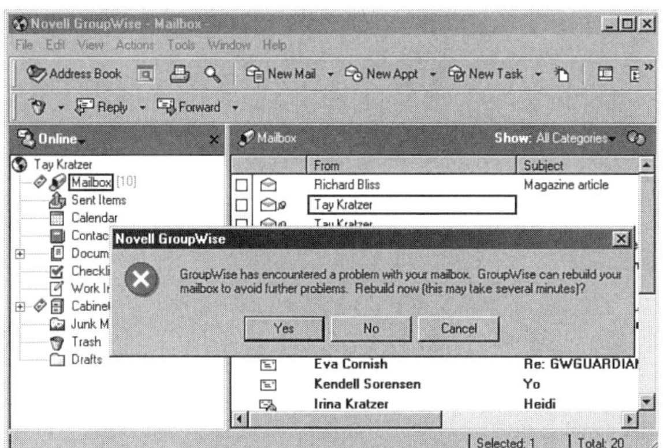

FIGURE 17.7
GroupWise 32-bit client GWCHECK alert.

Encourage your archive-savvy users to run these maintenance routines on their archive databases as a preventative measure. GroupWise archives are more likely to be damaged than the GroupWise information store is. Windows workstations are not quite the pillars of stability we would like them to be, and because the client writes to the archive directly, a GPF or blue screen of death can result in corrupt GroupWise archive data.

TIP

The GWCHECK operation that the client performs against the archive runs in two passes. The first pass is a Structure check on the user and message databases. The second pass is a Contents check on the user and message databases. The log files that contain the results of these GWCHECK operations are stored in the user's archive directory and are called OFCHECK1.LOG and OFCHECK2.LOG. You can review these log files to see the results of the GWCHECK operation.

GroupWise Caching Mode and Remote Mode Maintenance

The GroupWise 6.5 client can be installed with a GWCHECK version that will run against a caching/remote mode mailbox. This GWCHECK is installed and enabled only if the administrator indicated that it should be. The GWCHECK code can be installed and enabled via the SETUP.CFG when the GroupWise client is installed. This can be done by enabling the following three lines in the SETUP.CFG:

```
[GWCHECK]
InstallGWCheck=Yes
GWCheckEnabled=Yes
```

To learn more about configuring the SETUP.CFG file for the GroupWise installation, see Chapter 12, "Administering the GroupWise Client." If GWCHECK is installed and enabled, your users can run GWCHECK on their caching/remote mailbox by choosing Tools, Repair Mailbox. A scaled-down interface of GWCHECK will launch, as shown in Figure 17.8.

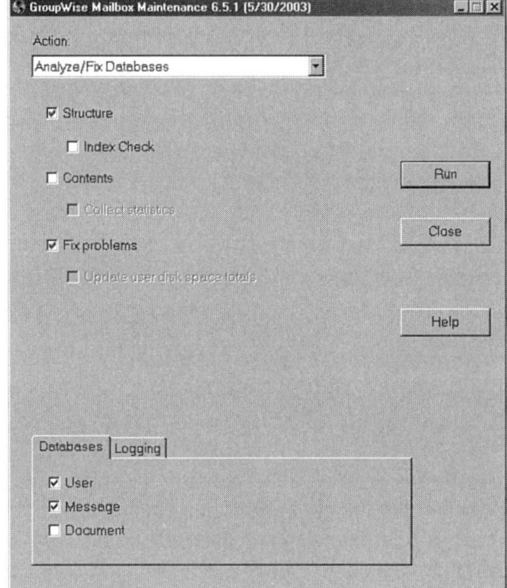

FIGURE 17.8
GroupWise Caching/Remote Mode GWCHECK screen.

Unfortunately, there's not an easy way to kick off a scheduled maintenance on users' caching and remote mode mailboxes. The users must do this themselves.

TIP

Users can also kick off a rebuild of their caching mode or remote databases by doing the following. Get out of GroupWise and then load the GroupWise client into caching or remote mode. Have the user hold down the Ctrl and Shift keys simultaneously while GroupWise is loading. Doing this will kick off a structural rebuild of their databases, before the GroupWise client even loads the GroupWise mailbox interface or prompts for the password. Figure 17.9 shows what the users will see when they are running a GWCHECK in this manner.

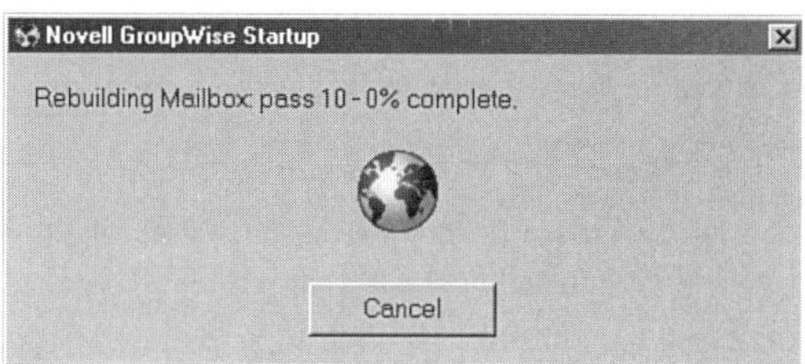

FIGURE 17.9
A client-based GWCHECK job using the Ctrl-Shift—then load mechanism.

When a user initiates the Repair Mailbox option from the client through the Tools menu, he sees a scaled-down GWCHECK options page. However, if you manually run the GWCHECK.EXE from the `C:\NOVELL\GROUPWISE` directory, you get the full GWCHECK interface. The client masks several of the GWCHECK options when GWCHECK is initiated from within the client to make it simpler for the user.

Troubleshooting Server-Based GWCHECK Problems

Sometimes you'll issue a GWCHECK job to execute on the POA, and the job won't seem to happen, you won't get a log, and so on. I've seen this before, and it's related to some corruption in the GWCHECK databases at the post office. Here are the steps you take to resolve this issue:

1. Bring down the POA.
2. Go to the post office directory (where the WPHOST.DB file is).
3. Rename the NGWCHECK.DB to NGWCHECK.OLD.
4. Go to the *<post office>*`\WPCSOUT` directory, and delete the subdirectory structure called `CHK`.
5. Restart the POA.

This method deletes all of the old GWCHECK data components at the post office, and gives the post office a fresh start. The POA will re-create these components when it reloads.

NON-GWCHECK/GroupWise Message Store Maintenance

There are two other maintenance settings on the POA that must be enabled to keep the message store in good shape. These maintenance settings are not

GWCHECK routines available to you from the GWCHECK or Mailbox/Library Maintenance interfaces. Here they are:

- *Perform User Upkeep:* This is a setting available from the Maintenance property page of the POA. Make sure this setting is enabled. The best time to have Perform User Upkeep execute is in the early-morning hours, for example 1:00 a.m. Performing User Upkeep, among other things, advances tasks in users' mailboxes and calendars. It also deletes trash items that might be set to expire according to the Client Options cleanup settings for the mailbox.
- *QuickFinder Indexing:* This setting is enabled from the QuickFinder property page of the POA. Make sure this setting is enabled. The best time to have QuickFinder Indexing run is during off-peak hours. My experience has shown that if you keep QuickFinder Indexing turned off, performance on your POA will slowly deteriorate. The reason for this is the POA must create real-time indexes anytime someone uses the features of a query folder in the GroupWise client. Without QuickFinder Indexing enabled, rather than the POA going to a pre-generated index, the POA must build an index on the fly, which can greatly impact the performance of the POA.

Maintaining GroupWise Directory Database Maintenance

GroupWise uses two repositories for directory information: Novell Directory Services (eDirectory) and the GroupWise FLAIM or GDS databases (as discussed in Chapter 3, "Understanding the GroupWise Directory").

Maintenance of Novell Directory Services (eDirectory) is beyond the scope of this book. Suffice it to say that if eDirectory is messed up, it can cause problems for GroupWise. This section focuses on maintaining the WPDOMAIN.DB and WPHOST.DB files.

My experience is that these files do not get corrupt nearly as often as information store databases. This is probably because they are not being written to as often as the information store databases. Thus it is not as critical that you run regular rebuilds of domain or post office databases.

The most important thing is that your WPDOMAIN.DB files—for all domains—are backed up regularly. Ideally, you should have this file backed up every day. Don't bother backing up the post office databases (WPHOST.DB), however. These files can be regenerated from the WPDOMAIN.DB file of the domain that owns the post office.

The single most important file in a GroupWise system is the primary domain's WPDOMAIN.DB file. I recommend that you run a recover-and-index rebuild of the primary domain monthly. This cannot be automated. Fortunately, you don't have to bring anything down in order to do this.

Here are the steps for a monthly maintenance of the primary domain's WPDOMAIN.DB:

1. Connect to the primary domain by choosing Tools, GroupWise System Operations, Select Domain. Select the domain database for the primary domain.
2. Highlight the primary domain and choose Tools, GroupWise Utilities, System Maintenance.
3. Select the action called Recover Database.
4. After the recover action is done, do a Rebuild Indexes for Listing action, which is also accessed from Tools, GroupWise Utilities, System Maintenance.

These operations are simple and take very little time to perform. Consider creating a monthly task item to remind you to perform these operations on the primary domain's WPDOMAIN.DB.

Summary

With the help of scheduled events, maintaining the GroupWise information store is easy. This chapter has shown you the events you need to schedule to ensure that your GroupWise information store stays healthy.

GroupWise directory databases maintenance must be done manually. Fortunately, the GroupWise directory databases are far less susceptible to damage, so they do not need to be checked as frequently as the information store.

CHAPTER 18

Using GroupWise Monitor

All GroupWise 6.5 agents have an HTTP-monitoring functionality. GroupWise Monitor takes your system beyond HTTP monitoring. Although HTTP monitoring of agents is a powerful tool, and some features are available only through HTTP monitoring, there is no alert mechanism. With the Windows-based GroupWise 6.5 Monitor, you can be alerted of problems without having to stare at a computer screen, waiting to see whether a problem is happening.

Installing GroupWise Monitor

The GroupWise Monitor Agent can be installed on a Windows NT-class operating system (2000, XP, and so on). Although you can install the GroupWise Monitor Agent on a Windows 95/98/ME computer, it loses some features, and so this chapter assumes you are installing GroupWise Monitor on a Windows NT/2000 computer.

You can install GroupWise Monitor on your own workstation; however I recommend installing GroupWise Monitor on an auxiliary Windows 2000 workstation or server computer that you intend to always keep running. By doing this, the GroupWise Monitor can monitor your system continually.

The GroupWise Monitor software has two separate components. They are the GroupWise Monitor Agent and the GroupWise Monitor Application. Here are some details about both of these components.

GroupWise Monitor Agent

- Runs only on the Windows platform.

- Provides all the features of GroupWise Monitor, except it does not support HDML (handheld device markup language for wireless telephones, typically) and simple HTML support.

GroupWise Monitor Application

- Runs on any Web server that supports the GroupWise WebAccess Application (the Monitor Application is normally installed on the same server as the WebAccess Application).
- Works only in conjunction with the GroupWise Monitor Agent.
- Provides HDML and simple HTML template support for the GroupWise Monitor Agent.
- Can act as a proxy server to access the HTTP information from each GroupWise agent.

The GroupWise Monitor Application cannot exist without the GroupWise Monitor Agent. The GroupWise Monitor Agent has no dependencies on the GroupWise Monitor Application.

Installing Windows SNMP Services

Before even trying to install the GroupWise Monitor Agent, you should install the SNMP services for Windows. The following are steps needed to install SNMP services on a Windows 2000 workstation machine:

1. Go to the Control Panel.
2. Select Add/Remove Programs.
3. Select Add/Remove Windows Components.
4. Choose the Management and Monitoring Tools option.
5. Click Next to allow Windows to install the SNMP.

To confirm that the SNMP service is installed and running, do the following:

1. Go to the Control Panel.
2. Select Administrative Tools.
3. Select Services.
4. Look for SNMP Service.

With SNMP services enabled, you can now proceed to the GroupWise Monitor installation.

Installing GroupWise Monitor Agent

The GroupWise monitor utility is located in your GroupWise 6 *<software distribution directory>*`\ADMIN\MONITOR` directory.

Following are the steps for installing the GroupWise Monitor Agent:

1. Run the SETUP.EXE program in this directory.
2. Proceed to the GroupWise Monitor: Components screen shown in Figure 18.1.

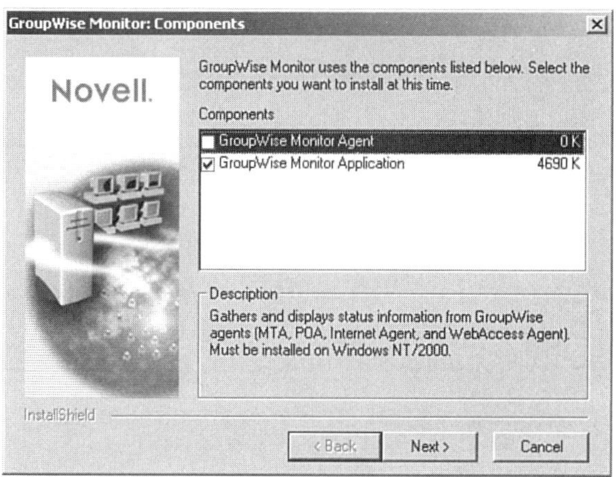

FIGURE 18.1 Choosing which GroupWise Monitor components to install.

3. Select the GroupWise Monitor Agent.

   Later in this chapter, you will install the GroupWise Monitor Application. It's generally easier to implement the agent first, and then implement the GroupWise Monitor Application as needed.

The GroupWise Monitor Agent is sufficient for monitoring your GroupWise system. The GroupWise Monitor Application allows an administrator to see the information on the GroupWise Monitor Agent from additional interfaces such as HDML and simple HTML. It also allows the administrator to drill down into each GroupWise agent's HTTP port from a single entry point.

4. Specify the correct IP address and port for the GroupWise Monitor utility, as shown in Figure 18.2, and then click Next.

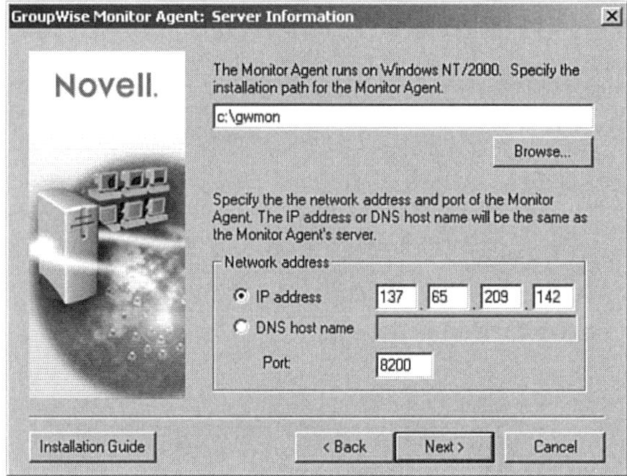

FIGURE 18.2 Entering the GroupWise Monitor Agent information.

NOTE **The GroupWise Monitor Agent can itself be accessed from a Web browser. That's the purpose of the Port field.**

5. Specify the path to a WPDOMAIN.DB in your system, which the GroupWise Monitor Agent can use to read configuration information about agents in your system, and then click Next.
6. Select the language you would like for GroupWise Monitor and click Next.
7. View the summary and make sure everything is correct, and then click Next. If it is not correct, you can use the Back button to correct things.

The GroupWise WebAccess Agent is now installed; you should further tune the WebAccess Agent, as explained in the next section.

Configuring Your System to Better Support GroupWise Monitor

GroupWise Monitor cannot be configured from ConsoleOne. However, the information that GroupWise Monitor uses to monitor your GroupWise system is spread all throughout your system. In order to make all the features of GroupWise Monitor work, you must enable three components:

- HTTP monitoring of GroupWise agents
- SNMP monitoring of GroupWise agents
- Message logging on GroupWise Message Transfer Agents (MTAs)

Enabling HTTP Monitoring

The chapters in this book regarding the GroupWise Post Office Agent (POA), MTA, GroupWise Internet Agent (GWIA), and WebAccess components all spoke of how to enable HTTP monitoring. To review, see each of those chapters. But in short, here's how you enable HTTP monitoring on all GroupWise agents.

Following are the steps for enabling HTTP monitoring of GroupWise agents:

1. Start ConsoleOne.
2. Go to the Properties of the agent (MTA, POA, WebAccess, or GWIA) you want to enable HTTP monitoring on, and go to the Network Address option under the GroupWise tab.
3. Enter the HTTP port value.

NOTE

Make sure that the HTTP port value is in fact the HTTP port on which your agent is actually listening. If you are using the `/HTTP*` switches in the startup files of your agents, you might not be using the same values as are specified in ConsoleOne. If a GroupWise agent has `/HTTP*` switches in its startup file, those switches take precedence over the HTTP values in ConsoleOne. The GWIA keeps the `/HTTP*` switches in its GWIA.CFG file. It is not recommended that you use the `/HTTP` startup switches in your agents, because managing them is more difficult than doing it through ConsoleOne.

Once you have completed adding HTTP monitoring support, you will need to restart the GroupWise agents for which you enabled HTTP monitoring.

Enabling SNMP Monitoring

All the GroupWise agents can be monitored via SNMP, and in fact, SNMP monitoring is a default on all GroupWise agents. The GroupWise POA can be configured to disable SNMP monitoring though, so here's how to enable SNMP monitoring on the GroupWise POA.

Follow these steps to enable SNMP support for a GroupWise POA:

1. Run ConsoleOne.

2. Go to the Properties of the POA object.
3. Go to the Agent Settings property page.
4. Slide down to the bottom of the Agent Settings property page and check the Enable SNMP check box, as shown in Figure 18.3.

FIGURE 18.3
Enable SNMP by checking the enable SNMP check box, and entering the GET string.

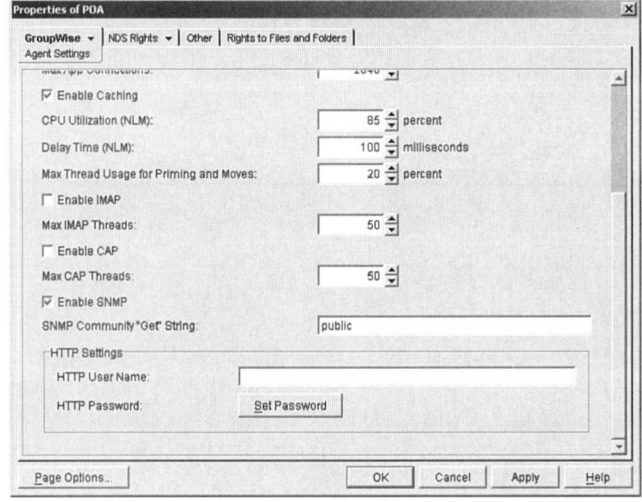

5. Enter the word **`public`** (case sensitive) in the SNMP Community Get String field below the SNMP check box.

NOTE **A discussion of SNMP community get strings is outside the scope of this book. You are welcome to change the SNMP Community Get String field according to your organization's SNMP guidelines.**

Enabling MTA Message Logging

To enable MTA message logging, follow these steps:

1. Run ConsoleOne.
2. Edit the properties of the MTA object.
3. Go to the Message Log Settings property page.
4. Change the Message Logging Level field so that it says Full.
5. Don't fill in the Message Log File Path field unless you want to change the Message Logging Path. By default, the MTA will place the message log files in the `<DOMAIN>\MSLOCAL\MSGLOG` directory.

6. Check all check boxes except the Track Administrative Messages. Rarely will you need to track ADMIN type messages through the system.
7. Determine a value, such as 30 days, for the Delete Report After field.

Figure 18.4 shows MTA message logging enabled.

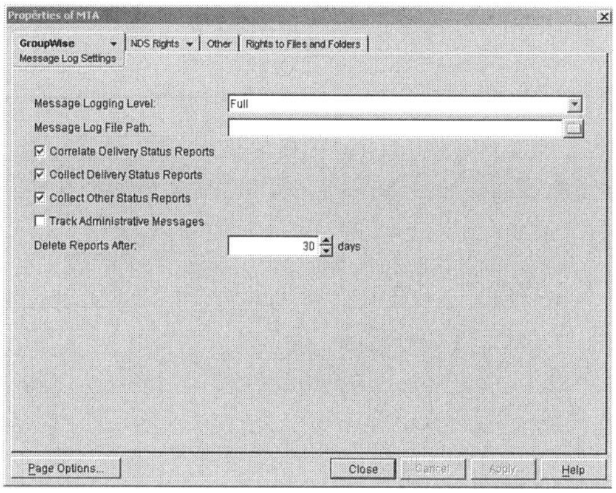

FIGURE 18.4
Enabling MTA message logging is accomplished from the Message Log Settings property page.

Now the MTA is logging information that is very useful when tracking message flow. These logs are separate from the typical MTA logs.

Starting and Using the GroupWise Monitoring Agent

The GroupWise monitoring agent is installed to the Start, Programs menu tree of the Windows computer where GroupWise Monitor Agent was installed. By default, GroupWise Monitor is installed in a folder under Start, Programs, Novell GroupWise Monitor.

The GroupWise Monitor Agent does not run as a Windows service. Thus, if the Windows machine that is running the GroupWise Monitor Agent is restarted, the GroupWise Monitor Agent will not run until someone logs into the Windows machine.

After starting the GroupWise Monitor Agent, you get a list of the agents that the GroupWise Monitor Agent was able to discover from your GroupWise system. This list is generated when the Monitor Agent reads the WPDOMAIN.DB for information about the system. By default, all agents will be placed in a folder in the left pane that is your GroupWise system name.

GroupWise Monitor is a very powerful and configurable tool. It's kind of like a piece of soft clay. You can mold GroupWise Monitor into many tools. Because of this, this chapter gives an explanation of some of the menu selections in GroupWise Monitor. There are no "best practices" for configuring GroupWise Monitor, so this chapter doesn't tell you how to configure GroupWise Monitor, or which fields to enable. Instead, it just explains the functional purposes of many of the features in the GroupWise Monitor. It is best to explore GroupWise Monitor and construct your own monitoring solution with GroupWise Monitor.

The whole idea of GroupWise Monitor is to allow you to view the state of your GroupWise system and notify you of problems or potential problems. The GroupWise 6.5 Monitor Agent introduced the concept of grouping your various agents together in whatever type of groups you want. This gives the administrator the capability to logically or physically organize all of the GroupWise agents in the system in whatever manor that makes sense for your particular GroupWise system. For example, you can create a folder for each site of your company. You can then create subfolders beneath folders to organize your agents. To create folders, right-click any parent folder and choose Create. You can then create a group or a folder to drag agents into. Figure 18.5 shows you the WorldWide Widgets Monitor, and illustrates how various folders have been created to organize the agents.

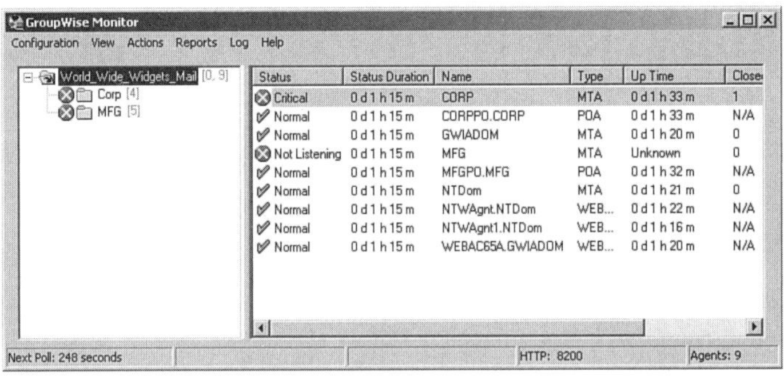

FIGURE 18.5 The GroupWise Monitor Agent displays the status of all GroupWise Agents.

TIP

When you drag and drop agents into various folders, they are moved into the destination folder. However, you can have parent folders display the agents contained in child folders by right-clicking the parent folder and selecting Show Subgroup Agents. This places a small black down arrow on the folder that signifies that this folder is set to view its subfolders agents.

When you load the GroupWise Monitor Agent, the agent will read the monitor.xml file to determine where the WPDOMAIN.DB file is. It will then connect into the WPDOMAIN.DB file to identify which agents you have in your GroupWise system. Next, it will attempt to open an HTTP connection to each agent. If your agents are password protected on their HTTP port, you might get a pop-up prompt for each agent in order to enter the agent's HTTP user and password settings. If you see this it is because the agent's HTTP user and password settings are not stored in the WPDOMAIN.DB file and are most likely set up in the agent's startup file. Because of this, it is much easier to define the HTTP user and password on your various GroupWise agents through ConsoleOne so that this information is in the WPDOMAIN.DB file, and the Monitor Agent can read this to authenticate to the agent. You can attempt to work around the pop-ups by using some startup switches on the Monitor Agent that feed the HTTP user and password settings into the various GroupWise agents for monitoring them.

The `/httpuser-` and `/httppassword-` switches are placed on the command line where you load the Monitor Agent. Here's an example of how this might look:

```
C:\gwmon\gwmon.exe /lang-us /httpuser-webmon /httppassword-
letmein
```

The next sections talk about how to enable three kinds of notifications:

- Visual notification
- Audio notification
- Remote notification

The following sections outline the steps for setting up notification.

Configuring Visual Notification: GroupWise Monitor Agent Windows Interface

The main GroupWise Monitor Agent screen, shown in Figure 18.5, gives you an eagle's-eye view of the state of your GroupWise system. The goal is to see green check marks next to each agent. If you see a red circle with an X through it, or a yellow circle with an exclamation mark in it, these are visual alerts that either an agent is down or GroupWise Monitor cannot get a hold of an agent for some reason. When an agent in a particular folder has a visual alert on it, the alert icon is placed next to the folder. This allows you to quickly identify whether any agents in any folder are in an alerted state.

You can get more information about any one of your GroupWise agents by double-clicking the agent. A details screen comes up, as shown in Figure 18.6.

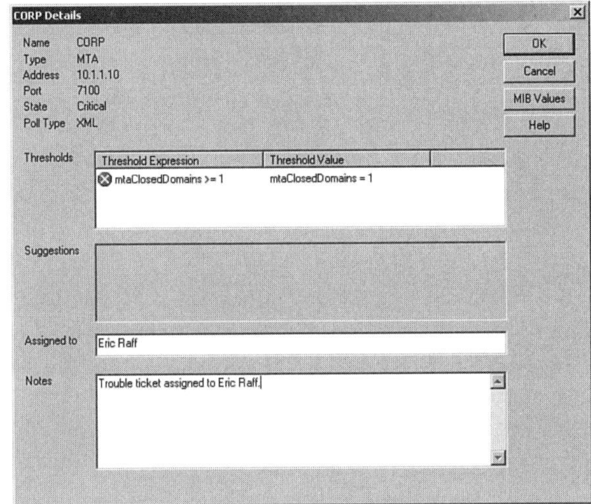

FIGURE 18.6
Agent Details shows why Monitor flagged an agent as having problems.

You can get even more details by viewing the SNMP values that the agent makes available. To do this, click the MIB Values button. Figure 18.7 shows the MIB values that come up on a POA agent.

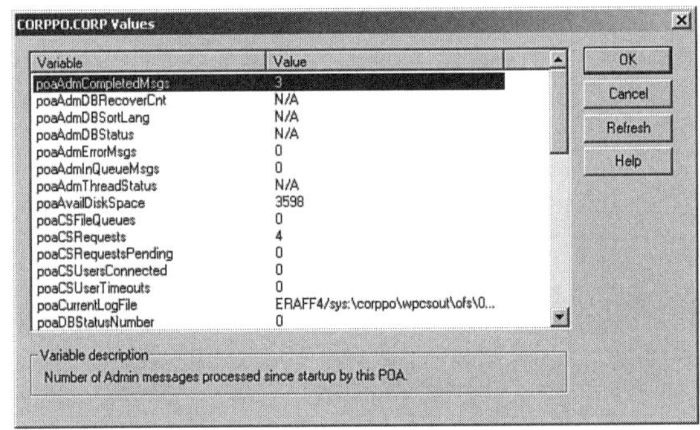

FIGURE 18.7
The SNMP/MIB values on a POA show which settings from a POA can be monitored with an SNMP request.

The SNMP/MIB values of an agent contain the information that you can monitor. By default, the Monitor Agent will query the agents via the HTTP port of the agent. If this port is inaccessible, it will revert to using SNMP to poll the agent. The Poll Type is identified on the agent details dialog box, as illustrated in Figure 18.6. If it is XML, the Monitor Agent is using the HTTP port to poll the agent. If you see the Poll Type of SNMP, you know the Monitor Agent is using the SNMP protocol to poll this particular agent.

Reports

With the Reports option, you can get real-time reports of configuration information, message flow, and so on. The reports features are pretty self-explanatory. What you should know though is that the user traffic, link traffic, and message tracking features all derive information from the message logs of the GroupWise MTAs in your system. These aren't the regular logs the MTA uses; these are the special logs that are enabled when MTA message logging is enabled. Enabling MTA message logging was explained earlier in this chapter.

Environment

The Environment report option will show you information about your entire GroupWise environment. It displays things like the agent name, the agent type, the agent version, the agent's IP address, the agent's port, and the server that the agent is running on. You can also opt to send this report to any e-mail address. When you click the Send icon when viewing the Environment report, you can enter the From and To e-mail address and the Monitor agent will act like an SMTP server to send the message out.

User Traffic

This report can track the messages sent by a particular user, within a time frame that you specify.

Link Traffic

This report tracks the amount of messages sent between domains in your system.

Message Tracking

This is a powerful but complex feature. As shown in Figure 18.8, this feature requires some investigation on your part.

First here's a scenario in which you might use this feature:

- `USERA` on `PO1.DOM1` sends a message to `USERB` on `PO2.DOM1`.
- `USERB` did not receive the message, and `USERA` shows the status of the message as pending.

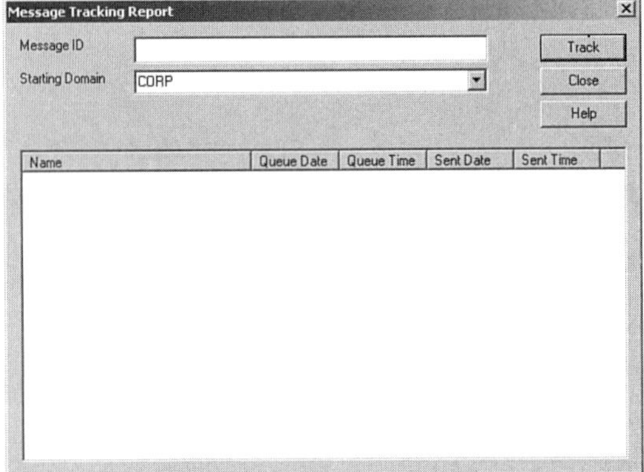

FIGURE 18.8
The Message Tracking Report feature allows you to search for a particular message to determine when it passed through the MTA.

You are the administrator; you want to know what happened to the message. Here is the information you would gather:

1. Have **USERA** go to his/her Sent Items folder.
2. Have **USERA** view the properties of the message sent to **USERB**.
3. Have **USERA** tell you the value on the line that reads Mail Envelope Properties located at the top of the properties page.

   The value you want is everything between the parentheses. For example, Figure 18.9 shows the properties of a mail message, with the Mail Envelope Properties being `3EF471C5.BCD : 15 : 41217`.

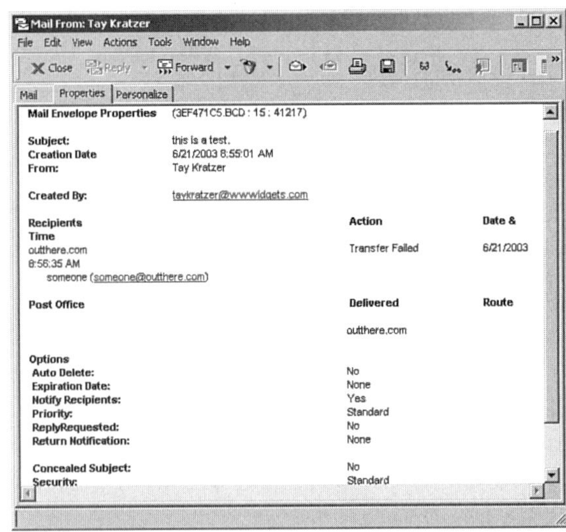

FIGURE 18.9
The properties of a GroupWise message reveal the message ID value.

4. After you have the Mail Envelope Properties value, you have the message ID value needed for the GroupWise Monitor message tracking report. Enter this same value in the message ID value, and select DOM1 as the starting domain.
5. Click the Track button to generate the report.

This section explained how to track a message. In order for a message to be tracked, it must be sent to at least one recipient outside the post office.

Link Trace

Link trace is a great tool that allows you to quickly and easily trace the link(s) from one MTA to another in your GroupWise system. Figure 18.10 displays the Link Trace tool with a link traced from the `CORP` domain to the `MFG` domain. You can see that the `CORP` domain is linked directly to the `MFG` domain, that the link is open, and that there are no queued messages waiting to be sent from `CORP` to `MFG`. In a large GroupWise system, this tool can be invaluable in identifying how the link configuration is defined on your system.

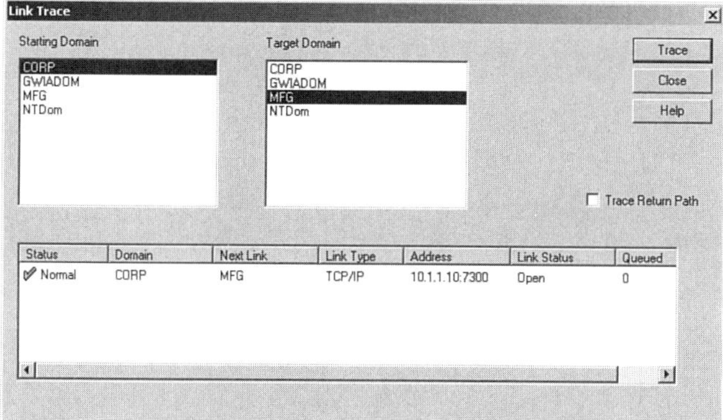

FIGURE 18.10
You can use Link Trace to trace MTA to MTA links.

You can also place a check box in the Trace Return Path option and the Link Trace tool will trace the links in both directions. For example, it will check the link from `CORP` to `MFG`, and then back from `MFG` to `CORP` in one step. This is useful to identify whether the two domains are configured correctly from the perspective of each MTA. One thing to note is that if there are problems in your link configuration, this tool will detect them and will show a visual alert.

Link Configuration

The Link Configuration tool is used when you need to know how an MTA talks to all other domains in the system. You can also use it to run a report on every MTA in the system, and what this MTA's link configuration is. Once again if there are problems such as link configuration loops in your system, this tool will identify them and alert you with a visual alert. Figure 18.11 shows the link configuration of the MFG domain. Notice that MFG's link to NTDOM is an indirect link through the CORP domain.

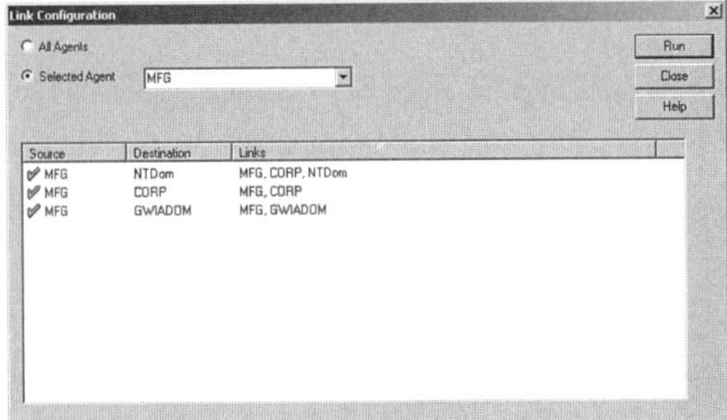

FIGURE 18.11 The Link Configuration tool can trace the speed of domain-to-domain links.

Configuring Visual Notification: GroupWise Monitor Agent HTTP Interface

The GroupWise Monitor interface allows you to define custom SNMP monitoring views of your GroupWise system. The GroupWise Monitor has a Web browser interface, and you can use GroupWise Monitor, even when you are away from the machine running the GroupWise Monitor agent.

To enable HTTP monitoring and to enable the HTTP interface to gain quick access to GroupWise agents, you need to define a user and password to access the HTTP port of the Monitor Agent. This allows you to check your GroupWise system by accessing the HTTP port of the agent directly. You can define the HTTP user and password on the agent by going to Configuration, HTTP and entering the option to Require authentication to browse GW monitor. Next, you define the user and password switches, and, if desired, you can define the intruder detection.

Specifying the HTTP Port for GroupWise Monitor Agent

The GroupWise Monitor Agent listens on a configurable port. You should check to see whether this port is enabled, and what it is enabled for. To do this, go to Configuration, HTTP in the GroupWise Monitor Agent Windows interface, as shown in Figure 18.12.

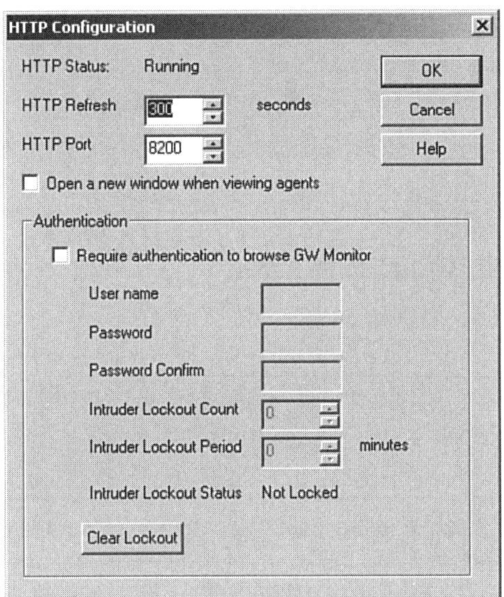

FIGURE 18.12
HTTP configuration for the GroupWise Monitor Agent can be configured using a number of settings.

Make sure that the HTTP port is filled in and make note of this port.

Accessing the HTTP Interface Through a Web Browser

Here is how you access the HTTP interface of the GroupWise Monitor Agent through your Web browser. Use the following line in your browser:

```
http://<monitor computer's IP address or DNS name>:<monitor's
HTTP port>
```

For example

```
http://137.65.32.63:8200
```

You should get an interface similar to the one in Figure 18.13.

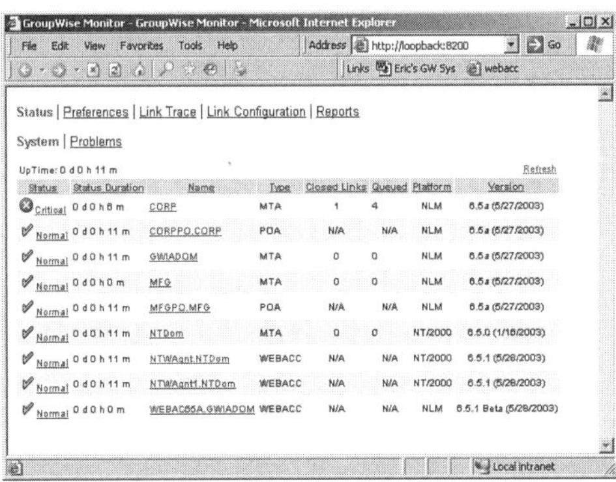

FIGURE 18.13
The GroupWise Monitor Agent as it appears in a Web browser interface.

Once you are in, you get an interface that is much like the Windows interface. There are two distinct advantages that I can see to this interface:

- HTTP access to GroupWise agents
- Custom views

HTTP Access to GroupWise Agents

From the main status screen in the Web browser interface of GroupWise Monitor, you can click any of the agents in the Name column, and you are immediately transported to the HTTP port of that agent and the resulting HTTP interface of that agent.

TIP

You can configure GroupWise Monitor to open the HTTP screen of agents in a new browser window. This way, you always have GroupWise Monitor, and you can access the HTTP interfaces of your other GroupWise agents at the same time. To do this, go back into the GroupWise Monitor's Windows interface and choose Configuration, HTTP. In the HTTP Configuration window, check the Open a New Window When Viewing Agents option.

Custom Views

With custom views, you can define the SNMP traps that you want to monitor (see Figure 18.14).

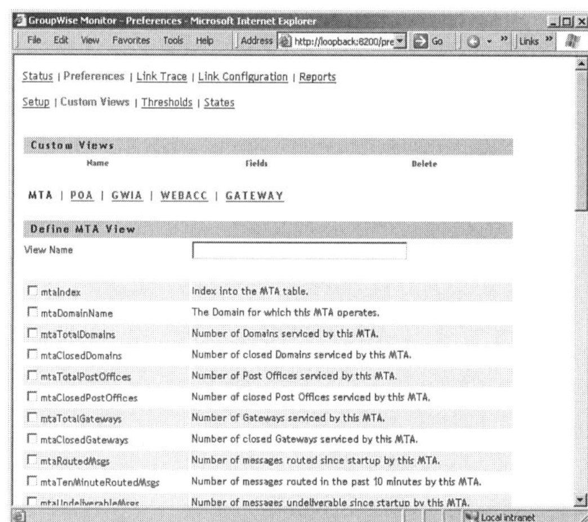

FIGURE 18.14 GroupWise Monitor offers the Custom Views option.

Rather than explain these traps (there's more than 200 of them), you can go to the status screen in the Web-browser interface and click an agent along the Status column. Here you will see each of the SNMP values filled in for that agent. With a little bit of thinking and matching, you should be able to determine the SNMP traps available to you. Now you can create an SNMP custom view:

1. Go back to the Custom View screen.
2. Select what type of agent for which you want to set up a custom view (MTA, POA, GWIA, WebAccess, or Gateway).
3. Select the SNMP traps that you are interested in. (The traps you see here are specific to the type of agent you are defining the trap for.)
4. Give the custom view a name by filling in the View Name field.
5. Click the Add View button at the bottom of the page. You have just created your own custom view that you can click to see just what you have defined.

This section explained visual notification by the WebAccess Agent. The next section explains how to get audio notification from the WebAccess Agent.

Configuring Audio Notification

The GroupWise Monitor Agent can play sounds when certain events have happened. This is useful if the GroupWise Monitor Agent is in earshot of your desk. To enable audio notification, choose Configuration, Notification, and then check the Play Sound option. To define the sounds you will hear with various thresholds, click the Sounds button, and you will see the window shown in Figure 18.15.

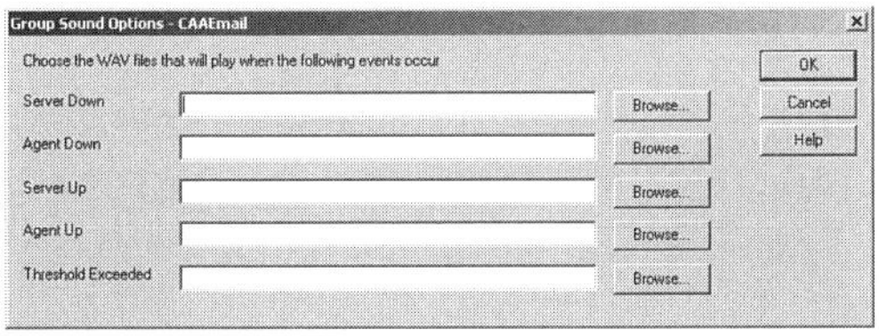

FIGURE 18.15 GroupWise Monitor sounds can be customized according to the nature of the event that causes Monitor to make an audible notification.

You can browse to find sound files that will play on the events shown in the Sound Options window.

Configuring Remote Notification

This is a powerful notification method. With remote notification, you can have GroupWise Monitor send a message to the Internet e-mail address for your pager, as well as to other e-mail addresses. Here's how to do it:

1. Go into the Windows interface of the GroupWise Monitor Agent.
2. Choose Configuration, Notification.
3. Select the Notification Events that you want to be notified of.
4. Enter the Notification list with e-mail addresses to send notification to, separating each address with a comma.
5. In the Mail Domain field, specify the mail domain name for your organization.

   My organization is `worldwidewidgets.com`.
6. For the Relay address, enter the IP address of a machine that will relay the notification onto the Internet for you.

   If you have enabled relaying on the GWIA, you can specify the IP address for your GWIA. However, you will most likely want to specify some other SMTP mailer in your system that you can relay off of in case the GWIA is down.

TIP

You can leave the Relay address blank and the Monitor Agent will send the e-mail directly to the destination SMTP mail servers. This works because the Monitor Agent has its own built-in SMTP server that allows it to send mail directly. You'll normally use a relay server only if the box that is running the Monitor Agent is not able to do the DNS lookup.

Figure 18.16 shows the GroupWise Monitor configured for remote notification.

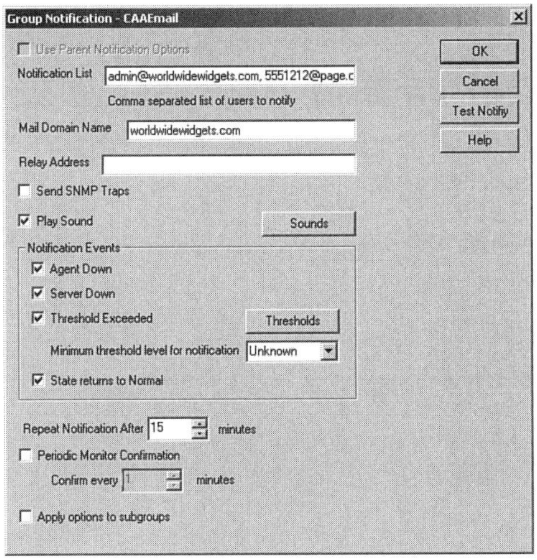

FIGURE 18.16 The Group Notification window shows that more than one e-mail can be notified by GroupWise Monitor.

Installing the GroupWise Monitor Application

The primary reason you would want to install the GroupWise Monitor Application is if you wanted to be able to monitor your GroupWise agents—down to the MTA, POA, GWIA, and WebAccess level securely from outside your corporate network. This means that if you are out of the office, and you get notified that there are problems with the GroupWise system, you can access the monitor application from a Web browser and actually drill down into the POA's HTTP port to check into things. The second greatest reason to install the Monitor Application is to broaden browser integration for your GroupWise Monitor Agent. The GroupWise Monitor Application can integrate the GroupWise Monitor Agent's interface into your Web server. A particular value to this is that you can leverage your Web server's outside availability on the Internet to broaden your access to monitoring your GroupWise agents. As if that isn't enough, the GroupWise Monitor Application also supports monitoring via simple HTML devices, such as a Windows CE device, or HDML-wireless devices, such as a cell phone with a micro-browser. The GroupWise Monitor also includes support for the PalmPilot Web-clipping platform.

Prerequisites to Installing the GroupWise Monitor Application

The GroupWise Monitor Application requires that you have a Web server. The GroupWise Monitor Application was written to support one of five Web servers:

- Netscape Enterprise Server for NetWare
- Apache Web Server for NetWare
- Netscape FastTrack/Enterprise Server for Windows
- Microsoft Internet Information Server (IIS) for Windows NT/2000 Server
- Apache Web Server for UNIX Solaris

You must have the GroupWise agent installed prior to installing the GroupWise Monitor Application.

Installing the GroupWise Monitor Application

Don't bother installing the GroupWise Monitor Application unless you have a GroupWise Monitor Agent installed and running.

Following are the steps for installing the GroupWise Monitor Application:

1. Run the SETUP.EXE program from the `SDD\ADMIN\MONITOR` directory.
2. Proceed to the GroupWise Monitor: Components screen shown in Figure 18.17.

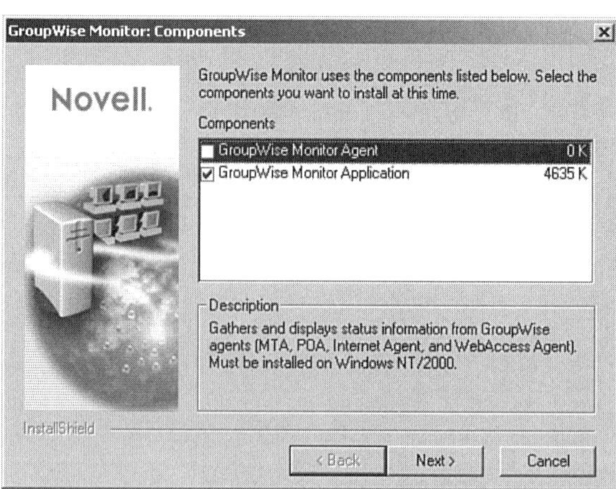

FIGURE 18.17 Choose which GroupWise Monitor components to install.

3. Select only the GroupWise Monitor Application and click Next.
4. At the next screen, enter the IP address and the HTTP port of the Windows NT/2000 computer that is running the GroupWise Monitor Agent.

   Figure 18.18 shows the screen on the GroupWise Monitor Agent where you can determine which HTTP port the GroupWise Monitor Agent is using. After filling out this dialog box, click Next.

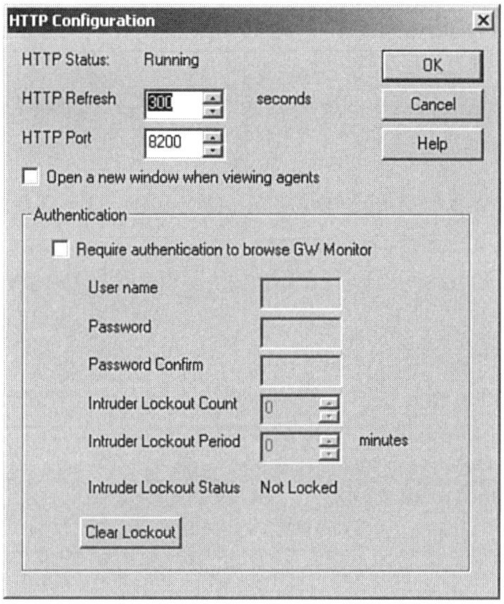

FIGURE 18.18 GroupWise Monitor Agent HTTP configuration information.

5. Now the installation wizard wants to know what type of Web server you will be installing the Monitor Application to. This can be the same Web server that you have the WebAccess Application installed to. In fact, using your WebAccess Application server for the Monitor Application is recommended because of the simplified management of both applications. Select which type of Web server you are running, and then specify the path to your Web server. Click Next.
6. You can now create the *.PQA file that you can use on your WebClipping enabled PalmOS device to access the Monitor Application. Enter the URL to your Web server where the Application will be running.
7. The next screen asks whether you want to make GroupWise Monitor your default Web server screen. Generally, you want to answer No to this question, and click Next.

NOTE

Because you will not be replacing the Web server's default Web page, you will need to access the GroupWise Monitor Application via the following location:

`http://<web server name or IP address>/servlet/gwmonitor`

8. The installation now wants to create a Novell directory on the Web server. The Novell directory is somewhat of a work directory for the GroupWise Monitor Application servlet. Click Next.
9. Next you are prompted about which servlet gateway to use. NetWare 5.1 and older servers will use the Novell servlet gateway, whereas NetWare 6 and newer servers will use the Tomcat servlet gateway. Select the appropriate servlet gateway and click Next.
10. Choose the language, and click Next.
11. Now you are prompted where in eDirectory to install the GroupWise Monitor Application configuration objects (see Figure 18.19). These objects are your administration points for the GroupWise Monitor Application. With these objects, the GroupWise Monitor Application is represented in eDirectory, and you can configure it from ConsoleOne. Click Next to proceed to the summary screen.

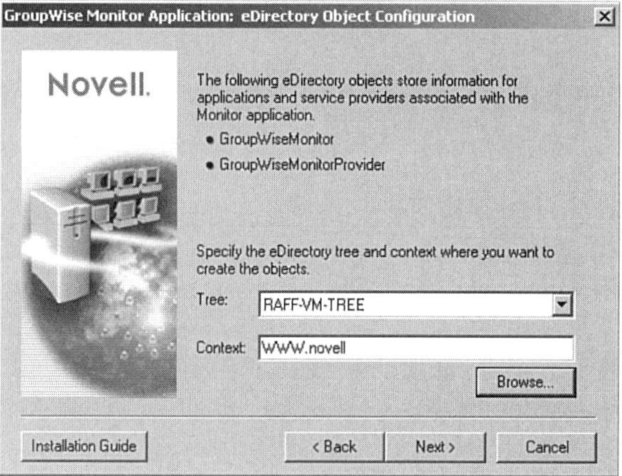

FIGURE 18.19
GroupWise Monitor Application eDirectory Object Configuration.

NOTE

The GroupWise Monitor Agent and Application are not in the GroupWise view in ConsoleOne, and they are not in the GroupWise WPDOMAIN.DB file. The GroupWise Monitor Agent is administered strictly from the agent itself. The GroupWise Monitor Application is administered from ConsoleOne in the NDS browser view.

12. You get a summary screen at the end of the installation. If everything looks correct, proceed to install the GroupWise Monitor Application software.

The GroupWise Monitor Application is now installed. The GroupWise Monitor Agent must be installed and running in order for the application to function.

Configuring the GroupWise Monitor Application

There really is not a whole lot to configure on the GroupWise Monitor Application. The GroupWise Monitor Application primarily needs to know the location of the GroupWise Monitor Agent. If ever you should need to configure the GroupWise Monitor Application to monitor a GroupWise Monitor Agent at a different IP address, you need to configure the GroupWise Monitor Application. To access the GroupWise Monitor Application, look in the NDS location where you installed it. You should find objects that look like the ones shown in Figure 18.20.

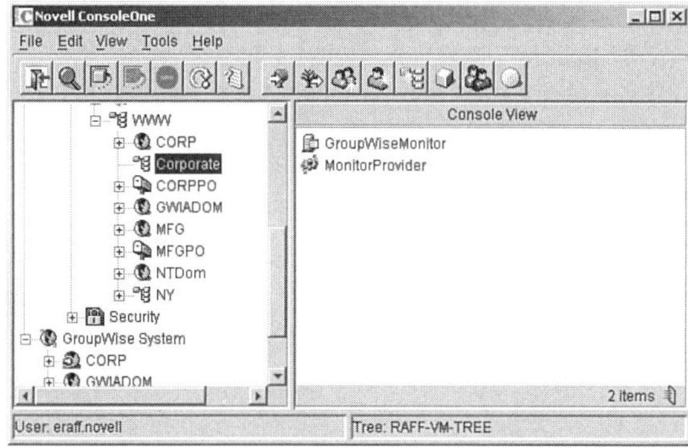

FIGURE 18.20 GroupWise Monitor Application Components as they appear in ConsoleOne.

The `MonitorProvider` object is where you indicate a different IP address for a GroupWise Monitor Agent.

The `GroupWiseMonitor` object has additional features such as how long a session will be terminated if it is inactive and the logout URL that a browser will be sent to when logging out of the GroupWise Monitor Application.

Starting the GroupWise Monitor Application

The GroupWise Monitor Application starts automatically when you start your Web server if you're using Netscape Enterprise Web server. Because the GroupWise Monitor Application is a servlet, you actually troubleshoot and configure the GroupWise Monitor Application as a part of your Web servlet and the servlet gateway. If you are using the Novell servlet gateway, the servlet-gateway administration can be accessed via a Web browser at the following location:

```
http://<web server name or IP address>/servlet/ServletManager
```

NOTE

The servlet gateway is case sensitive. Make sure you use the capital *S* and *M* (`ServletManager`) as shown.

You will be prompted for the password to administer the servlet manager before you can administer the Novell servlet gateway.

TIP

If you do not know the password needed to administer and troubleshoot the Novell servlet gateway and your Novell servlet gateway is running on a NetWare server, go to the `SYS:JAVA\SERVLETS` directory. Access the `SERVLETS.PROPERTIES` file and search for the word "password". You should find a line that specifies both the username and password that you should use. The username and password are case sensitive.

If you are running the Tomcat servlet engine on NetWare 6 or newer, you can simply kill any Java processes, exit Java, and then restart the Tomcat servlet engine. Follow these steps to accomplish this:

1. `Java -killall` (wait about 10 seconds)
2. `Java -exit`
3. `Tomcat33`

The Monitor application should now be started and ready to be accessed via a Web browser.

Utilizing the GroupWise Monitor Application

To access the GroupWise Monitor Application, go to the following location:

```
http://<web server name or IP address>/servlet/gwmonitor
```

You should get a screen similar to the one shown in Figure 18.21.

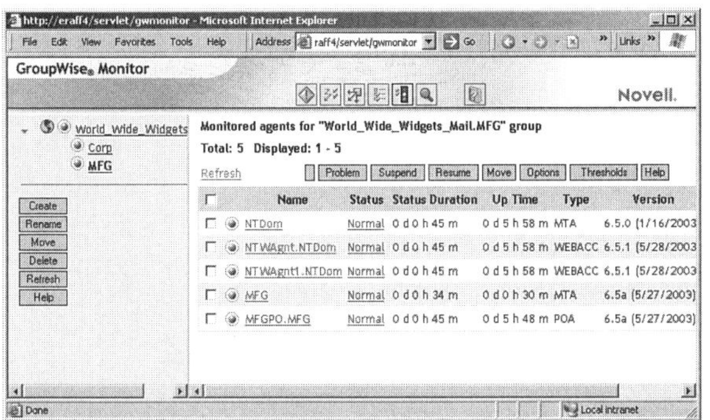

FIGURE 18.21
The GroupWise Monitor Application Client Interface as it appears in the HTML frames version.

If you use a Pocket PC to access GroupWise Monitor, the interface might look like the one in Figure 18.22.

FIGURE 18.22
The GroupWise Monitor Application Client Interface as it appears in the simple HTML version.

NOTE

The GroupWise Monitor Application also supports WAP devices, so you can access the Monitor Application from a phone as well.

The navigation buttons across the top of GroupWise Monitor HTML frames version allow you to switch to one of six views:

- **Problems:** This shows you the agents that have problems. It does not matter if the agent is in a particular group; it will display all agents in the system that have exceeded a threshold or are not reachable.
- **Link Trace:** This is a way of checking the status of a link from one domain MTA to another domain's MTA.
- **Link Configuration:** This option allows you to check the link configuration of a particular MTA. It will check all outbound links from the selected MTA, and list how this MTA communicates to all domains in the system.
- **Global Operations:** This option allows you to make basic configuration changes to the Monitor Agent from the Application Interface. You can change things such as the relay server, or the domain name, as well as when you send alerts.
- **States:** This allows you to view all states that the agents can be in. It also allows you to create custom states that you can apply to various thresholds.
- **Search:** This is a way of filtering for certain agents.

The online help in GroupWise Monitor is excellent and gives even more detail about how you might use these features.

Enabling Proxy Access to GroupWise Agents Through the Monitor Application

The Monitor Application and Monitor Agent can work together to allow you to access your GroupWise agent's HTTP interface through the application. You can access, say, a POA object's HTTP interface from outside your firewall with the Monitor Application acting as a proxy device. In other words, when you click a post office to drill down into its settings, the application will make the request to the agent in behalf of your browser, and will handle the information from the POA and send it down to your browser.

This functionality is not enabled by default. To enable it, perform the following steps:

1. Edit the shortcut to the Monitor Agent and add the `/proxy` startup switch. For example, the following would start the monitor agent:

```
C:\gwmon\gwmon.exe /lang-us /proxy
```

2. Shut down the Monitor Agent and then restart it.
3. Locate the GWMONITOR.CFG file located in the `\NOVELL\GWMONITOR` directory of your Web server. Open this file with any text editor.
4. At the very bottom of this file, you will find the following section:

```
#-------------------------------------------------------
-----------------
# Specify the access level for the web interface of GW
agents. The options are:
# 1. none - NO access to agent's web interface
# 2. basic - Access to agent's web interface from
inside the firewall
# 3. full - Access to agent's web interface from
outside the firewall
#-----------------------------------
Provider.GWMP.Agent.Http.level=basic
```

5. Edit the `Provider.GWMP.Agent.Http.level=basic` field to equal `full`. It should read like this:

```
Provider.GWMP.Agent.Http.level=full
```

6. Save the updated GWMONITOR.CFG file.
7. Shut down and restart the servlet gateway. If it's running on Netware 6 or later, you can issue the following commands at the NW Server console:
   - `Java -killall` (or issue `Java -show` and kill only the WebAccess process)
   - `Java -exit`
   - `Tomcat33`

   You can also use the `NVXWEBDN` and `NVXWEBUP` commands if you are using the Netscape Enterprise Web server.
8. Access the monitor application by going to `/servlet/gwmonitor` on your Web server. Everything will look the same now, except when you mouse over a hyperlink to an MTA, POA, GWIA, or WebAccess agent, the URL will not send your browser directly to this agent. Instead, the URL will reflect the fact that the Monitor Application will get the details of the agent for you. With this you can drill right down into various agents from outside your firewall. A GroupWise administrator's dream, right?

NOTE

If you're using any template other than the standard Frames template, when you browse down into your various GroupWise agents, a new browser window will try to open in the standard agent view. This is because the GroupWise agent's HTTP interface has not been ported into the various templates. If you are accessing the Monitor Application via a cell phone using WAP, you cannot drill down into the various agents because of this incompatible format on the WAP device.

WARNING

If you have not defined a HTTP user and password on the Monitor Agent, anyone will be able to access your Monitor Application without being prompted for a username and password. To secure your Monitor Application with a username and password, you need to go to your Monitor Agent's Configuration, HTTP settings. From there, you can enable the option to Require Authentication to Browse GW Monitor. Check this option, and then define a username and password. You can also enable intruder detection on the agent. If someone does try to guess the Monitor Agent username and password, you can lock out all access for a defined length of time. To reset the intruder lockout, you either wait the defined length of time or access the Monitor Agent directly and unlock the intruder detection from the HTTP configuration page. Of course, you will also want to enable SSL on your Web server so that your Monitor Agent's username and password are not sent over the network in clear text.

Summary

This chapter exposed the main functionality of GroupWise Monitor. GroupWise Monitor's strength is its capability to be customized and accessed from a broad variety of clients. Continue to explore GroupWise Monitor on your own, and see how you can customize it to your environment.

PART V

Applied Architecture

CHAPTER 19

Building Your GroupWise System Correctly

Back in 1993, when GroupWise was still WordPerfect Office, WordPerfect realized that poor planning had caused some of the worst problems administrators experienced with the product. Administrators often began installing and configuring their system without knowing in advance what they wanted it to look like.

The problems caused by failing to design the system correctly only got worse as the GroupWise product matured. This chapter helps you apply such architectural information as you plan your GroupWise system. The goals of this chapter are to help your installation run smoothly, and help you build a system that meets your needs. Most of all, though, your system should run the way you expect it to without you having to spend a lot of time or money on technical support.

General System Configuration

There are several basic principles of GroupWise system design that you should try to adhere to. If you cannot, you should at least understand why the principle is important, so you can knowledgeably work around the problems that your nonconformity introduces.

E-mail, Calendaring, and Document Management Are Mission-Critical

The first principle is a simple one. The system you are going to build (or you inherited) is going to be critical to the day-to-day work of your users. If GroupWise is down, your users will stop getting work done. If GroupWise performance is bad, your users will complain and will be less productive. If data is lost from the GroupWise system, that data will have to be re-created by users. These productivity hits will ultimately affect your bottom line. Your business will lose money when GroupWise is not running optimally.

The application of this principle is equally simple. If the system is mission-critical, if business cannot take place without it, you need to be prepared to spend money on the necessary infrastructure to support the system. This includes a solid LAN and/or WAN, a good Internet connection, and modern network file server hardware. That old NetWare 4.11 server running on the P100 box will run GroupWise, but not nearly as well as a NetWare 6 server with a XEON processor.

Mesh Message Transfer on the LAN

Message transfer agents (MTAs) can communicate via TCP/IP as they transfer messages between post offices. If you have multiple GroupWise domains on your LAN, you should probably avoid a star or hub configuration for network links. Allow every domain on the LAN to connect directly to every other domain. This will prevent bottlenecks, accelerate message transfer, and reduce the amount of network traffic.

Match WAN Message Transfer to WAN Topology

If you have more than one facility, or your offices are connected via wide area network technology (T2 or slower links), make sure that your MTA links match your WAN topology. This means that GroupWise domains should exist at the borders between the LANs. Use indirect connections between domains on one LAN and domains on another, allowing only a single pair of domains to communicate across the WAN. This will reduce network traffic on the WAN and prevent certain kinds of MTA problems, including TCP timeout errors.

Treat the Internet as part of the WAN. After all, your users will be swapping e-mail with Internet users with great frequency. You should dedicate a domain to this WAN link.

Applying System Configuration Principles in the Real World

This section looks at how the principles from the preceding sections can be put into practice by examining a hypothetical organization and designing a

GroupWise system for that organization according to the outlined principles.

The Scenario

All-American Widgets has corporate offices in Newark, Detroit, and Salt Lake City. They have regional sales offices in Atlanta and San Francisco. They have more than 11,000 employees.

In New Jersey, there are 2,500 employees, most of whom are in the sales, marketing, and engineering departments. These users are all connected to a 100MB fiber network.

In Detroit, there are 7,200 employees, all of whom are in the manufacturing division. Only about 1,000 of these users (the management team and a few stray engineers) have computers, but there are another 500 kiosks that are used by the employees on the plant floor.

There are 1,400 employees in Salt Lake City, in the service and support division. All 1,400 of them have computers, and they have a LAN similar to the one in New Jersey.

Finally, there are 15 employees in Atlanta and another 20 in San Francisco. These sales people all have mobile computers, and there's a solid network in their home office building. They do not, however, have a network administrator.

The Newark System

It should be pretty simple to arrive at a good design for the Newark portion of the system. All-American Widgets is not going to use caching mode on the GroupWise client in a broad manner. Newark has 2,500 users, so you should have five post offices, one for every 500 users. Each post office gets its own file server.

Newark will have three domains. One domain will own the five post offices. An auxiliary domain will own the GWIA and will handle communications with the other remote sites. The third domain will be an auxiliary domain for the WebAccess gateway and Web server. So, Newark gets eight file servers, five post offices, three domains, a GWIA, and a WebAccess gateway.

The Detroit System

Detroit is a little more complex. Detroit has a much larger user base, but most of them aren't regular computer users. The Detroit site creates three post offices and two domains. One domain will have all the post offices below it. The post offices will be for the 1,000 management folk. The third post office will have 6,200 mailboxes on it. We are breaking a rule here, but for good reason. These folks won't be using their mailboxes much. There are only 500 kiosks from which they can connect, so performance won't be a problem, and there will not be that much mail for them.

To simplify things, all the kiosks run WebAccess. That way, users don't have to worry about logging in and out of Windows to ensure that GroupWise Registry settings are correct.

Detroit will need two domains. One domain will own three post offices. The second domain will be an auxiliary domain to house WebAccess. So, Detroit gets five file servers, three post offices, two domains, one of which will house only the GroupWise WebAccess gateway, and the Web server.

The Salt Lake City System

Salt Lake City is going to look a lot like Newark, only smaller. The 1,400 users can be squeezed on to just two post offices in a single domain. Salt Lake City has its own Internet connection, and the repair technicians there will be sending a lot of Internet e-mail to customers they are supporting. A separate domain will handle WAN message transfer and will host the GWIA. Another auxiliary domain and server will host WebAccess and the Web server.

From the discussion on Internet addressing in Chapter 16, "Internet Addressing," you can probably guess that All-American Widgets is going to use overrides here. The Salt Lake City users will get a different Internet domain name (probably `user@support.allamericanwidgets.com`) and will use the local GWIA as their default GWIA.

The Remote Sales Offices

There are a couple of good options to handle smaller offices. First, you can place a post office in each location, but place the domain in the corporate office. This would give these users great client/server performance when they are in the office, but would require that somebody at least know how to reboot the server and load the remote console software so that it can be maintained from the corporate office.

A second solution is to put the sales people's mailboxes on post offices in Salt Lake City, Detroit, and/or Newark. These users would use the GroupWise client in caching mode all of the time, which won't be an inconvenience, because caching mode is optimal for users who are also on the road. This second solution is more ideal.

System Administration

With corporate headquarters in Newark, it makes sense that system administration is done from there. On a system of this size, you probably want to have a primary domain that does not own post offices. This means adding another server, and another domain, to the Newark site. You do not necessarily have to dedicate a server just for the primary domain, but it does help that the primary domain functions primarily as the GroupWise Directory Services relay location. In a GroupWise system, all updates to the GroupWise directory must replicate through the primary domain. There is no way to offload or load-balance the primary domain's job. Because of this, it's best that the primary domain have no other functions, such as servicing a post office, or a gateway, or even links between domains. In this perfect-world scenario, the primary domain will have mesh links to all other Newark domains, and nothing else to do but replicate GroupWise Directory Services administrative messages. It will connect indirectly to domains in Detroit and Salt Lake City via the routing domain that owns the GWIA.

Now you see why it's best to plan ahead. When you create a GroupWise system, the first thing you do is create the primary domain. But you cannot know where the primary domain is going until after you have the rest of the system plotted out.

Planning Your GroupWise System

Now you know the principles involved and you've looked at how they applied to a fairly large (hypothetical) organization. You are ready to begin planning your system.

Here are the common steps to use when planning your GroupWise system:

1. First, identify how many users you are going to be providing services for. Does everyone have a computer? Will everyone get an account, regardless of whether they have a computer?
2. Divide your user base into groups, based on your network topology first, and then on their departmental or workgroup affiliations. If you have a department with users in two different remote sites, those users probably get grouped separately.
3. Take these groups of users and divide them into post offices of between 400 and 2,000 users. If you plan to put anywhere between 1,000–2,000 users on a single post office, plan to spend top-dollar on file-server hardware, and be prepared for backups to take a while. Also if you plan on putting more than 1,000 users on a post office, it

is highly recommended that the users in this post office run in cache mode. This is a must in order to support this number of users in a single post office.

4. You should now have a list of post offices, and a rough list of which users belong to them. You are ready to begin assigning domains. On LANs, one domain can serve at least 10 post offices. For systems of more than 2,500 users, though, I recommend at least three domains: one primary domain, one post office domain, and one gateway domain.

5. Determine where your LANs interface with WANs. Plan for a routing domain at each of these locations.

6. Begin drawing the links, and compare this to a map of your networks. Make sure that it makes sense. Remember, your network links should follow your WAN topology. If a packet moving from site A to site C must be transferred across a T1 line to site B, and then across a 56Kbps line to Site C, you will want to have three domains involved, one at each site.

7. Plan your gateways and assign them to domains accordingly. The most important of these is the GWIA. Make sure that you know which domain it is going to belong to, and where it is going to reside. Know what the foreign ID is (your Internet domain name).

8. The WebAccess application should be running on a server that is dedicated to just run the Web server and the WebAccess application. Multiple WebAccess agents should be running throughout your system. Those agents can be running on the same servers as the post offices. If WebAccess agents that are running in protected memory abend, no harm is done to the server.

9. Now begin assigning names. Remember the discussion on naming conventions in Chapter 16. Post office and domain names should have numerical characters in them to unquestionably distinguish them from usernames. Try to keep names of domains and post offices short. This will make things simpler to manage.

10. Draw the system, complete with names, links, and user groups. Sleep on it. Run it by your boss. If you are the boss, run it by your spouse, significant other, fishing buddies, evil minions, or trusted lieutenants. Invite commentary and criticism. Listen.

11. Develop a standard for ports. This should include Message Transfer Ports (MTP) for Message Transfer Agents (MTAs) and Post Office Agents (POAs), as well as client/server ports for POAs. Also include

live remote ports for MTAs and plan for HTTP ports for all agents. An example of this is to have all client/server ports end in 7, such as 1667, 1677, 1687, and so on. If you ever have two post offices on the same server, you already know which client/server ports they will be using. HTTP ports could end in 1, for example 1671, 1681. An example of MTA MTP ports might be that they all end in 0, as in 7100, 7110, 7120, and so on. Make all POA MTP ports end in 1, as in 1661, 1671, 1681, and so on. It is nice to have a standard document in relation to all the GroupWise ports that are involved in a GroupWise system. Table 19.1 represents this type of port-numbering scheme.

TABLE 19.1

Example Port Number Scheme for GroupWise Agents

AGENT	MTP PORT	HTTP PORT	C/S PORT	POP PORT	IMAP PORT	CAP PORT	WEBACCESS PORT	MTA LIVE REMOTE
MTA	7100, 7200	7101, 7201						7107, 7207
POA	1670, 1680	1671, 1681	1677, 1687		143	1026		
WebAccess		7211, 7311					7205, 7305	
GWIA		9850		110/ 995	143/ 993			

Now that you have the basics of your GroupWise system design down, there are some other issues that you must deal with, particularly issues that affect data management.

Chapter 25, "Configuring a SPAM/Junk Mail Control Solution," discusses configuring GroupWise for SPAM control. You must have a SPAM solution in place.

Post Office Configuration

Most of what goes on in a GroupWise system also goes on at the post office. If you configure your GroupWise post offices correctly, your users will be far more satisfied with GroupWise.

E-mail Policies

E-mail policies might not seem technical, but they affect how you are going to configure elements of your post office. Your organization should have an e-mail policy that establishes rules such as the following:

- How long messages can be retained
- Whether users have disk space limits on their mailboxes
- The size of attachments that users can send within your organization and on the Internet
- Whether users can archive their mail messages
- Whether users can use POP3, IMAP4, or NNTP
- Whether users can share address books or folders with users outside their post office
- Whether users can send messages via S/MIME or PGP

By establishing an e-mail policy, the GroupWise administrator can do the following:

- Set GroupWise client options to mirror e-mail policies
- Do a better job of projecting the need for hardware resources
- Design the GroupWise GWIA to disallow huge-bandwidth-consuming attachments going on the Internet
- Set size restrictions on internal GroupWise links if needed
- Run reports to see who is hogging disk space, and encourage the abusers to delete certain sent- or received-mail items
- Automatically encourage users to curtail retaining too many messages

TIP

Even if your organization will allow users to retain messages for a long time, I strongly advise that your organization create a large-file-attachment policy. With GroupWise 6.5, you can control attachment size, right down to the post office level. So for example, you might decide that users cannot send files over 25MB. Furthermore, you could have a policy that requires that all files over 10MB be saved or deleted within seven days of receipt. To control attachment sizes, go into ConsoleOne, highlight a domain or post office, and choose Tools, GroupWise Utilities, Client Options, Send, Disk Space Mgmt. You can also control attachment size through Link Configuration. The difference in these two approaches is how the user is notified of the problem. When you use the client option, users get a notice when they click Send that the attachment is too large. When using link configuration, the user can send the message, but as soon as the messages hits

an agent (POA or MTA) that has a link configuration size limit imposed, this agent sends back an undeliverable message to the sender, letting them know that their message could not be sent because of the size limit.

E-mail policies have a important effect upon performance and server design.

Post Office Design

This section offers a few tips to consider when designing post offices for your GroupWise system.

When and Where to Create a Post Office

Every GroupWise post office has a certain amount of cost associated with its maintenance. A GroupWise post office will generally reside on a server by itself; that server should have a high-quality disk subsystem and be made by a reputable hardware manufacturer. A backup solution should also be implemented for this server.

It is best to create GroupWise post offices only when it is really warranted. In the past, GroupWise administrators often had to make small post offices to service regional sites. With the advancements of the GroupWise 6.5 WebAccess, and the GroupWise 6.5 client in caching mode, it's feasible to move users from small regional post offices into centralized post offices.

Where to Place Post Offices in eDirectory

When a user logs into GroupWise and if the NetWare client is loaded, GroupWise will look in eDirectory to discover information about the user's post office and POA. Because of this, it is best to put the GroupWise post office object in proximity to the users associated with the post office. If the users associated with a post office are in multiple eDirectory contexts, place their post office in an eDirectory Organizational Unit (OU) that is in the same replica as the majority of the users on the post office. Users should have browse, read, and compare rights to the post office object, as well as the POA associated with the post office.

NOTE

If you have LDAP authentication enabled, the Novell client is not used to query eDirectory, so these rules no longer apply. LDAP authentication effectively gives you more flexibility in designing the placement of your GroupWise post office objects in the eDirectory tree.

How Many Users to Place in a Post Office

If you have a good server and a fast network, GroupWise can scale nicely. The online client/server mode of the GroupWise client can be taxing on the server when a post office has several power GroupWise users. A GroupWise post office can easily sustain thousands of mailboxes; it's the number of users logged in at the same time that scale back the practical numbers of users on a post office. Take a close look at whether it is feasible to move to a distributed processing model; by using the GroupWise 6.5 client in caching mode, the GroupWise client is far less chatty and taxing on the GroupWise POA. The downside to caching mode is that users need enough disk space to accommodate a complete copy of the items in their master mailboxes on the server.

Other factors need to be considered when determining the number of users per server. For example, does your organization have an e-mail retention/expiration policy? If not, the message store is bound to grow and grow. Your servers might not have enough disk space to accommodate a message store for 1,000 users that just keeps growing. GroupWise is very efficient on disk space, but let's face it, e-mail is the layman's FTP utility. When considering post offices, think about the people who will be on the post office and what their job functions are. Marketing departments are likely to have lots of presentation files. Engineering might have CAD files. Therefore, you might want to put only 250 of these kinds of employees on a post office. Production people might not deal with attachments at all, so perhaps you could put 750 of them on a single post office.

Multiple Post Offices on a Server

This is a subject that somehow stirs strong emotions among GroupWise specialists. GroupWise is flexible enough to allow more than one GroupWise post office to reside on a server. Many customers have experienced plenty of success with more than one post office on a server. Others have not had success using this model. Success or failure often comes down to usage patterns. If you have two 700-user post offices full of power GroupWise users on one server in client/server mode, you might have performance problems. When two GroupWise POAs are loaded on a server, they are not cognizant of each other, and they have a tendency to hog the CPU if they feel they must do so. The result is that, at certain times, one of the POAs will not have the CPU time that it might need to adequately service users.

The GroupWise product suite is getting even more robust, with features such as document management and increased third-party integration. Because of this, users are more and more likely to be using GroupWise. This is good—productivity is going up. Just make sure that having two post offices on a server is not degrading the potential for good productivity.

Configuring the POA Object for Optimum Performance and Functionality

This section discusses some settings and their relationship to a successful POA configuration. If a setting has no bearing on regular performance or function in the GroupWise system, it is not mentioned.

Agent Settings Property Page

The Agents Settings property page is shown in Figure 19.1. The Agent Settings property page is where you fine-tune the POA.

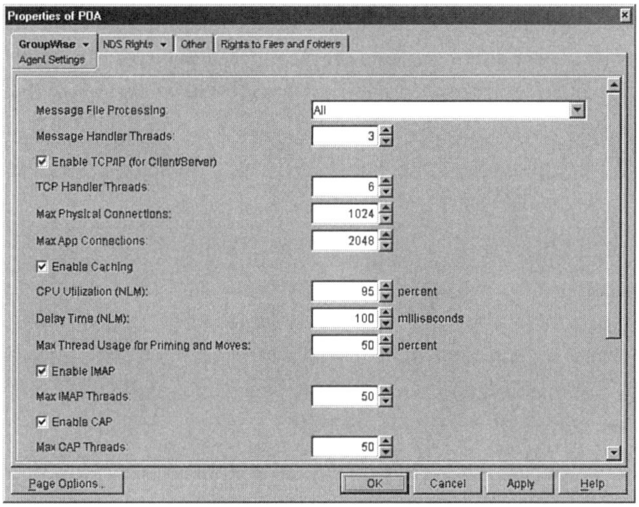

FIGURE 19.1
The POA Agent Settings property page allows you to fine-tune the POA.

Following are the parameters on the Agent Settings property page:

- **Message File Processing:** This should be set to All. In some cases, a GroupWise POA will be created for QuickFinder indexing. That POA would have message file processing set to Off. Don't set this to Low or High; if you do so, the POA will stop processing items in some of its queues.
- **Message Handler Threads:** Message handler threads should be set to about half the value of the TCP handler threads. If you have 16 TCP handler threads, the message handler threads should be set to 8.

- **Enable TCP/IP (for Client/Server):** Yep, you want this enabled for sure.
- **TCP Handler Threads:** This is a simple formula, as follows:

  A = Number of users

  B = The number of TCP handler threads that the POA should have allocated. The minimum value for B, though, should not go below six.

  B = A/25

  So if a post office has 400 users, the POA should be configured with 16 TCP handler threads. If a post office has 50 users, the post office should have six threads, not two. The POA should not be configured with less than six TCP handler threads.

  If your post office supports a significant number of users of a WAN link, even in Caching mode, you might want to monitor your TCP handler threads. You might need to increase the TCP handler threads to accommodate TCP connections that persist for a longer period of time
- **Max Physical Connections:** Allocate two physical connections per user. This is generally plenty. Setting this value to four per user is not going to cause any problems either. Just don't set it to some astronomical number, which chews up more memory than necessary.
- **Max App Connections:** Allocate at least four application connections for each member of the post office. More is fine, but much more is not necessary. This is one of those situations where not enough is bad, more than enough is fine, and much more than enough is not needed or helpful.
- **Enable Caching:** Caching mode can significantly improve POA performance. This setting allows the POA to cache various databases in server memory. The NGWGUARD.DB file is almost always a database that gets cached. The only time you should disable caching here is if your server is very unstable.

  Don't confuse this setting with the GroupWise client in Cache mode. This setting has nothing to do with whether or not users can use the client in cache mode.
- **CPU Utilization:** I personally like to set this to 90 to 95%. If the server crosses the CPU utilization threshold, it will not allocate more threads until the POA is below the threshold. If your POA is on a NetWare, 95% is generally fine. The beauty of NetWare is that it uses the CPU very efficiently and can regularly spike in the 90s without

users feeling any effect. Because GroupWise is mission-critical, it should get priority processing—greater than the default 85%. Having the value at 85% will probably be fine also, but likely should be the bottom threshold. I don't generally recommend going below 85%.

- **Delay Time:** The delay time correlates with the CPU utilization option. If the CPU utilization threshold has been exceeded, the delay time is the amount of the time the POA's NLM will wait before trying to get another thread, if needed. The default of 100 milliseconds is generally more than enough.
- **Max Thread Usage for Priming and Moves:** The default of 20 is pretty low. I personally like to set this to 50%.
- **Enable IMAP:** This is a new feature to the GroupWise 6.5 POA. Finally, your Outlook and other IMAP client users can have a client/server-based connection with a GroupWise POA. I would recommend that if you allow your MS-Outlook on user's desktops, you have a good virus-protection solution in place. A post office-based virus-scanning solution such as GWAVA (`www.gwava.com`) is a cost-effective solution to combat Microsoft Outlook–based viruses.
- **Max IMAP Threads:** The default is set at 50. That might seem high, and it is if you just have a few IMAP users. But if you have several users, 50 or more will be necessary. IMAP connections have more overhead because they are standards based, rather than proprietary. So the POA must accommodate inefficiencies in the IMAP protocol.
- **Enable SNMP:** If you are not using SNMP monitoring, turn this off. It saves a little overhead. The GroupWise monitor piece is an SNMP monitoring device, so if you intend to use GroupWise monitor, do not turn this off.
- **HTTP User Name and Password:** You definitely want to set an HTTP username for your GroupWise POA's HTTP monitoring feature. There are powerful actions that you can take from the POA's HTTP monitoring screen; you want to make sure that HTTP monitoring is secured.

Network Address Property Page

Not all of these settings necessarily affect the performance of the POA, but they do enable features that are important when monitoring your POA and extending its capabilities.

- **TCP/IP Address:** The TCP/IP address can be an IP address or a DNS name. The advantage to a DNS name is that if at some time the IP address changes for a post office, the change simply needs to be made in the DNS. This change is transparent to the users.

- **Proxy Server Address:** You can define a public IP address as the proxy IP address for the post office. This proxy server address is not bound to the server where the POA is; it is bound to a "proxy server" that's accessible from the Internet. The proxy server performs Network Address Translation (NAT) services from the public IP address and port to the internal IP address and port of the POA. This enables your remote and cache users to connect to the POA using the full GroupWise client from anywhere they have an Internet connection. They do not need to VPN in to your network first.
- **Message Transfer Port:** Domain MTA to post office POA communication can be configured in two manners—using UNC or TCP/IP. The UNC method is one in which the MTA moves files to the WPCSOUT queues off of a post office. Also, in UNC mode, the MTA fetches messages from a post office using a polling cycle. The POA looks in the WPCSOUT queues periodically to determine whether anything needs to be processed. The polling process is far less efficient, because the MTA and the POA are not really talking to each other; they are just dropping things off in queues. Each agent knows the other will look at the queues eventually.

  TCP/IP communication between the MTA and the POA is optimal. When a POA has something for the MTA, it hands it right to the MTA, and the MTA acts on the item immediately. It's the same when the MTA needs to give something to the POA. Quick handoffs are particularly helpful in time-sensitive functions. For example, when a user does a busy search on the calendar of a user on another post office, the busy search must pass from the POA to the MTA. Because the POA speaks directly to the MTA rather than placing the busy search request in a queue, the end-user has a far more interactive experience with the busy search. Even if a domain and post office are on the same server, it is still optimal to configure the post office and domain to communicate via TCP/IP.

  The message transfer port (MTP) is the IP port that the POA listens on for messages from the parent MTA of the post office. The MTP port should be different from the HTTP port and the client/server port.
- **HTTP Port:** The HTTP port on the POA should be filled in. This enables the POA to be monitored from a Web browser. There is some information that is available from the HTTP monitoring of the POA that is not available from the POA's console screen, such as the names

of users who are logged into the POA or the version of GroupWise client that they are using. Even if you have the `/HTTP` switches in the startup file of the POA, you still should fill in the HTTP port here. The GroupWise Monitor program discovers the HTTP port of the POA from this field.

- **HTTP SSL:** If you intend to monitor your POA via a Web browser across the Internet, you will want to use this option for security reasons. Enabling SSL is covered on Chapter 27, "Securing Your GroupWise System via SSL."
- **Local Intranet Client/Server Port:** It's important that the POA is listening on a unique client/server port. The port used doesn't matter as long as it's unique. The default port is 1677.
- **Internet Proxy Client/Server Port:** The internet proxy client/server port is new with GroupWise 6.5 support pack one (6.5.1). This port allows you to use the same proxy server address for all of your POAs in your GroupWise system. This is helpful because the proxy server address should be a public IP address. This Internet proxy client/server port can then be used to uniquely identify each post office in your system, which facilitates all user access to their post office through a single public IP address (the proxy server address). If your proxy server address is the same for all post offices, it is important that each POA have a unique Internet proxy client/server port defined.

  It is also important to note here that there is some additional configuration to make the proxy server address and Internet proxy client/server port to function. You must bind the proxy server address to a Layer 4 switch or some device that supports address translation (NAT), and possibly port address translation (PAT). This device must be accessible from the Internet. The device is then configured to translate the data that hits the proxy server address on a particular port (the Internet proxy client/server port) into the internal address *and* port of the correct POA.
- **IMAP Port:** Most likely you will want to keep the default port (143). IMAP clients look for an IMAP server connection on port 143 by default.
- **CAP Port:** Most likely you will want to keep the default port, which is 1026. CAP clients look for a CAP server connection on port 1026 by default. CAP allows a client to access a calendar much like a client can access their mailbox through the IMAP protocol. As of the writing of this book, there are few, if any, CAP-compliant clients on the market. GroupWise is ready to support CAP when there are clients that also support CAP.

Once you have configured your POA's ports, be judicious about making any changes. The changes are likely to affect users who connect to this post office.

QuickFinder Property Page

Let's look at how QuickFinder Indexing can affect the performance of your POA:

- **Enabled QuickFinder Indexing:** Make sure this option is checked. QuickFinder indexing is critical to GroupWise performance. If you turn this feature off, your post office will slowly experience more and more utilization, because the POA will have to perform real-time QuickFinder indexing operations whenever users use the Find feature in GroupWise.
- **Start QuickFinder Indexing Hours—Minutes:** This value should be set to however many hours after midnight that you want the QuickFinder indexing to occur. In most cases you want this process to happen after hours, as it can be a CPU-intensive process. Setting the value to 22 hours and 0 minutes causes QuickFinder indexing to start at 10:00 p.m. each night. Setting the value to 0 hours and 30 minutes causes QuickFinder indexing to start at 12:30 in the morning (30 minutes after midnight).
- **QuickFinder Interval:** In most customer environments, the QuickFinder indexing should happen once every 24 hours and 0 minutes. I recommend you keep this default unless you have a legitimate reason to change it.

It's important that you have QuickFinder tuned, and always enabled.

Maintenance Property Page

Following is a discussion of the Maintenance Property Page:

- **Enable Automatic Database Recovery:** If the POA discovers damage in a message-store database, having this option enabled allows the POA to kick off an immediate `GWCHECK` on the database.
- **Maintenance Handler Threads:** The default is 4, and the most you can specify is 8. You can get yourself into real trouble if you set the maintenance handler threads to 8, and then issue a post office-wide mailbox/library maintenance in the middle of the day. I did this once, and the maintenance handler threads were in a tug of war with the message handler threads to get access to the message store databases on the post office. So it's probably best to set this value to 4. If you

then need more power for mailbox/library maintenance after hours, crank this up to 8. You do not have to restart the POA when you change this setting, the POA will dynamically reread this setting. This gives you easy control over this feature.

- **Perform User Upkeep:** This should definitely be enabled. The Perform User Upkeep option performs seven tasks:
  - Advances uncompleted tasks to the next day.
  - Deletes expired items from users' mailboxes.
  - Deletes mail, appointments, tasks, and notes that are older than what's defined in the "client options" section.
  - Empties the trash based on client cleanup options
  - Synchronizes users' frequent contacts books with the system's address book
  - Clean Address Book Indexes
  - Expire References from the document folder

NOTE

When the POA actually executes the Perform User Upkeep code, the upkeep happens in two passes. In the first pass, the POA advances uncompleted tasks, and synchronizes users' frequent contacts books with the system address book. In the second pass, the POA deletes expired items from users' mailboxes, cleans address book indexes, and expires invalid references from the document folder (if you are using GroupWise document management).

- **Start User Upkeep:** Start User Upkeep should always be set to sometime after midnight to be effective. The Start User Upkeep option determines when the user-upkeep tasks occur. If you enable user upkeep to occur before midnight, it will not advance task items to the next day. If task items aren't advanced to the next day, the client's load-up time takes longer when the users log in the next day.
- **Generate Address Book for Remote:** You should definitely enable this setting. A better description for this is "Generate Address Book for Caching and Remote." If you have caching or remote mode users you definitely want to enable this setting. This process creates a file called WPROF50.DB in the `<post office>\WPCSOUT\OFS` directory. This file is then used when users request the system address book while in caching or remote mode. If the WPROF50.DB file is more than 24 hours old (which happens only if you do not have this setting checked), the POA will create it again on the fly. Generating this file is a CPU-intensive task, so it is best to create it after hours.

- **Start Address Book Generation:** Set this option to some time after business hours.
- **Disk Check Interval:** Enable this to occur every five minutes.

  The Disk Check Interval value corresponds with any disk check event that you have defined in scheduled events on the POA. The POA looks at the scheduled disk check events. The POA takes the appropriate action specified in the disk check events, if the disk space threshold has been crossed.
- **Disk Check Delay:** Leave this at two hours. If the POA has discovered that disk space is low, it won't take the actions in the disk check event until two hours have passed. This gives you a chance to respond to the low disk space problem.

Make sure that Perform User Upkeep is always enabled.

Log Settings Property Page

- **Log File Path:** Just keep this value blank. The POA will create the files in the `<post office>\WPCSOUT\OFS` directory.
- **Logging Level:** The Verbose setting is tremendously helpful when troubleshooting.
- **Max Log File Age:** The default of seven days is generally sufficient.
- **Max Log Disk Space:** The default of 65MB might not be enough. Crank this up as high as it will go if you have the space. This setting will go up to 1GB. You can then generally go back into the logs for several days in order to find information. The POA logs information such as what users deleted because of the junk-mail feature.

  Having this information for a few days is good. If someone mentions that he/she didn't get a message from someone on the Internet, you can search the logs of the POA and determine whether the message was junked by the recipient's junk-mail rules.

NOTE

The Max Log File Age and the Max Log Disk Space settings work together. If your log files can grow to 50MB, but you are storing only seven days worth of logs, this means that even if your logs only are taking up 20MB, they will be deleted after the seven days. Conversely, if the log disk space is reached, but logs are only five days old, the oldest log files will be deleted to make room for new log files. Also note that the Max Log Disk Space is cumulative of all the post office logs; it does not reflect how large one log file is. The POA cycles into the next POA log file when it reaches 1MB, or at midnight.

Log settings don't always have a direct impact on performance, but having correct log settings is very important for troubleshooting purposes.

Scheduled Events Property Page

Chapter 17, "Maintaining the GroupWise System," explains scheduled events, and how to construct them. You definitely want to enable scheduled events for mailbox/library maintenance events. Chapter 17 does not discuss disk space scheduled events though; that information is covered here instead.

If you left your Disk Check interval set at five minutes back on the Maintenance property page, a disk check event is spawned every five minutes. Also, the disk check event is defined on the Scheduled Events property page. Think this through for a moment. When do you want the red flag waved that disk space is low on a post office? I personally would like to be notified when 30% of my disk space is remaining. Here's what you do to create a notification mechanism that tells you when a volume that houses a GroupWise post office has dropped below 30%:

1. Make sure that the POA has the Disk Check interval set at a reasonable disk check number, such as five minutes.

   The Disk Check interval is a setting on the POA's Maintenance property page. Make sure that the Disk Check Delay setting is set at two hours, or some other value that you think is good enough. The Disk Check Delay option means that, when the POA has hit the trigger to start the action on the disk check event mentioned in the next step, it will wait another two hours before it kicks off the disk check event.
2. Go to the POA's Scheduled Events property page and create a new scheduled event or edit the Default POA Disk Check Event option that ships with GroupWise.
3. To edit the disk check event, make sure that the following settings are in place:
   - **Type:** Disk check
   - **Trigger:** 30%; don't use the "Stop mail processing" at option
4. To create an action for the scheduled event, do the following:
   a. Click the Create button.
   b. Give the action a name in the Name field.
   c. In the Action drop-down box, select Expire/Reduce Messages.

d. Enable the Reduce only check box, as well as the User and Message check boxes under the Databases tab.

e. Click the Results tab, and make sure that the results are sent to the administrator. You can also CC yourself if you are not defined at the administrator for the domain that owns this post office.

f. Click the Message button on the Results tab and compose a message that says something like, `"The post office has dropped below 30% in disk space; you will receive a message every two hours until this problem is resolved."`

5. Make sure that someone is defined as an administrator for the domain that owns the post office for which you are activating this disk check event.

   This person will get the message regarding low disk space. It's generally best to make the administrator a dummy user with rules that forward messages to several people in your IS department.

Now you have a low-tech mechanism for determining if the volume that houses GroupWise is running low on disk space.

Configuring the Post Office Object for Optimum Performance and Functionality

This section discusses some settings and their relationship to a successful post office configuration. If a setting has no bearing on performance or function in the GroupWise system, it is not mentioned.

Post Office Settings Property Page

Figure 19.2 shows the Post Office Settings property page.

Following are settings you can configure on the Post Office Settings property page:

- **Software Distribution Directory:** Chapter 12, "Administering the GroupWise Client," discussed the software distribution directory. The value you fill in here is important, but see Chapter 12 for a full explanation of the software distribution directory.
- **Access Mode:** This should be set to client/server only. Don't allow users to connect directly to the post office via a UNC connection, as this will open the message store to a much higher likelihood of corruption.

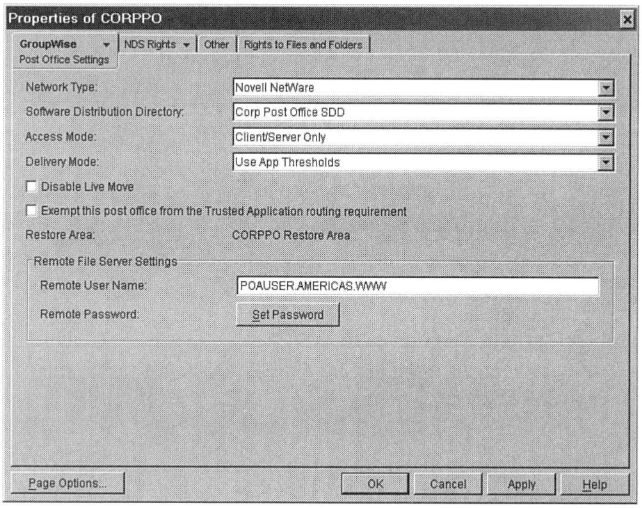

FIGURE 19.2
The Post Office Settings property page.

- **Disable Live Move:** Don't check this option unless you have good reason to do so. Live move is used when moving users. Live move is explained in more detail in Chapter 13, "Moving Users."

Client Access Settings Property Page

This one simple setting that most customers will want to enable:

- **Enable Intruder Detection:** You should enable this option.

NOTE

You can enable these settings anytime, and the POA will dynamically pick up the changes and apply them. You do not need to shut down the POA and restart it.

Security Property Page

This section offers a brief discussion of the most critical element of the Security property page.

For the Security level option, you want it set to high, with either the LDAP or eDirectory Authentication option checked. If you have users who do not have the Novell client installed, make sure the users have a password on a GroupWise account, or you'll need to enable LDAP authentication. The whole idea is that if the security level is high, GroupWise needs users to authenticate through a password-authentication process. The authentication will either be before the GroupWise client is started, which is the case with eDirectory authentication, or at the time GroupWise is loaded, which is the case with LDAP authentication or a GroupWise password.

With LDAP authentication enabled, if a user does not have the Novell client, or a user is using GroupWise WebAccess through a Web browser, the user can still use an eDirectory password. The POA will query eDirectory via LDAP in behalf of the user. Your implementation of eDirectory must be version 8.5 or better, with LDAP services enabled and configured. Chapter 26, "Configuring GroupWise Authentication via LDAP," discusses enabling LDAP authentication, the best authentication solution.

Default WebAccess Property Page

The idea of a default WebAccess is important to the performance of WebAccess. But it's way too much to explain in this chapter; read Chapter 11, "Configuring GroupWise WebAccess," for more information.

Configuring the GroupWise Client Options for Optimum Performance and Functionality

The GroupWise client comes with a bunch of settings. Your organization might want to control some of these settings so that your e-mail system is accomplishing its purposes.

GroupWise allows you to set client preferences and control features available to GroupWise clients. These preferences can be set at a domain level and excluded right down to a user level. There are a few features that, if used incorrectly, can generate more traffic in your system than you might want. Here are three client preferences to pay particular attention to:

- Wildcard addressing
- Status tracking
- Junk-mail handling

The client preferences can be modified in ConsoleOne by selecting a domain, post office, or user object and choosing Tools, GroupWise Utilities, Client Options.

Following is a discussion of the client preferences that affect performance:

- **Wildcard addressing:** Wildcard addressing is a great feature. With wildcard addressing, a user can send a message to all the recipients in a post office (that's the default), a domain, or even the GroupWise system and beyond that. The question then is do you really want your users to have that kind of power? You can turn off all users' capability to use wildcard addressing at the post office level. Then for those users who should be allowed this functionality, you can enable it individually. You can configure Wildcard addressing in ConsoleOne under Tools, GroupWise Utilities, Client Options, Send.

- **Status Tracking:** GroupWise has a great feature called status tracking. You can determine whether a message got to its recipient, and you can see when the recipient opened the message. Status tracking sets GroupWise apart from other groupware packages. Status tracking can be taken to the extreme, though. If your GroupWise system's client options for status tracking is set to all information, you will be generating a tremendous amount of data that does not need to be tracked. By requiring the GroupWise system to track all information, you impact the following:
    - GroupWise caching and remote users' downloads and uploads take longer.
    - When a user purges a large amount of messages from the trash, a tremendous amount of disk I/O is created.
    - Status messages are generated for just about every action to a message item, and rarely do people need that information.
    - Most customers will not want to enable all information. Check to see that this is not enabled somehow. Many customers will want to lock this feature down so that end-users cannot change the option to all information.

TIP

It's helpful to simply browse through the client options and think about what settings you might want to configure or even which features you might want to turn off.

Now that I've told you all the evils of using too much status tracking, let's consider a different perspective. If your post office is using caching mode, it can be very helpful from a troubleshooting standpoint for you to set the status tracking to all, and then lock it. This will force this option to take effect on all user's mailboxes and caching mailboxes. For troubleshooting purposes, the status tracking can be invaluable. With the All Information option enabled, you can see when a user's caching or remote mode client actually downloaded the message.

Tuning the NetWare Server for Optimum Performance and Functionality

Most customers have their GroupWise post offices on NetWare servers because of NetWare's prowess in file caching. This section focuses on fine-tuning your NetWare server for optimum performance.

- **GroupWise Only Volume:** When you place a GroupWise post office on a file server, it is best to create a volume that will only house the GroupWise post office. This just makes managing e-mail simpler; for example, you'll have a good picture of just how much disk space is being taken on a post office.
- **Compression:** Do not enable compression on the NetWare volume dedicated for GroupWise. GroupWise already compresses the message store, and does so even better than NetWare does. It's redundant effort on the part of the NetWare operating system to try to compress files in the GroupWise message store.
- **Immediate Purge:** GroupWise deals with a whole lot of files passing through queues off of the `WPCSOUT` and `WPCSIN` directories. Set these directories so that they are purged immediately. This allows the NetWare server to free up memory resources to optimize other parts of the NetWare server.
- **Server Set Parameters:** The syntax on these settings has been confirmed for NetWare 4.x through NetWare 6.0. The values here are the minimum; if you currently have your NetWare server tuned to use higher or faster values, you don't need to decrease the values.

  The STARTUP.NCF file should have the following set parameters in it:

  ```
  Set TCP defend land attack = off

  Set minimum packet receive buffers = 2000
  ```

  The AUTOEXEC.NCF file should have the following set parameters included in it:

  ```
  Set read ahead LRU sitting time threshold = 60
  Set maximum file locks = 20000
  Set minimum service processes = 100
  Set maximum service processes = 1000
  Set new service process wait time = 0.3
  Set maximum packet receive buffers = 5000
  Set new packet receive buffer wait time = 0.1
  ```

These set parameters will ensure that your server is more responsive than it would be otherwise.

Best Practices

What I really want to do here is encourage you to design your system on paper rather than in stone. Once you have created domains and named them, you cannot go back without starting over. Once users have mailboxes in one place, it is extremely tedious to move them to another place. It is especially annoying when you have to do this because your boss does not like the name of the post office, but more often than not I see this being done because post offices were too large to begin with.

Summary

Post office design is the biggest contributor to the success of your GroupWise system. There are many aspects to good post office design, namely the following:

- E-mail policies
- POA configuration
- Post office configuration
- GroupWise client option configuration
- Server configuration

CHAPTER 20

Troubleshooting Message Flow

This chapter explores GroupWise message flow in great detail. You get to look at the processes and store files involved in message creation, as well as the replication and transfer of messages between post offices.

The goal of this chapter is to enable you to troubleshoot GroupWise message flow through an understanding of the complete *signal path* for GroupWise messages.

Understanding Message Flow at the Database Level

To begin with, here is a look at the store files. When a user creates a message, one or more GroupWise information store files are written to. The particulars depend on the type of message. This section explores message flow using a few scenarios.

Each of the scenarios in this chapter follows the actions of USERA. USERA's GroupWise file ID (FID) is 123. Based on this FID, USERA is assigned to place all sent items in MSG17.DB.

GroupWise Information Store Concepts

Before proceeding, let's review some of the information store concepts. Most of this information is explained in Chapter 4, "Understanding the GroupWise Information Store," but for clarity's sake, this chapter reviews it.

GroupWise information (messages, address book info, rules, folders, and so on) is contained in the information store, which is composed of individual databases (also called store files). GroupWise information store databases are contained in each post office's `OFUSER` and `OFMSG` directories.

Databases are composed of records. Every record has a particular set of fields based upon the record type. Some GroupWise fields can exceed 2KB. Fields that do exceed 2KB are called external BLOB (binary large object) files. BLOB files are contained in the `post office\OFFILES\x` directories.

Every item in GroupWise—whether it is a mail message, a task, a document, or anything else that can be displayed in a user's mailbox—is just a record in a GroupWise information store database. Whenever a field within a record exceeds 2KB, that field is spun off to its own BLOB file outside of the database.

The User Database: USERxxx.DB

You might recall from Chapter 4 that every user has a user database. This file is named `USERxxx.DB`, where the *xxx* is replaced with the user's three-character file ID.

The easiest way to explain the user database file is that it is largely a pointer database. When `USERA` gets a message from `USERB`, the message isn't actually contained in `USER123.DB`. The message is contained in one of the message databases. A pointer to that message is created in the `USER123.DB` file.

The user database does contain records that represent complete items, however. For example, a user's folders and a user's personal calendar items are wholly contained in the `USERxxx.DB` file. Everything that you see from the GroupWise client is coming from the user database. You will never look at anything that is exclusively stored in the message database from the GroupWise client. Most of the items you see from the client are simply pointers to the full message in the message databases.

The Message Database: MSGn.DB

Every post office has 25 message databases, numbered `MSG0.DB` through `MSG24.DB`. All messages sent between users in a GroupWise post office are contained in one of the `MSGn.DB` files.

Group Items Versus Personal Items

When a user receives an e-mail message or an appointment, task, or note, that item is considered to be a *group item*. When a user creates an item in the calendar without sending it (that is, the item has no TO line), this is a *personal item*, also known as a *posted item*.

Message "Body" Parts

A GroupWise item is not just one record in a database. There are distinct body parts on a GroupWise message, and every body part has its own record.

Every GroupWise mail message has a handful of body parts and records. The *master record* and the *message properties record* are always present on group items (items that one user sends to another user).

The following explains the different types of body parts in a typical GroupWise message.

- **Master record:** The master record contains fields such as TO, CC, BC, and Subject. The master record also keeps track of all of the other records associated with the original message. If the TO, CC, and BC lines contain more than 2,048 bytes of data, the master record relies on the message properties record to hold the entire contents of the TO, CC, BC, and Subject lines.
- **Message properties record:** The message properties record shows the properties page of a message. If the contents of this record exceed 2KB (this happens often when sending to distribution lists), only the header of this record is kept in the `MSGn.DB` file. The remainder is spun off into a BLOB file in the `OFFILES` directory. Because the message properties record must contain the recipient list of the TO, CC, and BC lines, it becomes the master list for the TO, CC, and BC lines.
- **Message body record:** This record contains the text and attributes of the GroupWise message's message area. If the message text is more than 2,048 bytes in length, this record will be spun off into a BLOB file in the `OFFILES` directory.
- **Attachment record:** Each attachment has its own record. The attachment file is a field in the attachment record. If the attachment exceeds the 2,048-byte limit of the attachment field, it is spun off into the `OFFILES` directory.

Scenario #1: USERA Creates a Personal (Posted) Calendar Item

`USERA` creates a posted calendar appointment. The subject of the appointment is simply `"Test"`. There is no message body, nor are there any attachments. Here are some observations:

1. GroupWise puts the master record for the appointment in the USER123.DB file.
2. GroupWise creates a message body record for the body of the appointment. This also goes in USER123.DB.
3. A separate alarm record is written to the USER123.DB file. GroupWise Notify reads this alarm record.

NOTE **If an attachment had been made to the appointment, an attachment record will be created.**

Scenario #2: USERA Sends a Message to USERB on the Same PO as USERA

USERA creates a short message with no attachments and sends the message to USERB:

1. USERA's FID is USER123.DB. USERA's message database for outgoing messages is MSG17.DB.
2. GroupWise creates three records in MSG17.DB. In this example, the master record is record #12 in MSG17.DB, the message properties record is record #11 in MSG17.DB, and the message body record is record #13.
3. GroupWise creates a pointer in USER123.DB with a pointer to record #12 in MSG17.DB. GroupWise further indicates that this is a message sent by USERA.
4. GroupWise creates a pointer in USERB's database. USERB's FID is 789, so USERB's user database is USER789.DB. The pointer indicates that this is an inbox item. The pointer also indicates that the record is record #12 in MSG17.DB.
5. GroupWise successfully delivers the message to USERB, so GroupWise creates record #14 in MSG17.DB, which indicates that the message was delivered, and links record #14 to the master record, which is record #12. GroupWise also changes a value in USERA's user database to indicate that the delivery occurred and when it happened.

Here is a look at what happens when USERB opens the message from USERA:

1. GroupWise creates a new record in MSG17.DB, indicating that USERB opened the message.

2. GroupWise changes a value in the pointer record in USERA's user database, indicating that the item was opened and when it was opened.

Understanding Message Flow Outside the Post Office

If a GroupWise message is sent to a user on a different post office, it takes a specific route through file queues on its way to the destination post office. Understanding message flow through a GroupWise system is one of the most valuable troubleshooting tools you'll ever have.

This scenario follows a message from one post office to another. The detail at the message store level is even more explicit than the detail previously described in this chapter.

Scenario #3: Message Flow Between Post Offices

The messages between the post offices flow as follows:

- USERA is a user on PO1, which is a post office in DOMAIN1
- USERB is a user on PO2, which is a post office in DOMAIN1
- USERA's FID is 123
- USERB's FID is 789
- The MSGn.DB file for USERA is MSG17.DB
- All users connect to their post offices in client-server access mode
- PO1 is connected to DOMAIN1's Message Transfer Agent (MTA) via MTP (TCP/IP) between the MTA and the Post Office Agent (POA)
- PO2 is connected to DOMAIN1 via a UNC link

NOTE

I recommend that domain-to-PO connectivity be via TCP/IP; however this scenario uses a UNC connection from a domain to a post office so that you understand the message flow in case you are using a UNC connection.

The message store at PO1: USERA sends a message, with the subject "Test1". It contains a small message body and one attachment over 2KB. The byte size of the file is 93,812. The message is sent to USERB. Here's what happens:

1. The POA on PO1 creates the following records in MSG17.DB:

- A master record, which is record #385 in MSG17.DB.
- The DRN (domain record number), which is a unique identifier for the message 3827C415.FDE. The DRN for any GroupWise message can be viewed from the properties of a message. It will look much like this: `Mail Envelope Properties (3827C415.FDE : 17 : 65002)`.

NOTE **The 3827C415.FDE is the DRN, the 17 is the message database that the users use, and 65002 is a number that uniquely identifies the user. Every sent message that this user sends will have 17:65002 in the Mail Envelope properties.**

- A message properties record, which is record #384 in MSG17.DB.
- A message body record, which is record #382 in MSG17.DB.
- An attachment record, which is record #383 in MSG17.DB.
- A BLOB file called 382761a5.000 for the attachment that is created in the PO1\OFFILES\FD62 directory. The size of the BLOB file is 48,004 bytes. GroupWise compresses and encrypts BLOB files, which is why the file size decreased.

2. The POA also creates a record in PO1\OFUSER\USER123.DB with a pointer to record #385. This user database pointer record contains the following additional information:
   - The DRN for record #385
   - The date and time that the message was sent
   - To whom the message was sent
   - Other status-tracking information as appropriate (delivered, opened, and so on)

3. Now let's see what happens in the file queues at PO1. Because the message is destined for PO2, all records associated with the message having the DRN 3827C415.FDE are packed up into one file and placed in the PO1\WPCSIN\4 directory. The original name of the file is 482761a5.210. The file is 49,760 bytes. Because USERA sent the message with normal priority, it will travel through the 4 directory (where normal priority mail messages always flow).
4. The POA on PO1 transmits the file via TCP/IP to the MTA on its message transfer protocol (MTP) port.

5. Now let's see what happens in the file queues at DOMAIN1. The MTA receives the message on port 7100 and writes the file into the DOMAIN1\MSLOCAL\GWINPROG\4 directory. As the file is being received, it's called XEF34B5F.000. When the file is completely received, the MTA renames the file to 00000859.5P5. The MTA uses what's called an *MTP thread* to receive the message.
6. The MTA's MTP thread tickles the MTA's router thread (RTR) and notifies it about the message in the GWINPROG\4 directory. The router thread looks at the recipient post office for the message and determines that the recipient post office is PO2.

NOTE

The DOMAIN\MSLOCAL\GWINPROG\X directories are *memory queues.* This means that an MTA will fetch files from this directory only when it is prompted to by another subprocess of the MTA. These directories are scanned on startup or restart of the MTA, but that is the only time they get scanned. Sometimes though, you might find files stuck in the GWINPROG\X directories. If this is the case, just put them back into the DOMAIN\WPCSIN\0 directory. If you find a file with an X at the beginning of the filename and it's been there for a long time, don't bother moving the file. It's a casualty of a bad transmission. Just delete the file.

7. The MTA's RTR thread puts the file in the DOMAIN1\MSLOCAL\MSHOLD\PO25B46 directory, which is the FID for PO2.

NOTE

Every GroupWise object has a FID, be it a post office, a domain, or a user. To determine the FID for a post office, view the post office with GroupWise diagnostics and look for the attribute *File ID.*

When in verbose mode, the GroupWise MTA will report the message DRN. In this case, the MTA reported the following:

```
00:24:36 RTR: DOMAIN1: 00000859 Priority 4
3827C415.FDE:17:65002 : Transfer to DOMAIN1.PO2:OFS
```

8. Now let's go to the file queues at PO2. The MTA's RTR thread copies the file to the PO2\WPCSOUT\OFS\4 directory. The name that it gives the file is 482769C4.210. The byte size of the file is 49,820. The size of the file increased a bit from when it was on PO1 because the route the message took to get to PO2 is appended to the message.

NOTE **The WPCSOUT\OFS directories are the input queues for the POA process. Every POA has an FID of OFS, and so the input queue for the POA looks for work to do from the MTA in the WPCSOUT\<POA'S-FID>\X directory. The POA's FID is (or should always be) OFS. On rare occasions, the POA might have a different FID. If you discover this through GroupWise diagnostics, delete the POA and re-create it.**

9. Here's what happens at the message store at PO2. The POA picks up the file in the PO2\WPCSOUT\OFS\4 directory on its scan cycle and processes the file. The POA then commits the message to the message store at PO2.

10. The PO2 POA creates the following records in MSG17.DB:

    - A master record, which is record #4 in MSG17.DB.
    - The DRN for this master record is 3827C415.FDE, just like it was on PO1. When viewing the properties of the message, USERB sees the same DRN as the sender.

      ```
      Mail Envelope Properties  (3827C415.FDE : 17 :
      ➥65002)
      ```

    - A message properties record, which is record #3 in MSG17.DB.
    - A message body record, which is record #1 in MSG17.DB.
    - An attachment record, which is record #2 in MSG17.DB.
    - A BLOB file called 382774cd.000 for the attachment that is created in the PO2\OFFILES\FD62 directory. The size of the BLOB file is 48,004 bytes—the same size of the original file.
    - A status record, which is record #5 in MSG17.DB. The status record indicates that USERB received the message. This status record must be relayed back to PO1, which is coming up in a moment.

11. The PO2 POA creates a record in PO1\OFUSER\USER789.DB with a pointer to record #4. The USER database also indicates the following:

    - The DRN for record #4
    - The date and time that the message was received
    - Who sent the message to USERB

12. Here's what happens in the file queues at PO2. After the POA at PO2 delivered the message to USERB, it created a status message to be sent back to PO1. The status message is placed in the PO2\WPCSIN\5 directory. The name of the file is 582774CD.210. The file is 820 bytes.

NOTE

The WPCSIN directory structure is the input queue for the MTA. The MTA for DOMAIN1 is configured to talk to PO2 via a UNC connection, so the MTA will pick this file up. This is different from an MTP connection in that the POA pushes information from the PO\WPCSIN\X directory up to the MTA. The POA push method through MTP is preferred, however, because it is more efficient.

13. Here's what happens in the file queues at DOMAIN1. The MTA's RTR thread picks up the file from the PO2\WPCSIN\5 directory and places it in the DOMAIN\MSLOCAL\GWINPROG\5 directory. It then routes the file to the DOMAIN\MSLOCAL\MSHOLD\PO15B1E\5. The name of the file is 0000085C.001, and it is 860 bytes.
14. The MTA's router thread tickles the MTP thread and instructs the MTP thread to look in the MSLOCAL\MSHOLD\PO15B1E\5 directory for the file called 0000085C.001 to be processed.

NOTE

The MSLOCAL\MSHOLD queues are largely memory queues. This means that an MTA will fetch files from this directory only when it is given the file's specific name. The MSLOCAL\MSHOLD directories are scanned on startup or restart of the MTA.

15. The MTA's MTP thread transmits the status file to the POA at PO1. The POA's MTP thread (listening on port 7101) receives the status file into its WPCSOUT\OFS\5 directory. The name of the file is 582782F4.210, and it is 860 bytes.
16. The POA picks up the file and creates record #390 in MSG17.DB, linking that record to record #385, which is the original master record for this message.

NOTE

The last record used before the message was transmitted from PO1 to PO2 was #385. The reason the status record was #390 is that other records were written to the MSG17.DB file. GroupWise just picks the next available record number when writing a record into a message database.

Now you know what happens when messages are sent, which will help when troubleshooting message flow, or when trying to determine why you are seeing messages in a certain queue.

Important Architectural Concepts from Scenario #3

The previous section tracked a message as it moved between two post offices on the same domain, exposing most of the architectural methods involved in message delivery:

- Messages are either being submitted to a location or being sent out of a location.
- If the message is being submitted to a location by the MTA, it is placed in a `WPCSOUT\`*<Process-File ID>* directory. This is the MTA's *output* queue.
- If the message is being sent out of a location, it is placed in the `WPCSIN\X` directory. This is the MTA's *input* queue.
- Every message will pass through one of the eight queue directories, numbered 0-7. Here are the purposes of these queues (another review from Chapter 4):

  `0`: Live, interactive request messages (busy searches, remote library queries)

  `1`: Remote user update requests, shared folder, and shared address book replication messages

  `2`: Administration updates and high-priority messages

  `3`: Status messages from high-priority mail

  `4`: Normal-priority messages

  `5`: Status messages from normal-priority messages, mailbox/library maintenance requests

  `6`: Low-priority messages

  `7`: Status messages from low-priority messages

- When messages reach an MTA, the MTA receives the file into the `MSLOCAL\GWINPROG` directories and then places the file into the `MSLOCAL\MSHOLD\`*<Location-File ID>* directory. The file is then either transmitted (MTP via TCP/IP) or placed (UNC connectivity) at the destination. The file is then placed in the directory that corresponds to the FID of the process designed to process the message.
- When a message is sent from one GroupWise post office to the next, the message will retain its DRN, no matter which post office it is sent to. If a message is sent to a gateway, the DRN is taken off by the gateway.
- When a message is sent to more than one GroupWise post office, it is written to the same numbered message database on every post office—this is determined by the sender's FID.
- Elements of a GroupWise message are broken into separate records. Fields of certain record types can exceed 2KB. If a field exceeds 2KB, it becomes its own BLOB file.
- All elements of a GroupWise message are transmitted in one file when sent from one location to the next.

This section was heavily based upon the GroupWise post office message store and flow within the message store.

Scenario #4: Message Flow Between Domains

USER1 on PO1 at DOMAIN1 sends a message to USER2 on PO2 at DOMAIN2. Here's the file flow. This scenario follows this message all the way to PO2 and then follows the status message back to PO1. This scenario does not focus as much on records and databases as the previous scenario did.

The next section focuses more heavily upon message flow.

1. USER1 composes a low-priority message and sends it to USER2.
2. The POA on PO1 creates a message transport file in the PO1\WPCSIN\6 directory.
3. The POA at PO1 transmits the file from the PO1\WPCSIN\6 directory to the domain's MTA via TCP/IP, using port 7100.
4. The DOMAIN1 MTA receives the file and places it in the DOMAIN1\MSLOCAL\GWINPROG\6 directory.
5. The DOMAIN1 MTA moves the file to the DOMAIN1\MSLOCAL\MSHOLD\<DOMAIN2-File-ID>\6 directory.
6. The DOMAIN1 MTA transmits the file from the DOMAIN1\MSLOCAL\MSHOLD\<DOMAIN2-File-ID>\6 directory to DOMAIN2's MTA via TCP/IP, using port 7100.
7. The DOMAIN2 MTA receives the file and places it in the DOMAIN2\MSLOCAL\GWINPROG\6 directory.
8. The DOMAIN2 MTA routes the file to the DOMAIN2\MSLOCAL\MSHOLD\<PO2-File-ID>\6 directory.
9. The MTP portion of the MTA picks up the file in the DOMAIN\MSLOCAL\MSHOLD\<PO2-File-ID>\6 directory and transmits it via TCP/IP to the PO2 POA's MTP port 7101.
10. The POA on PO2 receives the file and writes it directly into the PO2\WPCSOUT\OFS\6 directory.
11. The POA processes the message and inserts it into the message store at PO2. The POA generates a status message and places it into the PO2\WPCSIN\7 directory.
12. The POA transmits the file in the PO2\WPCSIN\7 directory up to the DOMAIN2 MTA at TCP/IP port 7100.

13. The DOMAIN2 MTA receives the file into the DOMAIN2\MSLOCAL\GWINPROG\7 directory.
14. The MTA moves the file to the DOMAIN2\MSOCAL\MSHOLD\DOMAIN1-FILE-ID\7 directory.
15. The MTA transmits the file from the DOMAIN2\MSOCAL\MSHOLD\DOMAIN1-FILE-ID\7 directory to port 7100 on DOMAIN1's MTA.
16. The DOMAIN1 MTA receives the file into its DOMAIN1\MSLOCAL\GWINPROG\7 directory.
17. The DOMAIN1 MTA moves the file to the DOMAIN1\MSLOCAL\MSHOLD\<PO1-FILE-ID>\7 directory.
18. The DOMAIN1 MTA transmits the file to port 7101 on the PO1 POA.
19. The PO1 POA receives the file into the PO1\WPCSOUT\OFS\7 directory.
20. The PO1 POA places the status record into the GroupWise message store on PO1.

As you can see, message flow is logical and predictable. Understanding message flow at this level is very helpful when troubleshooting GroupWise.

Scenario #5: Message Flow Through the GroupWise Internet Agent (GWIA)

USERA is on PO1 at DOMAIN1 and wants to send a message to joe@acme.com via the Internet. PO1 connects with DOMAIN1 via TCP/IP. DOMAIN1 connects with DOMAIN2 via UNC. The GWIA is located on DOMAIN2. Here is the file flow:

1. The PO1 POA writes the appropriate item records to USERA's user database and assigned message database.
2. Because the destination is not on PO1, the PO1 POA drops a transport file in the WPCSIN\4 directory.
3. The PO1 POA transmits the file from the WPCSIN\4 directory at the post office to the DOMAIN1 MTA at the MTA's MTP port.
4. The domain MTA receives the file and places it in the DOMAIN1\MSLOCAL\GWINPROG\4 directory.
5. The domain MTA routes the file to the DOMAIN1\MSLOCAL\MSHOLD\<DOMAIN2-FileID> directory.

Note: You can determine a domain's file ID in a couple of ways. Perhaps the easiest way is by looking at the MTA's HTTP port and clicking Links. From there, you can click a particular link, and it will tell you what the hold queue directory is for the destination link. You can also go to the console for Domain1. Choose F10, Configuration Status, highlight DOMAIN2, and press Enter. The `Hold` directory contains the domain file ID.

6. Because `DOMAIN1` has a UNC connection to `DOMAIN2`, it does not transmit the message to `DOMAIN2` via TCP/IP. The `DOMAIN1` MTA places the message in the `DOMAIN2\WPCSIN\4` directory.
7. The message is destined for the GWIA on `DOMAIN2`, so the file is moved to the `DOMAIN2\MSLOCAL\MSHOLD\<GWIA-FileID>\4` directory.
8. The message is then moved to the `DOMAIN2\WPGATE\GWIA\WPCSOUT\<GWIA-FileID>\4` directory.
9. The GWIA will convert the GroupWise message to ASCII and drop the converted file into the `DOMAIN2\WPGATE\GWIA\SEND` directory. This is the input queue for the GWIA's sending daemon.
10. The GWIA generates a `Transferred` status message to be sent back to `USERA`. The GWIA places the transferred status message in the `DOMAIN2\WPGATE\GWIA\WPCSIN\5` directory.
11. The `DOMAIN2` MTA picks up the file from the `DOMAIN2\WPGATE\GWIA\WPCSIN\5` directory and moves it to the `DOMAIN2\MSLOCAL\GWINPROG\5` directory.
12. The `DOMAIN2` MTA tickles an RTR thread and notifies it about the file in the `GWINPROG\5` directory. The RTR thread looks at the message and determines that the message is destined for `DOMAIN1`. The RTR thread places the message in the `DOMAIN2\MSLOCAL\MSHOLD\DOMAIN1-FileID` directory.
13. The `DOMAIN2` MTA's RTR thread tickles the MTP thread and notifies it about the file in the `DOMAIN2\MSLOCAL\MSHOLD\DOMAIN1-FileID` directory. The `DOMAIN2` MTA transmits the file to the `DOMAIN1` MTA on MTP port `7100`.
14. The `DOMAIN1` MTA's MTP process receives the status message in its `DOMAIN1\MSLOCAL\GWINPROG\5` directory.
15. The `DOMAIN1`'s MTA tickles a RTR thread and notifies it about the file in the `DOMAIN1\MSLOCAL\GWINPROG\5` directory.
16. The `DOMAIN1` MTA's RTR thread routes the status message to the `DOMAIN1\MSLOCAL\PO1-FileID` directory.

17. The DOMAIN1 MTA's RTR thread tickles the MTP thread and notifies it about the file in the DOMAIN1\MSLOCAL\PO1-FileID directory.

18. The DOMAIN1 MTA's MTP thread transmits the status message to the PO1's POA on its MTP port.

19. The POA at PO1 receives the status message in the PO1\WPCSOUT\OFS\5 directory.

20. The POA at PO1 appends the status message to the message store at PO1.

This section was unique in that it showed message flow when a UNC path is used. A UNC path connection between domains or post offices is less efficient because a message must go through more queues, and because messages are picked up from their queue via a polling process. The method of polling queues isn't nearly as quick or efficient as the TCP/IP transfer method.

A Simplified View of Message Flow

Each of the previous three examples went into quite a bit of detail. This section outlines the file flow for the previous scenarios. Remember, the goal here is to reveal the GroupWise file flow system so that you will be able to troubleshoot problems with message delivery.

Scenario #1: PO1 to PO2 in the Same Domain

In this scenario, a user on PO1 sent a message to a user on PO2. Both PO1 and PO2 are in the same GroupWise domain.

Message: The message transport file passed through each of the following directories in order as it proceeded from PO1 to PO2 for delivery:

- PO1\WPCSIN\4
- DOMAIN1\GWINPROG\4
- DOMAIN1\MSLOCAL\MSHOLD\<PO2-FID>\4
- PO2\WPCSOUT\OFS\4

Status message: The status message transport file passed through each of the following directories as it proceeded from PO2 back to the sender's post office, PO1:

- PO2\WPCSIN\5
- DOMAIN1\GWINPROG\5

- DOMAIN1\MSLOCAL\MSHOLD\<PO1-FID>\5
- PO2\WPCSOUT\OFS\5

Scenario #2: PO1.DOMAIN1 to PO2.DOMAIN2

In this scenario, a user on PO1 sent a message to a user on PO2. PO1 and PO2 exist in different domains.

Message: The message transport file passed through each of the following directories as it proceeded from PO1 to PO2 for delivery:

- PO1\WPCSIN\4
- DOMAIN1\GWINPROG\4
- DOMAIN1\MSLOCAL\MSHOLD\<DOMAIN2-FID>\4
- DOMAIN2\GWINPROG\4
- DOMAIN2\MSLOCAL\MSHOLD\<PO2-FID>\4
- PO2\WPCSOUT\OFS\4

Status message: The status message transport file passed through each of the following directories as it proceeded from PO2 back to the sender's post office, PO1.

- PO2\WPCSIN\5
- DOMAIN2\GWINPROG\5
- DOMAIN2\MSLOCAL\MSHOLD\<DOMAIN1-FID>\5
- DOMAIN1\GWINPROG\5
- DOMAIN1\MSLOCAL\MSHOLD\<PO1-FID>\5
- PO1\WPCSOUT\OFS\5

Scenario #3: PO1.DOMAIN1 to GWIA.DOMAIN2

A user on PO1 sent a message to an Internet address. The GWIA resides on a different domain than the sender's post office.

Message: The message transport file passed through each of the following directories as it proceeded from PO1 to the GWIA. (The transmission of the message via SMTP and its ultimate delivery to the Internet recipient are not described here.)

- PO1\WPCSIN\4
- DOMAIN1\GWINPROG\4

- DOMAIN1\MSLOCAL\MSHOLD\<DOMAIN2-FID>\4
- DOMAIN2\GWINPROG\4
- DOMAIN2\MSLOCAL\MSHOLD\<GWIA-FID>\4
- DOMAIN2\WPGATE\GWIA\WPCSOUT\<GWIA-FID>\4

Status message: The status message transport file passed through each of the following directories as it proceeded from the GWIA back to the sender's post office, PO1. Keep in mind that this status message does not indicate that the message was delivered to the Internet recipient—only that the message was successfully transferred to the GWIA's SMTP daemon.

- DOMAIN2\WPGATE\GWIA\WPCSIN\5
- DOMAIN2\MSLOCAL\GWINPROG\5
- DOMAIN2\MSLOCAL\MSHOLD\<DOMAIN1-FID>\5
- DOMAIN1\MSLOCAL\GWINPROG\5
- DOMAIN1\MSLOCAL\MSHOLD\<PO1-FID>\5
- PO1\WPCSOUT\OFS\5

You will probably want to bookmark this page. This section's explanation of message flow is something you can refer to if you need to troubleshoot message flow.

Using File Flow for Troubleshooting

The previous sections provided you with a lot of detail about the flow of messages through the GroupWise system. This information might seem a little esoteric, though. This section applies the information to some scenarios in which the GroupWise administrator might need to troubleshoot problems with message flow.

Troubleshooting Scenario #1: Can't Send Internet E-Mail

The users in DOMAIN1.PO1 note that they can send e-mail within the post office, but can't send e-mail to recipients on the Internet.

Here are the typical troubleshooting steps taken to resolve this problem:

- The first thing the administrator does is check the GWIA on DOMAIN3. Obviously, to send to the Internet, users have to be able to send through the GWIA. It is up and running just fine, though. As a test, the administrator sends a quick message to a side myrealbox.com account. It is delivered.
- It occurs to the administrator that perhaps the users cannot send to anyone outside their post office. Rather than having one of these users send a test message, the administrator sends a message to one of the users in DOMAIN1.PO1, as well as to a user on DOMAIN2. The logic here is that by the time status messages have returned from DOMAIN2, they should also have returned from DOMAIN1.
- Checking the status of the message, the administrator sees that the message to DOMAIN1 remains in a *pending* state long after the message to DOMAIN2 showed up as being *delivered*. This means that something is blocking message flow to or from DOMAIN1.
- The administrator decides to focus on DOMAIN1.PO1 first (even though the problem might be with other post offices under that domain as well). Opening the PO1\WPCSIN\4 directory in Windows Explorer, the administrator finds nearly 300 files queued up for transport. The oldest file is nearly an hour old.
- The administrator checks the message transfer status on the POA console (see Chapter 8, "Configuring the Post Office Agent [POA]," for keystrokes, or view the POA through the HTTP interface to identify this), and the POA claims that the connection with the MTA is up and running. So the problem is not with the connection. However, in checking the message transfer status of the POA through the HTTP interface, the administrator notices that of the 300 files queued up for transport, the oldest file is 320MB.
- At this point, the administrator has determined the cause of the problem. Someone sent a huge message, and the POA and/or MTA could not handle the file. Even though these agents are multithreaded, all threads must use the same physical connection between MTA and POA, and in this case, the network link did not have the bandwidth to manage the transfer between the post office and the domain. All other messages sitting in the WPCSIN\4 directory are being held up behind this one.

The solution here is not likely to be pretty. The administrator could try to unload the POA to get it to release the file, but it is unlikely that it will unload cleanly. This means that the server will have to be downed and the file cleared out manually. Still, with the application of good message-flow principles, the administrator was able to resolve the problem without calling technical support.

TIP

Want to find out who in that post office sent that huge file? You can contact Novell GroupWise support for a utility called the GroupWise Post Master mentioned in TID # 10061973. This utility allows you to crack the header of these files that you find in the queues. It will tell you the sender's user ID, their source domain, post office, DRN, and message database. Pretty nifty. This utility was created just for such purposes. This utility does not include the recipient list, subject line, or any of the message body.

Lessons from Troubleshooting Scenario #1

There are some basic GroupWise troubleshooting principles that I'd like you to take from this scenario:

- **The people who report problems are rarely technicians.** Don't expect their information to be accurate. Was the information from the people on PO1 accurate? Well, yes, they couldn't send to the Internet, but the way they experienced the problem could lead you to believe that they were having problems only with Internet e-mail. They were, in fact, having problems sending to anyone outside the post office.
- **Focus at the first point of potential failure.** In this scenario, that meant focusing on PO1. If users on PO1 are complaining of a problem, log in as a test user on PO1 and witness the problem for yourself.
- **Think message flow.** Users say they cannot send to the Internet. What's the first place from PO1 that a message has to go in order to get to the Internet? The `POST OFFICE\WPCSIN\X` directories, which is therefore the first place to start looking. If there aren't files in the `POST OFFICE\WPCSIN\X` directory, keep looking upstream until you find the problem.

Troubleshooting Scenario #2: Can't Send Between Post Offices

Bob on PO1 complains that he cannot send to Mary Baker on PO2. He gets the mail message back with an error `D101` (user not found). The administrator troubleshoots by first sending to Mary Baker from his or her own mailbox on PO3. Mary gets the e-mail, and no errors are reported. Now the administrator must watch Bob send a message to Mary. Here's what happens:

- Bob starts typing Mary B and the name completion fills in the rest.
- The administrator has Bob open the address book. In the GroupWise address book, Mary Baker's entry is not grayed out. The administrator has Bob click the Frequent Contacts book. There he points out the entry for Mary Baker that has been grayed out. The administrator has Bob delete this entry from the frequent contacts list.
- Now the administrator has Bob send another message to Mary. Name completion executes as usual, and this time the message is delivered normally.

Lessons from Troubleshooting Scenario #2

Here are a couple more GroupWise troubleshooting principles to take home:

- **Watch your users, if you can.** The devil is in the details, as they say, and it is not likely that Bob would have reported the details of name completion to his administrator.
- **Isolate the problem.** This likely means running a quick test or two. In this scenario, the administrator had to determine whether it was just Bob who couldn't send to Mary, or whether it was everyone.
- **Once you've isolated the problem, apply your architectural knowledge.** In this case, an address book entry was incorrect, but it was not in the system address book. Knowing that the frequent contacts list is stored in the user database helped the administrator understand how one (and only one) user might get an error sending to one other user.

Troubleshooting Tips and Tricks

This section describes a few more troubleshooting scenarios that you might encounter, as well as how you might deal with them.

X-Locked Files

GroupWise uses a platform-independent mechanism for locking files in transit. When a transport file is in the process of being created, it is often created with a filename that starts with an X. This is called an *X-lock*.

A GroupWise agent will not touch any file that starts with an X. You are most likely to see X-locked files for an extended period of time when a big file is being transmitted, or when a link between a sending and a receiving site is slow. If you see a new file (created in the last five minutes or so) beginning with an X, it is most likely still in transit. If the file is more than a day old, however, it is most likely of no value and can be deleted. This was a failed attempt to transmit a file.

NOTE

Beginning with GroupWise 6.5 you will see files in the MTA's queues by the name of `XNSTORE`. These are not typical X-locked files. These are actually queue memory files. Here's how the MTA uses them. If the MTA comes up, and discovers that there's hundreds (or more) files in a queue, it will get a directory listing of the files in the queue, and write that directory listing to the `XNSTORE` file. This way, the MTA does not have to rescan the queue until it processed all of the files that are referenced in the `XNSTORE`. This is just one of those fine-tuning procedures that Novell developers do when they're trying to trim off milliseconds from message processing.

TCP/IP Troubles

Suppose for a moment that the POA is having difficulty talking to an MTA via MTP (TCP/IP). You suspect this because people on **CORP** complain that they cannot send to anyone outside the PO. You can see that the **PO1\WPCSIN\4** directory is full of files.

Where might you start? There's a set of logical places to look to determine the problem. Here's the scenario:

CORPPO -- POA	IP address 137.65.55.211	MTP inbound port 7101
CORP -- MTA	IP address 137.65.55.211	MTP inbound port 7100

Here are the troubleshooting steps you can take to resolve this problem:

1. Look at the POA and choose F10, Message Transfer Status.

   Figure 20.1 shows the message transfer status screen on the POA.

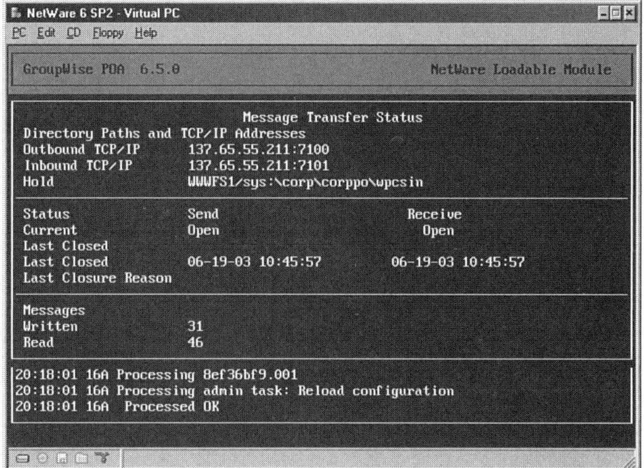

FIGURE 20.1
Message transfer status on a POA.

2. Look at the configuration status on the MTA by choosing F10, Configuration Status. Look at the connection to PO1. Figure 20.2 shows this screen.

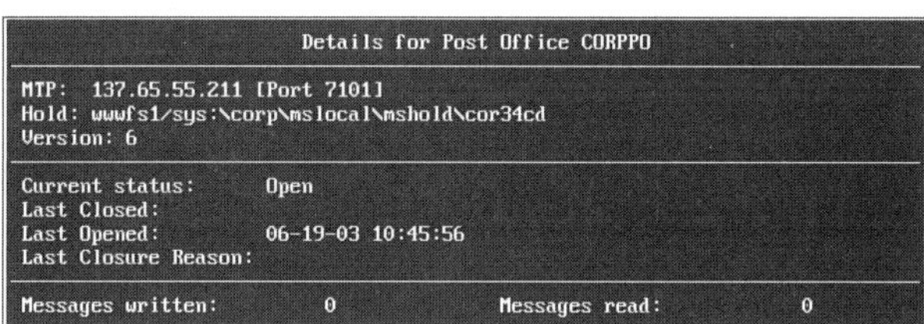

FIGURE 20.2
Configuration status on the MTA.

3. Confirm that the MTA is actually listening on port `7100` by loading TCPCON and choosing Protocol Information, TCP, TCP Connections. Ensure that the local host is using port `7100`. Figure 20.3 shows this screen in TCPCON.

4. Confirm that the MTA will receive connections at port `7100`.

   To do this, run a Telnet program. Make sure to turn on local echo in Telnet, which makes it easier to see what's going on, as shown in Figure 20.4.

Figure 20.4 is from a Windows 2000 workstation. The Telnet program on Windows NT and 9x is a GUI-based telnet. You set local from the Terminal, Preferences option.

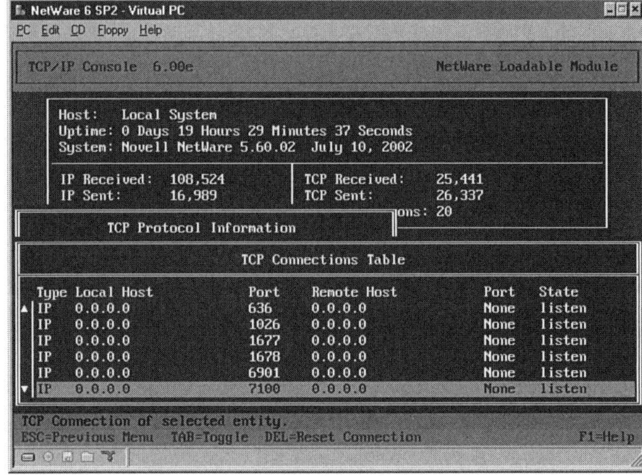

FIGURE 20.3
TCPCON information showing that 7100 is in use.

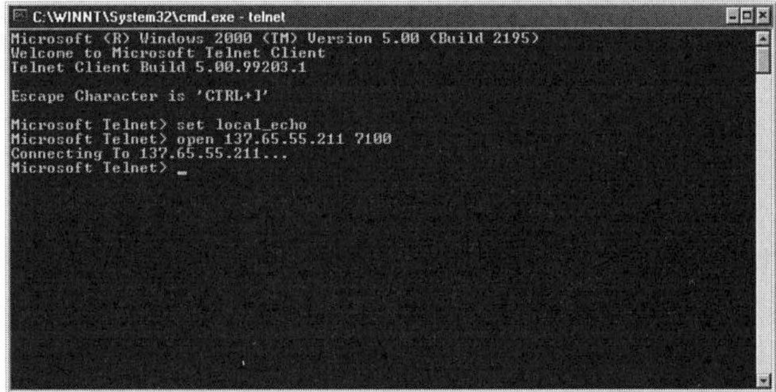

FIGURE 20.4
Telnetting to the MTA's port 7100.

5. If you get a connection to port `7100` (see Figure 20.4), enter some characters.

   You should then be disconnected. If you don't get disconnected, that's a problem. Perhaps you've found that the MTA is listening on port `7100`, but you have no guarantee that the POA can reach the MTA on port `7100`. See whether the file server running the POA can ping the server running the MTA. Be sure to change the byte size on the ping packet so that it represents a "normal" sort of transmission size (try 1,000 bytes).

6. On the file server running the POA, load ping and select the IP address for the box running the MTA, changing the packet size to 1,000 bytes.

7. Next, load the GWIP.NLM with the syntax `LOAD GWIP CONNECT 137.65.55.211 7100`.

The GWIP.NLM file can be obtained from Novell's support Web site. The name of the download file is GWIP.EXE. See Figure 20.5 for a successful GWIP session.

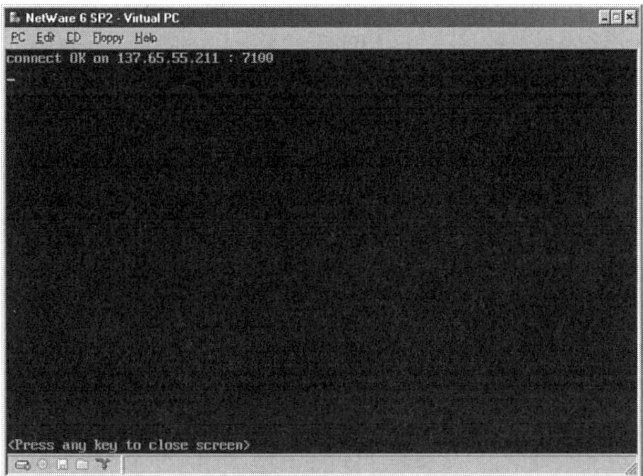

FIGURE 20.5
A GWIP.NLM session shows a successful connection.

Generally, you'll find the TCP/IP connectivity problem along the way as you use these steps. If the problem continues to elude you, try performing a *reinitialize system* on the box that houses the POA and the MTA. You *can* do this while people are connected to the POA.

Best Practices

As always, there are a few things that you can do ahead of time that will make your life (and your troubleshooting efforts) easier down the road:

- **Make sure that log files on your GroupWise agents can grow large enough and long enough to give you the diagnostic information you need when you need it.**
- **Look for message files in queue directories.** The mail message queue directories under a post office are the following:
    - `PO\WPCSOUT\OFS\0-7`: Incoming messages to the post office
    - `PO\WPCSIN\0-7`: Outgoing messages from the post office

The mail message queue directories under a domain are the following:

- DOMAIN\WPCSIN\0-7: These are incoming messages to the domain. These files are placed into the WPCSIN\0-7 directory if another domain has UNC connectivity to this domain.
- DOMAIN\MSLOCAL\GWINPROG\0-7: When a mail message is incoming to the MTA, it is initially created in these directories.
- DOMAIN\MSLOCAL\MSHOLD\XXXXXXXX\0-7: These are outgoing messages from the domain. Wherever a mail messages goes to a PO, to another domain, or to a gateway in this domain, it is first routed to the DOMAIN\MSLOCAL\MSHOLD*XXXXXXXX*\0-7 directory. The *XXXXXXXX* value corresponds with the FID of the object whose outgoing queue this represents.

TIP

In each of the DOMAIN\MSLOCAL\MSHOLD*XXXXXXXX* directories, there is a text file called MTANAME. If you open this file with any text editor, it will give you the full name of the domain or post office that this hold queue represents.

- DOMAIN\WPGATE\<gateway name>\WPCSOUT\<GATEWAY-FID>\0-7: When an MTA has a message to give to a gateway, it puts the message in this directory.
- DOMAIN\WPGATE\GATEWAY\WPCSIN\0-7: When a gateway has something to give the MTA, it puts the file in this directory.

- **If you use Windows Explorer to look at file queues, make sure Explorer is configured to give you the most accurate information.** Otherwise, you might not notice that a file in a particular queue is very large. Make sure that Windows Explorer is configured to do the following:
  - Show all files
  - Sort all files according to size
  - Show the details for files (so that you can actually see the file size)
- **Use the agent's HTTP monitoring interface to help troubleshoot message flow problems.** The GroupWise agents HTTP interface allows you to very quickly and easily determine if and where you are having link configuration problems. You can track the links through your system, and easily see whether there are any messages queued up in any of an agent's hold queues.

One other tip is that if you have message-logging enabled on the MTA and you see messages sitting in an `MSLOCAL\MSHOLD\XXXXXXXX` directory, you can actually click the messages. You can then determine who the sender of the message is.

Summary

This chapter covered a lot of information, but it can all be distilled into three basic troubleshooting principles. When you need to troubleshoot GroupWise message flow, you need to do the following:

- Check the queue directories for "stuck" files, backlogs, and so on.
- Check the POA and MTA logs for error messages, or track message DRNs.
- Check each of the connectivity points—TCP/IP connections between POAs and MTAs, links between MTAs on different domains, and any other links that are part of the signal path for the problem messages.

Remember, one of the easiest ways to check message flow is to send a message and then check its status. *Pending* status means that the flow has been blocked at some point. Any other status means that message flow is open between your mailbox and the destination mailbox.

CHAPTER 21

Moving Domains and Post Offices

This chapter walks you through the process of moving post offices and domains to new servers (new UNC paths), as well as moving their objects around within your eDirectory tree. This isn't something that you will do often, but you will not find these procedures documented in such detail in any other place.

Considerations Related to Moving a Domain

When moving domains, you are going to move a domain from one physical UNC location to another. Generally, the move is from one file server to another. This discussion assumes that the domain will be moved from one file server to another. Here is the scenario:

- Domain to be moved is `DOMAINX`
- `DOMAINX` is a secondary domain
- `DOMAINA` is the primary domain in this system
- The file server where `DOMAINX` originally resided is called `FS1`
- The file server where `DOMAINX` will reside is called `FS2`
- The old location of `DOMAINX` is `\\FS1\EMAIL\DOMAIN`
- The new location of `DOMAINX` is `\\FS2\EMAIL\DOMAIN`

That's the scenario; the next few sections talk about important preparatory steps to take.

Connectivity to the Primary Domain

One of the biggest concerns when moving a domain is the manner in which the new location for DOMAINX will be communicated to the rest of the system. Suppose that DOMAINX communicates to the rest of the GroupWise system via TCP/IP. The new file server, FS2, will have a different IP address than FS1. This needs to be communicated to the rest of the system, prior to moving DOMAINX. So the Message Transfer Agent (MTA) object for DOMAINX must be edited, and the network address field should indicate the IP address for FS2. Just as soon as the IP address for DOMAINX's MTA has been changed, the rest of the system expects to communicate with DOMAINX at the new IP address.

Any changes made to the IP address for the MTA on DOMAINX should be done with ConsoleOne physically connected to the WPDOMAIN.DB for DOMAINX. If you were to change the IP address for the MTA on DOMAINX while connected to the primary domain, your primary domain MTA would immediately restart but would not be able to communicate the change to DOMAINX's MTA if DOMAINX was not running on the new file server.

Communication between DOMAINX and the primary domain is the most important communications link. If the primary domain cannot communicate with DOMAINX in order to get the information about DOMAINX's new MTA IP address, no one is going to get the change. Make sure that DOMAINX can communicate with the primary domain.

Connectivity to Post Offices

When a domain is moved to a new IP address, its post offices must be informed of the change to the MTA's IP address in order for the Post Office Agent (POA) to be able to communicate with the MTA.

Moving a Domain to a New Server

The following is an example task list for moving DOMAINX. The discussion can help you apply these concepts to your own domain moves.

WARNING

If the domain that you want to move houses a GroupWise WebAccess gateway, you must delete the GroupWise WebAccess gateway first before moving the domain. A GroupWise WebAccess gateway cannot be moved along with its domain. You must reinstall and reconfigure the GroupWise WebAccess gateway.

DOMAINX is being moved from the file server called FS1 to the file server called FS2. DOMAINX has two post offices that it communicates with via TCP/IP. Another name for TCP/IP connectivity to a POA is MTP connectivity.

As a precautionary step, you'll want to sync DOMAINX with the primary domain.

Following are the steps for syncing a secondary domain with the primary domain:

1. In ConsoleOne, connect to WPDOMAIN.DB for the primary domain, highlight DOMAINX, and choose Tools, GroupWise Utilities, System Maintenance.
2. Select Sync Primary with Secondary and then click Run.

   Next, you'll want to install the GroupWise agents to FS2 (explained in step 3).
3. Go to the *<Software Distribution Directory>*\AGENTS directory and run INSTALL.EXE. Run all the way through the installation.

TIP

When you perform the agent install, you will be prompted to enter the domains or post offices that you are installing the agents for. If you do not enter or define any domains or post offices for the agent install, the installation process installs only the agent files. This is exactly what you want in this situation. In the next step, you will be copying the MTA's startup file. When you define the path to domain or post offices during the install routine of the agents, a new startup file is built by the install routine.

4. Copy the startup file for the GroupWise MTA from \\FS1\SYS\SYSTEM to \\FS2\SYS\SYSTEM.
5. Edit the MTA startup file in \\FS2\SYS\SYSTEM and make sure that the home switch points to the new domain directory.
6. If you intend to load the GroupWise MTA from the AUTOEXEC.NCF file of your NetWare file server, make sure you have a reference to this (for example, a reference within the file to GRPWISE.NCF). Make sure GRPWISE.NCF loads the GroupWise MTA in conjunction with the startup file you have configured for the MTA.
7. Load ConsoleOne and connect to DOMAINX in the GroupWise system view. This is done by going to Tools, GroupWise System Operations. Select Domain and then select the path to DOMAINX.

   Even though you haven't moved the domain, make sure DOMAINX and the primary domain can communicate. You can use 8 through 11 to confirm this is the case.

8. Edit DOMAINX's MTA and, on the Agent Settings property page, increment the Attach Retry option by one second. Usually this setting is 600; set it to 601.

9. Connect to the primary domain in ConsoleOne, edit DOMAINX's MTA, and find out whether the Attach Retry value changed on DOMAINX's MTA object.

TIP **The purpose behind incrementing the Attach Retry option specifically is that this value is not held in eDirectory. When you confirm that the change to this setting has actually replicated, you know GroupWise directory replication is working.**

Do not proceed to the next step until you confirm that this change has been replicated to the primary domain. Get in and out of the MTA object to verify the change.

NOTE **If you're moving the primary domain, you don't have to worry about whether there is communication with the primary domain, of course.**

10. In ConsoleOne, connectv back to DOMAINX's WPDOMAIN.DB file.

11. Edit DOMAINX's MTA and change the TCP/IP address in the network address option to reflect FS2's IP address (see Figure 21.1).

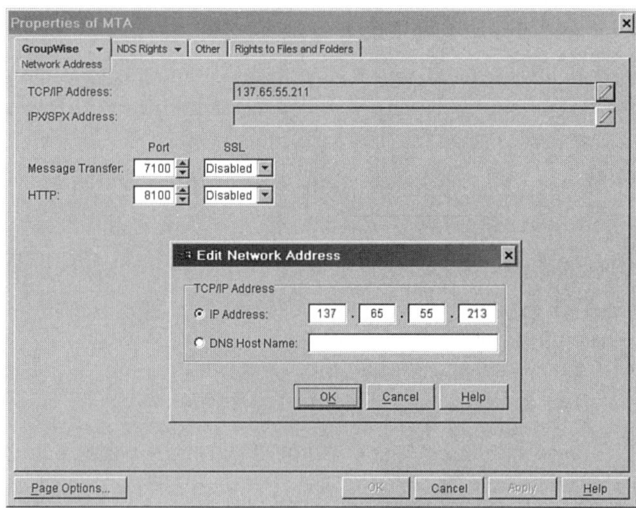

FIGURE 21.1
Change the network address on the MTA to reflect the new file server.

It might sound strange to change the IP address of an MTA to reflect the IP address on a server on which the MTA is not running; but don't worry, it will work. The whole idea is that the MTA that is currently running on FS1 communicate the change in the IP address before the MTA goes down. DOMAINX's MTA will be able to connect with the rest of the MTAs in the system, but they will lose connectivity to DOMAINX's MTA. This condition is just fine. Wait for about five minutes for this information to replicate before going to the next steps.

12. Exit ConsoleOne.
13. Bring down DOMAINX's MTA and any gateways running for DOMAINX.
14. Make sure no one is accessing WPDOMAIN.DB.

    Here is a simple test: Try to rename the WPDOMAIN.DB file to WPDOMAIN.REN and then back to WPDOMAIN.DB. If you can't rename the file, do not proceed until you can. NetWare server administrators can check file/open lock activity on the server monitor program to see which users still have a connection to the domain database. You then know who still has the domain database open. If the connection to the WPDOMAIN.DB happens to be 0, there is a process on the server that is holding the WPDOMAIN.DB file open.
15. Copy the domain directory from the old location to the new location.

    Copy the \\FS1\EMAIL\DOMAIN\ directory to \\FS2\EMAIL\DOMAIN using one of the following options:

    - Use a backup of the domain from FS1 and then restore it back to FS2.
    - Use NCOPY *.* /S /E. (NCOPY is superior to COPY or XCOPY because it performs a server-to-server copy, which is faster.)
    - Use XCOPY *.* /S /E.
    - Use Windows Explorer to copy and paste the directory, and then watch the flying pages!
16. Rename the WPDOMAIN.DB file on FS1 to WPDOMAIN.BAK.
17. Load ConsoleOne. You should get an error stating that the domain database for DOMAINX cannot be found. This is okay.
18. Connect to the now-relocated DOMAINX domain's WPDOMAIN.DB file and, when ConsoleOne asks you for the path to the domain, browse to the domain's new UNC location.
19. Edit DOMAINX's object as shown in Figure 21.2, and change the domain's UNC path to reflect the new path for DOMAINX.

FIGURE 21.2 Changing the UNC path to reflect the newly moved domain.

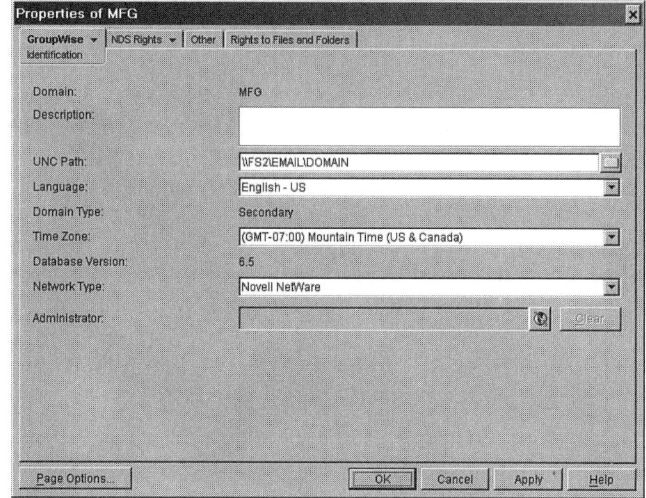

20. Edit `DOMAINX`'s MTA. Go to the Log Settings property page. If you have specified a path, make sure it reflects the UNC path where the domain is located. You should also check the Message Log setting and update this path if you have entered a path here.
21. Bring up the MTA for `DOMAINX` on `FS2`.
22. Get the POAs and the MTA talking via TCP/IP.

    You might have to restart the POA's MTP threads that service post offices that are in `DOMAINX`. Although the IP address for the MTA might have been communicated to the POA, the POA might not restart the MTP process to use the new address. The MTP process might show the domain being closed. The GroupWise 6.5 POA allows you to restart just the MTP threads. This is done through F10, Actions, Restart MTP threads.

    After restarting the MTP threads, see if it shows the new MTA's IP address. To do this, choose F10, Message Transfer Status.

    If the IP address is incorrect, you need to become a little bit more forceful with the POA. One option is to rebuild the WPHOST.DB file to force the information down to the post office. You can also use the information in the following tip for another resolution to this problem.

TIP

If you cannot get your POA to understand that the MTA has a new IP address, or you do not want to rebuild the WPHOST.DB file, you might want to just use the HTTP interface of the POA to edit the IP address and port. This can be done by accessing the POA's HTTP interface. Click the Configuration tab, and then scroll down and click the Message Transfer Protocol link. This will take you to a screen

where you can edit the in- and outbound IP address and port on which the POA listens. Edit the IP address you need here, and then make sure you click the Restart MTP option and click Submit. If you do not select the option to restart MTP, the change will not take effect.

If you are not using the HTTP interface option to the POA, you can also use the following switches in the POA's startup file to force the POA to cooperate:

```
/MTPINIP-<IP address of the POA>
/MTPINPORT-<MTP port of the POA>
/MTPOUTIP-<IP address of the MTA>
/MTPOUTPORT-<IP port of the MTA>

for example

/mtpinip-137.65.55.210
/mtpinport-7101
/mtpoutip-137.65.55.213
/mtpoutport-7100
```

23. Configure the NetWare server to run more efficiently with the new GroupWise domain by setting the following directories, and the subdirectories off of these directories, for immediate purge of deleted files:

```
\\FS2\EMAIL\DOMAIN\WPCSIN
\\FS2\EMAIL\DOMAIN\WPCSOUT
\\FS2\EMAIL\DOMAIN\MSLOCAL
\\FS2\EMAIL\DOMAIN\WPGATE\<gateway>\WPCSIN
\\FS2\EMAIL\DOMAIN\WPGATE\<gateway>\WPCSOUT
```

24. Finally, you must regraft the domain object. This will ensure that the domain's new UNC path is reflected in eDirectory. To do this, go to the eDirectory browser view (not the GroupWise view) and follow these steps:
    a. Highlight the eDirectory Organizational Unit (OU) that houses DOMAINX.
    b. Select Tools, GroupWise Utilities, GW/eDirectory Association, Graft GroupWise Objects.
    c. Select domains, post offices, and gateways.
    d. Proceed through the grafting wizard, and make sure to graft DOMAINX; you do not need to graft the users associated with DOMAINX.

Your domain should now be successfully moved. To test if it is, make sure you can connect to the domain in ConsoleOne, and that all other MTAs show this domain as open. You should also make sure that all post offices off of this domain show the domain as open.

Final Notes on Moving a Domain

The example in the preceding section is not a perfect fit for every situation. For example, some sites have implemented Domain Name Services (DNS) names for their MTAs rather than IP addresses. The DNS name simplifies the IP address change, because the only IP address that needs to change is in the DNS's translation table.

Also, if you have a gateway below a domain that needs to be moved, you will need to see that the gateway is configured for new changes to the IP address or the new UNC path for the domain. Consider, for example, a domain with a GWIA. If you are moving the domain that a GWIA is associated with, you have to do the following:

1. Copy the GWIA's executable code to the new server.

   To install the GWIA code to a new server without using the wizard to install a new GWIA, go to the software distribution directory and run the INSTALL.EXE file from the software distribution directory with the `/COPYONLY` switch. Here's the exact syntax:

   ```
   <SDD UNC PATH>\INTERNET\GWIA\install.exe /copyonly
   ```

2. Copy the GWIA.CFG file to the new file server—this file is typically in the `SYS:SYSTEM` directory on a NetWare server—and then modify the GWIA.CFG file so that it reflects the correct paths to the domain.
3. Modify the EXEPATH.CFG file to reflect the new path to the GWIA.CFG file.

   The EXEPATH.CFG file is in *<DOMAIN THAT OWNS THE GWIA>* `\WPGATE\`*<GWIA DIRECTORY>*.

NOTE

For more information on what's in the GWIA.CFG and EXEPATH.CFG files, see Chapter 10, "Installing and Configuring the GroupWise Internet Agent."

4. Edit the GWIA. Go to the Log Settings property page and make sure that the log path does not reflect the old UNC path.

Considerations Related to Moving a Post Office

First of all, it's impossible to move a GroupWise post office to a different domain. If you are reorganizing and need to move a post office to a new domain, you need to create the post office anew in the new domain and move all the users to the new post office. Have a look at Chapter 13, "Moving Users," if this is what you need to do.

This discussion talks about moving a GroupWise post office. You are going to be moving a post office from one physical UNC location to another. Here is the information from the scenario:

- Post office to be moved is called `PO-X`
- `DOMAINA` is the domain that owns post office `PO-X`
- The file server on which `PO-X` originally resided is called `FS1`
- The file server on which `PO-X` will reside is called `FS2`
- The old location of `PO-X` is `\\FS1\EMAIL\PO`
- The new location of `PO-X` is `\\FS2\EMAIL\PO`

That's the scenario; the next few sections talk about important preparatory steps to take.

GroupWise Client Connectivity

Most customers have configured their post offices to support client/server connections from the GroupWise client to the GroupWise POA. The GroupWise client knows that it must contact the GroupWise POA via an IP address. Each time the GroupWise client loads, it reads the IP address out of one of the following locations:

- eDirectory
- The Windows Registry where the GroupWise 32-bit client is installed
- In the USER.DB file for any GroupWise caching or remote client

If these locations don't provide the client with a valid IP address, it might check domain name services (DNS) for the `NGWNAMESERVER` POA.

NOTE

If the local machine has a value defined in the Registry at `HKLM\SOFTWARE\Novell\GroupWise\Client\5.0\DefaultIPAddress` and `DefaultIPPort`, the GroupWise client will not check NGWNAMESERVER to find a POA.

The trick is to communicate the new IP address to all GroupWise clients. If you specified the IP address for the POA using a DNS name (for example, `POA.POX.WORLDWIDEWIDGETS.COM`), the change is an easy one. Just change the DNS translation table for `POA.POX.WORLDWIDEWIDGETS.COM` so that it reflects the new IP address of the POA when running on `FS2`. In this way, the settings that the clients have stored will still be correct. The client will look to DNS to resolve the hostname the same way it did before the PO was moved, and DNS will give the client the new address.

If you have specified the IP address for the POA using numbers (which most customers do), for example 10.100.221.2, you have to depend on the client to perform an eDirectory lookup, or a DNS lookup for `NGWNAMESERVER`. This walkthrough shows you how to configure your system so that those lookups succeed.

Domain-to-Post Office Connectivity

The GroupWise MTA for `DOMAINA` has to know how to connect to the `PO-X` post office. Otherwise, messages will not move from the `DOMAINA` MTA to the POA running on `PO-X`.

GroupWise WebAccess and GWIA Connectivity

Your GroupWise WebAccess Agent needs to know about the change to `PO-X`'s location and/or IP address. If your GWIA is configured for POP3 or IMAP4 support, it will also need to know how to get a hold of the newly moved `PO-X` post office. These two gateways connect directly to the post office to provide alternative types of mailbox access, as discussed in Chapters 10 and 11. If they do not know about the post office's POA's new IP address, you will have WebAccess, POP3, or IMAP4 users who cannot get to their mail.

Libraries with Additional Document Storage Areas

If a library is contained in the post office you're moving, you might have an additional concern. Usually, you can simply copy the entire post-office structure, library directories and all, and be fine. The problem comes in when there are document storage areas (DSAs) defined outside of the post office directory.

If the DSA needs to be moved, consult Chapter 14, "Library and Document Administration." DSA moves can occur independently of post office moves. If the DSA does not need to be moved, all you need to do is make sure that, when the POA runs at the new location, it still has full access to the DSA.

WARNING

If you move a post office to a new location but keep the DSA at the old server path, you might have problems loading your GroupWise POA. You might get a `DF17` error, and the POA will not load. You need to correct the `DF17` error; but to get things up and running, you can add a `/noconfig` switch to the POA's startup file. You still must make sure that the POA can connect to the DSA.

The Software Distribution Directory (SDD)

Software distribution directories are similar to document storage areas in that they can be moved independently of the post office. You have three basic options with regard to your software distribution directory:

- **Assign the PO to a new software distribution directory.** It might be that with the PO move, a different server is used to deliver applications to users. If there is another SDD there, it makes sense to assign that one to the PO you are moving.

WARNING

If you assign a post office to a new software distribution directory, keep in mind the BUMP and BUILD numbers. If you do not want your users to get prompted to update the GroupWise client, make sure that the BUILD number is tweaked accordingly. See Chapter 12, "Administering the GroupWise Client," for more details on the BUMP and BUILD numbers.

- **Move the software distribution directory.** This should be your choice if the SDD resides on the same server as the users. In this case, you need to copy the SDD to the new server and edit the path of the SDD using the software directory management tool discussed in

Chapters 6, " Using GroupWise System Operations," and 8, "Configuring the Post Office Agent (POA)."

This section talked about all of the things to keep in mind when moving a post office. The next sections include an actual scenario for moving a post office.

Moving a GroupWise Post Office to a New UNC Path

Here is the scenario—the GroupWise post office `PO-X` is being moved from `FS1` to `FS2`. The file server housing `PO-X` isn't robust enough, so you must put the GroupWise post office on its own dedicated NetWare server. The `PO-X` post office communicates via TCP/IP to its owning domain, `DOMAINX`. All users access `PO-X` in client/server mode.

Moving the Post Office and Creating Domain-to-PO Connectivity

A few days before the post office move, let users know that the move of the post office will happen. If everything goes well, it should be rather seamless for most users. Unless you are using DNS names to identify where the POA is running, users who use GroupWise caching or remote mailboxes need to manually change the IP address to the POA under Accounts, Account Options, Properties, Advanced.

TIP

If when you rolled out your GroupWise clients, you defined the `DefaultIPAddress` and `DefaultIPPort` settings in the SETUP.CFG file to point to a DNS name of a post office, the cache and remote users will not need to reconfigure where their remote and cache clients attempt to connect to. The remote or cache client will attempt to connect to the old post office IP address. If this fails, and the Registry keys for `DefaultIPAddress` and `DefaultIPPort` are present on the machine, the remote or cache client will attempt to connect here before failing. This provides a great solution to your GroupWise remote and cache users. See Chapter 12 for more information on using the SETUP.CFG file with the `DefaultIPAddress` and `DefaultIPPort` parameters.

Here are the steps to follow:

1. Install the GroupWise POA software to `FS2`.

You can do this by running the agent install program, INSTALL.EXE, found in the AGENTS subdirectory of your GroupWise CD or SDD.

TIP

When you perform the agent install, you will be prompted to enter the domains or post offices that you are installing the agents for. If you do not enter or define any domains or post offices for the agent install, the installation will only install the agent files. This is exactly what you want in this situation, because in the next step you will be copying the POA startup file. When you define the path to domain or post offices during the install routine of the agents, a new startup file is built by the install routine.

2. Copy the POA's startup file from \\FS1\SYS\SYSTEM to \\FS2\SYS\SYSTEM.
3. Edit the POA's startup file and change the home switch to reflect the new UNC path for PO-X. Now you need to suspend connectivity from DOMAINA's MTA to PO-X.
4. Go to the MTA's screen at the NetWare console, press F10, and select Configuration Status.
5. Highlight the post office PO-X, press Enter, and select the Suspend option.
6. Bring down the POA that services PO-X.
7. Rename the WPHOST.DB file in \\FS1\EMAIL\PO to WPHOST.BAK.

   Do not proceed until you have done the rename successfully. If you cannot rename the WPHOST.DB file, there is either another POA running against the post office (maybe an indexer POA), or there are users logged in via direct mode who have a connection to it. Check file/open lock activity from the NetWare server monitor to determine who has a connection to the database.
8. Copy the contents and subdirectories of \\FS1\EMAIL\PO to \\FS2\EMAIL\PO, using one of the following options:
   - Use a backup of the post office from FS1 and then restore it to FS2.
   - Use NCOPY /S /E.
   - Use XCOPY /S /E.
   - Copy the data using Windows Explorer.
9. Load ConsoleOne and make sure you are connected to the WPDOMAIN.DB for DOMAINA.

10. Edit the post office object in ConsoleOne and change the UNC path to the post office, as shown in Figure 21.3.

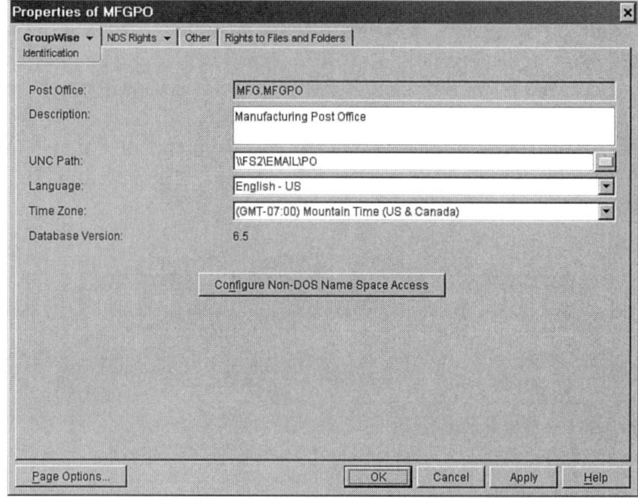

FIGURE 21.3
Changing the UNC path for the post office.

11. Edit the POA for the `PO-X` post office and change the IP address in the network address tab to reflect the IP address for `FS2`.

    Now you need to check the network links to `PO-X` to see if the change to the IP address made it to the link table.

12. Choose Tools, GroupWise Utilities, Link Configuration. Select `DOMAINA`, and then choose View, Post Office Links.

    You need to double-click the post office link to `PO-X` to make sure that it has the correct IP address.

13. Rebuild `PO-X`'s WPHOST.DB file by highlighting the post office, choosing Tools, GroupWise Utilities, and System Maintenance. Then, select Rebuild Database and click Run.

14. Bring down the MTA for `DOMAINA`, and bring it back up again.

15. Bring up the POA for `PO-X` on `FS2` to confirm that the POA can connect to the domain.

    The POA for `PO-X` is configured for MTP, so to test connectivity you do the following:

    - Go to the POA at the NetWare console.
    - Select F10 and then Message Transfer Status.
    - Confirm that the IP addresses are correct and that communication is established.

Now, you can confirm WebAccess and GWIA connectivity to the post office.

16. Edit the WebAccess gateway object.
17. Select the Post Office Links property page.
18. Highlight the link to `PO-X` and edit it, making sure that the link reflects `FS2`'s new information.
19. Edit the GWIA gateway object.
20. Select the Post Office Links property page.
21. Highlight the link to `PO-X` and edit it, making sure that the link reflects the new information for `FS2`.

    Finally, you can create client connectivity as explained in the next steps.

22. Make sure that all users have browse, read, and compare eDirectory object rights to the post office and POA objects.

    This way, if they are running the NetWare client and are in client/server–online mode, they will discover the location to the new POA. For users who do not have the NetWare client, you have hopefully set up the `DefaultIPAddress` and `DefaultIPPort` options in the SETUP.CFG file so they will use a DNS name to locate their post offices. If not, you will have to push out the IP address to the users in some other way. For example, if you have a method of changing the user's Registry, you can modify the Registry at the following location to reflect the new TCP/IP address:

    ```
    HKEY_CURRENT_USER\Software\Novell\GroupWise\
    Login Parameters\TCP/IP Address
    ```

23. Remember also that if you have not used the `DefaultIPAddress` and `DefaultIPPort` settings, the GroupWise caching and remote clients might need to manually change the IP address to the POA. You do this from Accounts, Account Options, Properties, Advanced.

You might need to take additional steps related to the post office move, as explained in earlier sections. And then your post office move is complete. The next section is not required as part of a post office move.

Moving a Post Office to a New OU

As your eDirectory tree evolves and grows, you might need to move a GroupWise post office object to a new OU. The GroupWise software does not readily allow for this, but this section shows you how to pull it off.

To begin, you need to disable the ConsoleOne GroupWise snap-ins by doing the following:

1. Get out of ConsoleOne.
2. From Windows Explorer, move the `GROUPWISE` folder and its contents from the `NOVELL\CONSOLEONE\<VERSION>\SNAPINS` directory into `C:\TEMP`, or some other location, as long as it's not under the ConsoleOne path.
3. Reconfirm that there is no longer a `GROUPWISE` folder in the `SNAPINS` folder.

   When ConsoleOne is unsnapped from GroupWise, all GroupWise objects show up with an icon that looks like a question mark on the right side of a 3D box, as shown in Figure 21.4.
4. Start ConsoleOne, and make sure that under the Tools menu there are no GroupWise menus, as shown in Figure 21.4.

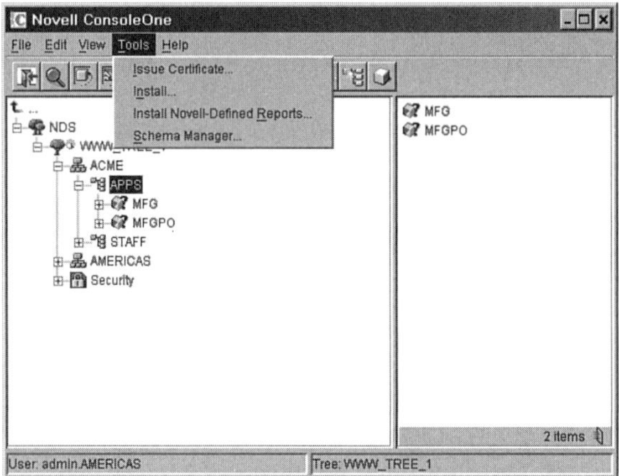

FIGURE 21.4
ConsoleOne without GroupWise snap-ins.

5. Delete the GroupWise POA object by highlighting and deleting the post office object, which appears to the right in Console View.

   Figure 21.5 shows the POA object.
6. Delete any GroupWise libraries that are associated with this post office.

   GroupWise libraries will be in the same eDirectory context as the post office object, so highlight a library and delete the object.
7. Delete the post office object from eDirectory (see Figure 21.6).

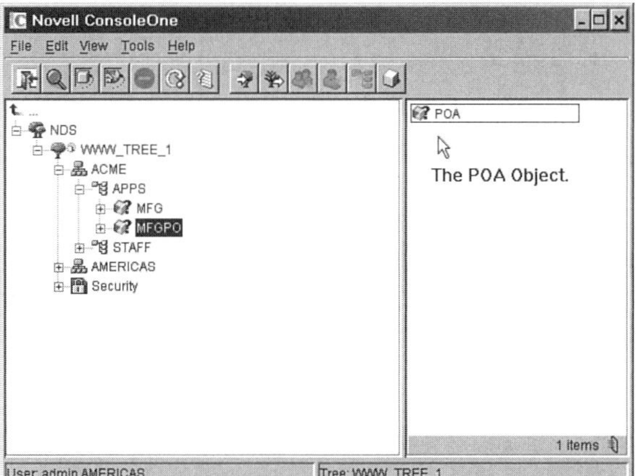

FIGURE 21.5
The POA object with ConsoleOne unsnapped from GroupWise.

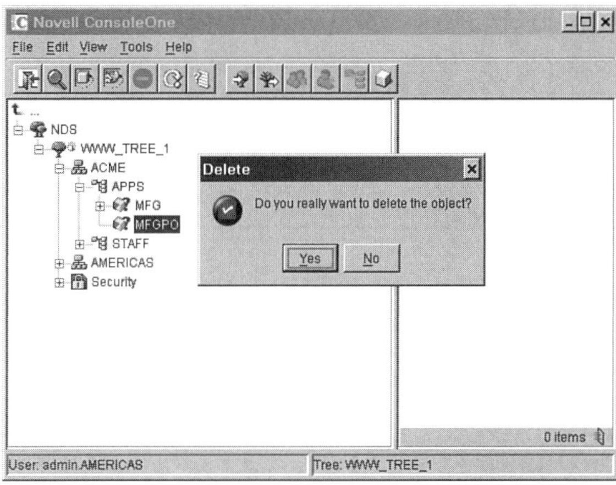

FIGURE 21.6
Deleting the GroupWise post office object.

8. Put the GroupWise snap-ins for ConsoleOne back into place by moving the `GROUPWISE` folder from the temporary location back to the `NOVELL\CONSOLEONE\<VERSION>\SNAPINS` directory.
9. Launch ConsoleOne. The GroupWise snap-ins should now be re-enabled.
10. Make sure to connect the domain owning the post office that you are moving.
11. Go into the eDirectory browser view and highlight the eDirectory OU that you want to move the post office into.
12. Choose Tools, GroupWise Utilities, GW/eDirectory Association, Graft GroupWise Objects.
13. Select domains, post offices, and gateways.

14. When prompted with the Select Domain window, select the domain that owns the post office you deleted from eDirectory.
15. Proceed to the Post Office Context window, as shown in Figure 21.7.

    Notice that the Edit Context button will not be grayed out when you highlight the post office that was deleted.

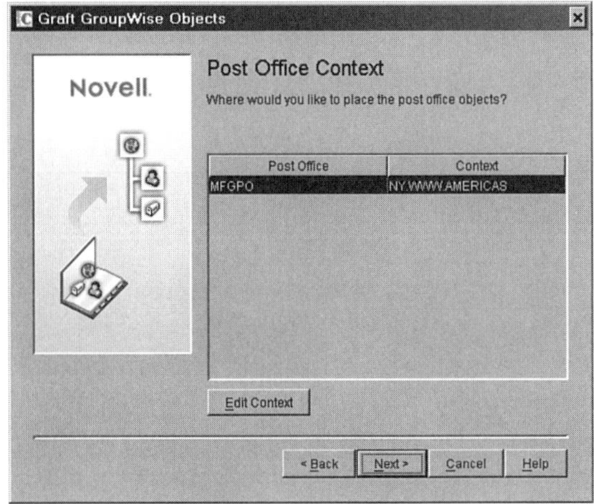

FIGURE 21.7 Post Office Context window in the Graft utility.

16. Edit the context and specify the new context for the post office object, if needed.
17. Click Next and then Finish.
18. Once the graft is finished, get out of the Graft utility, and then get out of ConsoleOne. Relaunch ConsoleOne.

TIP **Getting in and out of ConsoleOne gives ConsoleOne a chance to reread everything; otherwise ConsoleOne can become confused after a procedure such as this.**

19. Go to the eDirectory context that now houses your post office.
20. Now choose Tools, GroupWise Utilities, GW/eDirectory Association, Graft GroupWise Objects.
21. When the graft utility comes up, graft the users associated with the relocated post office by selecting users, resources, and distribution lists from the first graft screen.
22. Proceed through the Graft utility and follow the prompts, choosing the post office that you just moved to a new eDirectory OU as the post office for which the objects need to be grafted, as shown in Figure 21.8.

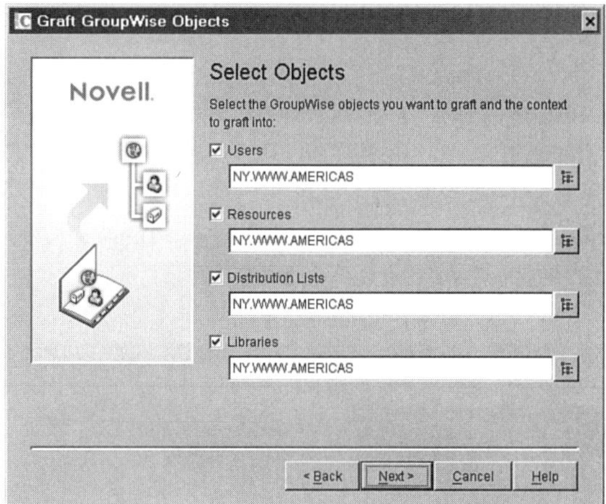

FIGURE 21.8 Selecting which objects associated with a post office to graft.

To determine whether your post office graft operation was successful, edit the post office object, and look at the Membership page. If you see the users on the post office in the Membership page, you know the graft was successful.

Moving a Domain to a New OU

As your eDirectory tree changes, you might need to move a GroupWise domain object to a new OU. As with the post office OU move explained earlier in this chapter, the GroupWise software does not have a built-in function to allow for this kind of a move. You'll do this just like you moved the post office to a new OU.

NOTE

When moving a GroupWise domain, the domain object must be deleted from eDirectory. The fact that the domain is deleted from eDirectory throws eDirectory off when trying to understand the GroupWise post office object. So when deleting a GroupWise domain object, you must also delete the post office objects along with the POAs and libraries.

Following are the steps for moving a GroupWise domain to a new eDirectory OU.

To begin, you first need to disable the ConsoleOne GroupWise snap-ins.

1. Exit ConsoleOne.
2. From Windows Explorer, move the `GROUPWISE` folder and its contents from the `NOVELL\CONSOLEONE\<VERSION>\SNAPINS` directory to `C:\TEMP`.

3. Reconfirm that there is no longer a **GROUPWISE** folder in the **SNAPINS** folder.

   When ConsoleOne is unsnapped from GroupWise, all GroupWise objects show up with an icon that looks like a question mark on the right side of a 3D box.

4. Start ConsoleOne and make sure that under the Tools menu there are no GroupWise menus, as shown in Figure 21.9.

FIGURE 21.9
ConsoleOne without GroupWise snap-ins.

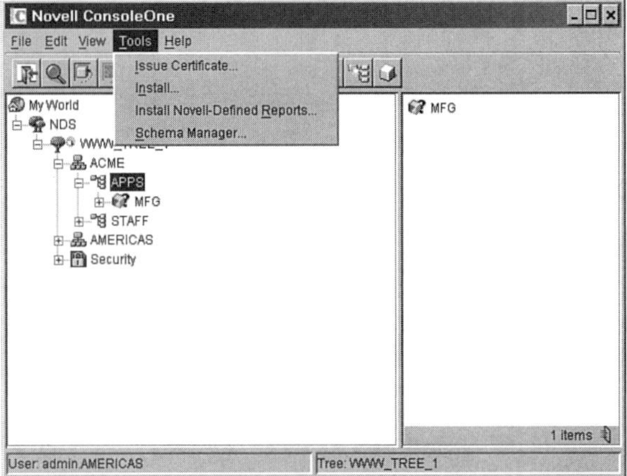

5. Delete the GroupWise MTA object of the domain that you moved.

   To do this, highlight the GroupWise domain object on the right side. The MTA will show up on the left side, as shown in Figure 21.10.

FIGURE 21.10
The MTA object with ConsoleOne unsnapped from GroupWise.

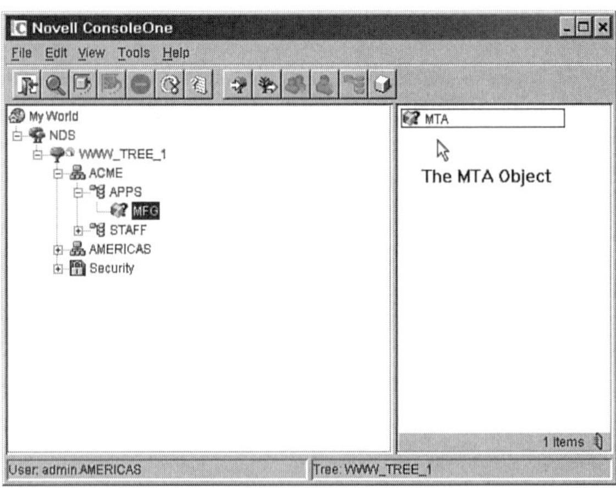

6. Delete any gateways or provider objects that are associated with this domain.

   Gateways and provider objects are shown on the right side, in the same place the MTA is.

7. Delete any GroupWise post offices that are associated with this domain.

   Refer to the section prior to this one entitled "Moving a Post Office to a New OU" for complete instructions on how to do this. You do not have to actually move the post office to a new eDirectory OU, but you must go through the process of removing the post office object from eDirectory, and then regrafting it to eDirectory.

NOTE

The GroupWise post office object might be in a different eDirectory organizational unit than the GroupWise domain.

You will need to delete all other objects subordinate to the domain being moved. The GroupWise post offices are not truly subordinate to the GroupWise domain in eDirectory. The GroupWise post office must still be deleted because eDirectory gets thrown off if information in the GroupWise post office points back to the deleted GroupWise domain. This *does not* mean that you need to delete the users; it just means that you'll have to delete the post office POAs subordinate to your post offices.

8. Delete the domain object from eDirectory.
9. Put the GroupWise snap-ins for ConsoleOne back into place by moving the `GROUPWISE` folder from the temporary location back to the `NOVELL\CONSOLEONE\<VERSION>\SNAPINS` directory.
10. Launch ConsoleOne. The GroupWise snap-ins should now be re-enabled.
11. Make sure you are connected to the domain that's moving.
12. Go into the eDirectory browser view and highlight the eDirectory OU that you want to move the domain object into.
13. Choose Tools, GroupWise Utilities, GW/eDirectory Association, Graft GroupWise Objects.
14. Select domains, post offices, and gateways.
15. When prompted with the Select Domain window, select the domain that you deleted from eDirectory.
16. Proceed to the Domain Context window, as shown in Figure 21.11.

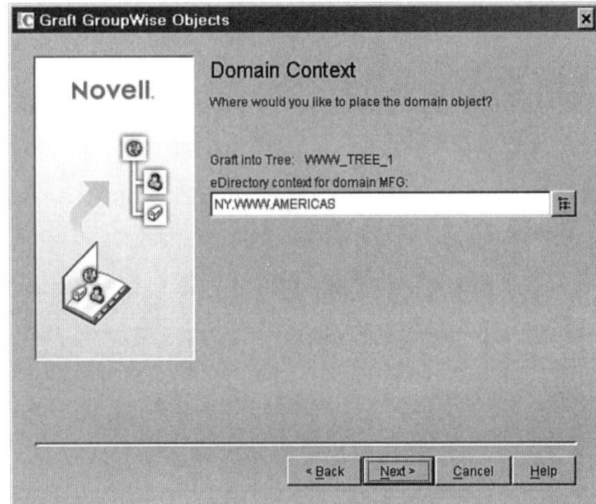

FIGURE 21.11 Domain Context window in the Graft utility.

17. Edit the context and specify the new context for the domain object. If you selected the correct context in step 11, the context should be correct here.
18. Now specify the context to place your post offices. Click Next and then Finish. Once again, if you have deleted the post office and POA eDirectory objects under this domain, the context will default to the same context as the domain. You might need to modify the context for each post office.
19. Once the graft is finished, get out of the Graft utility, and then get out of ConsoleOne and go back in.
20. Go to the eDirectory context that now houses your domain.
21. Now choose Tools, GroupWise Utilities, GW/eDirectory Association, Graft GroupWise Objects.

NOTE

Grafting users will not put them into the same context that the domain is in. Actually, you are just regrafting the users in their original contexts.

22. When the graft utility comes up, graft the users associated with all the post offices below the domain that you just moved. You do so by selecting users, resources, and distribution lists from the first graft screen.

TIP

You can simply graft the users for one post office at a time, if that would be easier.

Make sure to specify the correct context for resources and distribution lists. Any libraries will be placed in the resource context that you specify.

23. Finish grafting the users.

As this section showed, moving a domain to a new eDirectory OU is no small process. In order to move a domain to a new eDirectory OU, all post offices must be removed from eDirectory and then regrafted along with the domain.

Summary

Moving GroupWise domains and post offices around in a Novell eDirectory tree is difficult because there is a lot of detail you need to pay attention to. Make sure to perform all the steps mentioned in the walkthroughs, and your domain and post office moves should be trouble free.

You should also give consideration to who has what rights in the new eDirectory OU that now houses the moved domain or post office object.

CHAPTER 22

Troubleshooting the GroupWise Directory

CHAPTER 22

The GroupWise directory, sometimes referred to as GDS, is largely contained in the WPDOMAIN.DB and WPHOST.DB files. Typically, the most effective way to fix problems in GroupWise directory databases is by rebuilding them using system maintenance in ConsoleOne.

Using the Correct Tools

GroupWise administrators are often unclear about which tools to use to fix a GroupWise problem. When a problem appears in the system address book in the GroupWise client, running the Mailbox/Library Maintenance or GroupWise check (GWCHECK) will accomplish nothing. These are the wrong tools to use to fix GroupWise system address book/WPHOST.DB problems.

Reviewing the discussion of GroupWise architecture from Part I for just a moment, there are two kinds of GroupWise databases:

- **GroupWise directory databases:** WPDOMAIN.DB and WPHOST.DB files
- **GroupWise message/information store databases:** These are the *.DB files at any post office, excluding the WPHOST.DB file

Mailbox/library maintenance, or GWCHECK, is strictly for fixing message store databases. The tool for fixing the GroupWise directory databases is called system maintenance. As discussed in Chapter 7, "GroupWise Utilities and Diagnostics," you find this tool by choosing GroupWise Utilities from the Tools menu.

Fixing WPHOST.DB Files

In order to discuss repairing a post office database (WPHOST.DB), it's best to look at some examples. The scenarios in this section will help you explore the different options for system maintenance on a WPHOST.DB file.

System Maintenance: Validate, Recover, and Rebuild

For scenario #1, a Post Office Agent (POA) of a particular post office supporting 400 users is attempting to load. It will not load; instead, it produces a `C022` error.

When the GroupWise POA of any post office loads, it first interacts with the WPHOST.DB file, and then loads the NGWGUARD.DB file. The question is which one of those files is to blame for the `C022` error? Well, it's hard to tell. You might suspect the WPHOST.DB file is damaged. If you rebuild the WPHOST.DB file, there's a 50% chance you'll fix the problem. Your WPHOST.DB file is 48MB, and in the past, rebuilding this file has taken about an hour; an expensive proposition when you only *think* the problem is the WPHOST.DB file!

A better solution is to use the Validate Database option from the System Maintenance tool (see Figure 22.1).

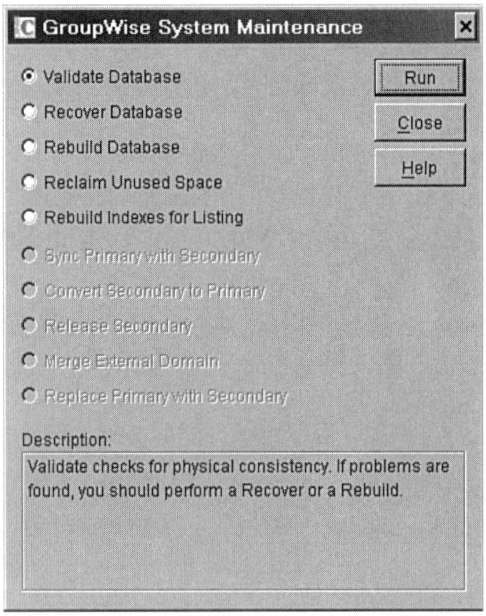

FIGURE 22.1 Validate Database is the first choice on the GroupWise System Maintenance menu.

TIP

Chapter 7 discusses how the choices in the System Maintenance menu can be used.

The Validate Database routine runs a quick structural analysis of a WPHOST.DB file to see whether it is physically consistent. The validate routine usually takes under a minute.

One possible outcome when you run the Validate Database routine is to get the error shown in Figure 22.2.

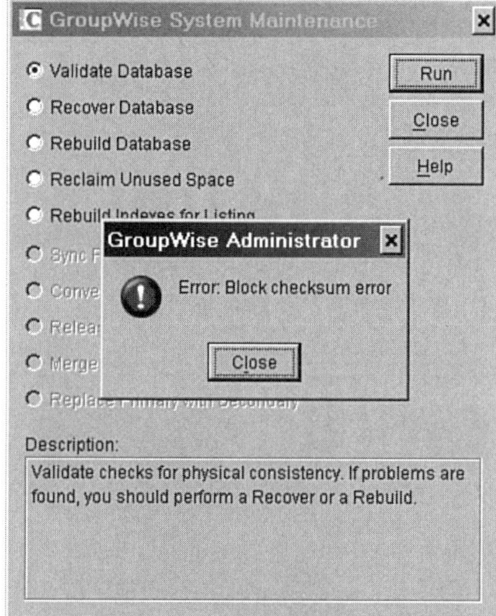

FIGURE 22.2
An error can occur while validating a WPHOST.DB file.

If this error appears, you know that your theory was right; the WPHOST.DB file is damaged, and rebuilding it is the appropriate course of action.

For scenario #2, Mary Smith's name has changed to Mary Jones. You changed her name, but in one post office's address book, Mary's name will not change to Mary Jones.

In this kind of a scenario, you should be less likely to immediately suspect gross structural damage to the WPHOST.DB file. It is more likely that, for some reason, Mary's change isn't being sent down to the post office. Perhaps there is a message-flow problem. The simplest course of action is the following:

1. Synchronize Mary's object. Highlight it, select the Tools menu, and choose GroupWise Utilities, Synchronize.

2. Watch the POA for the post office on which Mary's name did not change.

In this fictitious example, the POA reports a `DBxx` error (the *xx* represents any two characters) when trying to update Mary's object. The question becomes whether Mary's is the only object in this WPHOST.DB file that can't be updated. You need to determine whether you can change information about other users.

To troubleshoot this possibility, the administrator does the following:

1. Synchronize another user.
2. Watch the POA for the post office on which Mary's name did not change.

Suppose that the POA didn't report an error when rewriting this other user object to the WPHOST.DB file. However, upon further investigation in the POA log file, you do see other `DBxx` errors on user objects besides Mary's.

You can conclude that there is definitely a problem with Mary's object in this one WPHOST.DB file. The problem is not specific to Mary's object record, however. It is specific to the block of records in the same location in the WPHOST.DB where Mary's object record is. A few other users' object records are also located in that damaged block in the WPHOST.DB file, which accounts for the other `DBxx` errors.

You can assume that there is minor structural damage to the WPHOST.DB file at this particular post office that's getting the error.

Now, suppose that when you discover this problem, it's 10:00 a.m. on a Tuesday. To rebuild a WPHOST.DB file, the POA must be down so that you have exclusive access to the WPHOST.DB file.

Rebuilding the WPHOST.DB file to fix this problem is out of the question. It's not system-critical, because users aren't complaining. You've just stumbled across a problem that you know eventually must be resolved. Suppose also that at your organization you have a very involved procedure to follow if ever you must have downtime during business hours. You want to avoid that procedure.

The system maintenance routine to run in this scenario is called Recover Database.

Recovering a WPHOST.DB file does not require exclusive access to it. You run a Recover Database routine, and after doing so, synchronize Mary's object. There should no longer be errors when synchronizing Mary's object.

The Recover Database routine quite often does not fix WPHOST.DB damage. In the preceding case, all it did was remove the damaged block of records. Your synchronization of Mary's object was required to complete the fix, because the recover routine just cut out the mushy bad part of the database, but it didn't replace the records that were lost. This is because the Recover Database routine only extracts information from the same WPHOST.DB file that you are trying to recover. The Recover Database routine is working with an information source that you already know to be questionable. If you can use the Recover Database routine to help you get along, that's great, but it should be considered a Band-Aid approach to get you past business hours. After hours, you should rebuild the WPHOST.DB file.

The ultimate fix to your problem with a WPHOST.DB file is almost always to rebuild it. The reason you would use the other options under System Maintenance is because they are less intrusive (you do not have to bring the POA down). You must have exclusive access to the WPHOST.DB file in order to rebuild it or replace it. The POA is generally the only entity with this file open. However, bringing down the POA in some organizations is a big deal, and so you must try to limp along with a damaged WPHOST.DB file. The validate and recover options are really stop-gap measures until you can rebuild the WPHOST.DB file.

General Notes on Repairing Post Office Databases

The great thing about GroupWise architecture is that WPHOST.DB files can always be rebuilt, and with a guarantee against data loss. This is because everything written to the WPHOST.DB file is guaranteed to have been written to its owning domain's WPDOMAIN.DB file. When rebuilding a WPHOST.DB file, GroupWise administration is doing so from the perspective of the post office's owning domain.

The system maintenance routines are not the best way to resolve all GroupWise directory problems, however. For example, if a user's record is missing or incorrect from a post office's address book, synchronizing the user might be a simpler fix. Synchronizing a user's object, or any GroupWise object for that matter, repropagates that object to all GroupWise directory databases. This is far, far better than rebuilding every database on the system just to fix one record.

Fixing WPDOMAIN.DB Files

GroupWise WPDOMAIN.DB files should be approached differently than GroupWise WPHOST.DB files. Here are some concepts to keep in mind when repairing WPDOMAIN.DB files:

- Secondary domain databases are always rebuilt from the perspective of the primary domain's WPDOMAIN.DB file.
- The primary domain and its secondary domains might not always be in sync.
- In some circumstances (although rarely), accessing the backup WPDOMAIN.DB file might be the best solution.
- On some rare occasions, rebuilding a domain database might actually cause more problems than it fixes.

The best way to explore these concepts is through some scenarios.

For scenario #1, you are connected to the primary domain. You attempt to connect to `DOMAINC`, and when trying to do so, you get the error shown in Figure 22.3.

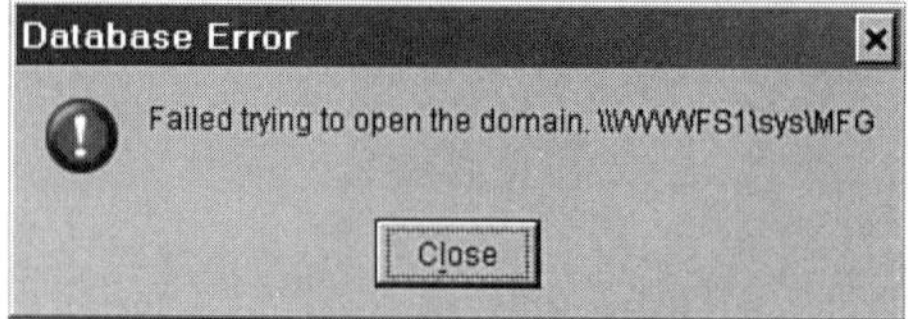

FIGURE 22.3
An error from a damaged WPDOMAIN.DB file.

This error is telling you that your attempt to connect to the WPDOMAIN.DB for `DOMAINC` could not be changed because of a problem with the WPDOMAIN.DB for `DOMAINC`. Upon further investigation, you also see that the Message Transfer Agent (MTA) for `DOMAINC` is not loaded. Things aren't looking good for `DOMAINC`'s domain database.

It's a safe bet that `DOMAINC`'s WPDOMAIN.DB file is corrupt beyond use. You can validate this theory by running a validate operation against `DOMAINC`. It will give some kind of an error, such as "Error opening database". The WPDOMAIN.DB file needs to be replaced. The question then is should the WPDOMAIN.DB file be replaced from backup tape, or should it be rebuilt?

Theory tells us that everything that is in a secondary domain's WPDOMAIN.DB file is replicated up to the primary domain. If there is no reason to believe that this process of replication was impeded, don't hesitate to rebuild the **DOMAINC** WPDOMAIN.DB file. The WPDOMAIN.DB for **DOMAINC** is rebuilt from the WPDOMAIN.DB of the primary domain.

The decision to rebuild a WPDOMAIN.DB file rather than bringing it back from backup largely depends upon your administration model. Suppose that you and one other person administer your GroupWise system. You both connect to the primary domain for administration purposes and connect to a secondary domain only occasionally. In this scenario, with an understanding of architecture, there is no reason to recover a secondary domain database from tape. The primary domain already knows about changes made to that secondary domain, because it proposed all of the changes.

Now consider the following twist: Suppose there is a damaged secondary domain that is in one of your field offices. A team in the field administers the secondary domain, and their Wide Area Network (WAN) link to you is often unreliable. You and the domain administrator already concur that some of the changes made to the secondary domain might never have made it to the primary domain. If the field office has a recent backup of the WPDOMAIN.DB file, their copy might be the most accurate regarding the objects they own.

If they recover their WPDOMAIN.DB from backup tape, you have a new procedure to consider. You can assume that their WPDOMAIN.DB file is accurate, minus any changes that they made in their domain since the backup. The secondary domain administrator can worry about remaking those changes. As long as they didn't add, rename, or delete any users, it's not a big deal. Unfortunately, this secondary domain's WPDOMAIN.DB database is not going to be accurate regarding the changes made to the rest of the GroupWise system. To make matters more confusing, the primary domain database is not going to be accurate regarding objects owned by this out-of-sync secondary domain.

If you rebuild this secondary domain, the field office will lose some changes that the primary domain never knew about, unless, of course, you synchronize the primary domain with the secondary domain first. Here is the procedure for synchronizing the primary domain with the secondary domain:

1. Highlight the secondary domain.
2. Choose Tools, GroupWise Utilities, System Maintenance.
3. Select Sync Primary with Secondary and click Run.
4. Once that procedure is complete, you can rebuild the secondary domain database.

NOTE **You will need file access to the secondary domain to go through this procedure. Because you are dealing with a field office with unstable WAN connections, consider bringing a copy of their domain database to your local site. When you are prompted for the path to the domain database to synchronize with, and later to rebuild, you can point to your local drive, or to a location on the network.**

You had to synchronize the primary domain with the secondary domain so that the primary domain knew about the changes made to the secondary domain. When a secondary domain is rebuilt, it is done from the perspective of the primary domain. The secondary domain database on disk is ignored altogether. The Sync Primary with Secondary operation took care of this for you, pushing up the secondary domain's information, on the objects it owns, to the primary domain. Then when the secondary domain is rebuilt just after the synchronize, the secondary domain will receive those objects back correctly. The secondary domain will also have all of the correct information about the state of the GroupWise objects throughout the rest of the GroupWise system.

For scenario #2, the primary domain WPDOMAIN.DB file is corrupted beyond repair. You know this because you cannot connect to the WPDOMAIN.DB in ConsoleOne, and the MTA for the primary domain will not load.

First of all, as a responsible network administrator, you should certainly have a backup of your primary domain. The question is whether restoring that backup is going to be the best thing to do. Typically, it is *not* the best solution.

The primary domain WPDOMAIN.DB file on your backup will quite likely be outdated, especially if your system is administered from multiple secondary domain sites. Your best hope is a secondary domain that you feel is likely to be in sync with the primary domain. Recall the GroupWise architecture. The GroupWise primary domain broadcasts all changes made to all domains to every other domain. In theory then, if everything is in sync, a secondary domain is just as well informed about the state of the GroupWise directory as the primary domain. You now need to generate a copy of the primary domain database from a secondary domain. Here is the procedure to generate a copy of the primary domain database from a secondary domain:

1. Make sure the primary domain MTA is unloaded and that nothing is accessing the primary domain's WPDOMAIN.DB file.
2. Rename the primary domain's WPDOMAIN.DB file to something that will indicate that this is the corrupt or bad database.

3. Connect to the secondary domain that is most likely to be in sync with the primary domain.
4. Highlight the primary domain.
5. Choose Tools, GroupWise Utilities, System Maintenance.
6. Select the Replace Primary with Secondary option, as shown in Figure 22.4.

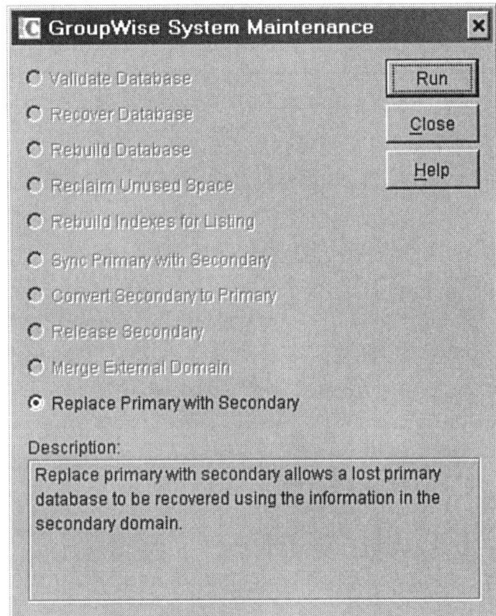

FIGURE 22.4
The Replace Primary with Secondary option allows you to recover a lost primary database.

You have now re-created the primary domain from the secondary domain. This solution is ideal because it does not require going to a backup solution.

Fixing GroupWise Directory Anomalies Without Rebuilds

There are other problems in the GroupWise directory that can't be readily fixed with system maintenance routines. In some cases, system maintenance routines could fix the problem, but you might want to avoid the downtime associated with rebuilding the databases.

I have seen cases where an object is acting stubborn. You might need to slap it around a bit to get it to behave. Usually, these kinds of problems occur with user objects.

NOTE **Technically, user objects cannot act stubborn. I simply enjoy the anthropomorphism more than I should. The cases described here usually result when a single field in a record is out of sync, and perhaps damaged. By repeatedly attempting to rewrite that record, the field problem can be corrected.**

Following are the actions that you can take with a user object to get it to behave. They are listed in the order of least drastic to most drastic measures. Most of the ideas here also apply to other GroupWise objects:

- Synchronize the user.
- Edit the user and make a minor change, click OK, and then remove the change.
- Remove GroupWise-specific eDirectory attributes on the user.

First, when zeroing in on an object, be sure to connect to the domain that owns that object. This will speed up your troubleshooting significantly, because GroupWise administration snap-ins will write the change directly, instead of passing the change through multiple MTAs.

Synchronize the User

Following are the steps for synchronizing a user object:

1. Highlight the user object.
2. Choose Tools, GroupWise Utilities, Synchronize.
3. Click Yes on the resulting dialog box.

This action rewrites the user's object to the WPDOMAIN.DB file, with much of the information coming from eDirectory. The synchronize also rebroadcasts the user's object record to all GroupWise directory databases. For a complete look at this process, refer to the synchronize section of Chapter 7.

Edit the User

This is much like synchronizing the user object because it re-propagates the record, but sometimes you'll have more success this way than by synchronizing the user. Follow these steps to edit the problematic user object:

1. Highlight the user object.
2. Right-click and select Properties.
3. Make an unobtrusive change to the object.

Don't change the object name, post office, or anything like that. Change a fax number, or something similar.

4. Click OK.

This action also repropagates the record to every domain and post office on the system. The difference here is that there is new record data involved, which might help solve the problem in some cases.

Remove GroupWise Specific eDirectory Attributes

This procedure uncouples a user's GroupWise Directory Service object from its eDirectory counterpart. After performing this step on a user, you will see that the user's object in the GroupWise view has a white shirt. The user's object in the eDirectory browser view will have a red shirt.

NOTE

You might need to exit ConsoleOne after performing this operation to see the shirt color difference.

Follow these steps:

1. Highlight the user object.
2. Choose Tools, GroupWise Utilities, GW/eDirectory Association, Disassociate GroupWise Attributes.

By uncoupling a user's GroupWise object from the eDirectory object, you eliminate one more factor. Sometimes your GroupWise Directory Services is perfectly healthy, but your eDirectory tree is having problems. Under these circumstances, you use the Disassociate GroupWise Attributes utility.

When you need to recouple a user's GroupWise object with the eDirectory object, do the following:

1. Highlight the user object in the GroupWise view.
2. Select Tools, GroupWise Utilities, GW/eDirectory Association, Associate Objects.
3. Choose the Select Existing eDirectory Object option.
4. Browse to the user's eDirectory object, and then click the OK button.

I often use these procedures when moving users. I disassociate the eDirectory object from the GroupWise object, move the user, and then reassociate the GroupWise object with its eDirectory counterpart.

How GroupWise Directory Changes and Objects Are Replicated

When troubleshooting the GroupWise directory, it's helpful to understand how changes replicate in the GroupWise directory. The following is an exhaustive discussion about how one object is replicated.

GroupWise object replication basically moves up from a secondary domain to the primary domain and from the primary domain to all other domains. Each domain is responsible for replicating objects to its respective post offices.

Objects and changes to objects or records in the GroupWise directory are replicated in the same manner.

Understanding a Scenario

Now for the long explanation, consider the following scenario:

- TKRATZER is the user
- DOMAINB is a secondary domain
- PO2 is the PO off of DOMAINB
- DOMAINA is the primary domain
- PO1 is the PO off of DOMAINA
- DOMAINC is a secondary domain
- DOMAIND is a secondary domain

A GroupWise administrator is connected to DOMAINB. The administrator creates TKRATZER. TKRATZER is added to PO2. Here's what happens:

1. TKRATZER's record is committed to the WPDOMAIN.DB file for DOMAINB by ConsoleOne.
2. TKRATZER's record is broadcast to PO2 by DOMAINB's MTA.

3. TKRATZER's record is broadcast to DOMAINA's MTA by DOMAINB's MTA.
4. PO2's POA accepts TKRATZER's record and commits it to PO2's WPHOST.DB file.
5. DOMAINA's MTA accepts TKRATZER's record and commits it to DOMAINA's WPDOMAIN.DB file.
6. DOMAINA's MTA broadcasts TKRATZER's record to its post office PO1.
7. PO1's POA accepts TKRATZER's record and commits it to PO1's WPHOST.DB file.
8. DOMAINA broadcasts TKRATZER's record to all other domains in the system besides DOMAINB. This includes DOMAINC and DOMAIND.
9. DOMAINC accepts the broadcast of TKRATZER and does everything that DOMAINA did with the object, except it does not broadcast TKRATZER to anyone outside its domain. That is DOMAINA's job, because DOMAINA is the primary domain.
10. DOMAIND does exactly what DOMAINC does.

Understanding the File Flow and Logic

The following is a very detailed scenario that illustrates the file flow and the logic of a user object creation. The names of the files are relevant only to the operation that took place on a test system. The names of the files created on your system will be different:

- TKRATZER is the user
- DOMAINB is the secondary domain
- PO2 is the PO off of DOMAINB
- DOMAINA is the primary domain
- PO1 is the PO off of DOMAINA
- DOMAINC is the secondary domain
- DOMAIND is the secondary domain

For this scenario, communication between all domains and post offices is via TCP/IP. Here's what happens:

1. Connected to DOMAINB, the administrator creates a user object, TKRATZER, under DOMAINB, PO2.
2. The change is committed to the DOMAINB WPDOMAIN.DB file.

3. There are two files created in the DOMAINB\WPCSIN\2 directory:

   File one is called A7D93EDD.000

   File two is called A7D93EDD.001

4. File one is picked up by DOMAINB's MTA and copied to the GWINPROG\2 directory using a router thread (RTR), and moved to the input queue for the MTP portion of the MTA.

   DOMAINB's MTA log reports the following:

   ```
   RTR: DOMAINB: 00000800: Routing
   comm3/sys:\domainb\mslocal\gwinprog\2\00000800

   RTR: DOMAINB: 00000800: Originator: DOMAINB.Domain
   ➥Message Server [ADS]
   RTR: DOMAINB: 00000800 Priority 10 :0:0 : Transfer to
   ➥DOMAINA

   RTR: DOMAINB: 00000800: Message queued:
   comm3/sys:\domainb\mslocal\mshold\dom3859\2\00000800.001
   ```

5. The MTP portion of the DOMAINB MTA finds the file and transmits it to DOMAINA, the primary domain. Note that the name of the thread is DOMAINA-IPS0 but that this is a thread created by DOMAINB's MTA.

   DOMAINB's MTA log reports the following:

   ```
   MTP: DOMAINA-ipS0: Connection established.
   ➥151.155.106.66
   MTP: DOMAINA-ipS0: Transmitting file
   comm3/sys:\domainb\mslocal\mshold\dom3859\2\00000800.001
   ```

6. A new copy of the message is also made for PO2, and queued up to the MTP process of the DOMAINB MTA.

   DOMAINB's MTA log reports the following:

   ```
   RTR: DOMAINB: 00000801: Routing
   comm3/sys:\domainb\mslocal\gwinprog\2\00000801

   RTR: DOMAINB: 00000801: Originator: DOMAINB.Domain
   ➥Message Server [ADS]

   RTR: DOMAINB: 00000801 Priority 10 :0:0 : Transfer to
   DOMAINB.PO2:ADS

   RTR: DOMAINB: 00000801: Message queued:
   comm3/sys:\domainb\mslocal\mshold\po23a0e\2\00000801.001
   ```

7. DOMAINB's MTA transmits the file to PO2 and reports the following in the log:

```
MTP: PO2-ipS0: Transmitting file
comm3/sys:\domainb\mslocal\mshold\po23a0e\2\00000801.001
```

8. PO2's POA MTP process reports the following about receiving the message from the domain:

```
MTP: Receiver thread started: 1 running
MTP: DOMAINB: Attention packet received
MTP: DOMAINB: Accepting connection
MTP: DOMAINB: Returning acknowledge (0)
MTP: DOMAINB: File transfer request received

MTP: DOMAINB: Received file: COMM3\SYS:/DOMAINB/PO2\
➥wpcsout\ofs\2\A7d950d6

MTP: DOMAINB: Returning acknowledge (3)

Processing a7d950d6.000
Domain Message Server.DOMAINB
Admin message processed: OK
MTP: DOMAINB: File transfer request received

MTP: DOMAINB: Received file: COMM3\SYS:/DOMAINB/PO2\
➥wpcsout\ofs\2\A7d950d8

MTP: DOMAINB: Returning acknowledge (3)
Processing a7d950d8.000
Domain Message Server.DOMAINB
Admin message processed: OK
```

9. The POA places the administration files in the WPCSOUT\ADS\2 directory. They are called 37D950D6.000 and 37D950D8.000.

10. The delivery thread on the POA then tickles the admin thread of the POA (this does not show in the log—the event takes place in the POA stack, behind the scenes).

    The admin thread reports the following:

```
ADM: Completed: Update object in Post Office -
User DOMAINB.PO2.TKRATZER (Administrator: (WWW_TREE_1)
tkratzer.WWW, Domain: DOMAINB)
ADM: Completed: Update object in Post Office - MTA
➥DOMAINB
(Administrator: (WWW) tkratzer.WWW, Domain: DOMAINB)
```

TIP

The GroupWise POA reports who made the change to the object. However, it is sometimes incorrect. The reason for this is that sometimes the GroupWise snap-ins do not update the Last Modified By field, and so a transaction will report in the log of the POA as being performed by ADMIN-A when the change was really performed by ADMIN-B.

11. Meanwhile, DOMAINA's MTA is receiving the file from DOMAINB's MTA.

    DOMAINA's MTA log reports the following:

    ```
    MTP: DOMAINB: Received file:
    comm3/sys:\domaina\mslocal\gwinprog\2\00000801

    RTR: DOMAINA: 00000801: Routing
    comm3/sys:\domaina\mslocal\gwinprog\2\00000801
    ```

12. DOMAINA's MTA identifies the message as an administrative message and queues the message up to its admin thread in the WPCSOUT\ADS\2 directory.

    DOMAINA's MTA log reports the following:

    ```
    RTR: DOMAINA: 00000801: Originator: DOMAINB.Domain
    ➥Message Server [ADS]

    RTR: DOMAINA: 00000801 Priority 10 :0:0 :
    Transfer to DOMAINA.Domain Message Server:ADS

    RTR: DOMAINA: 00000801: Message queued:
    comm3/sys:\domaina\wpcsout\ads\2\B7d94d48.00!
    ```

13. DOMAINA's MTA tickles the admin thread, and the admin thread reports the following:

    ```
    ADM: Completed: Update replica User DOMAINB.PO2.TKRATZER
    ```

14. DOMAINA's MTA then queues the message up to its post office, PO1.

    It does this in the exact manner in which the DOMAINB MTA queued up the change to PO2.

15. DOMAINA's MTA then broadcasts the administration message to both DOMAINC and DOMAIND in the same manner that DOMAINB broadcasts the administration message up to DOMAINA.

16. DOMAINC and DOMAIND's MTAs broadcast the administration message to their post offices, just as DOMAINB broadcasts its administration message to PO2.

A very simple operation in GroupWise administration becomes a file that must be replicated to all other GroupWise directory databases.

Best Practices for Working with the GroupWise Directory

For a large GroupWise system, here are some good rules to follow:

- **If you perform a large amount of operations, such as grafting or modifying multiple users on a domain, GroupWise administrator should be connected to the domain that owns the objects being modified.** If you do not do this, you will generate about 50% more administration traffic between domains than you need to. This means that not all of your administration will be done through the primary domain.
- **If your system has a lot of administration messages flowing through it, implement the 2nd Mail Priority Router on the primary domain MTA.** To do this, edit the MTA object, go to the Agents Settings page, and check the box named 2nd High Priority Router. This will provide an additional thread for processing admin messages, making bottlenecks at the MTA less likely.
- **Design your GroupWise system so that your primary domain is only doing administrative work.** If the primary domain is housing the GroupWise Internet Agent (GWIA), or is a routing hub for all other domains, it might not be efficient enough in servicing GroupWise administration changes. It is ideal to see to it that the primary domain has no post offices off of it.

These best practices should be more closely adhered to in systems with a few thousand or more users.

Bulletproofing the GroupWise Directory

The following practice is not widespread, but it is definitely worth mentioning. This idea came about when a customer's primary domain WPDOMAIN.DB file went bad. The idea of going to backup just wasn't all that pleasing because of all the changes made in the system since they performed their last backup. The customer needed to re-create the primary domain from a secondary domain.

The system maintenance feature, Replace Primary with Secondary, is a lifesaver, but it raises an important question—how do you guarantee the integrity of a secondary domain database, ensuring that you'll have a failsafe backup if your primary domain goes bad?

Here is a way to do just that:

1. Create a special purpose secondary domain, for example, a domain called `BACKUP-PRIMARY-DOMAIN`. Host it somewhere in your network, in close proximity of the primary domain.

   Ideally, it should be on a separate server, but on the same LAN segment as the server hosting the primary domain.

   You need to disable others from connecting to this WPDOMAIN.DB file with ConsoleOne. You do this by tricking all domains into thinking that this secondary domain is at a different UNC path than it really is. Steps 2 and 3 help you do this.
2. While connected to the primary domain, change the UNC path to the secondary domain `BACKUP-PRIMARY-DOMAIN` to make it invalid.
3. Restrict eDirectory object rights to this domain so that only a few people have such rights.
4. Establish MTA-to-MTA links so that only the primary domain can speak to this domain.
5. Establish a TCP/IP link between the two domains.

TIP

In order to connect to the `BACKUP-PRIMARY-DOMAIN` domain, you need to choose Tools, GroupWise System Operations, Select Domain, and then manually attach to the WPDOMAIN.DB for this domain. Right-clicking and choosing Connect won't work because the UNC path to the `BACKUP-PRIMARY-DOMAIN` is incorrect.

The system now has, in effect, a fully replicated version of the primary domain database, which is only about one minute out of sync with the primary domain. Should the primary domain database become irretrievably corrupted (in the case of a major disk failure, for instance), you have a secondary domain database that is the best possible candidate for use in a Replace Primary with Secondary operation. Just connect manually to WPDOMAIN.DB for the `BACKUP-PRIMARY-DOMAIN` and then perform the Replace Primary with Secondary system maintenance routine that was outlined previously in this chapter.

Understanding the Administration System

The administration of the GroupWise system goes hand in hand with the GroupWise directory. The administration system of GroupWise consists of two separates sets of software components:

- GroupWise administrator snap-ins to ConsoleOne
- The admin threads of the MTA and the POA

The GroupWise Snap-Ins

The GroupWise administration snap-ins are often misunderstood. Administrators are quite often cognizant of the version of the GroupWise client, or the version of the GroupWise agents. There is often little emphasis placed on determining the version of GroupWise administration.

The version of administration is especially important when you have implemented a patch or a new version of GroupWise, and you really want to leverage the new fixes or features in that patch or new version. As discussed in Chapter 7, in order to determine the version of GroupWise administration you are using, do the following:

1. Load ConsoleOne.
2. Choose Help, About Snapins. You should see the screen shown in Figure 22.5.
3. Click a snap-in to see its version information.

Is this the version you want to be running? Is this version of the GroupWise snap-ins on every file server or workstation where ConsoleOne is running?

Many of Novell's customers have a huge GroupWise installation that is managed by several administrators. It is important that everyone who runs ConsoleOne is using the latest GroupWise snap-ins, or at least the latest ones that have been approved for your organization. If this is not the case, someone might be causing problems in the GroupWise system—problems due to bugs that have been addressed in a later patch of the GroupWise administrator snap-ins.

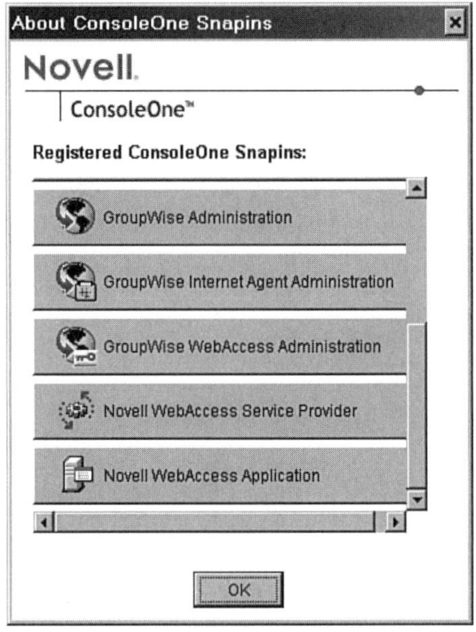

FIGURE 22.5 About Snapins in ConsoleOne.

TIP

The GroupWise 6.5.1 snap-ins allow you to restrict which version of snap-ins are allowed to connect to a GroupWise domain. This can be useful for preventing older snap-ins from accessing a WPDOMAIN.DB file and performing administration tasks. Define this setting from Tools, GroupWise System Operations, Admin Lockout Settings. From there, you can lock out older snap-ins. When administrators attempt to connect to a domain with older snap-ins, they will receive the error shown in Figure 22.6.

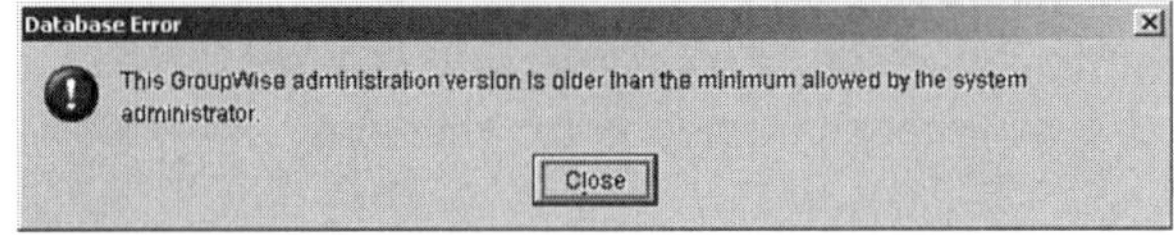

FIGURE 22.6 When you lock out older snap-ins, an error will occur, restricting access from older GroupWise snap-ins.

NOTE

Only the 6.5 and later snap-ins will honor the lockout setting. GroupWise 6.x and older snap-ins do not honor this setting; they can access the domain database even when this setting is in effect through the 6.5.1 snap-ins.

Understanding the GroupWise Admin Thread

Before GroupWise 5.5x and GroupWise 6.x, the admin thread was actually a separate agent. It was the administration agent, or ADA, in GroupWise 5.0 through 5.2. In GroupWise 4.1, the admin server was called ADS. It is helpful to know this because as you explore the GroupWise system, you will actually see the terms ADA and ADS used. In GroupWise 6.5, ADS, ADA, and ADM all refer to the admin thread.

In GroupWise 6.5, the admin thread is just a subprocess of the MTA and the POA. In the MTA and POA log files when the admin thread runs, it is logged as ADM. This chapter discussed this earlier, and this concept is also discussed in Chapters 8, "Configuring the Post Office Agent (POA)," and 9 "Configuring the Message Transfer Agent (MTA)."

The admin thread on an MTA or POA is responsible for updating its respective directory database. This admin thread has two input queues:

- **The ADS directory queue:** The first input queue for the admin thread is the `WPCSOUT\ADS\2` directory off of a post office or domain. The admin thread comes to life every minute. For example, when a POA's admin thread discovers a file in the `PO\WPCSOUT\ADS\2` directory, it makes a change in the WPHOST.DB file. If a domain MTA's admin thread discovers a file in the `WPCSOUT\ADS\2` directory, it makes the appropriate change to the WPDOMAIN.DB file.
- **The tickle queue:** The admin thread will also come to life when it gets a tickle from the POA or MTA that owns the thread. In GroupWise 6.5, although the admin thread comes to life every minute, when an MTA or POA gets an administration message via a TCP/IP connection, it queues the message up to the admin thread by a routine in memory. At the GroupWise domain/MTA level, quite often administration files do not go into the `WPCSOUT\ADS\2` directory. They are instead handed off to the admin thread while they are in the `MSLOCAL\GWINPROG` directory.

Summary

There are a variety of ways to fix a GroupWise directory problem. You need to determine what the problem is and determine the most expedient solution. With an understanding of the architecture, you will be better able to troubleshoot these problems and find the best solutions.

Always remember that the GroupWise synchronization process is complex, and that several GroupWise agents might need to be involved in order to replicate an object. Make sure every agent is communicating correctly before going further.

CHAPTER 23

Troubleshooting GroupWise

CHAPTER 23

Every application, or suite of applications, has its own particular set of error messages; GroupWise is no exception. As you administer your GroupWise system, you will inevitably see some errors. This chapter discusses the logic behind the errors and gives you some procedures to help you quickly arrive at the root of the problem that is plaguing you.

NOTE

For information specific to troubleshooting GroupWise message flow, refer to Chapter 20, "Troubleshooting Message Flow."

The Five Most Common GroupWise Errors

The following sections include a quick reference to the five most common errors seen in GroupWise, what they typically mean, and the actions to take to solve them.

D107—Record Not Found

Description: This error means that one record has a reference to a second record, and the second record is not found. This is typically considered a "content-related" problem in a message store database (rather than a structural problem). This typically happens when a pointer record in a user's database (USER*xxx*.DB) points to a record in a message database that no longer exists. Another possibility is that a master record in a message database (MSG*Xx*.DB) points to another record in the message database that does not exist.

Action: In the case of a message store database, usually a contents check of the database resolves the problem. The trick is determining which database to check. Chapter 20 explains where data is kept based upon the message type or who sent it. If you have questions as to which database to check, read Chapter 20.

TIP

You can run a contents check on a specific MSG*Xx*.DB file. To do so, run the standalone GWCHECK and enter the name of the MSG*Xx*.DB file in the User/Resource field. See Figure 23.1 for an example.

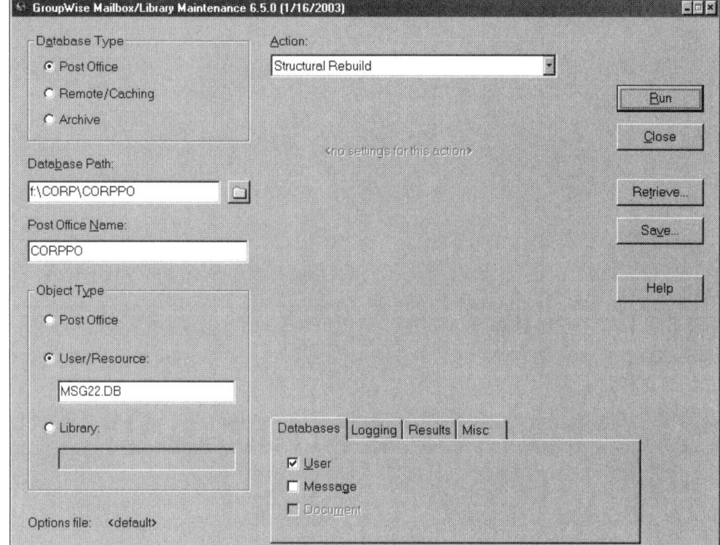

FIGURE 23.1
Running GWCHECK on an MSG*Xx*.DB file.

8209—Path to File Not Found

Description: In this case, GroupWise is trying to access a file and it cannot. This generally means that the path you specified is either incorrect, or the GroupWise software cannot reach the path because of assigned rights. If the software can reach the path, it cannot find the file it expects to find there.

Action: Indicate a correct path, put the file in place that GroupWise is looking for, and make sure that the GroupWise process has rights to the location indicated.

C05D—Dependent Store Does Not Exist on Disk

Description: Every database in the GroupWise message store is registered in the NGWGUARD.DB file. This error means that a database is registered in the NGWGUARD.DB file, but it is not physically in the location that the NGWGUARD.DB says the file should be. In the case of an NGWGUARD.DB on a post office, all USER*xxx*.DB files should be in the `<post office>\OFUSER` directory. If the Post Office Agent (POA) reports a C05D error on a file by the name of USER123.DB, this means that the NGWGUARD.DB file reports that the file is in the `<post office>\OFUSER` directory, but it cannot find the file there. If the POA complains of a C05D error on a MSGX*x*.DB file, that means it cannot find the file in the `<post office>\OFMSG` directory.

The GroupWise message store can also exist in a GroupWise archive, a GroupWise caching mailbox, or a GroupWise remote mailbox.

Action: Although the cause is easily stated, the action is not so easy to spell out. The solution varies based on the conditions in which you have the problem. This is best illustrated with a few scenarios:

Scenario 1—Issue: USERA moved from PO1 to PO2. However, the user's mail did not move to PO2. The administrator moved USERA back to PO1, fixed USERA's mailbox, and then attempted to move USERA to PO2. The POA at PO2 gives the error `C05D` with reference to USERA's USER*xxx*.DB file.

Scenario 1—Explanation: On PO2, a new USER*xxx*.DB file was created for USERA the first time USERA moved there. USERA might have even received a couple of messages from USERxxx.DB from the PO2 post office. When USERA was moved back to PO1, PO2 sent the few new message items to PO1, deleted the USER*xxx*.DB file from the post office, and unregistered it in the NGWGUARD.DB file. Everything is correct, but the POA has an old image of the NGWGUARD.DB cached in memory, and it hasn't reread the NGWGUARD.DB file. As strange as it might seem, the POA is the same one that deleted the reference to the USER*xxx*.DB file in the NGWGUARD.DB, but it doesn't even acknowledge that.

Scenario 1—Action: You need to bring the POA down and then back up so that it rereads the NGWGUARD.DB file. Then you must attempt to move USERA again. See Chapter 13, "Moving Users," for more guidance on trying to move a user when a move fails the first time.

Scenario 2—Issue: A user is attempting to archive a message, and receives a `C05D` error. You look in the Archive directory and there is only a NGWGUARD.DB and a MSG.DB file (there's no USER.DB file).

Scenario 2—Explanation: In the Archive directory (the `OFXXXARC` directory, whereby the *`XXX`* is the user's three-character FID), there is an NGWGUARD.DB file. This file is complaining that the USER.DB or the MSG.DB file in the `OFXXXARC` directory is not registered in the NGWGUARD.DB file.

Scenario 2—Action: Follow these steps:

1. Exit the GroupWise client as the user with the problem.
2. Go to the `<archive>OFXXXARC` directory.
3. Rename the NGWGUARD.DB to NGWGUARD.BAD.
4. Rename the MSG.DB to MSG.GOOD (if there is a MSG.DB).
5. Go into GroupWise as the user.
6. Have the user send one simple message to and from his/her e-mail address.
7. Archive that one message.
8. Exit GroupWise.
9. Go to the `<archive>OFXXXARC` directory.
10. Delete the newly created MSG.DB file.
11. Rename the MSG.GOOD file to MSG.DB.
12. Run the stand-alone GWCHECK on the user's archive, as shown in Figure 23.2. Perform the Re-create User Database action.

After doing this, all of the user's messages that were recovered from the MSG.DB file will have their pointers added to the USER.DB file. The messages will be placed in the Cabinet.

TIP

The shipping GroupWise 6.5.0 GWCHECK will not re-create a user's USER.DB file from the MSG.DB file in a user's archive. This problem is resolved in the GroupWise 6.5.1 (or better) GWCHECK for GroupWise 6.5.

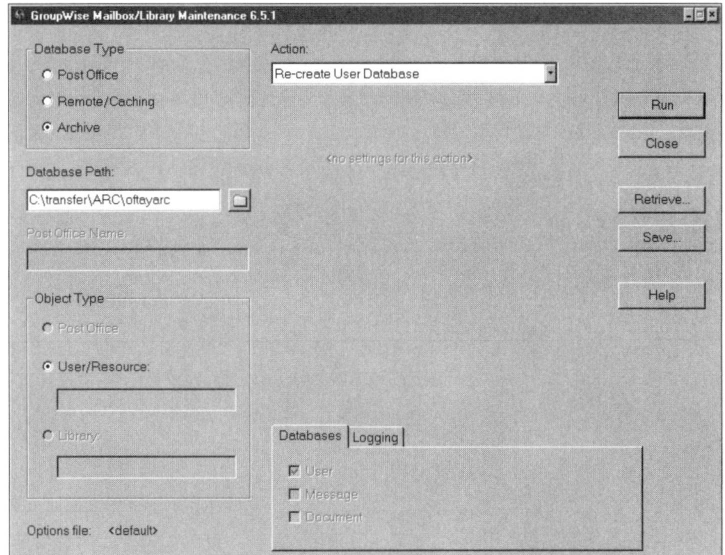

FIGURE 23.2
Running GWCHECK on a user's archive.

C067—Store Number Is Invalid

Description: This error means that a database in the GroupWise message store is physically located in the message store, but is not registered in the NGWGUARD.DB file. This error might be thought of as the reverse of the `C05D` error. This is generally evidence of the fact that the NGWGUARD.DB file is damaged, and therefore lost its reference to a database, or the file was placed back into message store area manually, but was not reregistered in the NGWGUARD.DB file.

Action: Once again, the action you take varies based upon the scenario. Here's an example of one scenario:

Issue: The user `TKRATZER` tries to log into his account. He cannot log in; he gets a `C067` error when trying to do so. The POA also reports a `C067` error in its log when user `TKRATZER` tries to log in.

Explanation: `TKRATZER`'s user database file (USERTAY.DB) is not registered in the NGWGUARD.DB file. It does exist in the `<post office>\OFUSER` directory. The NGWGUARD.DB file probably sustained some damage, and as a result the Registry for USERTAY.DB was lost from the NGWGUARD.DB.

Action: Follow these steps:

1. Go to the `<post office>\OFUSER` directory of the post office where `TKRATZER` resides.

2. Rename the file USERTAY.DB to USERTAY.GOOD.
3. Have the user `TKRATZER` log in, and then have user `TKRATZER` log out. Doing so will create a new USERTAY.DB file that is now registered in the NGWGUARD.DB file.
4. Rename the new USERTAY.DB file to USERTAY.NEW. (You might have to wait for several minutes to be able to do this because the POA has this file cached. Otherwise, you can bring the POA down and back up.)
5. Rename the USERTAY.GOOD file to USERTAY.DB.

The user `TKRATZER` should be able to log in now, without getting the `C067` error.

C022—Database Damage

Description: The database is damaged—structurally. This means that when GroupWise is attempting to read the database, it isn't finding the layout of the database to be standard. GroupWise cannot proceed in accessing the database, because it cannot guarantee consistent results. Tying this to an analogy—imagine you come into your bedroom in the dark and your other half has moved the furniture around. There's no guarantee you aren't going to stub your toe if you proceed.

Action: The database needs to be rebuilt. If the database is a GroupWise domain or post office database, it must be rebuilt from the System Maintenance utility. If it's a message store database, it must be structurally rebuilt from GWCHECK or from Mailbox/Library Maintenance.

Using the Scientific Method

Before beginning this discussion, it might not be a bad idea to review the scientific method. Most high school science students learn that this method has four important steps:

1. Observe
2. Hypothesize
3. Predict based upon the hypothesis
4. Test the hypothesis

The scientific method provides you with a very effective plan for troubleshooting. Too often, administrators are so wound up in their search for a solution, they shoot from the hip, hoping perhaps to stumble on the answer. Sometimes this works.

Sometimes, though, you'll encounter a real stumper of a problem, and the standard bag of tricks isn't going to help. This is when the scientific method can really help.

Observation Tools

The most important part of the scientific method is the observation phase. For the scientific method to work well, you need to have a good set of observation tools. You must carefully observe the conditions that are generating the errors in order to make meaningful predictions. The following sections cover some of the tools that allow you to take a close look at the components in your GroupWise system.

Windows Workstations/Servers

The following tools are for Windows-based systems:

- **WINIPCFG (Win95/98 only):** This utility tells you vital information about the IP configuration of the local machine.
- **IPCONFIG (Windows 2000):** This command-line version of the WINIPCFG utility tells you vital information about the IP configuration of the local machine.
- **PING:** The PING tool allows you to send small packets via TCP/IP to any host on the network or internetwork (or Internet, for that matter). If you can't connect to the POA, you should see whether you can ping it.
- **TRACERT:** The `tracert` command is used to determine how a network packet is being sent and received and the amount of hops required for that packet to get to its destination.
- **TELNET:** The TELNET tool allows you to open a TCP/IP connection on any port, to any host on the network or Internet. If you can't connect to the POA with the GroupWise client, perhaps you should see if you can connect to port `1677` (the client/server port) of the POA using the TELNET tool.
- **REGMON:** This utility tells you what calls are being made to the Registry. Although it takes some practice to use this tool well, it's great

for determining which Registry entries are causing a problem. You can obtain Registry Monitor (REGMON) from `www.sysinternals.com`.

- **FILEMON:** This utility is similar to REGMON, except that it tells you every file on a Windows platform that is accessed. You can obtain this utility from `www.sysinternals.com` as well.

NetWare Servers

These tools will work on your NetWare-based systems:

- **PING.NLM:** This is the NetWare version of the PING tool. It allows you to choose the packet size, and will even keep some simple statistical tallies as you ping hosts from the server console.
- **GWIP.NLM:** This tool is a little better than a ping, and almost as good as a TELNET. Because there is no true TELNET tool for a NetWare server, GWIP.NLM is an excellent addition to your troubleshooting toolkit. You can download it from `support.novell.com`. Search for GWIP.NLM in the knowledgebase.
- **IPTRACE.NLM**: This tool is the equivalent of the TRACERT tool on the Windows platform. It allows you to trace the IP route from a NetWare server.
- **TCPCON.NLM:** Load TCPCON and then go to Protocol Information, TCP, TCP Connections. You can determine whether a GroupWise agent is actually listening on a port.
- **MONITOR.NLM:** Here you can get an idea of how your system resources are faring. Look at things such as the Disk Cache Utilization and LRU Sitting time. (This is the menu tree on a NetWare 6.0 server.) This value should be well above 15 minutes. You can also determine which server processes are taking up the most CPU time. This is a very powerful and complex tool.

GroupWise Error Codes

Now that you have some observation tools in your scientific method toolbox, you need to know what the error codes mean. Most problems reported by GroupWise components are accompanied with some kind of a four-character error code, such as `8201` or `C05D`. These codes map to certain kinds of problems. Rather than memorize the individual mappings, however, it is useful to learn the families, or classes, of error codes.

82*xx* Errors

The `82xx` class of errors indicates some sort of file access or file I/O problem. Perhaps the POA is trying to access a database at a given path, but the database is not there (`8209`, path not found). A possibility is that file-system rights have not been granted to a Message Transfer Agent (MTA) that is attempting to poll a remote post office (`8201`, access denied).

89*xx* Errors

You will generally see `89xx` errors in conjunction with TCP/IP communication problems. For example, if a POA goes down, the GroupWise client will report an `8908` error. If the MTA times out on a communication with a POA, it might report an `8912` or an `8913` error. The `89xx` error suite also includes many errors outside of the realm of TCP/IP communications, but the non-TCP/IP errors do not crop up as often.

C*xxx* Errors

The `Cxxx` errors typically point to database structural integrity problems. For example, a user receives `C022` errors when creating any item in GroupWise. The error means that database integrity has been compromised. The `C04F` error indicates that the database checksum did not add up correctly. In either case, you know from the error class a GroupWise store file has structural damage.

There are two `Cxxx` -class errors that are a little bit different: `C05D` and `C067`. Both of these errors indicate structural damage to the information/message store, rather than just to one store file. This means that one or more store files are not correctly registered in the GroupWise guardian database. `C05D` indicates a registered store file that could not be found. `C067` indicates that a store file could not be created, because an unregistered version exists on disk.

D*xxx* Errors

The `Dxxx` class of errors points to database content problems. The problem might be a missing record, which will return a `D107` error. A missing user record (when the POA tries to deliver to a user who does not exist in the address book), might flag a `D101` error. The problem might not be that a record is missing, though. It might simply be that the data does not match what the GroupWise component was expecting to see, such as when the entered password does not match the one required (D109, access denied).

E*xxx* Errors

The Exxx class of errors changes the rules a bit. Instead of mapping to a database problem or I/O problem, E-class error messages indicate that the problem was found while using a document-management feature. The error state might actually indicate a normal situation, such as when a user tries to access a document that he or she has not been given rights to (E51B). It might also indicate a content problem with the document-management databases. A missing document record will return an E811 error.

Using the Error Classes

If you know what each error class means, you will still be missing an important piece of the puzzle. Most GroupWise errors tell you what kind of a problem was encountered, but do not tell you which component had the problem. For instance, if the GroupWise client is encountering structural problems working with the GroupWise archive, it will probably report a C022 or C04F error. Those are the same errors the POA would use to report problems with a message database in the post office directory. The same error can be reported by two different components, and it can be caused by a problem in any of several areas.

The only way you can know which component has the problem is to apply some of the architectural information available in the rest of the book. Here are some questions you can ask yourself that might help:

- **Which component reported the error?** For instance, if the POA reports a C022, you will see the error in the log. Check the log for any other information about the problem. Generally, the POA will report which database it's having a problem with.
- **Which components do not report the error?** Suppose the client reports an error, but the POA does not. This narrows the problem quite a bit. The databases that a client has exclusive access to that the POA does not have access to are the archive databases and the caching mode and remote databases.
- **Which pieces are touched by the component(s) that report(s) the error?** If you know, for instance, that the client reported an error, but the POA did not, you need to determine which pieces the client

touches that the POA does not. In client/server access mode, the problem would likely be the GroupWise archive. In direct access mode, the problem might be the master mailbox or the archive.

The Complete List of GroupWise Error Messages

As of this writing, Novell has not published a complete list of the error codes used by all GroupWise components. Fortunately, the more common errors have been well documented, and appear online at Novell's support connection Web site.

The Novell Support Connection

When you see an error message, you can look it up in the knowledgebase at `http://support.novell.com`. The odds are good that you are not the first person to see this message. This method is helpful for looking up messages one at a time, as you encounter them.

The Novell Online GroupWise 6.5. Documentation

You can access the GroupWise 6.5. online documentation to get a comprehensive list of most of the error codes in GroupWise. This site can be very helpful in identifying the various error messages' meanings. It is found at `http://www.novell.com/documentation/lg/gw65/index.html` under the Troubleshooting Guides section.

GroupWise Magazine

The GroupWise magazine is a great tool for administrators and users alike. I also write for this magazine. To access this magazine, go to one of the following locations:

`www.gwmag.com`
`www.novell.com/coolsolutions/gwmag/`

Use the Support Connection

Although the troubleshooting advice in this chapter is sound, here's the best advice of all—don't troubleshoot if you don't have to!

Novell has a world-class support site. Use the knowledgebase at `http://support.novell.com` before you begin racking your brain. In most cases, the exact set of conditions you are seeing has already been documented by

Novell Technical Services, and one or more ready-made solutions await you. Why re-invent the wheel?

Using Three-Step Mailbox Troubleshooting

On a large system, you might see mailbox-related errors often enough that you don't want to take the time to actually troubleshoot each one. Well, a GroupWise administrator I worked with passed along a gem. This administrator takes a standard approach to every problem he gets with a user mailbox, no matter what the error is. This approach fixes about 80% of the problems right off the bat.

The nice thing about this approach is that the operations you will be performing are not invasive or destructive. These actions can be performed on a healthy mailbox with no ill effects. This means that almost no matter what the problem, you can take these steps safely.

You could use this procedure to solve a myriad of problems:

- One user receives errors when trying to send new messages.
- Everybody receives errors when trying to send a message to one particular user.
- A user reports that messages he/she has read are showing up as unread.

This list could go on and on. Suffice it to say that if you think the problem is related in any way to the GroupWise message/information store, this procedure is a good place to start.

These steps must be completed in order:

1. Synchronize the user.
2. Run a structural rebuild on the user database using GWCHECK. (Server-based or stand-alone—see Chapter 17, "Maintaining the GroupWise System," for more details.)
3. Run an analyze/fix of the contents of the user database (do not include the message database).

The logic behind these steps is simple. First, make sure that the user object you want to work on is correctly represented in the post office database. The synchronize operation takes care of that.

Second, make sure that the user database for this user is structurally clean, with no damaged blocks or records for you to choke on. The structural rebuild operation takes care of this.

Finally, you want to make sure that all records in the user database correctly point to records elsewhere in the information store. The analyze/fix operation does this for you.

The rest of this section walks through each of these operations in turn.

Synchronize the User

The synchronize function, covered in Chapter 7, "GroupWise Utilities and Diagnostics," broadcasts a user's GroupWise object to the entire GroupWise system. Synchronizing is a fairly quick operation. To synchronize a user, do the following:

1. Load ConsoleOne.
2. Highlight the user in GroupWise view or in eDirectory browser view.
3. Choose Tools, GroupWise Utilities, Synchronize.

Structurally Rebuild the User's Database

Now that the user object has been synchronized, you are ready to issue a structural rebuild on that user's database.

1. Load ConsoleOne.
2. Highlight the user in GroupWise view or in eDirectory browser view.
3. Choose Tools, GroupWise Utilities, Mailbox/Library Maintenance.
4. In the Action drop-down list, select Structural Rebuild.
5. Under the Databases tab, select the User check box, making sure that the Message option is unchecked.

NOTE

Administrators are sometimes reluctant to do a structural rebuild on a user. They have a mistaken notion that a structural rebuild of a user database is a drastic, potentially destructive operation. It is not! A structural rebuild does not throw messages out of the folders or into the root of the cabinet. Don't mistake a structural rebuild with the process of re-creating the user database, which is an entirely different function. (Re-creating a user database will throw messages out of folders.)

Analyze/Fix and Repair the Contents of the User Database

When the POA analyzes the contents of a user database, it validates all the pointers in the database. The contents analysis also cleans up a user's personal address book. Here are the steps for running this operation:

1. In ConsoleOne, highlight the user in GroupWise view or in eDirectory browser view.
2. Choose Tools, GroupWise Utilities, Mailbox/Library Maintenance.
3. From the Action drop-down list, select Analyze/Fix Databases.
4. Select the Contents and Fix Problems check boxes, as well as the User check box under the Databases tab, making sure to uncheck all other check boxes.

Determining Problem Specificity

The steps in the preceding section could have taken care of a mailbox problem. If they did not, some very simple troubleshooting begins. Here is a systematic approach.

Determine Whether the Problem Is Machine-Specific

As the administrator, can you duplicate the problem from your own machine? Log in to the network as yourself and access the problem user's account by using the `/@u-?` switch. For troubleshooting purposes, have an extra GroupWise icon on your desktop. The icon should have a `/@u-?` switch after the GRPWISE.EXE. See Figure 23.3 for an example of this.

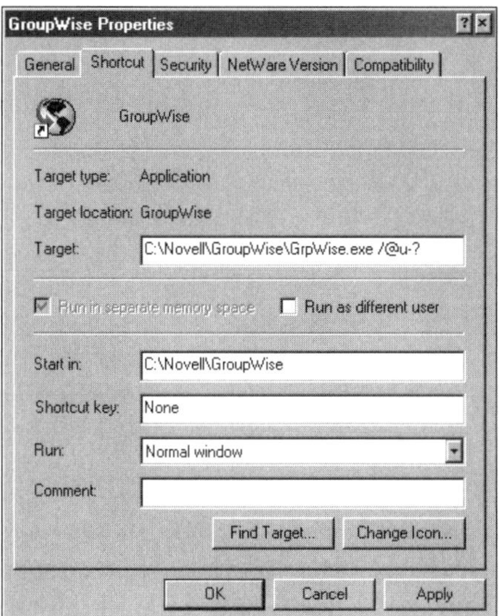

FIGURE 23.3 An extra GroupWise troubleshooting program shortcut.

TIP

You can use the free Nexic GroupWise Account Manager utility. It allows you to manage logging into various GroupWise accounts much more efficiently than the `/@u-?` **switch does. This utility is available from** `www.nexic.com`**.**

You must have GroupWise notify and the other GroupWise client software, such as the address book, unloaded in order to get into someone else's GroupWise account (the client suite can connect to only one account at a time). You will also need the user's password in order to enter the user's mailbox when using the `/@u-?` switch.

Troubleshooting Machine-Specific Problems

Suppose, however, that you can't duplicate the problem from your own machine. If this is the case, it's likely a machine-specific problem. Perhaps something has corrupted the GroupWise installation. At this point, I don't have a nice, numbered list of steps, but I do have a few suggestions, covered in the following sections.

Uninstall/Reinstall

One option is try uninstalling and reinstalling a few components:

- **Uninstall and then reinstall GroupWise.**

- **Reinstall Windows messaging.** Windows messaging can be reinstalled from the GroupWise 6.5 software distribution directory by running WMS.EXE from the `CLIENT\WIN32\WMS\xx` directory in your software distribution directory. For Windows 95, 98, and ME, run WMS from the 95 directory. For Windows NT/2000 and XP, run WMS.EXE from the NT directory.
- **Uninstall Windows messaging.** This can be hard to do on some machines because, although Windows messaging is installed, there's no uninstall option in the Windows Control Panel. This might sound funny, but you might have to run WMS.EXE to install Windows messaging before the Windows Control Panel will allow you to uninstall it.
- **Change Windows messaging profile information.** Delete the GroupWise profiles and then add them back in. The Windows messaging profile information is typically in the Control Panel under the Mail or Mail/Fax option. Sometimes this option isn't available. If you can load the GroupWise client, go to the address book and choose File, Services.

Troubleshooting TCP/IP from the Workstation

Perhaps the problem looks like a TCP/IP communication problem between the client and the POA (`89`*`xx`*-class errors). If so, try these steps:

1. Ping the server running the POA. If you can't ping successfully, fix that problem before going further.
2. Telnet to the POA. Run Windows Telnet by entering **`telnet`** from the Run prompt under the Start menu.
3. When using Telnet, turn on Local Echo.
4. Connect to the POA; the hostname should be the DNS name or IP address of the POA, and the port should be `1677`, or whatever your client/server port is. Figure 23.4 shows a Telnet session.
5. Upon successfully connecting to the POA's client/server port, you should be allowed to type characters and press Enter several times. Also, after holding the Enter key for several seconds, you should be disconnected from the POA. If you can't get the connection to the POA at the client/server port, you've got some kind of a TCP/IP problem.

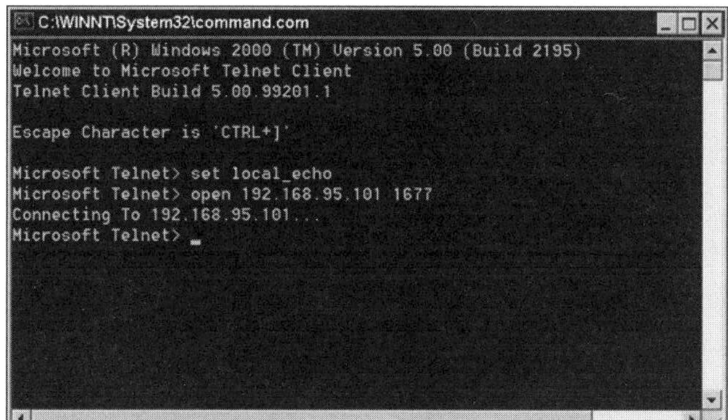

FIGURE 23.4
Telnet to the POA.

TIP

If you get a connection to the POA, hold down the Enter key, and then never get disconnected, that's actually an indication of a TCP/IP problem (for some reason, the POA cannot talk back to the client in order to close the connection).

If there are TCP/IP problems, it is appropriate to verify the TCP/IP settings or reinstall the TCP/IP services on the user's workstation. It might also be a good idea to break out the LAN sniffer and determine whether there is a network problem on this network segment.

NOTE

When using a LAN sniffer to help troubleshoot and diagnose problems between GroupWise components, you will not be doing any Application layer troubleshooting. This is because all data between GroupWise agents are encrypted. You will be looking for layer 2-4 problems on the TCP/IP stack when using a LAN sniffer to troubleshoot communication issues. An exception to this is SMTP traffic that is usually not encrypted.

Troubleshooting User-Specific Problems

If the problem can be reproduced on multiple machines, your problem is likely user-specific. Before you can classify a problem this way, however, you need to make sure the problem isn't specific to the post office or network segment.

A good test is to go to a machine on the same network segment, or on the same network switch as the machine that seems to be giving the user problems. From that machine, log in as a different user than the problem user, but one who is on the same post office as the problem user. Does the problem persist? If so, the problem really isn't user-specific, and it's not machine-specific. The problem is either post office-specific or network-specific.

Components Specific to Users

Imagine that a problem looks like it really is user-specific. It is still ideal to troubleshoot the problem away from the user's machine. There are just a few things that are truly specific to a user:

- **The user's object entry in the GroupWise directory:** Only the user interfaces with his/her object entry in WPHOST.DB file.
- **The user's master mailbox:** The USER*xxx*.DB database file in the GroupWise information store at the post office, and any other store files it references for item content.
- **The user's caching mode or remote databases:** If the user happens to use caching mode or remote, these files will be on the user's local drive. If you troubleshoot from a different workstation, GroupWise remote databases should not come into play.
- **The user's archive databases:** If the user is archiving to a local drive, troubleshooting from a separate workstation should isolate the problem.

Isolating GroupWise Archive Problems

The GroupWise client interacts with the archive databases on three occasions:

- When the GroupWise client first loads
- When reading items from the Archive mailbox
- When archiving a message item

The simplest way to determine whether a problem is an archive problem is to rename the user's Archive directory. To determine a user's Archive directory, do the following:

1. In the GroupWise client, go to Tools, Options, Environment, File Location.
2. Write down the Archive directory path.
3. Determine the user's three-character FID.

   In the GroupWise client, this information can be found under Help, About GroupWise. It's the three characters in the parentheses following the user's name, as shown in Figure 23.5.

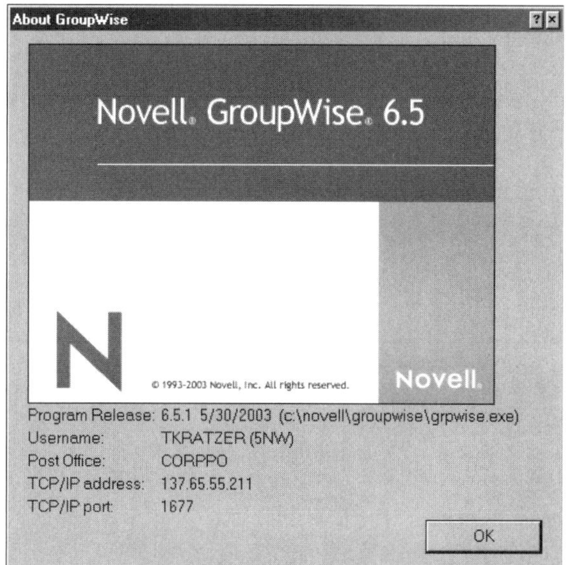

FIGURE 23.5
The GroupWise FID as shown from the GroupWise client.

The Archive directory is the file location of the archive plus `OF`*`xxx`*`ARC` (whereby *`xxx`* is the user's FID). If the user's Archive directory is `C:\ARCHIVE` and the user's FID is `123`, the Archive directory is therefore `C:\ARCHIVE\OF123ARC`.

TIP

It is always a good idea to back up GroupWise archives before working with them. In fact, Novell recommends that GroupWise archives be placed on network drives so that they are backed up automatically. Do not use Novell's iFolder to manage GroupWise archive backups. Novell's iFolder can corrupt GroupWise archive databases.

4. Rename this directory.

If this solves the problem, you know that the problem was with the user's GroupWise archive. You can now name it as before, and start taking steps to repair it using the standalone GWCHECK for Windows (GWCHECK.EXE).

The GroupWise client has GWCHECK within it. If you want to run a GWCHECK on an archive database, hold down the Ctrl and the Shift keys simultaneously, and then choose File, Open Archive.

Isolating GroupWise Master Mailbox Problems

Generally, a problem is either in a user's database or one of the message databases on the post office. The most likely culprit for problems is the user's USER*xxx*.DB file. Users can potentially destroy the contents of their USER*xxx*.DB files. For instance, a user can create a personal group with invalid addresses. If a user is complaining of a problem, and the problem is user-specific, begin by looking in the user's preferences and address book for clues about what is causing the problem.

If you already ran a structural rebuild on this user's database and you've reached this point, you might want some additional confirmation that you are looking in the right place. One way to do this is by renaming the user's user database. This is a common troubleshooting step:

1. Make sure the user is out of GroupWise.
2. Rename the user's USER*xxx*.DB file to USER*xxx*.OLD.

NOTE **You might have to bring the POA down to release this file. Just unload the POA, and then while the POA is unloading, go to the NetWare Console prompt and immediately reload the POA. Users who are in GroupWise will automatically reconnect to the POA, and there is generally a negligible interruption of service.**

3. Using the stand-alone GWCHECK utility, specify the following, as shown in Figure 23.6:
   - **Database Type:** Post Office
   - **Database Path:** Specify the path to the post office that the user is on
   - **Post Office Name:** Specify the name of the post office that the user is on
   - **Object Type:** User/Resource
   - **User/Resource:** The problem user's USER*xxx*.DB file
   - **Action:** Structural Rebuild (Not structure Analyze/Fix Databases)
   - **Databases**: User
4. Click Run.

   When GWCHECK runs, it will report, among other things, an error 26. This error is good. It means that GWCHECK will remove the registration of problem user's USER*xxx*.DB from the NGWGUARD.DB file. The system will now allow you to create a new USER*xxx*.DB file for this user.

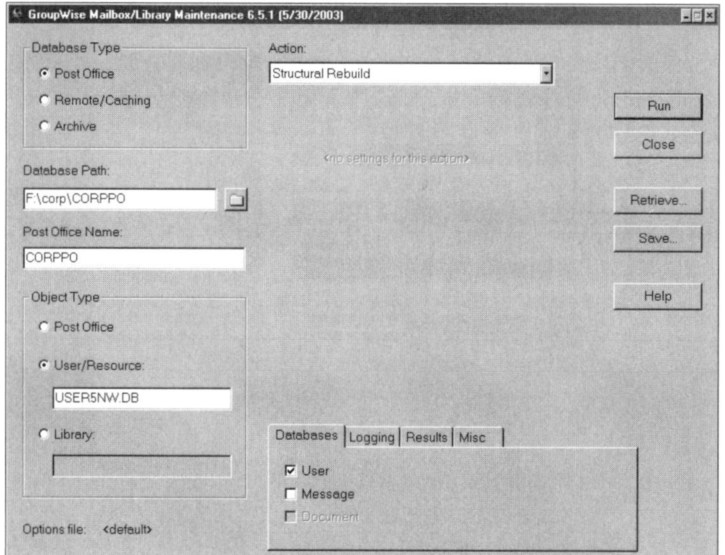

FIGURE 23.6
Using GWCHECK to drop a USER*xxx*.DB file from the guardian database.

You might have to bring the POA down again. When you go to load the GroupWise client, you could get a C05D error. A C05D error indicates that the USER*xxx*.DB file is registered in the NGWGUARD.DB file but is not on the disk. You just unregistered the USER*xxx*.DB file from the NGWGUARD.DB file, but the POA has it cached in memory. Bringing down the POA and bringing it back up fixes this issue.

5. Run GroupWise as the problem user.

   The e-mail box will be empty. Do the same action that caused a problem before. Does the problem still exist? If not, you know that the problem was wholly contained in the USER*xxx*.DB file that was renamed to USER*xxx*.OLD. If the problem does still exist, you are looking at a problem with the post office database, or perhaps you have not correctly ruled out machine- or network-specific problems.

6. Whether or not the problem was isolated to the user database you renamed, you should now rename the new USER*xxx*.DB file something else, and rename the USER*xxx*.OLD file back to USER*xxx*.DB.

   Again, you might need to unload and reload the POA to force the release of the file.

The next section gives more ideas on how to proceed, now that you know the problem is in the USER*xxx*.DB file.

Fixing Master Mailbox Problems

Suppose that in step 5 in the preceding section, you isolated the problem to this user's database. Now what should you do? The following are steps you can take:

- If you didn't synchronize the user object, do so now.
- If you didn't run a structural rebuild on the user's database, do so now.
- If you didn't run a contents check on the user's database, do so now.
- Run a Reset Client Options operation on this user from Tools, GroupWise Utilities, Mailbox/Library Maintenance.
- Run an index check on the user's database.
- Rid the user of the personal address book(s) and the entries in the frequent contacts address book list.

  You can export each of these books from the client, and then delete all the entries in each of these address books. When you have finished your testing and troubleshooting, you can re-import these entries.

  To export an address book, go into the GroupWise address book and choose File, Export. Make sure that you are not exporting the GroupWise system address book. Just export the frequent contacts and the user's personal address books.

If none of these steps resolves the problem, and the problem is really causing the user some headaches (which is to say, you cannot tell the user just to ignore the problem), you have two options:

- **Use the Re-create User Database option.** This routine could possibly fix the problem, but things will be pretty disorganized when the user goes back into his/her mailbox. All personal items will be thrown into the root of the mailbox Cabinet folder. The user's personal calendar items will also be lost.
- **Archive everything.** Archive everything that the user has, and then give the user a new, empty user database. Then unarchive the items into the new database.

Generating a Fresh User Database Without Losing Items

This walkthrough helps you create a new USER*xxx*.DB file for the user without losing any GroupWise messages and calendar items.

Exporting a User's Mailbox

Those of you familiar with the Archive feature might wonder why this section is called an *exporting* process. A user's mailbox isn't just composed of messages; it's also the folder structure they have created, their address books, their calendar items, even their trash items. People are rather sensitive about their mailbox—it can be an office of sorts. You won't be able to restore shared address books, shared folders, rules and personal preferences, but you should take care to restore everything you possibly can.

Configuring the Archive Directory

You first need to specify an archive location in order to create an Archive mailbox. Before I get into how to do this, take some precautions. I have had experience in the past with Windows caching data rather than writing it to the hard drive. When you are archiving so much data, it is often better to specify the archive path to a NetWare server. The NetWare client does a much better job than Windows does of handling data, which decreases the likelihood of corrupting the Archive mailbox when you're archiving a lot of data at one time.

Here are the steps for specifying the Archive directory:

1. From inside the user's mailbox, select Tools, Options, Environment, File Location, Archive directory.
2. Specify an Archive directory. Make sure to specify a new archive path; do not archive to an existing Archive mailbox. Using an existing mailbox would mix messages that the user intends for the Archive mailbox with messages intended for the master mailbox.

Configuring the Mailbox Folder Structure for Export

Many users have created an elaborate folder structure under their mailboxes and cabinets. When you archive messages, the folders containing messages are automatically created in the Archive mailbox. When you eventually unarchive the items, those folder names are re-created in the live mailbox. Folders containing no messages, however, will be lost. Again, the idea is to try to make the mailbox look as it did before it was deleted.

Following are the steps to preserving a mailbox folder structure:

1. Find one small message item in the user's mailbox that you will use for helping you to easily export the folders in this mailbox.
2. Highlight the item and select Edit, Move/Link to Folders.
3. In the resulting Move/Link Selections to Folder dialog box, place a check next to each folder within the Cabinet object. If the user has other folders under the mailbox that are not in the Cabinet, you can place check marks next to those. Figure 23.7 shows an example of this step.

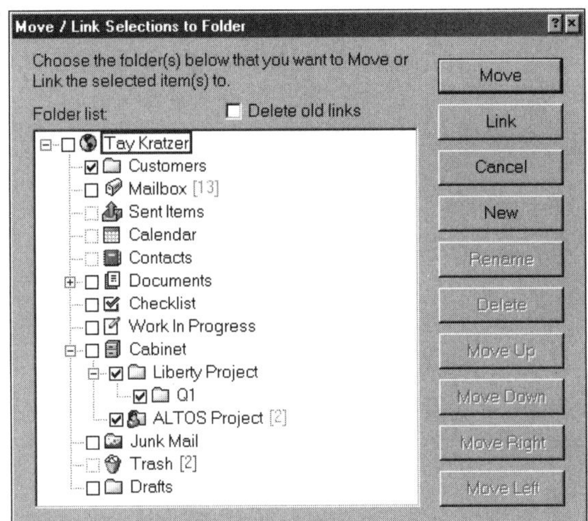

FIGURE 23.7
Linking a message item to all folders.

4. With the check marks in place, now click the Move button. This makes a virtual copy of this message in every folder in the mailbox. Get out of the Move/Link option. When you archive the folders, every folder will be created because there is an item in each of the folders.

Exporting All Messages Items

Now you are going to export the real meat of the mailbox. The easiest way to see that you get everything in the mailbox is to use the Find feature in the GroupWise mailbox.

When you issue a Tools, Find, make no additional selections from the Find dialog box, and click the OK button, you are actually telling GroupWise to find everything. And you'll see, everything will come up in the Find window. If this user is tidy, or you have an aggressive e-mail retention policy, perhaps you'll see just a few hundred items. However, you are more likely to see thousands and thousands of items. The problem with this is that the Find window will not display that many items. You might therefore need to alter your Find query to only find items in a certain time period or of a certain type.

You can, for example, alter the scope of the query by using the Date range section. You can specify a three-month range, and issue the Find, archive the items, and then modify the find from the Find window by selecting Tools, Modify Find. The idea is to get a maximum of about 4,500 items in the Find window, and then modify the Find window to get the next batch of items. Your goal is to eventually find, and then archive, all the message items in the user's mailbox.

Here are the basic steps for doing this; you might need to deviate from them in order to narrow the query a bit:

1. Inside the user' mailbox, select Tools, Find. Make sure the Find tab is active, not the Find by Example tab.
2. Accept the defaults and select the OK button. If you suspect that this user has more than 4,500 items in the mailbox, modify the find using the Date Range feature.
3. Select the first 500 or so items with a Shift-click of the mouse. Select Actions, Move to Archive.
4. Repeat step 3 (and possibly step 2) until all items are moved to the Archive mailbox.

This process of archiving the items from the Find query should find calendar items, be they group or personal calendar items, and all message items, whether sent or received. Ideally, this process will move all message items from the master mailbox to the Archive mailbox. When you get finished, the mailbox should look like a ghost town, perhaps containing a bunch of empty folders.

TIP

Although this process does archive the user's sent items, it doesn't create the Sent Items folder in the Archive mailbox. Don't worry though; sent items are still in the Archive mailbox. When you unarchive the message items, they will automatically be moved to the Sent Items folder.

The Sent Items folder is a *query folder*, which is a little different than other more traditional folder types, and consequently it is not created in the Archive mailbox when you archive items that are sent by the user. If you want to see the sent items from within the Archive mailbox, do the following:

1. Within the Archive mailbox, select Tools, Find.
2. In the resulting Find dialog box, select Sent in the Item Source area.
3. You should be able to see the sent items in the resulting Find folder.

When you unarchive the message items, they will automatically be moved to the Sent Items folder without any intervention on your part. What I'm saying is, don't worry; it'll all work like magic!

Exporting the Trash—It's Quick!

You might think this is crazy, but exporting the trash adds to the psychological effect of what you are doing. If you bring back the person's trash, they are going to think you performed wonders, yet it takes just a minute:

1. Create a new folder in the cabinet of the user's mailbox (not the Archive mailbox), called `trash2`.
2. Go to the trash and Shift-click to select all items. Drag them to the new `trash2` folder you created.
3. Go to the `trash2` folder you created under the cabinet, Shift-click to select all items, and select Actions, Archive.

NOTE **Later, you will move these trash items in the `trash2` folder back to the trash bucket in the user's live mailbox.**

Exporting the Address Book

Every user has at least two address books and quite often more than that. These two address books are the Frequent Contacts address book, and the address book named as the user's full name. The user you are working with might even have more. You can export their address books, and then later you will import them into the new mailbox.

Following are the steps for exporting personal address books:

1. Go to the GroupWise Address book by selecting Tools, Address Book.

2. Choose an address book to export by clicking the tab of the address book. (Not the Novell GroupWise address book; that's your system address book, not a personal address book.)
3. Inside the address book, choose File, Export, Entire Address Book. Figure 23.8 shows this dialog box.

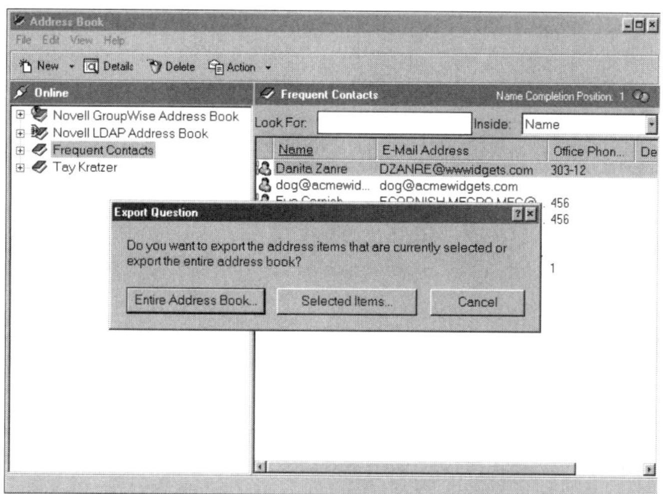

FIGURE 23.8
Exporting the GroupWise address book.

4. Save the file as a *.NAB file. You might want to name the *.NAB files according to the name of the address book. For example: `TKRATZER-Frequent Contacts.NAB`.

You've exported everything you possibly can. Now you need to rename the user's database and drop it from the guardian database (NGWGUARD.DB).

Following are the steps for removing a user's database, and dropping the user's registration from the NGWGUARD.DB file:

- **Note TKRATZER's FID:** Determine what TKRATZER's FID is. If GroupWise is loaded, and you're logged in as TKRATZER, choose Help, About GroupWise. The FID is in parentheses next to the user's name.
- **Rename TKRATZER's user database:** Now you need to rename TKRATZER's user database file. You know that TKRATZER's FID is 5NW. The file you are looking for, USER5NW.DB, is in the OFUSER subdirectory of the user's post office directory. Rename the file to USER5NW.OLD.

NOTE **As discussed earlier in the chapter, the POA might need to be unloaded before this database can be renamed.**

Renaming TKRATZER's USER*xxx*.DB file is not enough. The USER5NW.DB file is registered in the NGWGUARD.DB. Now you must "drop" the USER5NW.DB file (that you renamed to USER5NW.OLD) from the NGW-GUARD.DB. Following are the steps for doing this:

1. Run the stand-alone GWCHECK utility.
2. Specify the following:
   - **Database Type:** Post Office
   - **Database Path:** Specify the path to the post office that TKRATZER is on
   - **Post Office Name:** Specify the name of the post office that TKRATZER is on
   - **Object Type:** User/Resource
   - **User/Resource:** USER5NW.DB
   - **Action:** Structural Rebuild (Not a structure Analyze/Fix Databases!)
   - **Databases:** User
3. Click Run.

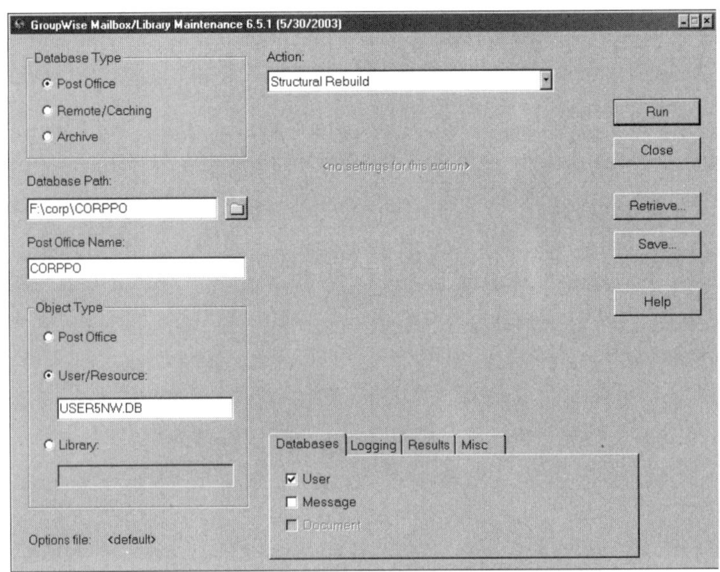

FIGURE 23.9
Using GWCHECK to drop a USER*xxx*.DB file from the guardian database.

The GWCHECK log will indicate an error `26`; you should expect and want this error. See Figure 23.10 for an example of this.

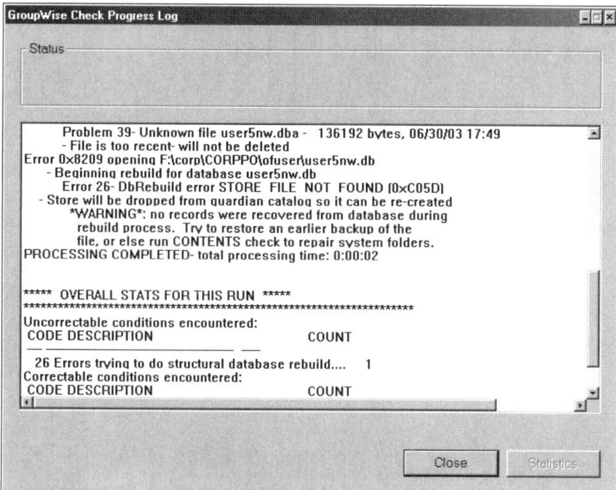

FIGURE 23.10
GWCHECK should give an error 26.

- **Access and test the clean mailbox:** It's time for a sanity check. Launch GroupWise as the user (using the `/@u-?` switch). The mailbox should be empty. Make sure that you can no longer duplicate the problem the user was having. If you can still duplicate the problem, this whole exercise is pointless. You probably did not correctly determine the specificity of the problem.

TIP

Remember, if you get a `C05D` error when loading the GroupWise client, you need to bring the post office's POA down and back up again.

- **Restore items from the archive:** Assuming the problem can no longer be duplicated, it is time to begin the process of moving items from the Archive mailbox back into the master mailbox. See the next section for how to do this.

Importing a User's Mailbox

When you get into `TKRATZER`'s live master mailbox, the steps are nearly the reverse of the export process steps, of course. First though, in order for the Find feature to work on the Archive mailbox, you must access the Archive mailbox, and then exit GroupWise. GroupWise needs to rebuild the QuickFinder index on the Archive mailbox. Exiting GroupWise after

GroupWise has discovered that it has new indexing to do causes the QuickFinder index for the Archive mailbox to be rebuilt, which helps the Find feature work properly.

Importing Mail/Folders and Trash Items

Following are the steps for importing folders and trash items from an Archive mailbox to a master mailbox:

1. Get into the user's live GroupWise mailbox.
2. Go into Tools, Options, Environment, File Location, Archive directory. Specify the Archive directory that you specified earlier in this chapter.
3. Go into the Archive mailbox by selecting File, Open Archive. Then exit GroupWise. (On older GroupWise clients, this allows GroupWise to re-index the Archive mailbox.) The index is essential when using the Find feature in step 4.
4. Get back into GroupWise and select File, Open Archive. From within the Archive mailbox, select Tools, Find. Find items in the same manner in which you did when you archived messages into the Archive mailbox. Make sure to select the Find tab, not the Find by Example tab. (If the Find feature does not find any items, try exiting GroupWise again.)
5. Select the items in the Find Results view and choose Actions, Move to Archive (this actually unarchives the items and moves them back to the master mailbox).
6. Repeat Step 5 until all items are unarchived. Get into the master mailbox (rather than the Archive mailbox). You should see your message items, and all the folders that were created. You still need to deal with the trash.
7. Make sure you're in the master mailbox, not the Archive mailbox. Go to the `Trash` folder under the cabinet. Delete this `trash2` folder under the cabinet, as well as all of the messages in the `trash2` folder. This will move the messages to the trash bucket on the master mailbox.

You restored/imported all of the message data, and it should show up in the master mailbox. There is more data that needs to be imported as explained in the next section.

Importing the Address Books

The import process is of course the opposite of the export process you did earlier.

Inside the GroupWise address book, you should see at least two personal address books. They are the Frequent Contacts address book, and the address book with the same name as the user's full name. Follow these steps to import them both:

1. Highlight one of the address book tabs for an address book you will import, and select File, Import.
2. Specify the correct *.NAB file for this address book. This is going to be the *.NAB file that you exported earlier.
3. If the user has more than the two default address books, you have to create the address book tabs for these address books before attempting to import the *.NAB file. To do this, select File, New Book and create the address book with the same name it had before.

Now the user's personal address books are imported.

Final Notes on the Import Process

The import process did not import the following less common attributes about a mailbox:

- Rules
- User preferences
- Saved Find folders
- Button bar settings

Earlier in the solution you might have linked a message item to several folders, in order to re-create the folder structure. You don't want that item linked to all the folders. Do the following:

1. Find one instance of that message item that is linked to all the folders.
2. Forward the message as an attachment from Tay Kratzer to Tay Kratzer. This way, the message isn't lost.
3. Archive the one item, and it will no longer be in all the folders. Then you can delete the archive; it's no longer needed at this time.

Here are the final things to pay attention to in order to set the mailbox as close to how it was before it was re-created:

- Set the archive path back to the original archive path that TKRATZER had, if they had an archive path. Do not select the option to move items.

- Set up proxy access.
- Set up shared folders.
- Request shared folders from others who have shared folders with TKRATZER.
- Set up shared address books.
- Request shared address books from others who have shared address books with TKRATZER.

Now you've completely re-created a mailbox database.

Summary

This chapter explained using the scientific method as a means of troubleshooting. The scientific method is a four-step process:

1. Observe
2. Hypothesize
3. Predict based upon the hypothesis
4. Test the hypothesis

This chapter discussed that problems are generally either one or the other of the following:

- User-specific
- Machine-specific

CHAPTER 24

Using Wireless and Handheld Devices with GroupWise 6.5 WebAccess

This chapter discusses using handheld devices and wireless access to the GroupWise mailbox. WebAccess was covered in Chapter 11, "Configuring GroupWise WebAccess," so you should be familiar with it and with its different components. If you have not already read Chapter 11, go back and do so before starting this chapter.

This chapter will help you better understand how access from wireless and handheld devices works through WebAccess. It will also give you an understanding of how modular and flexible GroupWise WebAccess is in regards to providing future support for all sorts of devices and protocols; one of the major advantages of the GroupWise WebAccess architecture.

Understanding Templates

GroupWise 6.5 WebAccess uses templates that facilitate access to the GroupWise mailbox from many different devices. Think of templates as a skeleton document that the WebAccess application stuffs the data into before displaying it to the connected client's device. This data is from the user's mailbox and is delivered to the WebAccess application from the WebAccess agent. If you are using a wireless phone to access your GroupWise mailbox through WebAccess, the application recognizes the type of device it is communicating with. As a result, when the data is received from the user's mailbox, the application will place this data (the mail items, for example) into a template that has been designed to work with wireless phones using the wireless access protocol (WAP).

The use of templates at the application level allows Novell development engineers to easily add support for additional devices. No coding changes need to occur at the agent level.

The WebAccess templates are stored on the Web server. On a NetWare 6 server running an Apache Web server and the Tomcat servlet gateway, the templates are found in the following location:

```
SYS:tomcat\33\webapps\ROOT\WEB-INF\classes\com\novell\
webaccess\templates
```

Out-of-the-Box Templates Included in GroupWise 6.5

The templates that ship with GroupWise 6.5 support the following devices or browsers:

- Web browser that supports HTML and frames.
- Web browsers that use simple HTML. This is usually what a Pocket PC is equipped with. The Web browser that comes in my Tungsten T, which is made by Novarra.com, also works nicely as a simple HTML browser.
- Wireless phone that supports WML (wireless markup language) through the WAP protocol (wireless access protocol).
- Palm OS devices, as well as other devices that support the Web clipping technology developed by Palm.

If you were to look at the template directories, you would note the following directories:

- *FRAMES*: The `Frames` directory contains the templates that most of the standard PC-based Web browsers will use (Netscape and Internet Explorer, for example).
- *HDML*: The `HDML` directory contains the templates that handheld devices use. HDML stands for the handheld device markup language. It is similar to HTML, but scaled down for handheld-device use. Many cell phone devices support HDML.
- *SIMPLE*: The `Simple` directory contains the templates for devices that use the simple HTML interface. A growing number of devices and browsers use simple HTML, including Pocket PC devices running the Microsoft Pocket PC/Windows CE OS. Another example of a simple HTML device is a Web TV appliance.

- *WEBCLIP*: Web clipping technology is used with the Palm OS products. The Palm OS version 3.5.1 through all Palm OS 4.x devices support the proprietary Web clipping technology created by Palm Inc. Palm OS 5 and going forward has dropped support for Web clipping.
- *WML*: The `WML` directory includes the wireless markup language templates and are used primarily by wireless phones. Another name for WML is WAP. WAP browsers exist for various platforms. For example, my Palm Tungsten T came with a WAP browser.

These are all the templates that currently ship with GroupWise 6.5, but as WebAccess supports more client types, there will be more templates. For instance, the GroupWise Cross-Platform (JAVA) will add templates to WebAccess when it is available to the public.

Managing Templates Through the GroupWise WebAccess Object

There are a few things that you as an administrator can configure regarding templates. You administer the GroupWise templates by accessing the properties of the GroupWise WebAccess object in ConsoleOne. From the Application property page, shown in Figure 24.1, select Templates from the drop-down list. From here, you can determine how the templates are configured.

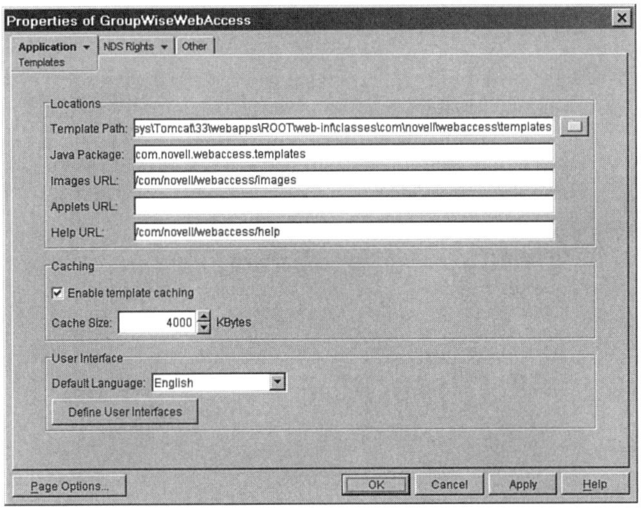

FIGURE 24.1
The WebAccess Application Templates property page allows you to define general information for the WebAccess Templates.

Following is an explanation of the Templates property page settings:

- *Template Path:* This is the path to the template directories. Under this path, you will see a directory representing each of the installed templates.
- *Java Package:* A Java package name is a directory path that uses the period (.) instead of a slash (\) to separate components of the path. Hence, this is really just a path that you are looking at here. Basically, this points to the same directory as the Template Path field, identifying the location of the template string tables. Unless you are a developer and creating your own custom templates, you will never need to modify this path.
- *Images URL:* This is the path to the image files. This path, under the Web server, contains the image files (*.GIF) that the different templates will display.
- *Applets URL:* This field allows you to define the path to any custom applets you are using. It is possible to use Java applets for some of the WebAccess components. This is most commonly seen if you want to develop custom address-book or calendar views.
- *Help URL:* This is the path under the root of the Web server to the location of the help files. You can move the help files to a different location, if desired.
- *Caching:* This option allows the WebAccess application to cache the templates in RAM the first time they are used, which increases performance.
- *Cache Size:* This value determines how much RAM the server will use to cache the templates.
- *Default Language:* This option determines the default language presented to users when they visit your Web server's home page.

There are even more settings related to templates; the next section discusses these.

Defining User Interface and Browser Integration

This section explains what the Define User Interfaces window, shown in Figure 24.2, allows you to do. It describes each of the three property pages and what they mean in relation to the templates.

User Interfaces

The User Interfaces tab in Figure 24.2 allows you to define the available templates. You can add references to templates, if needed. However, the templates have to be ones that you created; the five listed in Figure 24.2 ship with GroupWise WebAccess.

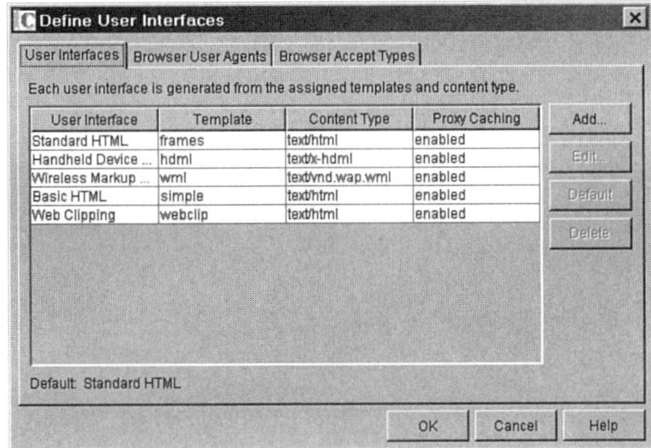

FIGURE 24.2 User interfaces are used to define the different templates available to the WebAccess Application.

Following is an explanation of the User Interfaces property page:

- *User Interface:* This defines the name of the template.
- *Template*: This is the actual name of the directory under the Template directory, as defined earlier.
- *Content Type:* This option defines the type of content this template can serve. In other words, it defines what type of content the receiving device can handle.

Generally you do not modify the information on this page. You will only do so if you introduce new templates to WebAccess.

Browser User Agents

The Browser User Agents tab shown in Figure 24.3 enables you to associate a user interface or template with a particular type of Web browser. The WebAccess application makes this association based on the browser identifying itself to the WebAccess application.

Just about every browser identifies itself with a Browser User Agent value. This can include the platform, version of browser, and so on. In other words, if a browser's user agent information includes Windows CE (this would be in the header of the data sent to the WebAccess Application from the user's browser), the application will use the basic HTML interface (or the simple templates) and not the default frames, which are defined under the User Interfaces tab.

The nice thing about this design is that you can easily add new browsers here.

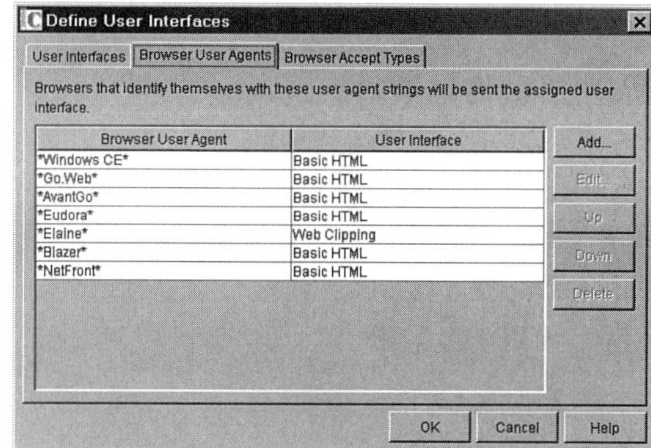

FIGURE 24.3
Browser User Agent defines popular browsers that are used on non-PC based devices.

Following is an explanation of the information on the Browser User Agents property page:

- *Browser User Agent:* Here, you identify what a browser can use to identify itself to the WebAccess application.
- *User Interface:* This column defines the template or user interface that will be delivered to the device when a match is made from the Browser User Agent list.

It is quite feasible that you might define additional Browser User Agents. The idea for doing this is explained later in this chapter.

Browser Accept Types

The Browser Accept Types tab also lets you associate a user interface or template with a particular type of Web browser. However, this association is based on the content type the browser will accept, not the browser identifying itself. For example, if a browser accepts `text/html` (one of the predefined entries), the WebAccess application will use the standard HTML interface (or the Frames templates). Most browsers will accept multiple content types, including `text/html` or `text/plain`. The content type identifies what type of information the browser can understand.

Many browsers accept more than one content type, such as both `text/html` and `text/plain`.

Following is an explanation of the information on the Browser Accept Type property page:

- *Browser Accept Type:* This option identifies what format the data can be in when the browser receives it.
- *User Interface:* This option defines the templates that deliver this type of content to the browser.

So, in a nutshell, the Define User Interfaces window allows you to identify and configure which set of templates are associated with different types of browsers—everything from standard browsers to wireless phones.

TIP

If you edit and make changes in the Define User Interfaces window, this information is written to the WEBACC.CFG file. The WebAccess application does not dynamically read this file. To get these changes to take effect, you must shut down and restart the WebAccess application.

How the WebAccess Application Detects Which Templates to Use

Given the numerous templates available, the WebAccess application needs to somehow know what templates to use. It must use the correct templates for the different types of browsers and devices that it supports.

When a device is directed to the URL that points to the `SERVLET\WEBACC` location on the Web server, it sends a small packet that contains header information about the browser that is being used. This header information contains information that helps to identify the Browser User Agent. An example of what a Pocket PC 2000 device might send is the following:

```
Mozilla/4.0 (compatible; MSIE 4.01; Windows NT Windows CE)
```

The WebAccess application then reads the cached information from the WEBACC.CFG file. This is how it determines what type of browsers it can support.

If the information from the browser contains the Browser User Agent name (Windows CE in this example), the application knows to use the associated template listed in the User Interface column.

If the browser has not provided the Browser User Agent name, the WebAccess application will try to determine what type of data the browser can understand. This information is configured in the Browser Accept Types options. If the browser identifies that it can understand `text/x-hdml`, the WebAccess application knows that it is probably talking to a wireless phone that is expecting data in the `x-hdml` format. The WebAccess application then checks the User Interface value to determines which templates to use when corresponding with the device.

If the WebAccess application still is not sure what type of device it is communicating with, it will go to the User Interface value and use the default template there.

This background should help you to understand how the WebAccess application works. The application understands what device or browser it is communicating with, as well as what set of templates to use when communicating to a device.

Accessing Your GroupWise Mailbox from Pocket PC Device

GroupWise wireless requires a Windows CE or Pocket PC device that supports IE version 4.0 or better. To determine the version of IE that comes with a Windows CE device, go to the Control Panel and the System icons.

To access the GroupWise WebAccess system from a handheld device running the Pocket PC or Windows CE OS, you must first have some way to get online with the device. There are a couple options you have to get online with your Pocket PC device. You can use a modem with the Pocket PC device and dial a traditional ISP to get Internet access. You can also use a wireless LAN card with the Pocket PC device, which places you on a corporate network, if this service is available to you. Many wireless phone providers also provide a card that allows you to access the Internet through their network. Check with your wireless phone provider to determine which solutions they offer in this arena.

Once you are online and have access to the Web server where the GroupWise WebAccess application is running, you can enter the URL of your WebAccess server. For example

```
http://groupwise.wwwidgets.com/servlet/webacc
```

The Pocket PC device should tell the Web server that it is a Windows CE user agent, and the WebAccess application will use the simple templates to display the mail. Figure 24.4 shows an example of what the simple interface looks like on a Pocket PC/Windows CE device.

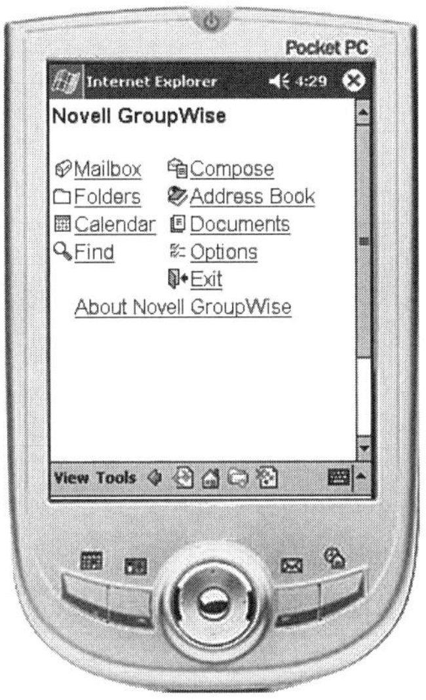

FIGURE 24.4
WebAccess simple HTML interface.

Notice from Figure 24.4 that you do not get all the graphics that the traditional GroupWise WebAccess frames view gives you. You will also notice that the simple templates are designed to fit on a much smaller screen. This is very helpful when using a Pocket PC device because it eliminates much of the scrolling across the screen to view the entire contents of the mailbox.

If you need to test whether the simple templates are working, but you do not have a simple HTML device, you can tell the WebAccess application which templates you want to use via the URL line. Here is an example of how to specifically tell the WebAccess application that you want to use the simple templates:

```
http://<yourwebserverver DNS name>/servlet/
webacc?User.interface=simple
```

NOTE

The "`User.interface=simple`" code is case sensitive.

When you press Return, the WebAccess application will display the login page using the simple templates. When you log in, the screen looks like Figure 24.5.

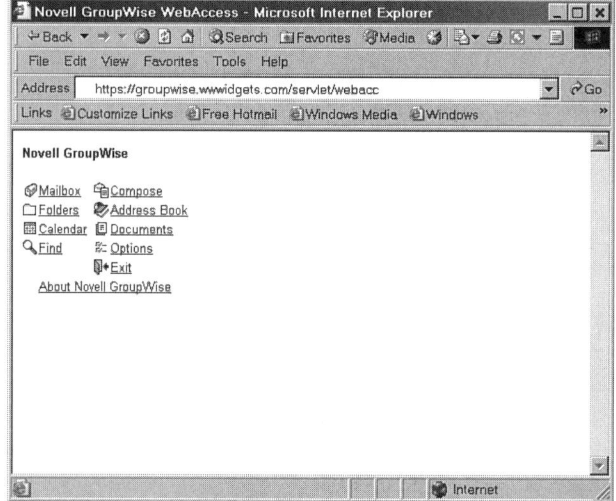

FIGURE 24.5 WebAccess simple HTML interface on a PC browser.

Defining a New Browser User Agent Type

Consider the following scenario, which illustrates the value of this information. A user has a Tungsten T which is a Palm OS 5 device. This device comes with a browser called Web Pro, made by Novarra. The Web Pro browser uses a proxy server, and the proxy server helps to make HTML pages digestable to the Web Pro browser. The Web Pro can either use normal HTML, with frames and the like, or it can use simple HTML. When the user uses the Web Pro browser to visit WebAccess using the simple HTML templates, the performance is much better than when using the regular HTML/Frames templates.

When the user first used GroupWise WebAccess with the Web Pro browser, the performance was very slow. You then instructed the user to change the URL on my Web Pro browser to indicate to WebAccess that the device was using a simple HTML browser. The WebAccess session's performance becomes much better. Following is the syntax the user used to force the WebAccess Application to serve up simple HTML:

```
http://groupwise.wwwidgets.com/servlet/
webacc?User.interface=simple
```

Typing this long URL once and then bookmarking it is not too difficult, particularly for a technical person. But imagine you have a bunch of users who want to access GroupWise WebAccess from their Tunsten T. Wouldn't it just be better to have GroupWise WebAccess detect the Web Pro browser type, and then give the users the simple HTML templates automatically? Of course. So here's how you can do this:

1. In ConsoleOne, edit the GroupWiseWebAccess Object from the eDirectory browser view. This is the WebAccess application's GroupWise WebAccess object.
2. From the Application tab, select the Templates property page.
3. Click the Define User Interfaces button.
4. Go to the Browser User Agents tab and click the Add button.
5. Enter **`*WebPro*`** in the Browser User Agent field.

   This means that if the browser identifies itself to the Web server with a string that contains "WebPro", the WebAccess Application correlates it with the Browser User Agent defined in step 5.
6. Change the User Interface drop-down list box to read as Basic HTML.

If a Web browser identifies its Browser User Agent information with a string that contains "WebPro", the WebAccess application use simple HTML templates.

You must stop and restart the Web server and the Java servlet gateway that are hosting the WebAccess application in order for these changes to take place.

Accessing Your GroupWise Mailbox from a Wireless Phone

To access the GroupWise mailbox from a wireless phone, there are a few prerequisites that must be met. First, the phone must support the wireless application protocol (WAP). WAP was designed to allow wireless applications to work across different wireless network technology types. It was developed by the WAP Forum, which consisted of various wireless venders. Think of WAP as the vehicle that carries the data to your cell phone.

To clarify why GroupWise WebAccess uses WML and HDML templates instead of a WAP template, you can think of WAP as the vehicle that brings WML or HDML content to a wireless device. WML (wireless markup language) and HDML (handheld device markup language) are the actual text documents that display content, and they sit on top of the WAP protocol. Hence, GroupWise uses the WML and HDML templates to create the content, which is delivered over the WAP protocol to the wireless device.

If you have a WAP-enabled phone, the next step is to make sure that the phone service provider provides WAP service to the phone. Otherwise, you have this nice gadget that is acting like a traditional cell phone. You will not be able to access the GroupWise mailbox from it because you have not subscribed to this service.

With a WAP phone and a subscription from the cellular phone service provider, you should be able to access the WebServer where your GroupWise WebAccess application is running. On the phone's browser, you enter the URL of the Web server that is running the WebAccess application.

NOTE

If the Web server does not have any WML or HDML pages to display, you will not be able to see the HTML Web page that is the default from a WML/HDML device. You need to enter the `/SERVLET/WEBACC` portion of the URL to direct the phone browser directly to the WebAccess application; for example, `<yourwebserverver DNS name>/servlet/webacc`.

When your phone accesses the `SERVLET/WEBACC` page, you will be presented with a prompt to enter the GroupWise user ID. After entering the user ID and selecting OK, you will be prompted for the GroupWise password. You will then be given a simple menu option consisting of Mail, Appointments, Tasks, Address Book, Compose, Documents, Options, and Logout. You can scroll through them to perform different tasks. Figure 24.6 shows GroupWise wireless on a cell phone.

As an administrator, you can test WebAccess to verify that you can access your mailbox from a WAP-enabled cell phone. Instead of just telling the Web browser to use the WML or HDML templates, you must use a WAP phone emulator. The reason for this is that the standard browsers out there do not support the WML or HDML protocols. WML was specifically designed for small handheld or wireless devices, and is not supported by the traditional Web browsers.

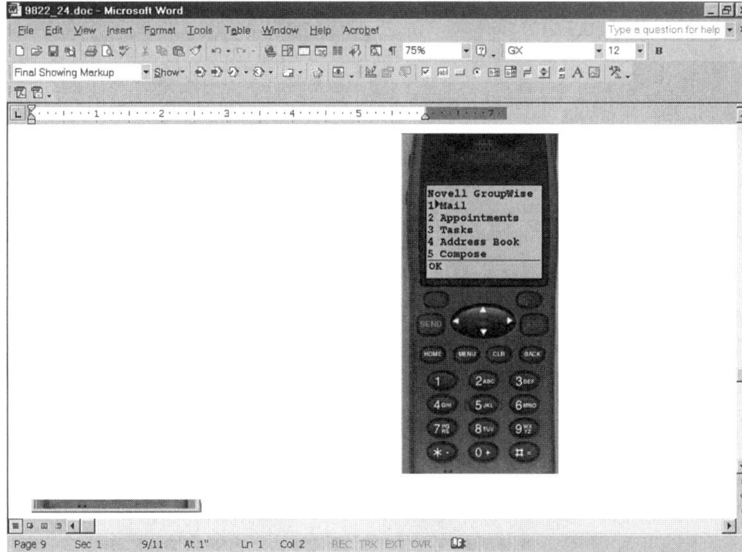

FIGURE 24.6
WebAccess simple WML interface.

To test with a WAP emulator running on any Windows OS platform, go to `www.openwave.com` and download the OpenWave software developer kit (SDK). The SDK has a very simple install process for installing the WAP phone emulator. Once installed, you can enter the URL in the GO field and press Return. It should connect you to the URL that you specified and allow you to log into the WebAccess mailbox.

Accessing Your GroupWise Mailbox from a Palm OS Device That's Web Clipping Compatible

The way that some Palm OS devices access the WebAccess system is by using a proprietary method called *Web clipping*. The device running the Palm OS must support Web clipping. If your Palm OS device does not have the built-in wireless functionality, you can purchase a product such as Palm's Mobile Internet Kit and a modem. You then install the Web clipping software, which enables you to dial an ISP, and then you use the Web clipping software to connect to the WebAccess server. The Palm OS version 3.5.1 through the Palm OS version 4.x devices support Web clipping.

With Palm OS 5, Palm dropped Web clipping support. Web clipping requires that users download a precompiled Palm Query Application (*.PQA file) to their Palm OS device. The *.PQA contains the IP address or URL of the Web server that is running GroupWise WebAccess. The *.PQA file was created when you installed the GroupWise WebAccess application.

TIP

The installation wizard that runs when you install GroupWise WebAccess places the GroupWise.PQA file on your Web server. On my server, which is a NetWare 6 server running Apache Web server, the English version of the GROUPWISE.PQA file is at: `SYS:Apache\htdocs\com\novell\webaccess\palm\en`**.**

Figure 24.7 shows a GroupWise WebAccess session on a Palm OS device.

FIGURE 24.7
WebAccess on a Palm OS device.

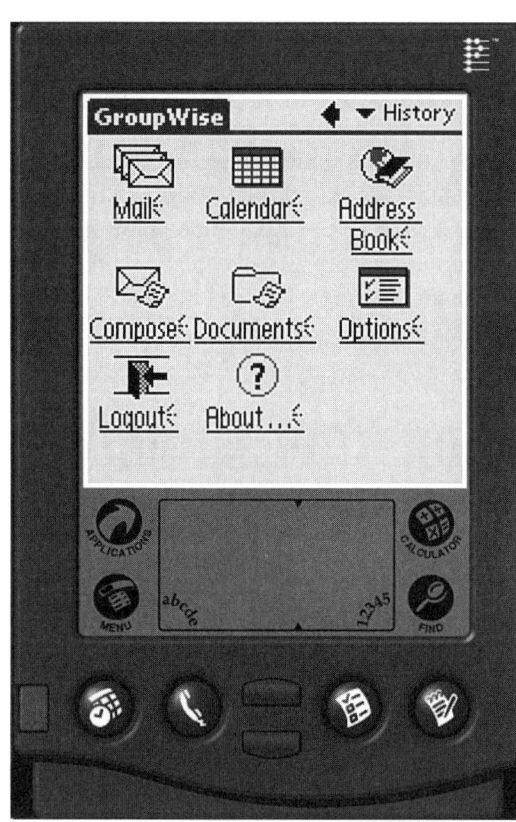

Generating a New Palm *.PQA File

If your *.PQA file seems to be misconfigured, you can regenerate it somewhat easily. Use the following steps:

1. Run the GroupWise WebAccess setup software with a `/PQA` option added at the end of the command to run SETUP.EXE. For example

   ```
   F:\GW65SDD\ADMINCD\INTERNET\WEBACCES\SETUP.EXE /PQA
   ```

2. Follow the short installation wizard, which will prompt you for the location to your Web server, and then ask you for the DNS or IP address that should go into the PQA.
3. After the Setup software is complete, you should be able to locate the newly created *.PQA files on the Web server. On my server that runs Apache Web server on NetWare 6, the *.PQA files are located at the following path:

   ```
   SYS:\Apache\htdocs\com\novell\webaccess\palm
   ```

Information Regarding SSL-ized Connections from Handheld Devices

Many installations of GroupWise WebAccess are using SSL to encrypt the data between the browser and the WebAccess application. This is advisable for security reasons. There are a few issues regarding this and using handheld or wireless devices to access WebAccess.

In order for the Web server to communicate with a Web browser, they must exchange certificates. As a result, the device that is accessing the WebAccess system must be able to support certificates. Most of the handheld and wireless devices come preconfigured with a set list of trusted root certificate authorities. What this means is that if you have used Novell's certificate server to generate a certificate for the Web server, you will not be able to use the handheld devices to access WebAccess. You must request and install a certificate from one of the certificate vendors that the device has in its trusted root list.

If you're using a cellular phone to access WebAccess that has SSL enabled on the Web server, you must check with the cellular phone service provider to ensure that its gateway has your Web server's certificate issuer on its trusted root list. Otherwise, the data will not pass through the cellular phone's network and down to your cell phone.

The safest thing is to have the Web server use a certificate that was obtained from a vendor contained in the trusted root list of the devices that will be used to access the WebAccess system. Chapter 27, "Securing Your GroupWise System via SSL," includes some pointers about how to enable a certificate on a NetWare platform Web server.

Summary

This chapter has described how WebAccess works with some of the more popular handheld and wireless devices on the market. There are many other devices that also work with WebAccess. If they support HTML, simple HTML, WML, HDML, or Web clipping, they should be able to access the GroupWise mailbox through WebAccess.

The wireless and handheld device support in GroupWise 6.5 WebAccess components is very impressive, and adds a lot of value for your users.

CHAPTER 25

Configuring a SPAM/ Junk Mail Control Solution

First let's define *SPAM*. The Coalition Against Unsolicited Email (CAUCE) defines SPAM as unsolicited commercial e-mail. In the CAUCE definition, SPAM includes commercial proposals for products, services, or as part of a money scam, and is overtly intended to trick recipients by making the e-mail seem relevant to them.

This chapter introduces the elements of GroupWise that can assist in handling SPAM. There are also some recommendations about solutions for managing SPAM that do not come with GroupWise.

Is SPAM Really a Problem?

Some folks don't think it is, and that's because they haven't given out their e-mail address, and a SPAMmer hasn't harvested it. SPAM is currently the biggest scourge of the Internet. Here are some of the hidden costs of SPAM:

- False-positives (pertinent messages are blocked)
- Identity theft
- Loss of productivity
- Security breaches (open relay attacks)
- Increased operation costs
- Downtime (denial-of-service attacks)
- Loss of reputation (placed on a Realtime Blacklist [RBL])
- Legal liabilities
- Lost employee confidence

The chapter introduces you to the features in GroupWise 6.5 that can act as a piece of your SPAM solution. However, it is important to note that you should not rely wholly upon the SPAM-control features in GroupWise; they are not sufficient to block the wide variety of SPAM messages out there.

I highly recommend that you look into a SPAM solution such as those from Novell's GroupWise partners. One such product receiving good customer reviews is MessageScreen by IntelliReach (`www.intellireach.com`). I have personally implemented a different product called GWGuardian available at `www.gwtools.com` with one of my customers. My customer found it to be very effective in controlling SPAM. The third product I recommend is called GWAVA; it's available at `www.gwava.com`. I have not implemented GWAVA as a SPAM solution, but I know that it can scan even down at the post office level. So GWAVA can also filter potentially inappropriate messages sent within your GroupWise system. I will not make a recommendation as to which product you should buy; I simply recommend that any one of these solutions is better than nothing.

First, let's discuss the GroupWise features available for controlling SPAM.

GroupWise 6.5 SPAM/Junk Mail Solutions

The following are actions you can take in GroupWise in an effort to control SPAM and junk mail. Let's cover the GWIA-based solutions first:

- Reject the mail if the sender's identity cannot be verified
- Protect against mail bombs
- Implement access control
- Utilize blacklists

In terms of client-based solutions, you can also implement a junk-mail handling procedure within GroupWise.

Implementing GWIA-Based SPAM Solutions

The following sections cover features of the GWIA that can be used to combat SPAM.

Reject Mail If Sender's Identity Cannot Be Verified

In the SMTP protocol, an SMTP host that is trying to transmit to another SMTP host identifies itself with a DNS name. SPAMmers' SMTP hosts often identify themselves incorrectly or do not identify themselves at all.

The GWIA can be configured to test the identity of an SMTP host. This configuration setting is called "Reject mail if sender's identity cannot be verified". This configuration feature is available on the Security Settings property page under the SMTP/MIME tab on the GWIA gateway.

There is a downside to this setting, however. Many legitimate SMTP hosts on the Internet will not identify themselves or at least not identify themselves correctly. This is a common issue with many SMTP hosts on the Internet. So if you enable this feature, be prepared for the fact that you might reject legitimate mail.

Mail Bomb Protection

This is another setting on the GWIA's Security Settings property page. It's called Mailbomb Protection. This setting is generally a safe setting to implement. Mail bombs are generally different from SPAM. The nature of a mail bomb is that SMTP HOSTA contacts SMTP HOSTB and sends messages to HOSTB in rapid succession. Generally, the goal of a mail bomb is for HOSTA (the mail bomber) to overpower HOSTB, causing the SMTP HOSTB to be overwhelmed by the volume of mail, and perhaps crash because of the volume. Most SPAMmers are not trying to make SMTP hosts crash, so they do not use mail bomb techniques.

Access Control

The features available under the Access Control tab are the most effective tools you have in GroupWise to curtail SPAMmers. The most important feature is called Prevent Message Relaying, as shown in Figure 25.1.

SPAMmers are constantly searching the Internet for SMTP hosts that will allow the SPAMmer to relay its messages. Relaying is a part of the SMTP protocol that allows HOSTA to relay a message it wants to get to HOSTC through HOSTB. HOSTB then sends the message to HOSTC. If you were to allow message relaying, your GWIA could be used like HOSTB in this example. The impact to you might be that other SMTP hosts on the Internet might identify your host as a SPAMming host. Because of this, your SMTP host might become *blacklisted*. (Blacklists are discussed later in this chapter, but in short, being on a *blacklist* means that many other SMTP hosts on the Internet will not receive messages from your site.)

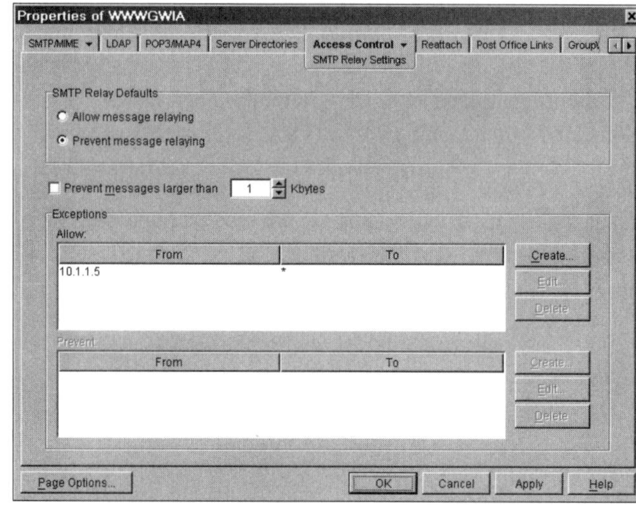

FIGURE 25.1 The Prevent Message Relay feature on the GWIA.

The GWIA will allow POP3 or IMAP4 users to relay through the GWIA, if they have already authenticated to the GWIA for a POP/IMAP session, prior to trying to relay off of the GWIA. If you have POP3/IMAP4 users, this kind of relaying is fine. It requires that a client that wants to relay through your GWIA have a mailbox within your system, and be authenticated to that mailbox, in order for the GWIA to allow the client to relay. It's important that your users configure their POP3/IMAP4 clients to authenticate before trying to relay. For example, in a popular POP3 client such as Microsoft Outlook Express, this is what you must do to enable authentication before relaying messages:

1. Select Tools, Accounts.
2. Highlight the Server definition/connection that represents the GWIA.
3. Click the Properties button.
4. From the Properties page, click the Servers tab.
5. Select the option My Server Requires Authentication.

These steps force Outlook Express to authenticate via the POP3 or IMAP4 credentials that the user has provided, each time the users tell their Outlook client to relay off of the GWIA.

You might have other devices in your organization that need to relay off of your GWIA, but are not sophisticated enough to authenticate. For these scenarios, it is often best to set up a special-purpose GWIA within your firewall. This GWIA can send messages out on the Internet, but no hosts on the Internet can contact this GWIA. This GWIA would be configured to "Allow message relaying". With this type of a configuration, only hosts on your Intranet would be able to relay off of the special-purpose GWIA.

Creating Blacklists

The GroupWise 6.5 GWIA supports the use of blacklists or RBLs (*realtime blacklists*). There are a couple of different kinds of blacklists. Those relevant to the subject of SPAM are *SPAM blacklists* and *Open Relay blacklists* (relaying was covered earlier in this chapter). Blacklists are lists compiled by hosts on the Internet that indicate which DNS addresses and IP addresses have SMTP hosts that are or could be used as SPAMming hosts on the Internet. Here is an explanation of how the GWIA utilizes RBLs:

1. HOSTA on the Internet contacts the GWIA and asks for an SMTP session.
2. The GWIA determines the IP address of HOSTA.
3. The GWIA queries its own DNS server for the reversed IP address of the sender appended to the blacklist server's DNS name. For example, if your GWIA was configured to use the blacklist server of `BL.SPAMCOP.NET` and the IP address of `HOSTA` were `134.55.65.213`, the DNS query would look like this:

   ```
   213.65.55.134.bl.spamcop.net
   ```

If the DNS system does not return a response to the request for the reversed IP address, that indicates to the GWIA that the address is not on that specific blacklist.

If a response for the DNS request is returned, the GWIA knows the host has been blacklisted.

What's clever about this architecture is that it does not require any special configuration of your local DNS server. This makes RBL checking compatible with virtually any DNS system.

In order to enable blacklists on your GWIA, you must go to the Blacklists property page under the Access Control tab of the GWIA object in ConsoleOne. Click the Add button, and add the correct host for a blacklist. For example, `BL.SPAMCOP.NET`, as shown in Figure 25.2.

FIGURE 25.2
A configured RBL.

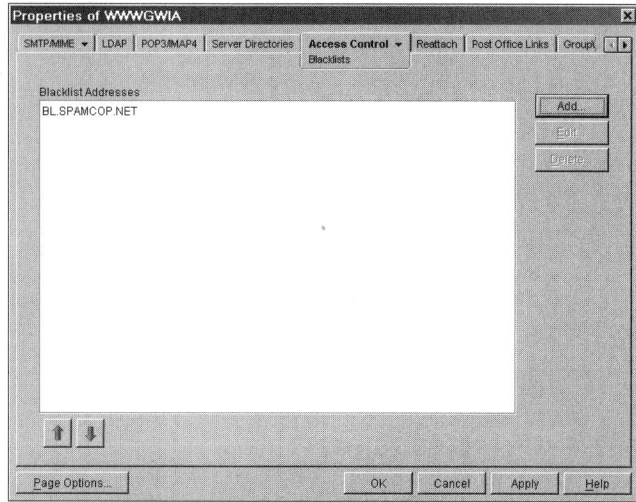

You can configure your own blacklist entries and "whitelist" entries if need be. On the Access Control tab on the GWIA object, if you select the Settings property page, you can edit the Default Class of Service profile. When you do so, there are two entry areas—one is titled Allow Messages From and the other is entitled Prevent Messages From. In this area you can indicate Internet domains that you do not want messages from. In the example shown in Figure 25.3, the GWIA has been configured to reject messages from the Internet domains named `spamrus.com` and `micromonopolysoft.com`. The `bob@deals.com` domain cannot send messages, and the SMTP host at `131.107.3.124` cannot send into the GWIA.

The Internet host `acme.com` was blacklisted by SPAMCOP accidentally. ACME is in the process of getting itself off of the blacklist, and in the meantime the WorldWide Widgets administrator added `acme.com` to the whitelist—which is the Allow Messages From field. This allows the GWIA to accept messages from `acme.com` even though it's blacklisted at the moment.

An important thing to note here is that you can override entries that your RBL hosts are saying should be blacklisted. You do this by creating an entry for the Internet domain in the Allow Messages From box.

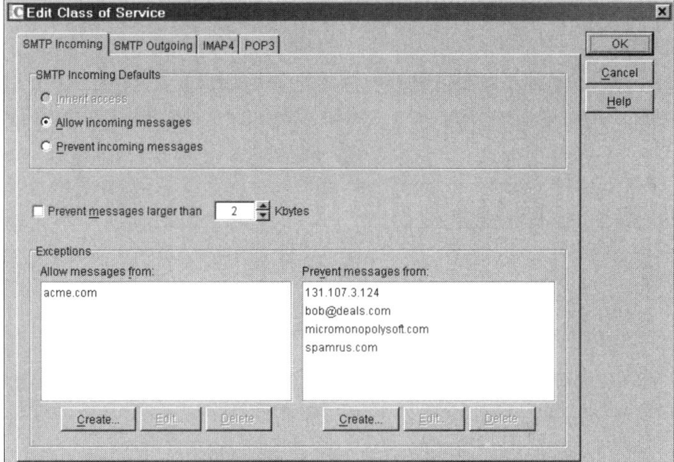

FIGURE 25.3 Configuring custom blacklists and whitelists.

My Experience with Blacklists

RBL filters are easy to configure and can be part of your SPAM solution. However, in my own testing in a live customer environment only about 1 in every 800 SPAM messages was caught by the SPAM RBL that we configured, which was caught via DNS queries to `bl.spamcop.net`. We had a SPAM solution in place that scanned for words that meant the message was SPAM after the messages came into the GWIA. Although the GWIA was doing RBL lookups on the messages, the GWIA in conjunction with SPAMCOP was able to detect only a small fraction of the messages that were SPAM. One thing to note, however, is that you can subscribe to multiple RBL servers. You will need to do your own research to determine which RBL services work the best for you. There are also free RBL services, as well as subscription RBL services available for use.

Implementing Client/Mailbox-Based SPAM Solutions

The capability for users to filter unwanted mail within their mailbox is built into the GroupWise 6.5 client. It's called the "Junk Mail" folder, not the SPAM folder. For the sake of this discussion, let's classify two kinds of unwanted mail—SPAM and junk mail. SPAMmers send SPAM mail, and they generally do so from random bogus Internet e-mail addresses and/or Internet domains. It's generally useless for users to use the junk mail feature in the GroupWise 6.5 client in an effort to prevent these kinds of messages.

They will never get a message from that SPAMmer again, with the same e-mail address or Internet domain. If GroupWise users do use the junk mail feature in GroupWise on SPAM messages, they are really creating more processing overhead on the POA for no good reason. The cumulative effect of hundreds of users on a large post office using the junk mail feature with hundreds (maybe thousands) of junk mail filters in each user database will drag the POA down over time.

Junk mail is a different kind of a message. Junk mail is when you go to a store, such as Sears, and you give them your e-mail address. Suddenly you start getting weekly mail messages from Sears. With the Junk Mail feature you can identify `weeklyoffers@sears.com` as a user whose messages you consider junk mail. This is the kind of scenario that best fits the junk mail feature in the GroupWise client.

You can control the junk mail feature from ConsoleOne, and perhaps even take the feature away from users. I am of the personal opinion that you should not enable this feature for users unless you have implemented a solution at your SMTP entry point or even at the domain or post office level that first filters out SPAM. I already established that SPAMmers rarely use the same identity. So if you have not implemented a SPAM solution prior to the messages getting to the user's mailbox, don't allow them to flag the SPAM using the junk mail feature. Perhaps the feature will make the user feel good, but in general this feature does not do anything for SPAM mail, but it does drag down the POA needlessly. The junk mail feature should be used for junk mail; not for SPAM.

In order to disable the junk mail feature, you can do the following:

1. In ConsoleOne, highlight a GroupWise domain.
2. Select Tools, GroupWise Utilities, Client Options.
3. Select Environment and uncheck the Enable Junk Mail Handling setting.
4. Click the padlock to the right of this setting, which will make this setting apply to all post offices under the domain.
5. Perform this action on all domains in your GroupWise system.

Figure 25.4 shows junk mail handling disabled.

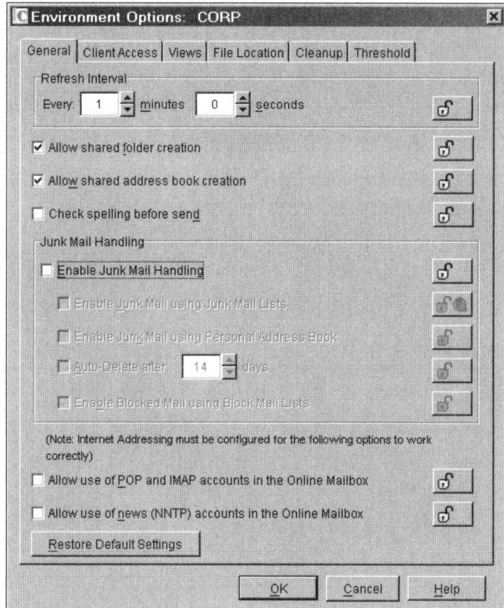

FIGURE 25.4 Disabling junk mail handling is done through Client Options in ConsoleOne.

Once you have implemented a server-based SPAM solution, whether it is SMTP-based or domain- or post office-based, and you are comfortable that the SPAM solution is filtering out about 95% of your SPAM, only then should you enable the junk mail handling feature.

It is important to note that junk mail handling is only an option for mail that comes in through your GWIA. Users are not able to "junk" mail that they receive from internal sources. The way that the POA knows if the mail came through the GWIA is if the view name on the message is "Internet". There might be a few customers out there that have changed the view name for inbound Internet messages. You can find out what the view name is for your inbound Internet messages by looking in the GWIA.CFG file for your inbound GWIA(s). Look for the section that says

```
/MailView-Internet
```

If your `/MailView-` switch says something other than Internet, users will not be able to use the junk mailing feature at the client.

So how does the POA process junk mail? The POA will perform several checks on the message to determine whether it matches settings that the user defined through junk mail handling. The POA uses the following algorithm to determine whether a particular Internet message should be junked or blocked based on the user's junk mail settings:

1. The POA looks for the sender's UserID to determine whether it's on the junk list or block list. If this field is not found, the POA will combine the sender's UserID field with the sender's Internet domain field and check both of these for a match.
2. Next, it examines the `FROM_TEXT` field and looks up that address in the junk or block lists.

   If no matches are found, the POA continues by looking for the domain name in the junk and block lists.
3. The POA checks the contents of the sender's Internet domain field against the SPAM lists. It also checks shorter versions of the domain name by trimming off the left portions of the name and trying each shortened name until there are only two segments left in the name.

For example, if the IDOMAIN was `pinball.games.microsoft.com`, the SPAM checker would first search for `pinball.games.microsoft.com`, and then for `games.microsoft.com`, followed by `microsoft.com`.

The SPAM checker tries to be fairly robust, checking all the versions of the address it can get its hands on.

Summary

This chapter explained ways for handling SPAM and junk mail. GroupWise has some strong built-in junk mail handling features. If you are serious about handling SPAM, though, you must turn to a third-party solution of some sort.

CHAPTER 26

Configuring GroupWise Authentication via LDAP

GroupWise client authentication can be configured to use an LDAP (Lightweight Directory Access Protocol) directory as the authentication method for accessing a GroupWise mailbox. The LDAP protocol is a means for getting information from a "directory" type database. In the case of GroupWise, LDAP is used for login credential information so that users can authenticate to GroupWise and access their mailboxes.

This chapter shows you how to configure GroupWise post offices to use LDAP authentication for Novell's eDirectory.

Understanding the Value of LDAP Authentication

In order for users to access their mailboxes, they need to use authentication credentials. In GroupWise the authentication credentials consist of the USERID/Mailbox ID and a password.

Here are the three most common conditions under which users do not need to enter a password in order to access their GroupWise mailboxes via the Windows client:

- The user has the Novell client installed, and is authenticated to eDirectory.
- The post office security level is set to Low.
- Novell's SecureLogin/Single Sign-On software is deployed, and so users must enter their GroupWise passwords just once, and Single Sign-On stores the GroupWise password.

Although with the GroupWise Windows client it might be easy to bypass the need to know, or even to create a GroupWise password, there are other circumstances that require the users to enter a password as part of their authentication credentials. These are some of the common circumstances:

- The Novell client is not installed on a user's computer, and the post office security level is set to High. Some customers are implementing environments in which core "NetWare" services are provided via iFolder and iPrint, and so they do not have the Novell client installed.
- The user needs to authenticate as a GroupWise WebAccess user.
- The user needs to authenticate as a GroupWise wireless user.

Without LDAP enabled, a user's password is a GroupWise password, which doesn't necessarily correlate with the user's eDirectory password. The downside to this is that users must then remember two passwords, one for eDirectory and one for GroupWise. This can be particularly confusing for users who regularly use the GroupWise Windows client—whereby they really do not need to know a GroupWise password. Users are faced with a GroupWise WebAccess login page, and they are dumbfounded why the password they enter—which is their eDirectory password—does not allow them to access GroupWise WebAccess.

With LDAP authentication enabled, users can now use their eDirectory password to authenticate to GroupWise. They do not need to remember a GroupWise password, they only need to remember their LDAP or eDirectory passwords for authenticating to GroupWise. There are some other potential benefits to GroupWise using LDAP for authentication credentials, as follows:

- eDirectory password expiration capabilities will also affect GroupWise (you can control this feature if you want).
- When a user changes their password in GroupWise, it can also change their eDirectory password (you can control this feature if you want).

NOTE

Most GroupWise customers will probably be using eDirectory's LDAP component to provide LDAP authentication services to the post office. However, GroupWise is flexible enough to allow you to use LDAP-compliant directories other than eDirectory.

LDAP Authentication and GroupWise External Entities

Before going further let's quickly address a special class of GroupWise users. GroupWise has a special kind of GroupWise object called a *GroupWise external entity*. An external entity is a full-blown GroupWise account that has an eDirectory object, but the object class is a GroupWise external entity and not an eDirectory user object. This kind of a GroupWise account cannot authenticate to eDirectory. The reason for this is because these type of users do not have "real" eDirectory user objects. They have a placeholder in eDirectory, but this object is far from a full eDirectory user class object. These users will still use a GroupWise password to authenticate. Enabling LDAP authentication will not break authentication for users who are external entities.

NOTE

It is possible to have external entities authenticate to an LDAP server other than eDirectory. You will see how this is done later in this chapter.

How LDAP Authentication Works

What follows is a high-level explanation of how GroupWise uses LDAP authentication to allow users to access their GroupWise mailboxes:

- GroupWise user loads the GW client (Windows, WebAccess, wireless, or other)
- The user sends his/her user ID and password to the Post Office Agent (POA)
- POA uses the LDAP protocol to query an external LDAP service provided database
- The LDAP requires a login or authentication
- The POA validates user credentials against the LDAP provided database
- The POA denies or grants access to the user depending on LDAP validation

As explained in this section, it's important to note that the LDAP authentication logic is all in the POA.

How to Configure LDAP Authentication

The following is a high-level explanation of how to configure LDAP authentication to GroupWise:

- Define LDAP server(s)
- Modify post office security
- Set security level to High
- Configure LDAP server settings

Step-by-Step Instructions for Enabling LDAP Authentication

Now roll up your sleeves; you are going to enable LDAP authentication. When you actually set up LDAP authentication in your system, it's a good idea to do so using a test post office and a few test users at first. This way, you can get familiar with the process of enabling LDAP prior to affecting your live GroupWise system.

Educate Users

When you are ready to cut over to LDAP authentication, educate your users about the fact that they now must use their eDirectory passwords instead of their GroupWise passwords.

In the following scenario, you are going to enable LDAP authentication for a post office called `CORPPO` on the `CORP` domain in the WorldWide Widget's GroupWise system.

Define the LDAP Server

Use these steps to define an LDAP server in the GroupWise system:

1. Load ConsoleOne, and connect to the primary domain. From the Tools menu select GroupWise System Operations, LDAP Servers.
2. In the Configure LDAP Servers menu, you might see an existing LDAP server. For example, in the WorldWide Widgets system, there is already an LDAP server defined called `LDAP CORP CORPPO`. The GroupWise 6.5 snap-ins create LDAP server definitions for new GroupWise post offices. However, if you have upgraded your system from a prior version of GroupWise, you might not have any LDAP servers defined in this dialog box.

3. Edit the existing LDAP server or add a new LDAP server for the CORPPO post office. In the WorldWide Widgets system, they use a naming convention such as `LDAP1 CORP CORPPO`. This naming convention is more logical for the *LDAP pooling* architecture, which is explained later in this chapter in the section "LDAP Server Pooling."
4. Each post office should have its own LDAP server defined for that post office, so the name of the LDAP server should correlate with the name of the post office. In the case of WorldWide Widgets, the name of the LDAP server is `LDAP CORP CORPPO`.

TIP

The name of the LDAP server must comply with the GroupWise domain naming standards. For example, you cannot use characters such as periods or commas.

5. Give the LDAP server a description; this can be the same description as the name of the LDAP server.
6. The next field is the Use SSL field. I strongly encourage you to enable SSL. Do so after you have tested this entire solution in a testing environment, without SSL. The instructions for enabling SSL are in Chapter 27, "Securing Your GroupWise System via SSL."
7. Fill in the LDAP server address, and keep the port of 389. When you enable SSL, the port will be 636.
8. Choose the user authentication method. Most customers will want to use Bind over Compare. These two methods are explained just a little later in the section titled "LDAP Bind and LDAP Compare."
9. Click the Select Post Offices button, and select the `CORPPO` post office. Only the `CORPPO` post office should use this LDAP server.

The LDAP server that you have configured should look similar to the one shown in Figure 26.1.

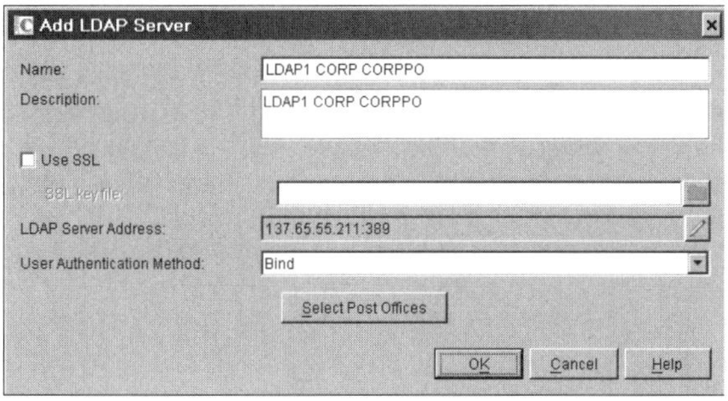

FIGURE 26.1
LDAP server configuration.

LDAP Bind and LDAP Compare

There are two user authentication methods available when adding an LDAP server. Most customers will want to use Bind instead of Compare. The following looks at each of these two methods:

The Bind method

- Uses the user ID and password supplied by the client/user to authenticate to the LDAP server.
- Requires that the POA make a connection to the LDAP server for each user logging in.
- Supports password expiration.

The Compare method

- Requires that the POA use the provided user ID and password to authenticate to the LDAP server.
- Allows the POA to make only one connection to the LDAP server.
- Does not support password expiration.

Enable LDAP Authentication at the Post Office

Now that the LDAP server is defined, you must enable LDAP authentication on the post office. Here are the steps for doing so:

1. Edit the properties of the `CORPPO` post office object (not the POA object below the post office).
2. From the GroupWise tab, select the Security property page.
3. The Security level should be set to High. Place a check mark next to the LDAP Authentication option.

NOTE

If you enable eDirectory authentication and LDAP authentication at the same time, the LDAP authentication is enforced. For example with both LDAP and eDirectory authentication enabled, if the GroupWise account does not have a password and you are authenticated to the network, you must still enter your LDAP password to gain access to the GroupWise mailbox. I have found that having both eDirectory and LDAP authentication checked has no real advantages over simply using LDAP authentication.

4. The LDAP User Name field needs to be filled out only if the LDAP server that you defined earlier in this section uses the Compare user authentication mode. The syntax for this field is as follows:

```
CN=<eDirectory USERID>,
<Organizational Unit - unless the user is at the root
➥of the tree>,
<Organization>.
```

For example

```
CN=LDAPUSER,OU=NY,OU=AMERICAS,O=WWW
```

The user does not have to be a super user with Admin equivalent rights. The user just must have Browse, Read, and Compare rights throughout the entire eDirectory tree, or at least in the OU or OUs that house the users that are associated with post office you are configuring.

5. The LDAP Password field is also only used when using the Compare user authentication mode. The password is the password for the user that you used in the LDAP User Name field.
6. The Disable LDAP Password Changing option is an important one. The default is to allow users to change their passwords within GroupWise, which changes their eDirectory passwords. There's not necessarily any harm done in allowing users to change their eDirectory passwords from GroupWise, unless you are using some other technology that may need to be apprised of eDirectory passwords. When a password changes in a GroupWise client, there might not be a way for other software to know of that password change. The needs of your environment will dictate whether you want to check the Disable LDAP Password Changing option.
7. The LDAP Pool Server Reset Timeout option has to do with LDAP server pooling option, which is explained later in this chapter.
8. Click the Select Servers button and make sure the `LDAP1 CORP CORPPO` LDAP server is in the Selected Servers column.

Figure 26.2 shows the `CORPPO`'s Security property page with LDAP authentication enabled for the post office. The post office supports Bind user authentication mode, and users can change their eDirectory passwords from within a GroupWise client.

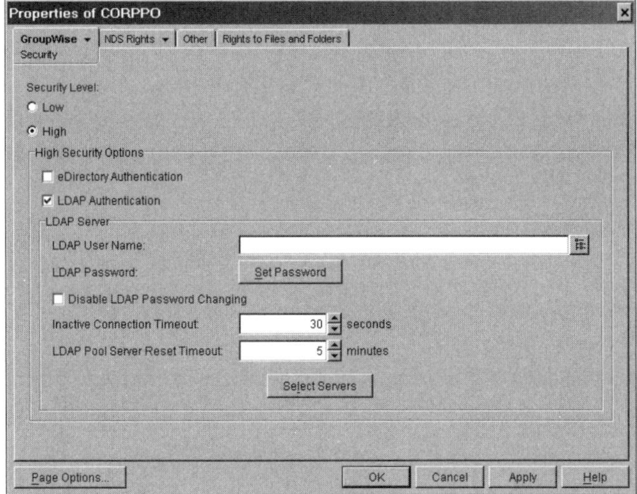

FIGURE 26.2
A post office with LDAP authentication configured.

eDirectory LDAP Server Tips

Although this isn't an eDirectory book, the following section provides a few tips for enabling LDAP on a NetWare server just the same:

- The NetWare server that you have configured to service LDAP requests must have the module NLDAP.NLM loaded.
- The NetWare server that services LDAP requests does not need any replicas on it; however, it is ideal that it have a copy of each eDirectory replica for every partition in the tree. By having eDirectory replicas for all partitions of the tree, the LDAP requests are serviced more quickly.
- The LDAP server must allow clear text passwords. By default, eDirectory's LDAP Group object is not configured to allow clear text passwords. You will encrypt those clear text passwords when you enable SSL, so there's no harm to do this at this point. Remember this setting is not enabled as the default, so you are going to need to check it. The following instructions for confirming that you have the Allow Clear Text Passwords option enabled assume that you have the LDAP snap-ins to ConsoleOne installed:

1. To confirm that your LDAP server supports clear text passwords, edit the object in your eDirectory tree called `LDAP Group - <Server Name>`. For example, in the WorldWide Widgets Tree, the object is called `LDAP Group - WWWFS1` and this object is in the same OU as the server called `WWWFS1`.
2. Edit the properties of the LDAP Group object. On the LDAP Group General properties page, make sure the Allow Clear Text Passwords option is checked.

NOTE

If you enable the clear text option, you do not need to unload and reload NLDAP. NLDAP will detect the changes in configuration, and update dynamically.

That's all that you need to do from an LDAP perspective on the eDirectory platform. You should of course make sure that your eDirectory tree is healthy, and available 100% of the time.

Testing and Confirming LDAP Authentication

Once you've configured everything, the easiest way to test the LDAP authentication is to do the following:

1. Create a test user on the `CORPPO` post office who has LDAP authentication enabled.
2. Go to the GroupWise Account property page for this user.
3. Select the Change GroupWise Password button. Change the password to something like `123`.
4. Now change the user's eDirectory password on the Restrictions—Password Restrictions property page. Make the password `abc`.
5. Now try to log into GroupWise as the user. When asked for the password, type `abc`. If you are allowed in using the eDirectory password, you know that LDAP authentication is working. If you cannot log in, you must troubleshoot the issue. See the next section for LDAP authentication troubleshooting tips.

Now you have configured the basics of an LDAP authentication infrastructure for a GroupWise post office.

LDAP Authentication Troubleshooting Tips

The GroupWise POA will log each time it attempts to authenticate a user to the LDAP server. Make sure the POA is on Verbose logging; Verbose logging shows you the POA user-authentication process. Figure 26.3 shows the user `TKRATZER` logging in, and the POA binding to the LDAP server at the IP address `137.65.55.211`.

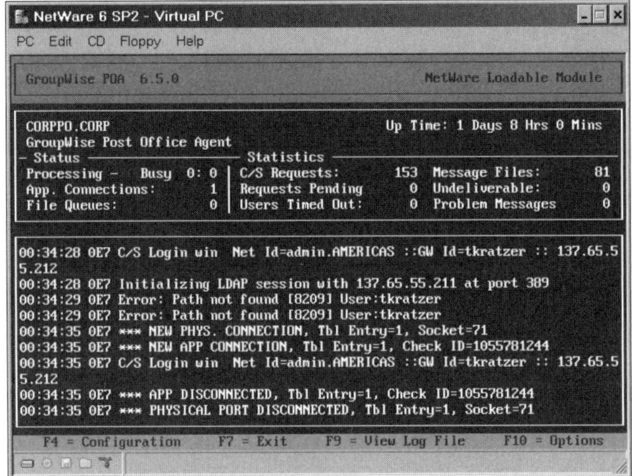

FIGURE 26.3
A POA log during LDAP authentication.

The POA's log is going to be one of your best mechanisms for troubleshooting LDAP authentication. Some of the things to check include

- Does the POA seem to have LDAP authentication enabled? If not, rebuild the WPHOST.DB for the post office.
- Is the server that is supposed to service LDAP requests running the NLDAP module?
- Does the user you are authenticating as have an eDirectory account? Is the user's GroupWise object grafted to that eDirectory account?
- Are there eDirectory problems that prevent the server running the NLDAP server from receiving information about the object? Perhaps using `DSTRACE` with LDAP filters will help to shake out this kind of a problem.

Creating Fault Tolerance

Although LDAP authentication is a great authentication method, if you don't take measures to make it fault tolerant, your users can all be locked out of their GroupWise accounts. If the LDAP server you have configured for your user authentication goes down, the POA cannot authenticate users, and so users will not be able to access their mailboxes. The solution to this potential problem is called *LDAP server pooling*. The next section talks about how to enable LDAP server pooling.

LDAP Server Pooling

LDAP pooling allows you to define a second (or even a third) LDAP server for the POA to roll over to if the first one is not available for some reason. Here are the steps for doing this:

1. Create a new LDAP server under Tools, GroupWise System Operations, LDAP Servers, just as you did earlier in this chapter.

   Take care to give the name of the LDAP server something slightly different than the first LDAP server you defined. For example, to be consistent with the naming standards at WorldWide Widgets, the second LDAP server, which is used for the `CORPPO` post office, is called `LDAP2 CORP CORPPO`.

   The IP address (or DNS address) should be different than the first LDAP server; because, of course, you want this to be a totally different server just in case the server defined as the first LDAP server goes down or is not available to service LDAP requests.

2. Edit the post office object, and go to the Security property page. Click the Select Servers button and make sure to add the second LDAP server to the Select Servers column, as shown in Figure 26.4.

NOTE

From the Select Servers button in the Select LDAP Servers dialog box, the order that the POA will access the LDAP servers is based upon the order in which the POA received the update of LDAP servers in its pool. The best way to view the LDAP pool state that the POA knows about is to access the POA's HTTP port. From there, you can click the Configuration tab, and then click the LDAP Authentication link. You will now see all the servers in the LDAP pool, as well as the state of the particular LDAP server. The LDAP server can be in a Starting, Good, or Bad state. Starting simply means that the POA has not really started to talk to this LDAP server. Good means that the POA has contacted this LDAP server, and Bad means the LDAP server is currently down. If an LDAP server is in the Bad state, you will see a second counter that lets you know when the POA will refresh this LDAP server to see whether its LDAP services are available again.

FIGURE 26.4
Selecting a second LDAP server.

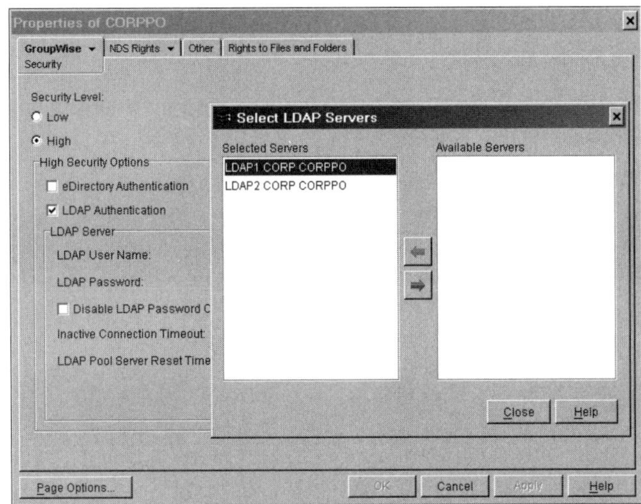

3. The LDAP Pool Server Reset Timeout value on the post office's Security property page governs how long an LDAP server is kept out of the LDAP server pool when the POA has determined it cannot obtain services from that LDAP server. You can adjust this setting to your liking; I prefer the default of five minutes.

Other LDAP Authentication Options

Let's take a deeper look at LDAP authentication in order to make an important point. The GroupWise POA identifies the user who is logging in based upon the User ID they fill in via the GroupWise client (be it the Windows, WebAccess, or wireless clients). In every user's record in the GroupWise directory (WPDOMAIN.DB and WPHOST.DB) there is a field called Network ID. There's another field that identifies the eDirectory tree the user is grafted into. These two values come from eDirectory based upon the eDirectory object that the GroupWise account is associated with. The POA uses these values to indicate which eDirectory context to look into in order to authenticate the users.

Now that you understand the architecture, imagine that your LDAP server is either in another eDirectory tree, or your LDAP server isn't even a Novell eDirectory LDAP server. What do you do then? You have two options, as follows.

Option 1

Each user object has a field on the GroupWise Account page called LDAP Authentication. This field allows you to indicate a different context or fully distinguished name. For example, you could enter

```
CN=ECORNISH,OU=EMPLOYEES,O=FLATTREEORGANIZATION
```

The fact that you enter the location for the user in another tree, means that the LDAP server defined to service this post office must also be in the other tree or LDAP directory.

Option 2

Leave the LDAP Authentication field blank, and make sure that the e-mail address attribute in the LDAP directory matches the eDirectory's e-mail attribute of the GroupWise user. You must then rename the LDAPX.NLM file found on the server where your POA is running and restart the POA. When you perform this step, the POA will not try to look up the eDirectory's distinguished name for the user, and because the LDAP Authentication field is blank, the POA will simply search against the LDAP server for the user's e-mail address. If it finds an e-mail address, it will then know the user's distinguished name, and will know how to authenticate to the other tree or LDAP directory as the correct user.

If you happen to have a *workforce tree* (an eDirectory tree created from another eDirectory tree via DirXML), and you want to use the workforce tree for LDAP authentication, refer to the following Technical Information Document at Novell's Web site:

```
http://support.novell.com/cgi-bin/search/searchtid.cgi?/
➥10067272.htm
```

I have also used the LDAP Authentication field to associate the user's login credentials with a different eDirectory user object. For example, I wanted to have the user `TKRATZER` to authenticate with the user `ADMIN`'s password. Here's what I did:

1. Edited the object `TKRATZER`.
2. Went to the GroupWise Account page for `TKRATZER`.
3. Entered the following in the LDAP authentication field:

   ```
   CN=admin,O=americas
   ```

4. Now when tkratzer logs into GroupWise, he types **`TKRATZER`** as the user ID, and the password for the object `ADMIN.AMERICAS` in the password field.

So, why do this? I did it to prove it could be done. You'll have to think of under what conditions you might find this useful.

This Technical Information Document talks about the details surrounding option 2. External eDirectory trees and DirXML are outside the scope of this book.

Summary

This chapter explained the benefits derived from GroupWise using LDAP authentication. This chapter also gave step-by-step instructions for enabling LDAP authentication for a post office.

Chapter 27 discusses enabling SSL for LDAP authentication.

CHAPTER 27

Securing Your GroupWise System via SSL

Every piece of a GroupWise system and a GroupWise messenger system can be secured via SSL (Secure Sockets Layer). SSL allows data to be encrypted via an industry-recognized protocol for encrypting data between two network hosts.

SSL is used only to encrypt data while it's "on the wire." SSL encryption is not used to encrypt data once it has traversed the network and is on a storage device such as a server or computer hard drive.

GroupWise has always used a proprietary 40-bit encryption scheme. In addition to that, the GroupWise 6.x revisions of GroupWise not only encrypt the data, but also compress it using another proprietary scheme. With the advent of government regulations and industry demands that require 128-bit encryption, GroupWise 6.5 supports SSL using 128-bit encryption. Setting up SSL encryption isn't all that difficult, it's just a matter of understanding some underlying concepts really well. You can then apply those concepts in a multitude of areas.

Understanding SSL Architecture

As an administrator, make sure that you read this section thoroughly; it's critical for you to understand how to enable SSL on your GroupWise system. In the following section, I'm going to give a very simplistic explanation of the pieces of SSL architecture that are pertinent to understanding how to logically set up SSL encryption in your GroupWise system.

SSL Encryption Using a Symmetric Key Method

The symmetric key method for encrypting data via SSL is one in which the hosts that communicate use the same encryption key. Security of the encrypted data between the two hosts is assured only if the encryption key is secret. In a GroupWise environment there is one scenario in which a symmetric key is used for SSL-izing data. The WebAccess Application to WebAccess Agent communication uses a symmetric key held in the COMMGR.CFG file. The key is editable via ConsoleOne. See Chapter 11, "Configuring GroupWise Web Access," for more details about the COMMGR.CFG file.

SSL Encryption Using Public Key Infrastructure (PKI)

SSL uses two types of keys in combination with one another. These keys are called

- Public keys
- Private keys

These keys allow Internet hosts to encrypt and decrypt data that will be sent to one another. If HOSTA wants to send encrypted data to HOSTB, HOSTA must obtain HOSTB's public key. Using HOSTB's public key, HOSTA encrypts its data to HOSTB. HOSTB uses its private key to decrypt the data. The same goes for how HOSTB sends encrypted data to HOSTA. HOSTB uses HOSTA's public key to encrypt data going to HOSTA. HOSTA then decrypts the data using its private key.

A public key must be signed by a certificate authority (CA). Once a public key is signed, it is considered a certificate. The private key is still considered a private key, or *the key*.

A certificate simply says that the public and private keys of HOSTA are certified by HOSTZ. HOSTZ is considered the certificate authority. HOSTB makes the decision as to whether to trust the certificate authority. If they do, the certificate for HOSTA is considered valid. HOSTB can send data using HOSTA's public key, with confidence that only HOSTA knows HOSTA's private key.

A certificate can also be *self-signed,* which means the host that creates the certificate also signs the certificate. A self-signed certificate is generally used for encryption when two hosts have already established a trusted relationship with one another, and they simply need to use public and private keys to encrypt and decrypt data. The GroupWise client and the GroupWise Messenger clients both use self-signed certificates for communicating with their supporting agents.

Public Key Infrastructure and a Novell Environment

With Novell's eDirectory software fully implemented, the pieces of PKI that are relevant to this discussion are already in place. They are

- **The certificate authority.** All eDirectory trees version 8.x or better have a certificate authority. Figure 27.1 shows the certificate authority in the WorldWide Widgets tree. The certificate authority (CA) in your Novell eDirectory tree can sign the public keys, which will validate the key.

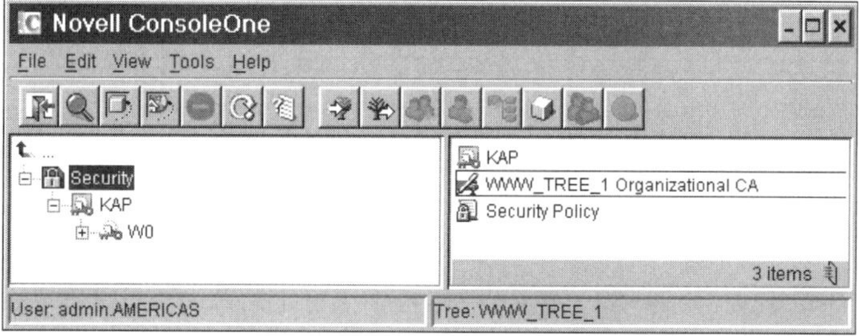

FIGURE 27.1 The certificate authority in an eDirectory tree.

- **Public Key Generation.** With Novell's Certificate Server and Certificate Server snap-ins in place, you can submit a private key. Certificate Server can generate a public key to be used in companion with the private key.

Configuring and Signing Certificates in eDirectory

This section assumes you have the following prerequisites:

- eDirectory 8.6.2 or better
- GroupWise 6.5

There are other prerequisites to fulfill in order to create signed keys (certificates), but the next section will explain how to fulfill those prerequisites.

Administrator's Workstation Prerequisites

The following are prerequisites for one administrator's workstation. Not everyone that uses ConsoleOne, or who is a network administrator, must have these prerequisites fulfilled.

Workstation NICI

Install the Novell International Cryptographic Infrastructure for Windows. At the time that this book was written, these are the instructions for doing this:

1. Go to `http://download.novell.com` and download the "Novell International Cryptographic Infrastructure" for Windows. This software will be installed directly on the machine from which you are going to use ConsoleOne. This software is necessary for the Novell Certificate Server snap-in, which you will install later, to work.
2. At the `download.novell.com` site, select the product [Novell International Cryptographic Infrastructure] and a platform [Windows 2000]. Choose the date of [<All Dates>] and the [English] language. At the writing of this article, the software is named "2.4.2 on Windows 95/98/NT/2000".
3. Run the *.EXE that you pulled down, and follow the installation wizard.

NICI is now installed, and the workstation does not even need to be rebooted for NICI to take effect.

Novell Certificate Console (PKI) Snap-ins for ConsoleOne

Although you have a CA and a PKI infrastructure already in place, it's possible that you do not have the Novell Certificate Console (PKI) snap-ins for ConsoleOne installed. The easiest way to determine what is installed is to load ConsoleOne, select Help, About Snapins. You need to make sure you have the "Novell Certificate Server Snapin version 2.21" or better. If you do not have these snap-ins, obtain them from Novell's Web site and install them. Here are instructions for doing that, at the time that this book was written:

1. Go to `http://download.novell.com`.

2. Obtain the latest PKI snap-ins for ConsoleOne by selecting [Certificate Server], platform [Windows 2000], choose the date of [<All Dates>] and the [English] language. At the time this chapter was written, the software was called "2.21 Snap-in on Windows 95/98/NT/2000".

3. This software does not have a README or an install routine. To install this software, run your UNZIP utility to expand the zipped file. When prompted for path to expand the software, indicate the path to ConsoleOne, such as `C:\NOVELL\CONSOLEONE\1.2`. Make sure to indicate the full path to the 1.2 directory. Figure 27.2 shows PKUNZIP with the correct extract path.

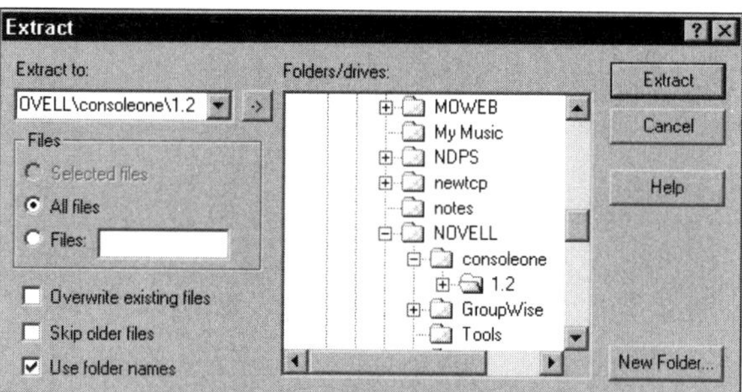

FIGURE 27.2
Installing the PKI snap-ins for ConsoleOne.

The PKI snap-ins for ConsoleOne will now load when ConsoleOne loads. These snap-ins will aid in the creation of certificates.

Generate a Private Key and a Certificate Signing Request for the Private Key

GroupWise 6.5 comes with a utility (GWCSRGEN.EXE) that can create a private key in the form of a file, and a CSR (certificate signing request) for that private key. Then the private key can either be signed by an external certificate authority such as Verisign or the certificate can be signed by the certificate authority in your eDirectory tree. This chapter assumes you will have the key signed by the certificate authority in your eDirectory tree.

You can find GWCSRGEN.EXE in the `<GroupWise 6.5 SDD>\ADMIN\UTILITY\GWCSRGEN` directory.

Following are the steps for using the GroupWise CSR Generation utility:

1. Run the GroupWise CSR Generate utility.
2. Fill in the fields of the CSR Generate utility, as shown in Table 27.1.

TABLE 27.1 **GroupWise CSR Generation Utility Configuration Instructions**

FIELD NAME	INSTRUCTIONS
Key filename	Name the file with an 8.3 name. The name doesn't matter to the software; I like to use a name with a *.KEY file name. For example, WWWIDGET.KEY.
Key password	This is a password that will be embedded inside the private key. This should be a password that you will not forget. If you do though, you will have to go through this entire procedure again.
CSR filename	The name and length of this file does not matter; it will only be used temporarily. I like to put a *.CSR extension on the file. For example, WWWIDGET.CSR.
Country	The two letter country code for the country you are in. For example, for the United States the country code is US. For Canada, it's CA.
City	Your city; you do not need to use abbreviations.
Organization	The full name of your organization. For example, WorldWide Widgets Corporation.
Division	The division of your organization that needs this certificate. For example, ITS.
Hostname	Technically, you define the DNS name for the server that will be using this certificate. However, in this example we will use the same certificate on all the agents, and in fact the DNS name need not be valid for GroupWise to use the certificates for encryption. You can just use the Internet domain name for your organization; for example, WWWIDGETS.COM.

Figure 27.3 shows the GroupWise CSR Generate utility with the aforementioned settings.

Generate a Public Key from the Certificate Signing Request

Following are the steps for generating a certificate from the CSR you made in the prior section:

1. Load ConsoleOne. This must be the same instance of ConsoleOne with the Novell Certificate Server snapins, as explained in the prerequisites section earlier in this chapter.

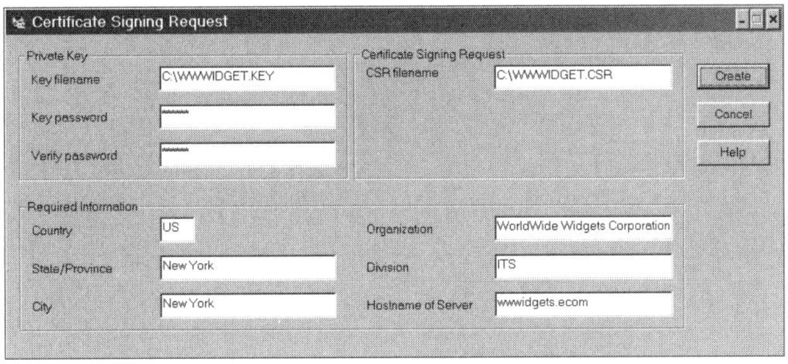

FIGURE 27.3
The GroupWise CSR Generate utility is used to create a private key, and generate a Certificate Signing Request.

2. Highlight any Organizational Unit, or Organization in your eDirectory tree browser view and select Tools, Issue Certificate.
3. You should get the Issue Certificate dialog box shown in Figure 27.4. Click the browse button to the right of the Filename field. Browse to the *.CSR file that you made in the instructions earlier in this chapter, and click Next.

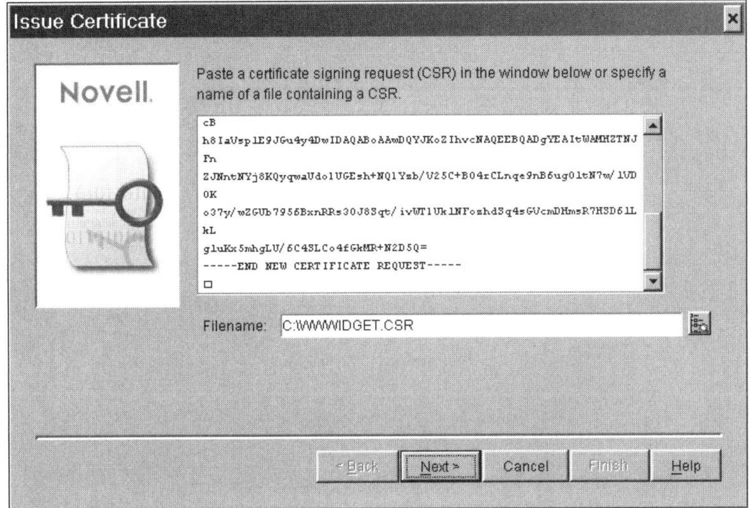

FIGURE 27.4
Specifying a CSR filename.

4. At the next page, you don't have any selection to make. Just click Next.
5. On the next screen, shown in Figure 27.5, you specify the key type. Select the following options and click Next:

    Custom

    Data encipherment

    Key encipherment

    Digital signature

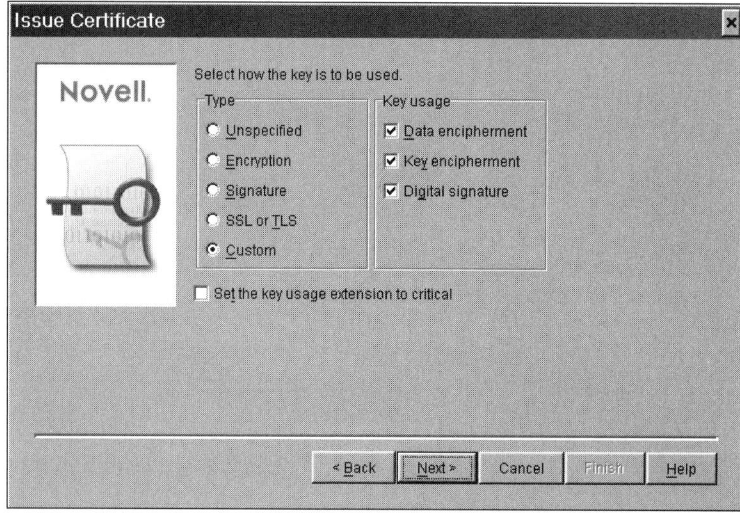

FIGURE 27.5
Specifying key type and usage.

6. At the next screen, you can choose the amount of years that the certificate is valid. Only you will be using these certificates; therefore, you might want to specify a period longer than the default, for example, five years. Then click the Next button.
7. On the review screen you get to see the configuration options your choose. Click the Finish button.
8. Lastly, you'll see the Save Certificate dialog box, as shown in Figure 27.6. Make sure to choose Base64 format for the file type.

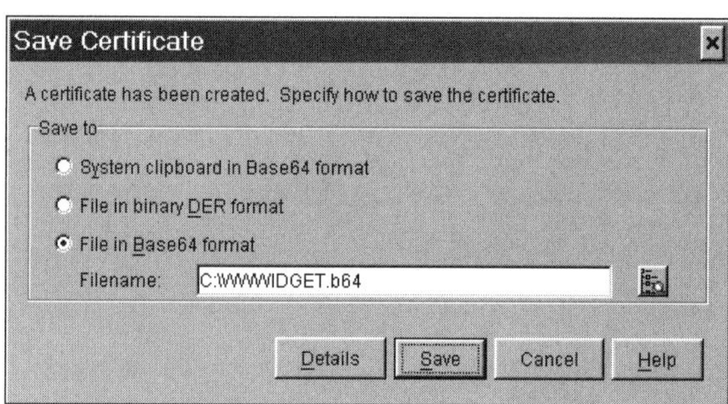

FIGURE 27.6
Saving the certificate in Base64 format.

Now you have generated and created a public key contained within a certificate which is the *.B64 file, a private *.KEY file. The private key is secured through the password that you assigned to the key when you used the GroupWise CSR Generate utility.

Securing GroupWise Agents That Use Certificates and Key Files

The instructions in the remainder of this chapter ensure that the following data is secured via SSL:

- GroupWise client to GroupWise POA communication
- GroupWise WebAccess agent to GroupWise POA communication
- GroupWise POA to IMAP client communication
- GroupWise POA to CAP client communication
- GroupWise POA to MTA communication via MTP
- GroupWise MTA to MTA communication via MTP
- HTTP monitoring of the GroupWise MTA
- HTTP monitoring of the GroupWise POA
- HTTP monitoring of the GroupWise WebAccess agent
- GroupWise Messenger Client to the Novell Messaging Agent
- GroupWise Messenger Client to the Novell Archive Agent
- HTTP monitoring of the Novell Messaging Agent
- HTTP monitoring of the Novell Archive Agent
- The GWIA's communications with other Internet hosts (that support SSL)
- The GWIA's communications with POP3 clients
- The GWIA's communications with IMAP clients

The public key, the private key, and the password for the private key can be used to fill in the fields. In ConsoleOne, you'll see the options to fill in the fields shown in Table 27.2.

TABLE 27.2 **Certificate Creation Configuration Instructions**

FIELD	INPUT
Certificate	The *.B64 file; the filename should not exceed the size of an 8.3 character filename.
SSL Key File	The *.KEY file; the filename should not exceed the size of an 8.3 character filename.
Set Password	This is the password you input earlier when using the GroupWise CSR Generate utility to generate the private key.

The path to the *.B64 and the *.KEY files should be a path on the server where the GroupWise agent is running. You have lots of flexibility as to where you place the certificates, it just needs to be somewhere on the server that is running the GroupWise agent. I like to use a model where I create a `CERT` directory off of the root data directory for that agent. Table 27.3 depicts my method for placing these files.

TABLE 27.3 **Recommended Certificate and Private Key Locations**

AGENT	CERTIFICATE AND KEY LOCATION
GroupWise MTA	Create the `CERT` directory off of the domain directory. The domain directory is the one that contains the file WPDOMAIN.DB.
GroupWise POA	Create the `CERT` directory off of the post office directory. The post office directory is the one that contains the file WPHOST.DB.
GroupWise WebAccess Agent	Create the `CERT` directory off of the `<Domain>\WPGATE>\<WEBACCESS GATEWAY DIRECTORY>`.
GroupWise Internet Agent	Create the `CERT` directory off of the `<Domain>\WPGATE>\<GWIA GATEWAY DIRECTORY>`.
Novell Messenger/GroupWise Messenger—Messaging Agent	Create the `CERT` directory off of the `SYS:NOVELL\NM\MA` directory.
Novell Messenger/GroupWise Messenger—Archive Agent	Create the `CERT` directory off of the `SYS:NOVELL\NM\AA` directory.

This method of placing the key and certificate under the root data directory for the agent is friendly to scenarios in which Novell Cluster Services is in place. Also, when you have the key and certificate files in close proximity to the root data directories of your agents, other folks with administrative rights to your servers are less likely to futz with these files because of their proximity to your GroupWise system's data directories. Figure 27.7 shows a GroupWise POA that has been configured to use a public and private key, and the password for the private key on the SSL Settings property page of the POA object. The password you use is the same one used when generating the private key in the GWCSRGEN.EXE utility.

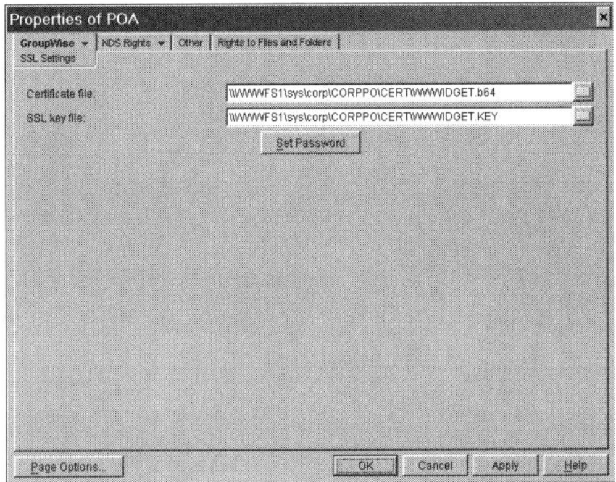

FIGURE 27.7
A Configured SSL Settings property page for a GroupWise POA.

Filling out the SSL Settings property page of a GroupWise agent is not all that you must do to enable SSL. You must also enable SSL encryption for the services that the agent provides. For example on the GroupWise POA, you might enable SSL encryption for client/server connections, MTP communication, and HTTP monitoring. Figure 27.8 shows a POA configured for these settings.

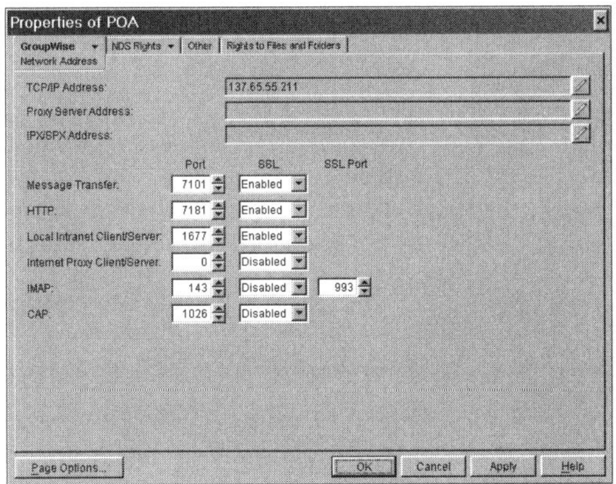

FIGURE 27.8
Specifying SSL for services the POA provides.

It's important to note that for some of the SSL fields on the POA you can set SSL to disabled, enabled, and required. The required option has the following impact. Suppose the POA is set for SSL Required for Local Intranet Client/Server. If a GroupWise WebAccess agent or client does not support SSL, that agent or client cannot log into the GroupWise POA. Note that only GroupWise client that supports SSL is the GroupWise 6.5 client. The GroupWise 5.x and 6.0x clients do not support SSL.

When a GroupWise client/server session is SSL-ized, a little padlock icon shows up in the lower-right corner of the GroupWise client. If a user hovers over the padlock with the mouse pointer, a simple dialog box displays that reads SSL Secured, as shown in Figure 27.9.

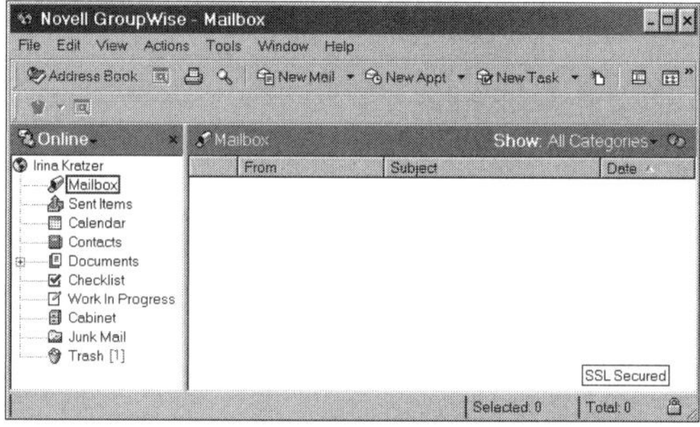

FIGURE 27.9 A GroupWise client/server sessions secured by SSL.

The location for configuring SSL certificates and keys is similar for all GroupWise agents. The GroupWise Messenger/Novell Messenger agents are slightly different. Table 27.4 lists the Agent type, explains where to configure the SSL certificates and keys, and indicates where to configure the services that are SSL-ized by that agent.

TABLE 27.4 How to Configure GroupWise Agents to Use SSL

AGENT TYPE	WHERE TO CONFIGURE SSL	WHERE TO CONFIGURE SERVICES
Agent	SSL Certificate and Key Configuration	SSL enabling services for this agent
POA	SSL Settings Property Page under the GroupWise tab	Network Address Property Page under the GroupWise tab
MTA	SSL Settings Property Page under the GroupWise tab	Network Address Property Page under the GroupWise tab

AGENT TYPE	WHERE TO CONFIGURE SSL	WHERE TO CONFIGURE SERVICES
WebAccess Agent	SSL Settings Property Page under the GroupWise tab	Network Address Property Page under the GroupWise tab
GroupWise Internet Agent (GWIA)	SSL Settings Property Page under the GroupWise tab	Network Address Property Page under the GroupWise tab
Novell Messenger/ GroupWise Messenger—Messaging Agent (MA)	Security Property Page under the Agent tab	Security Property Page under the Agent tab
Novell Messenger/ GroupWise Messenger—Archive Agent (AA)	Security Property Page under the Agent tab	Security Property Page under the Agent tab

Table 27.5 offers some important notes with regards to SSL-izing the agents:

TABLE 27.5

Troubleshooting Notes When Enabling SSL on GroupWise Agents

AGENT	NOTES
POA	If you "require" SSL connections you might end up denying connections to certain clients and WebAccess Agents. After enabling SSL, the POA generally picks up the changes and does not need to be restarted.
MTA	After enabling SSL, the MTA generally picks up the changes and does not need to be restarted.
WebAccess Agent	After enabling SSL, the WebAccess Agent (GWINTER) must be restarted.
GWIA	After enabling SSL, the GWIA must be restarted. The GWIA will only SSL-ize communication with other Internet SMTP hosts that also support Extended SMTP "STARTTLS" protocol. In Chapter 30, the section titled "Secure the SMTP Channel" talks more about STARTTLS.
Novell Messenger/ GroupWise Messenger—Messaging Agent (MA)	Make sure to enable the option called Enable SSL for Client/Server. After enabling SSL, the MA must be restarted.

Table 27.5 Continued

AGENT	NOTES
Novell Messenger/ GroupWise Messenger—Archive Agent (AA)	Make sure to enable the option Enable SSL for Client/Server. Make sure to enable the option Enable SSL for Message Transfer Protocol if the MA and the AA are configured to run on separate servers. After enabling SSL, the AA must be restarted.

NOTE

If you need to change the password on the key file, you normally need to restart the agent. Review the Agent log file to see whether it reports that it must be restarted because of a change to the key password.

The most important portion of GroupWise that should be secured through SSL is the GroupWise WebAccess application to Web browser conversation. This process is lengthy and is well documented in two articles that I have written. The first is in the October 2002 issue of *Novell Connection Magazine*. The second article is in the September/October 2003 issue of *Novell Connection Magazine*. *Novell Connection Magazine* is located on the Internet at `http://www.novell.com/connectionmagazine/`.

Enabling SSL for POA to LDAP Server Communication

Chapter 26, "Configuring GroupWise Authentication via LDAP," talks about how to enable the POA to perform LDAP authentication. Make sure to read that chapter first before trying to understand the steps in this section. Also, make sure to read all the material preceeding this section so that you more fully understand the steps you will be taking in this section.

In a Novell eDirectory environment, the LDAP server by default uses the SSL CertificateDNS—*<server name>* object in the same context as the server running LDAP services. This object is actually called a *key material object*. In order for the GroupWise POA to communicate with the LDAP server via SSL, the POA must use that same encryption key. The Novell LDAP server reads the key right out of eDirectory, but the GroupWise POA does not. The key, therefore, must be exported to a file so the POA can use it to send encrypted data to the Novell LDAP server. When you configure your GroupWise POA to speak to a specific LDAP server, you must have exported the key file that the LDAP server also uses. Read through this example scenario to understand how to configure the LDAP server and the POA to talk to one another via SSL.

Server Running the GroupWise POA for CORPPO Post Office (WWWFS1)

This is a NetWare 6 server running a GroupWise 6.5 POA.

Server Hosting Novell LDAP Services (WWWFS2)

There are three basic steps behind enabling SSL communications, as follows:

1. The first step is to make sure that your LDAP server is configured to speak correctly when using an SSL connection.
2. The second step is to export the encryption key file for the same Key Material Object in eDirectory that the LDAP server is currently configured to use. This way the POA can use the same encryption key from the key material object that the LDAP server is currently using.
3. The third step is to configure your POA to use the encryption key you obtained from the LDAP server.

The following sections walk through these actions.

Configuring the LDAP Server to Support SSL

The default settings for an eDirectory LDAP server do not allow for clear text passwords. If you enabled the LDAP server to allow clear text passwords, in order to set up and test your LDAP authentication without SSL, this is where you can now disable the option for clear text passwords. This ensures the security of your eDirectory usernames and passwords as now any service using NLDAP must use encryption to talk to the LDAP server. You should confirm the following configuration settings for the LDAP server:

- The port for LDAP SSL communication (which is 636 by default)
- That SSL is enabled for the LDAP server
- The LDAP server does not allow clear text passwords
- Determine which key material object the LDAP server is using

Here are the steps for checking out these settings. You might not have the correct LDAP server snap-ins, so rather than taking you through the process of obtaining the LDAP server snap-ins, this section instructs you about how to check these settings without the LDAP snap-ins. If you have the LDAP snap-ins for ConsoleOne, the settings I mention should be easy to find. I do not recommend modifying these attributes without the LDAP snap-ins. If you must modify them, you must find a copy of ConsoleOne that has the LDAP snap-ins enabled.

1. Highlight the eDirectory OU that contains the server that is running the LDAP services.
2. Edit the object called LDAP Server—*<server name of the server running LDAP services>*. In our example scenario this object is called LDAP Server—WWWFS2.

NOTE

You want to confirm that SSL is enabled for LDAP and that the SSL port is configured to 636. You also need to determine the key material object that the LDAP server is using.

3. From the Other tab (this is if you do not have the LDAP snap-ins), confirm the following:

   LDAP Enable SSL—Expand this attribute and make sure it says true.

   LDAP SSL Port—Expand this attribute and determine the port. It should generally read 636.

   LDAP:keyMaterialName—Expand this attribute, and determine the key that the LDAP server is configured to use. Generally the key is SSL CertificateDNS. If it's not, just make note of which key is being used.
4. Exit the LDAP server object you have been looking at, and find the object called LDAP Group—*<Server name of the server running LDAP services>*. In this example scenario, this object is called LDAP Group—WWWFS2.
5. Edit the LDAP Group object. Go to the Other tab and confirm the setting called LDAP Allow Clear Text Password. Expand this attribute and make sure it reads false.

Your LDAP server is now prepared to support SSL.

Obtain a Key File for the SSL CertificateDNS Object

In this section, you need to export a key file for the SSL certificate already in eDirectory—which the LDAP server is also using. By default, most LDAP servers are configured to use the SSL CertificateDNS—*<server name>* key material object. If your LDAP server is using a different key material object, just follow the instructions in this section with the appropriate key material object. This object is in the same context as the server, the LDAP server, and LDAP group objects mentioned in the prior section. In this scenario, the name of the object is SSL CertificateDNS—WWWFS2.

1. Load ConsoleOne. You must be using the ConsoleOne with the Certificate Server snap-ins mentioned in the prerequisites earlier in this chapter.

Usually if you run ConsoleOne from the `SYS:\Public\mgmt` directory, the Certificate Server snap-ins will be contained here.

2. Highlight the SSL CertificateDNS—*`<server name>`* object. In this example scenario, the name of the object is SSL CertificateDNS—WWWFS2.
3. Select the Certificates tab, and then choose the Trusted Root Certificate property page.
4. Click the Export button.
5. In the Export Certificate dialog box, *do not* export the private key with the certificate. Select the Next button.
6. In the next export screen, keep the file in *.DER format, and give the file a descriptive 8.3 character format. In the example shown in Figure 27.10, the file is saved as *`<fileservername>`*`.DER`. Click the Next button.

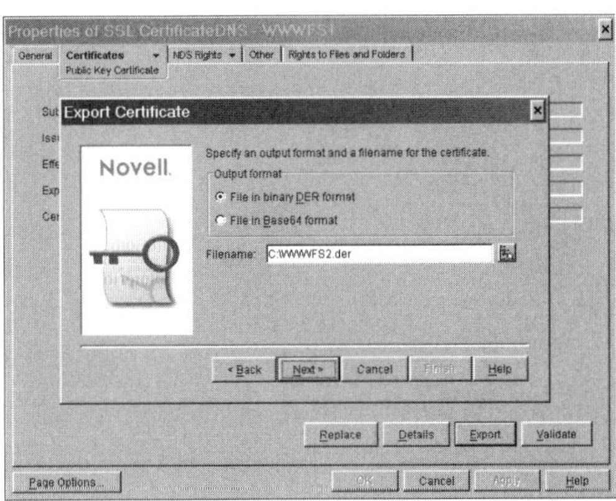

FIGURE 27.10
Exporting the public key into *.DER format.

7. On the summary screen, click the Finish button to export the key.
8. Make sure there is a directory under the post office called **CERT**. Copy the *.DER file that you just created to the **CERT** directory.

Now that you have placed the key file in the post office, you are ready to configure the GroupWise LDAP server definition so that it will support SSL. Follow these steps to do so:

1. In ConsoleOne, find your already configured LDAP server definition (or definitions if you are using LDAP server pooling) for the **CORPPO** post office. These are available under Tools, GroupWise System Operations, LDAP Servers.
2. Edit the LDAP server, and select the Use SSL check box.
3. Use the Browse button next to the SSL key file field to find the *.DER file that correlates to the LDAP server whose TCP/IP address is referenced in the LDAP server address field. In this scenario, it's the TCP/IP address for the file server WWWFS2. The *.DER file is WWWFS2.DER, as shown in Figure 27.11.
4. Click the pencil icon next to the TCP/IP address of the LDAP server in this dialog box. Change the port from 389 to port 636. Figure 27.11 shows a configured LDAP server.

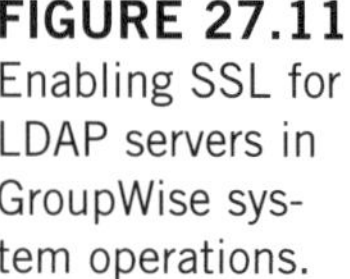

FIGURE 27.11
Enabling SSL for LDAP servers in GroupWise system operations.

5. The POA might need to be restarted in order for it to acknowledge the SSL settings for LDAP authentication that you just enabled.
6. Test to see whether LDAP over SSL is working using these benchmarks:

   Make sure the GroupWise POA is set to use verbose logging.

Log into GroupWise as a user on the post office where you have LDAP over SSL configured.

Observe the log of the POA; you should see something similar to the following example log:

```
13:13:11 1AB C/S Login win Net Id=irina ::GW Id=irina ::
137.65.55.212
13:13:11 1AB Initializing Secured LDAP session
with 137.65.55.211 at port 636 using SSL
Key file WWWFS1/sys:\corp\CORPPO\CERT\WWWFS2.DER
```

Now with SSL enabled for LDAP requests, users' passwords will no longer go across the wire in an unencrypted manner.

Enabling SSL for GroupWise Messenger to LDAP Server Communication

The steps to configure the GroupWise Messenger Agent's (MA) communication with the LDAP server over SSL are very similar to configuring the GroupWise POA. This section assumes that you already have the MA configured for LDAP authentication. In this section, you are merely enabling SSL.

In a Novell eDirectory environment, the LDAP server uses (by default) the SSL CertificateDNS—*<server name>* object in the same context as the server running LDAP services. This object is actually called a key material object. In order for the GroupWise POA to communicate with the LDAP server via SSL, the POA must use that same encryption key. The Novell LDAP server reads the key right out of eDirectory, but the MA does not. The key, therefore, must be exported to a file so the MA can use the key to send encrypted data to the Novell LDAP server. When you configure your MA to speak to a specific LDAP server, you must have exported the key file that the LDAP server also uses. Read through this example scenario to understand how to configure both the LDAP server and the MA to talk to one another via SSL.

Server Running the Novell Messenger/GroupWise Messenger MA (WWWFS1)

This is a NetWare 6 server running the Messaging Agent.

Server Hosting Novell LDAP Services (WWWFS2)

There are three basic steps behind enabling SSL communications:

- The first step is to make sure that your LDAP server is configured to speak correctly when using an SSL connection.
- The second step is to export the encryption key file for the same key material object in eDirectory that the LDAP server is currently configured to use. This way, the MA can use the same encryption key from the key material object that the LDAP server is currently using.
- The third step is to configure your MA to use the encryption key you obtained from the LDAP server.

The following sections walk through these actions.

Configure the LDAP Server to Support SSL

The default settings for an eDirectory LDAP server do not allow for clear text passwords. If you enabled the LDAP server to allow clear text passwords in order to set up and test your LDAP authentication without SSL, this is where you can now disable the option for clear text passwords. This ensures the security of your eDirectory usernames and passwords, because any service using NLDAP must use encryption to talk to the LDAP server. You should confirm the following configuration settings for the LDAP server:

- The port for LDAP SSL communication (which is 636 by default)
- That SSL is enabled for the LDAP server
- The LDAP server does not allow clear text passwords
- Determine which key material object the LDAP server is using

You might not have the correct LDAP server snap-ins, so rather than taking you through the process of obtaining the LDAP server snap-ins, this section instructs you about how to check these settings without the LDAP snap-ins. If you have the LDAP snap-ins for ConsoleOne, these settings are easy to find. I do not recommend modifying these attributes without the LDAP snap-ins. If you must modify them, you must find a copy of ConsoleOne that has the LDAP snap-ins enabled. Use these steps to view the settings:

1. Highlight the eDirectory OU that contains the server that is running the LDAP services.
2. Edit the object called LDAP Server—*<server name of the server running LDAP services>*. In this example scenario, this object is called LDAP Server—WWWFS2.

You want to confirm that SSL is enabled for LDAP and that the SSL port is configured to be 636. You also need to determine the key material object that the LDAP server is using.

3. From the Other tab (this is if you do not have the LDAP snap-ins), confirm the following:

   LDAP Enable SSL—Expand this attribute and make sure it reads true.

   LDAP SSL Port—Expand this attribute and determine the port. It should generally read 636.

   LDAP:keyMaterialName—Expand this attribute and determine the key that the LDAP server is configured to use. Generally the key is SSL CertificateDNS. If it's not, just make note of which key is being used.
4. Exit the LDAP Server object you have been looking at, and find the object called LDAP Group—*<Server name of the server running LDAP services>*. In this example scenario this object is called LDAP Group—WWWFS2.
5. Edit the LDAP Group object. Go to the Other tab and confirm the setting called LDAP Allow Clear Text Password. Expand it and make sure it reads false.

Your LDAP server is now prepared to support SSL.

Obtain a ROOTCERT.DER Key File from Server Running LDAP

In this section, you need to obtain the ROOTCERT.DER key file from the SYS:PUBLIC directory in which the LDAP services are running. The steps to perform are as follows:

1. Go to the `SYS:PUBLIC` directory of the server that is running your LDAP services. Obtain the ROOTCERT.DER file.
2. Make sure there is a directory under the MA root directory called `CERT`. Copy the ROOTCERT.DER file mentioned in step 1 to the `CERT` directory under the MA root directory.
3. Rename the ROOTCERT.DER file to something like the *<fileserver name of the file server running LDAP services>*.DER. The filename should be in the 8.3 format. For example, WWWFS2.DER.

Now you have put the LDAP server's key file in physical proximity to the GroupWise Messaging Agent so it can use the key file.

Configure the GroupWise LDAP Server Definition to Support SSL

Following are the steps for enabling LDAP authentication for the GroupWise Messaging Agent:

1. In ConsoleOne, find your already configured LDAP profile or profiles if you are using LDAP server pooling. The LDAP profiles are in the `LDAPContainer` object located under the `MessengerService` object.
2. Edit the LDAP profile object that you have already configured.
3. Under the LDAP Profile tab, go to the Connections Property page.
4. Edit the connection that represents the LDAP server you have obtained the public key for. Change the port to 636. Enable the SSL Enabled check box.
5. Use the Browse button next to the Root Certificate File field and select the *.DER file that correlates to the LDAP server whose TCP/IP address is referenced in the LDAP server address field. In this scenario, it's the TCP/IP address for the file server WWWFS2. The *.DER file is WWWFS2.DER, as shown in Figure 27.12.

FIGURE 27.12
The LDAP Connection window is where you define the LDAP server, as well as the key file associated with it.

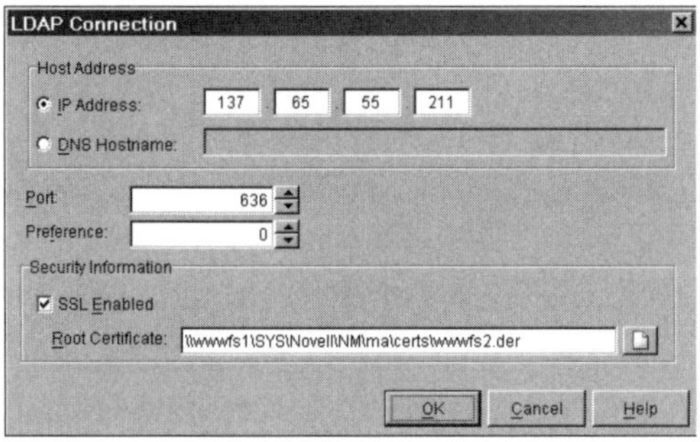

6. The Messaging Agent (MA) must be restarted in order for it to acknowledge the SSL settings for LDAP authentication that you just enabled.

Now with SSL enabled for LDAP requests and user's passwords, requests to LDAP will no longer go across the wire in an unencrypted manner.

Summary

This chapter reviewed how to enabled SSL communication on all GroupWise agents (except the Monitor agent, which cannot be SSL-ized). The encryption strength is 128-bit. In an average Novell environment, the process of enabling SSL is simple and cheap—free in fact!

CHAPTER 28

Restoring Deleted GroupWise Users

Have you ever restored deleted users? You were told to delete a user, you did, and then you were told to bring them back. Or maybe you deleted a user by accident! Either way, restoring a deleted user is a stressful task, so this chapter attempts to give you a complete solution to this scenario.

This chapter gives you step-by-step instructions, and it also tries to weave in some architectural explanations about what you are trying to accomplish within the various steps.

In order to restore a deleted user, you must use the Recover Deleted Account utility, which is new to GroupWise 6.5, or you must import the user. This process brings back only the user's object, not their messages. Then you must restore the user's messages. Restoring user's messages is also explained in this chapter.

The Scenario

Tay Kratzer's (TKRATZER) GroupWise account was accidentally deleted. You need to restore everything you possibly can of Tay's e-mail. Tay is on a GroupWise domain called CORP and a post office called CORPPO.

Here is a high-level view of the steps that you will take. There a two major methods for restoring a deleted user. The simplest method is called Recover and Restore. This method requires that you have a WPDOMAIN.DB file that existed prior to the user's deletion. The more complex method (and only slightly more thorough) is called Import and Restore or Archive. Following is a high-level explanation of both of these methods.

Recover and Restore

- Recover the user's object via the Recover Deleted Account utility
- Restore the user's mailbox via the Backup/Restore Mailbox utility

Sort and Restore or Archive

Following is a high-level discussion about this method of restoring a user:

- Import TKRATZER with the same USERID, FID, first name, and last name that TKRATZER used before he was deleted.
- Condition the WPHOST.DB file for Tay's post office so that Tay is a member of the post office, the post office security level is low, the post office supports client/server and direct connections, and WPHOST.DB has a new mailbox password for Tay.
- Place the WPHOST.DB file in the restored post office's directory, and get into GroupWise.
- Once in GroupWise, archive and export as much info as possible.
- Unarchive and import items into TKRATZER's live mailbox account.

You are welcome to mix and match elements of both of these solutions. For example, you can use the Recover method for re-creating the user's object (rather than the import method), and then use the Archive method for restoring the user's mailbox. There are two tasks that must take place—the user's account must be re-created, and the user's messages must be restored. How you accomplish these two tasks is up to you, and GroupWise is flexible enough to accommodate your particular situation.

Recover and Restore a User's Account

Bringing back a deleted user's account is the easier method. All of the needed utilities are built into GroupWise 6.5. If you cannot meet (or easily meet) the prerequisite mentioned in the next paragraph, which requires the WPDOMAIN.DB from backup, you will want to proceed to the method called Import and Restore or Archive. The Import and Archive method mentioned in the next major section brings back all that this method does, and more. The Recover and Restore method does not bring back the following:

- Personal address books
- Rules and proxy settings

If losing personal address books and the user's rules and proxy settings is not a problem, go ahead and use the methods explained in this section.

Prerequisites

You must have the following two components before getting started:

- A backup copy of the WPDOMAIN.DB for your system's GroupWise primary domain that existed prior to the time that TKRATZER was deleted. If you do not have this backup copy of the primary domain, you can use a backup copy of any secondary domain prior to the time that TKRATZER was deleted.
- A backup copy of the entire CORPPO post office prior to the time that TKRATZER was deleted.

Bringing the User Back

This section focuses on how to bring the user's eDirectory and GroupWise object back. You must have a backup copy of the WPDOMAIN.DB for the system's GroupWise primary domain, prior to the time that TKRATZER was deleted. If you don't have it, you can use a backup copy of any secondary domain prior to the time that TKRATZER was deleted.

1. Load ConsoleOne and connect to the primary domain.
2. From the Tools menu, select GroupWise Utilities, Recover Deleted Account.
3. To fill in the Backup Domain Path field, browse to the WPDOMAIN.DB that you brought back from backup.
4. Select the Account to Restore button, and select the deleted user TKRATZER. Figure 28.1 shows a configured Recover GroupWise Account dialog box.
5. Click Next, and proceed through the rest of the Recover GroupWise Account wizard.
6. After the account is recovered, confirm that the newly restored account can get into the GroupWise mailbox. The user's password is also recovered during this process.

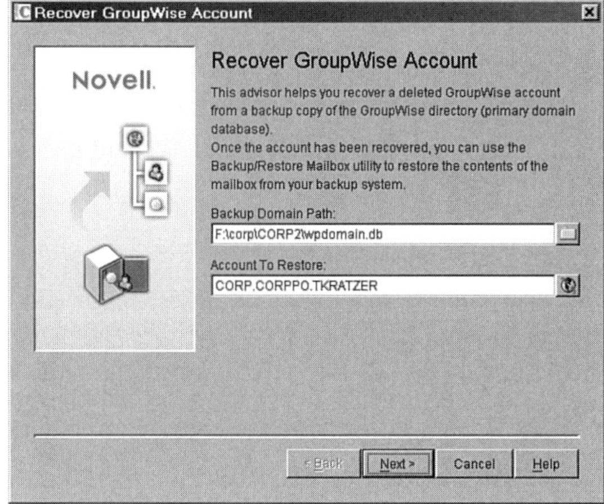

FIGURE 28.1 The Recover GroupWise Account wizard in ConsoleOne.

NOTE **At this time, the account is restored, but the messages in the mailbox are not.**

Restoring the User's Mailbox

In ConsoleOne you need to setup a *restore area* where the GroupWise message store of the post office that houses the deleted user can be restored and then accessed by users or the GroupWise Post Office Agent (POA) in order to restore deleted and purged e-mail.

You set up the post office's restore area within the GroupWise System Operations menu in ConsoleOne. Figure 28.2 shows that a restore area has been set up for the `CORPPO` post office.

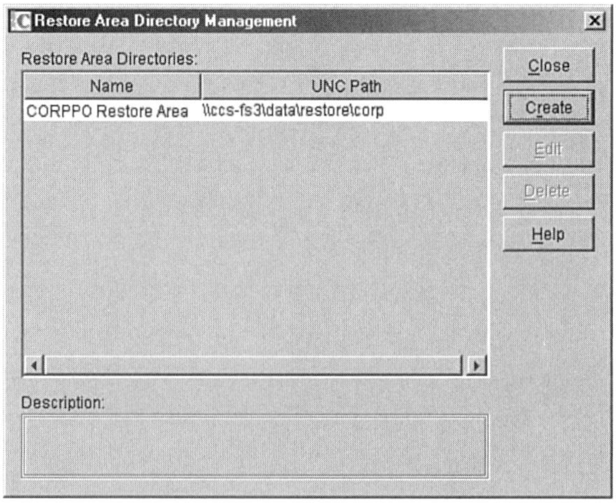

FIGURE 28.2 The Restore Area Directory Management dialog box in ConsoleOne.

To set up a restore area, follow these steps:

1. Load ConsoleOne.
2. Connect to the primary domain.
3. From the Tools menu, select GroupWise System Operations, Restore Area Management.
4. Type the name of the restore area. Type a description too if you want.
5. Create the directory structure you plan to use for the restore area. This should be a directory structure on a server that users can access (unless you are going to have the POA restore the user's mailbox). Either enter the UNC path in the restore area or browse to it.
6. Click the Membership tab to add users (or an entire post office) whose messages need to be restored.
7. Click Close to create the definition for the restore area.

NOTE

If in step 6 you added the post office to the Membership tab of the restore area, you can access the Post Office Settings property page to verify that the restore area is recognized and is ready for use. You will see the name of the restore area on the Post Office Settings page next to the field that reads Restore Area.

Once the restore area is set up and configured, you will need to find the backup that holds what is believed to be the correct post office message store prior to the time the user was deleted. You'll then prepare to restore it using your backup application. It's important to make sure that, in your restore area, you have sufficient space to restore the post office from backup.

Once a restore area is defined and the data is restored, there are two methods for restoring mail messages. The first method allows users belonging to the membership of a restore area to access their restored messages from within the GroupWise client. Users can then "cherry-pick" messages that they want to restore. The second method requires no effort on the part of your users. With this second method, the GroupWise POA restores the messages on behalf of the users.

It is important to note at this point that there is a slight difference between the users restoring their own mail, and the administrator performing this operation through ConsoleOne. If the user has been deleted and then re-created, their mailbox is now empty. They have no folder structure other than the default folders that any new account has. If the user is told to restore their mail as will be explained next, the mail that they choose to restore will not preserve the folder structure from the backup location into the production system *unless* the user manually creates their folder structure in the production system first.

If the Administrator kicks off the restore through ConsoleOne, and then the POA performs the entire restore operation, the POA will preserve the folder structure from the backup location into the production system. Therefore, if the user has been deleted and re-created, it's best to use ConsoleOne to restore the user's messages. On the other hand, if the user does not use many folders and does not mind if the restored messages end up in the Mailbox folder, either option works fine.

Before you actually restore the user's mail, you must verify that the production POA agent has Read, Write, Create, Erase, Modify, and File Scan rights to the restore area. If this is not set, you will see `8200` and possibly `8209` errors on the POA and on the client if the user is initiating the restore. The easiest way to verify this is to browse to go to properties of the restore directory in ConsoleOne. Click the Trustees tab, and make the POA object a trustee of this directory.

Restoring Messages—User and Windows Client-Based Message Restoration

Now that you've restored the message store to the restore area, you should notify and, if necessary, assist users to recover the deleted messages. At this point, you should have already assigned membership rights for the restore area to the user(s) who will be accessing the restore area. You should have also already made the user's POA object a trustee of the restore area.

TIP

If your users have any auto-delete or auto-archive preferences set up on their live mailboxes, you should disable those temporarily. If you do not, restored items that pass the time threshold defined in the user's mailbox will be deleted or archived just as soon as they are restored.

The steps in this operation are performed from within the GroupWise 6.x or later clients. Follow these steps to open the backup area and recover the deleted messages:

1. Start the GroupWise client and click the File menu.
2. Click the Open Backup command, as shown in Figure 28.3. The client will authenticate to the restore area. If the user has full rights to the restore area—and if the user is a member of the restore area—the backup mailbox will open.

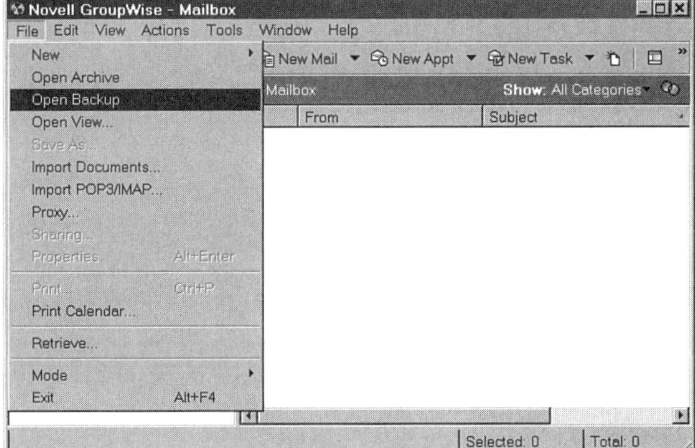

FIGURE 28.3
Accessing the restore area in the GroupWise Windows client.

3. Browse through the restorable messages and highlight the ones that need to be returned to the mailbox. You can select random messages with the Ctrl-click. You can select all messages by selecting the first message, moving down to the last one, and Shift-clicking the last message.
4. Once you've highlighted the messages, right-click one of them and choose the Restore command.
5. After the messages are restored, close the restore area by clicking the File menu and selecting the Open Backup command. You will be returned to the main mailbox and should see the recovered messages.
6. When restoring messages via the Windows client, you can also restore items that are in the trash of the Backup mailbox. In order to do this though, you must undelete the items from the trash in the Backup mailbox, and then restore the items. These items will not automatically move to the trash though; you must delete them yourself.

NOTE

When restoring mail through the client, the restored messages are placed in the mailbox folder unless the folder they are contained in also exists in the online mailbox. In other words, unless the online mailbox folder structure matches what is in the backup mailbox, mail that is restored will be placed in the mailbox folder.

This process of restoring messages works, but it isn't as slick as having the POA restore the user's messages, which is explained in the next section.

Restoring Messages—Administrator and POA-Based Message Restoration

This method has one distinct advantage over having the user perform the restore—the POA-based message restore will create any folders that do not exist in the online mailbox but that do exist in the backup location, and place the mail in the appropriate folder. This preserves the user's folder structure.

TIP

If your users have any Auto-Delete or Auto-Archive preferences set up on their live mailboxes, you should disable those temporarily. If you do not, restored items that pass the delete or archive time threshold defined in the user's mailbox will be deleted or archived just as soon as they are restored.

At this point you should have already assigned membership rights to the restore area for the user(s) (or post office) whose mailboxes are to be restored by the POA. This way when you issue a restore of a user's mailbox through ConsoleOne, the POA will correlate the user's membership to a restore area, and then know which UNC path to go to in order to access the backup of the post office. You must have also made the live POA object a trustee of the backup path with full rights. Follow these steps to task the POA with restoring a user's mailbox:

1. In ConsoleOne, highlight the user whose message items you need restored.
2. From the Tools menu, select GroupWise Utilities, Backup/Restore Mailbox. A dialog box similar to the one shown in Figure 28.4 should appear.

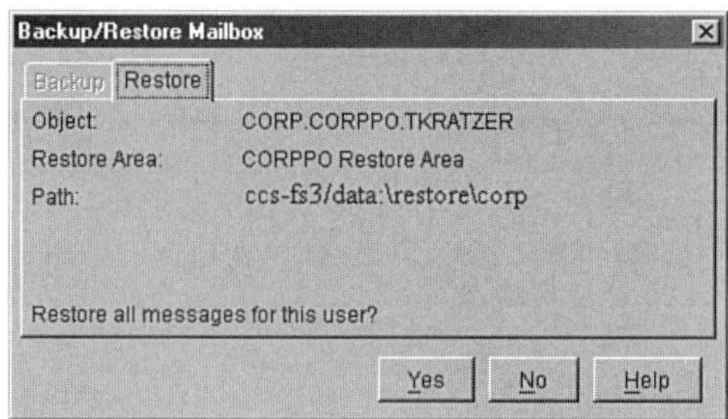

FIGURE 28.4
Issuing a mailbox restore from ConsoleOne.

3. Select the Yes button; this will send a message to the POA to restore the user's mailbox. Figure 28.5 shows the verbiage in the GroupWise POA's log when the user is restored. In this example, the logging level is set to verbose.

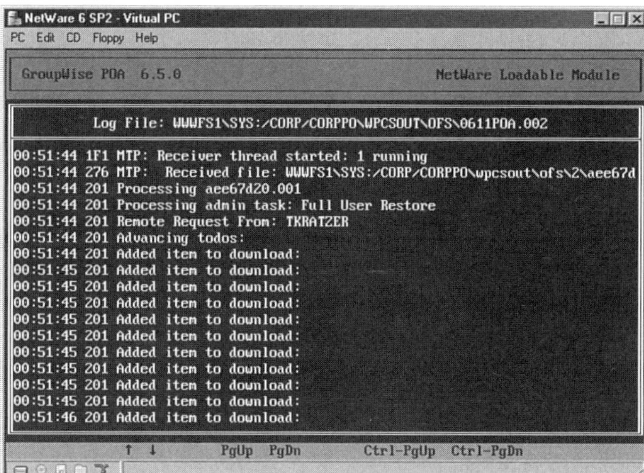

FIGURE 28.5
The GroupWise POA restoring a user's mailbox.

Now the user's account and mailbox are restored; they can begin functioning without any problems.

This is when you might see an `8200` or `8209` error. The most common cause of these errors is that the POA is not a trustee of the restore area, or that the POA cannot access the restore area for some reason. I have seen a few occasions in which the POA was reporting an `8209` error when it did have the necessary rights to the restore area. If you see this, you might find that it is best to place the restore area on the same server on which the POA is running.

Import and Restore or Archive a User's Account

The Import and Restore or Archive method of bringing back a deleted user's account is the most complete method. Not all of the needed utilities are built into GroupWise 6.5. The Import and Archive method brings back all of the items that the Restore and Recover method does, in addition to the following items:

- Personal address books
- Trash items (if you want them)
- Rules and proxy settings

The only attributes of the mailbox that this method does not restore are any preferences that the users set up in their mailboxes prior to their deletion.

Prerequisites

You must have the following three items before getting started:

- The most recent backup of the entire `CORPPO`'s post office directory structure, restored to a server somewhere in your network. If you don't have a backup, you can't go any further.
- The GroupWise 6.0 ConsoleOne snap-ins that allow you to do an Import/Export from ConsoleOne. You can obtain the GroupWise 6.0 Import/Export Utility on Windows 95/98/NT/2000 from `download.novell.com`.
- You also need to know the user's FID before he or she was deleted.

Bringing a GroupWise Post Office Back from Backup

You will need the entire post office directory structure and the contents of those directories in order to make this solution work. Sometimes, administrators think that just bringing the USER*xxx*.DB back from backup is enough; it's not!

When you bring the post office back from backup, you should place it in some other location other than where the current live post office is located. It can be on the same server, just a different location. Before you attempt to bring the post office back from backup, make sure you have sufficient space to do so.

Installing and Configuring the GroupWise 6.0 Import/Export Utility

GroupWise 6.5 does not ship with an Import/Export utility. The Import/Export Utility you are instructed to use was made during the GroupWise 6.0 period, but it can be installed into ConsoleOne and used with a GroupWise 6.5 environment. When the Import/Export utility is incorporated into the GroupWise 6.5 ConsoleOne snap-ins, you can skip this entire section.

Following are the steps for importing a user into the GroupWise directory:

1. Download GroupWise 6.0 Import/Export Utility on Windows 95/98/NT/2000 from `http://download.novell.com`.
2. Place the downloaded file "GWPORT32.EXE " in the CONSOLEONE\XX directory, for example, `C:\NOVELL\CONSOLEONE\1.2`.
3. Exit ConsoleOne.
4. Run the GWPORT32.EXE utility from the `C:\NOVELL\CONSOLEONE\1.2` directory. You should see a dialog box similar to the one shown in Figure 28.6.

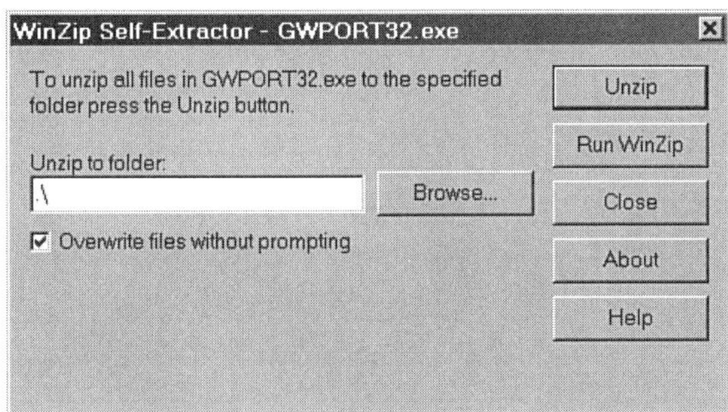

FIGURE 28.6
Extracting the GWPORT32.EXE utility.

5. Start ConsoleOne, select an Organization Unit (OU) in the eDirectory view, and then select Tools, GroupWise Utilities. You should see the Import and Export menu commands, as shown in Figure 28.7.

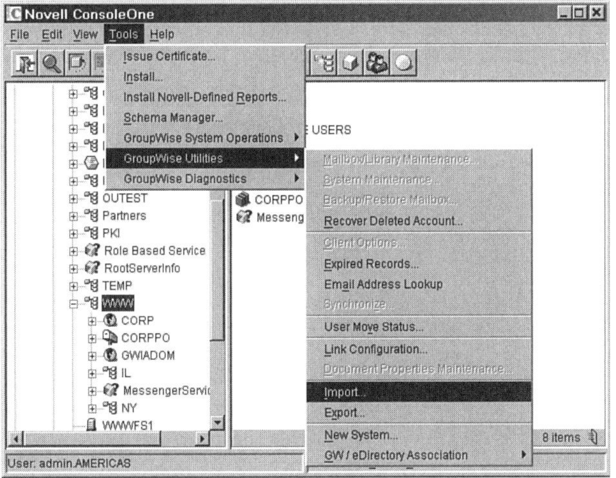

FIGURE 28.7
The GroupWise Import and Export utilities in ConsoleOne.

If you receive errors when trying to run the Import utility, delete the following Registry keys in your Windows Registry. This section can conflict sometimes with the Import/Export utility you just installed.

```
HKEY_CURRENT_USER\Software\NetWare\Parameters\
NetWare Administrator
```

And

```
HKEY_LOCAL_MACHINE\SOFTWARE\Novell\LIBRARY
```

Strategies for Determining a User's FID

In order to bring the user back, through an import that you will do soon in this chapter, you must know the user's three-character FID. Here are some ideas for determining the FID:

- Ask the user; there's a possibility he or she might know.
- Did the user have an archive directory? If, for example, their archive directory is `C:\ARCHIVE`, there will be a folder under `C:\ARCHIVE` with a name of `OFXXXARC`. The *XXX* is the user's FID.

Bringing the User Back

When bringing a user back from deletion, you must restore the user's directory object.

It's possible that you have already re-created the user so he or she has an account in the meantime. That's a common thing to do. However at this point, you cannot have a second account for the user before proceeding further. The person might have an eDirectory/NDS account, though. If the user has items in their new mailbox, get rid of their mailbox. You can have the user forward the message items to you or someone else for safekeeping.

Import the User's Object

1. Determine the following information about the user to be imported:
    - The user's last name.
    - The user's eDirectory common name. This is often referred to as the user's short name. For example, if my eDirectory name is `TKRATZER.NY.WWW`, my common name is `TKRATZER`.

- The user's GroupWise FID.
- The mailbox ID for the user if his or her mailbox ID *does not* match his or her eDirectory common name. The mailbox ID will not be used in the import file; it will be used if the mailbox ID and the eDirectory common name are different. You can make the change to the mailbox ID after importing the user.

Now you must create a user import file in an ASCII/text editor. Figure 28.8 shows and example of such a file in Notepad.

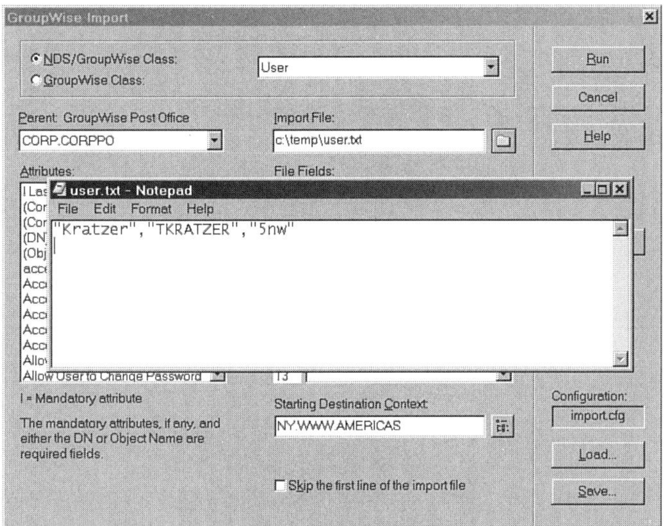

FIGURE 28.8
A user import file in Notepad.

2. Do not add any extra keystrokes; the import file follows a very strict format. The example user has a last name of "Kratzer", an eDirectory common name of "TKRATZER", and a FID of "5nw", followed by one carriage return (press Enter once).
3. Save the file as `C:\USER.TXT`.
4. Launch ConsoleOne.
5. Connect to the domain that owns the post office you are going to import TKRATZER to.
6. Launch the Import/Export utility. To do this, go to the eDirectory Browser view, highlight an eDirectory OU (any OU is fine), and select Tools, GroupWise Utilities, Import.

NOTE **It might take a long time for this utility to launch; just be patient.**

7. Inside the Import/GWPORT utility, do the following, as shown in Figure 28.9.

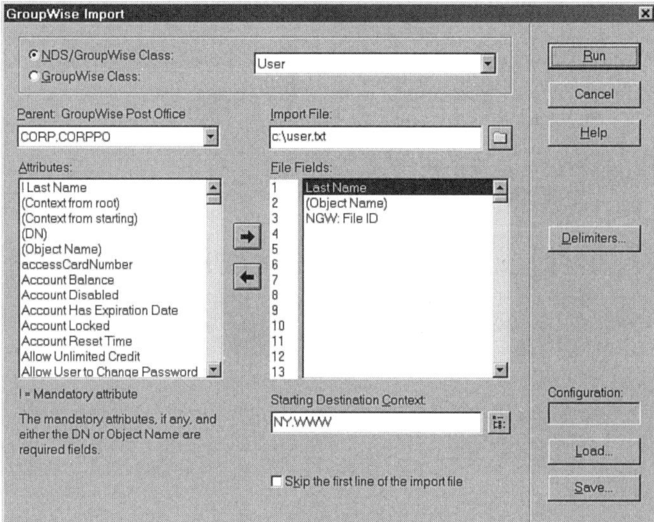

FIGURE 28.9
Importing a user.

- NDS/GroupWise Class: User.
- Parent: GroupWise Post Office. Select the post office this person will be associated with.
- Import File: `C:\USER.TXT`.
- Attributes (When you double-click these attributes they will be placed in the "File Fields" section): Last Name, (Object Name), NGW: File ID.
- Starting Destination Context: Select the context the user will be imported into. This user might already exist in eDirectory, but this does not matter.
- Do not make any other selections.

8. Select the Run button; this will import the user.

   When you click Run you get an Import dialog box. It might just stare at you for a while, but eventually it will come back. You might have to flip screens with the Alt-Tab keystroke sequence to get the import dialog box shown in Figure 28.10. The goal is for the Import utility to indicate that one user object was imported, as shown in Figure 28.10.

FIGURE 28.10 The Import dialog box is showing a successful import.

9. Select the Cancel button to get out of the Import utility. From ConsoleOne, finish the rest of this process.
10. Now edit the user's object in the eDirectory browser view, and enter the given name.
11. Now you can enter any other information about the user that you need to. Then exit out of the user's settings by clicking the OK button. You should now be able to see `TKRATZER` from the GroupWise view.
12. Confirm that `TKRATZER` actually has the FID that you specified. (I've seen situations in which the FID was `QXX`.) If you get this condition, make sure you are connected to the user's owning domain; then delete the user and try again.

It's easy to see when your import is successful. Importing can be difficult for some customers. The important thing to remember is the syntax in the import file. Make sure it is perfect, including just one carriage return at the end of the import file.

Obtaining Access to the User's Message Store on the Backup Post Office

You now have imported the user's object with their correct FID, so now you need to configure the post office so you can access the message store at the post office you brought back from backup. Every GroupWise post office has two security locks, so to speak. Those security locks are the WPHOST.DB file and the password on the user's USER*xxx*.DB file. In order to access the post office and the user's mailbox you restored from backup, you need to reconfigure the security locks to your advantage. On the post office database/WPHOST.DB file, you must

- Change the security level to low.
- Configure the post office to support direct connections. On the USER*xxx*.DB file, you must change the password to one that you know, in order to have access to the mailbox.

Here are the step-by-step instructions for accessing a user's message store (mailbox). You do not want to affect your live system with the changes you are going to make, so first you will have to spoof your system a bit:

1. From the domain directory, copy the WPDOMAIN.DB file for the domain that TKRATZER is now a member of from your live system to the C:\GWDOM directory. Also copy the GWPO.DC file from that same location to the C:\GWDOM directory.
2. In ConsoleOne, make sure the GroupWise snap-ins are connected to the WPDOMAIN.DB at the C:GWDOM directory. You can do this by selecting Tools, GroupWise System Operations. Select Domain. Specify the path as C:\GWDOM.
3. Edit Tay Kratzer's object, and on the GroupWise Account page, change Tay's GroupWise password to 123.
4. Edit the properties of the post office that Tay Kratzer is a member of (not the POA, the post office object):
    - Go to the Post Office Settings page under the GroupWise tab and change the Access Mode to Direct Only.
    - Now access the Security page on the GroupWise tab of the post office object. Change the security level to Low.

All the changes you made should not affect the live system because you are connected to the WPDOMAIN.DB on the local hard drive.

Now you need to build the WPHOST.DB file for the post office that TKRATZER is a member of. You will place this WPHOST.DB file in the post office directory that you brought from backup. To do so, follow these steps:

1. Highlight the post office object in the GroupWise view, and then select Tools, GroupWise Utilities, System Maintenance.
2. Select Rebuild Database and then click the Run button. When prompted for a path, specify the location of your backup post office directory.

You have been connected to the WPDOMAIN.DB file in the C:\GWDOM directory. It's important to make sure you disconnect ConsoleOne from this

WPDOMAIN.DB and connect to a WPDOMAIN.DB on your live system, which is on a server location. I suggest doing this right now. If you do not do this, the next time you load ConsoleOne, it will remember that you were connected to the domain on the `C:` drive, and will attempt to connect here. You might not notice that you are not connected to a production database, and all your administration changes will be for naught.

Now with the newly configured WPHOST.DB in place at the post office you brought from backup, you are just about ready to get in. You need to push Tay Kratzer's mailbox password of `123` down to the USER*xxx*.DB. Here's how to this:

1. Run the stand-alone GroupWise 6.5 GWCHECK.
2. Fill in the correct information in order to reset Tay Kratzer's password. Figure 28.11 shows you what settings to select.

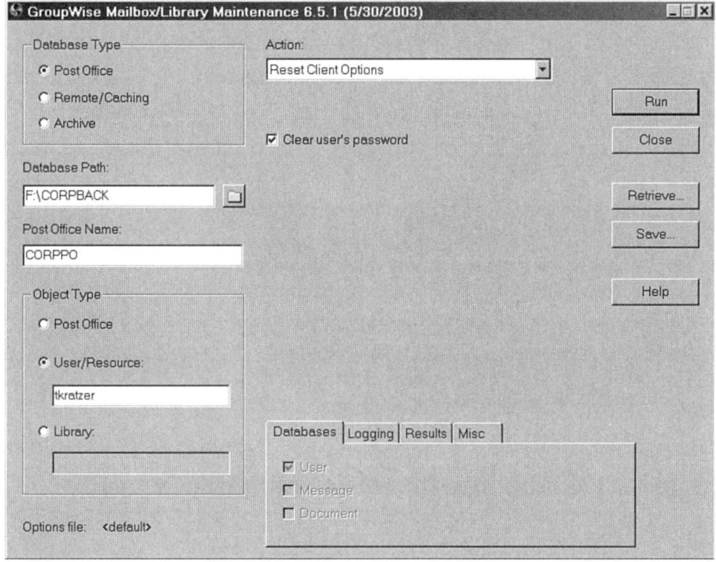

FIGURE 28.11
GWCHECK job is used to reset a password.

Now the user's message store is ready for you to access it. Here's what you do. Use the following command line in order to access the post office in direct mode:

```
GRPWISE.EXE /@U-<USERID> /PH-<PATH TO POST OFFICE >
```

For example

```
GRPWISE.EXE /@U-TKRATZER /PH-F:\CORPBACK
```

Exporting a User's Mailbox

Those of you familiar with the Archive feature might wonder why I refer to these next steps as exporting; there's more to it than just using the Archive feature. A user's mailbox doesn't contain only messages; it's the folder structure they have created, their address books, their calendar items, and even their trash items. Perhaps this is too sentimental a notion for you, but many users see their e-mail as an office of sorts. People are rather sensitive about their mailbox. You won't always be able to restore shared address books, shared folders, rules, and personal preferences, but if you are restoring the mailbox for an accidentally deleted user, you should take care to restore everything you possibly can.

Configuring the Archive Directory

First, you need to specify an archive location in order to create an Archive mailbox. Before doing this, you need to take some precautions. I have had experience in the past with Windows caching data rather then writing it to the hard drive. When you are archiving so much data, it might be better to specify the archive path to a NetWare server. The NetWare client does a much better job than Windows does of handling data. It decreases the likelihood of corruption to the Archive mailbox when archiving a large bunch of data at one time.

Here are the steps for specifying the archive directory:

1. From inside the user's mailbox, select Tools, Options, Environment, File Location, Archive directory.
2. Specify an archive directory.

Configuring the Mailbox Folder Structure for Export

Many users have created an elaborate folder structure under their mailboxes and cabinets. When you archive messages, the folders that have messages in them are automatically created in the Archive mailbox. When you eventually unarchive these items, the folder names are created again in the live mailbox. However, folders containing nothing at the time you performed the archive will be lost. Again, the idea is to try to duplicate the mailbox as closely as possible. Following are the steps for exporting the folder structure from a mailbox to the Archive mailbox:

1. Find one small message item in the user's mailbox. You'll use it to export the folders in this mailbox.

2. Highlight the item and select Edit, Move/Link to Folders.
3. In the resulting Move/Link Selections to Folder dialog box, check each folder within the Cabinet object. If the user has other folders under the mailbox that are not in the Cabinet, you can place check marks next to those. Figure 28.12 shows an example of this step.

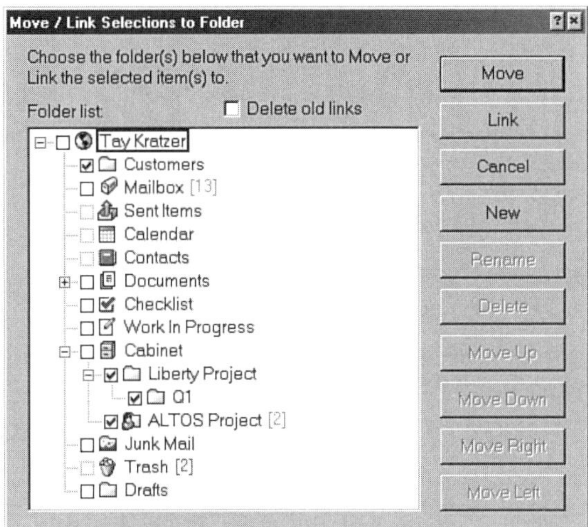

FIGURE 28.12
Linking a message item to all folders.

4. With the check marks in place, click the Move button. This creates a virtual copy of this message in every folder in the mailbox. Get out of the Move/Link option. When you archive, each of the folders will be created because there is an item in each of the folders.

Check in some of the folders and make sure all of them have a copy of the message you linked to the folders.

Exporting All Message Items—Even Sent Items and Personal/Posted Items

It is time to export the real meat of the mailbox. The easiest way to determine whether you archive everything in the mailbox is to use the Find feature in the GroupWise mailbox. Select Tools, Find, make no additional selections from the Find dialog box, and then click the OK button. This way, you are telling GroupWise to find everything. If this user is tidy or if you have an aggressive e-mail retention policy, perhaps you'll just find a few hundred items. However, many times you will find that there are thousands of items, maybe more.

The problem with this is that the Find window will not display that many items. So you might need to alter your Find query to only find items in a certain time period or of a certain type. When you choose Tools, Find, you can alter the scope of the query by using the Date Range section. You can also modify the results from the Find window by selecting Tools, Modify Find. I'll leave that to you. The idea is to get a maximum of about 4,500 items in the Find window, and then modify the Find window to get the next batch of items.

Your goal is to eventually find, and then archive, all of the message items in the user's mailbox. Here are example steps for doing this; you might need to deviate from these steps in order to pare down the results:

1. Inside the user' mailbox, select Tools, Find. Make sure the Find tab is active, and not the Find by Example tab.
2. Do not check or uncheck anything. Take the defaults by selecting the OK button. If you suspect that this user has more than 4,500 items throughout their mailbox, modify the find using the Date Range feature.
3. This process will find all message items. Select the first 500 or so items by Shift-clicking them. Then select Actions, Move to Archive.
4. Repeat step 3 (and possibly step 2) until all items have been moved to the Archive mailbox.

This process of archiving the items from the Find query should find calendar items, be they group or personal calendar items, and all message items if they are sent or received. Ideally, this process will move all message items from the master mailbox to the Archive mailbox. When the process finishes, the mailbox should look like a ghost town, perhaps with a bunch of empty folders.

TIP

This process of using the Find feature and archiving messages archives all of the user's Sent Items. Beginning with GroupWise 6.5, the Sent Items folder is no longer a find results folder. As a result, it is now created by default in the archive. So the user will see their sent items in the Sent Items folder by default. In earlier versions of the GroupWise client, this was not quite the case, and you had to create the Sent Items folder manually in the archive.

Exporting the Trash—It's Quick!

If you bring back the user's trash, he or she is going to think you performed wonders, and it takes just a minute. The steps to perform this are as follows:

1. Create a new folder in the cabinet of the user's mailbox (not the Archive mailbox), called `trash2`.
2. Go to the trash and Shift-click to select all items. Drag them to the new `trash2` folder you created.
3. Go to the `trash2` folder you created under the cabinet, Shift-click to select all items, and then select Actions, Archive.

NOTE

The section titled "Importing Mail/Folders and Trash Items" describes how to move these trash items in the `trash2` folder back to the trash bucket in the user's live mailbox.

Exporting the Address Book

Every user has at least two address books and quite often more than that. These two address books are the Frequent Contacts address book and the address book containing the user's full name. The user you are working with might even have more. You can export the user's address books, and then import them (at a later time) into the user's address book in the live mailbox. The following steps illustrate how to do this:

1. Go to the GroupWise Address book by selecting Tools, Address Book.
2. Choose an address book to export by clicking the address book in the left panel (not the Novell GroupWise Address Book; that's your system address book, not a personal address book).
3. Inside the address book, select File, Export, Entire Address Book. Figure 28.13 shows this dialog box.
4. Save the file as an *.NAB file. You might want to name the *.NAB files according to the name of the address book. For example, `TKRATZER-Frequent Contacts.NAB`.

Now you've exported everything you possibly can. You might want to check the user's rules and proxy settings and make a note of them. You will have to manually re-create them in the live system.

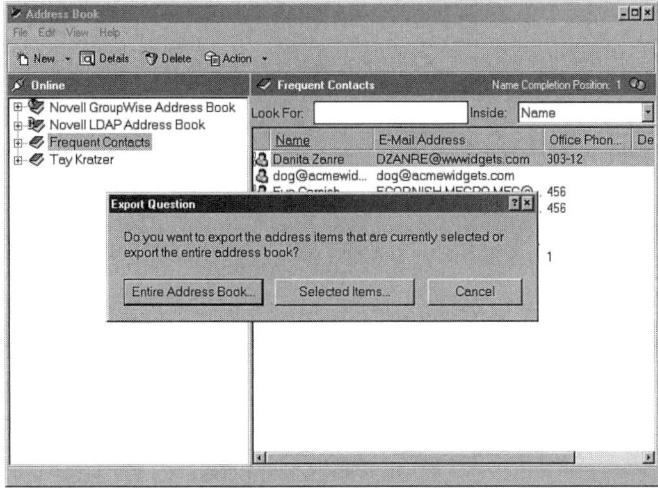

FIGURE 28.13
Exporting the GroupWise address book.

Next, you need to access the user's live mailbox and start the import operations.

Importing a User's Mailbox

You need to access the user's live mailbox, so you might need to reset TKRATZER's password in order to get in.

When you get into TKRATZER's live master mailbox, the process you follow is nearly the opposite of the Export process. First though, in order for the Find feature to work on the Archive mailbox, you must access the Archive mailbox, and then exit GroupWise. GroupWise needs to rebuild the QuickFinder index on the Archive mailbox. Exiting GroupWise after GroupWise has discovered that it has new indexing to do causes the QuickFinder index for the Archive mailbox to be rebuilt.

Importing Mail/Folders and Trash Items

Get into Tay Kratzer's live GroupWise mailbox, not the one on the backed-up post office, and perform the following steps:

1. Go into Tools, Options, Environment, File Location, Archive directory. Specify the archive directory that you specified earlier in this chapter. If prompted to move the archive, make sure you answer no.
2. Go into the Archive mailbox by selecting File, Open Archive. Exit GroupWise (on older GroupWise clients, this allows GroupWise to re-index the Archive mailbox). The index is essential when using the Find feature mentioned in the next step.

3. Get back into GroupWise and select File, Open Archive. From within the Archive mailbox, select Tools, Find. Find the items in the same manner in which you did when you archived messages into the Archive mailbox. Make sure to select the Find tab, and not the Find by Example tab. (If the Find feature does not find any items, try exiting GroupWise again.)
4. Select the items in the Find Results view and select Actions, Move to Archive (this actually unarchives the items and moves them back to the Master mailbox). Repeat this step until all items are unarchived.
5. Now enter the master mailbox (rather than the Archive mailbox). You should see your message items, and all the folders that were created. You still need to deal with the trash.
6. Make sure you're in the master mailbox, not the Archive mailbox. Delete the `trash2` folder under the Cabinet, as well as all of the messages in this `trash2` folder. This will move them to the trash bucket on the Master mailbox. Now the user's message data is imported, and should be available for you to view in the master mailbox.

Importing the Address Books

Importing is the opposite of the exporting you performed. Inside the GroupWise Address book, you should see at least two personal address books. They are the Frequent Contacts address book and the address book with the user's name. If they are there, follow these steps:

1. Highlight one of the address book tabs for an address book you will import, and select File, Import.
2. Specify the correct *.NAB file for this address book. This should be the *.NAB file that you exported earlier.
3. If the user had more address books than the two default address books, you will have to create the address book tabs for these address books before attempting to import the *.NAB file.

   To do this, simply select File, New Book and create the address book with the same name as before. Now you have imported all of the data that you can restore.

Final Notes About the Import Process

The import process does not import the following less common attributes about a mailbox:

- Rules
- User preferences
- Saved Find folders
- Button bar settings

You can go back into the backup mailbox and gather this data. You can try to re-create it in the live mailbox.

Additionally, earlier in the document you might have linked a message item to several folders, in order to re-create the folder structure. You don't want that item linked to all the folders, so

1. Find one instance of that message item that is linked to all the folders.
2. Forward the message as an attachment from Tay Kratzer to Tay Kratzer. This way, the message isn't lost.
3. Archive the one item, and it will no longer be in all of the folders. You can delete the archive; it's no longer needed.

Summary

This chapter discussed two methods for recovering a deleted user's GroupWise account. This chapter also covered two methods for recovering a deleted user's mailbox message items. GroupWise 6.5 makes it much simpler to re-create a deleted user and restore the user's settings. You can now perform all of these functions through ConsoleOne, and you don't even have to bother your users. The user's mail just appears as if by magic. Life is good.

CHAPTER 29

Configuring a GroupWise Messenger (Instant Messaging) System

GroupWise Messenger is a new collaboration system that first became available with GroupWise 6.5. The GroupWise Messenger software is rapidly evolving with new features and new architectural changes. In fact, GroupWise Messenger 1.0.1 has significant enhancements over GroupWise Messenger 1.0. And it's anticipated that the next support pack to GroupWise Messenger will also have significant enhancements. This chapter discusses the architecture of GroupWise Messenger without much focus on specifics. I recommend that you refer to the online documentation for GroupWise Messenger located at `http://www.novell.com/documentation/lg/gw65/` or the documentation that comes with your version of GroupWise Messenger.

NOTE

The instructions throughout this chapter assume you are using GroupWise Messenger version 1.0.1, which shipped in support pack 1 for GroupWise Messenger.

Architectural Basics

GroupWise Messenger is an instant messaging collaboration tool. A GroupWise Messenger system can run independent of your GroupWise system, and it has no dependencies upon GroupWise. As of the writing of this book, the only level of integration between GroupWise Messenger and GroupWise 6.5 is integrations at the client level. The GroupWise Messenger client can launch a new GroupWise message to compose, and the GroupWise 6.5 client can launch a GroupWise Messenger session. Although this integration exists, neither client has a dependency upon the other.

Client Software

The GroupWise Messenger client currently runs on the Windows desktop platform; it is anticipated that the GroupWise Messenger client will support other platforms in the future. The GroupWise Messenger client can be distributed along with the GroupWise 6.5 client installation, and this chapter explains how to do that.

The GroupWise Messenger client is currently not compatible with other instant messaging solutions, such as those provided by AOL or MSN.

Server Software

The server software is actually called "Novell Messenger" in the server interface for this software. As you install and work with your messenger system, you will see the Novell Messenger theme used often in the naming structure of files and directories. There are two server components for Novell Messenger—the Messaging Agent and the Archive Agent. The Messaging Agent relays IM (Instant Messenger) conversations between GroupWise Messenger clients. The Archive Agent, which you are not required to run, allows those conversations to be archived. Some customers will want to use the Archive Agent, particularly when GroupWise Messenger is used for conferencing sessions.

The GroupWise Messaging and Archive Agents run on the NetWare and Windows Server platforms.

Administration Software

GroupWise Messenger is configured through GroupWise Messenger snap-ins to ConsoleOne version 1.3.4 or higher. The GroupWise Messenger administration database is eDirectory. The GroupWise Messenger system in no way uses the GroupWise Directory Store (the WPDOMAIN.DB and WPHOST.DB files).

Directory Software

The GroupWise Messenger directory used is Novell eDirectory. GroupWise Messenger clients authenticate to eDirectory, and eDirectory is their directory in order to populate their GroupWise Messenger buddy list. eDirectory is also used to hold some user preferences. For example, a user's buddy list is held in eDirectory. Because of this, keep in mind the health of your eDirectory tree.

GroupWise Messenger users do not need to have the Novell client in order to use GroupWise Messenger, although they do need a full eDirectory account. I like to call this a "red-shirt" account. If your have users who are GroupWise *external entities* (the ones with green shirts), they will not be able to participate as GroupWise Messenger users. You must convert them to full eDirectory accounts in order for them to use GroupWise Messenger. Chapter 7, "GroupWise Utilities and Diagnostics," talks about how you can convert a GroupWise external entity into a full eDirectory user.

Configuration Files

The GroupWise Messenger agents have configuration files. However, many of the switches available in these configuration files can be modified through the ConsoleOne snap-ins. The most important switch for a GroupWise Messaging or Archive Agent is the one that tells it where in eDirectory its object exists. This is similar in function to the `/Home` switch on the GroupWise agents, but rather than pointing to a domain or post office database, it points to the eDirectory object that holds the configuration information for the agent.

Creating a Basic GroupWise Messenger System

GroupWise Messenger is very simple to install. This section states some obvious points and points out some potential trouble areas. I have significant experience with installing GroupWise Messenger as I implemented it at two customer sites during its 1.0 and 1.0.1 beta phases, so I'll try to pass along some of that wisdom while walking through the installation.

Preparation

There is no GroupWise Messenger administration view, like there is for GroupWise. So I recommend that you create a new eDirectory OU to house the components of your GroupWise Messenger system that you will be administering. You might call this OU IM or GWIM. Where you put the OU is not all that important from an eDirectory tree walking perspective. When your users populate their buddy lists, they will be adding data to the partitions they happen to be in. Your users do not need any eDirectory rights; the GroupWise Messenger logs in as sort of a "superuser" on behalf of all users. From an administration standpoint, you can control who users can see. So in effect you can make some users invisible to the GroupWise Messenger system.

Your eDirectory tree must be configured to support LDAP. The GroupWise Messaging Agent can run without LDAP support; however, I do not recommend it. I have found that not using LDAP causes the Messaging Agent to have difficulties authenticating users or searching eDirectory. LDAP is a lot faster and more efficient.

Your eDirectory tree must be healthy. If it's not, GroupWise Messenger will expose that fact. I recommend that you perform a basic eDirectory health check. I also recommend that you regularly check the health of your eDirectory according to Novell's recommendations. A good place to start this process is using Novell's documentation site, located at `www.novell.com/documentation`.

The GroupWise Messenger server software does not have a lot of overhead. Of course it's all relative to the number of users who you will have using GroupWise Messenger. Many organizations place their GroupWise Messenger Agents on a server that is dedicated for this purpose only. In fact, the GroupWise Messenger Agents are a good fit for Novell's clustering services. In many organizations, GroupWise Messenger will become a major collaboration solution. Users will expect telephone system type reliability from your GroupWise Messenger system. I speak from experience when I say that the GroupWise Messenger Agents have proven to be very stable. Part of the reason for this is that their primary function of relaying messages between clients is not very complex. It's still a good idea to use a dedicated server, if not a clustered server, for GroupWise Messenger.

The server that will run your GroupWise Messenger agents should have a DNS address: for example, `IM.WWWIDGETS.COM`. You might also want to consider making this server accessible through the firewall to service users on the road.

Server and Administration Installation

This section walks you through a basic GroupWise Messenger system installation. Your installation software might be different, because the GroupWise Messenger software is making rapid changes and improvements.

This scenario installs GroupWise Messenger to a NetWare server environment, as follows:

1. Insert the GroupWise Messenger CD.

   A screen similar to the one shown in Figure 29.1 will appear. If it doesn't, run SETUP.EXE at the root of the CD.

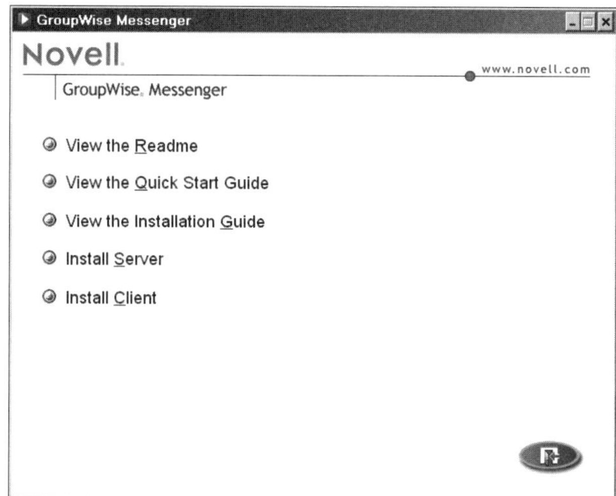

FIGURE 29.1
The GroupWise Messenger installation screen.

2. Select the Install Server menu choice.
3. Proceed to the Installation Options screen and choose Create or Update a System.
4. At the Server Information screen, choose a path to a NetWare server. This should be the path to a NetWare server that will be running your GroupWise Messenger Agents. A GroupWise Messenger Software Distribution Directory will also be created at this location. Click Next.
5. At the System Configuration screen, I recommend you keep all defaults and specify an eDirectory OU that you have created specifically to contain your GroupWise Messenger administration components. Click Next.
6. Allow the installation to extend the eDirectory schema of your tree, if needed.
7. From the Install Components screen, make sure to install the GroupWise Messaging Agent and the administration files. The Archive Agent is optional, although this example installs it. Click Next.
8. From the Directory Access Configuration screen, shown in Figure 29.2, indicate the IP address to your LDAP server. In a pure NetWare environment, this is the server that's running the NLAP.NLM. Keep the standard LDAP port of `389`, unless your LDAP server happens to be

configured to use a different port. It's important to fill in the Root Certificate field. LDAP requests are typically sent over the wire using clear text. However, the GroupWise Messenger will support SSL encryption of LDAP request if your GroupWise Messaging Agent has the root certificate from the Novell server that is running the NLDAP.NLM. In the UNC path, therefore, enter the path to the ROOTCERT.DER file on the server running your NLDAP.NLM. Click Next.

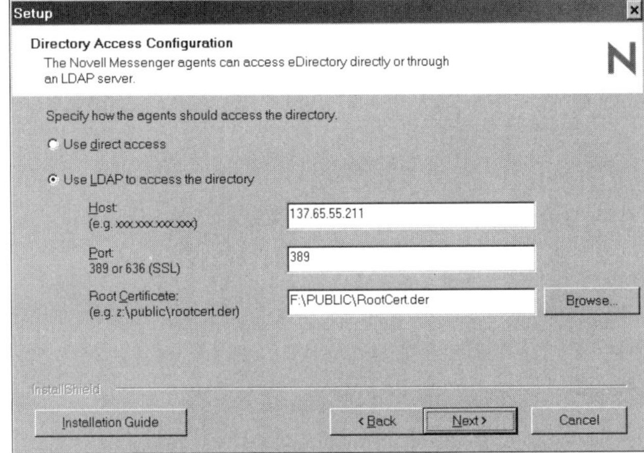

FIGURE 29.2 The Directory Access Configuration screen is used to specify which server is running LDAP in your eDirectory tree.

9. From the Directory Authentication screen, enter the authentication information for the "superuser". This user must have administrative-level rights. Figure 29.3 shows a superuser called `GWIMSUPERUSER` for this example. Click Next.

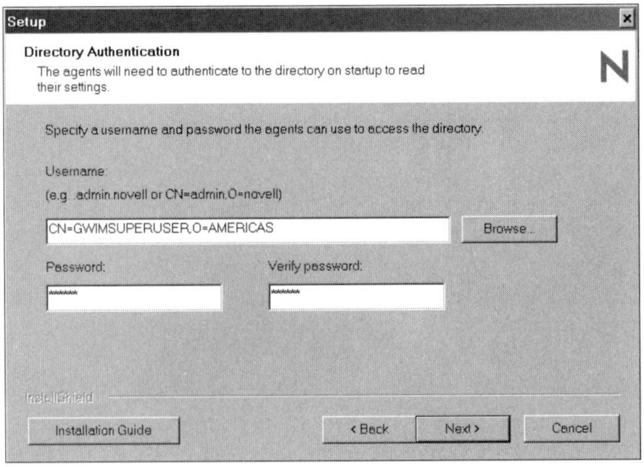

FIGURE 29.3 The Directory Authentication screen.

10. At the User Configuration screen, the best location for most customers is the organizational level sections at the top of the tree. You might also want to choose the Include Sub Contexts option. This will allow users in any part of the tree to authenticate to your GroupWise Messenger Agent, and it will also let users search for their buddies no matter where they are in your eDirectory tree. Click Next.
11. At the Server Address screen, you should most likely keep the defaults. If possible, you should use a DNS address rather than an IP address. DNS addresses are easier for users to remember. When you install the GroupWise Messenger client onto user's desktops, there is a way to configure the GroupWise Messenger client to know what the address of the GroupWise Messaging Agent is, so that you do not have to educate your users about this address. Click Next.
12. The Security Configuration screen allows you to enable SSL. You definitely want to do this. However, you can enable this later if you want. Chapter 27, "Securing Your GroupWise System via SSL," talks about how to enable SSL with GroupWise Messenger. Click Next.
13. At the Admin Configuration screen, indicate the path to ConsoleOne so that the installation can install the GroupWise Messenger snap-ins to ConsoleOne. Click Next.
14. Review the installation summary, and then click Next to allow the software to install.

You have now created a basic GroupWise Messenger system. It can function right away.

Starting Your GroupWise Messenger Agents

The command to start your GroupWise Messenger Agents is `NMSTART.NCF`. This NCF file is located in the `\NOVELL\NM` directory, wherever you installed the GroupWise Messenger software to. For example, `SYS:NOVELL\NM`. Here's an example NMSTART.NCF file:

```
load sys:\Novell\NM\ma\nmma.nlm @sys:\Novell\NM\ma\strtup.ma

load sys:\Novell\NM\aa\nmaa.nlm @sys:\Novell\NM\aa\strtup.aa
```

When I installed my GroupWise Messenger system just now for this chapter, and then tried to load the GroupWise Messenger Agents using the NMSTART.NCF file, the agents would not load. I got this error:

```
Agent configuration failure [0xAD2D]
Cause: LDAP Server is not available
```

Here's what I did to successfully resolve this error:

1. Edit the STRTUP.MA file.
2. Find the following two switches, and place a semicolon before them to disable these switches:

   ```
   ;/ldapipaddr-137.65.55.211

   ;/ldapport-389
   ```

3. Go into ConsoleOne. Find the `MessengerService` object and expand it, as shown in Figure 29.4.

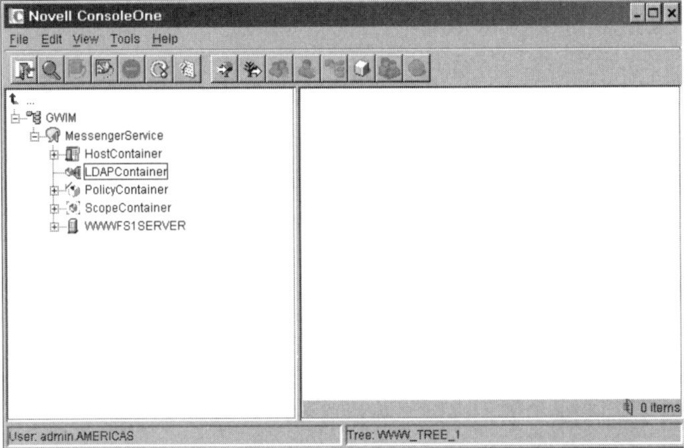

FIGURE 29.4 The MessengerService Object in eDirectory.

4. Highlight the `LDAPContainer` object. Right-click and select New, Object, nnmLDAPProfile.
5. Give a name to the new LDAP Profile. Select the Define Additional Properties check box.
6. On the General property page of the LDAP Profile that you just created, fill in the following fields:

   Base DN: This will often be the root organization of your eDirectory tree.

Username: In this scenario, the name of the user is `CN=GWIMSUPERUSER,O=AMERICAS`.

Here's another example: `CN=GWIMSUPERUSER,OU=NY,OU=WWW, O=AMERICAS`

Notice that there are commas that delimit the portions of the user's fully distinguished eDirectory name. LDAP uses commas, not periods, to delimit a user's full directory name.

Click the Set Password button and fill in the password for the user you just configured in the Username field.

Figure 29.5 shows the configuration of the example scenario.

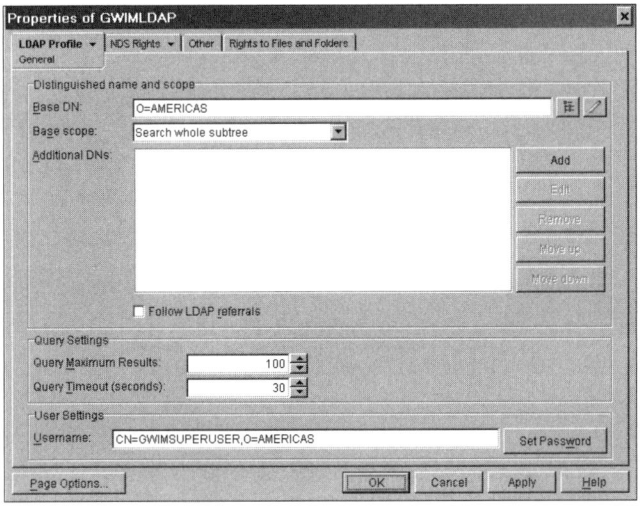

FIGURE 29.5
The LDAP Profile general screen.

7. Now go to the Connections property page under the LDAP Profile tab.
8. Click the Add button, and fill in the address to your LDAP server (enabling SSL is covered in Chapter 27). Figure 29.6 shows a configured LDAP server connection.
9. Click OK to save your settings. Now, when you run the NMSTART.NCF file, the GroupWise Messaging Agents should start. Figure 29.7 shows the GroupWise Messaging Agent console screen on a NetWare server.

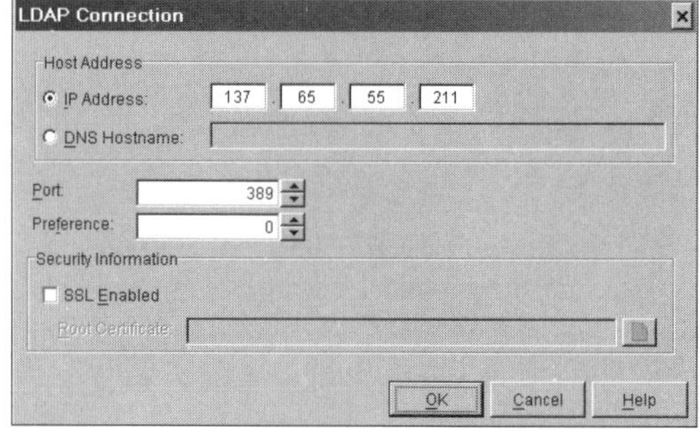

FIGURE 29.6
A configured LDAP server connection.

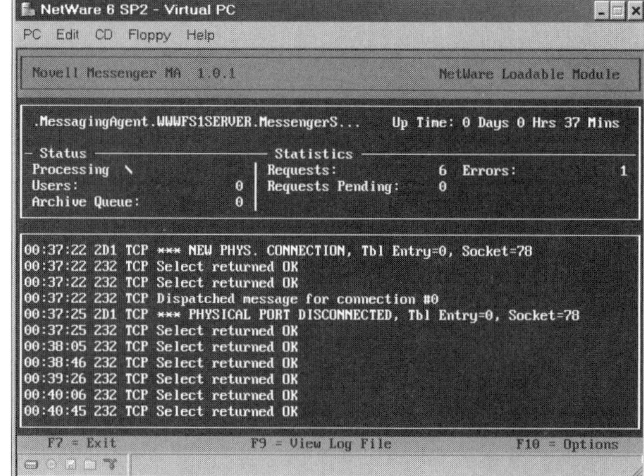

FIGURE 29.7
The GroupWise Messaging Agent console screen.

You have now defined an LDAP server for the GroupWise Messenger system to use. The LDAP services are necessary for users to authenticate, as well as add other users to their buddy lists.

Installing the GroupWise Messenger Client

The GroupWise Messenger client installation is actually very flexible. There are a variety of ways you can install the client, as follows:

- Installing the GroupWise Messenger from the GroupWise Messenger Software Distribution Directory.
- Enabling client installation from a Web browser to the GroupWise Messenger Agent.

- Installing the GroupWise Messenger client along with the GroupWise 6.5 Windows client installation.

This chapter covers all three of these GroupWise Messenger client installation methods.

Understanding the GroupWise Messenger Client Installation Files

The GroupWise Messenger installation created a Software Distribution Directory. Remember the `NOVELL\NM` directory? The GroupWise Messenger client installation SETUP.EXE utility can be found in the `\Novell\NM\ma\software\client\win32` directory. And much like the GroupWise 6.5 Windows client installation software, it contains a SETUP.CFG file. It is important that you configure the SETUP.CFG file, no matter which method you use to install the GroupWise Messenger client. The best kind of installation is one that does not require the users to answer any questions. In the chapter example, we will configure the SETUP.CFG without having to ask the users any questions.

Following are the steps for configuring the GroupWise Messenger's SETUP.CFG installation settings file:

1. Edit the SETUP.CFG file, which is located in the `\Novell\NM\ma\software\client\win32` directory.
2. Configure this file as shown:

```
[NMSetup]
Path=
ProgramFolder=
LaunchNow=No
LaunchOnStartup=No
ViewReadme=No
IconOnDesktop=Yes
RegKeyForDefaultPath=
RegKeyForDefaultFolder=Software\Novell\GroupWise\Client\
➥5.0\Folder
ServerAddress=im.wwwidgets.com
ServerPort=8300
ForceAddressAndPort=No
UseWindowsColors=

[ShowDialogs]
HideAllDialogs=Yes
```

```
SelectDestination=No
SelectProgramFolder=NoSetupComplete=No
```

3. Save the file. Now when your GroupWise Messenger installs, users will not be prompted with any installation questions. (Actually, if a user has already installed the GroupWise Messenger client, they will be prompted if they want to uninstall the GroupWise Messenger client.)

The SETUP.CFG is now configured so that users are not prompted with any installation questions when they install the GroupWise Messenger client.

Installing the GroupWise Messenger Client from the GroupWise Messenger Software Distribution Directory

This is a simple, yet manual, process necessary for your users to install the GroupWise Messenger client. You might consider launching the GroupWise Messenger installation from a login script if your users use the Novell client. Otherwise, follow these steps:

1. Make sure the SETUP.CFG file is configured how you would like it to be, as explained in the previous section.
2. Locate the `\Novell\NM\ma\software\client\win32` directory.
3. Run SETUP.EXE. The GroupWise Messenger client software will be installed.

The GroupWise Messenger client should install, without asking any installation questions.

Enabling Client Installation from a Web Browser to the GroupWise Messenger Agent

This is a slick way for your users to install the GroupWise Messenger client. Your users go to a location via their Web browsers and can install the GroupWise Messenger client from there. You don't even have to set up a

Web server to do this; you simply have to enable this feature on your GroupWise Messenger Agent along with a few other steps.

Configure the GroupWise Messenger Client Extractor File

This is an interesting concept. The GroupWise Messenger client is actually compressed into an *extractor* file called NVLMSGR.EXE. This file is located in the `\Novell\NM\ma\software\client\win32` directory. This file is a self-extracting zip file of the GroupWise Messenger client, including the SETUP.CFG and the SETUP.INI files.

The NVLMSGR.EXE file does not ship from Novell. It is actually generated the first time your GroupWise Messaging Agent loads. In fact, each time your GroupWise Messaging Agent loads, it checks to see that the client extractor NVLMSGR.EXE file is already created. The log will read as follows:

```
Client extractor already exists . . .
Client extractor successfully built . . .
```

Now, imagine that you made a tweak to your SETUP.CFG file. However, that change is not incorporated into the NVLMSGR.EXE file. To fix this, delete the NVLMSGR.EXE file, and then bring the GroupWise Messaging Agent down and back up. GroupWise Messaging Agent will re-create the file, and of course incorporate your newly created SETUP.CFG file. Here are step-by-step instructions for doing this.

1. Make sure the SETUP.CFG file is configured how you would like it to be, as explained earlier in this chapter.
2. Locate the file NVLMSGR.EXE, which is in the `\Novell\NM\ma\software\client\win32` directory.
3. Delete the NVLMSGR.EXE file.
4. Go to the GroupWise Messaging Agent console screen and unload the Messaging Agent by pressing F7.
5. Reload the GroupWise Messaging Agent. The command to do this is typically `NMSTART`.

The GroupWise Messaging Agent will generate a newly configured NVLMSGR.EXE file. You should see the Messaging Agent report that it built the client extractor. See Figure 29.8, which shows the Messaging Agent having built the GroupWise Messenger client extractor file.

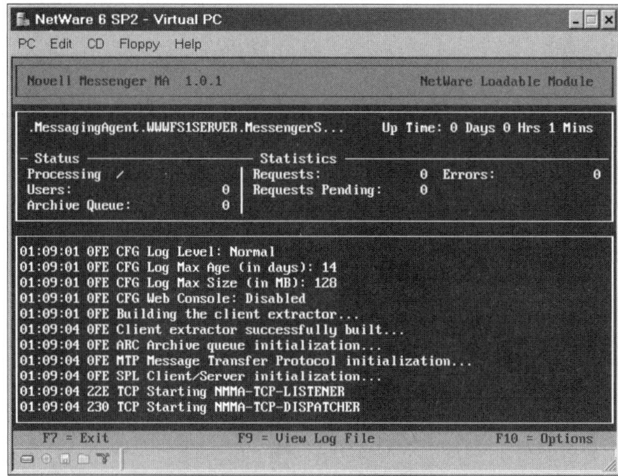

FIGURE 29.8
The GroupWise Messaging Agent builds the client extractor.

The GroupWise Messenger client extractor can now be used in a couple of ways. The next two sections talk about how to use the NVLMSGR.EXE file.

Install the GroupWise Messenger Client Through a Web Browser

This section walks you through the steps involved with installing the GroupWise Messenger client through a Web browser. Follow these steps:

1. In a Web browser, enter the IP address or DNS name of the GroupWise Messaging agent, followed by `8300`. For example, `http://im.worldwidewidgets.com:8300`.

NOTE **This can be a complex address for your users to enter. You might just want to send it to them in an e-mail message, which allows the users to then click the link.**

   Your users should see a screen similar to the one in Figure 29.9.

2. Click the Novell Messenger link and download the software.
3. Run the NVLMSGR.EXE file. The GroupWise Messenger software will install.

This method is slick in some ways, but it still has some manual elements to it. Users must download the *.EXE file and then run it. I like the next solution the best, because users aren't required to do much of anything.

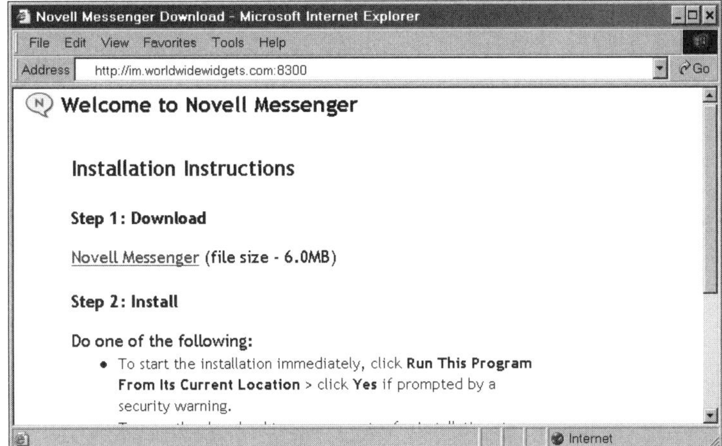

FIGURE 29.9 The GroupWise Messaging client Web browser installation screen.

Installing the GroupWise Messenger Client Along with the GroupWise 6.5 Windows Client Installation

This method requires no intervention on the part of your users. This method requires you to read Chapter 12, "Administering the GroupWise Client," and understand it. Chapter 12 deals with how to install the GroupWise client. This section dovetails into the solutions already explained in Chapter 12.

Installing the GroupWise Messenger Client Along with a GroupWise 6.5 Windows Client Mapped Drive Installation

As a prerequisite to this section, please read the prior section so that you can learn about how to generate a configured GroupWise Messenger client extractor file.

This method assumes you already have a GroupWise Software Distribution directory with a `CLIENT` directory that is already configured for installing the GroupWise 6.5 Windows client. After having done so, follow these steps:

1. Under the `CLIENT\WIN32` directory there should be an `ADDONS` directory. If there is not one, create it.
2. Create a directory under the `CLIENT\WIN32\ADDONS` directory called `GWMSGR`.
3. Copy the configured GroupWise Messenger client extractor file called NVLMSGR.EXE from the `\Novell\NM\ma\software\client\win32` directory to the `<SDD>\CLIENT\WIN32\ADDONS\GWMSGR` directory.

Rename the NVLMSGR.EXE file in the `<SDD>\CLIENT\WIN32\ADDONS\GWMSGR` directory to SETUP.EXE.

4. In the `\Novell\NM\ma\software\client\win32` directory, there is a file called ADDON.CFG. Copy this file to the `<SDD>\CLIENT\WIN32\ADDONS\GWMSGR` directory.

Figure 29.10 shows a GroupWise SDD configured to also support the GroupWise Messenger client installation.

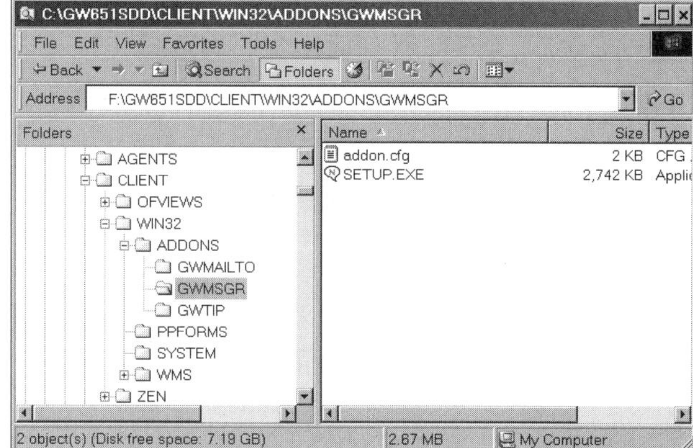

FIGURE 29.10 A GroupWise 6.5 SDD with GroupWise Messenger installation support.

When users run the SETUP.EXE file from the `<SDD>\CLIENT\WIN32` directory, it will install the GroupWise 6.5 Windows client, and it will automatically run the GroupWise Messenger installation.

Installing the GroupWise Messenger Client Along with a GroupWise 6.5 Windows SETUPIP Installation

As a prerequisite to this section, please read the section in this chapter, titled "Configure the GroupWise Messenger Client Extractor File," which explains how to configure a GroupWise Messenger client extractor file. This method assumes you already have already configured your Web server with a `GWCLIENT` directory (explained in Chapter 12). Follow these steps:

1. Under the `GWCLIENT\WIN32` directory on the Web server, there should be an `ADDONS` directory. If there is not one, create it.
2. Create a directory under the `GWCLIENT\WIN32\ADDONS` directory called `GWMSGR`.

3. Copy the configured GroupWise Messenger client extractor file called NVLMSGR.EXE from the `\Novell\NM\ma\software\client\win32` directory to the `GWCLIENT\WIN32\ADDONS\GWMSGR` directory on the Web server.

   Rename the NVLMSGR.EXE file in the `GWCLIENT\WIN32\ADDONS\GWMSGR` directory to SETUP.EXE.

4. In the `\Novell\NM\ma\software\client\win32` directory, there is a file called ADDON.CFG. Copy this file to the `<SDD>\CLIENT\WIN32\ADDONS\GWMSGR` directory.

Figure 29.11 shows a GroupWise SETUPIP GroupWise Client Distribution Directory configured to also support the GroupWise Messenger client installation.

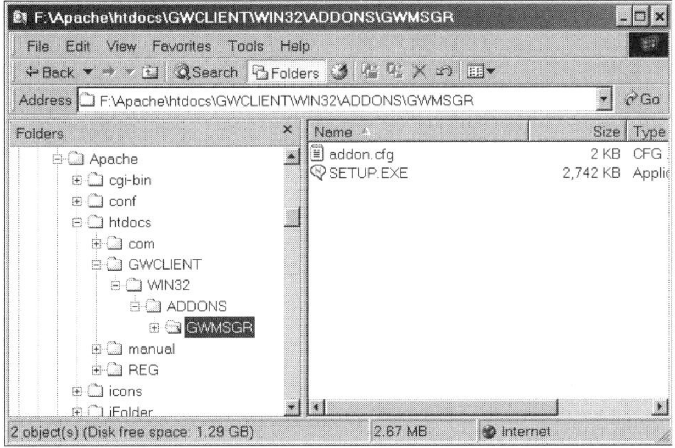

FIGURE 29.11
A GroupWise SETUPIP Installation with GroupWise Messenger installation support.

When users run the SETUP.EXE file from the `<SDD>\CLIENT\WIN32` directory, it will install the GroupWise 6.5 Windows client, and it will automatically run the GroupWise Messenger installation.

NOTE

You do not need to regenerate the SETUPIP.EXE file in order for this installation method to work.

There are some additional methods for installing the GroupWise Messenger client. You can distribute the NVLMSGR.EXE through a mail message, and tell users to right-click the attachment, and select Open. You can also put the NVLMSGR.EXE file on a Web site that your organization already has configured.

Summary

A GroupWise Messenger system can get very elaborate. The online documentation at `www.novell.com/documentation` will give you plenty of instruction on how to configure your GroupWise Messenger system. This chapter went further than that and exposed you to solutions and some real-world issues that the online documentation does not cover.

CHAPTER 30

Secure Messaging

Hundreds of millions of e-mails per day (according to some, soon even billions) are being sent through the Internet by using Simple Mail Transfer Protocol (SMTP). This protocol is indeed quite simple, especially when capturing and reading the information embedded in the message, thereby allowing you to access all kinds of valuable business information.

Have a look at your own GroupWise environment: Any GroupWise administrator can easily copy incoming or outgoing messages from the GWIA Sent or Receive directories, read the message and convert the attachment to its original format. Although this admin-ability might not be seen as a big issue, anybody on the Internet who can intercept your Internet traffic can capture your SMTP sessions and do the same. Figure 30.1 shows the vulnerability of SMTP sessions on the Internet.

Somewhere in the near future, somebody within your organization or within a recipient's organization is going to realize the impact of this security hole, and then will want you to fix it!

A growing number of organizations should already be implementing secure messaging solutions. For example, sending medical information regarding patients by regular Internet mail should not be legal. Other high-risk or high-security organizations, such as government agencies and financial institutions, are implementing policies to reduce or even remove the risk of information getting into the wrong hands.

Even as a private citizen, you should wonder what kind of information you're unwittingly sharing with the Internet community via Simple Mail Transfer Protocol (SMTP). It's really a bit like sharing all your private files on your hard disk with the entire Internet community, isn't it?

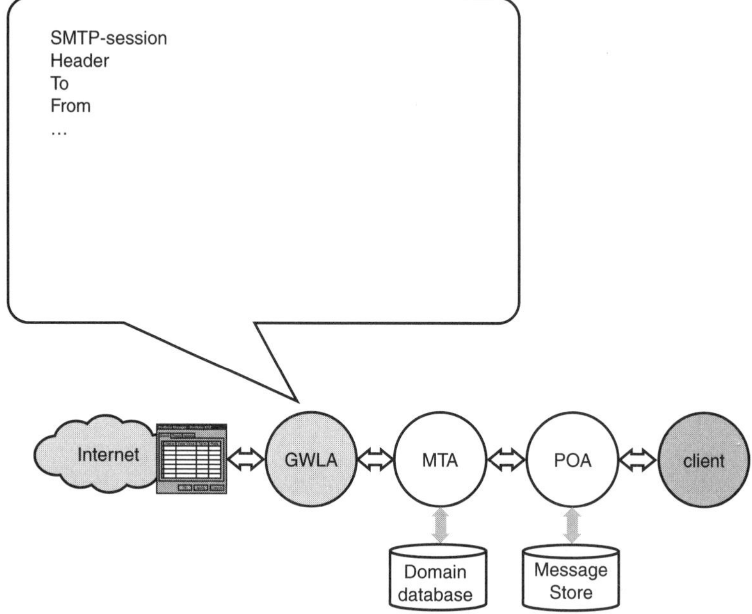

FIGURE 30.1 SMTP is not secure; messages are all easily readable as clear text.

This chapter provides you with the details of secure messaging, especially with regards to GroupWise. And really, in the end it isn't as complicated as it might look now. The first section of this chapter discusses some general ideas and techniques to secure your e-mail messages and then focuses on two important techniques—Pretty Good Privacy (PGP) and Secure MIME (S/MIME). The end of the chapter compares these two techniques and presents some general recommendations. For more information on secure messaging, try *Secure Messaging with PGP and S/MIME* written by Rolf Oppliger; it's really a bit like a Swiss army knife on this subject (and he's actually from Switzerland). It's not an easy read, but very concise and probably the only book that covers both PGP and S/MIME in depth. Please have a look at the reference list at the end of the chapter for more information.

Sending E-mail Across the Internet

There are two separate problems when sending e-mails via the Internet. The most well-known problem involves the unencrypted nature of SMTP. The other problem is probably as big and ugly—*identity spoofing* or *hijacking*, as shown in Figure 30.2

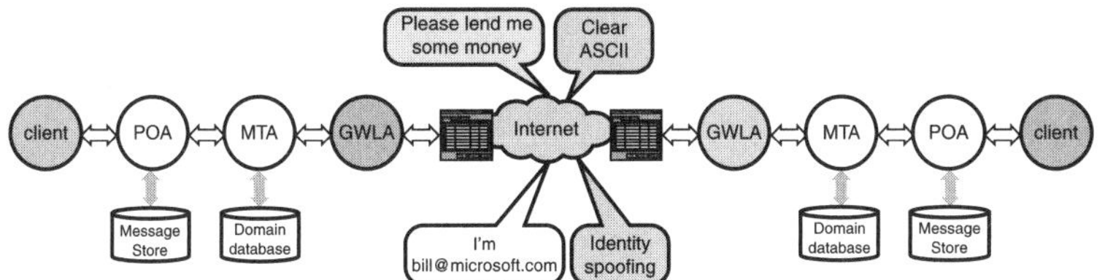

FIGURE 30.2 SMTP incorporates two problems—identity spoofing and clear text messages.

So you now have two problems to solve:

- **Reading unencrypted e-mails:** By simply collecting the right IP packets, anybody with the right tools can capture a complete SMTP session and easily read the plain ASCII information. The attachment will have to be converted from MIME-encoded to its native file format, but this is an easy task with so many tools available. Quite often, the local e-mail client can handle the conversion task.
- **Identity spoofing or hijacking:** It's rather easy to send an e-mail on behalf of somebody else. Just use your own SMTP server and add another Internet domain. Many recipients' sites will accept these kind of e-mails. In a world where more and more transactions and information exchanges are conducted via Internet e-mail, it's spooky to realize how simple it is to *hijack* somebody's e-mail identity.

Surprisingly, as will be shown in the next section, there are several ways to tackle the first problem, but these are more or less worthless if you don't tackle the much more difficult second problem.

Overview of How to Secure Messages

There are several ways to solve the problems mentioned previously; let's have a rather high-level look at some of these solutions:

- **Non-SMTP system connections:** Use GroupWise to GroupWise or GroupWise to foreign systems connections, effectively removing the need to use the SMTP protocol. Chapters 15 and 16, "Administering Multiple GroupWise Systems" and "Internet Addressing," respectively, talk about how to do this.
- **Secure SMTP:** Use Secure SMTP to set up a SSL-ized SMTP session between two SMTP servers, thereby creating a secure SMTP channel without any user intervention.

- **Web-based systems:** The sender's message is captured by an appliance, and a secured HTML link is sent instead to the recipient. An example of such a product is Message Protect from IntelliReach (`intellireach.com`).
- **Securing individual messages:** Use specialized additions to SMTP such as PGP or S/MIME to secure individual messages, which requires end-user participation.

These are just some of the solutions, there may well be others.

Non-SMTP System Connections

A GroupWise environment is internally secure from day one after setup. Security has always been one of the most important features of GroupWise and there is really no way a normal end-user or even a big-time hacker could simply access items in the message stream or the message store. Every bit of information in the message store is encrypted and messages sent between post offices via domains are encrypted with a proprietary 40-bit encryption. And as described in Chapter 27, "Securing Your GroupWise System via SSL," GroupWise 6.5 offers the capability to enhance this security by using 128-bit SSL encryption between all GroupWise components. Figure 30.3 shows how two GroupWise systems can speak securely to one another over the Internet.

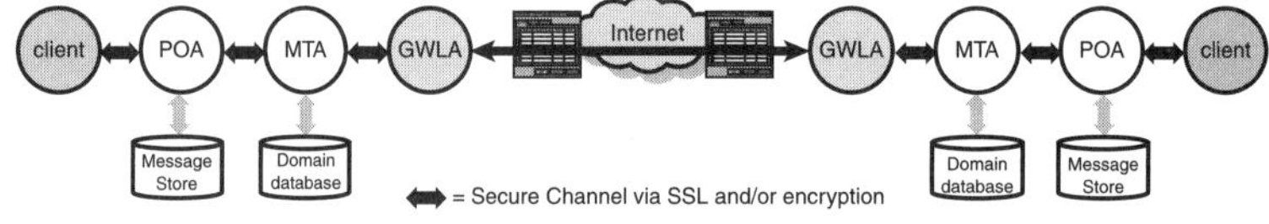

FIGURE 30.3 GroupWise to GroupWise connections via the Internet can be secure with SSL.

Predefined GroupWise to GroupWise Connections

If both the sending and the receiving environments are GroupWise systems, you can easily configure a *foreign domain connection*, enabling these to environments to transfer messages directly via MTA to MTA connection. The advantage of a predefined link is that you can also exchange address book information automatically. Setting up such a link is fairly simple and is described in Chapter 15.

Auto-Detected GroupWise to GroupWise Connections

Even without a predefined connection, an MTA to MTA connection can be established automatically, because with version 5.x, Novell can use Dynamic Internet Link to detect the possibility to connect to a foreign MTA. If you put the right information in the DNS, your MTA will be able to connect to a foreign MTA and exchange native GroupWise messages, which are of course encrypted by default. You can find more information in Chapter 16.

Predefined GroupWise to Foreign Systems

Another alternative to deliver secure and identity-checked e-mails is by using a high-level gateway between the two disparate systems, for example, from the GroupWise Gateway to Exchange or Domino. Although the tools are there and are relatively easy to set up, this will require diligent research and information exchange with the e-mail administrators at the other side and might therefore be too difficult to implement.

Reality Check

It's not a GroupWise-only world yet! Because so many organizations haven't made the decision yet to implement GroupWise as the best messaging system ever, it's important to cover other ways to solve the secure messaging problem. The chapter first covers the use of PGP, which according to some sources has the biggest market share yet, and then it dives into the newer S/MIME standard.

Although these non-SMTP high-level system connections solve the second problem by setting up a secure connection between the systems, not all of them completely solve the first problem—making sure the sender's identity is checked. This can only be solved with the predefined connections, all the while trusting each other's environments to be secured against this kind of fraud.

Securing the SMTP Channel

Theoretically, it would be rather simple to encrypt the complete SMTP session in between two SMTP servers. And the good news is that the stuff is already there with GroupWise 6.5.

The Extended Simple Transfer Protocol (Extended Simple—sic!) has some options to exchange information regarding capabilities of the two connecting ESMTP servers during the initial handshake. Based on the capabilities of both SMTP servers, the 6.5 GWIA will refuse to accept SMTP sessions that try to transfer messages of invalid recipients and/or a messages above a specified size. The two ESMTP servers can also detect if they both support SSL-ized SMTP sessions and will try to establish a SSL connection to transfer the SMTP message via this secure SSL-channel. This protocol is also referred to as StartTLS. Figure 30.4 illustrates how StartTLS is incorporated into SMTP mail.

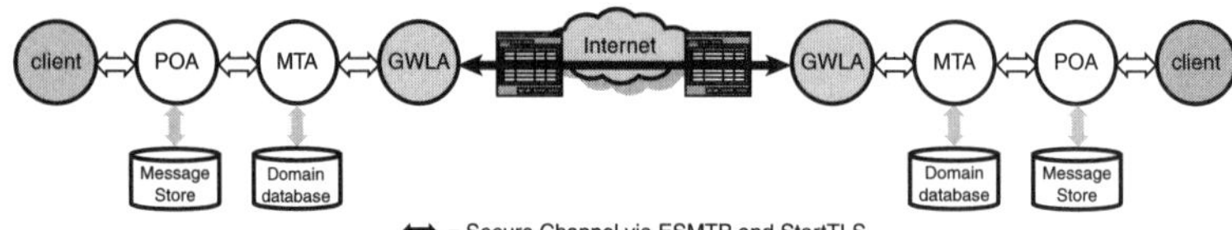

FIGURE 30.4 Securing messages via ESMTP and StartTLS.

In a perfect world, this would indeed solve at least the second problem, by encrypting the complete SMTP session and thus the e-mail within that session. However, only a very small percentage of the current SMTP-servers around the world can support this mechanism or are configured correctly to use it. And even so, you still haven't solved the second problem, because you can't ensure that no one within the sender's environment hijacked a sender's identity (imagine a big university with lots of students mimicking their professor's identity, raising their grades by simply sending some relevant messages).

Working with Web-Based Systems

When looking at Web-based secure messaging systems, you have to remember that market share is still small. Most solutions are single-vendor solutions. For example, `http://www.hushmail.com` is a great PGP Web-based solution, but corporations want to control such Web-based systems within the boundaries of their own IT environments and quite often don't want to host it externally. When looking at GroupWise environments, an enhancement of GroupWise WebAccess with PGP capabilities would be far more suitable than such external Web-based solutions.

NOTE

There are a few non-mainstream Web mail services offering secure messaging, for example Hushmail (`www.hushmail.com`) and ZipLip (`www.ziplip.com`). Hushmail uses a Java applet to create PGP encrypted e-mail. ZipLip is a Web mail service that sends an HTML message, which redirects the recipient to the ZipLip Web site to read the encrypted e-mail after asking for a password.

Securing Individual Messages

You can see now that most of the other methods don't solve all of your problems. It looks like you have to involve the users and give them some tools. First, let's have a closer look at the two problems. This section discusses the similarities between the two alternative solutions, PGP and S/MIME, and then zooms in on these two solutions.

Encrypted Messages

A message can be encrypted using various techniques; both PGP and S/MIME use private and public keys. The private key is stored in the sender's workstation environment and used to encrypt the message. The recipient can decrypt the message by using the sender's public key, to which she somehow needs to have access. This can be via a kind of lookup mechanism, for example based on LDAP, or by simply exchanging public keys and storing them in the recipient's environment.

A message is encrypted via an algorithm that generates a session key that is combined with the recipient's public key, transferred via the Internet, and decrypted by using the recipient's private key and the session key. This effectively means that as long as the keys aren't compromised, nobody in between the sender and the recipient can have access to the content of the message.

And now you have an interesting problem—really nobody or nothing, no processes at all, can touch this message, not even the corporate virus or content scanner! These messages will reside within your message store and travel through your message-flow like real untouchables. Both the sender and the receiver will have to rely on desktop virus scanning to process the unencrypted messages whenever the recipient or the sender opens such a message.

The big differences between PGP and S/MIME lie in how are keys generated; how these keys are validated and where are they stored. Let's focus on these in more detail in the upcoming paragraphs.

Digital Signatures

If you want to make sure that the users are who they say they are, you can do some basic checking on receipt of every SMTP message. Because most SMTP servers don't even do a basic reverse address lookup check (as described in Chapter 16), they really don't have any idea who the originator of a certain message is. Research has shown that most SMTP servers (estimated at 95%) don't even use this simple check. And yes, if you turn it on in your own environment you will reject e-mails from badly configured sender environments, so even if you're aware of the problem you might not be able to use this important feature.

And really, for the intents and purposes here, this check isn't good enough, because although it will make sure that you're connecting to the right SMTP server, you still don't know if the people on the other end are the lawful owners of the mailbox or if they are mimicking somebody else at the sending site.

Digital signatures can take away a lot of this discomfort and, if implemented and used properly, can give you an almost 100% certain guarantee that the sender (and the receiver) is genuine. The idea is based on the exchange of public keys and a method to check the validity of these keys against a Certificate Authority (CA, used by S/MIME and PGP) or a Web-of-Trust (used by PGP). When sending an e-mail the digital signature is added on request or automatically, and the receiving e-mail client can use this information to verify the validity of the signature and thus the identity of the sender.

Of course, you should realize that the handling of encrypted or digitally signed e-mail can obviously not be handled by any e-mail client For example, Gartner mentions in "E-mail encryption: multiple strategies needed" that almost 65% of the business recipients use e-mail software that could be configured to handle S/MIME messages. I will cover this aspect in more detail later.

Three Important Procedures

From an administrative viewpoint, there are actually three important tasks associated with the setup and maintenance of a secure messaging environment. Keys and certificates must be

- **Created:** Each user should somehow be able to get a copy of his or her private and public key. These keys are either generated individually (PGP) or centrally within a directory service in what is called a PKI (Public Key Infrastructure) in S/MIME and some of the newer implementations of PGP.
- **Distributed:** After the keys are created, the user must be able to store them in some kind of secret store. With PGP, this is a so-called PGP *key ring*. S/MIME most often uses the locally installed certificate, for example the Windows Certificate Store that is an integral part of Internet Explorer and/or Windows 2000/XP.
- **Revoked:** It's very important that keys be able to be revoked, either because they're compromised or become invalid for other reasons. For

example, when users leave the organization, they should not be able to send digitally signed e-mails on behalf of the organization. Within S/MIME this can be handled by mechanisms like the CRL (Certificate Revocation List) or the newer OCSP (Online Certificate Status Protocol) protocol, which will be briefly covered later, whereas PGP has some other mechanisms to handle revocation.

More of these differences and similarities between PGP and S/MIME are discussed in the section titled "PGP and S/MIME Compared."

Pretty Good Privacy (PGP)

In 1984 the Godfather of PGP, Philip Zimmermann, saw the need for encrypted communication for protecting rights overseas as well as for protecting political organizations at home. It was during the Reagan administration that in the eyes of Zimmermann and many others the right for privacy had to be extended to new means of communications that became available because of the Information age. His specific focus was electronic mail, but it also included digital documents and other digital data.

This process eventually resulted in the 1.0 release of a software product called PGP, an acronym that stands for Pretty Good Privacy. PGP version 1.0 was based on several encryption algorithms such as MD5, IDEA, and RSA. Soon after this first release, Zimmermann was faced with two problems. One of them was related to a U.S. patent; however, this issue was settled over time. The second problem was far more severe. Zimmermann was being accused of a federal crime, because the software became available as freeware outside the United States. At that time the United States had export restrictions that didn't allow cryptographic software to be exported to other countries without a license. U.S. courts finally dropped this case in 1996 and soon after that Zimmermann founded PGP Inc., which was acquired by Network Associates International (NAI) a year later.

At the end of 1999 export restrictions on cryptographic software were lifted during the last months of the Clinton administration and until then a very peculiar situation existed. In order to export PGP outside the United States, the source code had to be printed, shipped overseas, scanned in again and then OCR-ed in order to derive the original source code and to compile it back to the same binary code as the domestic version. This could be done because of a backdoor in the export regulations for cryptographic software, which covered encryption software only in electronic form and didn't prevent the export of printed source code of encryption software from the

United States. The PGP International (PGPi) project was a nonprofit initiative, which used this legal construction to export the source code from the United States, and they were responsible for the first clean PGP version outside the United States. Version 5.0i was one of the first versions that had legally been exported in the form of source code, covering 12 books with a total of 6,000 pages. Not only did PGPi derive the source code from the paper source, but the PGP International project also took care of translations.

The OpenPGP Working group of the Internet Engineering Task Force (IETF) started at the beginning of 1997 and in November 1998 they proposed RFC2440 for the OpenPGP Message Format. OpenPGP is a nonproprietary protocol that found its roots in the original PGP product. OpenPGP has become the standard for nearly all of the world's encrypted e-mail. Because of the IETF proposed standard, any company can implement OpenPGP without paying licensing fees. OpenPGP-compliant products can be found for numerous platforms, including Windows, Unix, Linux, Mac, Palm OS, and Pocket PC.

PGP Corporation acquired the PGP intellectual property from NAI in August of 2002. They also acquired the trademark PGP and Pretty Good Privacy, as well as the source code for that particular software implementation developed by Phil Zimmermann and his engineering team. But the name OpenPGP had been granted to the IETF for use as the name of the OpenPGP standard. The IETF allows any company that complies with that standard to use that name to describe their product. Any company can develop an independent implementation of the OpenPGP protocol without having to license it. PGP Corporation now of course is one of them.

PGP Products

If you want to have a look at the PGP products available on the market and on the Internet today, it's wise to have a look at the member list of the OpenPGP Alliance. Not only will you find Zimmermann & Associates LLC on the list (Zimmermann is now a consultant on cryptographic matters and an authorized reseller of the PGP products from PGP Corporation), but also members like GNU Privacy Guard. GnuPG is the OpenPGP implementation of the GNU project. Commercial support, consulting, and development are available through a German company called g10 Code.

This chapter focuses on the products of PGP Corporation. They not only provide the freeware version of PGP 8 for Windows and Macintosh, but also commercial versions of PGP 8 for Personal, Workgroup, and Enterprise use. The PGP Desktop and PGP Enterprise versions both support GroupWise, the Enterprise version also supports eDirectory integration. Both versions integrate the PGP 8 application with the GroupWise client by adding PGP buttons to the toolbar and by trapping certain GroupWise client events, such as when a user sends a message. This integration was being made in cooperation with The Messaging Architects (`www.gwtools.com`) that call this integration the GWSecure GroupWise plug-in. GWSecure works not only with a GroupWise 6.5 Win32 client, but also with GroupWise 5.5, 5.5e, and 6.0 clients.

NOTE

Because the integration is done via C3POs, which intercept the GroupWise Sent-button events, please be aware that other C3POs might try to catch the same event and could therefore cause a conflict.

For several years, Novell has had the OneNet vision. And OpenPGP is not tied into a specific platform like Windows or Macintosh. So you can use GnuPG on Linux from within Ximian Evolution or KMail. You can use Hushmail if you have only a Web browser, but still want to send PGP encrypted and/or signed mail. Novell recently added a new client to GroupWise—the GroupWise Cross-Platform Client. With a few adjustments, OpenPGP can integrate with it by using the GnuPG software. I'm eager to see how all this will evolve.

PGP Basics: An Overview

This section covers the basics in order to get you started with PGP from within the GroupWise client. It doesn't cover PGP in detail, because there are a lot of detailed publications out there, like *Secure Messaging with PGP and S/MIME* written by Rolf Oppliger, that cover PGP in much more detail. The article "How PGP works" on the PGP international Web site (`www.pgp.com`) is also helpful. Finally, the PGP help files are also of great value.

Encryption in general is a method with which you can transform some piece of information to a nonreadable encrypted format. Decryption can be done only if a valid recipient or owner of that information has a key to decrypt it.

One of the most famous simple encryption algorithms is the Caesar's Cipher, named after Julius Caesar. Caesar's Cipher is a simple substitution cipher that shifts letters in the alphabet with a predefined number of steps. Let's say you pick a Caesar key of 4. Then the word `NOVELL` would end up being `RSZIPP` by shifting the letters in the alphabet four places. The disadvantage of all this is that with some little analysis, you can crack the algorithm (Caesar) and the key (4). So, this is a very weak encryption method.

Public key cryptography combined with current strong encryption algorithms solved these problems to a certain degree. PGP is based on public key cryptography and conventional cryptography. With public key cryptography, the sender and receiver use different keys to encrypt and decrypt.

If you want to use PGP for communication, every user has to create a key pair that consists of a private and a public key. The public key can be sent out to whomever you choose to communicate with in a secure way. You can also store public keys in your Novell eDirectory tree if you extend your Novell eDirectory with the LDIF schema extensions (PGPschema.ldf) provided in the PGP Enterprise product. Public keys for internal use can then be stored in the directory and queried for by using LDAP from within the PGP keys application. If you allow the outside world to query your eDirectory tree by using LDAP, external users can also look up these PGP public keys.

The PGP Secret Key

The secret key, secured by a kind of password called a *passphrase*, has to be kept secret and stored in a place where no one except the owner has access. The collection of public and private keys is called a *key ring*, which is composed of two files being stored locally. Pubring.pkr and secring.skr are the two files being used by the PGP version for the Windows platform. Pubring.pkr contains all public keys being received and imported into the public key ring over time. Secring.skr contains all secret keys. The latter has to be secured in a proper way. The secret keys in the secret key ring can be used only if you know the passphrase. Nevertheless, it's advisable to store this file on a smartcard or on a compact flash (CF) card if you're a laptop user. If you are a desktop user with network access, the keys can be stored in your home directory on a server. Just don't put it on your local drive if possible—for security purposes, but also because computers are re-imaged now and then. Within PGP 8.0, the user interface (UI) to access both type of keys is called PGP keys; PGPKeys.exe is its filename.

The PGP Public Key

If two users want to communicate securely, they both need access to the public key of the recipient. PGP Public keys can be found in a number of ways, by using several public or private PGP servers, but users can also give each other their public keys by using traditional communication methods. PGP uses a direct trust model versus the hierarchical trust model of S/MIME. Basically anyone can provide with you a public key. It's up to the user to decide where to look for it and, after retrieval, whether the key is valid. After retrieving a public key from a user you want to communicate with, you can store it in your public key ring.

If user A wants to send an encrypted message to user B, user A needs user B's public key. After compressing the message, PGP creates a temporary session key. This session key encrypts the data. The session key is then encrypted to the recipient's public key. The session key and cipher text are then sent to the recipient. User B can then decrypt this encrypted message by using his or her secret key.

PGP also enables you to sign messages. You can compare this with a CRC (Cyclic Redundancy Check). The recipients of a PGP signed message can verify two facts. First of all, they can determine whether the sender sent the message, because only the sender can sign the message with his or her secret key. Secondly, the recipients can determine whether the message has been tampered with; if only one byte of the message is different from the original message, the digital sign will be broken and PGP will warn you about it. A big difference between signed messages and encrypted messages is that signed messages can be read and verified by anybody (if you have the right public key for it), whereas only the recipient can read an encrypted message.

Processing Messages: The PGP Digital Signature

When sending a digitally signed message, the sender must follow these steps:

1. The sender must use a one-way hash function to generate a message digest.
2. The sender must encrypt the message digest using one of his private keys (the encrypted message digest represents the digital signature for the message).
3. The sender must prepend the digital signature to the message.

The resulting message comprises a signature and a message part; both are sent to the recipient. On the recipient's side, two steps are required:

1. First, the recipient must decrypt the digital signature using the sender's appropriate public key to reveal the message digest. The key ID that is also included in the signature part of the message, in turn, identifies the appropriate key.
2. The recipient generates a new message digest for the received message and compares it to the revealed message digest. If the messages' digests match, the digital signature is verified and the message is accepted to be authentic.

Note that the recipient must have a way to get the sender's public key in an authentic form, as mentioned.

Processing Messages: PGP Data Encryption

When sending an encrypted message, the sender must follow these steps:

1. The sender must generate a random or pseudorandom number to serve as a session key for the message.
2. The sender's message is encrypted using the session key, for which several encryption algorithms can be used.
3. The session key is encrypted using each recipient's public key and the resulting encrypted session keys are prepended to the encrypted message.

Consequently, the resulting message comprises a session key part (for each recipient) and a message part. On the recipient's side, the procedure to unpack the digital envelope and decrypt the message includes two steps that can be summarized as follows:

1. The recipient extracts his encrypted session key from the session key part of the message. He then decrypts the encrypted session key with his private key.
2. The recipient decrypts the message using the decrypted session key.

Obviously, the second step reveals the message content to the recipient.

Installation of PGP Desktop 8

If you buy PGP Desktop 8 from the Web, you will receive a binary file called PGPDesktop.exe. This is the same binary code as the freeware version that comes as PGP8.exe. If you provide a valid license key during installation, modules like PGPMail for GroupWise and features like PGPDisk will be available. If not, PGP will run in freeware mode, without GroupWise integration.

If you want to install PGP, you have to execute PGPDesktop.exe. For a stand-alone installation the normal installation routine works just fine. You have to select several settings, which we will get to later in this chapter. With the right knowledge and documentation you will succeed in installing the product. From an administrator's perspective this is of less value. An administrator not only has to distribute the software to the users, preferably in a silent manner, but also has to provide a simple and consistent PGP configuration according to company policy.

For this purpose, you can find a tool called PGP Admin in the PGP Enterprise 8.0 version. The binary is called PGPAdmin.exe. PGP Admin has a feature called Create Custom Installer. With this you can repackage the PGPDesktop.exe binary based on options you select. This enables you to make an almost silent install with predefined settings like program files directory, PGP key length, and default key directory. PGP Admin also enables you to lock down menu options and certain settings.

Here are the steps to install this product:

1. Execute PGPDesktop.exe. After the welcome screen and the obligatory license agreement screen, the installation routine asks whether you already have PGP key rings that you want to use, as shown in Figure 30.5. Because you want to discuss a clean install, choose No, I'm a New User.

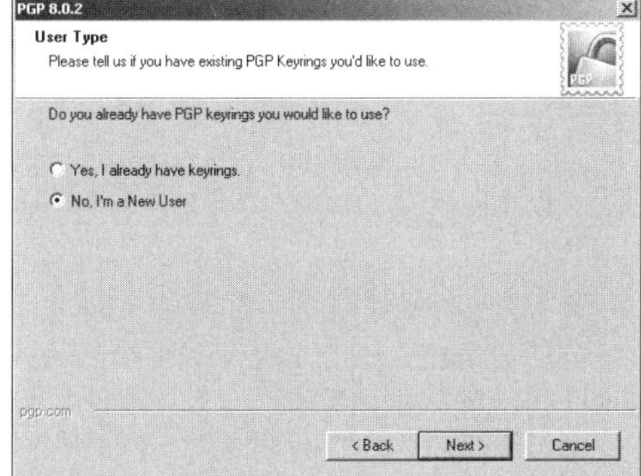

FIGURE 30.5
Defining a new PGP user.

2. Install directory. The default install directory for Windows 2000 workstations is `C:\Program Files\PGP Corporation\PGP` for Windows 2000. On a Windows XP workstation, it's `\C:\Program Files\PGP Corporation\PGP` for Windows XP. (I like to choose simple application directories. So instead of using the defaults, I choose `C:\Program Files\PGP`.)

3. Select components. Because I won't discuss other PGP related components like PGPdisk Volume Security, which you can combine with Novell's iFolder software by the way, I only choose PGPmail for GroupWise in order to install the integration with GroupWise, as shown in Figure 30.6. This integration consists of only one DLL called pgpgw.dll, which will be installed in the PGP directory and then registered in the Registry.

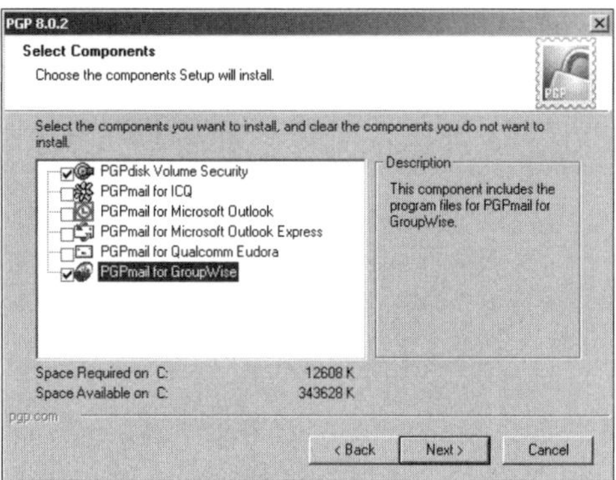

FIGURE 30.6 Choosing PGPMail for GroupWise.

4. After copying all necessary files to the `C:\Program Files\PGP` directory, PGPtray.exe will be added to your Startup folder. Restart your computer and log in again.
5. The PGP License Authorization screen will pop up. Enter your license information. You can change this license later if you need to, such as if you migrate from PGP Desktop to the PGP Enterprise version. All you have to do from within the PGPtray application is to select License, which not only enables you to see which PGP products have been installed, but also to change the license key being used.
6. The PGP Key Generation Wizard appears, as shown in Figure 30.7. It helps you create a secret and a private key. If you choose Export, you will be able to choose the key's size (1024–4096 bits), the encryption algorithms (Diffie-Hellmann/DSSm RSA or RSA Legacy), and an expiration date. Choose Next to use the defaults, which are 2048 bits and no expiration date.

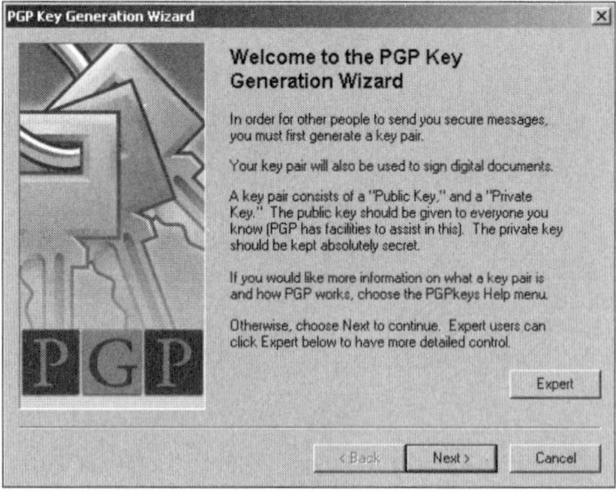

FIGURE 30.7 The PGP Key Generation Wizard is used to create pairs of keys.

7. Enter a full name in the appropriate field. Other PGP users will use this name to look you up in their PGP public key rings or on one of the PGP key servers you will store your public key at. A PGP key server is nothing more than a collection of PGP public keys. The PGP keys application discussed later uses two PGP keyservers by default: keyserver.pgp.com and europe.keys.pgp.com. Enter your e-mail address in the E-mail Addresses field, as shown in Figure 30.8. This will also be part of your public key pair. Other PGP users can search for this address to find the right PGP public key.

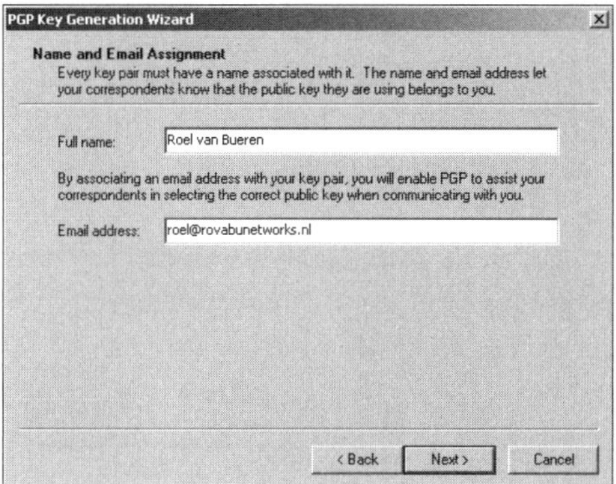

FIGURE 30.8
Fill in the e-mail address for PGP key generation.

WARNING

This address field is case sensitive. So there is a difference in `roel@rovabunetworks.nl` **and** `Roel@rovabunetworks.nl`**. Be sure to use the e-mail address defined in the GroupWise system.**

8. Passphrase assignment.

   A passphrase is a kind of password for your secret key, except it's much longer in length, and in most cases it contains multiple words. It's very important that you choose your passphrase wisely in order to circumvent dictionary attacks if your secret key gets lost. A passphrase has to be a minimum of eight characters long. Don't choose your own full name or your street address as your passphrase, because these are very simple to guess. Pick a line of one of your favorite books, and add some special characters to it, but still make it easy to remember. If you lose it, you can't use your secret key anymore and therefore can't read your encrypted messages anymore. Of course, never write it down on a piece of paper or on a sticky note. Figure 30.9 shows an example passphrase.

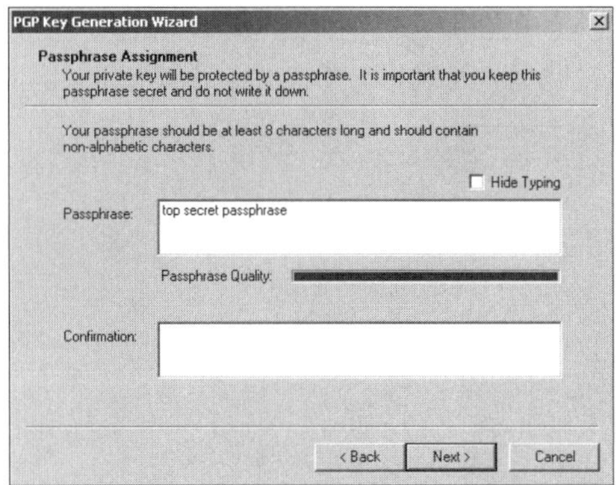

FIGURE 30.9
Creating a memorable passphrase.

PGP and the GroupWise integration have now been installed; you have also created a PGP secret key. During installation a PGP folder was added to your Programs menu in the Start menu and PGPtray was added to the startup group. PGPtray is just a little icon from which you can launch PGPkeys and PGPmail, but that you also can use to encrypt or sign data from any kind of Windows screen with text in it. You can also use PGPtray to encrypt or decrypt data from the Clipboard. PGPkeys enables users to manage their secret and public keys. I will not discuss PGPmail because this example uses PGP from within GroupWise.

Using PGP for GroupWise

It's time to start GroupWise in order to send your first encrypted e-mail message. If you take a close look at the main screen (shown in Figure 30.10), you will see two changes in the GroupWise client interface:

- A new drop-down menu PGP has been added between Actions and Tools. You can use it to start PGPkeys, as well as select PGP options.
- One new button has been added to the toolbar. You can start the PGPkeys application with this button.

Open a new e-mail screen by using File, New, Mail. Take a close look at this one too. This particular screen also has some new options, as shown in Figure 30.11:

- A new drop-down menu PGP has been added between Actions and Tools. This menu allows you to start the PGPkeys, as well as select whether the message has to be signed and/or encrypted when being sent.

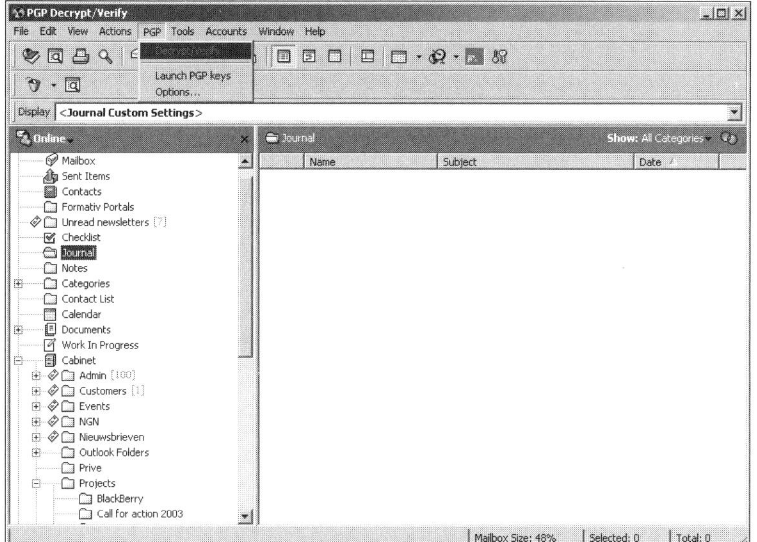

FIGURE 30.10
PGP integration with GroupWise.

- Three buttons have been added to the toolbar that perform the same actions as the menu options Encrypt on send, Sign on send, and Launch PGP keys. In fact, these buttons are automatically selected if you select the associated menu options.

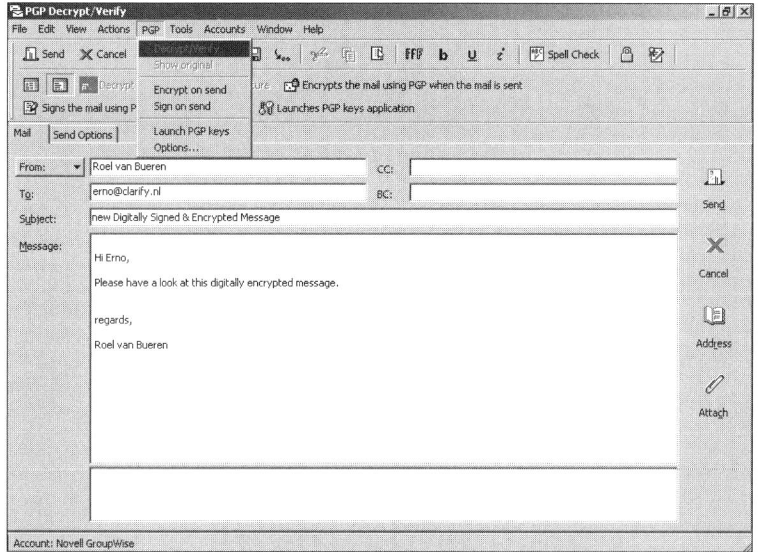

FIGURE 30.11
PGP integration when composing a message.

Sending a PGP Encrypted Message

Let's say I want to send an encrypted message to Erno de Korte. I put his e-mail address in the To field, enter the subject and message part of the e-mail message, select Encrypt the Mail Using PGP when the mail is sent and then press Send to send it to Erno, as shown in Figure 30.12.

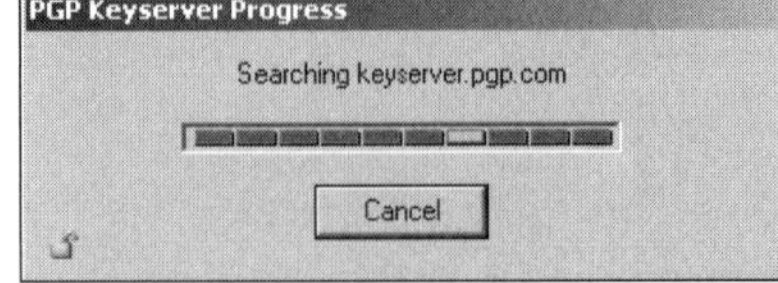

FIGURE 30.12 Sending a PGP encrypted message.

Then things start to get interesting. Because I haven't received a PGP public key from Erno yet, there isn't a public key for Erno de Korte `<erno@clarify.nl>` in my public key ring. I cannot encrypt the message with the public key of Erno yet, because I haven't received it.

If you start PGPkeys and take look at Edit, Options, Servers as shown in Figure 30.13, you will find two default key servers where PGP will look for PGP public keys. You can add more servers if you want to.

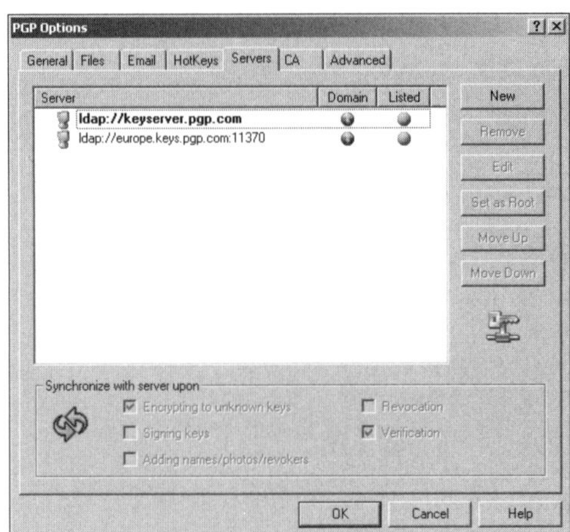

FIGURE 30.13 The default PGP servers created with the PGP client installation.

Because Erno published his public key to `keyserver.pgp.com`, I can retrieve his public key by using LDAP from within PGP. In the Recipient Selection screen, he will be listed as a recipient. Note the gray bullet under Validity, as shown in Figure 30.14.

If you select OK, the message will be encrypted and sent to `erno@clarify.nl`. Erno can then decrypt the message by using his secret key and the enclosed session key.

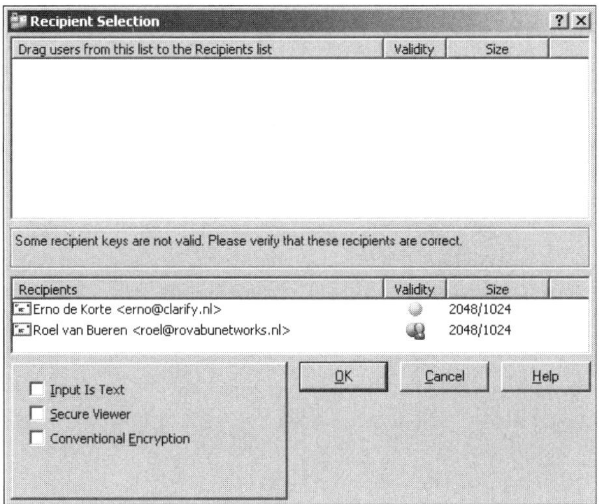

FIGURE 30.14
PGP recipient selection.

After sending the message, a screen will appear. You can import the PGP public key into your PGP key ring from this screen. It's a good idea to store a key locally if you're going to use it more often.

Before you do that, you will have to make sure that this is a valid key for `erno@clarify.nl`. Because there isn't a revocation method, the best way to verify a key is to call the person in question to verify his or her key. There are other methods, but this one is the most secure one.

Select the public key entry in the PGPkeys screen (Figure 30.15 shows Erno de Korte selected). Right-click the entry and choose Sign the selected public key after you have verified the fingerprint with the owner by using telephone or other communication methods. Select OK.

PGP Sign Key
By signing the selected user ID(s), you are certifying based on your own direct first-hand knowledge that the key(s) and attached user ID(s) actually belong to the identified user(s).
Before signing, make sure the key(s) were given to you in a secure manner by the owner or you have verified the fingerprint with the owner.

Key/User Name	Fingerprint
Erno de Korte <erno@clarify.nl>	298A 8971 16FF 33A6 D109 E737 BA7A 7F5F 23DB 56F7

Allow signature to be exported. Others may rely upon your signature.
More Choices
OK
Cancel
Help

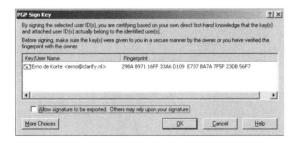

FIGURE 30.15
Signing a PGP key.

You are the only person who can approve this public key to be added to your public key ring. You do this by signing it with your own private key. Therefore you must enter your secret key's passphrase.

After you validate the public key, you will see a green bullet in the Validity column instead of a gray one.

You aren't done yet. We also have to trust the public key you just have validated. Select the public key entry in the PGPkeys screen again (in this case Erno de Korte). Right-click and choose Key Properties. In the lower right part of this screen you will find a slide button with which you can set a public key as untrusted or trusted. Slide it to the right (Trusted) and click OK. The key has also been trusted, as you can see that the rectangle icon underneath the column Trust has been darkened.

One can now communicate securely with Erno de Korte. Every time one sends a message from within GroupWise to erno@clarify or Erno de Korte, the GroupWise plug-in will select Erno's PGP public key from the public key ring.

If you take a look at the message in your Sent Items, you will see a screen similar to the one shown in Figure 30.16. An eavesdropper can't make any logic out of this text garbage. To say it in Dutch: je kunt er werkelijk geen chocola van maken.

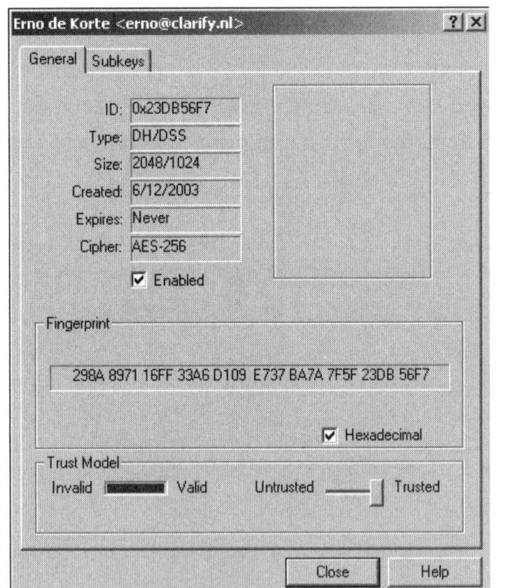

FIGURE 30.16
Viewing the properties of a PGP encrypted message.

If you want to read the message again, just open it and select Decrypt/Verify.

In case you can't find a public key on one of the key servers (you can add more key servers if you want; for example, if you do business with a company that runs its own PGP key server), you will see so in the Recipients Selection screen. Because Tay Kratzer hasn't published his PGP public key on one of the two default PGP key servers, a question mark appears before his name, as shown in Figure 30.17. His name itself will be crossed out. Until you remove the name from the recipient list or obtain his public key, you can't (of course) send him an encrypted message.

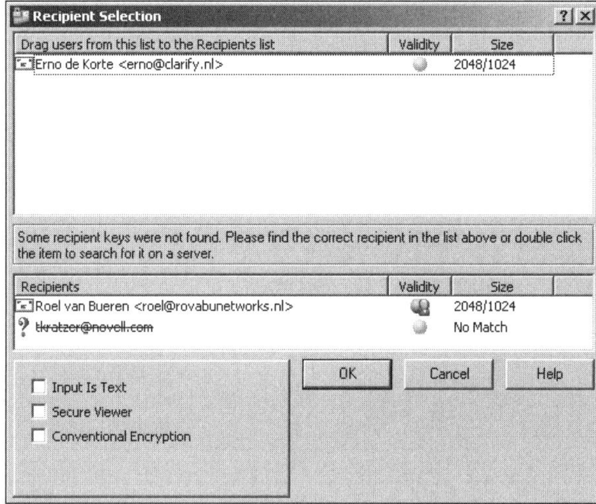

FIGURE 30.17
Cannot send to a user without a PGP key.

Receiving a PGP Encrypted Message

Let's look at what happens if you receive a PGP encrypted message. In the example that follows, I received a message from my long-time colleague Mark Ackermans, an expert on anti-virus software. In the past we discussed several possible vulnerabilities regarding MAPI, GroupWise, and Internet Explorer in order to secure our GroupWise systems. Because we didn't want anyone eavesdropping on such discussions, we shared each other's PGP public keys. Mark, however, doesn't use PGP 8.0; he uses PGP 6.5.8 (available at the PGP international Web site) with a plug-in for Netscape Messenger, because that's his default mail client. You can tell which PGP version he is using by looking at the first lines of the decrypted message.

Because PGP 6.5.8 is OpenPGP compliant, I can nevertheless decrypt the message he sent to me after encrypting it by using my public key. I can also use the Secure Viewer of PGP, shown in Figure 30.18. If you select Options,

E-mail from the PGPtray icon, you can select Always use secure viewer. By selecting this, every time a message encrypted with the Secure Viewer option is decrypted, the decrypted text appears on a secure PGP screen in a special TEMPEST attack prevention font. The TEMPEST attack prevention font is unreadable to radiation-capturing equipment. By default, the Use TEMPEST Attack Prevention Font option is selected. This option must be selected to securely view the decrypted text. The disadvantage of using the Secure Viewer is that you can't reply to a message from the default viewer. You will have to go back to the original encrypted message screen.

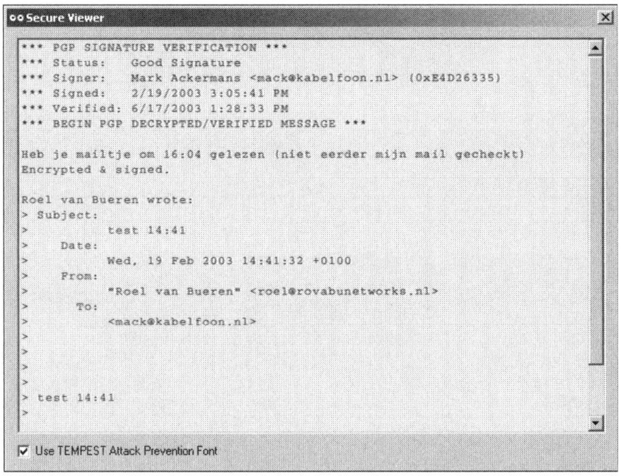

FIGURE 30.18
PGP Secure Viewer is used to view messages in a manner that they cannot be read by radiation-capturing equipment.

```
Secure Viewer
*** PGP SIGNATURE VERIFICATION ***
*** Status:   Good Signature
*** Signer:   Mark Ackermans <mack@kabelfoon.nl> (0xE4D26335)
*** Signed:   2/19/2003 3:05:41 PM
*** Verified: 6/17/2003 1:28:33 PM
*** BEGIN PGP DECRYPTED/VERIFIED MESSAGE ***

Heb je mailtje om 16:04 gelezen (niet eerder mijn mail gecheckt)
Encrypted & signed.

Roel van Bueren wrote:
> Subject:
>           test 14:41
>    Date:
>           Wed, 19 Feb 2003 14:41:32 +0100
>    From:
>           "Roel van Bueren" <roel@rovabunetworks.nl>
>      To:
>           <mack@kabelfoon.nl>
>
>
>
>
> test 14:41
>
[x] Use TEMPEST Attack Prevention Font
```

NOTE **Messaging Architects is the exclusive PGP reseller for the PGP GroupWise enterprise edition. It sells under the name GWSecure. The messaging architects can be found at** `www.gwtools.com`**. PGP also supports GroupWise WebAccess or even the upcoming GroupWise Cross-Platform (Java-based) clients. For cross-platform capabilities, PGP is superior to S/MIME.**

S/MIME

Just as with PGP, with S/MIME the user will use private and public keys to create and verify both signatures and encrypted e-mails. However, unlike PGP, the certificates used by S/MIME are centrally created and managed, either bought from an external third party such as Verisign, Entrust, Thawte, Globalsign, and various others or created within your own local Certificate Authority; for example the Novell Certificate Server, which is almost always an integral part in any environment that runs eDirectory.

Unlike PGP, no additional software is needed. GroupWise 6.5 natively supports S/MIME version 3.

The focus in this book is directed mainly at the Novell environment, but whenever possible, other solutions are briefly mentioned as well.

S/MIME Basics: An Overview

GroupWise utilizes other parts of your environment to create and distribute certificates/keys to your users, after which the users have to import their certificates within GroupWise just once. They will then be able to use the certificate for S/MIME, without any additional software needed, as well as have the option to use one or both of the special buttons on the toolbar (see Figure 30.19) to either digitally sign and/or encrypt the message.

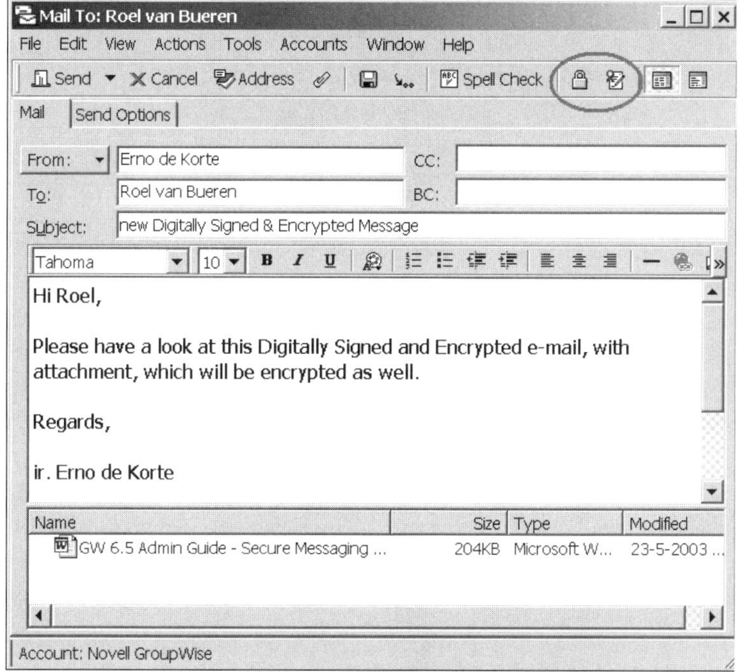

FIGURE 30.19 Digitally sign or encrypt a message.

The left button with the padlock presents the Encryption option; the right button with the small Certificate symbolizes the digital signature. Pressing these buttons without any preparation will present the users with one of several security errors and warnings.

You will have to prepare your GroupWise environment to be able to send a S/MIME message. We will investigate the details later; let's first have a high level overview of the process, which was taken from Rolf Oppliger's book.

Processing Messages: The S/MIME Digital Signature

When sending a digitally signed message, the sender must follow these steps:

1. The sender uses a one-way hash function to generate a message digest.
2. The sender encrypts the message digest using one of his private keys (the encrypted message digest represents the digital signature for the MIME entity).
3. The program prepares a block of sender information, that contains the sender's public key certificate, an identifier for the message digest algorithm, an identifier for the public key algorithm (that is used to encrypt the message digest), and the encrypted message digest.
4. The MIME entity and the block of sender information are concatenated to form a CMS-object of the type signed-data.

The resulting message is wrapped in MIME and sent to the recipient.

When message is sent with a digital signature the message body is still clear text, but the digital signature is added in a hashed format.

On the recipient's side, two steps must happen:

1. The recipient must decrypt the digital signature using the sender's appropriate public key, which is extracted from the block of sender information, to reveal the message digest.
2. The recipient must generate a new message digest for the received message and compare it to the revealed message digest. If the messages' digests match, the digital signature is verified and the message is accepted to be authentic.

If users try to send an S/MIME encrypted message without any preparation, the message won't proceed because the sender doesn't have a certificate with a private key available in his environment. Note that you don't need any information from the recipient for digital signing, because only the sender will add his or her digital signature, which can be verified by the recipient.

Processing Messages: S/MIME Data Encryption

When sending an encrypted message, the sender must follow these steps:

1. The sender (pseudo)randomly generates a content-encryption key that is appropriate for the encryption algorithm of choice.
2. The sender encrypts the MIME entity with the content-encryption key.
3. For each recipient, the sender encrypts the content-encryption key with the recipient's public key.
4. For each recipient, the sender prepares a block of recipient information that contains the sender's public key certificate, an identifier of the algorithm used to encrypt the session key, and the encrypted content-encryption key.
5. The encrypted MIME entity and the block(s) of recipient information are concatenated to form a CMS object encrypted enveloped data (in layman's terms: an encrypted message). In addition, a copy of the content-encryption key should be encrypted for the sender and included in the enveloped data.

The result of this operation is wrapped in MIME (as shown in Listing 30.1) and transmitted to the recipient. Please note that in step 3, the sender needs the recipient's public key. This might already be stored in his local secure store or can be harvested using LDAP for example, as you'll see later.

Listing 30.1 An S/MIME Encrypted Message

```
novell.com 16291
EHLO mail.clarify.nl
*S00001bbe* *Egroupwise.3EF381B1.FA3:a:fa3e:Y* *RH* MAIL
➥FROM:<erno@clarify.nl>
*NSF* *Osmtp;groupwise-TKRATZER@novell.com:1:1* RCPT
➥TO:<TKRATZER@novell.com>
DATA
Received: from Clarify-EXT-MTA by mail.clarify.nl
      with Novell_GroupWise; Fri, 20 Jun 2003 21:45:19 +0200
Mime-Version: 1.0
Date: Fri, 20 Jun 2003 21:50:41 +0200
X-Mailer: Groupwise 6.5
Message-ID: <20030620T215041Z_FA3E000A0003@clarify.nl>
From: Erno de Korte<erno@clarify.nl>
Subject: testing digital signature
To: Tay Kratzer<TKRATZER@novell.com>
Content-Type: multipart/signed; protocol="application/
➥x-pkcs7-signature";
```

```
    micalg=sha1; boundary="____IQLVNRRDMANYIVOBVWNJ____"

--____IQLVNRRDMANYIVOBVWNJ____
Content-Type: multipart/mixed; boundary=
➥"____RDFXQVUSLTRZHWFEOQYB____"

--____RDFXQVUSLTRZHWFEOQYB____
Content-Type: multipart/alternative; boundary=
➥"____QBAJWRNHWQNJYAINIUQI____"

--____QBAJWRNHWQNJYAINIUQI____
Content-Type: text/plain; charset=iso-8859-1
Content-Transfer-Encoding: quoted-printable

Hi Tay,

This message was digitally signed, please verify my signature!

Regards,

ir. Erno de Korte

MCNE/MCNI/MCSE/MCT
T +31-180-322300
M +31-629-016000
F +31-180-322340

--____QBAJWRNHWQNJYAINIUQI____
Content-Type: multipart/related; boundary=
➥"____XVYBEATNYECEPBTGWGYB____"
```

In the example shown in Listing 30.1, the message body is sent in a hashed format; only the sender, recipient, and subject are in clear text.

On the recipient's side, the procedure to decrypt the MIME entity includes two steps that can be summarized as follows:

1. The recipient decrypts his or her block of recipient information using his or her private key.
2. The recipient decrypts the message content with the session key.

Obviously, the second step reveals the message content of the recipient.

It's important to understand that any S/MIME compliant e-mail will be able to handle these steps and thus can process the digital signature and/or encrypted message. As Gartner (`www.gartner.com`) points out, nearly 65%

of business recipients use e-mail software that is capable of handling S/MIME, although many aren't configured properly to do so yet.

Preparing Your Environment

You need the following components in order to send secure messages in a Novell GroupWise environment:

- PKI S/MIME certificates for every user involved, either based on your directory services or bought from commercial vendors. In the case of a complete Novell environment, you need the following:
  - eDirectory, 8.6 or higher, which runs on almost any server-platform.
  - Certificate Server 2.0 or higher, which is an integral part of recent eDirectory implementations on almost any server-platform.
  - An LDAP server that's v3.0 compliant, in a Novell environment most commonly provided via the NLDAP NLM, as part of eDirectory. This is optional, but will increase user friendliness.
- S/MIME compliant e-mail client, such as GroupWise 6.5. GroupWise 5.5EP and 6.0 can also digest secure messages; however, the focus of this chapter is on the superior features of 6.5.
- A local desktop certificate store. Most likely, this will be available when the Internet Explorer or Netscape browser is installed. There may be additional certificate stores on your desktop, like the one from Entrust, but it's beyond the scope of this book to discuss this. This discussion assumes that IE 5.x or higher is installed and that the associated certificate store is functioning properly, as shown in Figure 30.20. More info on this subject can be found at the end of this chapter.

NOTE

Although it's perfectly feasible to install these browsers on the Windows 9x environment, experience has shown that the certificate stores on Windows 2000 or higher are far more stable than on earlier versions. A corrupt certificate store will most likely have to be reinstalled and all certificates might need to be imported again.

Because all information is stored in the Windows environment, you should consider using a roaming user strategy, as offered by ZENWorks (for example), otherwise the users will have to add the same information to the certificate store on any desktop they work on.

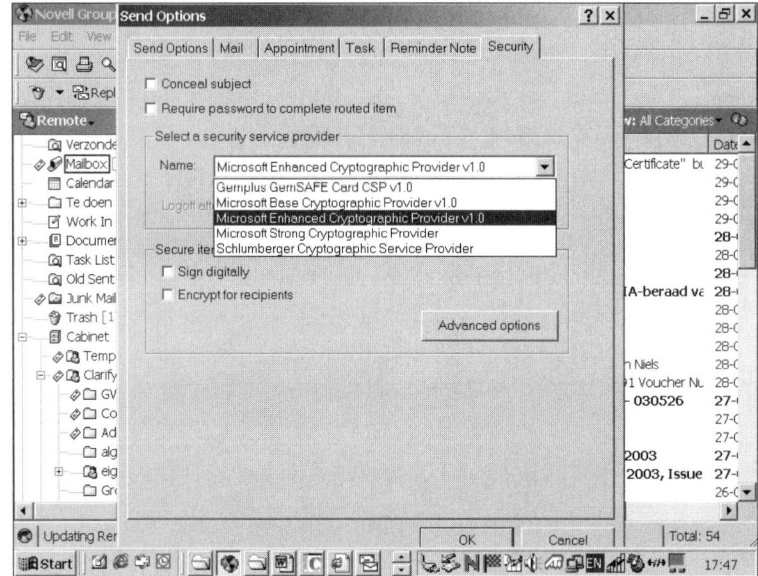

FIGURE 30.20 An example of a standard Windows 2000 environment with several Security Service Providers.

- ConsoleOne with the correct snap-ins, preferably version 1.3.4 or higher, with the snap-ins for both GroupWise 6.5 and the Certificate Server. The admin workstation will also need to have a recent NICI client installed, which is all part of the normal eDirectory 8.6.2 or higher install process. When using version GroupWise 6.5.0 (without any service packs), please make sure that you have installed the patch mentioned in TID2966245.
- GroupWise system without aliases. The GroupWise aliases aren't properly transferred into eDirectory (in fact, they're not transferred automatically at all). If you use aliases, you need the correct info in eDirectory. The eDirectory E-mail address field is being used to create the user certificate and/or for lookups via LDAP, so you have to get rid of the Gateway aliases and use the new GroupWise 6.5 Free Form Internet Address field instead.
- A proper firewall and DNS configuration that allows your senders to connect to external LDAP servers as well as allow external parties to collect Public Key info from your LDAP server. This is optional. Quite often you will also want to define an extra DNS-entry like `ldap.novell.com`, which will be easier than having to use the IP number of your (public) LDAP server.
- An LDAP-browser, recommended only for the administrator, to test the LDAP connection.

Most environments don't need anything extra to start sending S/MIME messages!

NOTE

Although using LDAP is optional, you will still need to make sure that all eDirectory user objects are properly filled in. It's especially important that the eDirectory field E-mail Address is properly filled in *before* generating the user-certificate, because the e-mail address will be embedded in the certificate info. Unfortunately, this is especially important if you use GroupWise gateway aliases, because normally these will *not* be filled into the proper eDirectory field. In general, it's not recommended to use gateway aliases with version 6.5, which has the FreeForm Internet Address field with some other advantages and is described in Chapter 16.

The requirements for S/MIME are generally not that difficult. Most customer environments have the S/MIME requirements already fulfilled.

Configuring Your Environment

The following eight steps show you how to prepare your environment for sending and receiving S/MIME messages. Step 1 describes an administrative procedure needed for every user; steps 2 and 3 need to be performed by the users before they can send a S/MIME message. Steps 1 and 2 can be skipped if you're using commercial certificates from Verisign and so on.

In step 4, you will be able to send your first digitally signed S/MIME message; step 5 demonstrates how to use LDAP lookup of public keys. Step 6 demonstrates what will happen if you receive and open a digitally signed message. Step 7 shows you how to send an encrypted S/MIME message. In step 8, you'll open such a message at the receiving side.

Step 1: Checking User Objects and Creating User Certificates in Your eDirectory Tree

Follow these steps to create certificates for eDirectory users:

2. Open the General tab and verify the e-mail address in the E-mail Address field (see Figure 30.21).

NOTE

As mentioned before, when using gateway aliases this information might not be filled correctly; as a general recommendation, first move away from gateway aliases to the new FreeForm Internet addressing format before starting to use S/MIME.

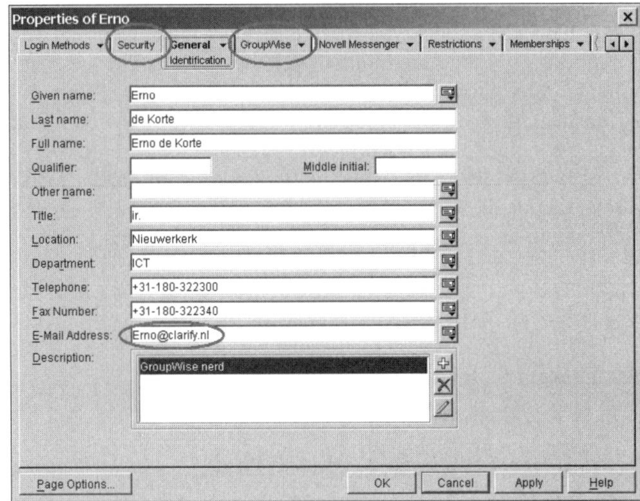

FIGURE 30.21 ConsoleOne—Checking Properties and Configuration tabs.

3. Click the Security tab.
4. If a user certificate is already present, make sure it was generated with the correct e-mail address embedded in the certificate. Also make sure the certificate is not expired.

NOTE **Do not replace the user certificate with wrong or old information without making sure that the user doesn't use it for something else. Creating a new user certificate will most of the time invalidate the old certificate.**

5. If not yet present, generate the certificate by using the Create button. You will be presented with the screen shown in Figure 30.22.

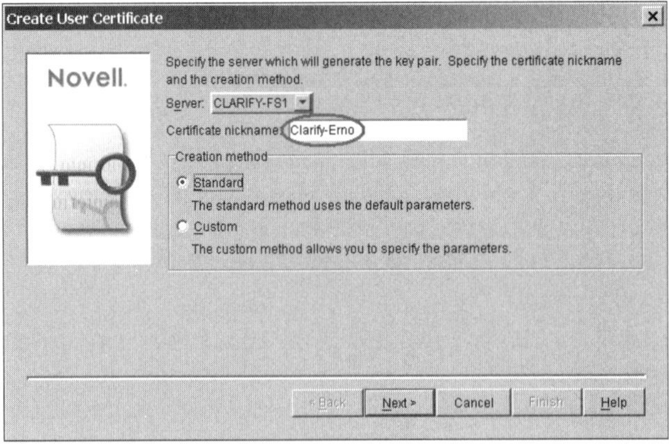

FIGURE 30.22 ConsoleOne—Specifying a user-friendly certificate name.

6. Specify a certificate nickname, preferably something user friendly, because this will be the default name that will be presented when the users save their certificates.
7. You can leave the creation method set to standard, which will create a certificate as needed. Click Next and you will see a screen similar to the one shown in Figure 30.23.

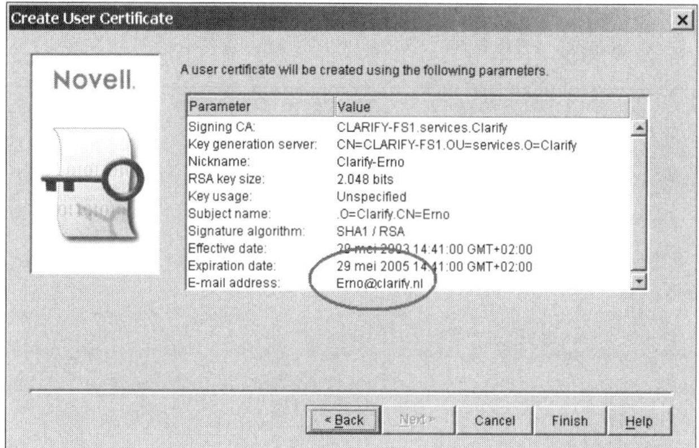

FIGURE 30.23
ConsoleOne—summary of creating a user certificate.

Check the information in the summary screen, especially the e-mail address field and the expiration date, and click Finish to create the certificate.

Here are some important notes:

- This certificate will contain both the private and the public key information for this user. However, as an administrator, you're *not* allowed to export the private key of any user object, other than your own account. You can only use the export function to export the public key.
- Keys are stored in Novell Certificate Server's secrets store in eDirectory and are therefore available to the user any time, any place. It's generally not recommended to let the user create a copy of the private key and store it in the file system, because this might compromise security. However, as you will see, you need a (temporary) copy of the private key to import into the user's desktop secret store. Currently, there is no way (yet) for GroupWise to access the certificates directly in eDirectory. However, Novell is considering creating a direct connection between GroupWise and Certificate Server as soon as all the APIs are available.
- The secret store within eDirectory can be used to safely store and distribute any PKI certificate, which might include commercial generated certificates from Verisign, Globalsign, and others, as shown in the next

step. As discussed, even PGP keys can be stored in eDirectory if the schema is properly extended. For more information, check the Novell online documentation.

The user's certificate is now created in eDirectory. GroupWise does not read certificates out of eDirectory, so the certificate must be exported. The next section explains how to do this.

Step 2: Exporting the Certificate from the eDirectory

This is an easy one; you can use a user tool called Novell Certificate Console to export the certificate and (temporarily) store the certificate into the file system. This tool can be found on most servers in the `SYS:PUBLIC\MGMT\CERTCONSOLE\BIN` directory. If not found there, you can download it from the Novell Web site (at `http://download.novell.com`). Select the Certificate Server product and click Submit Search.

NOTE

Theoretically, your users can start ConsoleOne and export their own public and private key and with more recent versions of Certificate Server. There are other ways to export the certificate from the eDirectory, for example via iManage. However, Novell Certificate Console offers a more user-friendly solution, works with any version of eDirectory, and can easily be offered to any user via ZENWorks.

Follow these steps to export a certificate from eDirectory using the Certificate Console utility:

1. Browse to the correct location to find CertCnsl.exe or click your ZENWorks object to open the Novell Certificate Console shown in Figure 30.24.

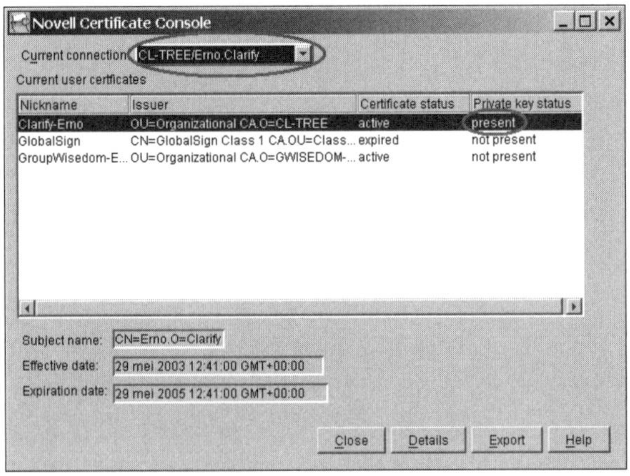

FIGURE 30.24
Certificate Console—Make sure the correct tree is selected and the private key is present.

There have been reports indicating that Certificate Console doesn't run on every workstation. In the rare case this might happen in your environment; just rename the (unneeded) module SYMCJIT.DLL in the `\CERTCONSOLE\BIN` directory and it should run fine.

As can be seen in this screen, this user has imported some additional certificates into eDirectory, so you need to make sure that you export the correct private key.

2. Make sure you're connected to the right tree by checking the Current connection. Check the Private Key status column to make sure your private key is available.
3. Select the appropriate certificate and click Export. You'll see the screen shown in Figure 30.25.

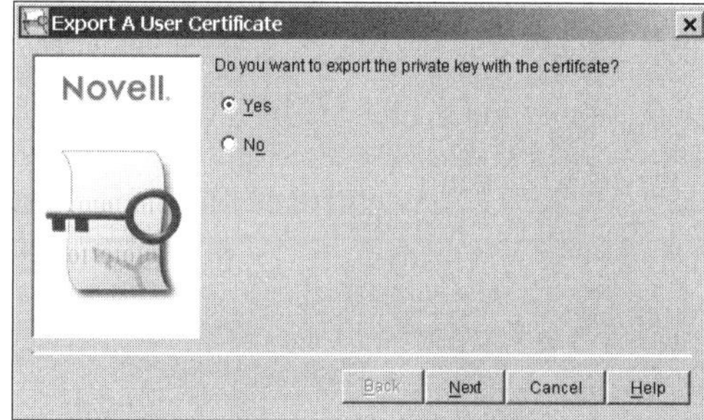

FIGURE 30.25
Certificate Console—Exporting the private key.

4. In this case, you do want to export the private key, so click Next and you will see the screen shown in Figure 30.26.

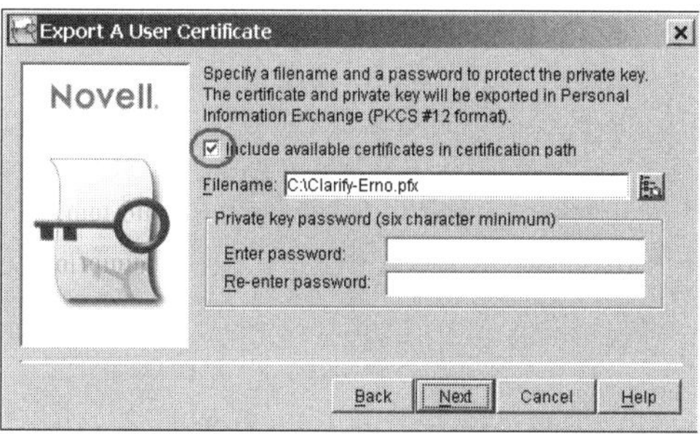

FIGURE 30.26
Certificate Console—Including the certificates in the certification path.

5. Make sure the check box called Include Available Certificates in Certification Path is checked; this will export the certificates from your Certificate Authority as well. Choose a proper file location, enter a secret password (sometimes called the passphrase), and click Next.

6. A summary screen will appear. Click Finish to export the certificate to a file.

The user's private key has to be guarded carefully and the file system might not be the proper place to store this certificate permanently. You should consider permanently deleting this (temporary) file after the next step. Your certificate information will still be safely stored in eDirectory and available any time and any place. However, bear in mind that if the users step away from their desks and their computers are still logged in, anybody can access the desktop and easily use the local certificate store to send secure e-mail on behalf of the users.

Step 3: Importing the Certificate in GroupWise

This step imports the certificate with private key information into the local Windows desktop certificate store. This process does not require you to exit from the GroupWise interface to access the certificate store. As mentioned, the certificate can come from any source, either from your own eDirectory tree or from a vendor.

1. Within the GroupWise client, click Tools, Options, Certificates, Import, as shown in Figure 30.27.

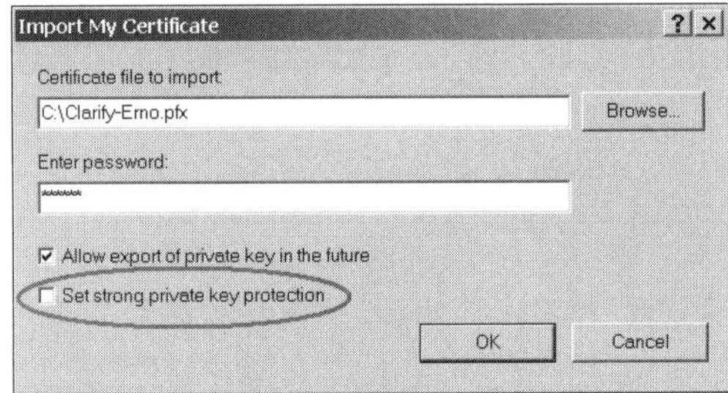

FIGURE 30.27 Importing the certificate into the local certificate store.

2. Browse to the location where you've (temporarily) stored your certificate, enter the password, and click OK. This will import the certificate in the local certificate store.

NOTE **In environments in which high security is a major concern, you might want to enable Set Strong Private Key Protection. This way, users are prompted for their secret passwords/passphrases every time they use the private key.**

3. If this is the first certificate you accept in this local certificate store for this organization, you will probably be asked whether you want to accept an organizational certificate in the root store.

NOTE

Novell uses a root certificate for the complete tree, which is used as a basis to create all other server and user certificates. Ideally, you need only one root certificate for your complete organization, which greatly reduces costs and gives you an enormous flexibility. Unfortunately, most commercial root-certificate vendors, such as Verisign, can only issue server or user certificates, which can't be used as a root certificate for your tree. The disadvantage of not having a commercially based root certificate lies in the fact that other organizations can't validate your organization's certificate against an external trusted party. The only current solution is to exchange root certificates and add them to the local certificate store, more or less the same procedure as you've just done by accepting the self-issued root certificate. Novell is currently investigating this problem and negotiating with several vendors to solve this issue.

4. Be sure to check the Expiration column and then click the Set As Default button, as shown in Figure 30.28. Otherwise, the GroupWise client doesn't know which certificate it needs to use, even if there is currently only one. A green checkmark will appear next to the default certificate. Bear in mind that when several users are using this desktop, there might be more than one certificate in the local certificate store, so a clear Certificate Name will help to identify which certificate to use.

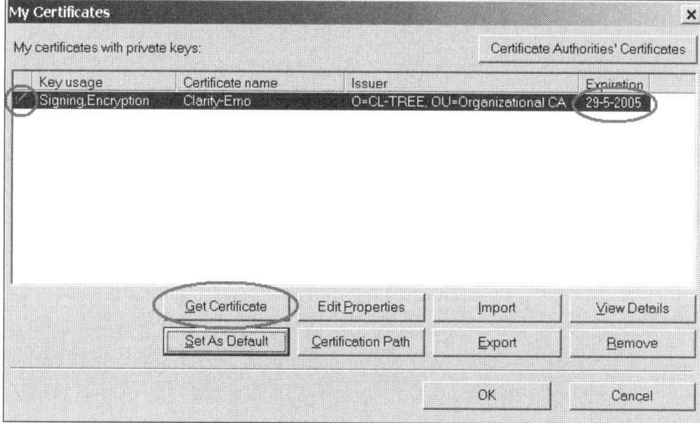

FIGURE 30.28
Imported certificate—Make sure Set As Default is set and the expiration date is valid.

Apart from the Import button, there is also a Get Certificate button. By default, clicking this button will direct you to a Novell Web page with instructions about how to get a certificate. You might want to consider changing this default behavior by changing an option in ConsoleOne. Right-click any domain, post office or user object, and then choose Client Options, Send Options, Security. Enter an alternative location on your intranet in the URL for certificate download field, which might present to-the-point information to your users.

When you use the newest version of Certificate Server, as delivered with Netware 6.5, you might also consider pointing this button to iManage, so users can export their certificates after logging in. In the future, Novell is considering integrating newer versions of Certificate Server and GroupWise more closely via this button, enabling you to directly import the certificate from eDirectory into GroupWise.

NOTE

This book is really an admin guide, so it doesn't cover every step for sending and receiving S/MIME messages. There is an excellent Appnote available at the Novell Web site; the second part of this Appnote includes a user guide at `http://developer.novell.com/research/appnotes/2003/may/02/a030502.htm`. **There is also some excellent user information available in the Novell online documentation (more info at the end of this chapter).**

Step 4: Sending the First Digitally Signed S/MIME Message

You are now ready to send your first S/MIME message, as follows:

1. Create a new message, choose any recipient, add a subject and some body text, and make sure you're message view is big enough to see all the buttons.
2. Activate the Digitally Sign button and click Send. That's all! How more user friendly do you want it?

NOTE

Remember, this was a digitally signed message, so the content is *not* encrypted. However, the recipient can now verify that the sender is who she says she is, so you've solved one of the earlier problems, the *identity-spoofing* problem.

If you get a warning that indicates that you haven't specified a default certificate, you might have forgotten to use the Set As Default button when importing the certificate. Review "Step 3: Importing the Certificate in GroupWise," to correct this.

NOTE

Before you can send your first encrypted message, you need some additional information. Remember, you're going to use the recipient's public key to encrypt the message, but you don't have this key yet. If you try to send a message to somebody without having the recipient's public key, you will get a message like the one shown in Figure 30.29.

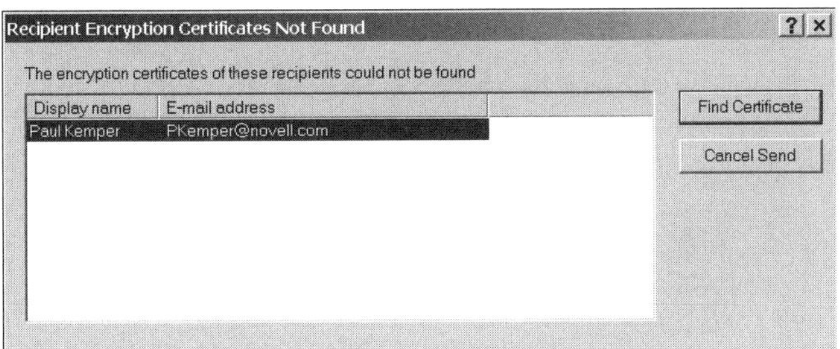

FIGURE 30.29 The dialog box you get in GroupWise when sending encrypted messages—when no public key is found for the recipient.

Without diving into this too deep, you can use several methods to get this information. Three of the most obvious methods are as follows:

- **Public key exchange:** You exchange the public key via e-mail or some other medium. Make sure that you know where this public key is coming from, which can be partly solved by the digital signature, and store the key in your local certificate store. You might end up with a large number of keys in your local certificate store and will have to make sure that they're properly transferred to other desktops that you will be working on.
- **Automatic public key retrieval:** You use a mechanism like LDAP to automatically retrieve the public key of the recipient. You will need some additional configuration in your environment, but in the end every recipient of these configured sources is automatically included. The Find Certificate button can find the information via LDAP in the recipient's environment.

You likely want as much automation as possible, so let's dive into the second option first. You will have to make sure that you can read the LDAP information from the recipient's side. The LDAP information should contain the public key information. For the first task you can use the normal GroupWise LDAP Address book option, but for the second task, it's better to use a full LDAP client (shown in Figure 30.30), like the ones from Novell or Softerra.

NOTE

Figure 30.30, taken from the Softerra client, shows the user object on the left side and the public key user info on the right side.

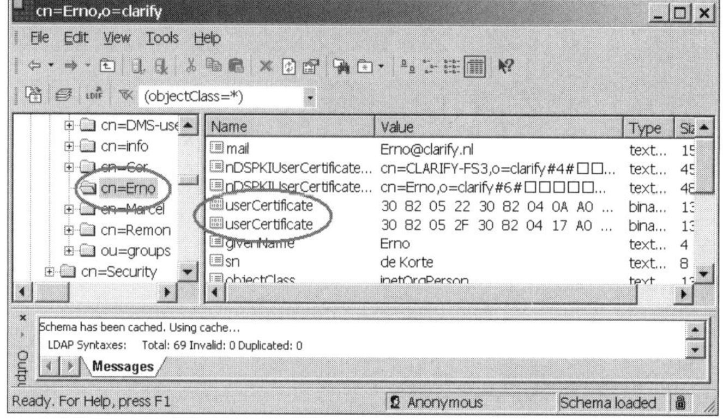

FIGURE 30.30 Softerra LDAP client—Verifying the availability of public key material via LDAP.

Step 5: Sending an Encrypted S/MIME Message with LDAP Public Key Lookup

You now need to configure the GroupWise client to use the LDAP Search Public Key option:

1. From within the GroupWise client, click Tools, Options, Send, Security, Advanced Options, as shown in Figure 30.31.

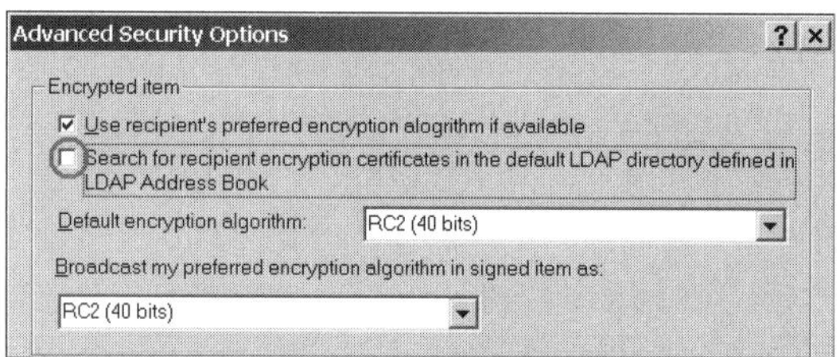

FIGURE 30.31 GroupWise client—advanced options—activating the search via LDAP option.

2. There are many interesting options on this page; the one you need to enable is the second option, called Search for Recipients Encryption Certificates in the Default LDAP directory. This option is not checked by default; make sure this option is checked. Click OK twice.

If you now add the recipient's environment to the GroupWise LDAP address book and set this as the default LDAP address book, everything will run nice and smooth. Follow these steps:

1. In the GroupWise address book, go to the Novell LDAP Address Book and click Directories.
2. You will see a list of defined LDAP address books (if any). Click Add to add an entry for your new recipient's environment. Enter a descriptive name on the first screen and click Next.

3. For this kind of information, most LDAP servers don't require you to log in, so you can just fill in the DNS name or IP address of the server and click Finish.
4. After returning to the list of defined LDAP servers, don't forget to use the Set Default button to point at the most often used LDAP source. Click Close.
5. You can now test your LDAP connection and should be able to get the same kind of information you've previously seen in your LDAP client.
6. You can now try to send your first encrypted message by addressing anyone in the recipient's environment with a valid certificate.

If everything is set up correctly, things will work like a charm. All the user has to do is click the Digitally Signed or Encrypt button to get things moving. Remember that the message was encrypted with the recipient's public key, so as long as the recipient's local certificate store is initialized with the correct private key from the same keypair, the message will open much like a normal message. The only difference is the little icon in front of the message in the message list and the same icon in the message itself.

This way, everything is set up and functioning correctly. Encryption becomes so easy, it can even become the default setting for every e-mail message.

NOTE

The advantage of this method is that the certificate is checked every time a message is sent. A second advantage is that any recipient with a valid public key can now receive encrypted e-mail; there's no need to configure anything extra. However, the client will have to connect to LDAP every time. Depending on your situation, the response when clicking the Sent button might be almost instantaneous or a bit slower than normal. Furthermore, when accepting a digitally signed message, the certificate will be stored in the local certificate store, making it unnecessary to use the online LDAP check. And of course, disconnected clients can't use the LDAP lookup and will have to rely on the local certificate store, which we will investigate next.

So what's going to happen if the recipient's side is not the default LDAP address book? The client won't be able to perform the lookup automatically (bear in mind that it could be a long list of LDAP servers) and will prompt for additional information, as shown in Figure 30.32.

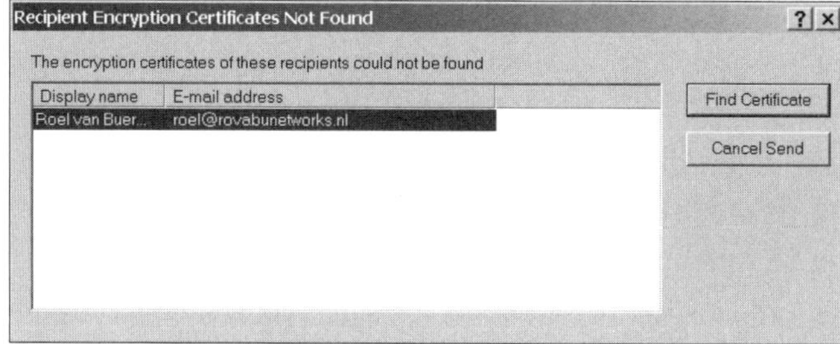

FIGURE 30.32 Sending encrypted messages without a default LDAP address book.

Follow these steps to find a user's public certificate from an LDAP server:

1. Click the Find Certificate button. The screen shown in Figure 30.33 will appear.

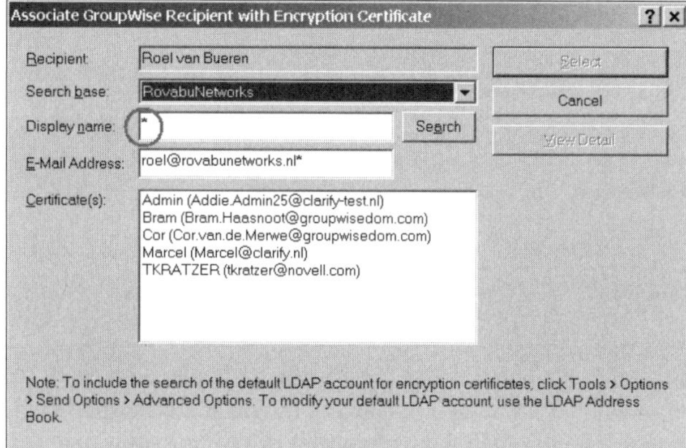

FIGURE 30.33 Using LDAP lookup—specifying search parameters.

2. By default, the Local Certificate Store will be selected, but by selecting the correct Search Base this can easily be changed in any of the defined LDAP servers. The E-mail Address field is already filled in; however, clicking the Search button will deliver no result.

WARNING

There seems to be an issue with the Display Name field. By default, an asterisk is placed into this search field; however, quite often the LDAP server will not give any results with this entry. When the asterisk is removed, the results are presented correctly.

3. Select the correct certificate, if there is more than one, and click Select. The message should now be sent directly!

You don't have to set up anything to receive a digitally signed message, the only thing we need is a correctly functioning local certificate store.

Step 6: Opening a Digitally Signed S/MIME Message

Just opening a digitally signed message from a new sender will present you with the screen shown in Figure 30.34.

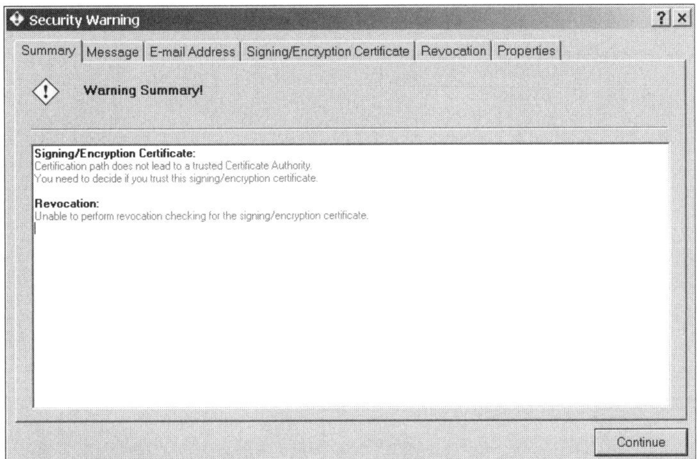

FIGURE 30.34
Receiving a digitally signed message from an untrusted recipient.

Follow these steps to accept a previously unreceived certificate:

1. You can click Continue to open the message, because it's not encrypted, but the next time you open this or another message from the same sender, the popup will reappear.
2. You can click the various tabs to see more of the info of this certificate, which for example will inform you of the fact that the embedded e-mail address is the same as the sender's e-mail. Another tab will inform you of the revocations status and you will have the option of checking the revocation status.

NOTE

With the Certificate Server 2.0, which was shipped with eDirectory 8.7 and earlier, it's not possible to use the revocation option for self-issued certificates, because these certificates are taken from your eDirectory and can't be compared against a Certificate Revocation List (CRL) or an OCSP server. The version of Certificate Server 2.52 that accompanies Netware 6.5 will have the CRL option. Novell is currently working on implementing the more modern OCSP in the next version of Certificate Server. You can check the revocation of most of the commercial certificates if you're online, because most of these certificates will have the necessary information embedded in the certificate.

3. If you've verified that this is a message from a trusted source, for example by calling the sender by phone, you can easily change the trust level of this certificate. Click the Signing/Encryption Certificate tab. You will have the option to Modify Trust or check the Certification path. This last button will present you with the complete certificate chain, as shown in Figure 30.35.

FIGURE 30.35
Determining the certification path.

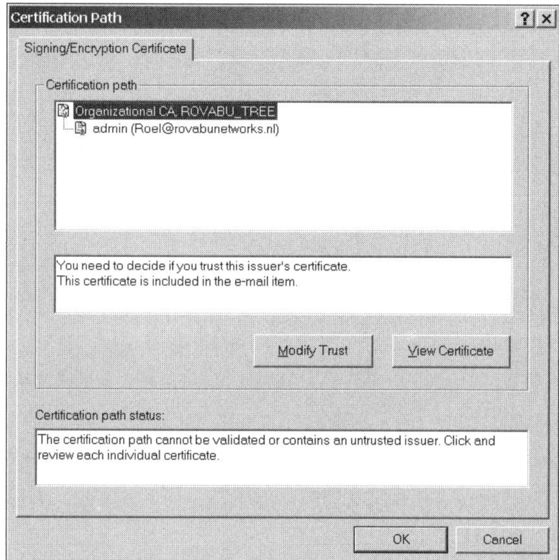

4. If you're sure this message comes from a trusted source, you can click the Organizational CA entry and modify the trust for the complete tree. This way, all future certificates coming from this sender's organization will have a valid root certificate. Accepting this certificate will have to be confirmed in the next screen. Recall that once such a root certificate is accepted, any other user-certificate coming from the same source will be validated automatically.

A very interesting improvement in GroupWise 6.5 is the way these user certificates are presented to the users. In previous versions and most other e-mail applications all the recipients will be presented in a long list, with possibly thousands of entries for every possible recipient you're communicating with. The address book of version 6.5 will sort all these entries and present them in a special certificate tab, shown in Figure 30.36, associated with the user object in the Address Book. This new feature makes the management of those certificates very neat and user friendly.

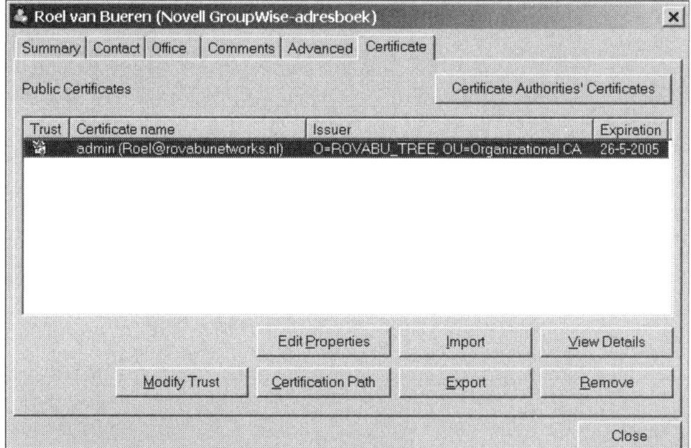

FIGURE 30.36
Using the GroupWise Address Book to view the details of the user certificate.

By accepting this certificate, every digitally signed message will be automatically accepted, without any popup screens.

NOTE

Because you've just accepted the public key from a user, you don't need LDAP anymore. Your own local certificate store now knows how to encrypt messages directed at this user, so sending encrypted e-mail will be very easy.

Step 7: Sending an Encrypted S/MIME Message with an Exchanged Public Key

This really is going to be an easy job; everything is set up to go! Because you've received a digitally signed message and accepted the user's public key, GroupWise will be able to find all the information it needs to send the message. Just try to send anything encrypted to anybody from whom you've accepted the public key and no questions will be asked.

Of course, if you didn't get a digitally signed message from a recipient yet, you will have to rely on LDAP or exchange keys first. Remember, encrypted messages cannot be sent without the recipient's public key.

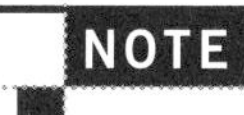

Remember that the sender will have used your public key, so the only thing you need is your corresponding private key, which is probably already in your local certificate store by now.

Step 8: Opening an Encrypted S/MIME Message

You can recognize an encrypted message by the icon in the message list and the icon on the subject bar. By clicking this icon you will get additional decryption information.

If for whatever reason your local certificate store doesn't contain your private key, you won't be able to open the message, and the warning in Figure 30.37 will be displayed. If this happens, you need to import the correct private key again (step 3) and you will be back in business.

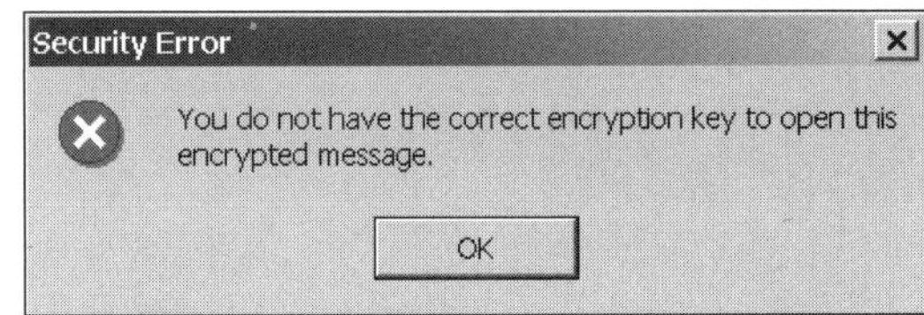

FIGURE 30.37
A security error appears when there is no private key in the local certificate store.

Combining Encryption and Digitally Signing S/MIME Messages

If everything is set up as described before you can easily combine digitally signing and encryption by just using the correct buttons, as long as you have the right keys available or if GroupWise can find them via LDAP.

Summary: What Do You Need to Do?

Regarding sending and receiving digitally signed and encrypted messages, always remember

- As a sender, you need your own private key to digitally sign a message.
- As a sender, you need the recipient's public key to send an encrypted message, either exchange keys, use LDAP lookup, or have the recipient send you a signed message so you can accept their public key (and you will need your private key in the local certificate store as well).
- As a recipient, you need your own private key to decrypt a received message, which is encrypted with your public key by the sender.
- As a recipient, you can open any digitally signed message without any additional key material, but you should make sure somehow that such a message is coming from a trusted source before changing the trust level.

Other points to bear in mind

- Checking the validity and the revocation of a key is (currently) a recipient's responsibility. This can either be done with Certificate

Revocation Lists (CRL) or with the more modern online OCSP protocol. For more info on these protocols, have a look at the URLs at the end of the chapter.

- As mentioned, only the users are allowed to handle their private keys. Within the Novell Certificate Console, ConsoleOne and iManage, the administrator can export the public key material from any user but himself.
- The eDirectory E-mail Address field must be properly filled in. GroupWise gateway aliases should be avoided when implementing S/MIME. Because these aren't properly represented within the eDirectory and user certificates, they might contain the wrong e-mail address.
- The certificate store on Windows 2000 and higher appears to be far more stable than Windows 9x, which also seems to be more vulnerable for security breaches.
- When properly set up, the S/MIME solution in GroupWise is exceptionally user friendly. User training might be limited; however, the Help desk should really understand the issues and must be thoroughly trained.

PGP and S/MIME Compared

So why does this chapter consider two solutions, not just one? Both of these solutions have market share and market potential. Even if you, as a GroupWise administrator, like one of these solutions more than the other, you might be forced to implement both, just because your users might need them both to communicate with certain customers.

Although S/MIME might be the preferred solution of many vendors, like Novell and Microsoft with their corporate collaboration solutions, PGP still has a bigger market share than S/MIME.

As you've seen, there are many similarities between PGP and S/MIME, one of the basic differences has always been how to handle trust. With PGP, a so-called web-of-trust will be created by the users by changing the trust level of user-certificates after some kind of verification. S/MIME relies heavily on a tree-structure, in which individual certificates can be trusted because they come from a trusted source.

Both PGP and S/MIME use public and private keys, but these keys are created rather differently. S/MIME has always been using PKI and X.509 certificates; PGP has only recently incorporated support for X.509. A PGP user can now choose between the web-of-trust model and the PKI tree model. Figure 30.38 shows these two models.

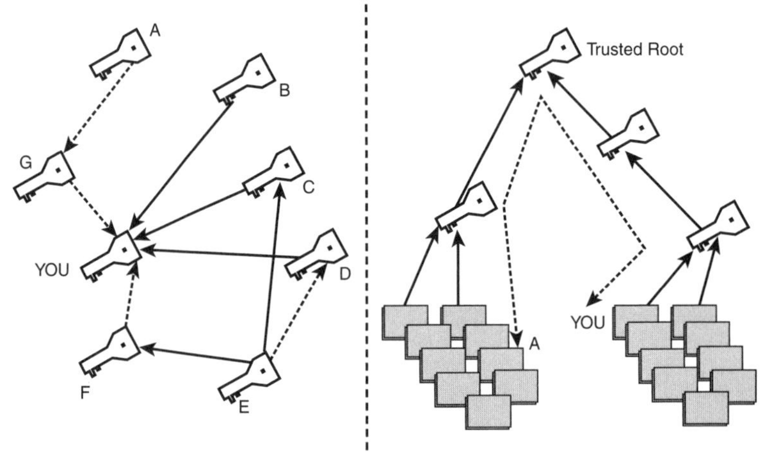

FIGURE 30.38 PGP's web-of-trust (left) compared to the PKI trusted tree model (right).

Table 30.1 offers a closer look at some of the differences and similarities between PGP and S/MIME.

TABLE 30.1 Comparing PGP and S/MIME

ELEMENT	PGP	S/MIME
Origin	Peer-to-Peer	Directory Services
Integration philosophy	Stand-alone with integration	Integrated client
GroupWise integration	Additional software needed, integration via C3POs.	No additional software needed, integral part of GroupWise and Windows OS.
Usage	Provides additional services like data encryption data.	
Security	Both provide basic message protection and use secure cryptographic algorithms. Both share the same security threads: poorly chosen pass-phrases and software-based attacks (like Trojan horses).	

ELEMENT	PGP	S/MIME
Scalability	Difficult if users don't know each other, especially with a large number of users. Recent versions of PGP can use the PKI tree model as well.	Tree model. As long as a recipient is part of a trusted tree, (s)he will be trustworthy.
Usability and Convenience in Use	Not completely integrated. User might need additional knowledge and skills.	Completely integrated; however, there might be differences in implementation between the different vendors. Not much need for additional knowledge, although the user should understand some basic principals.
Costs	Additional costs for additional software when used as an enterprise solution.	No additional software cost, although there might be setup costs.
Future prospects	Both are on a IETF standards track. PGP has limited support, might be the choice for private use.	S/MIME has received support from the major industry leaders.

Please bear in mind that PGP and S/MIME share one important feature: They both offer end-to-end encryption, which makes it virtually impossible to tamper with the messages in between the endpoints. This feature also makes it practically impossible to use virus scanning or SPAM handling in the message channel, which should therefore be handled at both ends of the line.

As you can see, there are many pros and cons to both approaches; let's hope that Oppliger's assumption of a merge between the two standards will soon become true. As long as you take the user-friendly approach, things should run smoothly for your users.

The Tovaris Solution: The Easy Way Out

The Tovaris SecureMail Gateway is plug-and-play e-mail security. It's truly a unique approach to PKI-enabled secure e-mail. The strength of Tovaris' design philosophy and the great flexibility of Tovaris' proxy server/network appliance approach enable the Tovaris SecureMail Gateway to integrate seamlessly with a wide variety of applications and architectures. For more info, go to `www.tovaris.com`.

For More Information on Securing Messaging

Some recommended reading follows:

- "E-mail encryption: multiple strategies needed", Gartner, J. Graff, September 13 2002
- "Secure Messaging with PGP and S/MIME," Rolf Oppliger, Artech, ISBN 1-58053-161-X
- "Digital Certificates, Applied Internet Security," Fegghi, Fegghi, and Williams, ISBN 0-201-30980-7
- "Understanding PKI," Carlisle Adams and Steve Lloyd, ISBN 0-672-32391-5
- "Secure E-mail: Innovation Strong, Interoperability Weak," Burton Group, James Kobielus, June 3 2003

Check out these relevant Internet standards:

- PGP—RFC2440, the RFC for the "OpenPGP Message Format" located at `http://www.ietf.org/rfc/rfc2440.txt`.
- S/MIME standards at `http://www.ietf.org/rfc/rfc2633.txt` and `http://www.ietf.org/rfc/rfc2634.txt`
- OCSP standards at `http://www.ietf.org/rfc/rfc2560.txt`
- CRL standards at `http://www.ietf.org/rfc/rfc3280.txt`

Here are some PGP-related links:

- The home page of the creator of PGP is at `http://www.philzimmermann.com/`

- Milestones in the history of PGP (the product), PGP (the technology), PGP Inc. (the original company), and the PGP Corporation (the current company) can be found at `http://www.pgp.com/company/pgphistory.html`
- The home page for The Messaging Architects's GWSecure is `http://www.gwtools.com/gwsecure`
- The home page of PGP Corporation is `http://www.pgp.com`
- The official PGP site for sales, support, and information on PGP products in Europe, the Middle East, and Africa (EMEA) is `http://www.pgpeurope.com/`
- The home page of the OpenPGP alliance is `http://www.openpgp.org/`
- The international PGP home page is `http://www.pgpi.org`
- The "How PGP works" article can be found at `http://www.pgpi.org/doc/pgpintro/`
- The GNU Privacy Guard is found at `http://www.gnupg.org/`

Here are some S/MIME-related links:

- For S/MIME interoperability testing, go to `http://www.rsasecurity.com/standards/sMIME/interop_center.html`
- For information on using S/MIME e-mail, go to `http://www.dartmouth.edu/~pkilab/pages/Using_SMIME_e-mail.html#Intro`

For Novell products and relevant articles, try these:

- Tay Kratzer's Appnote "Sending Secure and Encrypted Messages with GroupWise 6.5," found at `http://www.novell.com/coolsolutions/gwmag/features/a_send_secure_messages_appnote_gw.html`.
- GroupWise User Guide on S/MIME, by Tay Kratzer, found at `http://developer.novell.com/research/downloads.htm`.
- GroupWise Documentation—User Guide on S/MIME, found at `http://www.novell.com/documentation/lg/gw6/index.html?page=/documentation/lg/gw6/gw6_userguide/data/aaqe1hd.html`.
- Novell Certificate Server—product information, found at `http://www.novell.com/products/certserver/`.
- To download the Novell Certificate Console, go to `http://download.novell.com`. Choose the Certificate Server product and

click Submit Search. Download version 2.0 on Netware and extract the resulting CERTSERV.EXE to a directory. Locate the directory called `../files/PKIPUBLICFILES/CERTCONSOLE` and use SETUP.EXE to install Certificate Console (CERTCNSL.EXE) to a network directory.

- For the Novell user documentation regarding S/MIME messages, go to `http://www.novell.com/documentation/lg/gw65/gw65_userwin/data/aaqe1hd.html`.For information about LDAP browsers, try these sites:
  - For Softerra, go to `www.softerra.com` or `www.ldapbrowser.com`
  - For Novell Developer, go to `http://www.novell.com/coolsolutions/tools/1283.html`

Check out these commercial certification vendors:

- For Verisign, go to `www.verisign.com`
- For Thawte, go to `www.thawte.com`
- For Globalsign, go to `www.globalsign.com`
- For Entrust, go to `http://www.novell.com/coolsolutions/gwmag/html/a_in_entrust_we_trust_gw.html`
- For Comodo, go to `www.instantssl.com`

Summary

This chapter discussed how to send messages using two popular encryption methods—PGP and S/MIME. Customers who need encryption might find that the best thing to do is implement both PGP and S/MIME so that users are not limited to one solution.

CHAPTER 31

GroupWise Backup and Restore and Using the GroupWise TSA

Backing up your GroupWise system is a very important part of day-to-day administration of your messaging system. Hopefully you won't ever have to restore a component of your system. In the event you do need to, having a reliable, restorable backup is crucial. Due to the fact that e-mail systems typically have open files all the time (GroupWise normally holds the domain database open if you have gateways present in your system), you are presented with the challenge of how to get a restorable backup that includes those open files.

Open files aren't the only problem you can encounter, however.

Backing up your e-mail can also present problems of a different kind: legal ones. It is important to have a written policy dealing with how far back tapes with data and e-mail go. Without an explicit written policy that states exactly how long backup tapes holding e-mail or other data are kept, companies potentially open themselves up to big problems. As we've seen in some very public lawsuits, e-mail makes up the majority of evidence. Although the author of this book is not a lawyer, I strongly suggest your company create a policy clearly stating:

- How long e-mail is kept active in the message store
- Whether archive of e-mail by employees is allowed and how long archives will be kept
- How long e-mail backup tapes are kept
- What is done with backup tapes once the data on them expires—are they recycled or destroyed

With a clear, written policy about how e-mail is handled, you can prevent potential problems that might arise over legal issues.

This chapter discusses backing up your GroupWise system and how that process is easier and more reliable with the GroupWise Target Service Agent (GWTSA). The chapter begins with an overview of what a Target Service Agent is and does, and then moves onto the components that the GWTSA recognizes and backs up. The chapter then explains which backup solutions support the GWTSA and how to configure GWTSA and implement it on both backup media and remote servers. The chapter also explains how to back up GroupWise using three different backup software solutions: Veritas Backup Exec version 9 for NetWare, CA Brightstor ARCserve version 9 for NetWare, and Novell's Storage Management Services utility.

Next, the chapter also compares the GWTSA and other Open File (OF) agents and managers from third-party vendors. The chapter shows the restore process using each of the solutions and finally shows how the restore area and Restore Area Management works to restore deleted messages.

Backup Made Easier

Some e-mail administrators don't sleep well at night worrying about the safety and health of their systems. Their worries come from not knowing whether the e-mail system is getting backed up properly or if it could be restored in the event of major corruption or system failure. Using the GWTSA, along with a supported backup software solution, will definitely make administrators relax when it comes to getting the GroupWise system backed up properly.

There is almost no configuration of the GWTSA, as you will see throughout the rest of this chapter. The startup configuration file for the GWTSA is created at the time you install GroupWise agents onto the server, but is remarked out from loading. All you have to do is un-remark the `load` statement from the AUTOEXEC.NCF file so that the GWTSA will automatically load each time the server restarts. It can also be loaded manually at the command prompt, as you'll learn later.

The biggest downfall of the GWTSA is that it only runs on NetWare servers and can only back up local instances of GroupWise domains or post offices. Therefore, if one or more of your post offices are stored and run on a platform other than NetWare, you won't get the extra benefit that the GWTSA provides. In cases where post offices run on other platforms, open file agents or managers will be necessary in order to get complete backups.

The GWTSA currently runs only on NetWare servers as a NLM and it will only back up local instances. If your backup server is not your GroupWise server, you will need a remote agent from your backup vendor in order for the "media server" (where the tape drive and backup software are located) to back up GroupWise using the GWTSA.

What Is the GWTSA?

The GroupWise Target Service Agent or GWTSA is a NetWare-based program that communicates with several backup software solutions to provide GroupWise functionality to those software programs. The GWTSA does not have a user interface, but once it is loaded on a NetWare server, you will see GroupWise components listed as a backup agent. Figure 31.1 shows multiple backup agents running on servers hosting GroupWise domains and post offices, eDirectory, and the NetWare file system. You select one or more of the agents when configuring a backup job.

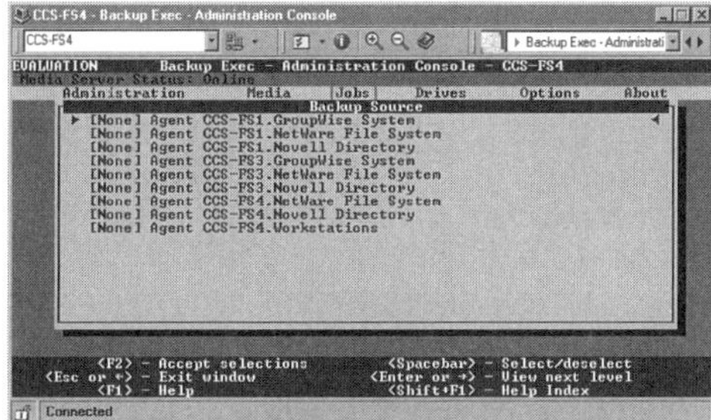

FIGURE 31.1
Backup agents registered in Veritas Backup Exec version 9 for NetWare.

The GWTSA backs up standard GroupWise files and directories found under both domain and post office directories. Those files are shown in Table 31.1.

TABLE 31.1 **Components of GroupWise Backed Up by the GWTSA**

FILES OR DIRECTORIES	RESULTS OF BACKUP WITH GWTSA
Domain directory	Domain database (WPDOMAIN.DB), .DC files, `mtaname` and `wpgate` directories
Post Office directory	Post office database (WPHOST.DB), NGWGUARD.* files, NGWCHECK.* files, *.DC files, the entire message store (`\OFUSER`, `\OFMSG`, `\OFFILES`)
Document Management directories	`<post office>\GWDMS` and all .DB files plus archive, index, and docs directories under each LIB000x directory

GroupWise 6 introduced the "SmartPurge" capability along with the GWTSA. If you use the GWTSA to back up GroupWise, it will timestamp each of the files that make up the message store (OFUSER, OFMSG, OFFILES) with the date of the successful backup. Messages that users delete and empty from their trash will then be purged from the message store because those messages have been successfully backed up. Later, depending upon your company's e-mail retention policy, you will be able to restore messages to the predefined restore area (see "Restore Area Management" later in this chapter) so those users can recover their own messages.

For those administrators who do not use the GWTSA, Novell includes the GWTMSTMP.NLM or GWTMSTMP.EXE files, which are used to timestamp the same message store databases and files so non-GWTSA backed up systems can take advantage of the SmartPurge.

How TSAs Work with Backup Products

The GWTSA is part of Novell's Storage Management Services technology. It works closely with other NetWare Loadable Modules (NLMs) to communicate with backup software. When you load your backup software on a NetWare server, you will notice that several Target Service Agents (TSAs) load. The GWTSA should be one of those TSAs, especially when the NetWare server has a post office or domain on it. Table 31.2 lists the SMS modules that work with GWTSA and your backup software.

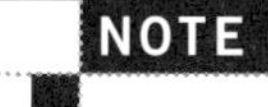

The GWTSA does not load automatically. You must either un-remark the load line for SYS:SYSTEM\GWTSA **in your server's AUTOEXEC.NCF or add the** LOAD GWTSA **line (with parameters) to the .NCF file that loads your backup software.**

TABLE 31.2

SMS, GroupWise, and Backup Terms

LOADING	COMPONENT DESCRIPTION
SMDR	Storage Management Data Requester is the communication module in the Storage Management Services architecture. It provides transparent access to SMS services by exposing a set of APIs, which can be used by backup software applications to access local or remote SMS services. Version 5.04 or later is protocol-independent when it communicates with other SMDRs.
GWENN4	This is the main GroupWise engine, providing API support for all GroupWise functions on the server. The GWTSA requires that it be loaded.
GWTSA	GroupWise Target Service Agent. It is installed and configured, but is remarked out; at the same time GroupWise agents are installed onto a NetWare server.
GWXIO10	GroupWise XIS integration module. This module provides a connection between the GWTSA and the XIS engine.
TSANDS, TSA600	Target Service Agents used to back up eDirectory and NetWare 6 file system.
CLIBAUX.NLM	CLIB shim that will allow the loading of GroupWise 6.x NLMs onto a NetWare 4.11 file server.
Media Server	The term that applies to the server where the backup software and the physical tape drive are located.
Remote Agent	Software provided by the backup vendor (Veritas, CA, and so on) to run on a server remote from where the backup tape device and media server software are running.
Open File Agent/Manager	Software available from backup vendors or third-party vendors that help backup software back up open files, such as the GroupWise domain database. Open file agents are used in place of the GWTSA to back up GroupWise components.

Backup Solutions That Support GWTSA

Currently, there are several major backup solutions that will use the GWTSA to help you get proper backups of your GroupWise system. These products include

- Veritas Backup Exec for NetWare
- Novell's Storage Management Services (SMS)
- Computer Associates BrightStor ARCserve for NetWare version 9
- Legato SnapShotServer for NetWare
- Syncsort Backup Express

Several vendors also offer Open File agents that either generically support GroupWise or specifically do so, as in the case of ARCserve/BrightStor. These agents are typically sold separately from the actual backup software.

- Open File Option (Veritas)
- Open File Manager (St. Bernard)
- GroupWise Agent (ARCserve)

NOTE

If you are backing up GroupWise 6.x with ARCserve, you can use the GWTSA. If you are backing up GroupWise 5.x, you need to purchase the GroupWise agent from CA.

Open File Options (OFO), Agents (OFA), or Managers (OFM) work very similarly to the way that the GWTSA works. Open file solutions either place files in temporary locations on a NetWare volume or take snapshots of files so that those files can continue to be open and in use. By default, the GWTSA places temporary files in the `sys:\system\temp` directory during the backup process. You can use the `/tempdir` switch to specify a different volume where more disk space is available for those temporary files. Each open file solution has specific switches and configuration parameters that you should consult if you plan to implement it.

When a backup job is running, the GWTSA takes a snapshot of the various GroupWise databases and places them in the `temp` directory. It does not take say, all the userxxx.db files, and place them in the `temp` directory. Because of this your `temp` directory does not need to equal the size of your post office or domain directory. There are only a few files in the `temp` directory at any one time. It is recommended to use the `/tempdir` switch so that the GWTSA `temp` directory is not on the `SYS` volume.

Installation and Configuration of the GWTSA

The GWTSA can be installed onto any server that you install GroupWise agents onto (the Message Transfer Agent [MTA] and Post Office Agent [POA]). At the time of the agent installation, you add the names and database paths of domains and post offices. Figure 31.2 shows the agent installation step where you input the domain and post office information to create the startup files. The name of the domain or post office and its database location are input as shown in Figure 31.3. This information goes into the agent startup configuration files (domain.mta and post.poa) and populates the `/home` switch that the agents use when loading on a server.

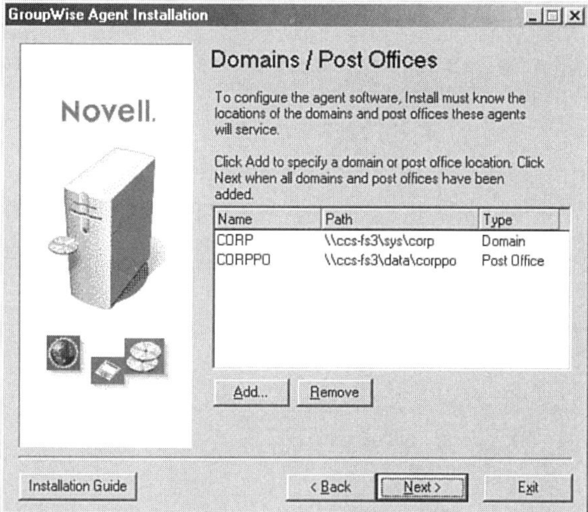

FIGURE 31.2
Add domains and post offices to agent installation.

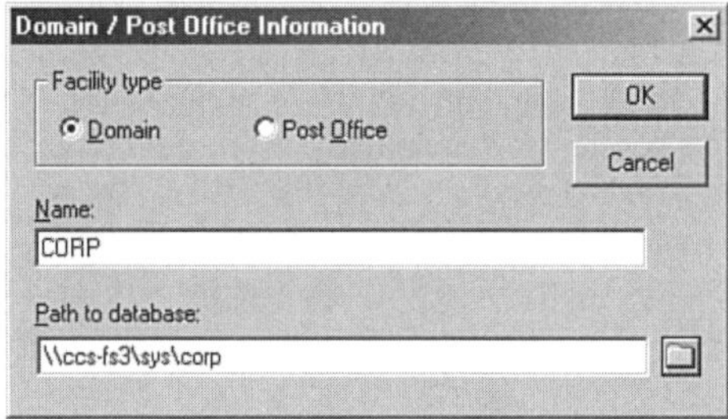

FIGURE 31.3 The Domain/Post Office Information window is where you specify domain or post office information.

The GWTSA.NCF file is created at the same time, using the database location(s) that you enter when you install the GroupWise agents. This NCF file is used when you load the GWTSA.NLM. Figure 31.4 shows the GWTSA.NCF file.

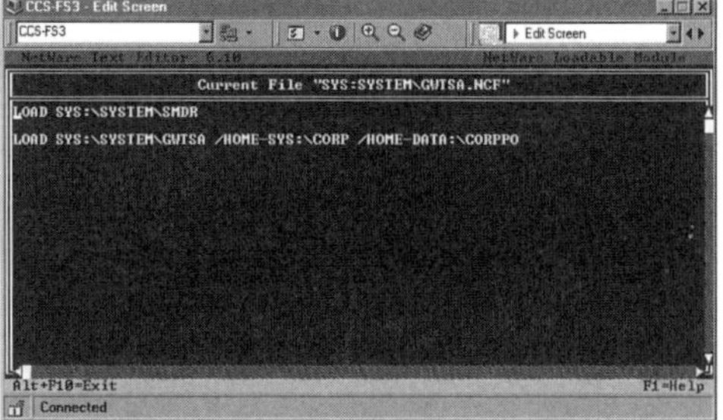

FIGURE 31.4 The GWTSA.NCF screen shown in the NetWare editor.

NOTE

The `"SYS:SYSTEM\GWTSA.NCF"` file is automatically added to the AUTOEXEC.NCF but is remarked (`REM`) out. You will need to remove the `REM` so that the GWTSA will load each time the server restarts.

You can load the GWTSA.NLM without using the .NCF file. Use the `/home` switch parameters for any domain and or post office running on the server you are loading the GWTSA on. The various command-line parameters for loading the GWTSA are shown in Table 31.3.

TABLE 31.3

Switches for the GWTSA

SWITCH	DESCRIPTION
/home	<*volume*>:*path* to domain or PO directory (or directories if there are more than two backup locations). Example: /home=DATA:\GW\CORPPO
/log	Enables GWTSA logging (default is off)
/ll	*log level* <normal or verbose> (default is normal) Example: /ll=verbose
/tempdir	<*volume*>:*path* where files will be copied temporarily during backup. Example: /tempdir=DATA:\GW\TSATEMP
/lang	<language in use> this is a two-character representation of the language you are using on the server and in the GroupWise system (default is US)
/help	Displays a help screen (on a NetWare 6 server, the help information is displayed in the LOGGER screen and not on the system console)

Once you've installed the agents onto a server and loaded the GWTSA along with the backup software components (either media server or remote agent), you are ready to begin backing up GroupWise. However, the installation of the agents and GWTSA leave out a critical file that is used during logging. This file, XISERR.XML, is the logging template file used by the GWTSA and the GWXIO10.NLM. If this template is not *manually* copied into the SYS:SYSTEM\TSA directory on the server where the GWTSA loads, you will get fatal errors and the backup job will not work.

To find and copy the XISERR.XML file, do the following:

1. Open the software distribution directory (SDD) and navigate into the <GW65SDD>\INTERNET\WEBACCES\NLM folder.
2. Copy XISERR.XML into the SYS:SYSTEM\TSA folder on the file server where the GWTSA will run.
3. Load the GWTSA using the GWTSA.NCF or manually using switches listed in Table 31.3. If GWTSA loads without any errors, you can proceed to the next section. Otherwise look at the log files mentioned in this section and troubleshoot.

Backing Up Your GroupWise System

This section details how to back up your GroupWise system using Veritas Backup Exec version 9 for NetWare, Computer Associates BrightStor ARCserve version 9 for NetWare, and Novell's Storage Management Services utility. Each solution begins with the assumption that you are running GroupWise 5.5 EP or later on one or more NetWare servers and that you are either planning to use or already using the GWTSA.

NOTE

If your GroupWise directories are located on a NetWare 4.11 server, you can use the GWTSA as long as you first load CLIBAUX.NLM. This NLM provides compatibility between this version of NetWare and GroupWise 6.x NLMs.

Veritas Backup Exec

Use the following steps to access Veritas Backup Exec in conjunction with the GroupWise TSA.

You can start configuring a backup job within either the server Administration console or the Windows Administration console. Figure 31.5 shows the Veritas Administration console on a NetWare server. To reach this point, do the following:

1. Select the Jobs menu.
2. Select the Backup command.
3. Select the Make Selections command.

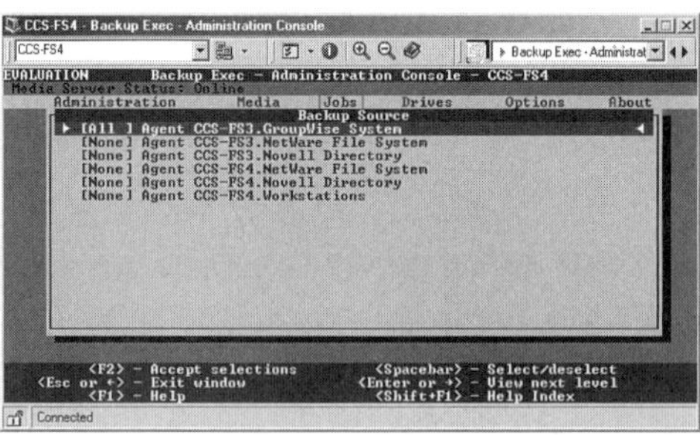

FIGURE 31.5
The GWTSA automatically registers with Backup Exec.

If you are using the Windows Administration console, follow these steps to set up a backup job:

1. Select the Jobs menu.
2. Select the Backup command.
3. Name the job (or use the default names) on the General tab of the dialog box that appears.
4. Click the Selections tab and then expand each of the agent sections so you can see the individual components of what a particular agent will back up.
5. Select the agent and its components. You will see green check marks appear in the various agent boxes. If you need to deselect a component (such as a directory or file), you will need to further expand the particular agent and remove the particular check marks.
6. Click OK to submit the job. By default, jobs set up with these steps will run once. Because configuring backup jobs in general is beyond the scope of this book, it's best to consult with the documentation that accompanies the product. The GroupWise agents are shown in Figure 31.6, selected and ready for a backup job to be submitted.

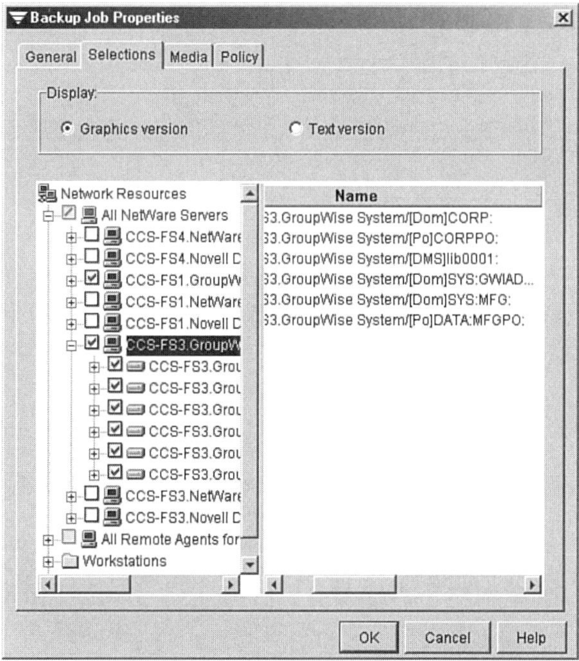

FIGURE 31.6
Backup job configured in the Veritas Windows Administration console.

If you use the GWTSA to back up GroupWise, you should deselect the various GroupWise directories and files that appear under the TSA500 or TSA600 agents, as shown in Figure 31.7. GroupWise directories should not be selected under the file system TSA. Otherwise, you might find you are backing up your GroupWise system twice.

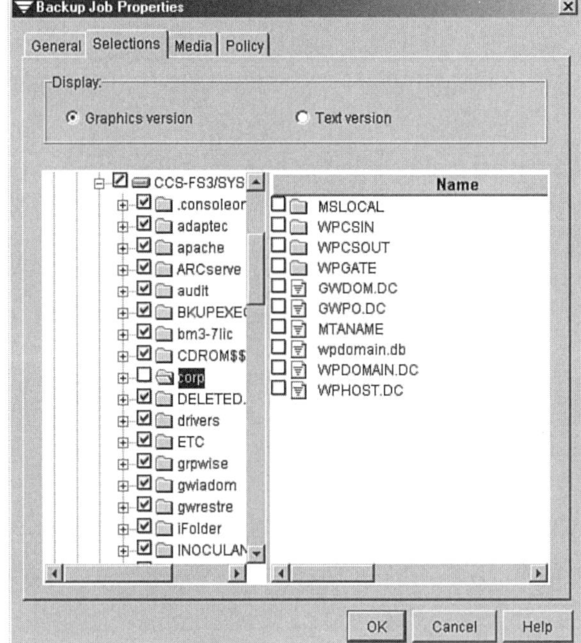

FIGURE 31.7
The GroupWise Domain directory should be unselected.

To verify that your backup job starts and backup of the GroupWise system begins, you might want to return to the server console, switch to the Veritas Administration console, and then look at Active Jobs (Administration menu, Active Jobs command). Figure 31.8 shows the backup of a GroupWise domain and post office in progress.

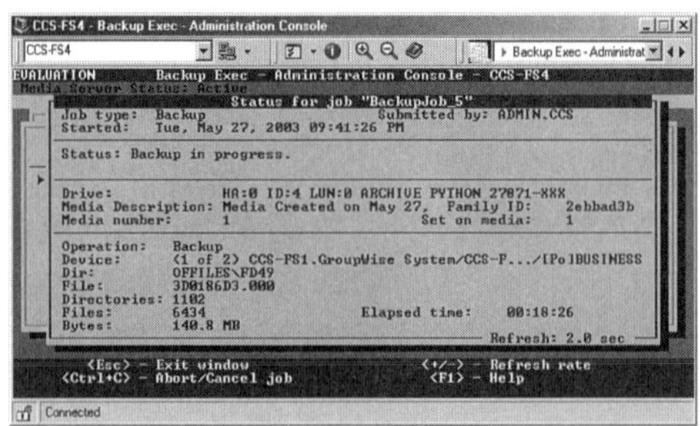

FIGURE 31.8
A backup job in progress.

When the backup job is completed, you should either look at the individual backup log or check the statistics screen that is shown in Figure 31.9. You will find the backup logs under the Administration menu or in the Jobs section of the Windows Administration console. Figure 31.9 shows the backup job completed "normally" and shows the amount of data backed up.

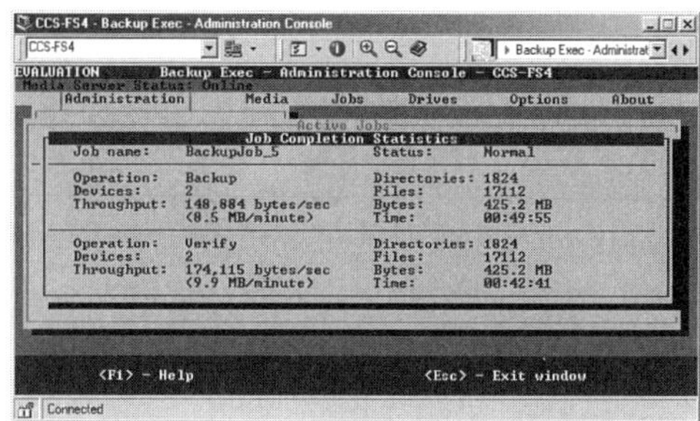

FIGURE 31.9
The job statistics screen shows the results of a backup job.

Prior to GroupWise 6 shipping with the GWTSA, CA made a GroupWise agent available and if you are using GroupWise 5.x and BrightStor ARCserve you will need to buy that agent from CA. If you are using GroupWise 6.x, the GWTSA will work with BrightStor ARCserve. However, it is only selectable from within the Manager utility that runs on Windows NT, Windows 2000, or Windows XP.

By default, GroupWise components aren't readily available for selection from within the Manager utility. You must add servers that host GroupWise components under the GroupWise System selection. Figure 31.10 shows the BrightStor Manager utility showing the GroupWise system selection prior to having GroupWise servers added.

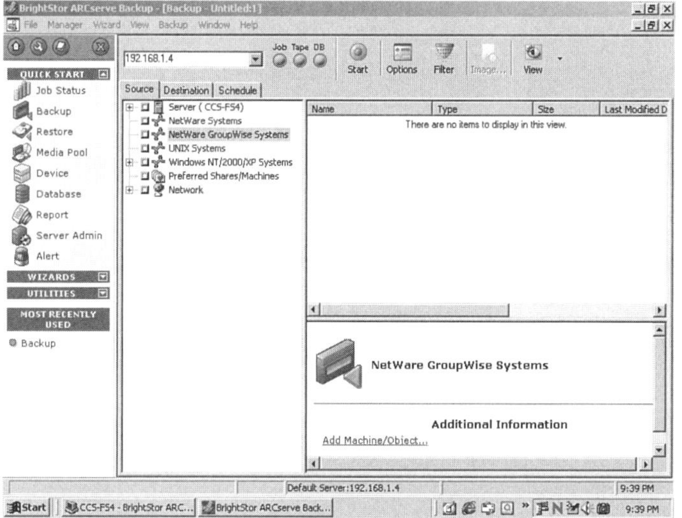

FIGURE 31.10
The BrightStor Manager utility.

To add a GroupWise server to the Manager utility, do the following:

1. Run the Manager utility. Once it is up and working, click the Backup link on the left of the screen.
2. Wait for the various agents to appear in the middle screen, as seen in Figure 31.10.
3. Right-click the GroupWise System and then click Add Machine/Object.
4. Enter the hostname (the name you want to see in the Manager utility) and the IP address of the server where the GWTSA is running. Click OK. You can add multiple machine/objects if you have multiple GroupWise servers to back up.

Once you have added one or more GroupWise servers to the list, you can begin to configure a backup job to back up your GroupWise system components. You can select GroupWise domains and post offices, as shown in Figure 31.11. Following are the steps to configure your backup job:

1. Click the newly added hostname of a GroupWise server. If you are prompted to authenticate, do so with the appropriate username and password.
2. Click the green boxes to select the GroupWise components you want to back up. You can select the server object added from the previous steps in order to select all GroupWise components on the server.
3. Verify that your backup destination is the correct tape drive. By default, configured jobs will run once unless you change the schedule and frequency (consult the vendor's documentation on changing the job schedule).
4. Click the Start button in the Manager utility to begin backing up your GroupWise components. The BrightStor will connect to the GWTSA you selected and begin backing up data. You can click the Job Status link on the left of the Manager utility to watch the status of the backup.

Figure 31.11 shows how GroupWise components are selected in the BrightStor ARCserve Manager console after servers are added under the GroupWise NetWare Systems section.

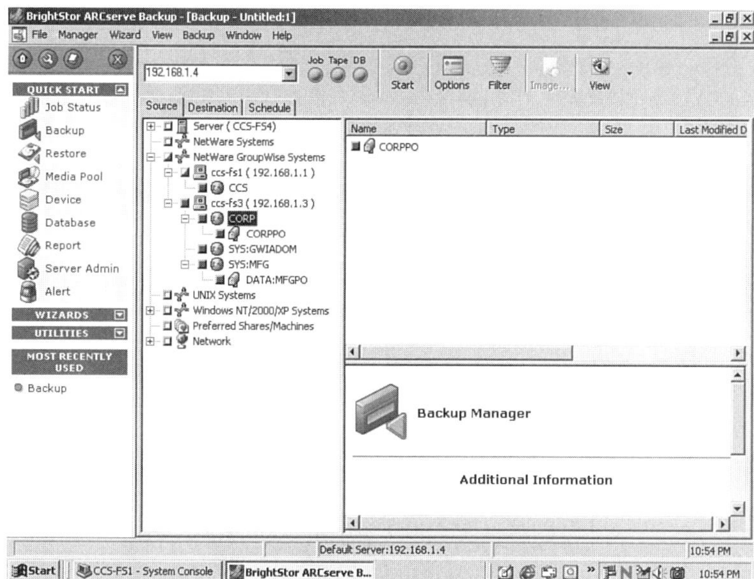

FIGURE 31.11 The BrightStor ARCserve Manager console.

Novell Storage Management Services

Novell ships its Storage Management Services backup utility with every NetWare server. Like the other backup solutions detailed in this chapter, it uses the GWTSA to assist in the backup of your GroupWise system. There is a server-based console (SBCON.NLM) and a Windows console available (NWBack32.exe).

The SMS console utilities recognizes TSAs and displays them after you select one of the registered servers, as shown in Figure 31.12. In this figure, the GroupWise System is shown in the NetWare SMS console (SBCON.NLM) prior to being selected for use in a backup job.

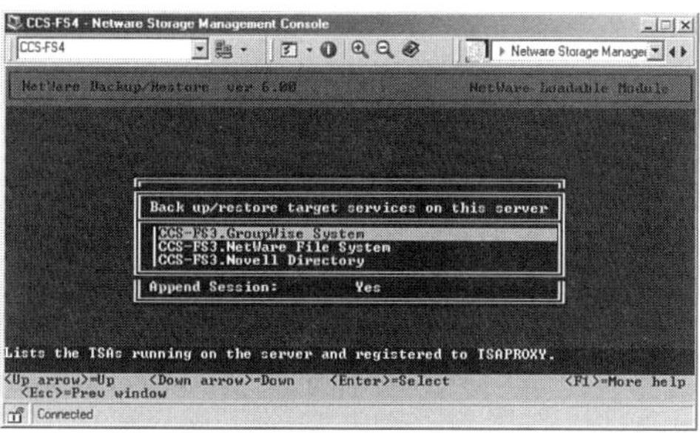

FIGURE 31.12 NetWare SMS console on a NetWare server.

You connect to the GWTSA by selecting it from the TSA list at the server or by choosing the GroupWise Database in the Windows utility. In either case, you will be required to authenticate with a username and password that is capable of backing up the selected system.

Once you've selected a file server and a GroupWise System (GWTSA) for backup, you need to specify a destination and a time to run the backup job. Like the other backup applications, the default runs the backup job once. However, it can be scheduled to repeat daily, weekly, or some other interval you choose.

Figure 31.13 shows the Windows console with components of a GroupWise system selected in the window on the left. If you select the GroupWise Mail Server, all GroupWise components will be backed up to the destination (as shown in the right window).

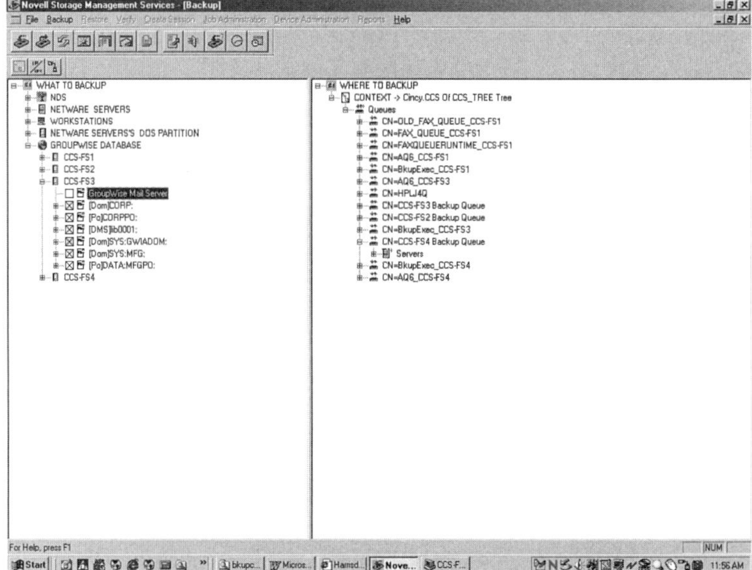

FIGURE 31.13
NetWare SMS console on a Windows workstation.

Follow these steps to submit a backup of GroupWise components to a SMS backup device using the server-based SMS utility:

1. Load the SBCON utility on your NetWare server where the tape backup device is installed.
2. Choose Job Administration (SBCON).
3. Choose Backup.
4. Select a server where the GWTSA is running.

5. Authenticate to the server by entering a username in a full distinguished name format (`.admin.americas`) that has access rights to back up the selected components.
6. Press Enter on "What to Backup" and then press Insert to see the GroupWise components you can back up. If you select GroupWise Mail Server, as shown in Figure 31.14, you will back up all GroupWise components on the server. GroupWise components can be individually selected or you can choose GroupWise Mail Server to back up all GroupWise components recognized by the GWTSA.

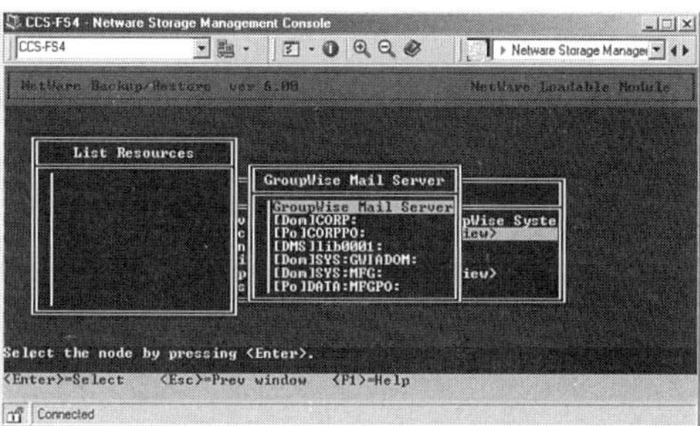

FIGURE 31.14 Choosing which GroupWise components to backup.

7. Select the Device/Media name to back up to (this is the recognized tape device).
8. If you want to set up scheduling for the job, choose the Advanced item.
9. Because you probably overwrite the contents of each backup tape, you should change the Append Session from Yes to No so the tape will be overwritten.
10. Finally, press Esc to be prompted to submit the job. This section has detailed how to submit backup jobs to three different backup applications: Veritas Back Up Exec version 9 for NetWare, Computer Associates BrightStor ARCserve version 9 for NetWare, and Novell's Storage Management Services backup utility. The next section explains how to set up the new GroupWise restore area, how to restore a GroupWise message store to the restore area, and how users can restore their own deleted e-mail from within the GroupWise client.

Restoring GroupWise

Restoring deleted e-mail is not a difficult task, but it is very time consuming. It is the amount of time required that makes restoring deleted e-mail difficult for a company to justify. If you need to restore messages that were cleaned up by an automatic emptying of the trash, accidentally deleted by a user, or might be needed to support a lawsuit, you will need to understand how to set up a restore area. You also must understand how to redirect a restore job from your backup software so the post office message store files end up in the restore area, and they don't overwrite your live post office databases.

Some users in your company will keep important e-mail in their mailbox's trash, and as we all know, the default cleanup setting within GroupWise will empty the trash after seven days. Unless you change the default cleanup settings and teach the users to not put important e-mail in the trash folder, you are probably going to be stuck restoring e-mail.

The e-mail retention policy briefly mentioned at the beginning of this chapter comes back into play here. If your company has a written policy about how e-mail is handled, you might not be even allowed to restore e-mail that users have deleted. If you are allowed to restore e-mail, how far back do backup tapes with message stores go? Can you afford to take the time to restore e-mail that "might" be in a mailbox that was backed up two years ago? Do you still use the same backup and restore technology (hardware and software) that you used when backup tapes were made five years ago?

Restore Area Management

Beginning with GroupWise 6, an item was added to the administrative Snapins to ConsoleOne that allowed you to set up a restore area where the GroupWise message store of a given post office could be restored and then accessed by users or the GroupWise POA in order to restore deleted and purged e-mail.

You set up the restore area for a post office within the GroupWise System Operations menu in ConsoleOne. As shown in Figure 31.15, a restore area is set up for the `CORPPO` post office.

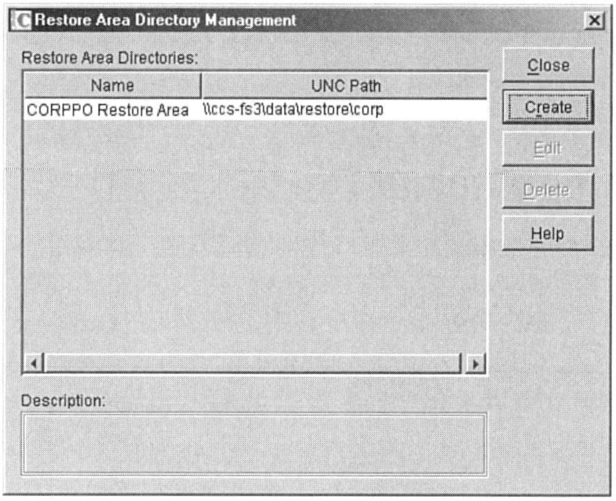

FIGURE 31.15
The Restore Area Directory Management dialog box in ConsoleOne.

To set up a restore area, follow these steps:

1. Load ConsoleOne.
2. Connect to the primary domain.
3. From the Tools menu, select GroupWise System Operations, Restore Area Management.
4. Type the name of the restore area. Optionally type a description.
5. Create the directory structure you plan to use for the restore area. This should be a directory structure on a server that users can access (unless you are going to have the POA restore the user's mailbox). Either enter the UNC path to the restore area or browse to it.
6. Click the Membership tab to add users (or an entire post office) whose messages need to be restored.
7. Click Close to create the definition for the restore area.

NOTE

If in step 6 you added the post office to the Membership tab of the restore area, you can access the Post Office Settings property page to verify that the restore area is recognized and is ready for use. You will see the name of the restore area on the Post Office Settings page next to the field that reads Restore Area.

Once the restore area is set up and configured, you will need to find the backup tape that holds what is believed to be the correct message store and prepare to restore it using your backup application. Following are the steps to restore a GroupWise message store to the restore area. To illustrate this process, this example uses Backup Exec to restore the message store.

TIP **Make sure that your restore area has sufficient space to restore the post office from backup.**

Restore Using Backup Exec

To restore a post office message store using Backup Exec, you need to have the tape the post office message store was backed up to. You can use either the Administration console at the server or the Backup Exec Java console on your Windows workstation. To restore a message store to the configured restore area, you must modify the restore job. Follow these steps to configure the restore job:

1. In the Veritas Java console for Windows, click the Jobs menu.
2. Click Restore.
3. Name the restore job in the Restore Job Properties dialog box.
4. Click the Selections tab and then double-click All Media.
5. Expand the back up device to show the TSAs used on the backup set.
6. Click the GroupWise post office component. It should expand to show the post office files and directories in the right window.
7. Click the Redirection tab and then double-click the backup set name/restore target name so that you can *override the restore location* into the restore area.
8. Once in the Restore Target dialog box, click the NetWare servers and then select the TSA representing the file system. This allows you to restore the files and directories that make up the post office message store to the separate restore area.

NOTE **BrightStor ARCserve version 9 and Novell's Storage Management Services utility (SBCON or NWBack32.exe) both work similarly when restoring a GroupWise message store to the restore area you set up in ConsoleOne. Follow each vendor's documentation on specific steps for setting up a restore job. In each case, you redirect the restored data to a different location (the GroupWise restore area).**

Once a restore area is defined and the data is restored, there are two methods for restoring mail messages. The first method described in this section allows users belonging to the membership of a restore area to access their restored messages from within the GroupWise client. They can then "cherry-pick" messages that they want to restore. The second method requires no effort on the part of your users. With this second method, the GroupWise

POA restores messages on behalf of the users. The potential downside to this method is that all messages in the user's mailbox are then restored to the live post office. If the message already exists in the live post office's message store (because the user did not delete it), however, the message will not be brought over again and duplicated. If the user's mailbox needs to be completely restored, no problem! If the user just needs a few messages back, it can be overkill to allow the POA to restore a user's mailbox.

Restoring Messages—User and Windows Client-Based Message Restoration

Now that you've restored the message store to the restore area, you should notify and, if necessary, assist users to recover the deleted messages. At this point, you should have already assigned membership rights to the restore area for the user(s) who will be accessing the restore area and restoring their messages.

TIP

If your users have any Auto-Delete or Auto-Archive preferences set up on their live mailbox, you should disable those temporarily. If you do not, restored items that pass the time threshold defined in the user's mailbox will be deleted or archived just as soon as they are restored.

These steps work for the GroupWise 6.x or later clients. Follow these steps to open the backup area and recover the deleted messages:

1. Start the GroupWise client and click the File menu.
2. Click the Open Backup menu command, as shown in Figure 31.16. The client will authenticate to the restore area and *if* the user has full rights to the restore area, the Backup mailbox will open.
3. Browse through the restorable messages and highlight the ones that need to be returned to the mailbox. You can select random messages with the Ctrl-click. You can highlight all messages by selecting the first message, moving down to the last, and Shift-clicking.
4. Once you've highlighted the messages, right-click one of them and choose the Restore command, as shown in Figure 31.17.

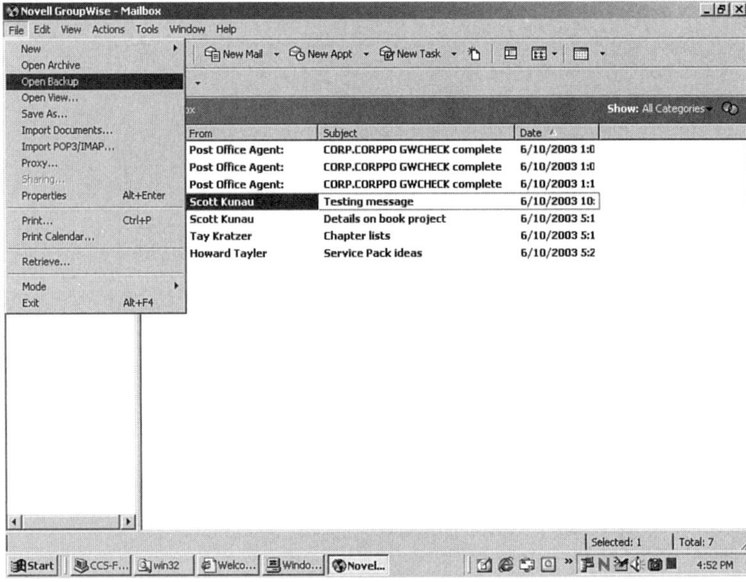

FIGURE 31.16 Accessing the restore area in the GroupWise Windows client.

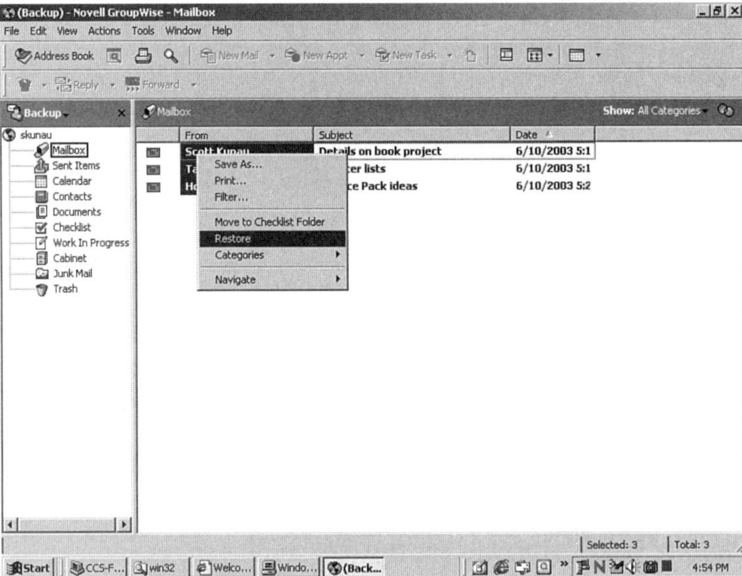

FIGURE 31.17 Selecting messages to restore.

5. After the messages are restored, close the restore area by clicking the File menu and selecting the Open Backup command. You will be returned to the main mailbox and should see the recovered messages.

Restoring Messages—Administrator- and POA-Based Message Restoration

My experience has been that sometimes the GroupWise POA on the NetWare platform requires that the restore area be on a volume on the same server where the POA is running against the live post office. The GroupWise POA on the Windows platform does not have this requirement.

TIP

If your users have any Auto-Delete or Auto-Archive preferences set up on their live mailbox, you should disable those temporarily. If you do not, restored items that pass the delete or archive time threshold defined in the user's mailbox will be deleted or archived just as soon as they are restored.

The POA object of the user's owning post office must have Read, Write, and File Scan rights to the restore area. If the POA object does not have at least these rights, the POA or the user will see an `8200` error and mail will not be restored. You might also need to add the `/user` and `/password` switches to the startup file of the POA in order to allow the POA to log into another NetWare server to access the restore area. At this point, you should have already assigned membership rights to the restore area for the user(s) and or the user's production POA agent whose mailboxes are to be restored by the POA. This way, when you issue a restore of a user's mailbox through ConsoleOne, the POA will correlate the user's membership to a restore area, and then know which UNC path to go to in order to access the backup of the post office.

Follow these steps to task the POA with restoring a user's mailbox:

1. In ConsoleOne, highlight the user whose message items you need restored.
2. From the Tools menu, select GroupWise Utilities, Backup/Restore Mailbox. A dialog box similar to the one shown in Figure 31.18 should appear.

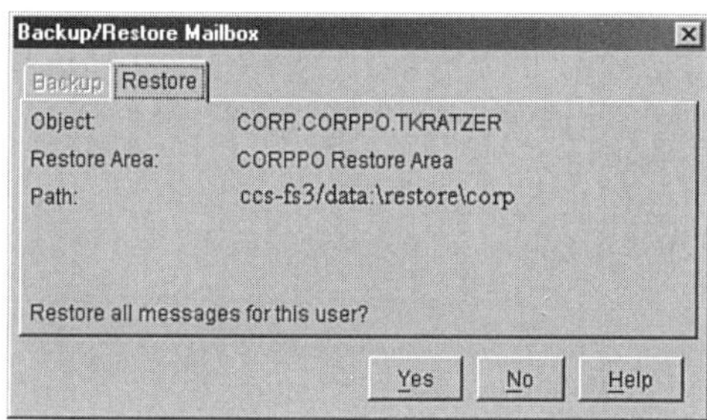

FIGURE 31.18
Issuing a mailbox restore from ConsoleOne.

3. Select the Yes button; this will send a message to the POA to restore the user's mailbox. Figure 31.19 shows the verbiage in the GroupWise POA's log when the user's mailbox is restored. In this example the logging level is set to Verbose, and the restore was initiated through ConsoleOne.

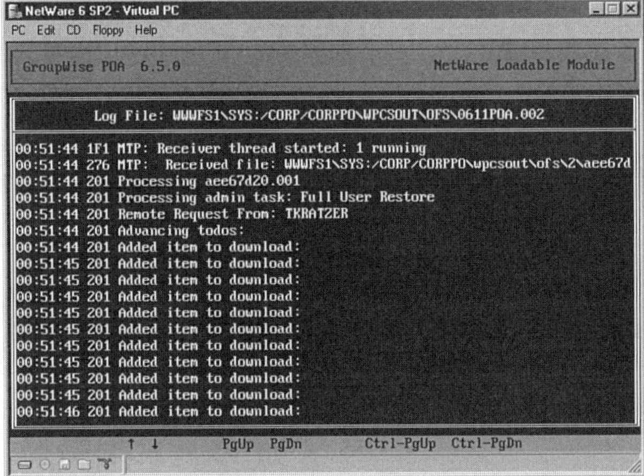

FIGURE 31.19
The GroupWise POA is restoring a user's mailbox.

NOTE

When a user restores an item from the client, the POA logs the information a little differently than when a restore is issued through ConsoleOne. Figure 31.19 shows the restore when initiated from ConsoleOne. When a client initiates a restore of mail, the POA logs it as a remote request:

```
03:10:09 138 Remote Request From: tkratzer
```

Summary

This chapter covered the importance of being able to back up and restore your GroupWise system. It discussed how the GroupWise Target Service Agent (GWTSA) works with backup applications to ensure that in-use files are properly backed up.

This chapter also covered restoring e-mail; both by allowing users to access their deleted and purged e-mail and restore them to their mailbox, and configuring the POA to restore a user's mailbox. Perhaps most importantly, this chapter discussed the need to have a written e-mail policy for your company.

INDEX

Symbols

A

B

C

D

E

F

G

H

I

M

N

O

P

S

T

U

V-W

X-Z